Technological Advancement in Developed and Developing Countries: Discoveries in Global Information Management

M. Gordon Hunter
University of Lethbridge, Canada

Felix Tan
Auckland University of Technology, New Zealand

Information Science REFERENCE

INFORMATION SCIENCE REFERENCE

Hershey · New York

Director of Editorial Content: Kristin Klinger
Senior Managing Editor: Jamie Snavely
Assistant Managing Editor: Michael Brehm
Publishing Assistant: Sean Woznicki
Typesetter: Carole Coulson, Sean Woznicki
Cover Design: Lisa Tosheff
Printed at: Yurchak Printing Inc.

Published in the United States of America by
Information Science Reference (an imprint of IGI Global)
701 E. Chocolate Avenue
Hershey PA 17033
Tel: 717-533-8845
Fax: 717-533-8661
E-mail: cust@igi-global.com
Web site: http://www.igi-global.com/reference

Library of Congress Cataloging-in-Publication Data

Technological advancement in developed and developing countries : discoveries in global information management / M. Gordon Hunter and Felix Tan, editors.
p. cm. -- (Advances in global information management series)

Includes bibliographical references and index.
Summary: "This book uses a multi-cultural approach to discuss many issues relating to information systems, and takes many different perspectives on this intriguing topic"--Provided by publisher.

ISBN 978-1-60566-920-5 (hardcover) -- ISBN 978-1-60566-921-2 (ebook) 1. Information technology--Management--Developed countries. 2. Information technology--Management--Developing countries. 3. Globalization. I. Hunter, M. Gordon. II. Tan, Felix.
HD30.2.T423 2010
303.48'33091724--dc22

2009044845

British Cataloguing in Publication Data
A Cataloguing in Publication record for this book is available from the British Library.

Table of Contents

Detailed Table of Contents

This chapter applies a technology-organization-environment framework to evaluate the determinants of the global information systems (GIS) strategies of foreign affiliates. The results indicate that IT maturity, parent resource dependency, cultural distance, restrictive regulations, and local competition are significant determinants of GIS strategy. This chapter also finds that the integration-responsiveness model can be applied to explain GIS strategies and their implementation. These findings provide additional insight into the complex relationship between headquarters and affiliates in GIS management. This chapter concludes by discussing the implications of these findings for both research and practice.

Risks evaluation is critical for the success of IT offshore outsourcing. Based on fuzzy group decision-making (FGDM) and variable precision fuzzy rough set (VPFRS), this chapter proposes a new integrated model, variable precision fuzzy rough group decision-making (VPFRGDM), to evaluate the risk in IT offshore outsourcing. This model can improve the capability to handle potential errors fairness and efficiency of risk evaluation, and is verified by a numerical case.

Despite the recent increased attention afforded malware by the popular press, there appears to be a dearth in user awareness and understanding of certain aspects of the security paradigm. This chapter presents a comparison of user awareness levels of rootkits, spyware, and viruses between U.S. and Chinese users. The results of a survey of 210 U.S. respondents and 278 Chinese respondents indicate that respondents' awareness and knowledge of rootkits is well below that of spyware and viruses. Data analysis further reveals that there are significant differences in Chinese and U.S. user perceptions with regard to spyware and computer viruses. However, there is no difference in cross-cultural awareness with regard to rootkits. Due to the ubiquitous nature of the Internet, rootkits and other malware do not yield at transnational borders. An important step to mitigate the threats posed by malware such as rootkits is to raise awareness levels of users worldwide.

Previously, Zhang and Lowry (2008) analyzed the issues, limitations, and opportunities in cross-cultural research on collaborative software in information systems. This chapter revisits the issues discussed in that paper and adds to them an analysis of the research done since their analysis which covered the years leading up to 2005. Five additional articles, published between 2005 and the end of 2008 have been added to their original analysis. Since the beginning of 2005, research has extended to new countries and cultures, and has covered a previously unexplored task type. New insights and opportunities are discussed. Previously, Zhang and Lowry (2008) found seven common failures in CSW-supported cultural research. This update analyzes five new papers against these seven failures and finds their recent research encouraging. The main contribution of this chapter is filling in the gaps that separate the current state of this particular area of research with the state of it as it was at the beginning of 2005 when the analysis of Zhang and Lowry was completed.

The off-shore software development companies in countries such as India use a global delivery model in which initial requirement analysis phase of software projects get executed at client locations to leverage frequent and deep interaction between user and developer teams. Subsequent phases such as design, coding and testing are completed at off-shore locations. Emerging trends indicate an increasing interest in off-shoring even requirements analysis phase using computer mediated communication. This chapter conducts an exploratory research study involving students from Management Development Institute (MDI), India and Marquette University (MU), U.S.A. to determine quality of such off-shored requirements analysis projects. The findings suggest that project quality of teams engaged in pure off-shore mode is comparable to that of teams engaged in collocated mode. However, the effect of controls such as user project monitoring on the quality of off-shored projects needs to be studied further.

The importance of consumer trust to the success of online businesses is well documented in the literature. Given the global nature of online transactions, an important question is whether trust and trust formation differ across cultures. This study compared Hong Kong and U.S. consumer trust in online businesses. Specifically, the study examined security and privacy risks related to the purchase of products as well as services. The results show that significant differences exist between consumers from the two countries regarding the perceived level of online business risks and the formation of trust via the transference process. These findings reiterate and underscore the significance of including national culture in studies of trust in e-commerce. The results also have potential implications for online businesses as well as third party certification and assurance services.

This chapter develops and tests a theoretical model that explains the impact of leadership style and interpersonal trust on the intention of information and knowledge workers in China to share their knowledge with their peers. All the hypotheses are supported, showing that both initiating structure and consideration have a significant effect on employees' intention to share knowledge through trust building: 28.2% of the variance in employees' intention to share knowledge is explained. The authors discuss the theoretical contributions of the chapter, identify future research opportunities, and highlight the implications for practicing managers.

By analyzing the survey data from 1211 firms across 14 industries and across various ownerships in Shanghai, the study examines factors that influence information technology (IT) usage in Chinese firms applying a technology – organization - environment framework and institutional theory. This study provides an in-depth investigation into the government's role in promoting Chinese firms' IT advancement. The finding suggests distinct paths where government actions affect firms' IT adoption and usage.

Preface

There is a story about someone from a poor developing country who was visiting a rich developed country. The visitor was amazed at the availability of technology and time saving devices. He was enthralled with the vast array of technology available to individuals in their daily work and personal lives. He was most impressed that almost everyone had a watch. After some contemplation he came to the realization that one of the major differences between his poor developing country and the rich developed country was that most everyone in his country may not have a watch but they had a lot of time. The moral of the story relates to determining if technology really provides what is truly required. It is necessary to decide on the appropriate use of technology.

Perhaps more importantly it is necessary to decide within a culture what the appropriate use of technology is. Indeed, when a cultural perspective is taken to investigating the use of technology two competing hypotheses emerge relating to convergence and divergence. (Ronen, 1986; Webber, 1969; and Yang, 1986).

The convergence hypothesis suggests cultures are becoming more similar because of the universality of technology. Further, education and the use of this common technology influences attitudes and values which underlie cultural characteristics. This convergence approach is reflected in a perspective which emphasizes technology and may be characterized by the idea behind the development of a global information systems profession with a standardized method for technology implementation.

The divergence hypothesis suggests cultures resist assimilation and strive to retain their distinctiveness. Thus, within a culture individuals will relate to one another through societal-based norms and there will be resistance to modify these norms through integration of other cultures. This approach is reflected in a perspective which emphasizes social interaction and may be characterized by the relationship established between information systems professionals and users; and their consequent culture-specific interpersonal interactions.

Beyond the convergence/divergence hypotheses dichotomy there exists a plethora of culture-related concepts which may be employed in a study of global information systems. These concepts may be viewed from various perspectives.

The management of global information systems necessitates a consideration for cultural aspects related to information system development, use, and maintenance. With respect to information systems development Leidner and Kayworth (2006) suggest that different cultures will perceive and approach the development of an information system in different ways. For instance some cultures may focus on the technical related issues while others might focus on personnel issues. Also, Leidner and Kayworth (2006) suggest use, depicted as adoption and diffusion will vary across cultures. As the use of information systems is inherently risky, risk-averse cultures will be more reticent at adopting and using new information systems.

General perspectives on technology vary across cultures. One view of an information system is that it consists of many related components which are organized to accomplish some task. These components include hardware, software, telecommunications, and people. Another view, commonly referred to as the socio technical perspective considers an information system to, in the first instance, be a social system, populated by personal interactions which are supported by technology. The discussion presented here is not meant to suggest which of the above two perspectives is more appropriate or correct. But, it is important that cross-cultural researchers realize that there are differing perspectives which should be taken into consideration when planning to conduct cross-cultural investigations.

The pervasive aspects of culture will impact how leadership and decision making is carried out within an organization. The Chief Information Officer (CIO) represents formal leadership and senior decision making of the information systems function within an organization. In his investigation of the CIO role Hunter (2007) determined that while the roles were similar, how they were operationalized varied across the cultures. He conducted in-depth interviews with CIOs in New Zealand, Taiwan, and the United States. The results of his investigation support earlier work (Hunter and Beck, 1996; Pearson and Chatterjee, 2003; and Pearson et al, 2003) which identified common roles that were carried out from different cultural perspectives. So, for instance, Hunter (2007) reported that, "...in Taiwan one of the CIOs indicated that the IT area provided leadership, expertise, and direction (expert) for the company. In New Zealand, however, the comment was more about how the IT area must attempt to work with (coach) the users." (Hunter, 2007:257).

A further area of investigation relates to cross-cultural research. As organizations expand internationally there is more interaction between individuals within the same company but from different cultures. This situation presents challenges requiring insights from a global perspective (Javidan and House, 2002). Researchers should be cognizant of the development of constructs to be employed in their research. Cross cultural research may take an emic or an etic approach (Pike, 1954; Berry, 1990; and Headland et al, 1990). An emic approach means that the constructs are developed within one specific culture and then their application is used to compare with another culture. The development of universal constructs based upon a number of different cultures is what is referred to as an etic approach. While the latter approach may represent a more multi-cultural approach to developing constructs, it requires a significant effort. Triandis (1972) has suggested a "pseudo-etic" approach which employs a limited number of cultures to attempt to develop a set of universal constructs. Early and Mosakowski (1995) have subsequently supported this development of quasi-universal constructs within the confines of a practical research project.

A common perspective offered for the comparison of culture is that proffered by Hofstede (Hofstede, 1980, 1983, and 1993; Hofstede and Bond, 1988; and Hofstede et al, 1990). This perspective suggests that culture will vary based upon the following dimensions:

- Individualism – Collectivism
  - Individualistic cultures emphasize independence, while Collectivist cultures emphasize mutual dependence and obligations.
- Power Distance
  - High Power Distance cultures accept an unequal distribution of power, while Low Power Distance cultures strive for an equal distribution.

- Uncertainty Avoidance
    - Strong Uncertainty Avoidance cultures have formal codes of behaviour, while Weak Uncertainty Avoidance cultures are less controlled.
- Masculinity – Femininity
    - Masculine cultures emphasize achievement, while Feminine cultures emphasize caring.

These dimensions will have a significant impact on the successful development and use of information systems in cross-cultural situations.

Yet another consideration resulting from globalization as companies expand internationally is the cause and affect dichotomy. That is, the implementation and use of an information system will change the business processes of an organization. As a consequence, the culture of the organization will change. The way business is carried out will be affected by the information system. From a broader perspective, the general implementation and use of many information systems across a significant number of organizations will affect culture in general. Alternatively, culture (both corporate and national) will affect how an information system is implemented and used. So, culture-based perspectives will come into play through the use of an information system. Thus, this cause and effect dichotomy of information system affecting culture and culture affecting the information system represents a rich area for research.

Conducting research in another culture will invariably involve another language. If the researcher is not bi-lingual it will be necessary for someone to speak in other than their first language or to involve an interpreter. The research participant may find it difficult to express their explanations of the topic being considered. Further, the interpreter may not be familiar with the topic content and may have difficulty accurately translating comments.

Beyond the consideration for language, conducting cross-cultural research involves more complex logistics than focusing on one geographical area. This raises the consideration for involving co-researchers. In turn, issues will emerge regarding researcher commitment and overall project co-ordination. Thus, it is important that all researchers involved in a cross-cultural investigation are made aware of and realize the benefits of both sharing the data gathered and completing the project. As with any group, but more importantly in cross-cultural research the concepts which support cohesion and team building will contribute to identifying and resolving any issues that may arise.

When gathering data from a research participant from another culture, the researcher must be aware of two generic categories of responses. First, the research participant may strive to provide the researcher with a response that is thought to be "right"; or what is thought by the research participant that the researcher wants to hear. So, the researcher must strive to impress upon the research participant that there is neither a right nor wrong answer and that the interpretive comments offered possess the real value to the interviewer. Second, the research participant may only want to focus on the "good news" and may not want to discuss aspects which may put the research participant of the representative culture in a negative light. In both cases extra time must be taken to develop a level of trust between the research participant and the researchers so that the research participant feels comfortable providing an honest and accurate response.

The field of information systems research incorporates both a technical perspective as well as social interactions. It is possible for those involved in the information systems profession to work with anyone, anywhere, especially as organizations expand their operations internationally. Individuals from different cultures will interact on a daily basis. It is thus incumbent upon the information systems researcher to remain cognizant of the aspects related to both the convergence and divergence hypotheses as well as the other aspects discussed above.

On a more positive note, new insights may be gained through conducting cross-cultural research. Rich data will be gathered reflecting cultural variability. Valuable perspectives will be gained on issues that transcend cultures. The similarities and differences from one culture to another will allow for researchers to compare and contrast research participant interpretations. These types of analyses will expand our understanding of information systems and their development and use in the global environment.

The research presented in the following chapters discusses many issues relating to information systems and takes many different perspectives on this intriguing topic.

GLOBAL THEMES

Chapter 1 by Hunter, Tan, and Tan discusses voluntary turnover factors of information systems professionals in New Zealand and Singapore. They identify universal factors that are culturally independent and those factors that are culturally sensitive. Understanding this variability will assist organizations to develop appropriate human resource policies. Trauth, Quesenberry, and Huang, in Chapter 2 conducted an analysis of career choices by women across multiple cultures including Australia, New Zealand, Ireland, and the United States. They identified themes relating to cultural influence on career choice attitudes. They propose that further research should take into consideration the variety of influences of career decisions by women and their varied responses. In Chapter 3, Lai identifies and evaluates the determinants of foreign affiliates' strategies relating to global information systems. The countries included in Lai's investigation include Canada, Japan, the United Kingdom, and the United States. They determined that global information systems strategy is more influenced by organizational and environmental factors than by industry or degree of globalization. These findings have implications for how assessing the complex relationship between head office and regional affiliates. Cong, Zhang, Chen, and Lai in Chapter 4 evaluate information technology offshore outsourcing. Their proposed model is based on a numerical analysis of a company in the United States that outsources software development to a firm in China. The model integrates risk assessment in the selection of an appropriate service provider. In Chapter 5, Schmidt, Johnston, Arnett, Chen, and Li assess awareness levels of computer security software between system users in China and the United States. They suggest the awareness level has not yet reached a critical mass sufficient for organizations to take proper precautions. Zhang, Gaskin, and Lowry in Chapter 6 examine the cultural impact on collaborative software systems. They rely upon many existing cross cultural publications. They provide a common taxonomy which they propose will support further necessary cross-cultural collaborative research. In Chapter 7, Nath, Sridhar, Adya, and Malik investigate requirements analysis for offshore projects. They compare results from investigations in India and the United States. They found that virtual teams develop their own control mechanisms and that the results are similar to face-to-face teams. Then, in Chapter 8, Greenberg, Wong-on-Wing, and Lui examine risks associated with products and services acquisition. They compared security and privacy aspects of consumer trust in online businesses in Hong Kong and the United States. They determined that there are cross-cultural differences in interpersonal trust which in turn will affect how e-commerce transactions are carried out.

REGIONAL THEMES

In this section the chapters focus on a specific location or small group of locations within a specific region. In Chapter 9, Huang, Davison, Liu, and Gu investigated the leadership style and interpersonal trust of knowledge workers in China. They determined that developing mutual trust will increase the knowledge sharing activity of knowledge workers. Cui and Zhang, in Chapter 10, examine the information technology adoption process in China and how government influences the process. They focus on firms in Shanghai. They conclude that government can support information technology adoption through the provision of information technology learning and practice information. Zhang, Sarker, and McCullough, in Chapter 11, focus on small to medium export firms in China to analyze their information technology capability. They determined that an innovative application of information technology will increase the small business' capability to perform globally. In Chapter 12, Chen and McQueen investigate small Chinese firms in New Zealand and their attitudes towards the adoption of e-commerce. They found that firms which used more advanced e-commerce possessed an innovative enthusiasm for e-commerce and were more tolerant of ambiguity and were more willing to take risks. Hsu and Wang, in Chapter 13, discuss the Taiwanese perspective on knowledge sharing policies and practices. They concluded that knowledge sharing policies and practices positively affect knowledge sharing effectiveness. In Chapter 14, Shih, Chiu, Chang, and Yen also focus on Taiwan in their investigation of the adoption of Radio Frequency Identification (RFID). They determined that this technology was adopted for operations and supply chain efficiency. Gerow, Galy, Thatcher, and Srite, in Chapter 15, investigate the use of information technology. They focus on the United States to assess acceptance and use of information technology while considering within culture variability. The results suggest that cultural values should be taken into account in order to respond to the resistance to the implementation of information technology. In Chapter 16, Shen, Zhao, and Huang investigate group decision making based upon a case related to the aftermath of Hurricane Katrina and its affect on New Orleans. The proposed approach provides valuable input mission-critical decision making tasks and group interaction. Finally, in Chapter 17, Quan focuses on firms in the United States to evaluate the link between e-business and performance. It was determined that superior firm performance occurred when the focus of assessments was on revenues rather than costs. Further, the results suggest that a long time horizon is necessary to determine an adequate evaluation of the investment in e-business.

REFERENCES

Berry, J. W. (1997). Impose-etics, Emics and Derived-etics: Their Conceptual and Operational Status in Cross-cultural Psychology. In T. N.Headland, K. L. Pike, & M. Harris (Eds.), *Emics and Etics: The Insider/Outsider Debate*. Newbury Park, CA: Sage Publications.

Early, P. C., & Mosakowski, E. (1995). A Framework for Understanding Experimental Research in an International and Intercultural Context. In B. J. Punnett, & O. Shenkaer (Eds.), *Handbook of International Management Research*. Blackwell Publishers.

Headland, T. N., Pike, K. L., & Harris, M. (1990). *Emics and Etics: The Insider/Outsider Debate*. Newbury Park, CA: Sage Publications.

Hofstede, G. (1980). *Culture's Consequences: International Differences in Work-Related Values*. Beverly Hills, CA: Sage Publications.

Hofstede, G. (1983). The Cultural Relativity of Organizational Practices and Theories. *Journal of International Business Studies*, 75-89.

Hofstede, G. (1993). Cultural Constraints in Management Theories. *Academy of Management Executive,7*(1), 81-94.

Hofstede, G. and M. H. Bond. (1988). "The Confucius Connection: From Cultural Roots to Economic Growth". *Organizational Dynamics*, Vol.16, No.4, pp.4-21.

Hofstede, G., Neuijen, B., Ohayv, D. D., & Sanders, G. (1990). Measuring Organizational Cultures: A Qualitative and Quantitative study Across Twenty Cases. *Administrative Science Quarterly*, 35,286-316.

Hunter, M. G. (2007). *Contemporary Chief Information Officers: Management Experiences*. Hershey, PA: IGI Publishing.

Hunter, M. G., & Beck, J. E. (1996). A Cross-cultural Comparison of 'Excellent' Systems Analysts. *Information Systems Journal, 6*, 261-281.

Javidan, M., & House, R. J. (2002). Leadership and Cultures around the World: Findings from GLOBE: An Introduction to the Special Issue. *Journal of World Business, 37*(1), 1-2.

Leidner, D. E., & Kayworth, T. (2006). A Review of Culture in Information Systems Research: Toward a Theory of Information Technology Culture Conflict. *MIS Quarterly, 30*(2), 357-399.

Pearson, C. A. L., & Chaterjee, S. R. (2003). Managerial Work Roles in Asia" An Empirical Study of Mintzberg's Role Formulation in Four Asian Countries. *Journal of Management Development, 22*(7/8), 694-707.

Pearson, C. A. L., Chatterjee, S. R., & Okachi, K. (2003). Managerial Work Role Perceptions in Japanese Organizations: An Empirical Study. *International Journal of Management, 20*(1), 101-108.

Pike, R. (1954). *Language in Relation to a United Theory of the Structure of Human Behavior*. Glendale, AZ, Summer Institute of Linguistics.

Ronen, S. (1986). *Comparative and Multinational Management*. New York: John Wiley.

Triandis, H. C. (1972). *Analysis of Subjective Culture*. New York: Wiley Interscience.

Webber, R. H. (1969). Convergence and Divergence. *Columbia Journal of World Business, 4*(3), 75-83.

Yang, K. S. (1986). Will Societal Modernization Eventually Eliminate Cross-Cultural Psychological Differences. In M. H. Bond (Ed.), *The Cross-Cultural Challenge to Social Psychology* (pp. 67-85). Newbury Park, CA: Sage.

Acknowledgment

On behalf of all the authors involved in the book we wish to express our gratitude for all the research participants who freely gave of their time, knowledge, and experience. Your involvement has made a significant contribution not only to this book but to our global information management field of study. To you we are indebted.

M. Gordon Hunter
Felix B. Tan
Editors
December 2008

Chapter 1
Voluntary Turnover of Information Systems Professionals:
A Cross-Cultural Investigation

M. Gordon Hunter
The University of Lethbridge, Canada

Felix B. Tan
Auckland University of Technology, New Zealand

Bernard C. Y. Tan
National University of Singapore, Singapore

ABSTRACT

This investigation examines the motivating factors associated with voluntary turnover decisions of information systems (IS) professionals within the context of two different cultures—Singapore and New Zealand. The narrative inquiry approach was employed to interview 35 IS professionals. Ninety-seven turnover episodes were identified, including 42 in Singapore and 55 in New Zealand. The findings indicate that there exist universal turnover factors which are culturally independent. However, there are also factors that are culturally sensitive, which should be considered by managers when dealing with an international workforce.

INTRODUCTION

The expansion of the global information economy and the consequent integration of information systems (IS) into core business functions have created issues regarding recruiting, retaining, and managing IS professionals (Segars & Hendrickson, 2000; Standbridge & Autrey, 2001). This situation is further exacerbated by companies attempting to identify and acquire the appropriate skills mix (Shah, Sterrett, & Wilmore, 2001). Also, the turnover rate for IS professionals exceeds that of other professionals, with estimates varying from 25& to 35% (Gionfriddo & Dhingra, 2000; Jiang & Klein, 2002). Voluntary turnover decisions can result in incurring significant expenses on the part of the company to find and replace necessary personnel.

Previous research into voluntary turnover decisions of IS professionals has focused upon a single culture (Madan, 2004; Theron, 2004). As business is increasingly conducted on an international basis, it seems appropriate to investigate the influence of national culture on the voluntary turnover decisions. The purpose of this investigation is to assess the impact that culture has on aspects of voluntary turnover of IS professionals. The turnover issues will be addressed from a cultural perspective. Thus, data are analyzed within the framework of Hofstede's (1991) cultural dimensions, which, while others exist (Hampden-Turner & Trompenaars, 2000; House, Hanges, Mansour, Dorfman, & Gupta, 2004; Trompenaars & Hampden-Turner, 1998) seemed the most appropriate for this research project.

The study reported here represents a contribution to knowledge as well as reporting on an innovative way of employing an accepted research approach and interview technique. The investigation of factors affecting job change, especially related to IS professionals, is relatively underresearched. The studies that are available relate to identifying either individual aspects, such as perspective (Crepeau, Crook, Goslar, & McMurtrey, 1992); attitude (Igbaria, Parasuraman, & Badawy, 1994); and personality (Wynekoop & Walz, 1998) or organizational factors such as environment (King & Sethi, 1998); organizational response (Benamati & Lederer, 2001); and skill sets (Feeney and Willcocks, 1998; Lee, Trauth, & Farwell, 1995). This study provides a better understanding of career-path impacts by combining individual and organizational factors through grounding the data in the interpretations of IS professionals and how they interact with their environment. Also, the studies listed previously used either special purpose or generic surveys as a research method. The research reported here employed narrative inquiry in an innovative way by conducting interviews (McCracken, 1998) based upon a research participant's résumé. This qualitative approach allows for an in-depth investigation of the subject and the gathering of rich biographical personal accounts of research participants' interpretations of specific career-path impacts.

This article is organized in the following manner. The next section presents a cultural perspective that provides the context to analyze the research results. Various turnover models are then reviewed to develop a research framework for this specific investigation. The next section presents a description of the adopted research method. The results are then presented, followed by a discussion of the findings. Finally, conclusions are drawn relative to the objectives of the project.

CULTURE PERSPECTIVE

Hofstede (1991) suggests that one social group is distinguished from another through the group's collective programming of the mind. Hofstede's (1991) cultural dimensions framework has been used extensively for multicountry comparisons (Ford, Connelly, & Meister, 2003). The framework has made a significant impact on international business studies (Chandy & Williams, 1994). Its contribution to theory development has been established by prior research (Carpenter & Fredrickson, 2001; Carter, 2000; Merritt, 2000; Moenaert & Souder, 1996; Png, Tan, & Wee, 2001). Further, support has been determined for the validity of the dimensions regarding cultural variability (Ronen & Shenkar, 1985; Shackleton & Ali, 1990). A number of IS investigations have also employed the dimensions for analyzing results (Earley, 1993; Hunter & Beck, 1996; Martinsons & Westwood, 1997; Straub, 1994; B. C. Y. Tan, Wei, Watson, Clapper, & McLean, 1998; B. C. Y. Tan, Wei, Watson, & Walczuch, 1998).

Hofstede's (1991) cultural dimensions are defined in the following Table 1.

Hofstede's (1991) cultural dimensions for Singapore and New Zealand are presented in Table 2.

In terms of Hofstede's (1991) cultural dimensions Singapore and New Zealand are different in some ways yet similar in others. The culture dimensions of Uncertainty Avoidance and Masculinity were not employed in the subsequent analysis of data obtained in this investigation.

- **Uncertainty avoidance**: Hofstede (1991) suggested this dimension relates to tolerance for ambiguous situations and a proclivity to avoid them. All turnover episodes involve uncertainly, and although different cultures may react differently, the focus of this investigation was more on the aspects of turnover episodes rather than how or whether turnover was approached.
- **Masculinity**: The index scores for this index are relatively similar (Singapore: 48; New Zealand: 58). In this case both cultures tend to emphasize achievement and assertiveness to the same degree.

Table 1. Hofstede's cultural dimensions

Cultural Dimension	Definition
Power Distance	The extent to which individuals expect and accept the distribution of power. High power distance cultures expect and accept unequal distribution of power. Low power distance cultures strive for an equal distribution of power.
Individualism-Collectivism	The extent to which individuals relate to each other. In individualistic cultures members emphasize independence with loose ties between individuals. Thus, members value personal time, decisions, and accomplishments. In collectivistic cultures, members emphasize mutual dependence and obligations. Thus, members tend to form into strong cohesive groups, taking actions and making decisions that support the well-being of the group.
Uncertainty Avoidance	The extent to which individuals deal with uncertainty. In strong uncertainty avoidance cultures, formal rules and regulations will be established. In weak uncertainty avoidance cultures, less control will exist and members will tend to be characterized by risk taking.
Masculinity	The extent to which individuals are assertive and competitive. Masculine cultures emphasize achievement focusing on tasks. Feminine cultures emphasize caring on interpersonal issues

Note. Adapted from Hofstede (1991)

Table 2. Hofstede's cultural dimension values: Singapore and New Zealand

Country	Power Distance Index (PDI)	Individualism Index (IDV)	Uncertainty Avoidance Index (UAI)	Masculinity Index (MAS)
Singapore	74	20	8	48
New Zealand	22	79	49	58
Mean Score (all countries)	57	43	65	49
Highest Score (all countries)	104	91	112	95
Lowest Score (all countries	11	6	8	5
Number of countries	53	53	53	53

The two cultures of Singapore and New Zealand are different based upon Hofstede's (1991) dimensions of Power Distance and Individualism.

- **Power distance**: Singapore's high Power Distance index of 74 indicates a culture that is relatively comfortable with unequal distribution of power. In New Zealand, however, a low Power Distance index of 22 suggests a preference for equal distribution of power among individual members of the culture.
- **Individualism**: In this case, Singapore's low Individualism index of 20 suggests a collectivist approach to working with other members of the culture. In New Zealand, a high Individualism index of 79 indicates members of the culture are expected to act independently.

Thus, the two cultures vary more significantly on the two dimensions of Power Distance and Individualism. These two dimensions will be employed later to analyze the results of the gathered interview data regarding voluntary turnover decisions of IS professionals from both cultures.

VOLUNTARY TURNOVER MODELS

Voluntary turnover, defined as "a conscious and deliberate willingness to leave the organization" (Tett & Meyer, 1993), has been the subject of considerable research and IS scholars in particular have long been interested in the turnover of IS professionals. Much of the main voluntary turnover literature is summarized in Table 3, which highlights the propositions of the leading theories carried out in the field of voluntary turnover and provides a discussion of the difference among them. The prime focus of all these empirical research has been to elaborate the antecedents of turnover, while theoretical efforts have largely been directed toward integrating the mass of findings into a model of turnover behaviour.

Most of these theories examine intent to turnover from an intra-individual perspective (Ang & Slaughter, 2004). Most of these turnover models have included job dissatisfaction as a primary catalyst for turnover (e.g., Rosse & Hulin, 1985). Many studies have focused on variations of Mobley's (1977) intermediate linkage model, which describes the decision steps between job dissatisfaction and turnover, including a search for and comparison with job alternatives (e.g., Hom et al., 1992). Several models have extended the breadth of antecedents beyond job satisfaction and job alternatives to include such aspects as organizational commitment (e.g., Bluedorn, 1982; Steers and Mowday, 1981); anticipated future satisfaction with the current organization (e.g., Forrest, Cummings, & Johnson, 1977; Mobley, Griffeth, Hand, & Meglino, 1979); and various antecedents of job satisfaction and perceived alternatives (e.g., Price & Mueller, 1981). Researchers have also recognized multiple decision-making paths leading to turnover (e.g., Steers and Mowday, 1981). In the theoretical model most employed to date, Lee and Mitchell (1994) integrated intermediate linkage models with image theory decision-making models. Besides traditional paths from job dissatisfaction, they proposed a process of matching or screening the current or an alternative job. In addition, actual turnover is also strongly influenced by internal labour market attributes such as promotability, wage levels, skills demand, and external labour market attributes such as mobility and availability of jobs (Kirschenbaum & Mano-Negrin, 1999; Trevor, 2001).

The widely acknowledged theories gleaned from the above discussion of voluntary turnover models indicate three general categories including *individual, organizational*, and *environmental* factors. The validity of each of the constituent factors has been substantiated in past studies on antecedents of turnover motivations for IS professionals (Madan, 2004; Theron, 2004) and

Table 3. Synthesis of main voluntary turnover literature

AUTHORS	CONTRIBUTIONS
March & Simon (1958)	• Organizational Equilibrium • Intentionally rational decision-making process • Main motivation factors are perceived alternatives and job satisfaction • Job satisfaction a multifaceted function of job attitudes like monetary rewards, types of supervision, autonomy, recognition
Mobley (1977)	• Sequential model • Job dissatisfaction → Intentions to quit → Evaluation of alternatives → Comparison → Quit • Included labour, organizational, job and personal variables • Introduction of micro-economic factors and expected utility of employee
Price & Mueller (1981)	• Job satisfaction shaped by pay, integration, instrumental and formal communication, and centralizations • Availability of alternative employment moderates relationship between satisfaction and turnover • Repetitive work reduces satisfaction and increases intention to stay
Steers & Mowday (1981)	• Extension to previous sequential model: Expectations met at work influence responses to job attitudes (job satisfaction, organizational commitment, and job involvement). • Significance of nonwork influences (e.g., family and personality) • Withdrawal behaviour/cognitions • Sequence differing across employees
Hulin, Roznowski, & Hachiya **(1985)**	• New perspective on effects of microeconomic factors • Multiple withdrawal paths: Alternative reactions to dissatisfaction (turnover, absenteeism, transfer, etc.) • Extra-work alternatives • Process of turnover differing across populations and types of employees
Hom, Caranikas-Walker, Prussia, & Griffeth **(1992)**	• Cost-benefit analysis in a quitting scenario • Affect of micro-economic moderators like unemployment rate, turnover base rates, types of population, etc. • Quitting without assured alternative or job search.
Lee & Mitchell (1994)	• Instinctual model based upon image theory (Beach, 1990) • Shock/event jarring assessment of current employment situation • Four different decision paths subjective to varying interpretations of work, levels of satisfaction, and availability of alternatives • Psychological processes • Decision paths unfold at different speeds, based on amount of mental deliberation

each will be further elaborated upon in the following section.

CATEGORIES OF VOLUNTARY TURNOVER FACTORS

Individual Level Factors

At the individual job level, voluntary turnover factors consists of *job satisfaction* and *reward and recognition.*

March and Simon (1958) described perceived desirability of movement as being primarily determined by job satisfaction. Lower levels of job satisfaction occur when people begin to feel, over time, that their jobs no longer provide the intellectual, emotional, or financial benefits they desire. In terms of job satisfaction, three main constituent variables are proposed, based loosely upon the job characteristics model by Fried and Ferris (1987): *job scope, autonomy,* and *skill variety.*

Job scope refers to the desire for interesting and challenging work that allows people to feel content and worthwhile. It comprises both task significance and task identity. *Task significance* is the degree to which a job has substantial impact on the organization and/or larger society, giving employees pride in what they have accomplished. *Task identity* is the degree to which a job requires completion of a whole or identifiable piece of work that fits into the whole product or service. Recognizable job scopes that are not just indistinguishable along the work chain but instead form a significant and inevitable component result in higher levels of job satisfaction (Levin & Rosse, 2001). The also suggest that IS professionals in general need a challenging and intellectually stimulating scope of work; desire to make a difference for others; want to see the value of their work; and like to be involved in the design of their work, so they feel part of what is happening. Research has shown that a more complex task would tend to induce higher cohesiveness among individualists than collectivists, as difficult tasks lead team members to unite together more strongly as a group (Tesluk & Mathieu, 1999), especially during critical periods. In line with Wagner's (1995) argument, because collectivists already exhibit a strong predisposition to work together as a group and have a more favorable perception of the working relationship with one another in an *in-group*, the effect of increased job complexity, although positive, is less prominent than for individualists. In contrast, individualists work better together when they encounter a difficult job and need to solve the problem. This shows that a way for managers to motivate individualistic employees and teams would be to assign them challenging work.

Autonomy is the feeling of freedom within one's job and the ability to make one's own choices about the work without the need for consultation with one's superiors. It is also linked to feelings of independence and responsibility. The negative relationship between job autonomy and turnover has been verified by Porter and Steers (1973) in their provision of studies that found leavers of a job reporting significantly lesser job autonomy than those who stayed (Ross & Zander, 1957). IS professionals tend to yearn for enough responsibility and authority, with opportunities to exhibit leadership and have direct accountability. Similarly, the finding that collectivists are less affected than individualists by an increase in job autonomy lends support to the reasoning that autonomy is a more salient and valued work attribute for the latter type than the former, who are more concerned with values relating to security and social relationships (Ronen, 1994; Triandis, 1995). Highly individualist people value freedom, personal time, self-sufficiency, and control over their own lives (Hofstede, 1991). Thus, individualists can also be assumed to favour autonomous work, since it offers them a feeling of freedom within one's job and the ability to make one's own choices about the work. Collectivists will adjust less well to the demands of increased autonomy as compared to individualists. When making decisions, collective concerns prevail over personal views (Hofstede, 1991). Driven by a strong sense of responsibility to the group and willingness to sacrifice themselves for others, they are more likely to go beyond their regular duties to help other colleagues when required instead of working independently. In addition, as suggested by prior researchers (Eylon & Au, 1999; Robert, Probst, Martocchio, Drasgow, & Lawler, 2000), power distance should affect the personal value of equal power sharing and hence the willingness of employees to accept and exercise discretionary power. Low power distance cultures expect relatively equal power sharing, limited dependence of subordinates on supervisors, and preference for employees being personally involved in decisions affecting their work. They would be envisaged to enjoy working without the need for consultation with one's superiors. Hence, decentralization is popular, and it might be argued that employees in such low power distance cultures will value autonomy to work independently with direct accountability to a greater extent as compared to employees in high power distance cultures.

Skill variety refers to the need to use different skills and talents to complete a variety of work activities. IS professionals tend to prefer opportunities to pick up new skills and dislike maintenance and routine operations. A negative relationship between skill variety and turnover has been determined by Porter and Steers (1973). Employees with a collectivistic inclination tend to harmonious relationships within the work group and work on the basis of trust. Being able to fully utilize skills and abilities on the job may be present as evidence of trust. Hence, we speculate that employees in collectivistic societies will value jobs with the need to the use of different skills and talents to complete a variety of work activities rather than sheer maintenance and routine operations.

Reward and recognition refers to competitive monetary compensation, bonuses, profit sharing, stock options, time off, and other perks of the job and has been identified as a factor shaping job satisfaction (Price & Mueller, 1981). Expressed recognition of a job well done in the form of remuneration and benefits serves to give an employee a sense of satisfaction, equity, and motivation for future job assignments. If people do not feel important or recognized for their efforts, they are not motivated to stay. The relationship between reward and recognition and turnover will be a negative one. In individualistic cultures, the employer-employee relationship is a business relationship, and the employee is committed to the organization to the extent that the individual feels that it is to his or her advantage (Allen, Miller, & Nath, 1988; Redding, Norman, & Schlander, 1994). The focus on the self creates a preference for autonomy and individual-based reward mechanisms, and people look primarily after their own interests, needs, and preferences. There is also a more calculative relationship to the firm, based upon an evaluation of what a person contributes and what is received in return (Hofstede, 1980). However, in a collectivistic society, people view their actions as an important contribution to their group's well-being, and they gain satisfaction and feelings of accomplishment from group outcomes. Moreover, more high power distance cultures allocate rewards differentially, on the basis of equity and performance inputs, whereas more low power distance cultures prefer equality to equity. A preference for equality in more low power distance cultures is likely to lead to employees in these cultures valuing remuneration and benefits to a larger extent and to a more equal distribution of power and wealth. Therefore, we can propose that cultures with low power distances that are highly individualistic will seek remuneration and job benefits to a greater extent, and such reward and recognition factors that incite turnover intentions will become more important.

Organizational Level Factors

At the organizational level, voluntary turnover factors include the *workplace environment* and *career commitment.*

Workplace environment refers to interactions between fellow employees and employers, respectively. Power distance is the extent to which society accepts the fact that power in institutions and organizations is distributed unequally. In a high power distance society, subordinates defer to superiors and rarely question their authority. Corporations in countries with high power distance tend to be hierarchical, with an unequal distribution of power and more authoritarian management practices (Jaeger, 1986). They are more centralized, and a few individuals make the majority of the decisions. Bochner and Hesketh (1994) also noted that individuals from high power distance countries tended to be more task than people oriented, because they were used to their managers initiating strategies and telling them what to do rather than asking them for their views. In low power distance societies, subordinates and superiors consider each other as essentially equal. The roles of supervisor and subordinate are flexible and change rapidly, so that your supervisor on one project may work along side you on another project. Moreover, countries with low power distance believe that everyone has basically the same rights, and people prefer being involved in decisions. Those with large power distance have an unequal distribution of rights, with those in power controlling the rights of the ordinary people. In individualistic cultures, the self is construed as independent—a unique entity, whose behaviour is organized primarily by reference to the individual's own thoughts, feelings, and actions rather than by reference to others (Markus & Kitayama, 1991). Employees focus less on social and interpersonal relations and will not really place good peer group relations as a high priority in a workplace environment. In a job, tasks prevail over relationships between friends and colleagues. On the other hand, in collectivistic cultures, the self is construed to be interdependent. Interdependence entails seeing oneself as part of an encompassing social relationship and recognizing that one's behaviour is contingent on what the individual perceives to be the thoughts, feelings, and actions of the important others, namely the in-group (Markus & Kitayama, 1991). Collectivists are integrated into strong cohesive in-groups, which consist of a group of people that shares a common characteristic or is bounded by a certain value system that is unique within the group; it is a group of people about whose welfare one is concerned, with whom one is willing to cooperate without demanding equitable returns, and the separation from whom leads to discomfort or even pain (Hofstede, 1991). Workplace environment consists of *peer-group relations* and *management relations.*

Peer-group relations refers to the relationship between colleagues and friends at the workplace. Klaus, LeRouge, and Blanton (2003) noted that employees with close friends at work are more inclined to stay with the organization. Chang (2002) proposed that social support (i.e., colleagues and supervisor) is positively related to job satisfaction and negatively associated to turnover intentions and that the relationship between social support and turnover intentions is moderated by an employee's social affiliation needs. Lack of support from coworkers to get work done also adds to office politics and poor peer-group relations. This is important in the context of IS professionals, because much of the work is in the form of projects requiring interactions with multiple team members.

Management relations refer to the ease with which employees have opportunities to gain mentor support for ideas, opinions, and values. Limited interaction with supervisors, frustration with many rules and regulations, and unfair treatment by supervisors may also cause employees to feel stifled and dissatisfied with the workplace environment. This may lead to a detachment from work assignments and may progressively erode an employee's motivation to perform well.

Career commitment relates to an individual's long-term association with his or her profession (Morrow, 1993). High career committed individuals are more motivated when their expectations are satisfied by the organization and are thus less likely to quit. Therefore, a negative relationship can be expected between career commitment factors and turnover. The basic motive structure of individualists reflects their internal beliefs and capacities, including the ability to effect change and to withstand social pressure (Triandis, 1995). As Triandis (1995) suggests, individualists always look for the best "deal" they can get, and they tend to emphasize the advantages and disadvantages of a particular situation with a goal of maximizing self-interest (Ting-Toomey, 1994). Individualists maintain relationships as long as they are in line with the individual's preferences and cost-benefit analyses, and they drop out of groups when personal and group goals become incompatible (Triandis, McCusker, & Hui, 1990). This likelihood to enjoy freedom of choice implies a higher degree of consciousness concerning their current job satisfaction and alternatives. An empirical study by Aycan and Fikret-Pasa (2003) showed that increased individualism is also reflected in the job-selection criteria, with employment settings that promote their career advancement being favoured. In highly collectivistic societies, employees would often view their organization as the entity that binds the group together. Employer-employee relationships as moral terms like a family link and hiring and promotion decisions take employees' in-group into account (Hofstede, 1991). They are therefore expected to be loyal and committed to the organization, and in return they hope to be looked after by the firm and have future opportunities afforded them. Lack of such potential opportunities would be presumed to more adversely affect collectivists as they expect this assurance of continuity and security at work and confidence in progressing within the firm. Such form of mutual cooperation is however unlikely in individualistic societies. In addition, employees with collectivistic inclinations tend to value the collective welfare, harmonious relationships within the work group, and fully utilizing skills and abilities on the job. Welfare in the form of training opportunities and good physical working conditions may be more attractive to such cultures, and a lack of them will be more likely to cause them to turnover. Career commitment consists of *career progression, future opportunities within the firm,* and *training opportunities.*

Career progression relates to accessing higher levels of responsibility and authority. This tends to be highly desired by IS professionals given their marketability and job skills. It is possible within the IS profession to progress both technically and managerially.

Future opportunities within the firm is the basis of assurance of continuity and security at work and confidence in progressing with the firm. Any indication about the future company plans will concern employees.

The need for *training opportunities* for the IS professional is particularly applicable and important to the IT industry. Rapid technological advances inevitably means that today's IT professionals must constantly update and educate themselves of the newest technology to ensure their employability and future marketability, for it is a certainty that their technological skills today will be obsolete tomorrow. A study by Agarwal, Ferratt, Moore, and Brown (1999) recognized that IT professionals thrive on technical opportunity, challenge, and growth. IT employees want to be frequently in contact with a range of new technologies and training opportunities to stay constantly updated and challenged so as to improve their capacity to perform a wide variety of jobs.

Environmental Level Factors

At the environmental level, factors that initiate turnover intentions are mainly *non-work factors,* which relate to *family/personal concerns.* Quality-of-life issues are becoming increasingly important to employees in today's fast-paced, active world. A substantial percentage of employees who quit their jobs due to non-work factors such as family and personal reasons or responsibilities (Porter & Steers, 1973) like marriage, pregnancy, an inheritance, family migration, pursuit of higher education, interests, and retirement. In an individualistic culture, people are particular about having a right to a private life and opinion and being independent from organizations (Hofstede, 1980). People in such cultures value freedom, personal time, self-sufficiency, and control over their own lives. Therefore, individualistic cultures are more likely to value their personal life over their work. In highly collectivistic national cultures, individuals look after an extended network or clan and are more willing to subsume their own interests to the needs of the collective. These societies are more tightly integrated and individuals are more embedded in their respective groups. In such societies, there is a stronger sense of personal obligation and we expect increased work centrality, which is the relative importance of work in relation to other areas in an individual's life.

METHOD

The method of narrative inquiry was employed to investigate how IS professionals make decisions for voluntary turnover and the factors which are taken into consideration given a set of circumstances. According to Bruner (1990), the narrative approach to conducting research involves the documenting and analyzing of individuals' stories about or personal accounts of a specific domain of discourse that are contextually rich and temporally bounded. The term *contextually rich and temporally bounded* relates to personal accounts of experiences that are vividly remembered and structured in a sequence with a beginning and an end. This structure is provided in this article through the adoption of McCracken's (1988) *long interview* technique and by employing the résumé as a guide to emphasize the sequence of the story. This approach is based on the premise that the narrative can be a powerful way to locate and understand their beliefs, concerns, values, experiences, and learning. By uncovering, shaping, and reflecting upon these professionals' stories of their career, we hope to illuminate some of the key issues and dilemmas associated with voluntary turnover. This method implies qualitative research, which assists researchers in their attempt to understand people and their social and cultural context. Research employing the narrative approach (Vendelo, 1998) has suggested that the sequence of the story elements (Bruner, 1990) contribute to the appropriateness of the method. Moreover, Swap, Leonard, Shields, and Abrams (2001) suggests that relating stories of personal experiences would be more memorable, be given more weight and be more likely to guide behaviour. Czarniawska-Joerges (1995) also further supports the importance of a sequential account when employing a narrative research approach.

Interviews were conducted with 17 Singapore-based and 18 New Zealand-based research participants who have been involved in the IS profession for some time and have been through at least one incident of voluntary turnover in their careers so far. During the interview, they were requested to tell their own story regarding events that lead to decisions to seek another position. They were also to describe any potential interventions the organizations could have used to prevent them from leaving their organizations. Subsequently, each turnover episode of such a decision to switch job formed one unit of analysis.

This research employed an innovative approach to conducting interviews using McCracken's (1988) long interview technique, based upon a research participant's résumé. Research participants were at various stages of their careers and the interviews focused on those aspects surrounding job changes. This technique allows research participants to reflect upon their careers in a relatively unbiased and free-flowing manner.

Individual résumés helped guide the interview, document the narratives and ground the discussion in the IS professionals' personal experiences (F. B. Tan & Hunter, 2003). The résumé was employed to assist research participants to reflect upon their experiences, especially those aspects surrounding job changes and report these experiences in a sequential account of events as they transpired throughout their careers. This approach has been used in previous IS research (Young, 2000). The résumé is readily available and an untapped source of data (Dex, 1991) as well as acting as a milestone reference to assist human memory recall (Baker, 1991). This process of recall is further supported by the fact that with episodic memory, relative important events are most readily remembered (Tulving, 1972). This approach allows for an in-depth investigation of the subject and the gathering of rich biographical personal accounts of research participants' interpretations of specific career-path impacts. These reflective biographies were gathered and analyzed regarding what the research participant considers to be important events that have led to moving from one employment position to another. These results represent a more thorough understanding of the turnover events within an individual's career path.

ANALYSIS OF INTERVIEWS TRANSCRIPTS

While analysis was an ongoing process, beginning during the course of gathering data, it formally begins by organizing the data. The interviews were tape recorded and later transcribed. The transcripts were mailed back to the respective interviewees for review. On approval, manual analysis of the interviews followed. Based upon review and thorough examination of the transcripts, the coded information was formulated by case analysis for each turnover episode. During coding, information was edited, redundancies were sorted out, and parts were fitted together. Noteworthy phrases and sentences were highlighted, and passages that seemed conceptually linked were grouped. The case data included background information, description of the settings, key events and processes involved, and observational issues supported by interview quotes.

The narrative analyses involved the identification of sequences and contexts. The case records for each interviewee were organized chronologically. Thompson (1997) suggested that interpretation of narratives is iterative and includes the two stages: understanding of each narratives and identifying emerging themes from amongst a number of narratives. Thus, data analysis involved searching of emerging themes first within an interview and then across a series of interviews—apart from studying each case study as an idiosyncratic manifestation, patterns, themes and commonalities across these cases were noted. Interpretation, which followed coding, entailed attaching significance to the observed patterns, offering explanations, drawing conclusions, extrapolating lessons, making inferences, building linkages, and dealing with data irregularities. This form of inductive analysis elucidated the voluminous interview transcripts. The process involved moving back and forth between emergent patterns in the data and the coded data to ensure validity and reliability, which resulted in a full descriptive analysis.

For the Singapore data set, 17 interviews lasting approximately 1 to 1 1/2 hours each were conducted, with all the interviewees having established their careers in Singapore. The interviewees consisted of 2 females and 15 males, with average age of 42.8 years. With regards to education, 4 obtained a bachelor's degree, 11 obtained masters' degrees, and 2 obtained a doctorate. Six of the interviewees obtained a master's in business administration after having completed undergraduate studies in engineering/computer-science stream. Overall, experience as an IS professional, average 18.1 years, and 2.5 turnover episodes per participant.

For the New Zealand data set, 18 interviews lasting approximately 1 to 1 1/2 hours each were conducted, with all the interviewees having established their careers in New Zealand. The interviewees consisted of 4 females and 14 males, with average age being 40.9 years. With regard to education, 4 of them completed secondary school, 7 obtained a bachelor's degree, and 6 obtained a master's degree. Overall, experience as an IS professional averaged 13.9 years and 3.1 turnover episodes per participant.

The results of the research are summarized in Table 4, which states the voluntary turnover factors along with the respective turnover episode numbers for each culture. Note that a turnover episode may include more than one constituent variable. That is, during the discussion of a voluntary turnover decision, multiple themes may have emerged, which were directly related to a constituent variable.

The common factors across all the turnover episodes were compiled for each country. The culture having the larger number of the turnover episodes for a particular turnover factor can be assumed to be the culture where IS professionals are affected or impacted to a greater extent by that factor. Constituent variables were considered different if the count of episodes was four or greater. This difference in frequency of the occurrences of the identified reasons among the coded turnover instances in the different cultures may be translated into the fact that these primary reasons for turnover are being moderated by either or both of the two specific cultural characteristics predominant in that country and studied in this research (i.e., power distance and/or individualism-collectivism).

DISCUSSION

Each of the 10 variables is reviewed in the following sections, relative to the number of turnover episodes and also whether Hofstede's (1980, 1991) cultural dimensions can provide support for a discussion of the comparison between the results obtained for Singapore and New Zealand.

Job Satisfaction

As evident from the results, the number of turnover episodes for the constituent variables of job satisfaction was more or less similar in Singapore and New Zealand, even though the skill variety numbers were on the verge of being considered "different." It is possible that this is due to the universal nature of the IT profession and also increasing entrepreneurship climate in Singapore.

The extremely competitive employment scene has IS professionals continually striving to keep up with the changing scope of technologies. The thrill of being continuously exposed to and challenged with new projects in varying fields of application keeps them motivated. Because the IS industry changes constantly, IS professionals feel satisfied and motivated when they are provided with ample opportunities to constantly update and upgrade themselves of the newest technological developments. Moreover, for almost all IS professionals, the main motivation to continue with a firm lies in the scope of work offering sufficient responsibility and getting acknowledged through involvement with new strategic projects which are vital to the organization. IS professionals are seen to enjoy leadership positions with direct accountability. The autonomy and freedom to be able to experiment with technology with a focused aim and to make decisions without having to go through a hierarchy to seek permissions is desirable.

Many of the turnover episodes that were due to a desire for greater job autonomy in Singapore were a result of joining a startup, moving into freelancing, or the setting up of a new department. In recent years, Singapore has promoted entrepreneurship and encouraged people to be innovative and improve the ability of firms to develop new ideas and businesses, tap new export markets, and broaden the economic base (Chew & Chew, 2001). IS professionals in Singapore are found to have strong desires to engage in jobs with greater responsibilities, authority, and entrepreneurship in spite of their perceived cultural traits.

Remuneration and Benefits

Remunerations and benefits were equally important to both cultures. They were neither seen as the primary motivator nor were they significantly more valued in either culture. Financial incentives such as pay, pension, health coverage, profit-sharing fringe benefits, and perks including cars and houses were stated as the added advantages in most of the turnover episodes; disincentives such as drop in current pay and unfair compensation schemes were push factors from former jobs.

A plausible reason for this finding could be that monetary incentives are more of a factor moderated by the career stages of IS professionals than is culture. Worth noting is the relatively more frequent occurrence of this factor among fresh graduates and professionals in the early stages of their career in both cultures. Therefore, in recruiting and retaining fresh talent in their early career phases, remuneration must be at par or above the competitive level for the area and industry to retain staff. Though, as stated earlier,

Table 4. Turnover episodes

TURNOVER FACTORS	CONSTITUENT VARIABLES	TURNOVER EPISODES		RESULTS
		Singapore	New Zealand	
Job Satisfaction	Job scope	1, 5, 6, 8, 9, 11, 13, 16, 18, 19, 22, 24, 25, 26, 29, 30, 33, 34, 35, 36, 37, 42 Total = 22	3, 5, 6, 7, 11, 14, 15, 16, 17, 18, 23, 30, 31, 32, 39, 43, 44, 45, 50, 52 Total = 20	Same
	Autonomy	1, 3, 4, 5, 8, 10, 15, 16, 27, 37 Total = 10	7, 19, 20, 28, 31, 39, 50, 53 Total = 8	Same
	Skill variety	4, 9, 10, 17, 19, 22, 24, 33, 37 Total = 9	7, 10, 18, 25, 38, 51 Total = 6	Same
Reward and Recognition	Remuneration and benefits	4, 7, 14, 18, 23, 30, 31, 32 Total = 8	1, 2, 17, 29, 47, 52, 55 Total = 7	Same
Workplace Environment	Peer-group relations	12, 15, 17, 21, 26, 41 Total = 6	9, 29 Total = 2	Different
	Management relations	4, 9, 15, 18, 23, 27, 36 Total = 7	5, 7, 14, 16, 25, 28, 29, 34, 35, 48, 49, 50, 54 Total = 13	Different
Career Commitment	Career progression	1, 3, 4, 7, 8, 10, 20, 21, 24, 25, 26, 28, 31, 33, 36, 38, 39 Total = 17	1, 3, 4, 7, 8, 11, 15, 16, 17, 18, 19, 20, 25, 35, 38, 39, 40, 43, 44, 51, 53 Total = 21	Different
	Future opportunities within the firm	2, 3, 4, 7, 10, 14, 16, 17, 20, 22, 24, 32, 40 Total = 13	1, 2, 3, 6, 10, 14, 21, 26, 29, 32, 34, 41 Total = 12	Same
	Training opportunities	7, 23 Total = 2	7, 10, 32 Total = 3	Same
Non-Work Factors	Family / personal concerns	1, 7, 8, 9, 21, 30 Total = 6	8, 11, 12, 19, 22, 24, 32, 33, 34, 37, 42, 44, 45, 46, 47, 49, 51, 52 Total = 18	Different

financial compensation does not account for primary reasons for turnover, nor is it usually the sole factor for any particular turnover episode. Thus, it may also be important to look at remuneration and benefits not as a standalone factor but also in tandem with other turnover factors.

Peer-Group Relations

Peer-group relations were a turnover factor that occurred more frequently in Singapore, a collectivistic culture. Most of the cases in the individualistic culture such as New Zealand did not really see peer-group relations as a strong reason for turnover. In the case of a collectivistic culture such as Singapore, a majority of turnover reasons were attributed to office politics as a push factor, while the remaining were attracted to favourable working relationships, common beliefs within the team, and collaborative teamwork at the workplace.

With regard to managerial implications, one suggestion would be for companies in more collectivistic cultures to foster better working relationships between fellow colleagues. Collectivists may benefit most from bonding sessions outside of work in the form of retreats, get-togethers, and training workshops, which will possibly help to build harmonious relationships with colleagues and thus enhance teamwork. Management support for employees and clear and fair guidelines in work attitudes, promotions, and compensation may also help to alleviate the problem of office politics.

Management Relations

Almost all of the turnover episodes from New Zealand, a low power distance culture, described poor management relations as a factor for quitting their jobs, as IS workers there expect relatively equal power sharing, believe that everyone has basically the same rights, and prefer being involved in decisions. Some of the issues faced with management related to interpersonal conflicts, personality and working-style clashes, disagreeable management ethics and policies, hierarchal management structure, internal politics required to move up in a career, sexual harassment and gender discrimination, unsupportive bosses, not listening to employees recommendations or advice, and poor people management.

Although it is important for all organizations, regardless of country, to improve their management styles for optimal performance, results from this study suggest that it becomes imperative for those within a workforce with a predominantly low power distance culture to look into cultivating good relations with employees. Only in this way can a better fit between the employee's personal values and the organization's culture lead to job satisfaction and employee retention. Therefore, management could place more emphasis on feedback from staff, taking into account their views not just as a formality but also with the intention to act on it and improve work processes if appropriate. A flat management structure with greater access to supervisors by subordinates will open the door to differences in working styles and policies. In this way, any problems faced can be discussed and the opportunity for mentor support will be highly valued by employees in low power distance cultures, as they prefer to resolve conflicts through personal networks and coalitions. If necessary, transferring employees to other departments, if there are differences or personal conflicts with their supervisors, could be done. Rules and regulations could also be less authoritative and instead be flexible and open to changes decided upon on consensus by both management and staff.

Career Progression

In a more individualistic culture like New Zealand, it is more likely turnover would result from a lack of career progression. The high marketability of IS professionals give them the liberty to be opportunistic and accept better offers that come their way. Unlike conventional practices, their careers are no longer reliant on the company performance. Instead, IS professionals may aggressively seek to create a sense of security, not by commitment to a single organization but by managing their careers to show continuous advancement and the acquisition of a set of highly refined job skills. These highly experienced professionals take the obvious career move toward more managerial roles with their focus changing from technical to business, as management roles provide the right advancement opportunities giving higher level of responsibility and authority. Such roles fulfill the aspirations of the professionals to have a say in critical business decisions in relation to integrated technology, to leverage off their much-valued knowledge in the field which they have gathered over the years.

Senior management in such individualistic cultures should continue providing expanded and flexible opportunities for those seeking mobility, understand the seriousness of the problems these employees face, increase utilization of individuals within their current jobs, enhance training and continue education programs, and broaden the rewards system so as allow their employees to achieve their fullest potential. In order to retain the best IS employees and promote those who are most promising, organizational policies should be directed towards provision of greater career opportunities possibly by establishing dual career paths, both managerial and technical, to expand the career options of IS professionals. Knowing opportunities in the current position, what jobs might be of future interest, suitability of the employee for these jobs, and the organization's willingness to work with the employee during a career planning process are pivotal to a successful human resource management system within the IS environment. Employees should also have the opportunity to discuss their needs and values with their bosses regularly to develop more suitable assignments and setting meaningful career goals. Such thought and effort within the organizations in charting out a progressive career path for IS employees, arranging periodic performance appraisal and acknowledging good work through due promotions should be facilitated. Given that individualists regard their career development as vital to a greater extent, a lack of confidence and failure by the employing firm to commit to an employee's career progress often result in turnover.

Future Opportunities within the Firm and Training Opportunities

The results for these two turnover variables suggest that IS professionals in general, regardless of nationality or culture, are just as likely to quit because of a lack of future opportunities within the firm or training opportunities, indicating the probable universal nature of this phenomenon across cultures. Although Singapore, a collectivistic country, is expected to value these opportunities more, a large number of turnover episodes in New Zealand, an individualistic country, indicated these reasons as well. Perhaps a suggestion for this observation is due to the economic nature of the country under study in this research. A large percentage of IS professionals in New Zealand stated lack of future opportunities within the firm as a reason for their turnover decisions. A closer look at this leads to a discovery that many of these firms were potentially closing down, or restructuring. This can result in concerns about one's own prospects and contribute to the push factors for the employee to seek job opportunities elsewhere.

Family/Personal Concerns

In individualistic cultures like New Zealand, the lives of IS professionals rarely revolves around only work and they place a greater emphasis on personal time, self-sufficiency and control over their own lives compared to collectivistic cultures like Singapore. Consequently, family and personal concerns as a cause of turnover are more likely to occur in individualistic cultures. In a collectivistic culture, it was found that family commitments formed all of the non-work factors that resulted in turnover intentions. Of the few turnover episodes, more than half of the reasons to change jobs were due to looking after aged or sick parents. The remaining reasons were with regard to spending more time with their families.

This result agrees strongly with the fact that collectivistic societies find people integrated into strong, cohesive groups, where they tend to take a team perspective in their actions and value the group's well-being more than individual desires (Hofstede, 1980). In this case, the family played an important role in determining the career decisions of these IS professionals. However in an individualistic culture such as New Zealand, although family commitments also played a significant part in turnover decisions, it was observed that personal desires seemed to be an important consideration as well. Besides factors such as spending time with parents, having a conducive location to raise a family, and closeness to family, personal concerns and lifestyle reasons such as marriage, health, migration, further studies, travel, and preference for a particular location due to its environment were also very common reasons. This is, again, in line with the fact that in individualistic cultures, people value personal time, individual decisions, and accomplishments, and these concerns play a major role in affecting turnover decisions.

The occurrence of non-work factors being more prevalent in individualistic cultures in this study serves as a timely reminder of the need for management in such cultures to create human resource policies that places a higher emphasis on the importance of a work-life balance. As the results show, the relatively high occurrences of family commitments, lifestyle choices, and pursuit of further education among the stated non-work factors organizations with an individualistic workforce could strive to be more family friendly, select location with a conducive environment, and perhaps even sponsor high-performance employees in their pursuit of further education. They can also mitigate the effects of stress from work overload and work-life conflicts by introducing nontraditional work scheduling arrangements like part-time, temporary, and contract jobs apart from increased multishift operations. The results obtained in this study also serves to shift management's focus; instead of constantly creating challenging and fulfilling working environments for employees, working environments should also emphasize giving sufficient freedom and respect to employees' non-work interests and commitments in such countries.

CONCLUSION

This study found that the impact of job scope, autonomy, skill variety, remuneration and benefits, future opportunities within the firm, and training opportunities as turnover factors not to be more significant in either high and/or low power distance and individualistic and/or collectivistic cultures. This finding is important because it demonstrates the dangers of drawing conclusions based on national culture without considering the possibility of other factors or characteristics of IS professionals that might outweigh the role of culture in turnover decisions.

The following limitations for this project are noted. A small number of interviews were conducted in two countries. While this is consistent with in-depth qualitative interviews to identify emerging issues, it is recognized that a more expansive investigation is warranted. Also, the two countries, Singapore and New Zealand, differ on only two of Hofstede's (1991) dimensions. A subsequent investigation should include cultures which vary upon more of the dimensions.

This study raises several issues for further research. First, replicating it in a wider range of national cultures can test the cross-cultural robustness of its findings. The extent to which the findings of this study are generalisable across different countries is unknown. To shed light on this issue, researchers have to replicate this study in a wider range of cultures. Countries high on power distance or individualistic (or both) can be explored to determine which factors affecting IS voluntary turnover have a greater impact in these national cultures. Conversely, countries low on power distance or collectivistic (or both) can be examined to see whether these factors remain the same and whether its effect is different. Beside the two cultural dimensions used in this paper, future studies can also include other cultural dimensions to be investigated as well to determine its impact and/or moderating effect on turnover factors.

Secondly, these results may have several important implications for prior and future IS turnover research and opportunities exist to refine and further develop these dimension in the context of voluntary turnover. Current theories and practices on managing voluntary turnover in the IT industry may need to be evaluated for their cross-cultural applicability and future studies on voluntary turnover may need to be qualified in terms of the cultural setting on which they are based. Only then can opportunities for organizations to break the turnover cycle be identified. Understanding the voluntary turnover process and identifying potential intervening points for IS professionals of different culture may result in practical solutions that benefit both the employee and the employer.

Further, other studies may more specifically identify subgroups within the IS profession such as system developers, database administrators, or Web designers and use a wider range of IS personnel for the study. Comparisons may be made with other professions to gain insight into the various possible career orientations and job motivations, since the available options and prospects differ. Studies must also include other potential in-demand professions such as engineering. The increase in scope may help to determine if IS professionals are truly unique or if the proposed theoretical model more accurately reflects other professions that are in high demand as well.

Overall, the findings of this study demonstrate the importance of culture in determining which causes of IS turnover are more important in different countries. The study affirms that cultural effects can moderate IS voluntary turnover factors such as family and personal concerns, management and peer-group relations, and career progression. These results provide an interesting contrast between high power distance/collectivistic and low power distance/individualistic nations. IS professionals with individualistic inclinations were found to possess a stronger likelihood to turnover because of family and personal concerns and career progression. Collectivistic IS professionals, however, are more likely to value peer-group relations more; turnover intentions due to management relations will be greater for those in low power distances.

In summary, this study suggests that some reasons for why IS professionals engage in voluntary turnover may be universal across national cultures while others may be specific to culture. Future IS turnover research can pursue this issue by examining current theories and practices on IS turnover in terms of the cultural setting on which they have been formulated and by evaluating these theories and practices for their robustness across national cultures. As businesses proliferate globally and the costs of higher staff turnover in the IT industry increase, it is imperative that a cultural perspective be added to existing theories and practices.

A cultural perspective to our understanding of the IS employees voluntary turnover process will provide knowledge of turnover factors that are culturally sensitive. Understanding the cultural implications of the IS voluntary turnover process can help organizations come up with appropriate human resource policies when managing their already limited IS workforce, so as to reduce the number of turnover episodes internationally. This research adds to our understanding in this direction.

REFERENCES

Allen, D. B., Miller, E. D., & Nath, R. (1988). North America. In R. Nath (Ed.), *Comparative Management* (pp. 23-54). Cambridge, MA: Ballinger.

Ang, S., & Slaughter, S. (2004). Turnover of information technology professionals: The effects of internal labour market strategies. *ACM SIGMIS Database, 35*(3), 11-27.

Agarwal, R., Ferratt, T. W., Moore, J. E., & Brown, C. V. (1999). Observations from "the front": IT executives on practices to recruit and retain information technology professionals. In *Proceedings of the SIGCPR* (pp. 102-112).

Aycan, Z., & Fikret-Pasa, S. (2003, Winter). Career choices, job selection criteria, and leadership preferences in a transitional nation: The case of Turkey. *Journal of Career Development, 30*(2).

Baker, M. (1991). *Research in marketing*. London: MacMillan.

Benamati, J., & Lederer, A. L. (2001, Spring). Rapid information technology change, coping mechanisms, and the emerging technologies group. *Journal of Management Information Systems, 17*(4), pp. 183-202.

Bluedorn, A. C. (1982). The theories of turnover: Causes, effects, and meaning. In S. B. Bacharach (Ed.), *Research in the sociology of organizations* (Vol. 1, pp. 75-128). Greenwich, CT: JAI.

Bochner, S., & Hesketh, B. (1994). Power distance, individualism/collectivism and job-related attitudes in a culturally diverse work group. *Journal of Cross-Cultural Psychology, 25*(2), 233-257.

Bruner, J. (1990). *Acts of meaning*. Cambridge, MA: Harvard University Press.

Carpenter, M. A., & Fredrickson, J. W. (2001). Top management teams, global strategic posture and the moderating role of uncertainty. *Academy of Management Journal, 44*(3), 533-545.

Carter, C. R. (2000). Ethical issues in international buyer-supplier relationships: A dyadic examination. *Journal of Operations Management, 18*(2), 191-208.

Chandy, P. R., & Williams, T. G. E. (1994). The impact of journals and authors on international business. *Journal of International Business Studies, 25*(4), 715-728.

Chang, B. L. (2002). The social context of turnover among information technology professionals. In *Proceedings of SIGCPR* (pp. 145-153).

Chew, S. B., & Chew, R. (2001). Public policy and entrepreneurship: The case of Singapore. *International Journal of Entrepreneurship and Innovation Management, 1*(2), 217.

Crepeau, R. G., Crook, C. W., Goslar, M. D., & McMurtrey, M. E. (1992). Career anchors of information systems personnel. *Journal of Management Information Systems, 9*(2), 145-158.

Czarniawska-Joerges, B. (1995). Narration or science? Collapsing the division in organization studies. *Organization, 2*(1), 11-33.

Dex, S. (1991). *Life and work history analyses*. London: Routledge.

Earley, P. C. (1993). East meets west meets mideast: Further explorations of collectivistic and individualistic work groups. *Academy of Management Journal, 36*(2), 319-348.

Eylon, D., & Au, K. Y. (1999). Exploring empowerment cross-cultural differences along the power distance dimension. *International Journal of Intercultural Relations, 23,* 373-385.

Feeney, D. F., & Willcocks, L. P. (1998). Core IS capabilities for exploiting information technology. *Sloan Management Review, 39*(3), 9-21.

Ford, D. P., Connelly, C. E., & Meister, D. B. (2003). Information systems research and Hofstede's culture's consequences: An uneasy and incomplete partnership. *IEEE Transactions on Engineering Management, 50*(1).

Forrest, Cummings, & Johnson. (1977). Organizational participation: A critique and model. *Academy of Management Review, 2,* 586-601.

Fried, Y., & Ferris, G. (1987). The validity of the job characteristics model: A review and meta-analysis. *Personnel Psychology, 40,* 287-322.

Gionfriddo, J., & Dhingra, L. (2000, May/Jun). *Human Resource Management International Digest 8*(4), 9-11.

Hampden-Turner, C. M., & Trompenaars, F. (2000). *Building cross-cultural competence: How to create wealth from conflicting values.* New York: Wiley.

Hofstede, G. (1980). *Culture's consequences: international differences in work-related values.* Beverly Hills, CA: Sage.

Hofstede, G. (1991). *Cultures and organizations: Software of the mind.* New York: McGraw-Hill.

Hom, P. W., Caranikas-Walker, F., Prussia, G. E., & Griffeth, R. W. (1992). A meta-analytical structural equations analysis of a model of employee turnover. *Journal of Applied Psychology, 77,* 890-909.

House, R. J., Hanges, P., Mansour, J., Dorfman, P., & Gupta, V. (2004). *Culture, leadership and organizations: The globe study of 62 societies.* Thousand Oaks, CA: Sage.

Hulin, C. L., Roznowski, M., & Hachiya, D. (1985). Alternative opportunities and withdrawal decisions: Empirical and theoretical discrepancies and integration. *Psychological Bulletin, 97,* 233-250.

Hunter, M. G., & Beck, J. E. (1996). A Cross-cultural comparison of "excellent" systems analysts. *Information Systems Journal, 6*(4), 261-281.

Igbaria, M., Parasuraman, S., & Badawy, M. K. (1994, June). Work experiences, job involvement, and quality of work life among information systems personnel. *MIS Quarterly, 18*(2), 175-197.

Jaeger, A. M. (1986). Organization development and national culture: Where's the fit? *Academy of Management Review, 11,* 178-190.

Jiang, J. J., & Klein, G. (2002). A discrepancy model of information system personnel turnover. *Journal of Management Information Systems, 19*(2), 240-272.

King, R. C., & Sethi, V. (1998). The impact of socialization on the role adjustment of information systems professionals. *Journal of Management Information Systems, 14*(4), 195-217.

Kirschenbaum, A., & Mano-Negrin, R. (1999). Underlying labour market dimensions of opportunities: The case of employee turnover. *Human Relations, 52*(10), 1233-1255.

Klaus, T., LeRouge, C., & Blanton, J. E. (2003). An examination of the relationships between select nature of work characteristics and organizational commitment of IT professionals. In *Proceedings of SIGMIS Conference* (pp. 147-149).

Lee, T. W., & Mitchell. T. R. (1994). An alternative approach: The unfolding model of voluntary employee turnover. *The Academy of Management Review, 19*(1), 51-79.

Lee, D. M. S., Trauth, E., & Farwell, D. (1995). Critical skills and knowledge requirements of IS professionals: A joint academic/industry investigation. *MIS Quarterly, 19*(3), 313-335.

Levin, R., & Rosse, J. (2001). *Talent flow: A strategic guide to keeping good employees, helping them grow and letting them go.* San Francisco: Jossey-Bass.

McCracken, G. (1988). *The long interview.* New York: Sage.

Madan, P. (2004). *Voluntary turnover: A study of IS professionals.* B. Comp. Honours Thesis, National University of Singapore.

March, J. G., & Simon, H. A. (1958). *Organizations.* New York: Wiley.

Markus, H. R., & Kitayama, S. (1991). Culture and the self: Implications for cognition, emotion and motivation. *Psychological Review, 98,* 224-253.

Martinsons, M. G., & Westwood, R. I. (1997). Management information systems in the Chinese business culture: An explanatory theory. *Information and Management, 32,* 215-228.

Merritt, A. (2000). Culture in the cockpit—Do Hofstede's dimensions replicate? *Journal of Cross-Cultural Psychology, 31*(3), 283-301.

Mobley, W. H. (1977). Intermediate linkages in the relationship between job dissatisfaction and employee turnover. *Journal of Applied Psychology, 62,* 237-240.

Mobley, W. H., Griffeth, R. W., Hand, H. H., & Meglino, B. M. (1979). Review and conceptual analysis of the employee turnover process. *Psychological Bulletin 86*(3), 493-522.

Moenaert, R. K., & Souder, W. E. (1996). Context and Antecedents of information utility at the R&D/marketing interface. *Management Science, 42*(11), 1592-1610.

Morrow, P. (1993). *The theory and measurement of work commitment.* Greenwich, CT: JAI Press.

Png, I. P. L., Tan, B. C. Y., & Wee, K. L. (2001). dimensions of national culture and corporate adoption of IT infrastructure. *IEEE Transactions on Engineering Management 48*(1), 36-45.

Porter, L. W., & Steers, R. M. (1973). Organizational, work and personal factors in employee turnover and absenteeism. *Psychological Bulletin, 80,* 151-176.

Price, J. L., & Mueller, C. W. (1981). A casual model for turnover for nurses. *Academy of Management Journal, 24,* 543-565.

Redding, S. G., Norman, A., & Schlander, A. (1994). The nature of individual attachment to the organization: A review of east Asian variations. In H. C. Triandis, M. Dunnette, & L. Hough (Eds.), *Handbook of industrial and organizational psychology* (2nd ed., Vol. 4, pp. 557-607). Palo Alto, CA: Consulting Psychologists Press.

Robert, C., Probst, T. M., Martocchio, J. J. Drasgow, F., & Lawler, J. J. (2000). Empowerment and continuous improvement in the United States, Mexico, Poland and India: Predicting fit on the basis of the dimensions of power distance and individualism. *Journal of Applied Psychology, 85,* 643-658.

Ronen, S. (1994). An understanding of motivational needs taxonomies: A cross-cultural conformation. In H. C. Triandis, M. D. Dunnette, & L. M. Hough (Eds.), *Handbook of industrial and organizational psychology* (2nd ed, Vol. 4, pp. 241-270). Palo Alto, CA: Consulting Psychologists Press.

Ronen, S., & Shenkar, O. (1985). Clustering countries on attitudinal dimensions: A review and synthesis. *Academy of Management Review, 10*(3), 435-454.

Rosse, J. G., & Hulin, C. L. (1985). Adaptation to work: An analysis of employee health, withdrawal and change. *Organizational Behavior and Human Decision Processes, 36,* 324-347.

Ross, I. C., & Zander, A. (1957). Need satisfaction and employee turnover. *Personnel Psychology, 10,* 327-338.

Segars, A. H., & Hendrickson, A. R. (2000). Value, knowledge, and the human equation: Evolution of the information technology function in modern organizations. *Journal of Labor Research, 21*(3), 431-445.

Shackleton, V. J., & Ali, A. H. (1990). Work-related values of managers: A test of the Hofstede model. *Journal of Cross-Cultural Psychology 21*(1), 109-118.

Shah, A. C., Sterrett, J. C., & Wilmore, J. (2001). Meeting the need for employee development in the 21st century. *Advanced Management Journal, 66*(2), 22-28.

Sondergaard, M. (1990). Hofstede's consequences: A study of reviews, citations and replications. *Organization Studies 15*(3), 447-456.

Spector, P. E., Cooper, C. L., & Sparks, K. (2001). An international study of the psychometric properties of the Hofstede values survey module 1994: A comparison of individual and country/ province level results. *Applied Psychology, 50*(2), 269-281.

Standbridge, J., & Autrey, R. (2001). Rapid skill obsolescence in an IT company: A case study of Acxiom corporation. *Journal of Organizational Excellence, 20*(3), 3-9.

Steers, R., & Mowday, R. (1981). Employee turnover and post decision accommodation processes. *Research in Organizational Behavior, 3,* 235-281.

Straub, D. W. (1994). The effect of culture on IT diffusion: E-mail and fax in Japan and the US. *Information Systems Research 5*(1), 23-47.

Swap, W., Leonard, D., Shields, M., & Abrams, L. (2001). Using mentoring and storytelling to transfer knowledge in the workplace. *Journal of Management Information Systems, 18*(1), 95-114.

Tan, B. C. Y., Wei, K. K., Watson, R. T., Clapper, D. L., & McLean, E. R. (1998). Computer-mediated communication and majority influence: Assessing the impact in an individualistic and a collectivistic culture. *Management Science, 44*(9), 1263-1278.

Tan, B. C. Y., Wei, K. K., Watson, R. T., & Walczuch, R. M. (1998). Reducing status effects with computer-mediated communication: Evidence from two distinct national cultures. Journal *of Management Information Systems, 15*(1), 119-141.

Tan, F. B., & Hunter, M. G. (2003, January 6-9). Using narrative inquiry in a study of information systems professionals. In *Proceedings of the 36th Hawaii International Conference on Systems Sciences (Hicss-36).*

Tesluk, P. E., & Mathieu, J. E. (1999). Overcoming roadblocks to effectiveness: Incorporating management of performance barriers into models of work group effectiveness. *Journal of Applied Psychology, 84*(2), 200-217.

Tett, R., & Meyer, J. P. (1993). Job satisfaction, organizational commitment, turnover intention, and turnover: Path analyses based on meta-analysis findings. *Personnel Psychology, 46*(2), 259-280.

Theron. (2004). *Voluntary turnover: A study of IS professionals.* B. Comp. Honours Thesis, National University of Singapore.

Thompson, C. J. (1997). Interpreting consumers: A hermeneutical framework for deriving marketing insights from the texts of consumers' consumption stories. *Journal of Marketing Research, 34,* 438-455.

Ting-Toomey, S. (1994). Managing intimate conflict in intercultural personal relationships. In D. D. Cahn (Ed.), *Intimate conflict in personal relationships.* Hillsdale, NJ: Erlbaum.

Trevor, C. O. (2001). Interactive effects among actual case of movement determinants and job satisfaction in the prediction of voluntary turnover. *Academy of Management Journal, 44,* 621-638.

Triandis, H. C. (1995). *Individualism and collectivism.* Boulder, CO: Westview.

Triandis, H. C., McCusker, C., & Hui, C. H. (1990). Multimedia probes of individualism and collectivism. *Journal of Personality and Social Psychology, 59*(5), 1006-1020.

Trompenaars, F., & Hampden-Turner, C. (1998). *Riding the waves of culture: Understanding cultural diversity in global business* (2nd ed.). New York: McGraw-Hill.

Tulving, E. (1972). *Organization of memory.* New York: Academic Press.

Vendelo, M. T. (1998). Narrating corporate reputation: Becoming legitimate through storytelling.

International Journal of Management and Organization, 28(3), 120-137.

Wagner, J. A., III. (1995). Studies of individualism-collectivism: Effects on cooperation in groups. *Academy of Management Journal, 38*(1), 152-172.

Wynekoop, J. L., & Walz, D. B. (1998). Revisiting the perennial question: Are IS people different? *Database for Advances in Information Systems, 29*(2), 62-72.

Young, J. (2000). *The career paths of computer science and information systems major graduates.* Unpublished doctoral dissertation, University of Tasmania.

This work was previously published in the Journal of Global Information Management, Vol. 16, Issue 4, edited by F. Tan, pp. 46-66, copyright 2008 by IGI Publishing (an imprint of IGI Global).

Chapter 2
Factors Influencing Career Choice for Women in the Global Information Technology Workforce

Eileen M. Trauth
The Pennsylvania State University, USA

Jeria L. Quesenberry
Carnegie Mellon University, USA

Haiyan Huang
Purdue University Calumet, USA

ABSTRACT

The increased cultural diversity emanating from the globalization of the IT sector presents challenges for gender research in the IT field. In an effort to address these challenges, this chapter presents an analysis of cultural factors influencing the career choices of women in the IT workforce. A review of the literature on cultural factors suggests the need for both greater analysis of cultural influences on women in the IT workforce and more nuanced theorizing about gender and IT. Hence, the authors employ the individual differences theory of gender and IT as a theoretical lens for examining, in greater detail, the variation in ways that perceptions of women's roles are embedded in a culture. The chapter then documents the influence of these perceptions on female IT career choices. Finally, the authors show how socio-cultural factors moderate these influences. The data employed in this chapter draws from a qualitative data set of interviews with 200 women from four separate studies of women in the IT workforces in Australia, Ireland, New Zealand and the United States. The themes that emerged from this analysis speak to the influence of cultural attitudes about maternity, childcare, parental care and working outside the home on a woman's choice of an IT career. The authors also saw evidence that other socio-cultural factors add further variation to gendered cultural influences: gendered career norms, social class, economic

DOI: 10.4018/978-1-60566-920-5.ch002

opportunity, and gender stereotypes about aptitude. These results lend empirical support to the emergent individual differences theory of gender and IT that theorizes within-gender variation with respect to issues related to gender and IT. They also point to areas where educational and workplace interventions can be enacted to address the under representation of women in the IT field.

INTRODUCTION

The twenty-first century is witnessing the emergence of a robust, globalized information sector. Countries around the world are recognizing the economic benefits that accrue from the development of an IT workforce capable of engaging in the deployment of computer hardware, software, and information services (Irwin, 2000; Shiva, 1989; Trauth, 2000). In addition, sophisticated networking technologies that have made both asynchronous and real-time communications between different regions and countries feasible, have enabled both new ways of working and increased collaboration (Huang and Trauth, 2006). This has led to an increasingly diverse IT workforce as more and more countries become equipped with a maturing IT sector and a pool of talented IT workers (Trauth et al., 2006a).

Ironically, there is also evidence of social exclusion in the IT sector (e.g. Finquelievich, 2003; Kvasny et al., 2009; Schienstock, 1999; Trauth and Quesenberry, 2006). This chapter examines one particular group – women -- who is under represented in all segments of the information technology career pipeline, from enrollment in secondary school and university courses, to positions in the IT workforce, to IT management positions (Camp, 2002; Margolis and Fisher, 2002; Teague, 2002; Women and Minorities in Information Technology Forum, 1999). In the U.S., for example, women comprise approximately half of the American labor force, yet the The Information Technology Association of America's (ITAA) Blue Ribbon Diversity Panel revealed that in 2004 women represented only 32.4 percent of the U.S. IT workforce, a figure down from 41 percent in 1996 (ITAA, 2005). The under representation of women is also documented by the gendered response to the dot.com bust. The data shows that men were far more likely than women to return to the IT profession as the market recovered. For example, from 2003 to 2004 the unemployment rate of skilled men in the IT field workers dropped 34.4 percent while the number of unemployed skilled women dropped only 5.15 percent (ITAA, 2005).

This phenomenon is replicated in other countries as well. The number of women working in IT occupations in Canada also declined from 28 percent in 2001 to 25 percent in 2003 (Downie et al., 2004). In India women account for only 14 percent of the IT industry (Pande, 2006). *Workforce Aging in the New Economy* (2004) reports that, in Europe, industry and policy initiatives to attract more women into the profession have not been met with success. In the UK and Germany, men outnumber women five to one in computing professions; in The Netherlands it is seven to one. In Australia the situation is the same. In 2001, women accounted for only 23.6 percent of the Australian IT workforce (Australian Bureau of Statistics, 2002). Based on the information compiled by Statistics New Zealand, Hembry and Presley (2006) noted that in New Zealand women accounted for only 11 percent of systems technician occupations and 16 percent of application engineer occupations in 2001. In the case of Ireland, in 1998, women accounted for near 31 percent of Irish IT workforce but this number dropped to 27.5 percent in 2004 (Organization for Economic Co-operation and Development, 2007). This review of workforce statistics shows that while the IT workforce may be diverse in terms of global representation, it is lacking sufficient diversity in terms of gender representation.

The under representation of women in a culturally diverse IT workforce presents a challenge to both practitioners and scholars. There is a need for more interventions to increase the representation of women. At the same time, there is a need for better theorizing of gender and IT and more data collection so as inform these interventions. Galpin (2002) suggests that the participation of women in the global IT workforce is influenced by complex cultural and societal factors that differ from country to country. As a result, he argues that when considering gender and IT issues it is important to take into account cultural context. Therefore, in an effort to contribute to both practice and theory, this chapter presents an analysis of cultural factors influencing the career choices for women in the IT workforce.

We begin by reviewing the literature about cultural influences on gender and IT. We then present a theoretical framework that has been employed in a multi-year, multi-country examination of the actual experiences of women in the IT workforce. Finally, we present the findings from our analysis of these field studies, and the implications for theory and practice.

CULTURAL INFLUENCES ON WOMEN AND IT

The under representation of women in the IT workforce has been a major concern of educators, practitioners, and researchers (e.g. Adam et al., 2002; Arnold and Niederman, 2001). Studies have shown that this is a worldwide phenomenon as manifested in enrollment in IT related disciplines and the number of women employed in the IT workforce (Galpin, 2002; Huyer, 2005; Rosser, 2005; Sanders, 2005). It has also been observed (Galpin, 2002) that there is wide variation in participation levels of women in IT with no clear pattern to explain these differences. Schinzel (1999) notes that this indicates a need to take a closer look at cultural influences on gender relations with respect to the IT field. In the sections below we consider the literature that has examined the ways in which cultural influences come into play in research on the topic of gender and the IT workforce. We categorize this literature into three themes: cultural influences within a country, multicultural influences within a country, and cultural influences across countries.

Cultural Influences on Women Within a Country

Frieze et al. (2006) argued that researchers and practitioners need to recognize the importance of cultural issues as these factors have a significant influence on the career options available to women. A wide variety of issues have been investigated regarding why women are underrepresented and how to narrow the IT gender gap within a given country. These studies of underlying cultural influences have produced a number of interesting findings about the role of family dynamics, and how gender identity and stereotypes are shaped by social and political ideology.

Several researchers have concluded that family dynamics and the role of parents are an important component of cultural influences on women and their relationship with IT (Burger et al., 2007; Creamer et al., 2007; Meszaros et al., 2007). Medeiros (2005) conducted a study of the decreasing participation of Brazilian women in IT-related activities and occupations. While women constitute 51 percent of Brazil's population and the amount of IT related work is increasing due to outsourcing, women are still under represented in computer related professions in the country. The author concluded that improving the participation of women in the IT workforce hinges on the family, since parental influence in Brazil plays a significant role in career choice and self image. Hence, there is a need for informal education of parents, which calls attention to the advantages of IT jobs for women.

In contrast, Adams et al. (2006; 2003) examined the role of cultural factors in Mauritius that have enabled an increasing number of women to study IT. The time period from 1990 to 2003 has shown a rapid increase in computer science and engineering enrollments in Mauritius. For instance, by 2003, the representation of women was 37 percent in computer science and engineering, 51 percent in information systems, and 49 percent in computer science and multimedia. The percentage of women graduating from computing programs has also increased. They believe that cultural factors were the major reasons for these increases. Specifically, the authors concluded that the following cultural dynamics were important: families that placed a high value on females having IT careers; a national culture that strongly promotes IT, and the single-sex high school system which allows girls to develop aptitude and interests towards technology in the absence of male peer pressure to conform to gender stereotypes about technology.

Researchers have also concluded that the social and political ideology about gender identity and stereotypes are an important component of cultural influences on women and their relationship with IT. Ecevit et al. (2003) studied professional women who work as systems analysts and computer programmers in Turkey. They found that Turkish women hold a higher share of computer related occupations compared to other male-dominated occupations such as law, medicine and engineering in the country. In addition, the presence of professional women in computer programming occupations in Turkey is also high compared to the statistics in the U.S. and the Netherlands. The historical, social, and cultural factors that contribute to this phenomenon include the emphasis on gender equality, the political ideology of Turkey with its attendant educational policies that support this ideology, and the family's encouragement of its daughters to be educated in science and technology fields. They also investigated various strategies used by professional women to reconcile professional and marital roles. Their conclusion is that it is critical to recognize women's own agency in shaping their own positions and responses to relationships with technology.

Multiple Cultural Influences on Women Within a Country

Researchers have also investigated the different cultural influences within a particular country on gender and IT. These studies show how the diversity of cultural backgrounds of women in a single country can result in wide variation in their relationships with IT. An example is the way in which geography and social class have been shown to influence women and their relationship with IT. Shen and Ge (2006) investigated technology adoption and IT careers among women in China. Their findings indicate that the number of Chinese female Internet users is increasing, yet the distribution is severely skewed with respect to age, region, and occupation. For instance, in China, the majority of female Internet users are younger in age (ranging from 15-30), reside in urban regions, are highly educated, and hold professional occupations. The authors add that while the social status of women is improving and the gender gap is becoming narrower in urban areas, there are still significant issues with respect to improving the participation of women in the IT workforce. Trauth et al. (2008b) investigated the influence of culture and economy on women in the IT workforce in three different regions of the US. Their findings revealed the influence of cultural factors such as attitude toward women, attitude toward women working and attitude toward women working in technical fields. They also showed the influence of economic factors such as the cost of living and the size of the IT sector relative to the regional economy.

Researchers have also found that race influences women's relationship with IT. Clarke and Teague (1994a; 1994b) analyzed interview data with Asian and Caucasian computer science and engineering students in Australia. The authors found that the Asian female students did not see computing as a male domain. Rather these students experienced direct encouragement from their families to pursue computing related secondary studies. Clarke and Teague's work mentioned earlier (1994b) pointed out that:

"... the differences within gender groups are greater than the differences between gender groups" [italics added] (p. 259).

In a later study, Nielsen et al. (1998) also investigated Asian and Caucasian female students enrolled in IT disciplines in Australia. Their study showed that both Asian and Caucasian females had similar views about the IT professions. However, Asian female students were more inclined to choose IT related subjects despite their negative perceptions of IT professions because of the future prospects of employment opportunities (Nielsen et al., 1999; 1998). The authors argued that this view is influenced by the collectivist characteristic of Asian culture and is based on practical considerations, as compared to the individualistic "free-choice" decision making model in most Western cultures. In a study of race in the US, Kvasny et al (forthcoming) documented the intersectionality of gender, race and socio-economic class in shaping women's involvement in the IT profession.

Researchers have also found that religion and ethnic identity account for variation in cultural influence on women and their relationship with IT. Eidelman and Hazzan (2006; 2005) examined the shaping effect of Arabic and Jewish cultural backgrounds on students in Israel. They found that the percentage of female high-school students who took advanced-level computer science courses was higher among Arab students in their study than their Jewish counterparts. The authors attributed this difference to cultural and familial differences between Arab and Jewish adolescents (Eidelman and Hazzan, 2006; 2005). Specifically, the authors argued that a collective characteristic of Arab culture is centered on strong family and peer influences that stress high scholastic achievement for social status improvement. On the other hand, the authors found that the influence of parents and friends is lower in the Jewish culture. They stressed that in order to not be inferior in the eyes of their family:

"... in particular and their society in general, it seems that Arab female students are highly motivated to study computer science since they consider these studies as a way to prove their skills and capabilities" (Eidelman and Hazzan, 2006 p. 1097).

Cultural Influences on Women across Countries

A number of gender researchers have conducted comparison studies across countries in order to identify variation by country and better understand the nuances of different socio-cultural influences on gender and IT. Minguez (2005) found political ideology to have an influence on women's relationship with IT. She compared statistics on computer and Internet use across several European countries and found unequal access to computing technologies based on gender to be more significant in Southern European countries, particularly in Spain. Minguez attributed this to the focus of the Franco regime on perpetuating the traditional family model of a male as primary bread-winner. She concluded that this ideology has, consequently, limited the opportunities for women to participate in the labor market.

Researchers have also found shifts over time in political ideologies with respect to influences on women and their relationship with IT. Hersh (2000) examined survey data from a research project on the changing position of women in engineering careers in 55 countries from the 1960-1997. The author stressed that women are still under represented in the engineering profession in the majority of countries despite significant increases in their participation over the last two decades. Yet, there are significant differences among the countries, and among different institutions within the same country. For example, the author reported that the participation of women in engineering careers in Eastern Europe has increased in recent years. The author explained that this growth was due to dramatic changes in economic development (i.e. the need for more engineers for industrial development) and ideological systems (i.e. the equal roles of men and women in the workplace in communist regions, the availability of child-care facilities, etc.):

"Thus, change in images and attitudes was facilitated by the changes in political climate and ideology from 1945 onward. It was probably, at least in part, due to the increasing importance of the development of industry in the state communist period, resulting in the need for more engineers and other technically qualified workers. This will have reinforced the ideological commitment to equalizing the roles of men and women in the workplace (at least at the lower levels). The availability of child-care facilities and the encouragement for women to enter paid employment will also have had an additional effect" (Hersh, 2000 p. 6).

Gender stereotypes related to IT have also been shown to vary by country. Durndell et al. (2000) compared computer self efficacy and gender of college students in Scotland and Romania. Their findings showed that for within-country comparisons, males were more confident about their computer skills than females in both Scotland and Romania. Yet, for across-country comparisons both males and females in Romania were more confident about their advanced computer skills than their Scottish counterparts. Likewise, Makrakis and Sawada (1996) studied 773 ninth-grade students in Japan and Sweden in order to measure and compare male and female attitudes towards computers. Their findings show that males in both countries reported higher scores of usefulness, aptitude and interest in computers. They also found differences in the perception of computers and mathematics among males and females. Japanese students perceived more strongly than Swedish students that computers and mathematics are male domains. Swedish students' gender stereotypes appeared to be less strong than was the case for Japanese students. According to these authors the differences reflect the Japanese cultural norm of "good wife, clever mother,"[1] which affects Japanese girls' choice of a gender stereotypical education suitable for a wife and mother. This is the case in spite of the fact that, in principle, there seem to be equal opportunities applied to both genders in Japanese society.

Cultural analysis of the first exposure to computers across China and the UK has also revealed an important difference in the influence on women and their relationship with IT. Li and Kirkup (2007) investigated underlying cultural factors for both similar and different use patterns of the Internet by women in China and the UK. Their results indicate that gender differences in computer ownership may no longer exist for young adults at universities in China and the UK. The authors felt that the situation in China could be attributed to the parental value placed on education and computing skills. The authors felt that in the UK, the findings could be attributed to the pervasiveness of the computer. They also found that gender differences within the British group were more significant than those within the Chinese group. The authors argued that it might be due to the differences in first time computer use. The British women in their study tended to have negative computer experiences in the early stage of computer use. On the other hand, the Chinese women in their study were typically exposed to computers for the first time at school where the educational setting helps to provide equal opportunities for students of both genders. However, their findings indicate that in spite of the increase of computer ownership, there were significant gender differences in computer and Internet usage in both Chinese and British groups.

Men in both countries were more likely to use the computer and the Internet for personal interests such as playing games and/or using chat rooms, and they were more confident about their computer skills as well.

Cultural analysis of technology use among young children in China and the US has also revealed an important difference in the influence on women and their relationship with IT. Jackson et al. (2008) conducted a study of 600 Chinese and 600 US children and found that US children used computers and the Internet more than did Chinese children, with Chinese females being the least intense users. They also found that young boys played videogames more than did young girls. Further, they concluded that racial and ethnic group differences indicate that diversity within cultural groups among subcultures must be considered in understanding children's IT use.

Finally, technophobia, or the perceived fear of computers, was found to vary with respect to its relationship to gender and IT. Weil and Rosen (1995) examined the level of technophobia among first year university students from 23 countries, including the U.S., western and eastern European countries, Israel, and countries in Asia, South America, and Africa. Their results indicated that gender was only mildly correlated with technophobia and appeared in less than one-fourth of the countries. In addition, past experiences with computers decreased the appearance of technophobia in the majority of the countries. According to their results, females in Israel and Hungary showed more computer anxiety than males in these two countries, and males in Thailand, Italy and Kenya showed more computer anxiety than females in these three countries. Hence, the authors concluded that "there is no worldwide consensus on who are more technophobic – males or females" (p. 102). Rather, they concluded that the country's cultural characteristics serve as one of the important factors affecting the level of technophobia in that country.

Summary of Research about Cultural Influences on Women and IT

Research on cultural influences on career choices for women in the IT workforce can be classified into three categories. One stream of research focuses on studying the relationships between gender and IT in a particular national context in order to reveal the underlying cultural influences (e.g. Adams et al., 2006; 2003; Ecevit et al., 2003; Medeiros, 2005). Another stream of research considers the multiple cultural influences on gender and IT within a specific societal context while studying how the diverse cultural backgrounds of different women may influence their relationships with IT (e.g. Clarke and Teague, 1994a; 1994b; Eidelman and Hazzan, 2006; 2005; Kvasny et al., 2009; Nielsen et al., 1999; 1998; Shen and Ge, 2006; Trauth et al., 2008b; Varma et al., 2006). The third stream of research consists of comparison studies that investigate how and why women's participation in IT varies across countries (e.g. Durndell et al., 2000; Hersh, 2000; Siddiqui, 2008; Li and Kirkup, 2007; Makrakis and Sawada; 1996; Minguez, 2005; Varma, 2007; Weil and Rosen, 1995).

This extensive body of research has produced two important results. First, it shows that culture is highly relevant in the consideration of factors affecting gender and IT. Second, while there are some common themes there is also wide variability across different countries, or across different groups within a given country. Thus, the research to date demonstrates that both gender and IT are socially constructed, and historically and culturally shaped (Huang, 2006; Li and Kirkup, 2007; Trauth et al., 2006b). At the same time, there is also wide variation in the ways in which culture shapes women and the particular factors at work.

Thus, several issues remain with respect to research on culture, gender, and IT. First, there is a need for additional research that articulates how cultural factors influence the image of gender, the image of technology, and gender relations with respect to technology. Without in-depth understandings of the influential factors from the surrounding socio-cultural contexts, solutions intending to improve the social inclusion of women in IT may only have limited effect and may not be far reaching. Second, while those studies acknowledge the diverse relationships between gender and IT across different countries, there is limited research recognizing that such diverse relationships also exist within gender groups in the same country. Gender is only a part of an individual's social identify. Gender interacts with other social constructs such as race, ethnicity, age, and social class. Third, it is important to recognize that these streams of research are mutually informative, particularly with the increasing trends of globalization of the IT industry, offshore outsourcing, and the mobility of the IT professions. Frieze et al. (2006) argued that appropriate local interventions in the micro-culture may have a large effect. We conclude this discussion of the research to date with the observation that just as the topic of diversity in the IT sector is not simple, research about this topic cannot be simplistic.

THEORETICAL FRAMEWORK: THE INDIVIDUAL DIFFERENCES THEORY OF GENDER AND IT

One common theme that runs through these three streams of research is that perceptions of women's roles in society and in the IT sector are socio-culturally constructed. As shown in the review of the literature presented above, these perceptions vary across countries. Another cultural dimension emphasized in the literature is the influence of family on women's career choices. Thus, the research literature demonstrates the need to understand the nuances of different socio-cultural influences on gender and IT both within a country and across different countries. This recognition, in turn, suggests the need to incorporate this understanding into the development of interventions to improve women's participation in IT that fit with a specific socio-cultural context. Finally, the literature points to the need to conduct theoretically-informed investigations of these nuances. However, what appears to be missing in cultural studies of gender and IT is sufficient gender and IT theorizing that can help to explain this variation in cultural influences.

In response, Trauth has developed the *individual differences theory of gender and IT* (Trauth, 2002, 2006; Trauth and Quesenberry, 2006; Trauth et al., 2004), to explain the variation in factors that account for gender representation in the IT field. To date, the theorizing has focused on variation in the ways women experience and respond to characteristics of IT work, the IT workplace and societal messages about women and IT.[2] The theory addresses the need for greater nuance in the examination of gender and IT in that it conceptualizes women and men as individuals, having distinct personalities, experiencing a range of socio-cultural influences, and therefore exhibiting a range of responses to the social construction of IT. More specifically, the theory examines the gender variation as a result of both personal characteristics and environmental influences in order to understand the participation of women and men in the IT profession. Hence, the individual differences theory of gender and IT focuses on the differences *within* rather than *between* gender groups through the understanding of specific influencing factors (Howcroft and Trauth, 2008; Quesenberry and Trauth, 2008; Trauth, 2002; Trauth and Howcroft, 2006; Trauth and Quesenberry, 2007; 2006; 2005; Trauth et al., 2008a, 2008b).

The reason for placing theoretical focus on within-gender variation in response to societal-level gender influences regarding IT is to address the question of why some women persist in the IT field in the face of systemic gender biases in both education and the workplace while others do not. The theory posits that the answer can be found in the combined influence of endogenous and exogenous factors that influence an individual's personal development and subsequent IT career decisions (Trauth et al., 2004). That is, while all females in a particular society may be exposed to similar messages about gender roles and IT, both the interpretation of these messages and the response to them will vary as a result of individual factors. Thus, the individual differences theory of gender and IT searches for the causes of the gender imbalance by examining the factors that account for the varied ways that individuals internalize and respond to gendered messages. It seeks to understand the sources of individual agency that enable some women to overcome systemic negative influences.

According to this theory, an understanding of individual responses to common societal influences can be obtained from an understanding of the combination of personal characteristics and environmental influences. The theory also views women as individuals who possess different technical talents and inclinations and respond to the social shaping of gender in unique and particular ways. This theory acknowledges that common social shaping messages are conveyed to subgroups in a culture (e.g. to women by age, race, etc.). But at the same time it also takes into account the varied influence of individual background and critical life events that result in a range of responses to those uniform messages (i.e. not all women of a certain age group respond in the same way to commonly received messages).

This theory is comprised of three sets of constructs that, together, explain women's decisions to enter and remain in the IT field. The *individual identity construct* includes both personal demographic items (e.g. age, race, ethnicity, nationality, socioeconomic class, and parenting status) and career items (e.g. industry in which one currently does or will work, IT discipline – e.g. computer science, information systems or information science – one is studying). The *individual influence construct* includes personal characteristics (e.g. educational background, personality traits and abilities) and personal influences (e.g. mentors, role models, experiences with computing, and other significant life experiences). Finally, the *environmental influence construct* includes cultural attitudes and values (e.g. attitudes about IT, about women in IT, about race/ethnicity) related to the geographic area in which one lives, as well as economic and policy influences in that region/country. The individual differences theory of gender and IT posits that, collectively, these constructs account for the differences among women in the ways they relate to the IT field, and societal messages about women and IT. Research to date has employed this theory to investigate gender variation with respect to: social networks (Morgan et al., 2004); regional and national gender influences (Trauth et al., 2008a, 2008b; 2006b; 2005); work-life balance (Quesenberry and Trauth, 2005); motherhood (Quesenberry et al., 2006); responses to power (Howcroft and Trauth, 2008; Trauth and Howcroft, 2006); the interpretation of gender messages about IT careers (Trauth and Quesenberry, 2006); the intersectionality of race, gender and class (Kvasny et al., forthcoming) and career motivations (Quesenberry and Trauth, 2007, 2008).

In this chapter the theory is used to illuminate the investigation of cultural influences on gender and IT by facilitating examination of possible connections between cultural factors and the experiences of women in the IT workforce. This theoretical application allows for analysis of women *in a societal context.* The argument for considering women's experiences in a societal context stands in contrast to research which de-contextualizes women's experiences by generalizing from a single data set to all women everywhere. Researchers have demonstrated that investigations of gender as a single construct can be problematic (e.g., Llewellyn and Usselman, 2001; Woszczynski et al., 2004). As an alternative, this chapter illustrates the benefit of considering the *relationship* between two constructs such as gender and societal context.

In this chapter we address two important issues. One is the ways in which IT career choice is affected by perceptions of a woman's role that are embedded in a particular culture. The other is how other societal factors might moderate these influences.

RESEARCH METHODOLOGY

We examined four datasets of interviews conducted between 1990 and 2006 with women working in the IT workforce in four countries: Australia, New Zealand, Ireland and the U.S. These investigations were all conducted by the first author.[3] The dataset about women working in Ireland comes from two separate field studies of women in Ireland's IT sector. The first of these datasets came from interviews conducted in 1990 as part of a larger, Fulbright sponsored, investigation of the influence of socio-cultural factors -- culture, economy, infrastructure and economy -- on the evolution of Ireland's information economy (Trauth, 2001; 2000; 1999). Gender was one among many factors examined in this study.[4] The questions about gender that were part of the interviews focused on the role of women in Irish society at that time and the subsequent effect on women's potential for participation in the information economy (Trauth 2000 pp. 101-141; 1995).

The second Irish dataset came from interviews conducted in 2003 as part of a Science Foundation Ireland funded study of socio-cultural impacts of Ireland's information economy. The purpose of these interviews was to note differences in perceptions about a woman's role in Irish society, participation in the Irish information economy, and the effect of Ireland's new found economic health on the position of women.

The third dataset came from an investigation of women working in IT in Australia and New Zealand that was conducted in 2000. This study was also part of a larger study. It was carried out in conjunction with an Australian Research Council funded investigation -- Women and IT (WinIT) -- that was being conducted at Griffith University in Brisbane, Australia (Trauth, 2002; Trauth et al., 2003). The purpose of these interviews was to investigate the ways in which individual identity and individual influences helped to moderate negative societal messages about women's participation in the IT sector.

The final dataset came from a multiyear, National Science Foundation funded investigation of women in the U.S. IT workforce (2002-2007). The purpose of these interviews was to collect empirical data in order to develop and test an emergent theory about the role of individual differences in the social shaping of gender and IT. The goal was to better understand the factors that help to account for the under representation of women in the American IT sector.

All four of these projects were carried out as interpretive field studies in which the first author conducted face-to-face, open-ended interviews with female IT practitioners and academics. Strategic, convenience sampling techniques were used to facilitate geographical representation of the women in the studies.[5] Women were asked to talk about their educational backgrounds, work experiences and about family and socio-cultural factors that influenced them to become IT professionals. The women were also asked about factors that have either enhanced or inhibited their participation in the IT sector (see Appendix A).

The results of the first Irish study inspired the subsequent gender studies. While gender was one among many socio-cultural factors examined in the first Irish study, gender was the explicit focus of the Australian/New Zealand study. The theoretical insights resulting from that study, in turn, formed the basis of the U.S. study and the second Irish study was conducted contemporaneously with it.

All of the interviews lasted between 60 and 180 minutes in length[6]. A total of 200 interview transcripts were analyzed for this paper. Forty-six of these interviews were conducted in Ireland, 31 were conducted in Australia/New Zealand, and 123 were conducted in the United States (see Table 1). The interviews were recorded and transcribed in

Table 1. Interviews by country of residence

COUNTRY OF RESIDENCE	YEAR(S) CONDUCTED	# OF INTERVIEWEES
Australia/New Zealand	2000	31
Ireland	1990	25
Ireland	2003	21
United States	2002-2006	123
Total	**1990-2006**	**200**

order to facilitate coding and analysis. Transcripts from the first Irish study were coded by the first author. Themes that emerged from the first Irish study, relevant gender literature and the constructs of the emergent individual differences theory of gender and IT formed the basis for the coding of the Australian/New Zealand interviews,[7] those from the U.S. study, and the interviews from the second Irish study. The second Irish study and the U.S. study were coded by all three authors. Generic database software[8] was used to facilitate computer-based analysis of the dataset from the first Irish study. The other three datasets employed the same special purpose qualitative analysis software[9] for analysis. Analysis of the interviews was supplemented by participant observation notes about the women and their socio-cultural environment as well as by literature about the culture of the regions/countries in which the interviews were conducted. These notes were compiled by the first author who lived in each country while conducting the interviews.

RESEARCH FINDINGS

These women represent considerable variation with respect to demographics and personal characteristics. The women range in age from 21 to 65 years old with a median age of 41 years.[10] Twenty-six of the women are single, 106 women are married or in a partnered relationship, 11 women are divorced (not remarried) and one woman is widowed (not remarried).[11] Sixty-six of the women have no children, 20 women have one child, 40 women have two children, and 18 women have three or more children.[12] The women have pursued a range of (IT and non-IT related) educational paths and (undergraduate and graduate) degrees. The women also represent a diverse background with respect to IT work experience. Collectively, they include roles in: academia; information and requirements analysis; systems design and development; quality assurance; systems administration and support; consulting; training and management.

Considerable cultural variation exists in this combined data set. First, cultural differences are represented by virtue of the four countries in which the participants were living. Second, the participants in each of these countries come from a range of racial and ethnic backgrounds including: Asian (China, Korea, Japan, Taiwan, Vietnam, India), Pacific Islander (Fiji, Australia, New Zealand), Caribbean (Jamaica, Trinidad, St. Thomas and Puerto Rico), Hispanic / Latino, Middle Eastern (Lebanon, and Egypt) eastern European (Poland, and Bosnia and Herzegovina), western European (France, Germany, Italy, Ireland and the UK) (See Table 2). As a result, these women embody a rich variety of cultural influences that are manifested in a variety of ways in their professional lives.

To investigate how cultural factors are manifested in the lives of female IT practitioners and academics, we explored the perceptions of women's role in society that are embedded in a culture and how this influences career choice. In doing so, we investigated the following themes: mater-

Table 2. Participant racial / ethnic identity by country of residence

PARTICIPANT RACIAL / ETHNIC IDENTITY BY COUNTRY OF RESIDENCE	# OF PARTICIPANTS
American Participants	**123**
White American	**99**
Black American	**10**
African American	7
Afro-Caribbean	3
Asian American	**10**
Vietnamese	1
Chinese	3
Taiwanese	1
Japanese	1
Korean	1
Indian	3
Hispanic / Latino	**2**
Middle Eastern	**2**
Egyptian	1
Lebanese	1
Australian Participants	**31**
Australian Caucasian	12
New Zealand Caucasian	9
American Caucasian	1
Asian Australian	4
Indian	1
Chinese	1
South Korean	1
Fiji	1
European Australian	5
Bosnia and Herzegovina Caucasian	1
Irish Caucasian	1
Polish Caucasian	1
United Kingdom Caucasian	2
Irish Participants (1990)	**25**
Irish Caucasian	25
Irish Participants (2003)	**21**
Irish Caucasian	21
TOTAL	**200**

nity, child care, perceptions of women working outside of the home and parental care responsibilities. During this analysis a number of additional themes about cultural influences emerged from the data. These themes center around cultural factors influencing career choice determinates among women. Specifically, these were grouped into the following categories: choosing a career you *want* to do versus what you *can* do, social class influences, economic opportunities, and gender stereotypes about aptitude. These themes are discussed in more detail in the remainder of this section.

Perceptions of a Woman's Role in Society

A prevalent manifestation of cultural influence on the experiences of women in the IT workforce relates to maternity and motherhood. One aspect of this theme is how societal messages about it change over time. A common theme in the first Irish study was the ambivalence the women, particularly mothers, felt about working outside the home. As Patricia explained:

"This is a very traditional society... It is still frowned upon for a mother to work" [Patricia].

Likewise, Siobhann explained that in the 1980s a 'marriage tax' in Ireland made it very difficult for married women to work because they did not have a personal tax free allowance:

"[The Irish tax rates were very high and the laws] added together the husband and wife's salaries and taxed them as one. So, the husband got all the tax free allowances and the wives would not get any. [As a result] every hourly salary is taxed at the high rate" [Siobhann].

A decade later, the sentiment in the 2003 interviews was distinctly different. Many of the Irish women that were interviewed this time felt the position of women in their country has improved. Norah believed that the position of women is "definitely better" and there are more opportunities for women particularly in the sciences. Dymphna explained that working women are no longer viewed as taking a job away from a man who is supporting a family. In her view, this was because people have learned that dual-income couples are necessary in the new economic reality of increased costs and mortgages. Although, the position of women has improved, barriers to their participation in the IT workforce still remain however. For example, Iaobh recognizes that it is more difficult for women to climb the corporate ladder of success:

"I think [climbing the corporate ladder] depends on children. I think that is one thing that can hold some women back. ... But I think that is changing, men are getting more involved" [Iaobh].

Another theme about motherhood and careers that was raised by women in our studies relates to how the economic regime shapes societal views about women working outside of the home. For example, Anita, who is from Bosnia and Herzegovina, explained that communist and socialist ideologies, as opposed to capitalist ideologies, typically have a different view of female employment. She felt that former Soviet Union and other communist countries had very little gender segregation in high paying careers because of an importance placed on gender equality issues. Likewise, Charlene, an Australian woman who grew up in communist Poland, felt that communist and socialist ideologies were more open to women working because of pure economics. She felt this paradigm was a result of a "different society structure" where both women and men had careers and shared domestic responsibilities:

"I feel coming from a communist country, I was raised in a little bit different way than girls are raised [in capitalist western cultures]. There was more expectation on us to get to any field we wanted and gender was not really an issue. And because of economical reasons, our mothers had to work. As such, they were also our bread

winners as much as our fathers. I guess, there was a bigger awareness or let's say, acceptance of women [working]" [Charlene].

However, greater opportunity to work outside the home doesn't necessarily lead to greater equity regarding work inside the home, as the first author learned. In the course of giving research presentations about gender and IT during 2008 in conjunction with a Fulbright award, she was informed by women from two former communist countries – the Czech Republic and Romania -- that while women in communist regimes may have had more opportunity to work outside the home, they still had full responsibility for the unpaid work inside the home.

Many women also spoke about the role of government-provided child care and maternity leave. Brianna, an Irish woman, felt that the Irish national policies on maternal and paternal leave are extremely beneficial for working mothers. By taking a short amount of paid leave from work, mothers and/or fathers are able to spend quality time with newborn children, but are not punished when returning to the workforce. Two other Irish women, Iaobh and Dearbhla, believed that there has been an increase in the acceptability of mothers working outside of the home in Ireland in recent years.

A theme raised by many participants was the influence of family dynamics on their careers. These women explained how their families influenced their perceptions of the acceptability of women working outside of the home. Jada, an India woman working in America, said that her parents always encouraged her to have a career outside of the home:

"The message you got from your mother and father was always that you were going to have a career and get to go to college?" [Interviewer].

"Oh absolutely, yeah. And one of the things, the key things, that I tell people when I am talking about my influences is that for us college was not optional. It was always expected" [Jada].

At the same time, other women spoke about their cultures being more family-centered than work-centered. For Rose, who is Japanese American, her parents' traditional values dictated that she become a stay-at-home mother:

"The Japanese culture in particular does not put a lot of emphasis on women, in particular, going out of the household. There was a lot of emphasis on the Japanese women staying home and taking care of the children and as well taking on certain kinds of duties like finances and keeping, certain traditions alive" [Rose].

She went on to explain that being raised in America gave her a hybrid view of the role of women: a traditional Japanese view mixed with an assimilated American view. Another Asian American, Samantha, also felt her cultural impressions about the role of women working outside of the home are influenced by her traditional Korean background and her assimilated American upbringing.

The women, particularly those who spoke about female family responsibilities, also revealed a number of options available to them to help balance work and family. For example, Karen, an Indian woman working in America, explained:

"Traditionally in an Indian environment, when the girl is pregnant, when she is in her 3rd trimester, she would go to her mom's place and have the baby there. And come back after the baby is a few months older. It is a very traditional thing to do, because the mom's side of the family offers a lot more support" [Karen].

Mitul, an Australian woman who was born and educated in India, explained that the grandparents typically care for a child while the parents are at work. Otherwise, child care facilities are available, although this option can be costly. Furthermore, as observed by the third author of this chapter who is Chinese, it is not uncommon for Chinese women studying or working in America to send their newborn babies back to China to be raised by the grandparents during the initial stages of infancy.

With respect to work-life balance, several Asian women spoke about the expectation to care for their parents and in-laws as they get older. Carol, a Chinese American woman, explained that in China domestic responsibilities include taking care of your children, and "taking care of your parents and your husband's parents." When asked if this perception differed from that of her American co-workers, she responded:

"I think [a] difference is that probably they do not have to take care of their parents. That is the big difference I can see" [Carol].

The women also noted that pleasing parents and in-laws factored into the choice of career and lifestyle. Several Asian women spoke about the expectations that their parents and in-laws would be involved in decision making about whom to marry, where to work, and when to have children. Karen explained that it would have been "impossible" to marry her husband if his parents would not have been supportive. Mitul considered herself to be lucky because her parents and her in-laws did not object of her working once she had a child. She added that if they had objected it would have been a difficult situation and she "probably would not have gone against their wishes."

Socio-Cultural Moderators of Gender Influence

One theme that repeatedly surfaced in the interviews was the difference in career choice decision factors. Women in the U.S. study felt the American societal message of career choice centers on what you *want to be*. Yet, in other countries the societal message of career choice centers on what you *can be* or what you *should be.* For instance, Cynthia, an Australian woman from China, explained that in China the decision to enter a certain career depends more on strong academic marks than a particular interest in the subject. She explained that she did not have an interest in the IT field per se, but was encouraged to pursue a career in the field because she performed well on university entrance exams. Karen explained that she wanted to pursue a career in the humanities, but was discouraged because she earned very strong grades in school. When asked if she was oriented toward sciences, she replied:

"Yes. Although, that is not where my passion lies. It was more because I was compelled to take sciences in India. Humanities and arts were not considered something that smart kids would do. Although I was more interested in literature and the arts, my mom wanted me to go into engineering, although I wanted to do journalism" [Karen].

Rosalie, who grew up in Taiwan also felt that pursuing a career in the IT field would be prestigious for her parents. She explained that she was the youngest daughter so she had a lot of freedom in her career decisions, but she wanted to make her parents proud of her career decision by entering an esteemed field. Mitual echoed these sentiments. She explained that in India she was a "topper," a high scoring student on exams:

"I was really intelligent. I was a topper. So that is why [people said I would become a doctor]... I had good marks, [but not enough to go into medicine]... I didn't want to give up. I wanted to be a professional" [Cynthia].

Mitul added that, in India, exam scores only determine what a woman can be, but social class determines what a woman should be. She explained that in the highest social class, the expectation is that women will not work, in contrast to women in middle or lower classes who are expected to work. As a result, Mitul felt it might be easier for Indian women from the middle class to enter the IT workforce than those from the upper class.

Another career choice theme that was expressed by a few women from Ireland and China centers on the idea of "clean" work. Some women explained that traditional factory or agrarian careers required a large amount of physical labor in which workers were expected to get their hands dirty. The emergence of information work has brought a shift in the nature of work. A career in the IT workforce is generally consider "clean" since an employee does not interact directly with dirt or factory machinery. For example, Deirdre explained that when choosing a career her Irish school counselor and her father persuaded her to select an IT career because you do not "get dirty." In addition, Carol, a Chinese American, explained that her parents encouraged her to pursue an IT career because she could work in an office on a computer rather than being exposed to harsh conditions out-of-doors, as is the case with some careers. Likewise, Sibyl, who grew up in China, first became interested in an IT career because of her experience in financial accounting, which she believes is perceived as an "ideal profession for girls in China."

Yang, an Australian woman from South Korea, and Sue an Australian Caucasian, offered insights into how the differences in societal messages about career choice can be manifested. They believe women in Australian technology courses at their universities are typically Asian because they are preparing for high paying careers in their home countries. Since IT careers are in demand in many nearby countries (Malaysia, Thailand, Singapore, Indonesia and the Philippines) a larger number of the students come to Australia to seek an IT education.

A final theme noted by a number of women related to the varying messages about gender aptitude stereotypes surrounding IT. In some cultures the societal stereotype is that women are not well suited for technical work. Yet, in other cultures the stereotype is the opposite. This conflicting depiction of women's relationship with IT was frequently discussed in the interviews. For instance, Linda, an American woman from India, explained that she was never "blocked" when she pursued IT as a field of study. In addition, Carol explained that in China it is not viewed as inappropriate for women to work in IT as she feels it is in the U.S. Likewise, Haiyan, also a Chinese American, explained that women in her school in Hong Kong were encouraged by teachers to pursue studies in math and science. She also explained that this attitude was consistent among teachers in China, Hong Kong and Taiwan, although other cultural differences often exist among them. In addition, Cynthia spoke at great length about the differences between Chinese and Australian perceptions of women doing technical work:

"I think more women in China study engineering than [in Australia]. In China, our country says a woman and a man are equal. There is no [stereotype that IT] is men's work" [Cynthia].

The conflicting stereotypes about aptitude are further complicated by cultural messages about gender, race, and class. Some of the women felt that gender was not the primary distinguishing factor in stereotypes in their countries. Rather, members of a particular race and class were typically the primary targets of stereotypes in a country. For example, Allison, an American woman from Jamaica, explained that negative stereotypes in Jamaica are not focused on gender. She explains that because the country is so diverse "the issue is not race and gender, it is status and money." As a result she has a difficult time reconciling race or gender discrimination she faces in the U.S. In addition, Candace, an Australian woman from Fiji, explained that gender is not the primary factor in societal stereotypes. She explained that ethnic background such as European, Fijian or Indian is the primary distinguishing factor in Fiji:

"To be honest, nobody really cared that much about male-female [differences], because the main focus was between Fiji and Indian culture [differences]. That was the huge cultural dichotomy that existed. ... Everything else kind of paled in comparison to that" [Candace].

Lu, a Vietnamese American, spoke about how the gender stereotypes are compounded by ethnic stereotypes in the U.S. She explained that she likes math and hence, many people associate her with the stereotype that Asians are good at math:

"The majority of [my family and Asian American friends] are good at math and we excel at math and science. I think that it is kind of funny. I mean I know some people who do not fit in that stereotype whatsoever - the studious, hard working science oriented person. But I think that almost all of my family fits in that so it just kind of makes me laugh when I think about it" [Lu].

Another aspect of gender aptitude stereotypes centers on the interpretation of the term "geek." Carol explained the differences in America and China with respect to women being geeks. She feels that in the U.S. it is generally considered insulting to refer to females as geeks. As a result, a number of young girls she has met do not want the negative label associated with an interest in IT and chose not to pursue IT careers. Yet in China, Carol adds it "is just the opposite" since referring to a female as a geek is a positive comment and, in many ways, a complement.

DISCUSSION

The results presented in this chapter show the importance of including a cultural perspective in gender and IT research. We present evidence that differences in nationality and ethnicity produce varying cultural influences on women in the IT field. Further, we classified the manifestation of these cultural influences into two themes found in prior literature about cultural influences on women. These are: perceptions of women's role *that are embedded in the culture* of a society influencing IT career choice; and socio-cultural moderators of those cultural influences.

With regard to perceptions of women's role that are embedded in a society, themes about maternity, childcare, parental care, and women working outside of the home emerged from the data. With regard to socio-cultural moderators, themes about gendered career norms, social class, economic opportunity, and gender stereotypes about aptitude emerged from the data. Our analysis demonstrates how the varied perspectives on these themes produce variation in female IT career choice by culture within a country, by cultural differences within a country and by culture across multiple countries. (This analysis is depicted in Figure 1).

Our analysis shows that while themes related to parenting, family and economics might be evident in studies of women in each societal context; the *ways* in which these themes are experienced by the women vary across cultures. That is, not all women experience economic or parenthood issues in the same ways. Finally, the results of this research have clear implications for the theoretical underpinnings of gender and IT research. The evidence of varying cultural influences on women in the IT labor force and varying responses by women to common experiences such as parenthood, suggest the need for deeper examination of factors affecting women's recruitment into and retention in the IT field.

We explored these themes for several reasons. First, the themes build on prior work with the individual differences theory of gender and IT by adding to our understanding of the influence of environmental context on women in the choice of IT careers. In doing so, we explored historical and current economic and cultural factors present in the environmental context. Second, the themes, when holistically examined, represent a range of

Figure 1. A model of cultural factors influencing career choices for women in the it workforce

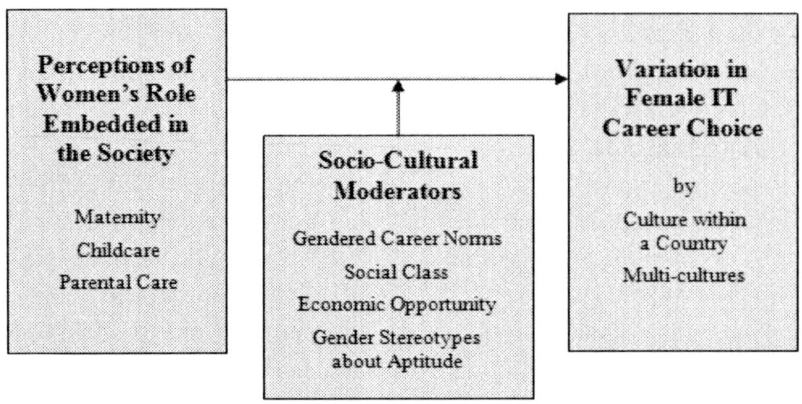

diverse influences such as the effects of: political, economic, and geographical context on gendered messages in the culture, family dynamics and expectations on career choice, and differences in support structures on career enactment. Finally, these themes demonstrate the importance of considering cultural factors when conducting gender and IT research inasmuch as they appear to significantly influence women's choice about an IT career. Doing so will become increasingly important as the IT field continues to globalize and the cultural diversity of the domestic IT workforce continues to grow.

The findings presented in this study make a contribution to both research and practice. With respect to research, our analysis points to areas of cultural influence that warrant further academic study. In addition, our findings make a contribution to theory by lending further empirical support for the theoretical insights offered by the individual differences theory of gender and IT. This theory challenges essentialist assumptions that do not consider context when concluding that the reasons for the under representation of women can be found within women themselves. That is, this theory challenges the assumption that women either are not interested in or not capable of achieving in the IT field. At the same time, evidence that different cultures exert different influences on women also adds nuance to the social construction of 'female roles' and 'gendering of IT' as they relate to the choice of a career in the IT field. We believe this theoretical lens addresses the knowledge gap about under representation in the IT field by offering a means of better understanding and articulating the varied influences on women's career choices, brought about in part, from cultural factors.

This work also makes a contribution to practice. The problem for practice relates to IT employers, policy makers, and IT educators. First, IT workforce employers need to develop interventions to increase the under representation of women that focus on recruitment and retention. One important implication of our findings is that these interventions must take into account the varied cultural influences on women. Thus, childcare provisions, alone, may not be sufficient in some countries; elder care or telecommuting provisions may be needed as well. In addition, multinational corporations may need to consider whether their human resource policies are consistent with cultural pressures on women in a particular country. It is also critical to recognize women's own agency in shaping their positions and responses to cultural factors and their subsequent relationships with technology. As the women in this study have shown, a "one size fits all" approach can be problematic.

Second, public policy can serve to enhance or hinder the recruitment of women into and their retention in the IT field in very practical ways. Our findings suggest the need to (re)visit maternity, child care and elder care policies. As pointed out in the first Irish study, tax laws provided a disincentive for some women to participate in the labor force. Policy makers interested in redressing the gender imbalance in the IT fields of their countries can look to the role that work leave, tax, antidiscrimination and other such policies might be playing in either enhancing or inhibiting women's participation.

Finally, pre-college educators play a crucial role in increasing the under representation of females in the IT field. Employers and IT educators need to work in collaboration with primary and secondary educational institutions to conduct outreach programs for students and their parents. By providing a 'face' of the IT worker to whom these young women and their parents can relate, we may be able to change both the image and the composition of the IT profession.

CONCLUSION

The research presented in this chapter supports an argument for reexamining the discourse regarding diversification of the IT workforce in a critical and broad sense: what diversity means and how to address diversification issues from multiple integrated perspectives. Trauth et al. (2006a) suggest that we should take a comprehensive view of diversity that builds upon the notion of "diversity as difference," and include in our consideration not only demographic differences, but also socio-cultural and individual differences. Other researchers have also pointed out that the IT gender gap is not an isolated phenomenon and stress the need to address the gender issues in conjunction with other issues such as class, race, ethnicity, etc. (Kvasny, 2003; Kvasny et al., 2009; Naryayan, 1998).

Our results contribute to the growing body of IT workforce research literature that is focused on cultural variation in gender and IT issues. The analysis of two themes (perceptions of women's role in society and socio-cultural moderators) reveals a wide range of influences on women's choice of an IT career based upon nationality and ethnicity. These results reinforce the need to move away from theoretical lenses that reinforce monolithic analyses of gender and IT and that assume a common experience for all women. Instead, we argue for the need to move toward more robust and nuanced analyses that take into account the wide variation of both influences on women in the IT field and women's varied responses to them.

ACKNOWLEDGMENT

This research was funded by a grant from the National Science Foundation (NSF EIA-0204246, 2002-2007), two Fulbright awards (Ireland, 1989-1990; Austria, 2008), a Science Foundation Ireland distinguished visitor award (2003), and a grant from the Australian Research Council (2000). Earlier versions of this work appeared in Trauth et al. (2006b, 2008a).

REFERENCES

Adam, A., Howcroft, D., & Richardson, H. (2002). Guest Editorial. *Information Technology & People*, *15*(2), 94–97.

Adams, J. C., Baichoo, S., & Bauer, V. (2006). Women Embrace Computing in Mauritius. In E.M. Trauth (Ed.), *Encyclopedia of Gender and Information Technology* (pp. 1258-1266). Hershey, PA: Idea Group Publishing.

Adams, J. C., Bauer, V., & Baichoo, S. (2003). An Expanding Pipeline: Gender in Mauritius. In *Proceedings of ACM SIGCSE Conference, Reno, Nevada, February 19-23, 2003* (pp. 59-63). New York: ACM Press.

Arnold, D., & Niederman, F. (2001). The Global Workforce. *Communications of the ACM, 44*(7), 31–33. doi:10.1145/379300.379306

Australian Bureau of Statistics. (2002). Special Tabulation. Unpublished. Cited in Staehr, L., Byrne, G. and Bell, E. (2006). Gender and the Australian IT Industry. In Trauth, E.M. (Ed.), *Encyclopedia of Gender and Information Technology* (pp. 467-473). Hershey, PA: Idea Group Publishing.

Burger, C. J., Creamer, E. G., & Meszaros, P. S. (Eds.). (2007). *Reconfiguring the firewall: Recruiting women to information technology across cultures and continents*. Wellesley, MA: AK Peters Publishing.

Camp, T. (2002). Reprints: The incredible shrinking pipeline. *ACM SIGCSE Bulletin, 34*(2), 129–134. doi:10.1145/543812.543846

Clarke, V. A., & Teague, G. J. (1994a). Encouraging girls to study computer science - Should we even try? *Australian Educational Computing, 9*(1), 17–22.

Clarke, V. A., & Teague, G. J. (1994b). A psychological perspective on gender differences in computing participation. In *Proceedings of the ACM SIGCSE 1994 Conference* (pp. 258-262). New York: ACM Press.

Creamer, E. G., Lee, S., & Meszaros, P. S. (2007). Predicting women's interest and choice in a career in information technology: A statistical model. In C.J. Burger, E.G. Creamer & P.S. Meszaros (Eds.), *Reconfiguring the firewall: Recruiting women to information technology across cultures and continents*. Wellesley, MA: A K Peters, Ltd.

Downie, R., Dryburgh, H., McMullin, J., & Ranson, G. (2004). A profile of information technology in Canada. *Workforce Aging in the New Economy International Report, Number One*. Retrieved from http://www.wane.ca/PDF/IR1.pdf.

Durndell, A., Haag, Z., & Laithwaite, H. (2000). Computer self efficacy and gender: A cross-cultural study of Scotland and Romania. *Personality and Individual Differences, 28*, 1037–1044. doi:10.1016/S0191-8869(99)00155-5

Ecevit, Y., Gündüz-Hoşgőr, A., & Tokluoğlu, C. (2003). Professional women in computer programming occupations: The case of Turkey. *Career Development International, 8*(2), 78–87. doi:10.1108/13620430310465480

Eidelman, L., & Hazzan, O. (2005). Factors influencing the shrinking pipeline in high schools: A sector-based analysis for the Israeli high school system. In the *Proceedings of the ACM SIGCSE Conference, St. Louis, MS, February 23-27, 2005* (pp. 406-410). New York: ACM Press.

Eidelman, L., & Hazzan, O. (2006). The shrinking pipeline in Israel high schools. In E. M. Trauth (Ed.), *Encyclopedia of gender and information technology* (pp. 1092-1098). Hershey, PA: Idea Group Publishing.

Finquelievich, S. (2003). Civil society and the new economy. Social Science Research Council. Retrieved from http://www.ssrc.org/programs/itic/publications/knowledge_report/memos/finquelievichmemo2.pdf

Frieze, C., Hazzan, O., Blum, L., & Dias, M. B. (2006). Culture and environments as determinants of women's participation in computing: Revealing the "women-CS" fit. In *Proceedings of the ACM SIGCSE Conference, Houston, TX, March 1-5, 2006* (pp. 22-26). New York: ACM Press.

Galpin, V. (2002). Women in computing around the world. *ACM SIGSCE Bulletin, 34*(2), 94–100. doi:10.1145/543812.543839

Hembry, O., & Presley, A. (2006). IT proves to be a turnoff for women. Retrieved from http://www.nzherald.co.nz/topic/story.cfm?c_id=498&objectid=10370311

Hersh, M. (2000). The changing position of women in engineering worldwide. *IEEE Transactions on Engineering Management*, *47*(3), 345–359. doi:10.1109/17.865903

Howcroft, D., & Trauth, E. M. (2008). The implications of a critical agenda in gender and IS research. *Information Systems Journal*, *18*(2), 185–202. doi:10.1111/j.1365-2575.2008.00294.x

Huang, H. (2006). The cross-cultural dimension of gender and information technology. In E. M. Trauth (Ed.), *Encyclopedia of gender and information technology* (pp. 147-153). Hershey, PA: Idea Group Publishing.

Huang, H., & Trauth, E. M. (2006) Cultural diversity challenges: Issues for managing globally distributed knowledge workers in software development. In P. Yoong & S. Huff (Eds.), *Managing IT professionals in the Internet age* (pp. 254-276). Hershey, PA: Idea Group, Inc.

Huyer, S. (2005, June 12-14). Women, ICT and the information society: Global perspectives and initiatives. In *Proceedings of the International Symposium on Women and ICT: Creating Global Transformation,* Baltimore, MD. New York: ACM Press.

Information Technology Association of America (ITAA). (2005). *Untapped talent: Diversity, competition, and America's high tech future – Executive summary*. Retrieved from: http://www.itaa.org/eweb/upload/execsummdr05.pdf

Irwin, L. (2000). Gender inequities in technology in developing nations: Females and computers in traditional cultures. *Intercultural Education*, *11*(2), 195–200. doi:10.1080/713665242

Jackson, L. A., Zhao, Y., Qiu, W., Kolenic, A., Fitzgerald, H. E., Harold, R., & von Eye, A. (2008). Culture, gender and information technology use: A comparison of Chinese and US children. Comput. *Human Behavior*, *24*(6), 2817–2829. doi:10.1016/j.chb.2008.04.007

Kvasny, L. (2003). Triple jeopardy: Race, gender and class politics of women in technology. In M. Mandviwalla & E.M. Trauth (Eds.), *Proceedings of the 2003 ACM SIGMIS Conference on Computer Personal Research, Philadelphia, Pennsylvania, USA* (pp. 112-116). New York: ACM Press.

Kvasny, L., Trauth, E. M., & Morgan, A. (2009). Power relations in IT education and work: The intersectionality of gender, race and class. *Journal of Information . Communication and Ethics in Society Special Issue on ICTs and Social Inclusion*, *7*(2/3), 96–118.

Li, N., & Kirkup, G. (2007). Gender and cultural differences in Internet use: A study of China and the UK. *Computers & Education*, *48*(2), 301–317. doi:10.1016/j.compedu.2005.01.007

Llewellyn, D., & Usselman, M. (2001). *Ethnic differences in female applicants to engineering and IT majors*. American Educational Research Association Conference (AERA), Seattle, Washington.

Makrakis, V., & Sawada, T. (1996). Gender, computers and other school subjects among Japanese and Swedish students. *Computers & Education*, *26*(4), 225–231. doi:10.1016/0360-1315(95)00085-2

Margolis, J., & Fisher, A. (2002). *Unlocking the clubhouse: Women in computing*. Cambridge, MA: MIT Press.

Medeiros, C. B. (2005, June 12-14). From subject of change to agent of change – Women and IT in Brazil. In *Proceedings of the International Symposium on Women and ICT: Creating Global Transformation,* Baltimore, MD. New York: ACM Press.

Meszaros, P. S., Lee, S., & Laughlin, A. (2007). Information processing and information technology career interest and choice among high school students. In C.J. Burger, E.G. Creamer, and P.S. Meszaros (Eds.), *Reconfiguring the firewall: Recruiting women to information technology across cultures and continents*. Wellesley, MA: AK Peters Publishing.

Minguez, A. M. (2005, June 12-14). New technologies as social fact: Gender and digital divide in Spain in compared perspective. In *Proceedings of the International Symposium on Women and ICT: Creating Global Transformation,* Baltimore, MD. New York: ACM Press.

Morgan, A. J., Quesenberry, J. L., & Trauth, E. M. (2004). Exploring the importance of social networks in the IT workforce: Experiences with the 'boy's club.' In J. Luftman (Ed.), *Proceedings of the Americas Conference on Information Systems, New York* (pp. 1313-1320).

Naryayan, U. (1998). Essence of culture and a sense of history: A feminist critique of cultural essentialism. *Hypatia: A Journal of Feminist Philosophy, 13*(2), 86-107.

Nielsen, S., von Hellens, L., Pringle, R., & Greenhill, A. (1999). Students' perceptions of information technology careers: Conceptualising the influence of cultural and gender factors for IT education. *GATES, 5*(1), 30–38.

Nielsen, S., von Hellens, L. A., Greenhill, A., & Pringle, R. (1998). Conceptualising the influence of cultural and gender factors on students' perception of IT studies and careers. In *Proceedings of the 1998 ACM SIGCPR Conference,* Boston, MA, (pp. 86-95). New York: ACM Press.

Organization for Economic Co-operation and Development (OECD). (2007). ICTs and gender. Retrieved from: http://www.oecd.org/dataoecd/16/33/38332121.pdf

Pande, R. (2006). Digital divide, gender and the Indian experience in IT. In E.M. Trauth, (Ed.), *Encyclopedia of gender and information technology* (pp. 191-199). Hershey, PA: Idea Group Reference.

Quesenberry, J. L., & Trauth, E. M. (2005). The role of ubiquitous computing in maintaining work-life balance: Perspectives from women in the IT workforce. In C. Sorensen, Y. Youngjin, K. Lyytinen, & J.I. DeGross (Eds.), *Designing ubiquitous information environments: Socio-technical issues and challenges* (pp. 43-55). New York, Springer.

Quesenberry, J. L., & Trauth, E. M. (2007). What do women want?: an investigation of career anchors among women in the IT workforce. In *Proceedings of the ACM SIGMIS Computer Personnel Research Conference, St. Louis, Missouri, April* (pp. 122-127). New York: ACM Press.

Quesenberry, J. L., & Trauth, E. M. (2008). Revisiting career path assumptions: The case of women in the IT workforce. In *Proceedings of the International Conference on Information Systems* (Paris, France, December).

Quesenberry, J. L., Trauth, E. M., & Morgan, A. J. (2006). Understanding the 'mommy tracks': A framework for analyzing work-family issues in the IT workforce. *Information Resources Management Journal, 19*(2), 37–53.

Rosser, S. V. (2005, June 12-14). Women and ICT: Global issues and actions. In *Proceedings of the International Symposium on Women and ICT: Creating Global Transformation,* Baltimore, MD. New York: ACM Press.

Sanders, J. (2005, June 12-14). Gender and technology in education: What the research tells us. In *Proceedings of the International Symposium on Women and ICT: Creating Global Transformation,* Baltimore, MD. New York: ACM Press.

Schienstock, G. (1999). *Social exclusion in the learning economy.* Presented at the European Socio-Economic Research Conference, Brussels. Retrieved from http://www.uta.fi/laitokset/tyoelama/sowing/report/SocExcLearningEcon.pdf

Schinzel, B. (1999, July 29-31). The contingent construction of the relationship between gender and computer science. In *Proceedings of International Symposium on Technology and Society: Women and Technology,* New Brunswick, NJ, (pp. 299-311).

Shen, C. Y., & Ge, J. (2005, June 12-14). Women and ICT: from the Chinese perspective. In *Proceedings of the International Symposium on Women and ICT: Creating Global Transformation,* Baltimore, MD. New York: ACM Press.

Shiva, V. (1989). *Staying Alive: Women, Development, and Ecology in India.* London: Zed Press.

Siddiqui, H. N. *(2008).* Investigation of intention to use e-commerce in the Arab countries: A comparison of self-efficacy, usefulness, culture, gender, and socioeconomic status in Saudi Arabia and the United Arab Emirates. *Doctoral Thesis.*

Teague, J. (2002). Women in computing: What brings them to it, what keeps them in it? *SIGCSE Bulletin, 34*(2), 147–158. doi:10.1145/543812.543849

Trauth, E. M. (1995). Women in Ireland's information industry: Voices from inside. *Eire-Ireland, 30*(3), 133–150.

Trauth, E. M. (1999). Leapfrogging an IT labor force: Multinational and indigenous perspectives. *Journal of Global Information Management, 7*(2), 22–32.

Trauth, E. M. (2000). *The culture of an information economy: Influences and impacts in the Republic of Ireland.* Dordrecht, The Netherlands: Kluwer Academic Publishers.

Trauth, E. M. (2001). Mapping information-sector work to the workforce: The lessons from Ireland. *Communications of the ACM . Special Issue on The Global IT Workforce, 44*(7), 74–75.

Trauth, E. M. (2002). Odd girl out: An individual differences perspective on women in the IT profession. *Information Technology & People, 15*(2), 98–118. doi:10.1108/09593840210430552

Trauth, E. M. (2006). Theorizing gender and information technology research. In E.M. Trauth (Ed.), *Encyclopedia of gender and information technology* (pp. 1154-1159). Hershey, PA: Idea Group Publishing.

Trauth, E. M., & Howcroft, D. (2006). Critical empirical research in IS: An example of gender and IT. *Information Technology & People, 9*(3), 272–292. doi:10.1108/09593840610689859

Trauth, E. M., Huang, H., Morgan, A. J., Quesenberry, J. L., & Yeo, B. (2006a). Investigating the existence and value of diversity in the global IT workforce: An analytical framework. In F. Niederman & T. Ferratt (Eds.), *Managing information technology human resources* (pp. 331-360). Hershey, PA: Information Science Reference.

Trauth, E. M., Nielsen, S. H., & von Hellens, L. A. (2003). Explaining the IT gender gap: Australian stories for the new millennium. *Journal of Research and Practice in IT, 35*(1), 7–20.

Trauth, E. M., & Quesenberry, J. (2006). Are women an underserved community in the information technology profession? In *Proceedings of the International Conference on Information Systems, Milwaukee, Wisconsin, December.*

Trauth, E. M., Quesenberry, J., & Huang, H. (2006b, April 13-15). Cross-cultural influences on women in the IT workforce. In *Proceedings of the 2006 ACM SIGMIS CPR Conference, Claremont, California, USA* (pp. 12-19). New York: ACM Press.

Trauth, E. M., Quesenberry, J., & Huang, H. (2008a). A multicultural analysis of factors influencing career choice for women in the information technology workforce. *Journal of Global Information Management, 16*(4), 1–23.

Trauth, E. M., Quesenberry, J., & Yeo, B. (2008b). Environmental influences on gender in the IT workforce. *The Data Base for Advances in Information Systems, 39*(1), 8–32.

Trauth, E. M., & Quesenberry, J. L. (2005, June, 23-24). Individual inequality: Women's responses in the IT profession. In G. Whitehouse (Ed.*), Proceedings of the Women, Work and IT Forum, Brisbane, Queensland, Australia.*

Trauth, E. M., & Quesenberry, J. L. (2007). Gender and the information technology workforce: issues of theory and practice. In P. Yoong & S. Huff (Eds.), *Managing IT professionals in the Internet age* (pp. 18-36). Hershey, PA: Idea Group Publishing.

Trauth, E. M., Quesenberry, J. L., & Morgan, A. J. (2004). Understanding the under representation of women in IT: Toward a theory of individual differences. In M. Tanniru, & S. Weisband (Eds.), *Proceedings of the 2004 ACM SIGMIS Conference on Computer Personal Research, Tucson, Arizona, USA* (pp. 114-119). New York: ACM Press.

Trauth, E. M., Quesenberry, J. L., & Yeo, B. (2005). The influence of environmental context on women in the IT workforce. In *Proceedings of the ACM SIGMIS Computer Personnel Research Conference, Atlanta, Georgia, April* (pp. 24-31).

Varma, R. (2007). Changing borders and realities: Emigration of Indian scientists and engineers to the United States. *Perspectives on Global Development and Technology, 6*(4), 1–18. doi:10.1163/156914907X253224

Varma, R., Prasad, A., & Kapur, D. (2006). Confronting 'socialization' barrier: Cross-ethnic differences in undergraduate women's preference for IT education. In J. McGrath Cohoon & W. Aspray (Eds.) *Women and information technology: research on underrepresentation* (pp. 301-323). Cambridge, MA: MIT Press.

Weil, M. M., & Rosen, L. D. (1995). The psychological impact of technology from a global perspective: A study of technological sophistication and technophobia in university students from twenty-three countries. *Computers in Human Behavior, 11*(1), 95–133. doi:10.1016/0747-5632(94)00026-E

Women and Minorities in Information Technology Forum. (1999). *Causes and Solutions for Increasing the Numbers in the Workforce Pipeline*. Women and Minorities in Information Technology Forum, Old Dominion University, Hampton Virginia.

Workforce Aging in the New Economy (WANE). (2004). *Europe, phase one: A selection of initial findings on employment diversity*. Retrieved from http://www.wane.ca/PDF/EUBriefing.pdf

Woszczynski, A., Myers, M., Beise, C., & Moody, J. (2004, August 5-8). Diversity within the ranks: How ethnicity affects choices in IT. In *Proceedings of the Tenth Americas Conference on Information Systems (AMCIS)*. New York.

ENDNOTES

1 The Japanese cultural norm of "Ryosai Kenbo" (translated to "good wife, clever mother") can be traced back to the late 1800s during the Meiji reign. It is still influential

today for Japanese girls from all social classes to pursue an education that is suitable for a good wife, and clever mother.

2 While the research, to date, has applied this theory to the study of women, it is intended that this theory is also applicable to men.

3 The second and third authors were involved in the data analysis for the U.S. and the second Irish studies.

4 For a complete set of factors examined in this larger study see Trauth (2000 pp. 387-390).

5 In the case of the two Irish studies and the Australian/New Zealand study women throughout the country were interviewed. In the case of the American study the geographical representation was limited to three states: Massachusetts, North Carolina and Pennsylvania. This was done because of the size of the American population in contrast to that of Ireland, Australia and New Zealand. Limiting the geographical representation, thus, facilitated more focused socio-cultural analysis. (See, for example, Trauth et al., 2008)

6 The norm was 90 minutes.

7 The Australian/New Zealand transcripts were coded by the first and second authors.

8 A retrieval system based on Foxpro was developed.

9 QSR N6.

10 Age data was not collected for all participants in the original Ireland and Australian studies. Hence, the age statistics do not include information for 25 Irish women and 10 women from the Australian/New Zealand study.

11 Relationship status was not collected for all participants in the original Ireland and Australian/New Zealand studies. Hence, the relationship statistics do not include information for 25 Irish women and 31 Australian/New Zealand women.

12 Motherhood status was not collected for all participants in the original Ireland and Australian/New Zealand studies. Hence, the motherhood statistics do not include information for 25 Irish women and 31 Australian/New Zealand women.

APPENDIX A: INTERVIEW TOPICS

First Irish Study (1990)

Demographic background (country of origin, country of residence at time of interview)
Personal background (educational background, IT work experience)
Experiences as a woman working in the IT field in Ireland

Australian/New Zealand Study (2000)

Demographic background (country of origin, country of residence at time of interview)
Personal background (educational background, IT work experience)
Experiences as a woman working in the IT field in Australia or New Zealand

U.S. and Second Irish Study (2002-2006, 2003)

Demographic background (age, race/ethnicity, country of origin, country of residence at time of interview)
Personal background (relationship status, parenthood status, educational background, IT work experience)
Experiences as a woman working in the IT field in the US or Ireland

Note: While for the two earlier studies the question about experiences as an IT professional in the country was asked in a very open-ended fashion, for these two studies the questions were more directive. That is, participants were specifically asked to discuss significant influences on career progression such as people and experiences in their lives. Nevertheless, women in each study were asked to relate their experiences as an IT professional to the societal and cultural context in which they lived, studied and worked. Thus there was consistency in the data that was collected that was used in this paper.

Chapter 3
The Information System Strategies of MNC Affiliates:
A Technology-Organization-Environment Analysis

Vincent S. Lai
The Chinese University of Hong Kong, Hong Kong

ABSTRACT

This article applies a technology-organization-environment framework to evaluate the determinants of the global information systems (GIS) strategies of foreign affiliates. The results indicate that IT maturity, parent resource dependency, cultural distance, restrictive regulations, and local competition are significant determinants of GIS strategy. We also find that the integration-responsiveness model can be applied to explain GIS strategies and their implementation. These findings provide additional insight into the complex relationship between headquarters and affiliates in GIS management. We conclude by discussing the implications of our findings for both research and practice.

INTRODUCTION

Today's globalized business environment has motivated multinational corporations (MNCs) to establish affiliates in foreign markets to achieve economies of scale and critical mass, reduce risk, and facilitate effective resource sharing (Neo, 1991). This means that MNCs must rely on information technology (IT) to manage, control, and plan their operations to compete effectively on a global level. Although many MNCs have global business strategies to guide their expansion into foreign markets, few have corresponding global information systems (GIS) strategies, despite how critical they are to the coordination and integration of worldwide business operations (Karimi & Konsynski, 1991; Lai, 2001; Lai & Wong, 2003). With the increasingly widespread use of international networks and global databases, information is now moved and shared globally, with the result that GIS have become a prime source of competitive advantage (Grover, Segars, & Durand, 1994).

Over the last decade, many MNCs have adopted enterprise resource planning (ERP) systems to integrate their worldwide business functions, including production, planning, purchasing, manufacturing, sales, distribution, accounting, and customer service. These ERP systems have emerged as complete business software systems that, ideally, facilitate enterprise-wide integration of information by connecting MNC headquarters, affiliates, and partners worldwide without geographical restrictions (Sheu, Yen, & Krumwiede, 2003). In practice, however, ERP implementation is complex and has a low success rate of 10% (Zhang, Lee, Huang, Zhang, & Huang, 2005). ERP success is even harder to achieve when MNCs and affiliates must deal with cultural issues in their business operations (Dar & Balakrishnana, 2006). Considering that most ERP systems have been developed in Europe and North America and have built-in value bias reflecting Western cultures, foreign affiliates operating in China, for example, often find it hard to accept them (Xue, Liang, Boulton, & Snyder, 2005). Consequently, they turn to domestic ERP systems to find a 'fit' between ERP functionality and business culture (Liang, Xue, Boulton, & Byrd, 2004; Xue et al., 2005; Sheu, *et al.*, 2005; Wang, 2006). This misalignment of ERP systems in supporting affiliate IS activity represents an unanticipated GIS issue that MNCs must tackle (Madapusi & D'Souza, 2005).

Not only has ERP been extensively implemented to support integrated GIS IT infrastructure and information architecture, but many MNCs have also outsourced or offshored part or all of their IT functions as a solution to their GIS strategies (Doh, 2005). Though outsourcing and offshoring offer MNCs benefits such as lower costs, improved productivity, higher quality, higher customer satisfaction, faster time to market (Dhar & Balakrishnan, 2006), and an ability to deal with international conflicts and cultural differences (Lai, 2001), the effectiveness of these strategies in resolving GIS issues remains unexplored, particularly in the internal governance that ensures the offshore components strictly adhere to corporate worldwide procedures and rules.

Undoubtedly, globalization and IT advancement have already made GIS strategic design more + and offshoring, which have already shattered the traditional wisdom of GIS management, continue to reshape the IT architecture and information infrastructure that support GIS operation and management (Madapusi & D'Souza, 2005; Wilcocks & Feeny, 2006). Consequently, GIS strategy must be flexibly designed to overcome organizational, cultural, political, and political issues. The evolution of affiliates and their local IS strategies complicates GIS strategy design. In the past, it was commonly assumed that the GIS strategy of MNCs, including GIS cross-border activities, was decided at headquarters, with foreign affiliates being limited to decisions regarding local IS operating environments (Luo, 2003; Roth & O'Donnell, 1996). However, the increasing competitiveness in the global economy now requires MNCs to adopt more decentralized GIS strategies that can enable faster responses and more flexibility in local environments (Karimi & Konsynski, 1991; Lai & Floyd, 1998; Rosenzweig & Nohria, 1994). This development has drastically redefined the role of foreign affiliates in GIS management, which now encompasses the responsibility for developing individual information technology (IT) capacities appropriate for the original and distinctive markets in which they operate (Papanastassiou & Pearce, 1997). In other words, foreign affiliates now have the option to build up technological capacity within their own operations or to collaborate with other affiliates or headquarters to attain a more integrated IT capability (Lai & Wong, 2003). Many foreign affiliates go through creative transitions in which local environments and IT processing needs increasingly differentiate their positions within their MNCs, which makes it even more difficult to formulate GIS strategies appropriate to their new roles.

Against this background, we find that only a few studies have investigated various GIS strategies and their relative effectiveness (Lai & Wong, 2003). These investigations suggest that GIS strategy can be shaped by an MNC's organizational characteristics, management intentions (Tractinsky & Jarvenpaa, 1995), IT architecture, affiliates' strategic roles (Karimi & Konsynski, 1991), national differences and cultural distance (Morosini, Shane, & Singh, 1998; Sheu et al., 2003); local regulations (Lai 2001; Lai & Wong 2003), and international strategy (Taylor, Beechler, & Napier, 1996). These research variables can be divided into three categories: IT architecture, organization characteristics, and local and international environment. Hence, a technology-organization-environment (TOE) framework provides an appropriate research model for future investigations of global IS strategy issues and effectiveness. It should be noted, however, that Shore (2006) has adapted the integration-responsiveness (IR) perspective of Prahalad and Doz (1987) to argue that GIS strategy may be the consequence of an MNC responding to two pressures: the pressure to decentralize to improve local responsiveness and the pressure to centralize to improve global business integration. Unfortunately, this IR model has not been evaluated in the context of IS research.

These previous studies have undeniably contributed significantly to the understanding of GIS strategy, but most are conceptual explorations and do not validate their propositions and frameworks with empirical data. Even where empirical data are available, they have been collected from MNCs that are headquartered in the United States. This bias gives rise to two problems. First, the findings from these studies represent the perspective of headquarters, and thus do not shed light on the role of foreign affiliates in deciding GIS strategy or on the impact of GIS strategy on local IS management. It is therefore doubtful whether the results can be extended to foreign affiliates. Second, the findings can only explain the IS operations of U.S. organizations in overseas markets, and again have limited applicability in the international business context.

This study has two specific objectives: to validate the applicability of the IR model to IS, not only because of its rich theoretical foundation but also because of its limited application thus far to any strategy-related IS research, and to apply the TOE framework to systematically organize the determinants that contribute to the formulation of GIS strategy from an international and affiliate perspective. The results of this study will provide both insight and guidance for those involved in GIS implementation. In generating guidelines for the design of a GIS strategy, we make a number of important contributions. First, we acknowledge the relative importance of local conditions, IT characteristics, and organizational characteristics in shaping an affiliate's GIS strategy. More significantly, the model and propositions that are developed in this study represent an important step toward providing a theoretical and empirical research framework to give researchers a better understanding of the determinants of GIS management among foreign affiliates.

THEORETICAL BACKGROUND

In this study, two models are adopted to evaluate GIS strategy. The TOE framework is applied to systematically evaluate the critical determinants of GIS strategy formulation and the IR model is then used to classify the various types of strategies for managing GIS operations.

Technology-Organization-Environment Framework

In 1990, Tornatzky and Fleischer (1990) proposed the technology-organization-environment framework in an attempt to provide a more systematic and structured approach to exploring the impact of technology, organization, and environment on the adoption and implementation of IT. The TOE framework identifies three aspects of a firm's context that are relevant and critical to IT in business operations: the *technology context*, which describes the internal and external technologies that are relevant to a firm, the *organization context*, which describes the nature and characteristics of a firm, and the *environment context*, which describes the arena in which a firm conducts its business (Zhu & Kraemer, 2005; Zhu, *Kraemer, & Xu*, 2003).

The TOE framework has been applied to investigate the adoption of a wide variety of IT, such as EDI (Iacovou, Benbasat, & Dexter, 1995; Thong, 1999), open systems (Chau & Tam, 1997), and electronic business (Yap, 2006; Zhu & Kraemer, 2005; Zhu et al., 2003). Although specific TOE factors are employed in these investigations, the findings provide consistent empirical support for the appropriateness of the TOE framework in innovation research (Zhu et al., 2003). In the context of the international business strategy of MNCs, a growing body of literature (for example, Garfield & Watson, 1998; Lai & Wong, 2003; Straub, 1994) indicates that TOE factors are important determinants of strategy formulation and performance, although both theoretical and empirical concerns abound. It is likely that the TOE framework can be extended to investigate the dynamics of GIS strategy, because GIS strategy is determined by technological competency and maturity, driven by organizational vision and characteristics, and influenced by global and local IT processing requirements and environments.

Integration-Responsiveness Model

The IR model of Prahalad and Doz (1987), which grew out of earlier evolutionary MNC development theories, has been proven to be a robust framework for the evaluation of MNC strategy at the headquarters and affiliate level (Venaik, Midgley, & Devinney, 2004). Initially, three environmental pressures confronting MNCs were identified in the IR model: the global integration of activities, global strategic coordination, and local responsiveness. However, due to the high correlation between the first two pressures, Prahalad and Doz combined them to create two pressure dimensions: the pressure for global integration and the pressure for local responsiveness. Global integration incentives include economies of scale and scope, which lower the cost and standardization of IS management, implementation, and development. Incentives for local responsiveness, in contrast, include customization and adaptation to local markets or cultural settings to ensure the viability and prosperity of the organization. Only through carefully crafted adaptation to the local environment can MNC foreign affiliates develop unique competitiveness-enhancing IS organizational competencies and routines. These combined pressures constitute the IR model, which has been successfully applied to explain the fit between strategy and environment and its relationship to the performance of MNCs.

A clearer explication of these pressures is given in Figure 1, in which each pressure is represented as a separate axis that comprises a 2 x 2 matrix. Based on this matrix, GIS strategies can be classified into three categories: (1) *globally integrative*, with an emphasis on global strategic coordination, (2) *locally responsive*, with an emphasis on the domestic level, and (3) *multi-focal*, with an emphasis on both global collective operations and domestic responsiveness (Prahalad & Doz, 1987).

The IR model has also been suggested as a model for distinguishing affiliate types, and the work of Jarillo and Martinez (1990) has been inspirational in this regard. They found that there are three classes of affiliate (see Figure 1) that correspond to the three IR strategies: *active affiliates*, which are highly integrated and highly responsive, *autonomous affiliates*, which are highly responsive but poorly integrated, and *receptive affiliates*, which have a low level of re-

Figure 1. Integration-responsiveness model at the affiliate level

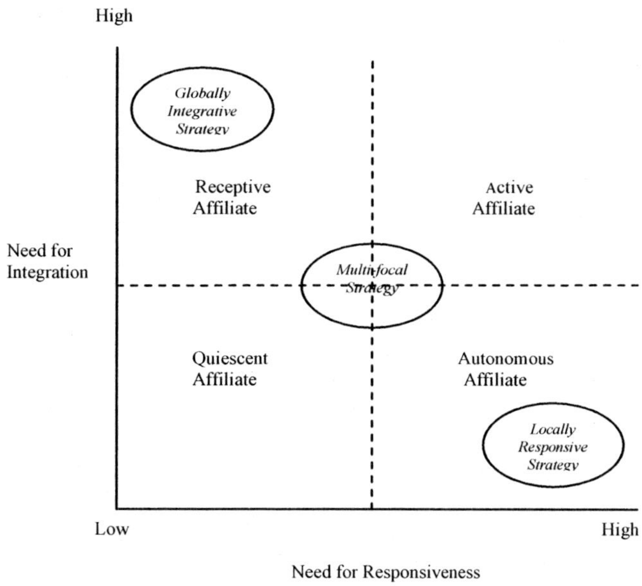

sponsiveness but are highly integrated. In a later study, Taggart (1997) identified a new class of affiliate: *quiescent affiliates*. These affiliates are located in the last quadrant of the IR matrix, and are characterized by poor integration and a low level of responsiveness. To date, much research effort has been devoted to the investigation of the characteristics of these four classes of affiliate (for example, Hannon, Huang, & Jaw, 1995; Roth & Morrison, 1992; Taggart, 1997). However, in this study we focus on GIS strategy type, rather than affiliate type, and thus the IR model is only used to guide our classification of GIS strategies.

RESEARCH MODEL

The research model that is illustrated in Figure 2 is used explicitly to examine the determinants of GIS strategy at the affiliate level. Although researchers strive to develop comprehensive research models that incorporate all potentially important variables, this is often not possible. Such attempts often prove unwieldy, fail to provide any additional insight, or result in restricted data analysis due to sample size constraints (Premkumar & King, 1992). Therefore, our study focuses on a parsimonious TOE framework that includes only those variables that are relevant to TOE factors and that are deemed relevant in the GIS setting.

The dependent variable of our research model is GIS strategy. According to the IR model, GIS strategies can be classified as locally responsive, globally integrative, or multi-focal. The TOE determinants in the model include IT maturity, the formalization and centralization of the MNC, the cultural distance and resource dependency between parent and affiliate, local regulations, and local competition. To control the effects of firm size, industry type, and country that might affect GIS strategy decision, these three variables are designed as control variables in our study.

In the technology context of the TOE framework, IT maturity is critical to GIS strategy selection. To fulfill the IT processing requirements of both headquarters and local offices, the IS department of an affiliate needs to monitor and maintain

Figure 2. TOE research framework for GIS strategy selection

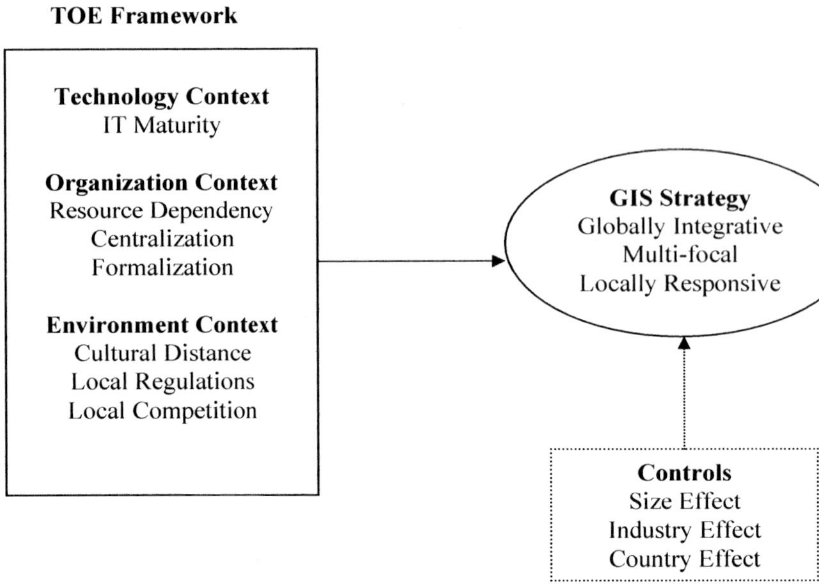

the operational efficiency and effectiveness of the organization's global IT infrastructure, including networks, hardware, and software. It also needs to upgrade and integrate its software and hardware systems to ensure the competitiveness of the corporate IT architecture. Hence, the maturity of the IT infrastructure has a significant impact on an affiliate's GIS strategy selection. Many previous TOE studies (for example, Thong, 1999; Zhu & Kraemer, 2005) have adopted IT maturity and sophistication as the critical technology variables in examining the adoption and implementation of innovation, and mostly conclude that technology competency and sophistication are related to the adoption, implementation, and success of IS.

In the organization context, organization size, scope, financial commitments, centralization, formalization, and management support are some of the most frequently investigated TOE variables (Thong, 1999; Zhu & Kraemer, 2005). Of these, centralization and formalization are critical to shaping the organizational norms necessary to establish a GIS strategy that is either centrally integrated, distributed, or locally independent. The parent-affiliate relationship has also been validated as a determinant of strategy formation and selection in many international strategy studies. Of all the reported types of parent-affiliate relationship, resource dependence between headquarters and local affiliates seems to be the most relevant to our study. For a GIS strategy to be effective, IT professionals worldwide must orchestrate the planning, design, management, and control of an MNC's IT activities to attain optimal performance. However, the effectiveness of such parent-affiliate collaborations is affected by resource support and availability, which in turn may change an MNC's GIS strategy. Hence, it is important to include resource dependence alongside organizational centralization and formalization as the organization variables in the TOE model.

The environment context has been identified by international strategy researchers to include local culture and values, local regulations, and local competition. GIS researchers (Lai & Mahapatra, 2004; Lai & Wong, 2003) have also argued that restrictive regulations, the cultural distance between headquarters and an affiliate, and local business competitiveness are both determinants and moderators of GIS strategy and its effectiveness. GIS researchers have suggested that MNCs with overseas operations are exposed to local pressures that derive from market demand, government regulations, and local competitors and force them to adjust their GIS strategies to make them more adaptive and flexible to the host country. Affiliates also need to consider their cultural distance from headquarters, as a wider cultural gap requires a greater effort to adapt to local cultural values and may create additional burdens (Tihanyi, Griffith, & Russell, 2005). It is therefore important to empirically investigate the effects of local regulations, local competition, and cultural distance on GIS strategy in the presence of conflicting pressures for local responsiveness and global integration.

RESEARCH HYPOTHESES

Technology Context

The ability of an affiliate's IS function to integrate its IT infrastructure in support of globally collaborative business models is critical to the selection of a GIS strategy (Andriole, 2006). IT infrastructure is difficult to configure, because it incorporates a diverse set of complex IS questions, such as the distribution of data and applications both at headquarters and among foreign affiliates, the standards that are adopted in processing and communication in the international context, the data architecture that guides future worldwide systems development, the heterogeneity of IT platforms across all IS processing sites, and the shared databases that support the information requirements of current global business processes (Lai & Mahapatra, 2004). A firm with a mature IS function is likely to have an integrated and sophisticated IT infrastructure so that it can take full advantage of the benefits offered by IT. In the technology assimilation model (McFarlan, 1984), IT maturity is defined as the last phase in the IT diffusion process. Firms that are classified as being in this phase have generally disseminated IT benefits and experience to all units within the firm, are almost at the end of the IT learning curve, emphasize the formal and long term planning of IT, and have installed an integrated IT infrastructure.

A number of researchers have conceptually explored the relationship between IT infrastructure and GIS strategy, but no empirical evidence has been reported to support this relationship. The effects of IT maturity on IS have also been investigated by a number of researchers (such as Karimi & Konsynski, 1991; Lai, 2001). Raymond (1990), for example, provides confirmatory evidence that a higher level of IT sophistication and maturity positively influences the success of IS within an organization, and that greater sophistication in the use of IT (in terms of hardware and software technology) leads to significantly better system and organizational performance. The successful implementation of a GIS strategy requires an MNC and its affiliates to have a mature, well developed, and diverse IT infrastructure, and as GIS strategy determines the policies and technologies that dictate the deployment and use of IT within an affiliate, the success of such a strategy is likely to be determined by the maturity of the IT infrastructure. If an affiliate does not have a mature IT infrastructure, then it lacks the flexibility to devise an optimal GIS strategy that can respond to the conflicting pressures of global integration and the demand for local responsiveness. This is particularly true in the case of globally integrative strategies, which require a mature IT infrastructure to ensure and support IT integration across systems and countries. Silvestro and Westley (2002) believe that a mature cross-functional integrated IT infrastructure improves collaboration between functions and the alignment of organizational objectives, which are factors that favor a global IS strategy. Kim (1994) argues that an integrated and mature IT infrastructure helps organizations to focus on their strategic goals and that the IS function does not require additional effort or resources directed toward reengineering IT infrastructure to fit organizational strategy. This implies that foreign affiliates with a more mature IT infrastructure are less likely to deviate from the IS strategy of headquarters or design their own. We therefore postulate the following hypothesis:

H1: *Affiliates with a more mature IT infrastructure will adopt a globally integrative GIS strategy, rather than a locally responsive or multi-focal GIS strategy.*

Organization Context

Affiliate's Dependence on the Parent

Luo (2003) suggests that parent-subsidiary links exert a strong and positive influence on the performance and strategy of subsidiaries or affiliates. Frequently, MNCs control their corporate resources (such as capital, technology, and management) to influence the GIS strategy of their affiliates.

Hannon et al. (1995) state that affiliates that are more dependent on the parent MNC for technology and management resources are more susceptible to the influence of the parent's international strategies. Martinez and Ricks (1989) have also found that the influence of the parent firm over the global policies of its affiliates is positively related to the extent to which the parent provides resources to affiliates. This is because when there is an increase in the resource flow between affiliate and parent, the level of resource dependence—and thus the need for control—increases (Pfeffer & Salancik, 1978; Taylor et al., 1996). When this is the case, it is logical to argue that affiliates that are more reliant on the parent for IS technical and managerial know-how are more heavily influenced by the IS practices of the parent, and hence follow a more globally integrated or multi-focal GIS strategy. Based on these views, we hypothesize the following:

H2: *Affiliates that are more dependent on their parent for resources will follow a globally integrative, rather than a locally responsive or multi-focal, GIS strategy.*

Affiliate Organizational Characteristics

International business researchers have pointed out that the organizational structure (such as centralization and formalization) of an MNC is the key to its global strategy. Egelhoff (1982) states that to operate successfully in the global environment, the organizational structure and GIS strategy of an MNC should match, and that an MNC should select the most efficient or lowest cost structure that satisfies the information processing requirements inherent in its strategy. This theoretical assumption implies that an MNC's GIS strategy and information processing requirements must be aligned with its organizational structure and information processing capabilities.

Centralization is the degree to which power and control are concentrated in the hands of relatively few individuals (Rogers, 1983). Egelhoff (1988) argued that worldwide organizational structure tends to centralize strategic decision making, but this structure tends to be less sensitive to local political and economic conditions. Therefore, Karimi and Konsynski (1991) suggest that the GIS strategy of MNCs with a more decentralized organizational structure should aim to be more responsive to the local markets of its affiliates. This means that strategic decisions are decentralized and headquarters is mainly responsible for monitoring the results of the operations of affiliates. Lai and Floyd (1998) share this perspective, and believe that decentralized affiliates are more inclined to pursue a locally responsive GIS strategy to reap data processing benefits, but are careful to select one that creates the fewest problems with global information exchange. In accordance with the previous studies, we propose the following hypothesis:

H3a: *The affiliates of more decentralized MNCs will follow a more locally responsive GIS strategy, rather than a globally integrative or multi-focal GIS strategy.*

Formalization is the degree to which an organization emphasizes rules and procedures in the role performance of its members (Rogers, 1983). The correlation between formalization and IT adoption has been heavily investigated in IS research, but seemingly lacks conclusive findings. Most researchers (such as Burns & Stalker, 1961) argue that more informal organizations tend to adopt new technologies more readily than do formal organizations because high degrees of formalization can restrict innovation adoption by inhibiting exploration. Other researchers (such as Grover & Goslar, 1993; Lai & Guynes, 1998), however, do not support this finding and suggest that the level of formalization has no impact on the adoption of innovations.

In the context of GIS strategy research, the relationship between formalization and local GIS strategy has been found to be negative in most cases. As Sullivan explained (1992/1993), formalization has been adopted to create standards and ensure predictability, but differing conditions across markets have threatened the idealized consistency of formalization. Stopford and Wells (1972) also suggested that though formalization is integral to reducing ambiguity caused by differentiated subsidiaries, local directives should still take precedence. In fact, coordination and control between headquarters and affiliates is achieved through personal relationships, rather than by written rules, procedures, or a formal organizational structure. Therefore, it is expected that less formalized organizational characteristics encourage affiliates to be more liberal in adapting to local IS expectations and practices (Garfield & Watson, 1998; Karimi & Konsynski, 1991). Hence, we postulate that:

H3b: *The affiliates of less formalized MNCs will follow a more locally responsive GIS strategy, rather than a globally integrative or multi-focal GIS strategy.*

Environment Context

Cultural Distance between Parent and Affiliate

National culture and cultural distance have a significant influence on strategic decisions (Kashlak, 1998). Cultural distance is defined as the degree to which the cultural norms of one country are different from those of another (Kogut & Singh, 1988; Morosini et al., 1998). Holmstrom, Fitzgerald, Agerfalk, and Conchuir (2006) suggest that cultural distance is a complex dimension that involves organizational culture, national culture and language, politics, and individual motivations and work ethics. A greater cultural distance leads to greater differences in organizational and administrative practices, employment expectations, and the interpretation of and response to strategic issues (Kogut & Singh, 1988; Park & Ungson, 1997).

In the context of GIS, culture has a strong influence on the viability in a given country of strategies and IS that were developed in another country (Hofstede, 1993). The alignment of cultural norms and technology policies thus plays a major role in shaping GIS policy (Garfield & Watson, 1998). Taylor et al. (1996) argue that the more similar the host country's culture to that of the home country, the easier it is for an affiliate to follow the practices of its parent. They believe that greater similarity between cultural values and norms reduces the barriers to employing strategies and practices that were developed at headquarters. Roth and O'Donnell (1996) indicate that when the cultural distance between an affiliate and its corporate headquarters is greater, the affiliate should be allowed more responsibility in formulating and determining strategy. In the context of GIS, it is always preferable to maintain a homogeneous processing environment worldwide to take advantage of standard IT maintenance, acquisition, data exchange, and application development. As Lai (2001) points out in his GIS study, the smaller the cultural distance between parent and affiliate, the easier it is for an affiliate to achieve internally consistent GIS practices. This is especially true when a parent MNC establishes brand-new affiliates that do not present employee resistance or institutional pressure to utilize local IS policies and practices. In addition, the costs and uncertainty associated with affiliates are likely to be greater in culturally dissimilar host countries than in culturally similar countries (Padmanabhan & Cho, 1996). We thus hypothesize the following:

H4: *Affiliates with a smaller cultural distance from the parent may follow a globally integrative GIS strategy, rather than a locally responsive or multi-focal GIS strategy.*

Restrictive Local Regulations

Overseas affiliates are frequently impeded by host country laws and regulations, which determine the extent to which local government restricts affiliate business activities, including cross-border data flow and IS processing (Luo, 2003). Steinbart and Nath (1992), in their research on global network operations, report that almost 70% of MNCs have encountered at least one type of local political constraint, including the use and choice of networks, hardware, and software. Such restrictions are often compounded by a lack of international uniformity in laws and regulations, which prevents MNCs and their affiliates from formulating effective IS strategies to support GIS practices that benefit parent-affiliate collaboration.

The emergence of restrictive local regulations has proven to be a catalyst for change in the way MNC manages their affiliates. Sambharya and Phatak (1990), for example, report that MNCs with a centralized GIS strategy are more affected by local restrictions than those with a distributed or decentralized GIS strategy. Wang (1993) also believes that local regulations will create major barriers for GIS management, thus recommends seven strategies to deal with this problem. These include the reduction of data activities, the use of remote computing services, and change the GIS strategy to become more decentralized and distributed. After all, a locally responsive approach allows affiliates' local processing needs to be met more readily and flexibly, particularly in the presence of locally enacted restrictive regulations. Hence, we hypothesize the following:

H5: *Affiliates that operate in a more restrictive local environment will follow a locally responsive GIS strategy, rather than a globally integrative or multi-focal GIS strategy.*

Local Competition

IT can fundamentally alter the basis of competition (Applegate, 1996) and competition can have a significant impact on the formulation of GIS strategy (Lai, 2003). Porter (1990) argues that competition drives the process of initiation and upgrading capability, and that the level of local competition has a positive influence both on an affiliate's own competitiveness and on its contributory role in local markets. In a highly competitive environment, the success of an affiliate depends more on how well it fits into the host country than on the level of support it receives from headquarters (Hannon, 1995). Consequently, the affiliate's IS platform should differ from that of its parent in functionality, data architecture, hardware platform, or even customer, order, and sales support (Jarvenpaa & Ives, 1994).

Li, Murray, and Efendioglu (2002) believe that to bring costs down, a successful global strategy must include not only top-quality products but must also be supported by aggressive localization. These notions can also be applied to GIS management in arguing that locally responsive strategies enable affiliates to compete more effectively, for example, by allowing them to handle IT resources more flexibly. IS strategies can then be more responsive to local problems, systems development and maintenance better tailored to local processing needs, and business problems more readily resolved. Choi and Nailer (2005) also suggest that pursuing a local strategy in a competitive environment may save significant costs. The key elements of localization-based cost reductions include tariffs, management, software development, personnel, and operations. We thus hypothesize the following:

H6: *Affiliates that operate in a more competitive local environment will follow a locally responsive GIS strategy, rather than a globally integrative or multi-focal GIS strategy.*

RESEARCH METHOD

Data Collection

The empirical data were collected through a postal questionnaire that was sent to four independent samples, each of which contained 250 MNC foreign affiliates that operated in Canada, Japan, the United Kingdom, or the United States. These four countries were selected for two reasons. First, they have a large number of MNCs operating overseas. Second, they allowed us to build a comparative index for each parent-affiliate country pair (e.g., U.S. MNCs with affiliates in Japan, U.K., and Canada; Japan MNCs with affiliates in the U.K., Canada and the U.S., etc.), which was required for the operationalization of cultural distance. These selection criteria consequently allow us to collect data only from developed countries.

Affiliates were randomly drawn from the *Worldwide Branch Locations of Multinational Companies*, *International Directory of Corporate Affiliations*, *Directory of Foreign Investment in the U.S.*, and *Foreign Affiliated Companies in Japan*, using two selection criteria. The first was that the headquarters of the MNCs had to be located in one of the aforementioned countries, and the second was that the headquarters had to own at least 51% of the affiliate.

Before conducting the survey, a local survey representative was appointed in each country to manage and coordinate the local survey activities. These local representatives were also responsible for identifying the contact information of the IS directors of the affiliates and for making follow-up phone calls if any of the directors failed to respond to the survey. In the first mailing of the survey, the questionnaire, along with a covering letter that explained the purpose of the study, was sent to the IS executive responsible for managing the affiliate's GIS. A month later, the local survey representatives made follow-up phone calls and mailed additional questionnaires to the IS executives who did not respond to the initial communication.

Operationalization of the Variables

Variables in the model were measured with Likert-type items with which the respondents were asked to agree or disagree on a 7-point scale. Most variables were adapted from earlier empirical work on innovation and strategy, and only a few items were constructed for the specific purpose of this investigation.

The dependent variable, *IR*, was operationalized by the eleven-item scale developed by Prahalad and Doz (1987), the first six items of which determine the extent of global integration and the last five items the degree of local responsiveness.

This construct has been adopted and validated in many IR studies with largely positive results (Taggart, 1997).

IT maturity was captured using a construct that was developed by Raymond and Pare (1992). This is a multi-dimensional construct that measures the aspects of technological diversification, processing diversification, the number of IS specialists, and the formality of planning. Raymond, Pare, and Bergeron (1994) later adapted this construct to study organizational performance.

Centralization was evaluated by using the multi-item measures of Hage and Aiken (1967), including the extent of the participation of subordinates in decision and policy making, the flexibility of decision making, and the extent to which individual decision making is encouraged. To measure *formalization*, the respondents were asked to assess "rule codification," that is, the extent to which rules were employed, and "rule observance," or the degree to which the conformance of employees to company standards was supervised. Similar centralization and formalization measures have been used by Hage and Aiken (1967), Grover (1993), and Grover and Goslar (1993).

Dependency on the parent was measured by a scale that was adapted from the work of Liu et al. (1998) and Hannon et al. (1995). This scale consisted of questions about the degree to which the parent firm's technology was used, the degree to which the parent's management system was shared, the degree of reliance on the parent's IS research and development support, and the amount of integration between the affiliate's IS activities and those of other parts of the MNC.

Cultural distance was measured using the four original attributes (individualism, masculinity, uncertainty avoidance, and power distance) identified by Hofstede (1991). Using these indices, a composite index for each parent-affiliate country pair (for example, U.S.-Japan) based on the deviation in each of the four cultural dimensions was formed to generate the measure of cultural distance. The deviations were corrected for variance for each dimension, and were then arithmetically averaged. This equation for cultural distance calculation was originally developed by Kogut and Singh (1988), and has been successfully used on several other occasions (see Arora & Fosfuri, 2000; Erramilli, 1996; Kashlak, 1998; Padmanabhan & Cho, 1996; Roth & O'Donnell, 1996).

The magnitude of *local restrictions* was measured by the level of data restrictions on GIS operations, which include restrictions on privacy law, business records, personal information export, data creation, and databank registration. This approach was adopted by Sambharya and Phatak (1990) and Lai and Floyd (1998) in studying the impact of trans-border data flow restrictions on GIS management among MNCs. *Local competitiveness* was measured by using a three-item scale that rated the intensity of domestic business competition, competition among local partners, and competition among local competitors.

Three controlled variables are used in our study: firm size, industry type, and country of operation. *Firm size* was measured by the affiliate's annual sales and number of employees, and *industry type* was classified into finance, manufacturing, IT, insurance, and health. Our research only investigated affiliates operating in the U.S., the U.K., Japan, and Canada. These four countries naturally become our *country types*.

Data Analysis

The data analysis was conducted in two stages. In the first stage, cluster analysis was used to identify the discrete categories of the sample based on the two aggregated dimensions of global integration and local responsiveness. After the clusters were established, the between-cluster variance and *F*-values were assessed to cross-validate the solution, which comprised three clusters. In the second stage, an ANOVA analysis was performed to evaluate the significant differences in the TOE variables across the three-cluster solution. This procedure was followed by a series of *post hoc*

Scheffe's multiple-range tests to validate the hypothesized differences in the GIS strategic dimensions.

This two-stage analysis is a frequently used statistical approach to strategy classification and the testing of differences in the chosen variables among strategy groups, and has been used in several IR strategy studies, including those of Hannon et al. (1995), Jarillo and Martinez (1990), Roth and Morrison (1992), Taggart (1997), and Venaik et al. (2004).

Validity and Reliability

A number of measures were taken to ensure the validity and reliability of the instrument. First, content validity was established through the careful selection and adaptation of items from previously validated instruments. Second, the construct was pilot tested by two business professors with expertise in survey research and three IS executives with varying degrees of GIS management experience. Feedback from the pilot test was used to improve the readability and quality of the questions in the instrument. Third, measurement reliability was checked by computing the Cronbach's alpha, with items with a low correlation being dropped. The results, which are presented in Table 1, show that the Cronbach's alpha values for the variables were significantly higher than the 0.7 range that is recommended by Nunnally and Bernstein (1994) for the early stages of basic research. Fourth, a factor analysis was performed to test the construct validity of the instrument. This determined whether the measurement items loaded in accordance with the *a priori* theoretical expectations. Only those items with factor loadings of greater than 0.5 were used in the study. The results of this analysis are also given in Table 1.

Table 1. Factor analysis of GIS strategic variables

	Cronbach's Alpha	Factor Loading	Eigenvalue
Global Integration	0.87		1.43
IS decisions worldwide		0.78	
IS specifications developed by HQ		0.76	
Affiliate services world-wide		0.82	
Centralization of technology development		0.87	
Dependence of affiliate on internal network		0.77	
Centralization of IS planning		0.89	
Local Responsiveness	0.77		1.38
Heterogeneity of customers and their needs		0.79	
Level of IS sophistication		0.71	
Stability of technology		0.78	
Product line and IS process		0.84	
Heterogeneity of executive group		0.78	

continued on the following page

Table 1. continued

IT Maturity	0.83		1.73
Technological diversification		0.77	
Processing diversification		0.72	
Number of IS specialists		0.81	
Formality of planning		0.73	
Dependence on parent resources	0.78		1.63
Information technology		0.78	
Management system		0.84	
IS research and development support		0.72	
Degree of parent-affiliate integration		0.78	
Centralization	0.84		2.11
Participation of subordinates in decision making		0.82	
Action taken before decision approval		0.77	
Discouragement of decision making		0.84	
Participation of subordinates in new policy		0.79	
Formalization	0.86		1.89
Freedom to work as desired		0.81	
Own rules formulated		0.74	
Employees checked for rule violations		0.72	
Comprehensive rules exist for routine operations		0.83	
Local Regulations	0.81		2.45
Privacy protection laws		0.85	
Business records		0.78	
Export of personal information		0.87	
Database creation		0.82	
Registration of databanks		0.76	
Local competition	0.86		4.14
Domestic business		0.84	
Local partners		0.89	
Local competitors		0.80	

RESULTS

Profile of the Respondents

Of the 1,000 affiliates in the sample, 312 (87 from Canada, 72 from Japan, 69 from the United Kingdom and 84 from the United States) responded, yielding an effective response rate of 34.2%, which was better than expected. This high response rate can be attributed to the use of local survey representatives and the follow-up phone calls. Replies were tested for non-response bias by comparing sales and number of employees of the firms of the respondents from the first mailing, the second mailing, and the non-respondents. There were no statistical differences between the three categories of samples, which offer some assurance of the representativeness of the responding affiliates.

According to the respondent profiles, which are given in Table 2, over 39% of the foreign affiliates were in the finance and manufacturing sectors. The sales of these affiliates ranged from U.S. $1.8 million to over U.S. $2 billion, with the average sales level being around U.S. $150 million. The affiliates represented 229 different corporate parents, all of which were headquartered in the studied countries. As for the respondents themselves, 87.8% were senior IS executives. The seniority of the respondents means that the quality of the data is high, which is important given that the study focuses on the analysis of IS strategies.

Cluster Analysis of GIS Strategies

A cluster analysis was performed to evaluate the dimensions of the various GIS strategies by following a three-step approach of preliminary cluster solution, selection of candidate number of clusters, and final cluster solution (Punj & Stewart, 1983). In the first step, a three-cluster solution analysis was initially performed to determine whether the IR model of Prahalad and Doz was supported by our study. The results, which are shown in Table 3,

Table 2. Characteristics of respondents

	Canada	Japan	U.K.	U.S.	Total
1. Industry					
Finance	19	14	16	20	69 (22.1%)
Manufacturing	14	10	11	18	53 (17.0%)
Computer/IT	12	12	7	15	46 (14.7%)
Insurance	7	6	6	9	28 (9.0%)
Medical/health	5	7	9	6	27 (8.7%)
Other	26	21	16	15	78 (25.0%)
Missing	4	2	4	1	11 (3.5%)
2. Title of respondents					
Senior VP or VP of IS	10	9	8	9	36 (11.5%)
CIO	12	19	8	15	54 (17.3%)
Director of IS	32	23	27	36	118 (37.8%)
Manager of IS	21	15	12	18	66 (21.2%)
Other	10	4	13	5	32 (10.3%)
Missing	2	2	1	1	6 (1.9%)

indicate that a three-cluster solution is appropriate for our dataset. The cluster means suggest that Cluster 1 predominantly confronts the pressure for global integration, Cluster 3 predominantly confronts the pressure for local responsiveness, and Cluster 2 simultaneously confronts both pressures. After the clusters were established, an ANOVA was conducted, the *F*-statistics of which show the means of all of the IR proxies to be significantly different from each cluster.

In the second step, solutions with 2, 4, and 5 clusters were developed. Each solution's between-group variance and *F*-value was evaluated to determine the best clustering. The results, based on the between-group variance analysis, show the two-, three-, four-, and five-cluster solutions to have a variance of 46%, 59%, 61%, and 64%, respectively. From this finding, it is obvious that the proportion of variance increases very slowly after the three-cluster solution, which suggests that a three-cluster solution is the most appropriate. In the *F*-values analysis, we observed a significant decline in *F*-value as the three-cluster solution was changed to a two-, four-, or five-cluster solution, which reinforces the appropriateness of the three-cluster solution.

In the last step to confirm the cluster solution, we performed a t-test on all of the clusters to determine whether the clustering was due to industry-specific differences. The findings show that the proportion of respondents from the three clusters does not vary significantly according to industry type, and we can thus be confident that the differences between our respondents in terms of IR pressures are related to strategy.

Validation of the Hypotheses

The ANOVA procedure was carried out to compare the means of the TOE variables using the three-cluster solution. Of the seven proposed TOE variables, which are shown in Table 4, five were found to vary significantly among the three strategy clusters. These five variables were further assessed by using Scheffe's multiple range tests, and the results were used to validate the postulated hypotheses.

Table 3. Cluster analysis: three-cluster solution

Industry variables	Cluster 1 (n = 58)	Cluster 2 (n = 73)	Cluster 3 (n = 82)	F-value
IS decisions worldwide	4.51	3.12	3.07	38.3*
IS specifications developed by HQ	4.02	3.28	3.10	17.9*
Affiliate services worldwide	3.79	3.27	2.08	24.7*
Centralization of technology development	3.51	3.18	2.54	16.1*
Dependence of affiliate on internal network	4.24	2.56	2.08	27.8*
Centralization of IS planning	5.21	2.82	2.54	30.1*
Heterogeneity of customers and their needs	3.02	3.41	4.01	24.3*
Level of IS sophistication	3.61	3.39	4.83	15.4*
Stability of technology	2.46	3.32	4.32	9.7*
Product line and IS process	2.84	3.26	3.82	30.3*
Heterogeneity of executive group	2.42	3.01	3.44	10.4*

* *Significant at the $p \leq 0.01$ level.*

As is indicated in the last column of Table 4, the affiliates pursuing a globally integrative strategy have a more mature IT infrastructure than those following a multi-focal or locally responsive strategy, which supports our hypothesized relationship (*H1*) between these two variables. Affiliates adopting a globally integrative strategy also have a greater extent of parent-affiliate resource dependence, which supports our hypothesis (*H2*) that affiliates with a greater dependence on the parent for resources follow a globally integrative GIS strategy. However, the organizational variables, including both centralization and formalization, do not differ significantly across the three GIS strategies, and thus propositions *H3a* and *H3b* are not supported.

We find the cultural distance between parents and affiliates to be an important variable in determining GIS strategy. As is indicated in Table 4, global strategies are statistically different from local strategies in terms of cultural distance, which supports our hypothesis (*H4*) that affiliates that are culturally closer to the parent follow a globally integrative strategy, rather than a locally responsive strategy. However, the affiliates pursuing a locally responsive strategy are found to operate in a more restrictive local environment than those following a globally integrative or multi-focal strategy, which supports our hypothesis (*H5*) that a more restrictive local environment favors a more locally responsive GIS strategy. Compared to the globally integrative and multi-focal strategies, locally responsive strategies are also found to be more extensively adopted in local environments that are more competitive. This validates our hypothesis (*H6*) that a more competitive local environment is likely to favor the application of a locally responsive GIS strategy. Between the global and multi-focal strategies, our findings suggest that affiliates in a more competitive environment prefer a global strategy over a multi-focal strategy.

Finally, the effects of the three control variables (firm size, industry type, and country) on GIS strategy are examined. The use of these variables in our model helps control for firm-, industry-, and country-level differences that might affect GIS strategy selection. Of these three control variables, only country has a significant impact on GIS strategy, suggesting that affiliates operating in different countries would have different preferences of GIS strategies. These findings imply that affiliate selection of GIS strategies is not determined by firm size or industry type

Table 4. Comparison of GIS variables in the three-cluster solution

GIS variables	Globally integrative (1)	Multi-focal (2)	Locally responsive (3)	*p*-value	Contrast[1]
IT maturity	5.47	5.11	4.76	0.00**	1>2,3; 2>3
Dependence on parent resources	4.91	4.23	4.12	0.00**	1>2,3
Decentralization	4.31	4.38	4.45	0.14	--
Formalization	4.90	4.81	4.88	0.21	--
Cultural distance	2.19	2.32	2.46	0.03*	3>1
Local regulations	4.01	3.92	5.01	0.00**	3>1,2
Local competition	4.31	3.98	4.96	0.00**	3>1,2; 1>2

* *Significant at the* $p \leq 0.05$ *level.*

** *Significant at the* $p \leq 0.01$ *level.*

[1] *Based on Scheffe's multiple range test*

difference, but rather by country difference in business operation.

DISCUSSION AND IMPLICATIONS

We find that the IR model is applicable to explain GIS strategy in situations in which MNCs are confronted with diverse and often conflicting environmental pressures as they undergo international expansion. Our study also finds that GIS strategy is not determined by industry or by degree of globalization, but by the organizational and environmental forces that confront affiliates, a notion that is generally consistent with the categorization that is suggested by the IR model. Although MNCs may react differently to the same IR pressures, the TOE framework serves as a good basis for the elaboration MNC responses to underlying IR pressures.

In general, the TOE framework provides a good guideline for the assessment of affiliate GIS strategies. Although centralization and formalization do not vary significantly across the three types of GIS strategy, our findings (Table 4) indicate that the direction of the correlations is aligned with the relationships that we hypothesized. In the global environment, a GIS strategy may take a long time to develop, and may be altered directly or indirectly by various organizational and environmental factors. Such factors may have overpowered the relevant structural factors during the period that is covered by this study, and thus a statistical test of direction may prove more meaningful than a test of magnitude of the effects. Affiliates with more decentralized and informal structures are found to be more inclined to adopt a locally responsive strategy rather than a globally integrative strategy. This relationship is not statistically significant, but takes the direction that we proposed in our hypotheses.

We also find two significant correlations that were not hypothesized. The first is that affiliates with a more mature IT infrastructure are more likely to adopt a multi-focal strategy than a locally responsive strategy. This relationship makes sense, as affiliates pursuing a multi-focal strategy place emphasis on both local responsiveness and global integration, and, like affiliates pursuing a globally integrative strategy, must have a mature platform in place to be able to coordinate with headquarters and their sister affiliates effectively and efficiently. The second unexpected finding is that affiliates which operate in a more competitive local environment prefer a globally integrative strategy to a multi-focal strategy. This finding is contradictory to the results of many previous studies, but may be explained by the need for more control and cost saving in highly competitive environments, in that an affiliate may implement a standardized and centrally developed IS to create a more controlled environment for the ease of management and to achieve economies of scale.

Implications for Practitioners

Our findings validate that IT maturity is a determinant of the adoption of a globally integrative GIS strategy. In today's business environment, most affiliates have already moved toward the adoption of sophisticated and integrated IT to ensure smooth data exchange and application interoperability. Our findings confirm that for MNCs and their affiliates to take advantage of the benefits of a globally integrative strategy, such as cost savings, standardized IS management, compatible information architecture, and optimized IS performance, they must first have a mature IT infrastructure in place. To sustain the success of a globally integrative strategy, IS professionals should continue to invest in more globalized and sophisticated IT. In other words, IS professionals must be the prime movers in developing planning processes that link information strategies to the IS processing needs of parent and affiliates and in encouraging investment in IT that is aligned with the organization's GIS strategy. They should devote more effort and resources to the assimilation of emerging innovative IT and the improvement of standards to ensure a mature IT infrastructure that ensures reliable and secure IS services worldwide.

The insignificance of the organizational variables in this study suggests to IS professionals that the selection of a GIS strategy is determined by the correct matching of an affiliate's IT capability and its IS and business operating environment. Of course, the existence of organizational norms that support decentralized and informal decisions and IS structures may encourage an MNC and its affiliates to consider a more localized GIS strategy. However, affiliates must be aware that the characteristics of their organization are of less importance than environmental and IT factors in determining GIS strategy. Our study finds that affiliates in distinct business contexts require distinct GIS strategies that respond to their IS needs. A correct match between context and strategy thus guarantees the overall feasibility and effectiveness of the chosen GIS strategy. A mismatch may lead to inefficient GIS operations and will eventually oblige the affiliate to rebalance context and strategy to cope with the pressure to survive and the pressure to sustain a competitive edge. Consequently, IS professionals need to focus on evaluating their IS requirements and environment in shaping an appropriate GIS strategy.

Our findings suggest that the cultural distance between parent and affiliate exerts a powerful influence on GIS strategy selection, which signals to IS professionals that culture is a critical determinant in the formulation of a GIS strategy. If an affiliate's IS platform is to be operated in a very different culture from that of the parent firm, then it may be a good idea to outsource implementation to a partner that can make sense of the foreign environment and handle culturally sensitive tasks.

The findings of this study offer support for those who contend that locally restrictive regulations favor the adoption of a locally responsive GIS strategy. The implication of this finding for IS professionals is clear—local restrictions can affect the GIS operations of an affiliate, which in turn can lead to a wide range of IS design and management issues. To deal with these issues effectively, a locally responsive GIS strategy is preferable to other strategies in terms of handling of data control, application development, maintenance, and other IS activities. In addition, it may also be advisable for local IS professionals to cultivate good relationships with local regulatory authorities, both personally and on behalf of the organization, to minimize the likelihood of regulatory interference. Another alternative for dealing with local regulations is the establishment of collaborative relationships with local service providers and the utilization of their capabilities. To ensure the success of such collaborations, IS professionals must be trained to acquire skills critical to vendor relationship management. Of course, foreign affiliates must also attempt to establish internal strategies to resolve regulatory issues, such as the adaptation of IT products to local requirements, learning from the affiliates of other leading MNCs or customers, keeping abreast of foreign technologies, and maintaining access to local skilled IT professionals.

Implications for Researchers

This study confirms that the IR model is applicable to GIS strategy, which implies that MNCs seek a variety of ways of co-opting the assistance of their foreign affiliates to alleviate the pressures of IS integration and responsiveness. However, this study does not investigate the roles that headquarters and affiliates play in the formulation of GIS strategy, which leaves us uninformed as to whether this process is uni-, bi-, or multi-directional. Furthermore, it is also doubtful whether foreign affiliates play an active role as sentient agents that are able to develop and implement their own local IS strategy that they can sell to headquarters and that fulfills their IS objectives. In general, a GIS strategy must be adapted to the worldwide business environment, which changes over time. This means that it is critical for researchers to investigate the corresponding evolution of GIS strategy and the role of each TOE dimension in strategy shifts. Follow-up investigations could look at the most and least volatile GIS strategies and could undertake detailed studies to evaluate the pattern of change in each type of strategy and the variables that initiate that change.

The significance of the environmental variables (cultural distance, local regulations, and local competition) on GIS strategy calls for research into how a locally responsive strategy should be implemented. Previous studies suggest that a locally responsive strategy includes the use of local vendors and partners in the form of joint ventures, outsourcing, or any other form that is beneficial to all of the parties that are involved. Of these forms, outsourcing seems to be most prevalent among affiliates, perhaps because of its cost effectiveness. If affiliates are moving toward outsourcing as a strategy, then research is needed to explore the outsourcing strategies that best fit a given GIS strategy. For example, it must be determined whether total outsourcing would better fit a locally responsive strategy and partial outsourcing a multi-focal strategy. Inevitably, research is also needed on the impact of GIS strategy on outsourcing strategy and its subsequent effect on the IS performance of parent and affiliates. As different affiliates may have different IS processing capabilities, it would be logical to evaluate whether IS specialization, based on certain combinations of IS needs and cultural, social, and technological variables, could be developed by an affiliate in house. If both outsourcing and in-house approaches are feasible GIS strategies, then researchers should propose guidelines for their adoption, implementation, and management.

Among affiliates that adopt locally responsive GIS strategies, it is natural that some will develop distinct technological competencies, both internally and through organized cooperation with external business partners in the host country. The experiences of the development of such competencies, along with the competencies themselves, are crucial to overall IT competitiveness. MNCs must seek ways to tap into these competencies and integrate them to improve their IT infrastructure to support their GIS operations. However, the assimilation of local IS competencies is not an easy task, particularly when affiliates are only marginally integrated with each other. Thus, research is needed to investigate how IS competencies are generated in the global context, the extent to which such competencies are transferred back to headquarters and to sister affiliates, how this competence can be successfully assimilated and diffused throughout an MNC, and the factors that influence the level of integration of competencies between headquarters and affiliates. Obviously, future research should also investigate the strategic role of affiliates in the knowledge transfer process.

A somewhat unanticipated finding of this study is the lack of influence of organizational characteristics (decentralization and formalization) on affiliate GIS strategies. Previous studies have consistently argued that affiliates need to be more flexible in dealing with the local culture and environment, possibly through the adoption of a local strategy and the practice of local hiring. These studies suggest that affiliates also need to be empowered to deal with local conflicts, that they should be encouraged to create norms to cope with changes, and that affiliates that adopt a locally responsive strategy should be more decentralized and informal. Future research should investigate the validity of this postulation and assess the extent to which organizational structure and characteristics influence GIS strategy.

The sample in our study only covers developed countries, the economic structure of which is influenced by the U.S. business environment. Therefore, the findings may not be applicable to non-U.S. business contexts. Conceptually, developing and underdeveloped countries configure their business practices differently due to differences in culture, economy, and politics. Given today's globalized business environment, this study should be extended to investigate the GIS strategy of the affiliates of MNCs in South America, Africa, and Eastern Europe, particularly in relation to the adaptation of Western practices in formulating GIS strategy. Some key starting points for such research could include patterns of business agreements, religion, traditions, features of social and business customs, crime rate and corruption levels, social structure, and attitudes towards foreigners. The results would assist MNCs both in the selection and development of appropriate business and IS solutions in response to the conflicting pressures for global integration and local responsiveness that they face.

REFERENCES

Andriole, S. J. (2006). The collaborate/integrated business technology strategy. *Communications of the ACM, 49*(5), 85-90.

Applegate, L. M., McFarlan, F. W., & McKenney, J. L. (1996). *Corporate information systems management.* Irwin.

Arora, A., & Fosfuri, A. (2000). Wholly owned subsidiary versus technology licensing in the worldwide chemical industry. *Journal of International Business Studies, 31*(4), 555-572.

Burns, T., & Stalker, G. M. (1961). *The management of innovation.* London: Tavistock Publications.

Chau, P., & Tam, K. Y. (1997). Factors affecting the adoption of open systems: an exploratory study. *MIS Quarterly, 21*(1), 1-21.

Choi, C. J., & Nailer, C. (2005). The China market and European companies: pricing and surviving the local competition. *European Business Review, 17*(2), 177-190.

Dhar, S., & Balakrishnan, B. (2006). Risks, benefits, and challenges in global IT outsourcing: perspectives and practices. *Journal of Global Information Management, 14*(3), 39-69.

Doh, J. (2005). Offshore Outsourcing: Implications for International Business and Strategic Management Theory and Practice. *Journal of Management Studies, 42*(3), 695-701.

Egelhoff, W. (1982). Strategy and structure in multinational corporations: an information processing approach. *Administrative Science Quarterly, 27*(3), 435-458.

Egelhoff, W. (1988). Strategy and structure in multinational corporations: A revision of the Stopford and Wells Model. *Strategic Management Journal, 9*(1), 1-14.

Erramilli, M. K. (1996). Nationality and subsidiary ownership patterns in multinational corporations. *Journal of International Business Studies, 27*(2), 225-248.

Garfield, M. J., & Watson, R. T. (1998). Differences in national information infrastructures: the reflection of national cultures. *Journal of Strategic Information Systems, 6*, 313-337.

Grover, V. (1993). An empirically derived model for the adoption of customer-based interorganizational systems. *Decision Sciences, 24*(3), 603-640.

Grover, V., & Goslar, M. D. (1993). The initiation, adoption, and implementation of telecommunications technologies in U.S. organizations. *Journal of Management Information Systems, 10*(1), 141-163.

Grover, V., Segars, A. H., & Durand, D. (1994). Organizational practice, information resource deployment and systems: a cross-cultural survey. *Journal of Strategic Information Systems, 3*(2), 85-106.

Hage, J., & Aiken, M. (1967). Relationship of centralization to other structural properties. *Administrative Science Quarterly, 12*(2), 72-92.

Hannon, J. M., Huang, I. C., & Jaw, B. S. (1995). International human resources strategy and its determinants: the case of subsidiaries in Taiwan. *Journal of International Business Studies*, 531-554.

Hofstede, G. (1991). *Cultures and organizations: software of the mind.* New York: McGraw Hill.

Hofstede, G. (1993). Cultural constraints in management theories. *Academy of Management Executive*, *7*(1), 81-94.

Holmstrom, H., Fitzgerald, B., Agerfalk, P., & Conchuir, E. (2006). Agile practices reduce distance in global software development. *Information Systems Management*, *23*(3), 7-18.

Iacovou, C., Benbasat, I., & Dexter, A. (1995). Electronic data interchange and small organizations: Adoption and impact of technology. *MIS Quarterly*, *19*(4), 465-485.

Jarillo, J. C., & Martinez, J. L. (1990). Different roles for subsidiaries: the case of multinational corporations in Spain, *Strategic Management Journal*, *11*, 501-512.

Jarvenpaa, S., & Ives, B. (1994). The global network organization of the future: information management opportunities and challenges. *Journal of Management Information Systems*, *10*(4), 25-57.

Karimi, J., & Konsynski, B. R. (1991). Globalization and information management strategies, *Journal of Management Information Systems*, *7*(4), 7-26.

Kashlak, R. J., Chandran, R., & Benedetto, C. (1998). Reciprocity in internal business: a study of telecommunications alliances and contracts. *Journal of International Business Studies*, *29*(2), 281-304.

Kim, B. O. (1994). Business process reengineering: building a cross-functional information architecture. *Journal of Systems Management*, *December*, 30-35.

Kogut, B., & Singh, H. (1988). The effect of national culture on the choice of entry mode. *Journal of International Business Studies*, *19*, 411-432.

Lai, V. (2001). Issues of international information systems management: a perspective of affiliates. *Information and Management*, *38*, 253-264.

Lai, V., & Floyd, S. (1998). The impact of transborder data flow restrictions on international information systems management. *Decision Support Systems*, *22*, 121-134

Lai, V., & Guynes, J. (1997). An assessment of the influence of organizational characteristics on information technology adoption decision: A discriminative approach. *IEEE Transactions on Engineering Management*, *44*(2), 146-157.

Lai, V., & Mahapatra, R. (2004). Re-engineering the organization: an evaluation of the role of information system function. *Internal Journal of Production Research*, *42*(12), 2357-2382.

Lai, V., & Wong, B. (2003). The moderating effect of local environment on a foreign affiliate's global IS strategy-effectiveness relationship. *IEEE Transactions on Engineering Management*, *50*(3), 352-361.

Li, Z., Murray, L., & Efendioglu, A. (2002). Marketing PCs to China. *Business Horizons*, *45*(6), 60-66.

Liang, H., Xue Y., Boulton, W., & Byrd, T. A. (2004). Why Western vendors don't dominate China's ERP market. *Communications of the ACM*, *47*(7) 69-72.

Liu, S. J., Huang, T. L., & Chen, Q. H. (1998). International development of Taiwan's information industry: an empirical study on human resource strategy of overseas subsidiaries. *IEEE Transactions on Engineering Management*, *45*(3), 296-310.

Luo, Y. (2003). Market-seeking MNEs in an emerging market: How parent-subsidiary links shape overseas success. *Journal of International Business Studies, 34*, 290-309.

Madapusi, A., & D'Souza, D. (2005). Aligning ERP systems with international strategies. *Information Systems Management, 22*(1), 7-17.

Martinez, Z. L., & Ricks, D. A. (1989). Multinational parent companies' influence over human resources decisions of affiliates: U.S. firms in Mexico. *Journal of International Business Studies, 20*(3), 465-487.

McFarlan, W. F. (1984). Information technology changes the way you compete. *Harvard Business Review, May-June*, 98-103.

Morosini, P., Shane, S., & Singh, H. (1998). National cultural distance and cross-border acquisition performance. *Journal of International Business Studies, 29*(1), 137-158.

Neo, B. S. (1991). Information technology and global competition: a framework for analysis. *Information and Management, 20*, 151-160.

Nunnally, J.C., & Bernstein, I.H. (1994). *Psychometric theory* (3rd ed.). McGraw-Hill.

Padmanabhan, P., & Cho, K. R. (1996). Ownership Strategy for a foreign affiliate: an empirical investigation of Japanese firms. *Management International Review, 36*, 45-65.

Papanastassiou, M., & Pearce, R. (1997). Technology sourcing and the strategic roles of manufacturing subsidiaries in the U.K.: local competences and global competitiveness. *Management International Review, 17*(1), 5-25.

Park, S. H., & Ungson, G. R. (1997). The effect of national culture, organizational complementary, and economic motivation on joint venture dissolution. *Academy of Management Journal, 40*(2), 279-307.

Pfeffer, J., & Salancik, G. (1978). *The external control of organizations: a resource dependence perspective.* New York: Harper & Row.

Porter, M. E. (1990). *The competitive advantage of nations*. New York: Free Press.

Prahalad, C. K., & Doz, Y. L. (1987). *The multinational mission: balancing local demands and global vision*. New York: Free Press.

Premkumar, G., & King, W. R. (1992). An empirical assessment of information systems planning and the role of information systems in organizations. *Journal of Management Information Systems, 9*, 299-125.

Punj, C., & Stewart, D. W. (1983). Cluster analysis in marketing research: review and suggestions for application. *Journal of Marketing Research, 20*, 134-148.

Raymond, L. (1990). Organizational context and information systems success: a contingency approach. *Journal of Management Information Systems, 6*(4), 5-20.

Raymond, L., & Pare, G. (1992). Measurement of information technology sophistication in small manufacturing business. *Information Resource Management Journal*, 4-16.

Raymond, L., Pare, G., & Bergeron, F. (1994). Matching information technology and organizational structure: an empirical study with implications for performance. *European Journal of Information Systems, 4*(1), 3-16.

Rogers, E.M. (1983). *The Diffusion of Innovations*. New York: The Free Press

Rosenzweig, P. M., & Nohria, N. (1994). Influences on human resource management practices in multinational corporations, *Journal of International Business Studies, 25*(2), 229-251.

Roth, K., & Morrison, A. L. (1992). Implementing global strategy: characteristics of global subsidiary mandates. *Journal of International Business Studies, 23*(4), 715-735.

Roth, K., & O'Donnell, S. (1996). Foreign subsidiary compensation strategy: an agency theory perspective. *Academic Management Journal, 39*(3), 678-703.

Sambharya, R. B., & Phatak, A. (1990). The effect of transborder data flow restrictions on American multinational corporations. *Management International Review, 30*(3), 267-289.

Sheu, C., Yen, H. R., & Krumwiede, D. W. (2003). The effects of national differences on multinational ERP implementation: an exploratory study. *TQM and Business Excellence, 14*(6), 641-657.

Shore, B. (2006). Enterprise integration across the globally distributed service organization. *Communications of the ACM, 49*(6), 102-106.

Silvestro, R., & Westley, C. (2002. Challenging the paradigm of the process enterprise: a case study analysis of BPR implementation. *Omega, 30*(3), 215-225.

Steinbart, P. J., & Nath, R. (1992). Problems and issues in the management of international data communications networks: the experiences of American companies. *MIS Quarterly, 16*(1), 55-76.

Stopford, J., & Wells, L. (1972). *Managing the multinational enterprise.* New York: Basic Books.

Straub, D. W. (1994). The effect of culture on IT diffusion: e-mail and fax in Japan and the U.S. *Information Systems Research, 5*(1), 23-47.

Straub, D., Keil, M., & Brenner, W. (1997). Testing the technology acceptance model across cultures: a three country study. *Information and Management, 33,* 1-11.

Sullivan, D. (1992/3).Organization in American MNCs: The perspective of the European regional headquarters. *Management International Review, 32*(3), 237-250.

Taggart, J. H. (1997). An evaluation of the integration-responsiveness framework: MNC manufacturing subsidiaries in the UK. *Management International Review, 37*(4), 295-318.

Taylor, S., Beechler, S., & Napier, N. (1996). Toward an integrative model of strategic international human resource management. *Academy of Management Review, 21*(4), 959-985.

Thong, J. (1999). An integrated model of information systems adoption in small businesses. *Journal of Management Information Systems, 15*(4), 187-214.

Tihanyi, L., Griffith, D. A., & Russell, C. J. (2005). The effect of cultural distance on entry mode choice, international diversification, and MNE performance: a meta-analysis. *Journal of International Business Studies, 36*(3), 270-283.

Tornatzky L., & Fleischer (1990). *The process of technological innovation.* Lexington, MA: Lexington Books.

Tractinsky, N., & Jarvenpaa, S. L. (1995). Information systems design decisions in a global versus domestic context. *MIS Quarterly, 19*(4), 507-529.

Venaik, S., Midgley, D., & Devinney, T. (2004). A new perspective on the integration-responsiveness pressures confronting multinational firms. *Management International Review, 44*(1), 15-48.

Vestring, T., Rouse, T., & Reinert, U. (2005). Hedge your offshoring bets. *MIT Sloan Management Review, Spring,* 27-29.

Voordijk, H., & Stegee, R. (2005). ERP and the changing role of IT in engineering consultancy firms. *Business Process Management Journal, 11*(4), 418-430.

Wang, E., Klein, G., & Jiang, J. (2006). ERP misfit: Country of origin and organizational factors. *Journal of Management Information Systems, 23*(1), 263-292.

Wang, P. (1993). Information systems solutions for transborder data flow problems for multinational companies. *International Journal of Information Management, 13*(1), 29-41.

Willcocks, L. P., & Feeny, D. (2006). IT outsourcing and core IS capabilities: Challenges and lessons at Dupont. *Information Systems Management, 23*(1), 49-56.

Xue, Y., Liang, H., Boulton, W., & Snyder, C. (2005). ERP implementation failures in China: case studies with implications for ERP vendors. *International Journal of Production Economics, 97*, 279-295.

Yap, A., Das, J., Burbridge, J., & Cort, K. (2006). A composite-model for e-commerce diffusion: integrating cultural and socio-economic dimensions to the dynamics of diffusion. *Journal of Global Information Management, 14*(3), 17-38.

Zhang, Z., Lee, M., Huang, P., Zhang, L., & Huang, X. (2005). A framework of ERP systems implementation success in China: an empirical study. *International Journal of Production Economics, 98*, 56-80.

Zhu, K., & Kraemer, K. (2005). Post-adoption variations in usage and value of e-business by organizations: cross-country evidence from the retail industry. *Information Systems Research, 16*(1), 61-84.

Zhu, K., Kraemer, K., & Xu, S. (2003). Electronic business adoption by European firms: a cross-country assessment of the facilitators and inhibitors. *European Journal of Information Systems, 12*(4), 251-268.

This work was previously published in the Journal of Global Information Management, Vol. 16, Issue 3, edited by F. Tan, pp. 74-96, copyright 2008 by IGI Publishing (an imprint of IGI Global).

Chapter 4
A Variable Precision Fuzzy Rough Group Decision-Making Model for IT Offshore Outsourcing Risk Evaluation

Guodong Cong
Huazhong University of Science and Technology, China

Jinlong Zhang
Huazhong University of Science and Technology, China

Tao Chen
Huazhong University of Science and Technology, China

Kin-Keung Lai
City University of Hong Kong, China

ABSTRACT

Risks evaluation is critical for the success of IT offshore outsourcing. Based on fuzzy group decision-making (FGDM) and variable precision fuzzy rough set (VPFRS), this article proposes a new integrated model, variable precision fuzzy rough group decision-making (VPFRGDM), to evaluate the risk in IT offshore outsourcing. This model can improve the capability to handle potential errors fairness and efficiency of risk evaluation, and is verified by a numerical case.

INTRODUCTION

Offshore outsourcing is impacting many industries especially in information technology (IT). According to the Meta Group IT consulting firm's forecasting, the annual offshore outsourcing rate will continue to grow at 20%, reaching $10 billion in 2005 (Rottman, 2006). Offshore outsourcing brings up opportunities and changes for both companies and many countries. Its benefit, as literally and practically illustrated, includes substantial cost savings, increased productivity, better access to new technology, and higher quality of service. However, there have been reported a lot of unsuccessful cases, for example, cost exceeding, deterioration in service quality, or even cultural conflict, and so forth. The Gartner IT consulting firm estimates a 50% failure rate for offshore outsourcing initiatives (Rottman, 2006).

To some extent, IT offshore outsourcing is more risky than IT outsourcing. IT offshore outsourcing inherits naturally risks of IT outsourcing, such as information dissymmetry, high dependency on service providers, and contains some unique characteristics. The first one is cost, as IT offshore outsourcing means much higher expense on selecting providers and instructing transaction, which might even offset the expected savings from outsourcing; the second one is culture, as IT offshore outsourcing involves potential conflict in region, moral, or even history between two countries in addition to differences between two company styles. Moreover, there might be more risk and difficulty in policy, law, security, and intellectual property, and so forth. The complication mentioned results in more difficulty to achieve objectives of cost, quality, and schedule. In order to guarantee the success of offshore outsourcing, risks need to be evaluated and managed more precisely due to the unique challenges posed by geographical, cultural, and other differences.

IT offshore outsourcing risk attracts much research interest and is discussed at great lengths. Rottman (2006) suggests that both the people involved in offshore projects and the projects themselves must be treated differently from internally developed projects, and instructs to establish processes that ensure successful delivery and protection of its intellectual property. Verhoef (2005) identifies the most prominent quantitative input needed to close goal-driven outsourcing deals, forwards five executive issues enabling rational decision making concerning cost, duration, return, ,financing, and especially risk aspects of outsourcing. Doh (2005) suggests that international labor and environmental standards and corporate codes of conduct could mitigate some of the most intense concerns raised about offshoring. Kliem (2004) believes that the risks should be managed throughout the life cycle of the offshore outsourcing projects to achieve benefits, and provides a framework of risks associated with outsourced projects and a process that can be used to develop a matrix of risks and controls appropriate for the project's objectives. Qu and Brocklehurst (2003) outline a framework for analyzing transaction costs and uses the framework for pinpointing where China is unable to compete with India. Nair and Prasad (2004) utilize a SWOT analysis technique for identifying a potential IT offshore outsourcing location. Carmel and Nicholson (2005) examined the factors using transaction cost theory (TCT) three stages, identify nine mitigation approaches to reduce transaction costs for small firms. Bahli and Rivard (2005) validated measures of risk factors based on transaction cost theory, which are adopted in this article.

The papers mentioned focus mainly on identification, analyzing framework, prioritization, and management planning of IT offshore outsourcing risks; yet further emphasis is needed on quantitative methodology for analyzing and assessing risks in order to support decision-making in uncertain environments. As literally and applicably demonstrated, IT offshore outsourcing risk evaluation is a complex, unstructured, or semi-structured decision-making process involving linguistic assessment and ambiguity. Additionally, IT related technology, product, and service evolve too fast for any decision-maker to handle. Consequently, a synthetic methodology is needed, which is able to utilize both experts' knowledge and historical data, able to handle the ambiguity involved in data evaluation, able to eliminate bias of possible personal preference or discrimination, and the capability to handle potential errors..

FGDM is not only fit for handling the ambiguity involved in data evaluation and the vagueness of linguistic expressions (e.g., very high, high, middle, low, very low), but is also fit for alleviating bias arising from particular evaluator's personal preferences, which has been applied in propulsion/maneuvering system selection (Ölçer & Odabasi, 2005) and selection among computer integrated manufacturing systems (Bozdağ, Kahraman, & Ruan, 2003) and so on. Meanwhile, variable precision fuzzy rough set (VPFRS) forwarded by Mieszkowicz-Rolka & Rolka (2004), which inherits the advantages of both VPRS (Ziarko, 1993) and fuzzy rough set (FRS) by Dubois and Prade (1992). With a given upper limit u, VPFRS admits some level of misclassification, which is useful in analysis of fuzzy knowledge with uncertainty in inconsistent decision tables. Therefore it is reasonable to incorporate VPFRS and FGDM to risks in evaluate IT offshore outsourcing.

This article proposes a new integrated model called variable precision fuzzy rough group decision-making (VPFRGDM) to evaluate IT offshore outsourcing risk. After the historical knowledge is represented in a fuzzy decision table (FDT), based on recent work on FRS (Shen & Jensen, 2004) and VPFRS (Mieszkowicz-Rolka & Rolka, 2004), the model is utilized as follows: under a certain upper limit u of admissible inclusion error, it derives the weight of each feature to guide the subsequent process, turns linguistic evaluation given by evaluators into triangular fuzzy number (TFN), and then rates and ranks the aggregative risks of alternatives with the fuzzy technique for order performance by similarity to ideal solution (TOPSIS) approach in FGDM. Finally, it evaluates the risk on the whole admissible inclusion error interval to optimize decision-making. The model enhances the reasonableness of FGDM, further reduces bias possibly caused by preferences of evaluators, and improves the efficiency with better flexibility and comprehensiveness in IT offshore outsourcing risk decision-making.

This article is organized as follows: The second section first summarizes the theoretical background of basic ideas of VPFRS and TFN that are relevant to this work. Then it describes the proposed model in detail. The third section, based on the work of Bahli and Rivard (2005), newly develops main metrics of the risk index system and briefly explains the reason of selecting those metrics. The fourth section, in order to demonstrate the applicability of the model, provides a numerical case of a synthetic evaluation of IT offshore outsourcing risk. The fifth section then provides the final concluding remarks and future work required.

THE MODEL

At the beginning of this section, some basic definitions, notations, and principles will be reviewed briefly. They will be used throughout this article, until otherwise stated.

Basic Ideas of VPFRS

As shown in Shen and Jensen (2004), let $I=(U, A)$ be an information system, where U is a non-empty set of finite objects (the universe of discourse); A is a non-empty finite set of features. Let $C \bigcup D = A$ and $C \bigcap D = \varnothing$, where C is the set of conditional features and D is the set of decision features.

Basic Concepts of the Rough Set Theory (RST)

For any $P \subseteq A$, $IND(P)$ represents an indiscernible relation where

$$IND(P)=\{(x, y)\square U^2 | \forall a \square P, f(x)=f(y)\} \quad (1)$$

The partition of U, generated by $IND(P)$ is denoted as U/P. Let $X \subseteq U$, the P-lower approximation of a set is defined as

$$\underline{P}X = \{x \mid IND(P) \subseteq X\} \quad (2)$$

Let P and Q be equivalence relations over U, then the positive region is defined as

$$POS_p(Q) = \bigcup_{X \in U/Q} \underline{P}X, \quad (3)$$

which is the set of all elements of U that can be uniquely classified into different classes of the partition U/Q, by the knowledge in features P.

Fuzzy Lower Approximations of FRS

For typical FRS applications, the decision values and the conditional values may all be fuzzy. The fuzzy P-lower approximations could be alternatively defined as:

$$\mu_{\underline{P}X}(x) = \sup_{F \in U/P} \min(\mu_F(x), \inf_{y \in U}\{\mu_F(y)\mu \rightarrow_X(y)\}), \quad (4)$$

where "→" stands for fuzzy implication and $\mu_F(x)$ is the membership degree of an object $x \in F$.

The membership degree of an object $x \in U$, belonging to the fuzzy positive region, can be defined as:

$$\mu_{POS_P(Q)}(x) = \sup_{X \in U/Q} \mu_{\underline{P}X}(x), \quad (5)$$

which means that object x will not belong to the positive region only if the equivalence class it belongs to is not a constituent of the positive region.

Using the definition of the fuzzy positive region, the dependency function can be defined as follows:

$$\gamma_P'(Q) = \frac{|\mu_{POS_P(Q)}(x)|}{card(U)} = \frac{\sum_{x \in U} \mu_{POS_P(Q)}(x)}{card(U)}, \quad (6)$$

where $card(U)$ stands for the cardinality of set U.

The Mean Rough Fuzzy u-Approximation of VPFRS

It is natural to bring VPRS into the fuzzy environment. A way of evaluating the variable precision fuzzy rough approximations is introduced (Mieszkowicz-Rolka & Rolka, 2004). Consider a fuzzy compatibility relation R, and denote it by compatibility class X_i on universe U. Any given fuzzy set F defined on the universe U can be approximated by the obtained compatibility classes. In order to evaluate the inclusion degree of a fuzzy set A in a fuzzy set B regarding particular elements of A, a new fuzzy set is obtained in a way, which is called the fuzzy inclusion set of A in B and denote by A^B. To this end an implication operator → is applied as follows:

$$\mu_{A^B}(x) = \begin{cases} \mu_A(x) \rightarrow \mu_B(x) & \text{if } \mu_A(x) > 0 \\ 0 & \text{otherwise} \end{cases} \quad (7)$$

Only the proper elements of A (support of A) are considered as relevant. Herein the "→" stands for the fuzzy implicator. There are many kinds of definitions of fuzzy implicators, the Lukasiewicz implicator is adopted for its advantage (Mieszkowicz-Rolka &Rolka, 2004), where $x \rightarrow y = min(1, 1 - x + y)$.

With the well known notion of α-cut, by which for any given fuzzy set A, a crisp set A_α is obtained as follows:

$$A_\alpha = \{x \square X: \mu_A(x) \geq \alpha\} \text{ where } \alpha \in |0, 1|. \quad (8)$$

With a given upper limit u, for the u-lower approximation of the set F by R is a fuzzy set on X/R with the membership function, which is defined as follows:

$$\mu_{\underline{R}_u F}(X_i) = \begin{cases} f_{i_u} & \text{if } \exists \alpha_u = \sup\{\alpha \in (0,1]: \; e_\alpha(X_i, F) \le 1-u\} \\ 0 & \text{otherwise} \end{cases}$$

where

$$f_{i_u} = \inf \inf_{x \in S_{i_u}} \mu_{X_i}(x) \to \mu_F(x), \; S_{i_u} = \operatorname{supp}(X_i \cap X^F_{i_{\alpha_u}}) \quad (9)$$

The set S_{i_u} contains those elements of the approximating class X_i that are included in F at least to the degree α_u provided that such α_u exists. The membership f_{i_u} is then determined using the "better" elements from S_{i_u} instead of the whole class X_i. The given definition helps to prevent the situation when a few "bad" elements of a large class X_i significantly reduce the lower approximation of the set F. The measure of α-inclusion error $e_\alpha(A,B)$ of any nonempty fuzzy set A in a fuzzy set B:

$$e_\alpha(A,B) = 1 - \frac{power(\operatorname{supp}(A \cap A^B_\alpha))}{power(A)} \quad (10)$$

where $power(F) = \sum \mu_F(x_i) (\forall x_i \in U)$.

Triangular Fuzzy Numbers

Fuzzy numbers are a fuzzy subset of real numbers, representing the expansion of the idea of the confidence interval. TFN are adopted to characterize the membership function of the linguistic terms. According to the definition (Laarhoven & Pedrycz, 1983), a TFN should possess the following basic features:

A fuzzy number $\tilde{A}$ on R would be a TFN if its membership function $\mu_{\tilde{A}}: R \to [0, 1]$ is equal to:

$$\mu_{\tilde{A}}(x) = \begin{bmatrix} (x-L)/(M-L) & L \le x \le M \\ (U-x)/(U-M) & M \le x \le U \\ 0 & \text{otherwise} \end{bmatrix} \quad (11)$$

TFN can be denoted by $\tilde{A} = (L, M, U)$, where L and U stand for the lower and upper bounds, respectively, of the fuzzy number $\tilde{A}$, and M stands for the middle value. As shown in (Chen, 2000), the sum of two fuzzy numbers $\tilde{A}_1 = (L_1, M_1, U_1)$ and $\tilde{A}_2 = (L_2, M_2, U_2)$ is:

$$\tilde{A}_1 \oplus \tilde{A}_2 = (L_1, M_1, U_1) \oplus (L_2, M_2, U_2) = (L_1 + L_2, M_1 + M_2, U_1 + U_2). \quad (12)$$

The distance between two TFNs can be calculated as follows:

$$d(\tilde{A}_1, \tilde{A}_2) = \sqrt{\frac{1}{3}[(L_1 - L_2)^2 + (M_1 - M_2)^2 + (U_1 - U_2)^2]} \quad (13)$$

The Model and Analysis

In FGDM, one of the most popular methods to evaluate alternatives is FTOPSIS (Chen, 2000). That is, the chosen alternative should have the biggest relative closeness to the ideal solution. In the model, VPFRS is initially utilized as a pre-processor for FGDM. Assume that there are a total of m features, denoted as C_i ($i=1, 2,..., m$). In fact, IT offshore outsourcing risk evaluation on alternatives can also be dealt with as a FGDM problem, which may be described by means of the following sets:

i. a set of n evaluators called $E = \{E_1, E_2,..., E_n\}$
ii. a set of N possible alternatives called $A = \{A_1, A_2,..., A_n\}$
iii. a weight vector of feature $\tilde{W}_C = (W_{C_1}, W_{C_2},..., W_{C_m})$, derived from fuzzy decision table; and that of evaluator $\tilde{W}_E = (W_{E_1}, W_{E_2}, ..., W_{E_n})$, attained from distance
iv. a matrix of fuzzy evaluations $\tilde{E} = (\tilde{E}_{ij})$, where $\tilde{E}_{ij} = (LE_{ij}, ME_{ij}, UE_{ij})$ is the evaluation of feature j of alterna-

tive i and $\tilde{E}_{ij} = (LE_{ij}, ME_{ij}, UE_{ij}) = (\sum_{k=1}^{n} LE_{ij}^{k} W_{E_k}, \sum_{k=1}^{n} ME_{ij}^{k} W_{E_k}, \sum_{k=1}^{n} UE_{ij}^{k} W_{E_k})$. (14)

Herein, $(L_{ij}^{k}, M_{ij}^{k}, U_{ij}^{k})$ is the TFN given by evaluator k to feature j of alternative i.

v. The fuzzy positive-ideal solution (FPIS, denoted as $\tilde{A}^{*}$) and fuzzy negative-ideal solution (FNIS, denoted as $\tilde{A}^{-}$), are preset beforehand or calculated from evaluations. In this article, they are represented as TFN matrix and are obtained as follows:

$$\tilde{A}^{*} = (\tilde{A}_1^{*}, \tilde{A}_2^{*}, \ldots, \tilde{A}_m^{*})^{T},$$
where $\tilde{A}_j^{*} = (LA_j^{*}, MA_j^{*}, UA_j^{*})$
$$= (\underset{1 \le i \le N}{MAX}\{LE_{ij}\}, \underset{1 \le i \le N}{MAX}\{ME_{ij}\}, \underset{1 \le i \le N}{MAX}\{UE_{ij}\}). \quad (15)$$

$$\tilde{A}^{-} = (\tilde{A}_1^{-}, \tilde{A}_2^{-}, \ldots, \tilde{A}_m^{-})^{T},$$
where $\tilde{A}_j^{-} = (LA_j^{-}, MA_j^{-}, UA_j^{-})$
$$= (\underset{1 \le i \le N}{MIN}\{LE_{ij}\}, \underset{1 \le i \le N}{MIN}\{ME_{ij}\}, \underset{1 \le i \le N}{MIN}\{UE_{ij}\}). \quad (16)$$

With a given FDT, rating and ranking of the risk of each alternative, in the model, involves four steps: Firstly, under a certain upper limit u, calculate the weight of each feature. Secondly, calculate the weight of each evaluator. Thirdly, rate and rank the risk of each alternative. Fourthly, utilize the mean method to evaluate the risk on the whole admissible inclusion error interval and make the final decision.

Step 1: Calculate the Weight of each Feature

Assume that there are m conditional features and one decision feature in FDT in all, denoted as C_i (i=1,2...m) and D respectively. Then set $P = \{C_i\}$, $Q = \{D\}$, according to equations (8) ~ (10), the dependency of each feature will be calculated individually.

Definition 1. *The u-dependency function of feature D on feature C_i is*

$$\gamma_{C_i}^{u}(D) = \sup_{X_j \in U/C_i} \sup_{F \in U/D} \{\mu_{\underline{R}_u F}(X_j)\}. \quad (17)$$

Referring to Shen and Jensen (2004), for any $x \in U$, if the definition of lower approximation in equation (4) is alternatively defined as follows

$$\mu_{\underline{P}X}(x) = \sup_{F \in U/P} \{\min(\mu_F(x), \mu_X(x))\}. \quad (18)$$

Then equation (6) will be:

$$\gamma_{C_i}'(D) = \frac{\sum_{x \in U} \mu_{POS_{C_i}(D)}(x)}{card(U)}$$
$$= \frac{\sum_{x \in U} \sup_{X_j \in U/C_i} \sup_{F \in U/D} \{\min(\mu_F(x), \mu_{X_j}(x))\}.}{card(U)} \quad (19)$$

There is a linkage between the two definitions in equations (17) and (19), namely, under certain conditions, the two definitions are equivalent as shown in proposition 1, which means $\gamma_{C_i}'(D)$ can be calculated by either definition.

Proposition 1. *For a given upper limit u, if* $\exists \mu_{\underline{R}_u F}(X_j) > 0$ ($\forall X_j \in U/C_i$, $\forall F \in U/D$), *then*

$$\gamma_{C_i}'(D) = \frac{\sup_{X_j \in U/C_i} \sup_{F \in U/D} \{card(\mathrm{supp}(X_j \cap F)) \times \mu_{\underline{R}_u F}(X_j)\}}{card(U)} \quad (20)$$

Proof.
According to equation (5), (18) & (19):

$$\gamma_{C_i}'(D) = \frac{\sum_{x \in U} \mu_{POS_{C_i}(D)}(x)}{card(U)}$$
$$= \frac{\sum_{x \in U} \sup_{X_j \in U/C_i} \sup_{F \in U/D} \{\min(\mu_F(x), \mu_{X_j}(x))\}}{card(U)}$$

According to equation (9),

$$f_i = \frac{power(X_i \cap F)}{card(\mathrm{supp}(X_i \cap F))}$$
$$= \frac{\sum_{x \in U} \min(\mu_F(x), \mu_{X_i}(x))}{card(\mathrm{supp}(X_i \cap F))}$$

That is $card(\text{supp}(X_i \cap F)) \times f_i = \sum_{x \in U} \min(\mu_F(x), \mu_{X_i}(x))$

According to equation (9):

$\mu_{\underline{R}_u F}(X_i) = f_i$ or 0,

and if $\exists \mu_{\underline{R}_u F}(X_i) > 0$ ($\forall F \in U/C_i$, $\forall X_j \in U/D$), which means $\mu_{\underline{R}_u F}(X_i) = f_i$,
then $card(\text{supp}(X_i \cap F)) \times \mu_{\underline{R}_u F}(X_i) = \sum_{x \in U} \min(\mu_F(x), \mu_{X_i}(x))$

Since $\sup\{a, 0\} = a$, $\forall a \geq 0$, thus:

$$\sup_{X_j \in U/C_i} \sup_{F \in U/D} \{card(\text{supp}(X_j \cap F)) \times \mu_{\underline{R}_u F}(X_j)\} =$$

$$\sup_{X_j \in U/C_i} \sup_{F \in U/D} \sum_{x \in U} \min(\mu_F(x), \mu_{X_i}(x)) =$$

$$\sum_{x \in U} \sup_{X_j \in U/C_i} \sup_{F \in U/D} \min(\mu_F(x), \mu_{X_j}(x)) =$$

$$card(U) * \gamma'_{C_i}(D)$$

This completes the proof.

Since the dependency degree implies the importance of a conditional feature for the decision feature, the weight of each conditional feature can be calculated on the basis of the dependency function. Then the weight of feature C_i will be calculated as follows:

$$W^u_{C_i} = \frac{\gamma^u_{C_i}(D)}{\sum_i \gamma^u_{C_i}(D)} \quad i = 1, 2, \ldots m \cdot \tag{21}$$

After the weight of the feature is calculated, the weight of the item is calculated through AHP, within the same hierarchical feature. The reason is, compared to the weight of the feature that is critical to the evaluation result, the weight of the item is small enough to deny the bias. Though it could also be determined by calculating TFN, and so forth, it is efficient and practical to calculate them through AHP. While all the weights are calculated, they are fixed in the system and guide the whole rating and ranking process.

Step 2: Calculate the Weight of each Evaluator

After the weight of the feature is calculated, it is time to determine the weight of each evaluator, which will be calculated through the distance from each other (Xie, Zhang, & Lai, 2005). Based on equation (13), the distance between evaluator k and l will be a weighted Euclidean distance defined as follows:

$$d^u(E_k, E_l) =$$

$$\sum_{i=1}^{N} \sqrt{\sum_{j=1}^{m} {w^u_{C_j}}^2 \{[LE^k_{ij} - LE^l_{ij}]^2 + [ME^k_{ij} - ME^l_{ij}]^2 + [UE^k_{ij} - UE^l_{ij}]^2\}} \tag{22}$$

In order to reflect the difference between each evaluator and others, construct the distance matrix D' as follows:

Box 1.

$$d^u(\tilde{A}, \tilde{A}^*) = \sqrt{\sum_{j=1}^{m} {W^u_{C_j}}^2 [(LE_{ij} - LA^*_j)^2 + (ME_{ij} - MA^*_j)^2 + (UE_{ij} - UA^*_j)^2]}$$

$$= \sqrt{\sum_{j=1}^{m} {W^u_{C_j}}^2 [(\sum_{k=1}^{n} W^u_{E_k} \times LE^k_{ij} - LA^*_j)^2 + (\sum_{k=1}^{n} W^u_{E_k} \times ME^k_{ij} - MA^*_j)^2 + (\sum_{k=1}^{n} W^u_{E_k} \times UE^k_{ij} - UA^*_j)^2]} \tag{26}$$

$$D' = \begin{bmatrix} 0 & d^u(E_1,E_2) & d^u(E_1,E_3) & \cdots & d^u(E_1,E_n) \\ & 0 & d^u(E_2,E_3) & \cdots & d^u(E_2,E_n) \\ & symmetrical & 0 & \cdots & \\ & & & \ddots & \\ & & & & 0 \end{bmatrix} \quad (23)$$

Let $d_k^u = \sum_{j=1}^{n} d^u(E_k, E_j)$. (24)

which reflects the difference between evaluation of evaluator k and of the others. The less is d_k^u the more similar is the evaluation of evaluator k to those of the others.

Thus, weight of evaluator k will be:

$$W_{E_k}^u = \frac{1/d_k^u}{\sum_{k=1}^{n}(1/d_k^u)} \quad (25)$$

It is easy to see that $\sum_{i=1}^{m} W_{C_i}^u = 1$□$\sum_{k=1}^{n} W_{E_k}^u = 1$.

Step 3: Evaluate the Risk of each Alternative under a given Upper Limit *u*

After all the weights are calculated, the distance of each alternative to FPIS ($\tilde{A}^*$) and FNIS ($\tilde{A}^-$) respectively will be calculated.

The distance of alternative i to FPIS ($\tilde{A}^*$) will be seen in Box 1.

Similarly, the distance of alternative i to FNIS ($\tilde{A}^-$) will be seen in Box 2.

The relative closeness to the ideal solution of alternative i is:

$$RC_i^u = d^u(\tilde{A}_i,\tilde{A}^-) \Big/ [d^u(\tilde{A}_i,\tilde{A}^-) + d^u(\tilde{A}_i,\tilde{A}^*)] \quad i = 1,2,\ldots,N. \quad (28)$$

And the larger RC_i^u ($i = 1, 2,\ldots, N$) is, the better the alternative will be. Additionally, if there were two or more alternatives very close to each other by RC_i^u, there will be a complementary standard that, the larger $d^u(\tilde{A}_i,\tilde{A}^*)$ is, the better the alternative will be.

Step 4: Evaluate the Risk on the Whole Admissible Inclusion Error Interval

Since the ranking of results is calculated under certain u, it is reasonable to consider the mean relative closeness to the ideal solution on the whole interval [γ, 1]. From the process, it is easy to know that $W_{C_i}^u$ is piecewise constant function of u, and $W_{E_k}^u$ a linear function of u ($\forall i \in [1, m]$, $k \in [1, n]$) Since the TFNs are fixed, then functions $d^u(\tilde{A}_i,\tilde{A}^*)$ and $d^u(\tilde{A}_i,\tilde{A}^-)$ are Riemann integral and the mean distance will be shown in Box 3.

Thus, the mean risk of alternative i will be:

$$RC_i = \overline{d(\tilde{A}_i,\tilde{A}^-)} \Big/ \left[\overline{d(\tilde{A}_i,\tilde{A}^-)} + \overline{d(\tilde{A}_i,\tilde{A}^*)} \right], \quad i = 1,2,\ldots,N \quad (31)$$

Box 2.

$$d^u(\tilde{A}_i,\tilde{A}^-) = \sqrt{\sum_{j=1}^{m} W_{C_j}^{u\,2}[(LE_{ij} - LA_j^-)^2 + (ME_{ij} - MA_j^-)^2 + (UE_{ij} - UA_j^-)^2]}$$

$$= \sqrt{\sum_{j=1}^{m} W_{C_j}^{u\,2}[(\sum_{k=1}^{n} W_{E_k}^u \times LE_{ij}^k - LA_j^-)^2 + (\sum_{k=1}^{n} W_{E_k}^u \times ME_{ij}^k - MA_j^-)^2 + (\sum_{k=1}^{n} W_{E_k}^u \times UE_{ij}^k - UA_j^-)^2]} \quad (27)$$

Box 3.

$$\overline{d(\tilde{A}_i,\tilde{A}^*)}=\frac{1}{1-\gamma}\int_\gamma^1 d^u(\tilde{A}_i,\tilde{A}^*)\,du$$

$$=\frac{1}{1-\gamma}\int_\gamma^1 \sqrt{\sum_{j=1}^{m} {W_{C_j}^u}^2[(\sum_{k=1}^{n} W_{E_k}^u \times LE_{ij}^k - LA_j^*)^2+(\sum_{k=1}^{n} W_{E_k}^u \times ME_{ij}^k - MA_j^*)^2+(\sum_{k=1}^{n} W_{E_k}^u \times UE_{ij}^k - UA_j^*)^2]}\,du \tag{29}$$

and

$$\overline{d(\tilde{A}_i,\tilde{A}^-)}=\frac{1}{1-\gamma}\int_\gamma^1 d^u(\tilde{A}_i,\tilde{A}^-)\,du$$

$$=\frac{1}{1-\gamma}\int_\gamma^1 \sqrt{\sum_{j=1}^{m} {W_{C_j}^u}^2[(\sum_{k=1}^{n} W_{E_k}^u \times LE_{ij}^k - LA_j^-)^2+(\sum_{k=1}^{n} W_{E_k}^u \times ME_{ij}^k - MA_j^-)^2+(\sum_{k=1}^{n} W_{E_k}^u \times UE_{ij}^k - UA_j^-)^2]}\,du \tag{30}$$

THE INDEX SYSTEM OF IT OFFSHORE OUTSOURCING RISK

Categorizing IT offshore outsourcing risks is not only the initial phase but is also the deterministic factor of the correctness of risk evaluation. There have been other offshore outsourcing risk index systems focusing on risk origin, such as financial, technical, and legal (Kliem, 2004). However, it is confusing and controversial to analyze and evaluate risk this way due to different viewpoints or standards of different groups, as well as due to the difficulty in validating the index system and so on. To solve the problem, the TCT is a better option. The reasons are manifold. First of all, since the primary reason for outsourcing IT operation is to reduce cost, the cost should undoubtedly be the first objective to consider. Moreover, as any outsourcing deal shows, typical challenges and associated risks mainly consist of how to collaborate the resources among two organizations that are geographically or culturally spread apart. That is to say, risks from the process of transaction are the key to outsourcing risks. Finally, if risks in outsourcing are analyzed with just one uniform measurement, it will be more efficient, less controversial, and easily understood, as demonstrated in the case of Intel in measuring IT value. All in all, particular requirement is investigated in IT offshore outsourcing, and the index system is established on the basis of the work (Bahli & Rivard, 2005). That is, IT offshore outsourcing risk is divided into three features, with 10 items altogether. The more important is, for the convenience of monitoring and measuring, the main metrics for each item are newly developed, as shown in Table 1.

The newly developed metrics for each risk item are briefly explained as follows:

1. Asset specificity refers to investments in physical or human assets that are dedicated to providing a specified service. In order to guarantee and enhance the capability of service providing, suppliers should focus on what the clients need and require. Since safety failure is always the most hazardous threat, suppliers should trace the threats and invest in safety related hardware and software. Needless to say, financial condition, human resource structure, and training are the basics to ensure normal operation and efficient work.
2. Multiple sources will reduce the risk in switching suppliers, which offer the client sufficient space to control and collaborate

Table 1. Risk factors in IT offshore outsourcing operations

Risk features	Risk items	Main metrics (newly developed)
Transaction	Asset specificity (A1)	Software/hardware for the highest level of safety of supplier investment
		Financial condition of supplier
		HR structure of supplier
		Training to be provided by supplier
	Small number of suppliers (A2)	Reputable suppliers>4
		Trustworthy suppliers>2
	Uncertainty (A3)	Technology obsolescence and effect on safety
		Times of client requirement changing in main task
	Internal relatedness (A4)	Quantity of affected internal process and possible loss
	External relatedness (A5)	Degree of interdependency among outsourced operations and possible loss
	Measurement problems (A6)	Percentage of unclearly defined jobs
		Agreement on degree of satisfaction, cost saving
Client	Degree of expertise with the IT operation (B1)	Qualification of end users
		Performance of IT department
	Degree of expertise with outsourcing (B2)	Maturity of project management
		Degree of understanding service level agreement (SLA) within end users group
Supplier	Degree of expertise with the IT operation (C1)	Qualifications of the service team
		Quantity of successful projects
		Matching degree of business and IT architecture
		Level of service oriented architecture (SOA)
	Degree of expertise with outsourcing (C2)	Communication ability
		Maturity of project management

with suppliers. The two numbers listed in Table 1 are the bottom-line for the client to keep this kind of risk within an appropriate degree, though the cost might increase slightly.

3. Uncertainty reflects human limitations to predict changes in environment, no matter where the changes come from. As the fast evolving technology is one of the most important characteristics of the IT offshore industry, and changes in client's requirements pose tremendous challenge and will affect the performance of IT offshore outsourcing, it is necessary and reasonable to concentrate on the effect of changes in technology and the resultant changes in requirements.
4. Relatedness, which is sometimes called interdependence or connectedness, refers to the interconnections between tasks, business units or functions, and even processes (Doh, 2005). Relatedness is universal and complicated, which increases the difficulty

in analyzing and measuring it. A practical way to measure the relatedness risk among main processes is to assess approximately the probability and possible loss, which is similar with the generally used method for measuring of risk exposure.

5. Two types of measurement problems have been identified (Alchian & Demsetz, 1972): one is the team production, where it is impossible to evaluate individual contributions of the parties; the other is the measure of the fair value of these contributions. As a matter of fact, disagreement over measurement may bring negative effect on provider's morale and attitude, which will lead to service deterioration. Based on a detailed and flexible SLA, the first topic for both client and supplier to bear in mind is how to measure satisfaction. Meanwhile, unclearly defined jobs often trigger disagreement and need much attention.
6. Expertise is defined as "special skill or knowledge that is acquired by training, study, or practice" (Sinclair, 1992). End users and IT department are more than the receivers of service, since they play an important role in evaluation and even judgment of service. Moreover, IT service involves so many intangible and ambiguous factors, for example, satisfaction, that it is indispensable and beneficial to require their qualification, including technical, managerial, and even moral. Furthermore, IT department usually manages IT assets of the whole organization and offers aid for both users and providers, its performance should be taken into account because of its effect on the performance of IT offshore outsourcing.
7. IT offshore outsourcing is executed via projects, which requires outstanding ability of project management. Just as mentioned, end users are important in the offshore outsourcing process, so the better they understand SLA, the better they will cooperate with suppliers, which will certainly propel and enhance IT offshore outsourcing.
8. The requirements for suppliers are different from, and undoubtedly more strict than, the client. The team, namely, the executor and implementer of service, should possess sufficient expertise accumulated in similar projects. Deep insight, clear understanding, and professional expression of the client's business process are critical for service quality. Besides maturity of project management, communicating skills of the supplier can be seen as one of the principal deterministic factors of successful project management, especially for the existence of culture difference and language obstacle.

A NUMERICAL CASE

FSC is one of the biggest semiconductor companies in the U.S., about $6B in annual revenue. This time, they want to develop a kind of embedded software, so they will select a supplier from three companies in P.R. China, who have provided similar IT service for FSC.

The generation of FDT is fulfilled among CIO and experts from the IT department and the business department, by analyzing the historical data in most representative cases, both successful and failed. Based on Table 1, the team generated FDT as shown in Table 2. In Table 2, feature 'Transaction' is denoted as 'A,' 'Client' as 'B,' 'Supplier' as 'C,' the risk of the decision as 'D;' 'L' represents 'low,' 'M' 'medium,' and 'H' 'high.' Every data is the membership degree of an object belongs to the class 'low,' 'medium,' or 'high,' within the feature.

Risk Rating and Ranking

The evaluators are divided into five groups of evaluators, including CIO, IT department, two user groups, and experts from a consulting company.

Table 2. Fuzzy decision table of risks in outsourcing IT operations

U	A			B			C			D		
	L	M	H	L	M	H	L	M	H	L	M	H
1	0.8	0.2	0	0	0.3	0.7	0.7	0.3	0	0.85	0.15	0
2	0.75	0.25	0	0.2	0.8	0	0.75	0.25	0	0.8	0.2	0
3	0.6	0.3	0.1	0.25	0.65	0.1	0.65	0.35	0	0.6	0.4	0
4	0.2	0.7	0.1	0.1	0.7	0.2	0.9	0.1	0	0.7	0.3	0
5	0.25	0.75	0	1	0	0	0.65	0.35	0	0.7	0.3	0
6	0	0.85	0.15	0	0.1	0.9	1	0	0	0.3	0.7	0
7	0.25	0.75	0	0.65	0.35	0	0.1	0.6	0.3	0.1	0.8	0.1
8	0	0.25	0.75	0.9	0.1	0	0.8	0.2	0	0.5	0.5	0
9	0	0.3	0.7	1	0	0	0.85	0.15	0	0.1	0.5	0.4
10	0	0.2	0.8	0	0.8	0.2	0.2	0.7	0.1	0	0.2	0.8

Table 3. Evaluation to each item

E	Alt	A1	A2	A3	A4	A5	A6	B1	B2	C1	C2
	1	L	VL	L	L	H	M	L	M	L	L
1	2	L	VL	M	M	L	L	M	M	L	L
	3	L	M	L	VL	M	L	L	VL	M	H
	1	M	L	VL	M	M	L	L	M	M	VL
2	2	M	L	L	L	M	M	M	M	VL	M
	3	L	M	L	H	M	M	M	VL	L	H
	1	M	M	L	VL	M	M	M	M	L	VL
3	2	M	L	M	M	L	L	L	M	M	M
	3	L	M	L	L	M	VL	M	L	M	L
	1	M	L	M	M	VL	L	L	L	M	L
4	2	L	M	L	L	M	M	M	M	L	M
	3	L	M	L	M	M	VL	M	L	M	L
	1	L	M	VL	M	H	M	M	L	M	M
5	2	L	M	L	L	M	M	M	M	L	VL
	3	L	M	VL	L	M	M	L	L	L	M

Herein γ=0.4, namely $u \in [0.6, 1]$. The process is described as follows:

Herein five linguistic values are used, namely, very high, high, medium, low, and very low; and they are abbreviated into VH, H, M, L, and VL respectively. To improve the accuracy, each evaluator will give a TFN to each item and the TFN of each feature will be the weighted sum of the items. The evaluation of each evaluator is shown in Table 3. In Table 3, the linguistic values seem to be the same among different evaluators, but the value is different from each other. TFN of each evaluator to each linguistic term are shown in Table 4, which reflect the difference among

Table 4. Linguistic value of evaluator

E	VH			H			M			L			VL		
1	30	40	50	40	50	60	60	75	85	75	85	90	90	95	100
2	35	45	55	50	60	70	65	75	80	80	85	90	85	92	98
3	30	40	50	45	55	65	65	75	80	80	88	90	85	95	100
4	25	35	50	40	50	60	60	70	80	70	80	85	80	90	100
5	30	40	55	40	55	65	65	75	88	75	85	90	85	95	100

Table 5. The TFN evaluation of each feature by evaluators

E	Alt	A			B			C		
		L	M	U	L	M	U	L	M	U
1	1	69.4	80.45	87.25	65.25	78.5	86.75	75	85	90
	2	71.5	82.85	89.7	60	75	85	78.75	88.75	93.75
	3	75.6	85.75	91.6	84.75	91.5	96.5	55	68.75	78.75
2	1	74.5	82.42	87.68	70.25	78.5	83.5	70	79.25	84.5
	2	72.7	81	86.2	65	75	80	80	87.75	93.5
	3	70.15	78	83.8	78	86.05	91.7	72.5	78.75	85
3	1	71.8	81.48	85.9	65	75	80	81.25	89.75	92.5
	2	71.8	81.08	84.9	70.25	79.55	83.5	65	75	80
	3	79.65	88.55	91.8	74.75	83.45	86.5	68.75	78.25	82.5
4	1	68.1	78.2	85.55	70	80	85	62.5	72.5	81.25
	2	66.6	76.7	83.8	60	70	80	67.5	77.5	83.75
	3	72.5	82.6	91.65	66.5	76.5	83.25	62.5	72.5	81.25
5	1	69.75	80.35	89.58	71.5	81.5	89.3	65	75	88
	3	73.75	83.85	92.18	65	75	88	77.5	87.5	92.5
	4	73.75	83.85	92.18	75	85	90	72.5	82.5	89.5

evaluators' opinion on the linguistic terms. In the tables, 'evaluator' will be abbreviated into 'E' and 'alternative' into 'Alt,' and they will be used throughout this article, until otherwise stated.

The TFN evaluation of each feature, after calculation and transformation, is shown in Table 5.

Step 1: Calculate the Weight of each Feature

According to equations (8) ~ (10), (21) & (24), the weight of each feature will be calculated, for example, when u= 1, the weight vector of each feature will be $(W_{C_1}, W_{C_2}, W_{C_3})$=(0.46,0,0.54).

Similarly, all the weight of each feature under variable u can be calculated; the results are shown in Table 6.

Table 6. Weights of features under various u

u	W_{C_1}	W_{C_2}	W_{C_3}
[0.6,0.67)	0.321	0.302	0.377
[0.67,0.79)	0.327	0.288	0.384
[0.79,1]	0.46	0	0.54

It is easy to see that the weights vary with u. When u is big, they vary violently but they get stable after u is small enough ($0.6< u <0.79$). It demonstrates that, the risk of mistaken classification is significant when u is big, but the risk will be under control when u is small enough.

The weight vector of items is calculated through AHP and maintain unchanged as follows:

$(W_A^1, W_A^2, W_A^3, W_A^4, W_A^5, W_A^6) = (0.24, 0.06, 0.20, 0.15, 0.10, 0.25)$
$(W_B^1, W_B^2) = (0.35, 0.65)$, $(W_C^1, W_C^2) = (0.75, 0.25)$

Step 2: Calculate the Weight of each Evaluator

According to equation (22) ~ (25), when $u = 1$, the weight vector of each evaluator is:

$(W_{E_1}, W_{E_2}, W_{E_3}, W_{E_4}, W_{E_5}) = (0.202, 0.218, 0.173, 0.192, 0.214)$.

Table 7. Weight of evaluator under various u

u	W_{E_1}	W_{E_2}	W_{E_3}	W_{E_4}	W_{E_5}
[0.6,0.67)	0.194	0.224	0.178	0.184	0.22
[0.67,0.79)	0.195	0.224	0.178	0.184	0.219
[0.79,1]	0.202	0.218	0.173	0.192	0.214

Table 8. The rating and ranking results under various u

u	Alt	P-dis	N-dis	RC_i	Rank
[0.6,0.67)	1	4.163	3.061	0.424	3
	2	5.233	4.507	0.463	2
	3	4.499	5.306	0.541	1
[0.67,0.79)	1	4.086	3.05	0.427	3
	2	5.019	4.597	0.478	2
	3	4.589	5.098	0.526	1
[0.79,1]	1	3.89	3.557	0.478	2
	2	2.062	6.573	0.761	1
	3	6.562	2.418	0.269	3

Similarly, all the weights vectors of each evaluator under various u can be calculated; the results are shown in Table 7.

It is easy to see that weights of evaluators vary with u less violently than the weights of the features. However, there occurs a subtle fluctuation, which will affect the evaluation result too.

After all the weights are calculated, according to equation (28) ~ (31), the risk of each alternative will be calculated. The evaluation results, according to various u, are shown in Table 8, and the results of the mean method in Table 9, where 'positive distance' and 'negative distance' are abbreviated into 'P-dis' and 'N-dis' respectively. Based on Table 9, the final decision-making is to select alternative 2 and designate alternative 1 as backup.

To demonstrate the advantage of the model, this article will also employ three other methods: the fuzzy evaluating algorithm (EFWA) presented by Ngai (2005), the possibilistic method by Carlsson and Fuller (2001), and FTOPSIS (Chen, 2000). For convenience and ration, the evaluation data are all from Table 5, the weight of each evaluator is assumed be the same, and the weights of each feature is (0.321, 0.302, 0.377) when u falls in (0.6, 0.67).

Then the overall risk level and result of the three alternative obtained with EFWA algorithm is shown in Table 10, where the rate is Linguistic Value. And the result with the possibilistic method and FTOPSIS are shown in Table 11 and Table 12 respectively.

Table 9. Final result of alternatives with the mean method

Alt	P-dis	N-dis	RC_i	Rank
1	3.296	3.318	0.502	2
2	2.618	5.619	0.682	1
3	4.852	3.727	0.434	3

Table 10. The result with EFWA algorithm

Alt	L	M	U	Rate
1	70.027	79.907	86.525	L
2	70.025	80.059	86.638	L
3	71.728	81.111	87.454	L

Table 11. The result with the possibilistic method

Alt	LE	ME	UE	AR	σ^2	RANK
1	70.027	79.907	86.525	79.363	11.343	3
2	70.025	80.059	86.638	79.483	11.502	2
3	71.728	81.111	87.454	80.605	10.305	1

Discussion

With the results in Table 8 compared, it is easy to see that the ranks of the alternatives are varying. The reason of these variations is the violent fluctuations in weights of features when u is big. When u>0.79, the weight of supplier's expertise is zero, which is inconsistent with common sense. The fact is, from the client's view, its own expertise is indeed less important and less relevant than the supplier's. However, the weight, namely, the importance of client's expertise, should never be denied. The extraordinarily small weight demonstrates the fact that, even though fuzzy method has been adopted to alleviate possible errors in data preprocessing, there might still exist significant classification errors, which might even be hazardous enough to cause negative influence leading to mistaken decision-making.

When u<0.79, either the weight or the evaluation turns stable and more reasonable. It is the evidence that the classification error and its associated negative influence are under better control. The final result in Table 9 is clear and convincing, which demonstrates the effectiveness of the mean method to eliminate bias. The risk of the 2nd alternative is the lowest, which takes all possible u into consideration and is more reliable.

Table 12. The result with the method FTOPSIS

Alt	*P-dis*	*N-dis*	RC_i	Rank
1	4.030	3.272	0.448	3
2	5.207	4.395	0.458	2
3	4.388	5.283	0.546	1

With the results in Table 10~12 compared, it is uneasy or even impossible to distinguish the best alternative from others, even mistaken rank occurs. However, this is not an issue in Table 9, which demonstrates the advantage of the model.

The model is capable of dealing with all possible precision u and all possible evaluation is incorporated into just one model. It is also clear and 'transparent' enough for decision-makers to find out the stable and reasonable subinterval of u, that is, the convenience to probe into all ways of evaluation under variable precision requirements. In other words, they can easily decide which precision level to select in order to make a satisfactory resolution. Additionally, the process of calculating weight is simplified. Consequently, the decision-making efficiency is improved.

CONCLUSION

This article focuses on facilitating evaluation of IT offshore outsourcing risk, and proposes a model to evaluate IT offshore outsourcing risk, which is applied to select the most appropriate service supplier. The index system based on the TCT integrates risk features into three categories, which is easy to measure, and highlights the characteristics of IT offshore outsourcing. Furthermore, in the model, the weight of feature is derived directly from the fuzzy decision table, the weight of the evaluator is attained by distance, the rating and ranking of risk is achieved with the FTOPSIS approach, and the final decision is made on the whole admissible inclusion error interval. The model further enhances the capability to handle potential errors, improves fairness and efficiency in IT offshore outsourcing risk measurement and decision-making, which is verified by the provided numerical case.

As demonstrated in this article, the model is not only particularly suitable for FGDM in analyzing IT offshore outsourcing risk, it could also be generalized to other domains and other industries. Furthermore, VPFRS could certainly be more helpful in FGDM. For instance, since the greatest advantage of FRS is the capability to induct fuzzy rules, further research may be conducted in searching for fuzzy rules and fuzzy reasoning, which might be another tool to solve universal problems in evaluation of, and knowledge discovery in, risk. Thus, the decision-making process in risk management could be fulfilled by multiple methods and the decision-making could also be more efficient and reliable.

ACKNOWLEDGMENT

The work described in this article was fully supported by the grant from National Natural Science Foundation of China (No. 70571025).

REFERENCES

Alchian, A. A., & Demsetz, H. (1972). Production, information cost and economic organization. *American Economic Review, 62*(1), 777-792.

Bahli, B., & Rivard, S. (2005). Validating measures of information technology outsourcing risk factors. *Omega, 33*, 175-187.

Bozdağ, E. C., Kahraman, C., & Ruan, D. (2003). Fuzzy group decision making for selection among computer integrated manufacturing systems. *Computers in Industry, 51*(1), 13-29.

Carlsson, C., & Fuller, R. (2001). On possibilistic mean value and variance of fuzzy numbers. *Fuzzy Sets and Systems, 122*, 315-326.

Carmel, E., & Nicholson, B. (2005). Small firms and offshore software outsourcing: High transaction costs and their mitigation. *Journal of global information management, 13*(3), 33-54.

Chen, C. T. (2000). Extensions of the TOPSIS for group decision-making under fuzzy environment. *Fuzzy Sets and Systems, 114*, 1-9.

Doh, J. P. (2005). Offshore outsourcing: Implications for international business and strategic management theory and practice. *Journal of management studies, 42*(3), 695-704.

Dubois, D., & Prade, H. (1992). Putting rough sets and fuzzy sets together. In R. Slowinski (Ed.), *Intelligent decision support: Handbook of applications and advances of the rough sets theory* (pp. 203-232). Dordrecht: Kluwer Academic Publishers.

Kliem, R. (2004). Managing the risks of offshore IT development projects. *Information systems management, 21*(3), 22-27.

Laarhoven, P. J. M., & Pedrycz, W. (1983). A fuzzy extension of Saaty's priority theory. *Fuzzy Sets System, 3*, 229-241.

Mieszkowicz-Rolka, A., & Rolka, L. (2004). Variable precision fuzzy rough sets. In J. F. Peters et al. (Eds.), *Transactions on rough sets I, LNCS (3100)* (pp. 144-160). Berlin Heidelberg: Springer-Verlag.

Nair, K. G. K., & Prasad, P. N. (2004). Offshore outsourcing: A SWOT analysis of a state in India. *Information systems management, 21*(3), 34-40.

Ngai, E. W. T., & Wat, F. K. T. (2005). Fuzzy decision support system for risk analysis in e-commerce development. *Decision Support Systems, 40*(2), 235-255.

Ölçer, A. I., & Odabasi, A. Y. (2005). A new fuzzy multiple attributive group decision making methodology and its application to propulsion/maneuvering system selection problem. *European Journal of Operational Research, 1*, 93-114.

Qu, Z. H., & Brocklehurst, M. (2003). What will it take for China to become a competitive force in offshore outsourcing? An analysis of the role of transaction costs in supplier selection. *Journal of information technology, 18*(1), 53-67.

Rottman, J. W. (2006). Successfully outsourcing embedded software development. *IEEE Computer, 39*(1), 55-61.

Shen, Q., & Jensen, R. (2004). Selecting informative features with fuzzy-rough sets and its application for complex systems monitoring. *Pattern Recognition, 37*, 1351-1363.

Sinclair, J. (1992). *Collins Co-build English language dictionary.* London: Collins.

Verhoef, C. (2005). Quantitative aspects of outsourcing deals. *Science of computer programming, 56*(3), 275-313.

Xie, G., Zhang, J. L., & Lai, K. K. (2005). A group decision-making model of risk evasion in software project bidding based on VPRS. (*LNAI 3642*, 530-538). Springer-Verlag GmbH.

Ziarko, W. (1993) Variable precision rough sets model. *Journal of Computer and System Sciences, 46*, 39-59.

This work was previously published in the Journal of Global Information Management, Vol. 16, Issue 2, edited by F. Tan, pp. 18-34, copyright 2008 by IGI Publishing (an imprint of IGI Global).

Chapter 5
Discovering Computer Security Awareness Levels Among U.S. and Chinese Computer Users

Mark B. Schmidt
St. Cloud State University, USA

Allen C. Johnston
University of Alabama at Birmingham, USA

Kirk P. Arnett
Mississippi State University, USA

Jim Q. Chen
St. Cloud State University, USA

Suicheng Li
Xi'an University of Technology, China

ABSTRACT

Despite the recent increased attention afforded malware by the popular press, there appears to be a dearth in user awareness and understanding of certain aspects of the security paradigm. This chapter presents a comparison of user awareness levels of rootkits, spyware, and viruses between U.S. and Chinese users. The results of a survey of 210 U.S. respondents and 278 Chinese respondents indicate that respondents' awareness and knowledge of rootkits is well below that of spyware and viruses. Data analysis further reveals that there are significant differences in Chinese and U.S. user perceptions with regard to spyware and computer viruses. However, there is no difference in cross-cultural awareness with regard to rootkits. Due to the ubiquitous nature of the Internet, rootkits and other malware do not yield at transnational borders. An important step to mitigate the threats posed by malware such as rootkits is to raise awareness levels of users worldwide.

DOI: 10.4018/978-1-60566-920-5.ch005

INTRODUCTION

In order to increase efficiency and effectiveness, organizations are increasingly reliant on computer based information systems. Paradoxically, this increased use and reliance on information systems has lead to increased incidents of computer abuse (see Dhillon & Backhouse, 2000). In fact, the most recent CSI/FBI report, which was based on feedback from 522 computer security practitioners representing a diverse slice of corporate America, found that 43% of the respondents reported some form of malicious attack within the past year. This figure is down from 46% the previous year (Richardson, 2008). Yet another metric that attempts to enumerate the number of attacks comes from iDefense where they report monitoring more than 27,000 attacks last year, of which more than half were designed to covertly steal information or take over computers (Brenner, 2005). The under reporting of computer attacks is prevalent for many reasons, and most of these reasons center on a desire to avoid negative press. Given the corporate world's propensity to under report, other efforts and strategies are needed to examine threats and continue to raise awareness of these threats. Before such efforts can begin, a baseline of awareness levels can be used to establish an appropriate starting place.

Primarily because of today's reliance on computer networks and the Internet we note that more attention is afforded to security issues that affect computer networks and the Internet. This coverage is apparent in the popular press as well as academic literature. Many journals include security articles or have special issues devoted to security and malware. For example, the August 2005, Communications of the ACM was devoted to spyware (Stafford, 2005).

Despite the recent increase in attention given to the information systems security milieu, there is a puzzling dearth of scholarly research regarding rootkits. It is possible that this shortage has more to do with publication delay than a lack of interest among security researchers. Although rootkits have been around for 10 plus years, they have only recently appeared in the news. This is due to their invasion of the Windows world and recent high profile events such as the SONY rootkits and the early discovery of attack vector used to slip unsigned drivers past Windows Vista release candidate security.

A recent survey of 301 IT executives found that security concerns are increasing on the ranking of managements' most important concerns (Luftman & McLean, 2004). In efforts to mitigate the threats posed to information systems security concerns, IT officials are finally beginning to devote an increasing amount of resources to threat detection and amelioration (Whitman, 2003). The appropriate steps that may be taken to counteract security threats include increasing the number of formal security audits, providing financial commitments to holistic security practices, and increasing interest in security awareness training (Gordon, Loeb, Lucyshyn, & Richardson, 2004).

PURPOSE

The purpose of this paper is twofold. The first purpose is to provide an understanding of the concept and potential damage of rootkits. In doing so, it is hoped that users will become cognizant of the rootkit phenomenon, thereby taking a first step in the struggle to effectively cope with the threat. The second purpose of this paper is to present a cross-cultural comparison of rootkit awareness levels among end users in the United States and China. The data representing the level of awareness among users in the United States was initially published in 2006 (see Schmidt, Johnston, & Arnett, 2006), whereas the data from Chinese users was obtained specifically for this study. The insights derived from this study will provide a baseline awareness level of rootkits and will empirically test the self-reported familiarity levels of rootkits.

MOTIVATION FOR U.S. AND CHINA COMPARISON

China, the world's fastest growing economy, has maintained an average 9.4% GDP growth rate for the last 27 years (Zheng, 2005). Even faced with the current global economic slowdown, China's GDP growth rate in the first three quarters of 2008 was 9.9% (Li, 2008). After a late start, Chinese business and public computer usage has increased dramatically. The output of computer hardware industry grew from RMB 5 billion in 1990 to RMB 124 billion (approximately $15.5B U.S.) in 1998 ("The Whole-View Scanning of the Electronic Information Industries in China," 1998). It is estimated that the GDP of information industries will be as high as RMB 6 trillion in 2010 ("China Will Become the Biggest Market for Electronic Information," 1998). As the economic reform continues, more and more Chinese businesses realize the crucial importance of using information technology and of protecting their information assets. By the end of June 2008, China Internet users had reached 253 million surpassing the U.S. (estimated 218 million) to become the world largest Internet user population. (www.cnnic.net.cn). More than four fifths (84.7%) of the Chinese netizens have broadband access and more than 68 percent of the netizens are under 30 years old.

As more and more Chinese use computers and the Internet, computer security is becoming a serious concern. According to a security report released by Microsoft (), Chinese Internet users have become chief targets for online criminals. The report reveals that attackers favor hiding malicious programs in seemingly innocent Web browser applications to record users' keystrokes, steal passwords, credit cards numbers, and banking information. The attackers often succeed because many of Chinese netizens are not savvy to tricks and traps, which is often true among fledgling Internet users in developing countries. Outside firms doing business in China are not immune to the security attacks. As more U.S. businesses enter the Chinese market, a study of Chinese computer user's awareness of security threats should provide useful information to both U.S. and Chinese business alike.

Another important reason to compare U.S. and China security awareness levels is the very different cultures of the two countries. Hofstede uses five indexes to measure culture differences: PDI (Power Distance Index) measures the degree of equality between people in a society. IDV (Individualism) measures the degree to which a society reinforces individual or collective achievement and interpersonal relationships. MAS (Masculinity) focuses on the degree a society reinforces the traditional masculine work role model of male achievement, control, and power. UAI (Uncertainty Avoidance Index) measures the level of tolerance for uncertainty and ambiguity within a society. LTO (Long-Term Orientation) measures the degree a society embraces long term devotion to traditional, forward thinking values (Hofstede, 2003).

Figure 1 shows the scores from Hofstede's studies between the USA and China on the five cultural dimensions. With the exception of the MAS index, China and U.S. scores depict two very different cultures. China has much higher scores on PDI and LTO, which indicates greater inequalities of power and wealth among its people. This is reflected by centralized decision making in Chinese society, where the rich and powerful dominate the country. The higher LTO indicates the people values long-term commitment and less likely to adopt changes that may deviate from its tradition or normal practices. This explains why Chinese have a high tolerance for injustice and inequality. They hope time will bring them justice. Meanwhile, China gets much lower scores on IDV and UAI, which indicate that Chinese culture values collective achievements and community effort. A low score on UAI is indicative of a culture where people are used to following many rules and instructions.

Figure 1. China and U.S. scores on Hofstede's culture dimensions (Hofstede, 2003)

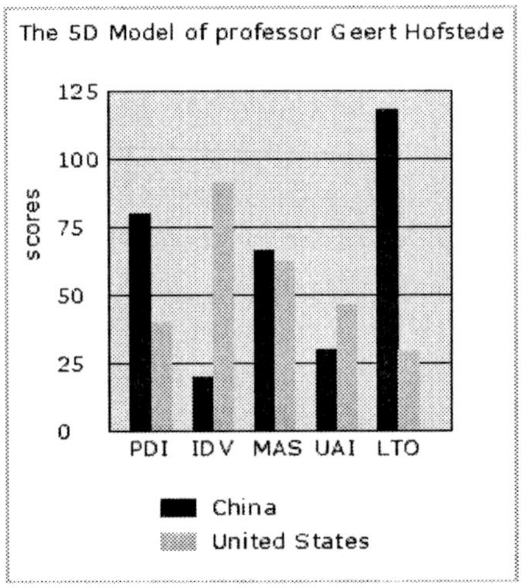

Culture influences how security policies are formulated and implemented. Culture also determines how a society will perceive computer security threats. It is our speculation that many Chinese organizations/businesses adopt centralized security measures which shield their users from viruses and spyware attack. For example, server-side software may block most malicious attacks, closely monitor a user's computing habits, and enforce stringent security rules on software downloading and installation. Chinese computer users may view these rules as perfectly acceptable and necessary, while in the U.S. such an environment may face opposition and cause privacy concerns among users. It is also speculated that when it comes to self reporting their knowledge of security threats, Chinese users may exhibit greater modesty in relation to their U.S. peers.

Although this study investigates awareness levels of three types of malware, including spyware, viruses, and rootkits, a more detailed description is presented of the rootkit concept, as it is a more recent phenomenon and hence less well known. A thorough discussion of rootkits and their potential effects follows this introduction. The following section provides a detailed description of the survey and both the American and Chinese respondents. Next, an analysis of the data is presented. Conclusions and a call to action are presented at the end of this manuscript.

ROOTKIT DETAIL

A rootkit is a "type of Trojan that keeps itself, other files, registry keys and network connections hidden from detection. It runs at the lowest level of the machine and typically intercepts common API calls. For example, it can intercept requests to a file manager such as Explorer and cause it to keep certain files hidden from display, even reporting false file counts and sizes to the user" (TechWeb, 2005). A more concise definition can be found at rootkit.com, "a rootkit is a tool that is designed to hide itself and other processes, data, and/or activity on a system" (Hoglund, 2006). The origins of rootkits can be found in the Unix world, and because they allow access at the lowest (or root) level, the term rootkit was coined.

Originally targeting Unix machines, rootkits were developed circa 1995 and, until recently, have been relatively rare on Windows machines (Roberts, 2005). The first notable rootkit targeting Windows NT, was introduced in 1999 by Greg Hoglund who also maintains rootkit.com, a popular website for disseminating information about rootkit exploits (Dillard, 2005). More recently, computer criminals and even global multinational corporations such as Sony have developed rootkits to beleaguer systems running Microsoft Windows. It seems a certainty that malware developers will continue to develop Windows rootkits (Seltzer, 2005).

Rootkits can exert several effects on a computer system. They can hide files, processes, or registry data, most often in an attempt to mask intrusion and to surreptitiously gain administrative rights to a computer system. Further, rootkits can provide the mechanism by which various forms of malware, including viruses, spyware, and Trojans, attempt to conceal their existence from detection utilities such as anti-spyware and anti-virus applications. A blended threat refers to two of more malware programs, such as rootkits, spyware, viruses, and worms, acting in a symbiotic relationship in delivering a payload. A blended threat contains many advantageous features for the attacker. For instance, a spyware/rootkit blended threat would include the data gathering capabilities and performance degradation capacity of spyware (Arnett & Schmidt, 2005) with the stealth like nature and persistence of a rootkit. Not only is the resulting threat likely to cause more problems for the user, it is also more difficult to detect and remove than single threats (Levine, Grizzard, & Owen, 2008).

Recently, rootkits have become progressively more prevalent in the networking world (Roberts, 2005). There have been companies such as Sony, which exploit rootkits for commercial purposes (Cass, 2006; Gibbs, 2005; Graham, 2005). Another recent use of rootkits was seen in a scheme at a university in California to obtain names and social security numbers of approximately 59,000 past, current, and potential faculty, staff, and students (Rosencrance & Vijayan, 2005). Due to the nature of the rootkit threat, more academic study is warranted.

The following section describes the details of the survey. The survey was administered to IT users at three institutions of higher learning in the United States as well as users at an institution of higher learning in China. Data analysis and results are detailed in subsequent sections.

THE SURVEY

The survey used in this study is based on the survey used in two previous studies (Jones, Arnett, Tang, & Chen, 1993; Schmidt & Arnett, 2005). Both of these studies examined relatively new malware as it emerged on the computing landscape. The original study (Jones et al., 1993) focused on users perceptions of computer viruses. In the second study, Schmidt and Arnett (2005) utilized a similar instrument to assess users' perceptions of spyware. The study described herein was similar in that it investigated the relatively new phenomena of rootkits. Specifically, this study examined IT users' perceptions of rootkits, spyware, and viruses. It further compared the perceptions of users in the United States and China. The following section describes the survey, its subjects, and the analysis process that followed.

The survey used a five-point Likert scale (1 = Strongly Disagree, 3 = Neutral, 5 = Strongly Agree) for the research items and contained additional demographic items including gender, age, computer experience, education, and occupation. The subjects were college students who were enrolled in institutions during the 2005-06 academic year. It is worth noting that, given the respondents are college students, they possibly posses a higher level of knowledge of technology than the average computer user. Previous studies have shown that majority of the computer users are young and with college backgrounds ("17th Statistical Survey Report on The Internet Development in China," 2006). A survey of such a major computer user group will provide a reasonably good understanding of the computer security awareness level. Further, these college students were readily accessible and their participation, while not required, was near 100% in both settings. This allows for currency in the reporting of the results.

In total, the U.S. survey was conducted with 210 subjects from three public institutes of higher learning from various geographical regions. To provide a basis for the cross cultural comparison, 278 college subjects in China completed the questionnaire. Figure 2 presents a summary of the respondents by gender and country.

The majority of the US respondents were male (57%). Forty five (45%) of the respondents had 5-10 years of computer experience; while the Chinese respondents were evenly split in terms

Figure 2. Respondents by country and gender

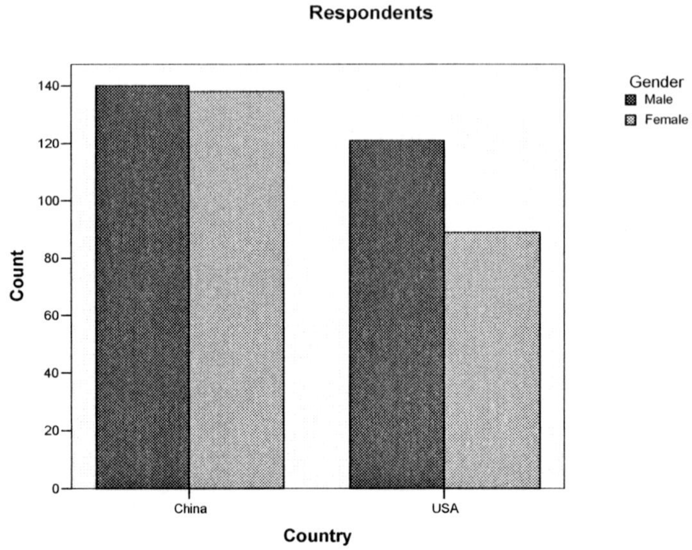

of gender and were somewhat less experienced with computers (53% had 2-5 years experience). A large number (94%) of US respondents own at least one computer while fewer (63%) of Chinese respondents reported that they owned at least one computer. Table 1 presents selected demographics.

RESULTS AND ANALYSIS

Survey responses indicate that 83.7% of U.S. and 81.3% of Chinese users have not even heard of rootkits. Not surprisingly, user knowledge of viruses was much higher. In fact, every U.S. user (100%) and 98.2% of Chinese users have known of viruses for at least one year. Spyware appears to have a high level of awareness with 83.8% (U.S.) and 38.4% (Chinese) of users having known of spyware for more than one year. These findings indicate the relative newness of rootkits and lack of awareness from the user perspective. As one may suspect, this general lack of awareness of rootkits is reflected in security practices as only 2.5% (U.S.) and 3.2% (Chinese) of users report using Rootkit Revealer detection software.

Depicted in Table 2, comparisons of responses provided by U.S. and Chinese users suggests that there are significant differences in how the two user groups report their familiarity of rootkits, spyware, and viruses in general. For example, U.S. and Chinese users report similar levels of familiarity with rootkits; while U.S. users report higher levels of familiarity with spyware and viruses than their Chinese counterparts. Included in the analysis is a fictitious threat, "Trilobyte," which was introduced to the study simply as a means for ascertaining the quality of the survey responses. U.S. users report higher levels of familiarity than Chinese students with the "Trilobyte" virus, although neither group reports more than low to moderate familiarity. Interestingly, both groups believe their familiarity of the "Trilobyte" virus to be greater than that of rootkits. Also included in Table 2, perceptions of familiarity with the very real "Melissa" virus were similar among the user groups, with both groups reporting a moderate level of familiarity.

As depicted in Table 3 and interpreted in Table 4, ANOVA techniques were used to determine if the differences between U.S. and Chinese users regarding their awareness levels of viruses,

Table 1. Selected profile of respondents

	Response category	USA respondents	Chinese respondents
Age	18 to 29 30 to 39 40 to 49 50 to 59 60 and over	82.6% 8.0% 8.5% 1.0% 0%	99.3% .4% 0% .4% 0%
Gender	Female Male	42.4% 57.6%	49.6% 50.4%
Computer experience	< 1 year > 1 year to 2 years > 2 years to 5 years > 5 years to 10 years > 10 years	2.5% 2.5% 20.6% 45.2% 29.1%	6.5% 14.7% 53.2% 24.5% 1.1%
Occupation	Full time student Part time student IT professional Other	81.5% 7.3% 6.8% 4.4%	96.0% 1.4% .7% 1.8%
How many personal computers (or laptops) do you own?	0 1 2 3 4 or more	6.2% 47.1% 31.4% 7.1% 8.1%	37.1% 50.4% 11.5% .7% .4%

spyware, and rootkits were in fact significant. The results indicate that there are significant differences between U.S. and Chinese users on four of the eight dimensions under consideration. Results indicate that for spyware and virus familiarity, U.S. and Chinese self-reported levels differ significantly ($P<.001$); yet for rootkits, the two groups' familiarity levels are similar.

Respondents from both countries were more familiar with spyware and viruses than they were with rootkits. We believe that it takes some time for the awareness levels of new malware to reach a point where IT users are cognizant of the threats to such a level where they can and will adequately protect themselves. A historical view of viruses finds that 79.6% of respondents were aware of viruses for one or more years when viruses were approximately 10 years old (Jones et al., 1993). Schmidt & Arnett (2005) found that even though the concept of spyware was less than 10 years old, only 6% of respondents were aware of spyware for less than a year. It follows that as time progresses, users are more aware of malware in its early stages. It further appears that the time period from the introduction of a particular type of malware to widespread awareness of it is becoming compressed. Even the best prognosticative efforts reveal that only time will tell as to whether or not this pattern holds with rootkit awareness.

The U.S. respondents consider themselves more aware of spyware and viruses than do Chinese respondents. This is expected, given China's relatively lower score on Hofstede's IDV dimension of the cultural index. There are several possible explanations for the relatively low level of awareness among Chinese respondents. First, a relatively small percentage of Chinese population owns and uses computers because computers and internet access are still expensive for most Chinese. Even if people have computers, they do not use them regularly. Therefore, computer viruses and spyware are not as widely reported in China as they are in United States. Second, Chinese business and marketing firms use TV and paper media as their major advertising tools. Use of spyware for business advertising is lim-

Table 2. Respondent perception

Item		N	Mean	Std. Deviation
Familiar with rootkits	USA	209	1.44	0.950
	China	278	1.44	0.851
	Total	487	1.44	0.894
The "average" person at my institution is familiar with rootkits	USA	210	1.94	0.952
	China	278	1.96	0.985
	Total	488	1.95	0.970
Familiar with Spyware	USA	210	4.13	1.034
	China	277	1.92	1.174
	Total	487	2.87	1.562
The "average" person at my institution is familiar with spyware	USA	210	3.85	0.903
	China	277	2.29	1.079
	Total	487	2.97	1.269
Familiar with viruses	USA	210	4.21	0.799
	China	275	2.40	1.244
	Total	485	3.19	1.400
The "average" person at my institution is familiar with viruses	USA	210	4.12	0.858
	China	277	2.62	1.092
	Total	487	3.27	1.242
Familiar with the fictitious "Trilobyte" virus	USA	208	1.95	1.107
	China	274	1.80	1.073
	Total	482	1.86	1.090
The "average" person at my institution is familiar with the fictitious "Trilobyte" virus	USA	209	2.31	0.957
	China	276	2.25	1.160
	Total	485	2.27	1.076

ited due to the small computer user base. Third, computer security breaches are under-reported in China. The under-reporting is largely due to the limited free flow of information and the lack of efficient business news reporting channels. Most news media in China are state owned. Strict rules are imposed on news media. The government uses the media as propaganda tools to publicize government policy. Unless a security breach is sufficiently severe it is difficult to obtain news media's attention.

Given the relative maturity of the computer virus concept, the belief was that awareness levels would be higher. Even with the increase in popular press reports of incidents involving rootkits, awareness regarding the pervasiveness and threats posed by rootkits remains low in both groups.

The limited awareness and knowledge of rootkits is especially alarming considering recent high-profile viruses, the Sony rootkit debacle, spyware, and other forms of malicious software in the headlines. IS journals are affording more and more coverage to computer security issues. For instance, the August 2005 issue of *Communications of the ACM* was devoted to the topic of spyware (Stafford, 2005). To adequately prepare for the future of secure computing, the first step is to make users aware of the challenges that

Table 3. ANOVA results

Item		Sum of Squares	Df	Mean Square	F	Sig.
Familiar with rootkits	Between Groups	0.001	1	0.001	0.001	0.975
	Within Groups	388.196	485	0.800		
	Total	388.197	486			
The "average" person at my institution is familiar with rootkits	Between Groups	0.037	1	0.037	0.039	0.843
	Within Groups	457.879	486	0.942		
	Total	457.916	487			
Familiar with Spyware	Between Groups	582.325	1	582.325	467.765	0.000
	Within Groups	603.781	485	1.245		
	Total	1,186.107	486			
The "average" person at my institution is familiar with Spyware	Between Groups	290.669	1	290.669	286.686	0.000
	Within Groups	491.738	485	1.014		
	Total	782.407	486			
Familiar with viruses	Between Groups	391.942	1	391.942	339.653	0.000
	Within Groups	557.357	483	1.154		
	Total	949.299	484			
The "average" person at my institution is familiar with viruses	Between Groups	266.785	1	266.785	267.902	0.000
	Within Groups	482.977	485	0.996		
	Total	749.762	486			
Familiar with the fictitious "Trilobyte" virus	Between Groups	2.889	1	2.889	2.441	0.119
	Within Groups	568.074	480	1.183		
	Total	570.963	481			
The "average" person at my institution is familiar with the "Trilobyte" virus	Between Groups	0.376	1	0.376	0.324	0.569
	Within Groups	560.152	483	1.160		
	Total	560.528	484			

they face. Given the nature of rootkits, spyware, viruses, blended threats, and yet to be developed computer malware, we may be just beginning what will prove to be a constant battle for control of the modern computing paradigm.

CONCLUSION

It takes time for the level of awareness to reach a critical mass in respect to any malware. Until this point is reached, it is unlikely that users will take the proper precautions to protect themselves from this type of malware. Users in the U.S. appear to be reasonably aware of viruses and spyware. However, there is much to be done in terms of achieving that level of awareness for rootkits in both the U.S. and China. Rootkits are particularly threatening as they have the potential to cause a great deal of harm because they are designed not only to conceal themselves but also to conceal other symbiotic malware such as viruses and spyware (Seltzer, 2005). Because of the Chinese culture's position on Hofstede's cultural dimensions index, (i.e. relatively high in PDI and LTO and simultaneously low in IDV and UAI) Chinese organizations may be very successful in implementing centralized prevention, detection, and remediation

Table 4. Interpretation of differences

Item	U.S. Mean	Chinese Mean	Interpretation
I am familiar with how rootkits work	1.44	1.44	No significant difference. Amazingly both groups reported exactly the same, albeit low, awareness level with rootkits. Much work is needed to raise users' awareness in both countries in an effort to provide an adequate level of protection.
The "average" person at my institution is familiar with rootkits	1.94	1.96	No significant difference. Once again the groups reported a very similar awareness level. Interestingly, both groups envision that the average person in their organization is more aware of rootkits than there are themselves.
I am familiar with spyware	4.13	1.92	U.S. respondents have a self-reported "better" knowledge of spyware. This is possibly due to the recent coverage afforded spyware in the popular press.
The "average" person at my institution is familiar with Spyware	3.85	2.29	U.S. respondents believe the average person in their organization is reasonably aware of spyware (but less aware then they themselves are). Chinese respondents believe their contemporaries are more informed than they regarding spyware.
I am familiar with computer viruses	4.21	2.40	U.S. respondents have a higher self-reported knowledge of viruses than do Chinese users. Because awareness is a critical step in prevention, it is somewhat discouraging to find the level so low among Chinese users.
The "average" person at my institution is familiar with computer viruses	4.12	2.62	U.S. respondents believe the average person to have a solid level of familiarity with viruses whereas; the Chinese report a lower awareness level. Again the U.S. respondents have indicated that their knowledge is above the average persons' knowledge whereas, Chinese users provide opposite findings.
I am familiar with the "Trilobyte" virus	1.95	1.80	No significant difference. It is encouraging to see that both groups reported a low to moderate awareness of the "Trilobyte" virus as this is a fictitious virus.
The "average" person at my institution is familiar with the "Trilobyte" virus	2.31	2.25	No significant difference. Interestingly, both groups envision that the average person at their institution knows more about this fictitious virus than they, themselves, do.

procedures. Comparatively, home users in China need to become more aware of security threats in today's rapidly changing computer security paradigm. MAS appears to be similar for both countries, thus minimal differences in security policy development is necessary based on this dimension. Considering the large discrepancy in LTO between countries, it might be necessary to exert more effort to convince Chinese uses of the long term benefits of a rigorous security policy. Given China's relatively high score in PDI, it is possible that there will be many in that culture that do not have access to computing resources, Therefore, it would be important to consider the implications of the digital divide when developing security policies and conducting computer security policies.

In many cases awareness is the first step to providing security (Goodhue & Straub, 1989; Im & Baskerville, 2005; Siponen, 2000; Straub & Welke, 1998). Unfortunately, consumers are not demanding rootkit detection and removal methods and antivirus software developers have been slow to add rootkit features to their protection tools. There are, however, some notable exceptions. For instance, F-Secure (http://www.f-secure.com) now includes "BlackLight," a rootkit detection tool with its "F-Secure Internet Security 2006" security suite. It seems obvious that as awareness increases, perhaps due to recent high profile rootkit abuses such as the Sony debacle, that user awareness of rootkits will increase. When the knowledge levels increase it is then logical to assume consumers will demand more adequate protection tools and that those demands will be met by security and other vendors.

The 2005 Global Information Security Survey, conducted by Accenture, found that Chinese organizations suffer more than U.S. organizations from the effects of malware (D'Antoni, 2005). Consequently, there is no surprise that Chinese users indicated less awareness regarding spyware and viruses relative to the U.S. users. Perhaps because fewer Chinese respondents (62.9%) compared to 93.8% of U.S. respondents own one of more computers, their exposure to threat may be limited because the owner rather than the user is responsible for computer security of the machines in question. It should be expected that these levels will increase over the next few years as malware becomes more prevalent in the computing milieu.

It is evident to many that malware poses significant threats to computer security. Given the current levels of awareness and knowledge within the user community, there are steps to be taken to increase awareness of rootkits in both the U.S. and China as well as both spyware and viruses in China. Unfortunately, it is likely that security professionals' attempts to mitigate the threats posed by malware will encounter many challenges. The first of these challenges appears to be the awareness levels among users. Unfortunately, a lack of knowledge of malware negatively effects an organization's ability to counter the effects that malware is likely to cause (Straub & Welke, 1998). Given the aforementioned findings, it is with great anticipation that effective widespread malware amelioration will be common in the computing environment.

All malware including rootkits, spyware, viruses, and blended threats are potentially very dangerous to the computing environment. Fortunately, users needn't suffer the full effect of malware if the security community can raise awareness to the point where end users will utilize appropriate detection and removal tools as part of their overall computing protection paradigm. The first step in this call to action is to use the baseline awareness levels described herein in the development of a program to increase awareness levels of malware in both countries to the appropriate level so users are prepared to understand, detect, and remove malware. It has been suggested that solid policy formulation to mitigate security risk from malware such as spyware needs to be a global effort (Warkentin, Luo, & Templeton, 2005). In order for such a global effort to be successful, global awareness levels need to by measured and, in many cases, be raised. This paper provides a baseline measurement of specific malware awareness levels for users in two prominent countries.

REFERENCES

Arnett, K. P., & Schmidt, M. B. (2005). Busting the Ghost in the Machine. *Communications of the ACM*, *48*(8), 92–95. doi:10.1145/1076211.1076246

Brenner, B. (2005). Botnets are more menacing than ever. Retrieved September, 2005, from http://searchsecurity.techtarget.com/originalContent/0,289142,sid14_gci1068871,00.html

Cass, S. (2006). Antipiracy software opens door to electronic intruders. *IEEE Spectrum*, *43*(1), 12–13. doi:10.1109/MSPEC.2006.1572337

China Top Target for Computer Attacks. Microsoft. Microsoft Security Report, November 3, 2008. Retrieved December 2, 2008 from http://www.spacewar.com/reports/China_top_target_for_computer_attacks_Microsoft_999.html.

China Will Become the Biggest Market for Electronic Information (1998, May 11). *People's Daily*.

D'Antoni, H. (2005, October 31). IT Security in China Shows Cracks. *InformationWeek,* 47-51.

Dhillon, G., & Backhouse, J. (2000). Information System Security Management in the New Millennium. *Communications of the ACM, 43*(7), 125–128. doi:10.1145/341852.341877

Dillard, K. (2005). Rootkit battle: Rootkit Revealer vs. Hacker Defender. Retrieved from http://wwwSearchWindowsSecurity.com

Gibbs, M. (2005, November 14). More on Sony's rootkit. *New World (New Orleans, La.), 22*, 82.

Goodhue, D. L., & Straub, D. W. (1989). *Security Concerns of System Users: A Proposed Study of User Perceptions of the Adequacy of Security Measures.* Paper presented at the Proceedings of the Twenty-Second Annual Hawaii International Conference on System Science (HICSS), Kailua-Kona, HI.

Gordon, L. A., Loeb, M. P., Lucyshyn, W., & Richardson, R. (2004). *2004 CSI/FBI Computer Crime and Security Survey.*

Graham, J. (2005, November 16). Copy-protected-CD flap raises questions. *USA Today.*

Hofstede, G. (2003). Cultural Dimensions. Retrieved August 12, 2006, from http://www.geert-hofstede.com/geert_hofstede_resources.shtml

Hoglund, G. (2006). The Definition of a Rootkit. Retrieved February 17, 2006, from http://www.rootkit.com/blog.php?newsid=440

Im, G. P., & Baskerville, R. L. (2005). A Longitudinal Study of Information System Threat Categories: The Enduring Problem of Human Error. *The Data Base for Advances in Information Systems, 36*(4), 68–79.

Jones, M. C., Arnett, K. P., Tang, J. T. E., & Chen, N. S. (1993). Perceptions of computer viruses a cross-cultural assessment. *Computers & Security, 12*, 191–197. doi:10.1016/0167-4048(93)90101-A

Levine, J., Grizzard, J., & Owen, H. (2004). A methodology to detect and characterize kernel level rootkit exploits involving redirection of the system call table. In *Proceedings of the Second IEEE International Information Assurance Workshop*, 2004.

Li, X. C. (2008). National Economy: Steady and Fast Growth in the First Three Quarters of 2008. National Bureau of Statistics of China. Retrieved December 2, 2008 from http://www.stats.gov.cn.

Luftman, J., & McLean, E. R. (2004). Key Issues for IT Executives. *MIS Quarterly Executive, 3*(2), 89–104.

22rd Statistical Survey Report on The Internet Development in China [Electronic (2008). Version]. Retrieved December 2, 2008 from http://www.cnnic.net.cn

Richardson, R. (2008). *2008 CSI/FBI Computer Crime and Security Survey.*

Roberts, P. F. (2005, October 17). Rootkits sprout on networks. *eWeek, 22,* 25.

Rosencrance, L., & Vijayan, J. (2005, March 21). University Computers Hacked on Each Coast. *Computerworld, 39*, 57.

Schmidt, M. B., & Arnett, K. P. (2005). Spyware: A Little Knowledge is a Wonderful Thing. *Communications of the ACM, 48*(8), 67–70. doi:10.1145/1076211.1076242

Schmidt, M. B., Johnston, A. C., & Arnett, K. P. (2006). An Empirical Investigation of Rootkit Awareness. *Business Research Yearbook: Global Business Perspectives, 13*, 153–158.

Seltzer, L. (2005). Rootkits: The Ultimate Stealth Attack. *PC Magazine*, *24*, 76.

Siponen, M. T. (2000). A Conceptual Foundation for Organizational Information Security Awareness. *Information Management & Computer Security*, *8*(1), 31–41. doi:10.1108/09685220010371394

Stafford, T. F. (2005). Spyware. *Communications of the ACM*, *48*(8), 34–35. doi:10.1145/1076211.1076235

Straub, D. W., & Welke, R. J. (1998). Coping With Systems Risk: Security Planning Models for Management Decision Making. *MIS Quarterly*, *22*(4), 441–469. doi:10.2307/249551

TechWeb. (2005). Retrieved October 29, 2005 from http://www.techweb.com/encyclopedia/

The Whole-View Scanning of the Electronic Information Industries in China. (1998, August 10, 1998). *People's Daily*.

Warkentin, M., Luo, X., & Templeton, G. F. (2005). A Framework for Spyware Assessment. *Communications of the ACM*, *48*(8), 79–84. doi:10.1145/1076211.1076244

Whitman, M. E. (2003). Enemy at the Gate: Threat to Information Security. *Communications of the ACM*, *46*(8), 91–95. doi:10.1145/859670.859675

Zheng, J. (2005). China's GDP Grows 9.5% In First Half [Electronic Version]. *National Bureau of Statistics (NBS)*. Retrieved May 1, 2006 from http://www.china-embassy.org/eng/gyzg/t204319.htm

Chapter 6
Revisiting Issues, Limitations, and Opportunities in Cross-Cultural Research on Collaborative Software in Information Systems:
A Critical Literature Update

Dongsong Zhang
University of Maryland, Baltimore County, USA

James Gaskin
Case Western Reserve University, USA

Paul Benjamin Lowry
Brigham Young University, USA

ABSTRACT

Previously, Zhang and Lowry (2008) analyzed the issues, limitations, and opportunities in cross-cultural research on collaborative software in information systems. This chapter revisits the issues discussed in that paper and adds to them an analysis of the research done since their analysis, which covered the years leading up to 2005. Five additional articles, published between 2005 and the end of 2008 have been added to their original analysis. Since the beginning of 2005, research has extended to new countries and cultures, and has covered a previously unexplored task type. New insights and opportunities are discussed. Previously, Zhang and Lowry (2008) found seven common failures in CSW-supported cultural research. This update analyzes five new papers against these seven failures and finds their recent research encouraging. The main contribution of this chapter is filling in the gap between the current state of this particular area of research and the previous state at the beginning of 2005 when the analysis of Zhang and Lowry was completed.

DOI: 10.4018/978-1-60566-920-5.ch006

INTRODUCTION

Globalization has affected business by increasing marketplace competitiveness, restructuring organizational boundaries, and creating new challenges for managers who deal with multinational companies or international alliances. Businesses often use multicultural collaborative groups working in distributed environments to cope with uncertainty, change, ambiguous problem definitions, and rapidly changing information (e.g., Vick, 1998). A critical need exists for managers "to develop a new repertoire of skills and abilities to manage and/or work with people whose cultures and value systems can be significantly different from those at home" (Tung, 1995, p. 485). Thus, "understanding the potential advantages and disadvantages of this diversity is important for organizations" (Staples & Zhao, 2006, p. 403).

Improving group processes and outcomes has been one of the most highly investigated research issues of the past two decades. The advance of information technologies makes it possible for distributed teams to be supported through collaborative technologies such as group support systems (GSS) and computer-mediated communication (CMC), which are collectively known as collaborative software (CSW). CSW refers to computer systems that combine communication and decision-support technologies to facilitate the formulation and execution of various group activities. These distributed, computer-supported groups are often referred to as virtual teams.

In this study we are primarily concerned with cultural effects on virtual teams. Information technology is not "culturally neutral and may come to symbolize a host of different values driven by underlying assumptions and their meaning, use, and consequences" (Leidner & Kayworth, 2006, p. 359). Only a small number of studies have empirically and theoretically examined cultural effects. To advance this knowledge, we review and critique existing research that specifically addresses cultural effects on CSW-supported group processes and outcomes. We hope that our attempts at assimilation and analysis of existing studies will stimulate further research along this line.

The scarcity of literature in this area makes meta-analysis infeasible. Thus, our review and discussion are offered from a descriptive and critical perspective that aim to provide a roadmap for researchers. In addition, we focus only on studies that include (1) participants from different cultures, (2) the use of CSW in face-to-face (FtF) and/or distributed settings, and (3) culture as a key conceptual construct. Our coverage includes papers published before 2009 in the following journals and conference proceedings in information systems (IS) and management fields (Table 1).

In the remainder of the chapter, we discuss underlying cultural theories, research methodologies, and findings of the studies we reviewed. We then provide insights into the limitations of existing studies and highlight some directions for future research.

CULTURE AND COLLABORATIVE SOFTWARE

In general, CSW has been proven useful in alleviating problems associated with intercultural communication primarily by reducing many behaviors that might offend members of other cultures (Aiken, Martin, Shirani, & Singleton, 1994; Gray & Olfman, 1989). Few studies both advance theories involving culture and employ empirical data to test assumptions and hypotheses. In an earlier review of 230 CSW studies (Fjermestad & Hiltz, 1999), only nine were found that included culture as either an independent variable (IV) or a moderator. The benefits of CSW identified mostly from research on Western cultures may not be manifest in different cultures under the same circumstances. For example, Kim et al. (1990) report that some incentives used to motivate North American workers can be counterproductive in collectivistic cultures.

Table 1. Literature review coverage

Journals	Academy of Management Journal
	Academy of Management Review
	Communications of the ACM
	Decision Sciences
	Decision Support Systems
	Group Decision and Negotiation
	Information and Management
	Information Systems Research
	Journal of Global Information Management
	Journal of Management Information Systems
	Management Science
	MIS Quarterly
	Small Group Research
	International Journal of Computers, Systems and Signals
Conferences	International Conference on Information Systems (ICIS)
	Hawaii International Conference on System Sciences (HICSS)
	Americas Conference on Information Systems (AMCIS)
Digital Libraries	ACM digital library
	IEEE digital library

This chapter discusses CSW studies on cultural influence from several perspectives, as depicted in Figure 1. These studies primarily involve the following independent variables: culture, task type, conflict management style, and technology support. We examine the effects of cultural differences on group processes (including group participation equity, production blocking, group polarization, status effects, and majority influence) and outcomes (including group consensus, perceived satisfaction, group productivity, and quality of results). Culture can also be used as a moderator while studying group process and final group outcome (Samarah, Paul, Mykytyn, & Seetharaman, 2003). We discuss the reviewed studies in terms of independent variables (IV), dependent variables (DVs), and major findings and limitations.

Independent Variables

Culture. Individuals are socially conditioned by their culture (Zakour, 2004). Based on previous culture literature (Groeschl & Doherty, 2000; Hofstede, 1991; Kluckhohn, 1962), we define culture as a system of implicit and explicit beliefs, values, norms, preferences, and behaviors that are stable over time, are held in common by a group of people, and distinguish one group from others.

The majority of cultural theories focus on group value orientations such as value dimensions of national culture or the competing values framework at an organizational level (Leidner & Kayworth, 2006). Among many culture theories that have been developed (Hall & Hall, 1990; Hofstede, 1984; H. Triandis, 1972), most CSW studies that focus on the impacts of culture rely on Hofstede's (1991) model of national culture, which was developed based on a large body of

Figure 1. An overview of independent and dependent variables used in CSW studies

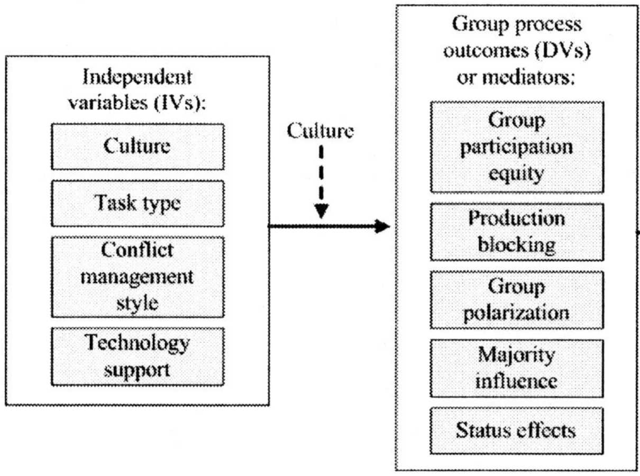

survey data about the values held by people in more than fifty countries. His model defines five generalizable cultural dimensions based on value orientations that are considered important and are shared across cultures: power distance, individualism and collectivism, masculinity-femininity, uncertainty avoidance (UAI), and Confucian dynamism. Hofstede's model has been widely validated by theoretical and empirical evidence (Usunier, 1998). In our literature review, almost every empirical study adopted one or more cultural dimensions of Hofstede's model.

As far as representation, all of the studies we reviewed involved at least one culture other than U.S.[1] culture, as summarized in Appendix I. Since the beginning of 2005, several national cultures that previously received no attention have now been studied, including South Africa, the Middle East, New Zealand, Sweden, Canada, Central America, and South America. The majority of existing cultural research on CSW outside of the U.S. involves Asian and European countries, and Australia. The lack of research on South America and Central America may be attributable to the relatively rare adoption and use of CSW in those regions due to economic, political, and technological barriers. Unexplained is the apparent lack of research on Canada (one study), Japan (no studies), and, to some extent, India (two studies). The growing CSW usage in these three countries, along with strong academic traditions, makes the lack of research on them even more puzzling.

So far, IS researchers have not developed models or theories for the cultural effects on CSW-supported group work. Some of the studies we surveyed failed entirely to base their hypotheses on any previous cultural model (e.g., Aiken, Hwang, Magalhaes, & Jeanette, 1993; Daily & Steiner, 1998; Daily, Whatley, Ash, & Steiner., 1996; Lin, Standing, & Liu, 2008).

Although Hofstede's model is the dominant cultural model used in existing IS studies, the individualism-collectivism dimension of his model has received more attention in cross-cultural CSW research than other dimensions (Leidner & Kayworth, 2006). This dimension delineates stark differences between cultures and can be cleanly operationalized for observations between cultures in a controlled setting. Conversely, the cultural dimensions of masculinity-femininity, UAI, power-distance, and Confucian dynamism in Hofstede's cultural model have been rarely adopted in cross-cultural CSW research, possibly due to the difficulty in operationalizing these dimensions.

Technology support. Cultural studies on CSW often use technology support as an IV, concentrating on how group processes and outcomes differ with and without CSW support (Daily & Steiner, 1998; Daily, et al., 1996; El-Shinnawy & Vinze, 1997; Hardin, Fuller, & Davison, 2007; Ho, Raman, & Watson, 1989; Lin, et al., 2008; Mejias, Shepherd, Vogel, & Lazaneo, 1997; Quaddus & Tung, 2002; Reinig & Mejias, 2003; Staples & Zhao, 2006; Tan, Wei, Watson, Clapper, & McLean, 1998; Tan, Wei, Watson, & Walczuch, 1998;Tung & Quaddus, 2002;Watson, Ho, & Raman, 1994). These studies have mainly compared three work modes: (1) traditional FtF groups without CSW support; (2) FtF, synchronous groups supported by CSW; and (3) distributed, anonymous groups supported by CSW. To our best knowledge, few CSW studies have examined culture in distributed, asynchronous, and CSW-supported groups; distributed and identified groups; or distributed, culturally heterogeneous groups— likely because of the great technical and logistic challenges in carrying out empirical studies in such environments. Since the beginning of 2005, a series of "collaborative trials" done by Clear and Kassabova (2005) has been published, in which they had students from New Zealand and Sweden (geographically distributed) collaborating in virtual teams to accomplish preference and cognitive-conflict tasks.

Different communication media provide different levels of information cues (Daft & Lengel, 1986), social pressure, and immediacy of feedback (i.e., synchronous versus asynchronous communication). Given previous research on the topic, we argue that the cultural influence on group process may vary according to different amount of social presence afforded in various types of communication media. *Social presence* is "the degree to which a medium facilitates awareness of the other person and interpersonal relationships during the interaction" (Fulk, Schmitz, & Steinfield, 1990). According to Social Presence Theory (Miranda & Saunders, 2003; Short, Williams, & Christie, 1976), FtF communication typically offers the highest level of social presence, while CSW-supported communication is typically low in social presence.

Several studies use the anonymity feature of CSW as an IV to examine its effect in different cultures (Atkinson & Pervan, 1998; Hardin, et al., 2007; Mejias, et al., 1997). Anonymity works better in an individualistic culture than in a collectivistic culture, because individualistic cultures encourage free exchange of ideas, egalitarian decisions, and creativity (El-Shinnawy & Vinze, 1997; Tung & Quaddus, 2002). Collectivists are accustomed to conforming and restricting their ideas by following the group majority or the group leader's preferences—even when using CSW. Thus, the use of the anonymity feature may induce more conservative decision making and reduce participation equity in a collectivistic culture.

Task type. Groups primarily exist to complete collaborative tasks, and the choice of group tasks in collaboration research is critical because it may account for 50% of total group performance (Poole, Seibold, & McPhee, 1985). Most cross-cultural CSW studies use McGrath's task circumplex (1984) as outlined in Table 2.

As shown in Table 2, creativity and preference tasks are the most popular ones selected, followed by intellectual and cognitive-conflict tasks. The other four task types have never been used in previous culture-focused[2] CSW research. Among the reviewed studies, five used task type as an IV (Clear & Kassabova, 2005; Quaddus & Tung, 2002; Tan, Wei, Watson, Clapper, et al., 1998; Tan, Wei, Watson, & Walczuch, 1998; Tung & Quaddus, 2002). The preliminary findings suggest that group members with diverse cultures behave differently while performing different tasks. It is interesting to note that although tasks in *negotiate* and *execute* categories are common in real life they have almost never been used in previous studies. Prior to 2005, no studies had been done using cognitive-conflict tasks; it is good to see that researchers are branching out and are finding ways to use this very common group task.

We believe that because most participants in these studies were university students, they lacked sufficient knowledge and experience with these

Table 2. Use of McGrath's task circumplex

Task category	Task type	Task description	Used in previous studies
Generate	Type 1: planning tasks	Generating action-oriented plans (e.g., problem-solving tasks)	None
	Type 2: creativity tasks	Generating ideas (e.g., brainstorming tasks and idea generation)	(Aiken, et al., 1993; Aiken, Kim, Hwang, & Lu, 1995; Atkinson & Pervan, 1998; Daily & Steiner, 1998; Daily, et al., 1996; De Vreede, Jones, & Mgaya, 1999; Kunene, 2005; Mejias, et al., 1997; Mejias, Vogel, & Shepherd, 1997; Quaddus & Tung, 2002; Tung & Quaddus, 2002)
Choose	Type 3: intellective tasks	Solving problems with a correct answer; such tasks have a demonstrable right answer, and the group task is to invent/select/compute that correct answer	(Tan, Wei, Watson, Clapper, et al., 1998; Tan, Wei, Watson, & Walczuch, 1998; Vogel, Davison, & Shroff, 2001; Vogel, Van Genuchten, et al., 2001)
	Type 4: decision-making tasks or preference tasks	Dealing with tasks for which the preferred or agreed upon answer is the correct one; tasks for which a demonstrably correct answer does not exist and for which the group's task is to select, by some consensus, a preferred alternative (e.g., tasks used in choice shift, and polarization studies; mock juries)	(Clear & Kassabova, 2005; De Vreede, et al., 1999; El-Shinnawy & Vinze, 1997; Griffith, 1998; Hardin, et al., 2007; Ho, et al., 1989; Morales, Moriera, & Vogel, 1995; Quaddus & Tung, 2002; Reinig & Mejias, 2003; Souren, Priya, Imad, & Mykytyn, 2004; Staples & Zhao, 2006; Tan, Wei, Watson, Clapper, et al., 1998; Tan, Wei, Watson, & Walczuch, 1998; Tung & Quaddus, 2002; Watson, et al., 1994)
Negotiate	Type 5: cognitive-conflict tasks	Resolving conflicts of viewpoint; tasks where members of the group do not just have different preferences but have systematically different preference structures (e.g., some jury tasks)	(Clear & Kassabova, 2005; Lin, et al., 2008)
	Type 6: mixed-motive tasks (resolving conflicts of interest)	Resolving conflicts of motive-interest (e.g., negotiation and bargaining tasks, mixed–motive dilemma tasks)	None
Execute	Type 7: contests/ battles/ competitive tasks	Resolving conflicts of power; competing for victory (e.g., wars, winner-take-all conflicts, competitive sports)	None
	Type 8: performances/ psycho-motor tasks	Executing performance tasks; psychomotor tasks performed against objective or absolute standards of excellence (e.g., many physical tasks)	None

other tasks. As a result, those types of tasks may be inappropriate for typical university students, but should be used in field studies, or should include the ever growing population of executive MBA and executive doctorate of management (EDM) students[3].

Conflict management style. Conflict refers to situations in which group members believe their needs cannot be mutually satisfied, reconciled, or integrated. Conflict among group members can emerge for various reasons, including a group's cultural composition (Reinig & Mejias, 2003). Different ways of handling internal group conflict are termed "conflict management styles" (Souren et al., 2004). They include avoidance, accommodation, competition, collaboration, and compromise (Rahim, 1983).

Conflict management styles often vary by culture. Hofstede's dimensions of power-distance, individualism-collectivism, and UAI can help explain how conflict is managed differently in different cultures. In high-power-distance cultures, low-status individuals depend on high-status individuals to make final decisions; thus open conflict is uncommon. Collectivists are more inclined to reach consensus and resolve conflicts by following majority views than are individualists (Tan, Wei, Watson, Clapper, et al., 1998; Zhang et al., 2006; Zhang, Lowry, Zhou, & Fu, 2007). In high-UAI cultures, people fear ambiguous situations; groups are more likely to suppress deviant ideas and behavior. As a result, conflicts are more easily resolved in high-UAI groups.

Some studies have shown how culture affects conflict management styles. Samarah et al. (2003) investigated whether the cultural heterogeneity of a group influences the styles of conflict management adopted by group members. Their study used a fuzzy task (e.g., Campbell, 1988) to examine the behavior of U.S. homogeneous, Indian homogeneous, and U.S.-Indian culturally heterogeneous groups. Results showed that group heterogeneity as well as the interaction between collaborative conflict management style and cultural diversity had positive moderating effects on perceived decision quality and the degree of group management. Another study (Souren et al., 2004) used conflict management style as an IV to examine its effect on group performance using homogeneous and heterogeneous groups consisting of U.S. and Indian members. The study found that the culturally heterogeneous groups had a lower level of collaborative conflict management style than did homogeneous groups. In addition, the collaborative conflict management style positively influenced user satisfaction with the decision-making process, perceived decision quality, and perceived participation.

Dependent Variables

We discuss DVs in two categories: (1) group *process* variables that assess group process gains or losses and (2) group *outcome* variables that evaluate the final results of group interaction.

Process: Group participation equity. *Group participation equity* is defined as equal and effective group participation (Steiner, 1972). Barriers to group participation equity often result from cultural and social norms (Hofstede, 1984; Robichaux & Cooper, 1998; Steiner, 1972). Because CSW encourages participation through anonymity and simultaneity, participation equality is often greater in groups supported by CSW than those without support (Reinig & Mejias, 2003; Staples & Zhao, 2006).

The findings from our review further establish the notion that the use of CSW, by alleviating status effect and avoiding direct confrontation, should encourage equal participation and reduce individual dominance (Ho et al., 1989; Reinig & Mejias, 2003). In American culture, openness and directness in communication are often considered a virtue. In contrast, people from high power distance and low individualism cultures (such as Singapore and Hong Kong (e.g., Ho et al., 1989) or Mexico (e.g., Reinig & Mejias, 2003) tend to be modest and nonconfrontational with others through direct, open communication. On the one hand, the use of CSW can encourage participation particularly from those low-status group members from cultures with high power distance and low individualism. Conversely, high-status members in such cultures may be unhappy because they feel they lose the power and influence over other group members because of CSW, which poses challenges to their authority and changes traditional social norms. As a result, those high-status members may be uncomfortable with or even resist the adoption and use of CSW in support of group tasks.

Process: Production blocking. Production blocking refers to productivity loss in brainstorming groups when group members must take turns to express their ideas. This interferes with idea generation in two possible ways. First, it disrupts the generation of ideas when delays are relatively long. Second, it reduces the flexibility of idea generation when delays are unpredictable. Because CSW enables parallel input from group members, it can significantly reduce production blocking that is common in FtF groups without CSW support.

Three studies have explicitly used production blocking as a DV, either examining whether the use of CSW reduces production blocking or comparing levels of production blocking between Asian and U.S. groups (Aiken et al., 1993; Aiken et al., 1995; Reinig & Mejias, 2003). They all found that CSW reduced production blocking in both U.S. and Asian groups. Non-Western participants supported by CSW often experience significantly more production blocking than Western users of CSW did (Chung & Adams, 1997; Reinig & Mejias, 2003). This is likely because collectivism influences CSW users to contribute in a slower, more reserved manner.

Process: Group polarization. *Group polarization* is the tendency of individuals in a group to engage in more extreme decisions than their original individual inclinations (Moscovici & Zavalloni, 1969). CSW may alter group polarization because it allows people to participate in group discussion with reduced social presence in comparison to FtF verbal communication. To date, only one study has examined the impact of technology and culture on group polarization (El-Shinnawy & Vinze, 1997). That study used persuasive arguments theory (PAT) (Pruitt, 1971) to study group behavior in a CMC setting and in a FtF, non-CMC setting that included two cultures—the U.S. and Singapore. The power-distance and individualism-collectivism dimensions of Hofstede's model were used as the theoretical basis. It was found that Singaporean groups polarized in a riskier direction, whereas U.S. groups polarized in a more cautious direction. This phenomenon may be explained by the concept of Groupthink (Janis, 1971; Janis, 1972), which states that a group averse to confrontation (e.g., collectivists) will tend to agree with whatever notions are presented, regardless of personal disposition and preferential conflict. Thus, risky, polarized conclusions are less likely to be challenged.

Process: Status effects. *Status effects* occur when high-status members negatively dominate or marginalize the contributions of low-status members (Berger, Fisek, Norman, & Zelditch, 1977). Cultures that emphasize the status or power differences among members can increase evaluation apprehension and conformance pressure. Cultural norms dictate that critical remarks should be avoided in order to steer clear of conflict (Robichaux & Cooper, 1998). In high-power-distance cultures, status differences among individuals are prominent; individuals with higher status are powerful and exude excessive influence during group communication; people strive to maintain harmony; and relationship concerns tend to prevail over task concerns (Earley, 1994).

Only one cultural study on CSW has examined status effects (Tan, Wei, Watson, & Walczuch, 1998)[4] The study used Singaporean and U.S. groups and two different tasks (intellective versus preference tasks). Results showed that the task type and communication medium (FtF verbal communication versus CMC) had significant main effect on both status influence and perceived influence, whereas national culture had a nearly significant main effect. National culture, task type, and communication medium had significant effects on sustained influence. Status influence and sustained influence were higher in preference task groups than in intellectual task groups. CMC was able to reduce status effects in both U.S. and Singapore CSW groups.

Process: Majority influence. *Majority influence* is the attempt by a majority of members in a group to impose their common position upon group dissenters during a decision-making process (Levine & Russo, 1987). When CSW replaces verbal and visual communication, group majorities may exercise less normative influence on minorities (Ridgeway, Berger, & Smith, 1985), likely due to anonymity. Several empirical studies conducted in North America have examined the effects of CSW on majority influence (e.g., Clapper, McLean, & Watson, 1991; Connolly,

Jessup, & Valacich, 1990; Gallupe, Bastianutti, & Cooper, 1991; Jessup, Connolly, & Galegher, 1990; Zigurs, Poole, & DeSanctis, 1988). Some argue that minority members are more likely to oppose a majority viewpoint when they use CSW, especially when working anonymously (Dennis, Hilmer, & Taylor, 1998). One possible explanation, according to the Media Richness Theory (MRT) (Daft & Lengel, 1986), is that CSW is a lean medium that results in lower levels of social presence and conformance pressure than experienced in traditional FtF communication.

Outcome: Consensus. *Consensus* refers to the achievement of group solidarity in decision making. Collectivistic cultures are more oriented toward consensus and less tolerant of conflict and discord (Kim, Triandis, Kagitcibasi, Choi, & Yoon, 1994) than individualistic cultures are. Research results vary as to the relationship between CSW use and different levels of group consensus in various cultures. Overall, results indicate that collectivistic groups may favor a more defined approach to convergence and agreement in comparison to U.S. groups, and individualists may be more adept at accommodating divergent viewpoints than collectivists are (Mejias, et al., 1997; Reinig & Mejias, 2003; Watson, et al., 1994).

Outcome: group productivity. CSW can increase group productivity in terms of time spent (Dennis, 1994), idea production (Gallupe, DeSanctis, & Dickson, 1988; Kunene, 2005), and document length (Lowry & Nunamaker Jr., 2003). A few cultural studies on CSW have investigated group productivity in terms of idea generation and reported mixed results. In (Atkinson & Pervan, 1998), participants from high-power-distance cultures who used the anonymity feature of CSW derived a higher level of productivity than those from low-power-distance cultures (i.e., Malaysia > Indonesia > Singapore > Australia). Conversely, Mejias et al. (1997), as well as Quaddus & Tung (2002), found just the opposite; namely, that low-power-distance cultures were more productive in idea generation tasks than high-power-distance cultures (U.S. >. Mexico, and Australia > Singapore).

Daily et al. (1998; 1996) compared the productivity of culturally homogeneous and culturally heterogeneous groups. Among groups using CSW, culturally heterogeneous groups produced a significantly higher number of unique ideas than culturally homogeneous groups did. A possible explanation for this finding is that CSW may aid in conflict management and diffuse intergroup conflict in culturally diverse groups, thus increasing productivity. According to Triandis et al. (1965), when a culturally heterogeneous group employs a process to reduce stress and communication problems, it becomes more creative than a homogeneous group. A culturally heterogeneous group also brings to the table more unique perspectives than a homogenous group, thus increasing the likelihood of unique ideas surfacing.

Outcome: quality of group outcome. CSW can increase the quality of group outcome by providing group members with equal opportunities to contribute instantaneously and anonymously (George, Easton, Nunamaker, & Northcraft, 1990). Three cultural studies investigated the effects of CSW on the decision quality but reported contrasting findings. Daily et al. (1996) found no significant differences in the quality of solutions produced by culturally homogenous and culturally heterogeneous groups supported by CSW; Samarah et al. (2003) and Souren et al. (2004), however, reported that the interaction of collaborative conflict management style and cultural diversity of groups supported by CSW had a significant effect on perceived decision quality. Kunene (2005) also reported on outcome quality, but the independent variable was task decomposition. Kunene found that CSW-supported tasks that were broken up into smaller parts resulted in significantly higher quality decisions than the same tasks given as a single task.

Outcome: satisfaction. User satisfaction reflects perceived individual goal attainment, as well as perceived future gains (Briggs, de Vreede, & Reinig, 2003). Results of traditional CSW studies on user-perceived satisfaction are mixed, with some showing higher satisfaction (George et al., 1990) and others lower (Gallupe et al., 1988). Because cultures may differ in the nature of individual goals, results of user satisfaction in previous studies are also mixed. Some studies find that Western users of CSW have higher levels of satisfaction than non-Western users (Reinig & Mejias, 2003). Yet more studies report that CSW evokes feelings of comfort and satisfaction among participants from non-Western cultures (Vreede et al., 1999; Mejias et al., 1997; Morales et al., 1995). For example, Mejias et al. (1997) reported that Mexican groups supported by CSW perceived higher levels of satisfaction than their U.S. counterparts did. This difference might be caused by the interactive effect between the culture factor and experimental treatment factors.

A recent study by Staples and Zhao (2006) tests the effect of cultural heterogeneity on team satisfaction and performance in a CSW-supported setting. The findings show that even though *satisfaction* of CSW-supported, culturally heterogeneous teams is significantly lower than satisfaction of culturally homogeneous teams, team *performance* does not differ significantly.

Lin et al. (2008) performed a meta-analysis of 50 studies (carefully selected from a group of 251 virtual team and decision support studies), in order to understand the various factors that affect virtual team performance and satisfaction. Culture was found to be an insignificant factor. They also performed a field experiment and a survey (based in Australia) to better understand their research questions. They found *performance* to be a direct predictor of *satisfaction*, and *coordination* to be a direct predictor of *performance.* Other significant antecedents of *satisfaction* were *communication, cohesion, and relationship building*. Because culture did not surface as significant in the meta-analysis, it was not included in the field experiment or survey. Future research may be needed to investigate if culture is a moderating construct in Lin et al. (2008)'s model. For example, do group members in some cultures have a greater tendency to build relationships in group task situations? Do people in some cultures tend to communicate more than those in other cultures? Do individualistic groups tend to lack cohesion more than collectivistic groups?

Culture as a Moderator

Although the majority of previous studies considered culture as an independent variable, culture may also be a moderator of other factors (Tan, Wei, Watson, Clapper et al., 1998; Samarah et al., 2003). For example, the effect of communication media may be moderated by culture (Tan, Wei, Watson, Clapper et al., 1998). Thus, if we assume that collectivistic cultures value relationship building and openness and that distributed communication tends to decrease satisfaction in general groups, then it is possible that the degree of collectivism would moderate satisfaction in distributed groups. Other moderation relationships are possible and remain largely unexplored.

DISCUSSION: LIMITATIONS, EXTENSIONS, AND NEW OPPORTUNITIES

In the previous section, we reviewed the existing literature and analyzed various issues regarding cultural differences and their impact on group settings supported by CSW. This section seeks to highlight major limitations of current research and provides some insights into future research opportunities and methods.

Existing research has barely begun to address fundamental research questions. More empirical research needs to be conducted to fully examine whether and how the effective use of CSW is contingent upon cultural norms. Since culture is a prominent factor in general IT adoption (Hasan

& Ditsa, 1999), it also likely affects the adoption and use of CSW. Research suggests that groups are more likely to adopt a technology if their own values match or fit the values embedded within the technology or those associated with its development (Leidner & Kayworth, 2006). One might thus assume that the use of CSW would be more suitable in a collectivistic culture than in an individualistic culture, but that is not necessarily true (Davison, 1996). In collectivistic cultures, the use of CSW that incorporates anonymous communication may have dysfunctional effects (Watson et al., 1994). Furthermore, in collectivistic cultures in which public dissent is discouraged and early consensus is encouraged, members have a social obligation to conform to rules that place national or group interests higher than individual interests. Although the structure and anonymity of CSW can facilitate expression of conflict in North American groups, they may not help collectivistic groups because CSW forces group members to be direct and open. This feature is undesirable in collectivistic cultures in which people prefer to express disagreement indirectly in order to preserve group harmony. Therefore, the degree of fit between a group's social values or norms and the values embedded in the CSW is an important construct for studying the relationship between cultural values and the adoption of CSW.

To guide future empirical research, we highlight seven major limitations identified in existing research and discuss potential future research opportunities. This section concludes with an analysis of how the five new articles from 2005-2008 have fared against the seven failures.

1. **Lack of theory.** Related literature clearly shows that culture matters but does not fully and consistently explain and predict *why* culture matters. Some authors simply note the observed differences among subjects from different countries and label them as "cultural differences" without linking those differences to specific cultural beliefs or values and/or without having any cultural theory as a theoretical foundation (Gallivan & Srite, 2005). Failing to answer "why" may be the greatest limitation of existing research and the greatest opportunity for future research.
2. **Singular focus on national culture.** The logic that "Americans will behave in a certain way while citizens of another country X will behave in another way" is the dominant paradigm in prior research. Straub et al. (2002) and Myers and Tan (2002) highlight and criticize the focus of previous research that leans on nationalistic definitions of culture. They assert that with globalization, culture aligns itself less with the definition of a nation-state because many countries are melting pots of various cultures. In addition, culture may not be static. It becomes increasingly difficult for any cultural group to remain isolated and uninfluenced by other cultures. Over time, societies may experience attitude changes towards gender, environment, race, family life, and religion, although these changes would rarely happen as fast as technological changes. Thus, defining a culture by nation may be too simplistic. We suggest that when a researcher uses national culture as an IV manipulation, it is important to validate the cultural characteristics of recruited participants to ensure that expected cultural differences exist. There should be a manipulation check of participants' cultural characteristics.
3. **Limited sampling.** Because of difficulty in recruiting participants with different cultural backgrounds, many studies have the small sample size problem. It is common in previous studies to have less than six groups in each experimental condition (e.g., Aiken et al., 1993; Aiken et al., 1995; Atkinson & Pervan, 1998; Daily & Steiner, 1998; Daily et al., 1996; Kunene,

2005; Quaddus & Tung, 2002; Souren et al., 2004; Walther, 1997). Such small sample size, though understandable given the challenging nature of conducting this type of research, may significantly weaken the validity and generalizability of findings. Small sample size is also the likely cause of some mixed findings of previous studies.

4. **Lack of research on group heterogeneity.** With globalization, more tasks are being accomplished by distributed teams consisting of members from varied cultural backgrounds, making it imperative to examine such groups. More research needs to be conducted to examine how diverse team members value compliment or contradict each other (Leidner & Kayworth, 2006). Specifically, it would be useful to investigate how group processes and outcomes can be improved in both culturally homogeneous and heterogeneous groups supported by CSW within a broader context of diversity management.

Several research issues related to culturally heterogeneous groups are worth investigating in future research. One is the potential difference in the level of status effect and majority influence (two of the most common phenomena in group work) on group members from different cultures, which can be reflected by their behavior during a group task. Furthermore, would group members from different cultures behave differently under status effect and majority influence in FtF and distributed communication environments? Will the use of CSW reduce (or increase) such influences? Will the individualistic members dominate in a group task? How can managers encourage equal participation in culturally heterogeneous groups? These are all practical and interesting questions to be answered. Language barriers could also significantly prevent team members who speak different native languages from communicating with each other effectively (Clear & Kassabova, 2005).

5. **Too much focus on FtF groups.** Although work mode is one of the major IVs in previous research, participants in most prior studies worked only in FtF mode. We argue that findings in the FtF environment may not be applicable to a distributed environment. So far, only a few studies examined the effects of culture in distributed groups (Clear & Kassabova, 2005; Montoya-Weiss et al., 2001; Vogel et al., 2001; Vogel et al., 2001; Walther, 1997). However, the findings about distributed work in general may provide some theoretical and empirical foundation for theory development and experimental design for research that explores the relationship between culture and distributed work. Watson et al. (1994) suggests that although FtF, anonymous meetings are suitable for individualists, asynchronous and distributed meetings may be more suitable for collectivists. Future studies should extend to other work modes such as distributed and asynchronous working environments.
6. **Singular focus on small groups.** Almost all studies we reviewed used only small groups (i.e., consisting of three to five members), yet it is well recognized that group size affects group outcomes and the degree of conflict within a group's structure (Steiner, 1972; Valacich, Wheeler, Mennecke, & Wachter, 1995). Small groups are more likely to resolve opinion differences, whereas in larger groups consensus is more difficult to achieve (Hare, 1981). In traditional FtF groups without CSW support, increasing group size can significantly increase process losses (Bouchard & Hare, 1970; Steiner, 1972). CSW has been shown to be effective in support of larger groups (e.g., Dennis, 1994; Gallupe et al., 1992; Valacich et al., 1995). Future research needs to examine cultural effects in groups of different group sizes and to

Table 3. Five new studies against the seven failures

Authors	Absurdity test	Grouping by Nation	Limited Sampling	Homogeneous groups	Just FtF	Small Groups	Lack of Realism
Clear and Kassabova (2005)	X						X
Hardin et al. (2007)							
Kunene (2005)	X		X	X	X		X
Lin et al. (2008)				X			X
Staples and Zhao (2006)						X	X

* X = *presence of the failure*

determine whether the group size has a moderating or mediating effect on cultural influence.

7. **Lack of realism.** All of the reviewed previous studies except Morales et al. (1995), Vreede et al. (1999), and Calhoun et al. (2002) used students working on hypothetical tasks as opposed to organizational members engaging in real-world tasks. There are a few potential problems with employing lab experiments using student subjects. First, students may not be representative of their culture. Second, some culture values examined, such as power distance, are unlikely to be reflected by participants with equal status. Although the relative homogeneity of student participants prevents a source of uncontrolled variance, their motivation to maximize the quality of group tasks is sometimes questionable. Also, an interaction might exist between types of participants and the effectiveness of technology (Fjermestad & Hiltz, 1999). Likewise, most research is conducted on groups that have no working history. Existing relationships between group members established prior to carrying out group tasks set conditions for a group's interaction (McGrath, 1984; Watson et al., 1994). Future studies should examine the performance of established groups versus ad hoc groups. To increase realism, researchers should consider using nonstudent participants performing realistic work tasks.

Five Papers and the Seven Failures

This section briefly evaluates the five new studies against the seven failures just discussed. Overall, the five new studies have mostly avoided the pitfalls of previous cross-cultural, CSW supported research (see Table 3). See Appendix II for a more detailed table with explanations).

The only consistent failure among those five studies is the lack of realism. Four out of the five studies used rather unrealistic tasks involving students. Hardin et al. (2007) used students, but the project tasks "had a significant impact on students' grades" (p. 140). Tasks were typical team projects in a work environment, and for all purposes, they were realistic. Those tasks covered an entire semester, unlike most studies whose tasks only lasted 40 minutes or so in a lab environment. For example, the task in Lin et al. (2008) was a timed and fictitious case task, virtual team communication was restricted to text chat only; all participants were asked to participate by professors, and they had no vested interest in the outcomes of the tasks (i.e., no effect on their grade, no reward for good performance).This example clearly fails the realism test.

Failure to pass the absurdity test (to explain *why* culture did/did not have an effect) was exhibited by two of those five new studies (Clear & Kassabova, 2005; Kunene, 2005). Clear and Kassabova (2005), for example, stated that "It appears there is a cultural influence on the motivation for this grouping where one perseveres with the task at hand regardless of the negative perception" (p. 54). No further explanation was given. There are no other explanations of possible cultural effects. Thus, they observed an effect, but did/could not explain why such an effect was present.

Based on those five new papers, it appears that using heterogeneous groups in CSW-supported research is getting more common place. Staples and Zhao (2006) used participants from Hong Kong and the U.S. in culturally homogenous and heterogeneous groups in both FtF and CSW-supported teams in a 2 * 2 factorial design.

Using small groups, limited sampling, and focusing on FtF communication alone were only present in one of the five studies. Staples and Zhao (2006) only had five members in each of their 79 groups. Kunene (2005) only used two groups. Kunene (2005) used collocated CSW-supported groups.

We were pleased to find that none of the new studies made generalized quality statements about cultures based on the country of origin. Hardin et al. (2007) did group students from Hong Kong together and students from the U.S. together, but only after performing a manipulation check to ensure collectivist and individualist scores were truly good measures based on the country of origin. Staples and Zhao (2006) also used collectivism/individualism to describe the difference among participants, but did so on an individual basis instead of on a cultural (country) basis.

CONCLUSION

With increasing globalization, CSW is recognized as an important family of technologies supporting collaborative work. In this update to Zhang and Lowry (2008), we analyzed five new papers published between 2005 and the end of 2008. This chapter makes several contributions by providing a common taxonomy of CSW research that examines the impact of culture on group collaboration. Our review and analysis lead to four general conclusions. First, interest in research on cross-cultural collaboration appears to be increasing. However, compared to hundreds of papers published in the field of CSW research, only a limited number of studies have examined the impact of culture. The body of relevant literature is too small to be able to draw any significant and general conclusions. As Ford et al. (2003) point out, the prior research in this area has been conducted in a manner that resists building a cumulative tradition. Findings obtained within specific contexts are difficult to generalize. Second, existing studies have investigated only limited types of group outcomes within limited contexts. The effects of cultural differences on many important constructs have yet to be investigated. Third, prior research shows that culture affects group processes and outcomes; however, the findings are still inconsistent. Part of this inconsistency may arise from the research using CSW with different features and design goals, different group tasks, and varying statistical power. Fourth, as an emerging area of research, this line of research lacks comprehensive and empirically validated theories. Researchers should realize that no single solution is universally applicable to all organizational, cultural, or social problems. Many factors can affect the performance of groups supported by CSW. It is imperative that practitioners introducing collaborative technologies into groups with disparate cultures understand cultural differences and their impact. Developing a deeper theoretical understanding of differences in cross-cultural groups will go a long way toward assisting global organizations to manage their groups more effectively. More advanced and validated theories need to be built, and better-designed empirical research needs to be conducted. The five new papers exhibited relatively few common failures. We hope this is a trend indicating higher quality research to come.

REFERENCES

Aiken, M., Hwang, C., Magalhaes, R. D., & Jeanette, M. (1993). A comparison of Malaysian and American groups using a group decision support system. *Journal of Information Science*, *19*(6), 489–491. doi:10.1177/016555159301900608

Aiken, M., Kim, D., Hwang, C., & Lu, L. (1995). A Korean group decision support system. *Information & Management*, *28*(5), 303–310. doi:10.1016/0378-7206(95)00003-F

Aiken, M., Martin, J., Shirani, A., & Singleton, T. (1994). A group decision support system for multicultural and multilingual communication. *Decision Support Systems*, *12*(2), 93–96. doi:10.1016/0167-9236(94)90009-4

Anderson, W. N., & Hiltz, S. R. (2001, January 3-6). *Culturally heterogeneous vs. culturally homogeneous groups in distributed group support systems: Effects on group process and consensus.* Paper presented at the 34th Hawaii International Conference on System Sciences (HICSS), Maui, HI.

Atkinson, D., & Pervan, G. (1998, June 4-6). *Group support systems and productivity in four national cultures.* Paper presented at the Sixth European Conference on Information Systems, Aix-en-Provence, France.

Berger, J., Fisek, M. H., Norman, R. Z., & Zelditch, M. (1977). *Status Characteristics and Social Interaction*. Amsterdam: North-Holland.

Bouchard, T., & Hare, M. (1970). Size, performance, and potential in brainstorming groups. *The Journal of Applied Psychology*, *54*(1), 51–55. doi:10.1037/h0028621

Briggs, R. O., de Vreede, G. J., & Reinig, B. A. (2003, January 6-9). *A theory and measurement of meeting satisfaction.* Paper presented at the 36th Hawaii International Conference on System Sciences (HICSS), Big Island, HI.

Calhoun, K. J., Teng, J. T. C., & Cheon, M. J. (2002). Impact of national culture on information technology usage behavior: An exploratory study of decision making in Korea and the USA. *Behaviour & Information Technology*, *21*(4), 293–302. doi:10.1080/0144929021000013491

Campbell, D. J. (1988). Task complexity: A review and analysis. *Academy of Management Review*, *13*(1), 40–52. doi:10.2307/258353

Chung, K., & Adams, C. R. (1997). A study on the characteristics of group decision making behavior: Cultural difference perspective of Korea vs. US. *Journal of Global Information Management*, *5*(3), 18–29.

Clapper, D. L., McLean, E. R., & Watson, R. T. (1991). *An experimental investigation of the effect of a group decision support system on normative influence in small groups.* Paper presented at the Twelfth Annual International Conference on Information Systems (ICIS), New York.

Clear, T., & Kassabova, D. (2005). *Motivational patterns in virtual team collaboration.* Paper presented at the 7th Australasian Conference on Computing Education, Newcastle.

Connolly, T., Jessup, L. M., & Valacich, J. S. (1990). Effects of anonymity and evaluative tone on idea generation in computer-mediated groups. *Management Science*, *36*(6), 689–703. doi:10.1287/mnsc.36.6.689

Daft, R. L., & Lengel, R. H. (1986). Organizational information requirements, media richness and structural design. *Management Science*, *32*(5), 554–571. doi:10.1287/mnsc.32.5.554

Daily, B. F., & Steiner, R. L. (1998). The Influence of Group Decision Support Systems on Contribution and Commitment Levels in Multicultural and Culturally Homogeneous Decision-Making Groups. *Computers in Human Behavior*, *14*(1), 147–162. doi:10.1016/S0747-5632(97)00037-X

Daily, B. F., Whatley, A., Ash, S. R., & Steiner, R. L. (1996). The effects of a group decision support system on culturally diverse and culturally homogeneous group decision making. *Information & Management*, *30*(6), 281–289. doi:10.1016/S0378-7206(96)01062-2

Davison, R. (1996). National cultures, organisational forms and group support systems Retrieved September 28, 2004, from http://www.is.cityu.edu.hk/Research/WorkingPapers/paper/9607.pdf

De Vreede, G., Jones, N., & Mgaya, B. J. (1999). Exploring the application and acceptance of group support systems in Africa. *Journal of Management Information Systems*, *15*(3), 197–234.

Dennis, A. R. (1994). Electronic support for large groups. *Journal of Organizational Computing*, *4*(2), 177–197. doi:10.1080/10919399409540222

Dennis, A. R., Aronson, J. E., Heninger, W. G., & Walker, E. D. (1999). Structuring Time and Task in Electronic Brainstorming. *MIS Quarterly*, *23*(1), 95–108. doi:10.2307/249411

Dennis, A. R., Hilmer, K. M., & Taylor, N. J. (1998). Information exchange and use in GSS and verbal group decision making: Effects of minority influence. *Journal of Management Information Systems*, *14*(3), 61–88.

Dennis, A. R., & Wixon, B. H. (2001). Investigating the moderators of the group support systems use with meta analysis. *Journal of Management Information Systems*, *18*(3), 235–257.

Earley, P. C. (1994). Self or group? Cultural effects of training on self-efficacy and performance. *Administrative Science Quarterly*, *39*(1), 89–117. doi:10.2307/2393495

El-Shinnawy, M., & Vinze, A. S. (1997). Technology, culture and persuasiveness: A study of choice-shifts in group settings. *International Journal of Human-Computer Studies*, *47*(3), 473–496. doi:10.1006/ijhc.1997.0138

Fjermestad, J., & Hiltz, S. R. (1999). An assessment of group support systems experimental research methodology and results. *Journal of Management Information Systems*, *15*(3), 7–149.

Ford, D. P., Connelly, C. E., & Meister, D. B. (2003). Information Systems Research and Hofstede's Culture's Consequences: An Uneasy and Incomplete Partnership. *IEEE Transactions on Engineering Management*, *50*(1), 8–25. doi:10.1109/TEM.2002.808265

Fulk, J., Schmitz, J., & Steinfield, C. (1990). A social influence model of technology use. In J. Fulk & C. Steinfield (Eds.), *Organizations and Communication Technology* (pp. 117-142). Newbury Park, CT: Sage.

Gallivan, M., & Srite, M. (2005). Information technology and culture: identifying fragmentary and holistic perspectives of culture. *Information and Organization*, *15*, 295–338. doi:10.1016/j.infoandorg.2005.02.005

Gallupe, R. B., Bastianutti, L. M., & Cooper, W. H. (1991). Unlocking brainstorms. *The Journal of Applied Psychology*, *76*(1), 137–142. doi:10.1037/0021-9010.76.1.137

Gallupe, R. B., Dennis, A. R., Cooper, W. H., Valacich, J. S., Bastianutti, L. M., & Nunamaker, J. F. Jr. (1992). Electronic brainstorming and group size. *Academy of Management Journal*, *35*(2), 350–369. doi:10.2307/256377

Gallupe, R. B., DeSanctis, G., & Dickson, G. W. (1988). Computer-based support for group problem-finding: An experimental investigation. *MIS Quarterly*, *12*(2), 277–298. doi:10.2307/248853

George, J. F., Easton, G., Nunamaker, J. F., & Northcraft, G. (1990). A study of collaborative group work with and without computer-based support. *Information Systems Research*, *1*(4), 394–415. doi:10.1287/isre.1.4.394

Gray, P., & Olfman, L. (1989). The user interface in group decision support systems. *Decision Support Systems*, *5*(2), 119–137. doi:10.1016/0167-9236(89)90002-X

Griffith, T. L. (1998). Cross-cultural and cognitive issues in the implementation of new technology: Focus on group support systems and Bulgaria. *Interacting with Computers*, *9*(4), 431–447. doi:10.1016/S0953-5438(97)00033-7

Groeschl, S., & Doherty, L. (2000). Conceptualizing culture. *Cross Cultural Management - . International Journal (Toronto, Ont.)*, *7*(4), 12–17.

Hall, E. T., & Hall, M. R. (1990). *Understanding Cultural Differences*. Yarmouth, ME: Intercultural Press.

Hardin, A. M., Fuller, M. A., & Davison, R. M. (2007). I Know I Can, But Can We? *Small Group Research*, *38*(1), 130–155. doi:10.1177/1046496406297041

Hare, A. P. (1981). Group size. *The American Behavioral Scientist*, *24*, 695–708. doi:10.1177/000276428102400507

Hasan, H., & Ditsa, G. (1999). The impact of culture on the adoption of IT: An interpretive study. *Journal of Global Information Management*, *7*(1), 5–15.

Ho, T., Raman, K., & Watson, R. (1989, December 4-6). *Group decision support systems: The cultural factor.* Paper presented at the Tenth Annual International Conference on Information Systems, Boston, MA.

Hofstede, G. (1984). *Culture's Consequences: International Differences in Work Related Values*. London: Sage Publications.

Hofstede, G. (1991). *Cultures and Organizations: Software of the Mind*. Berkshire, England: McGraw-Hill Book Company Europe.

Janis, I. L. (1971). Groupthink. *Psychology Today*, *5*(6), 43–76.

Janis, I. L. (1972). *Victims of Groupthink*. Boston, MA: Houghton Mifflin.

Jessup, L. M., Connolly, T., & Galegher, J. (1990). The effects of anonymity on GDSS group process with an idea-generating task. *MIS Quarterly*, *14*(3), 313–321. doi:10.2307/248893

Kim, K., Park, H., & Suzuki, N. (1990). Reward allocations in the United States, Japan and Korea: A comparison of individualistic and collectivistic cultures. *Academy of Management Journal*, *33*(1), 188–198. doi:10.2307/256358

Kim, U., Triandis, H. C., Kagitcibasi, C., Choi, S. C., & Yoon, G. (1994). *Individualism and Collectivism: Theory, Methods and Applications*. Thousand Oaks, CA: Sage Publications.

Kluckhohn, C. (1962). *Culture and Behavior*. New York: The Free Press of Glencoe.

Kunene, K. N. (2005). A Field Experiment on the Effect of Task Decomposition on the Quality of Decision in a Group Support Environment. *International Journal of Computers . Systems and Signals*, *6*(2), 13–25.

Leidner, D., & Jarvenpaa, S. (1995). The Use of Information Technology to Enhance Management School Education: A Theoretical View. *MIS Quarterly, 19*(3), 265–291. doi:10.2307/249596

Leidner, D. E., & Kayworth, T. (2006). A Review of Culture in Information Systems Research: Toward a Theory of Information Technology Culture Conflict. *MIS Quarterly, 30*(2), 357–399.

Levine, J. M., & Russo, E. M. (1987). Majority and Minority Influence. In C. Hendrick (Ed.), *Group Processes* (pp. 13-54). Newbury Park, CA: Sage.

Lin, C., Standing, C., & Liu, Y. (2008). A model to develop effective virtual teams. *Decision Support Systems, 45*(4), 1031–1045. doi:10.1016/j.dss.2008.04.002

Lowry, P. B., & Nunamaker, J. F. Jr. (2003). Using Internet-based, distributed collaborative writing tools to improve coordination and group awareness in writing teams. *IEEE Transactions on Professional Communication, 46*(4), 277–297. doi:10.1109/TPC.2003.819640

McGrath, J. E. (1984). *Groups: Interaction and Performance*. Englewood Cliffs, NJ: Prentice-Hall, Inc.

Mejias, R. J., Shepherd, M. M., Vogel, D. R., & Lazaneo, L. (1997). Consensus and perceived satisfaction levels: A cross-cultural comparison of GSS and non-GSS outcomes within and between the United States and Mexico. *Journal of Management Information Systems, 13*(3), 137–161.

Mejias, R. J., Vogel, D. R., & Shepherd, M. M. (1997, January 7-10). *GSS meeting productivity and participation equity: A US and Mexico cross-cultural field study.* Paper presented at the Thirtieth Hawaii International Conference on System Sciences (HICSS), HI.

Miranda, S., & Saunders, C. (2003). The Social Construction of Meaning: An Alternative Perspective on Information Sharing. *Information Systems Research, 14*(1), 87–106. doi:10.1287/isre.14.1.87.14765

Montoya-Weiss, M. M., Massey, A. P., & Song, M. (2001). Getting it together: Temporal coordination and conflict management in global virtual teams. *Academy of Management Journal, 44*(6), 1251–1262. doi:10.2307/3069399

Morales, B., Moriera, H., & Vogel, D. R. (1995, January 4-7). *Group support for regional development in Mexico.* Paper presented at the 28th Hawaii International Conference on System Sciences (HICSS), HI.

Moscovici, S., & Zavalloni, M. (1969). The group as a polarizer of attitudes. *Journal of Personality and Social Psychology, 12*, 125–135. doi:10.1037/h0027568

Myers, M. D., & Tan, F. B. (2002). Beyond Models of National Culture in Information Systems Research. *Journal of Global Information Management, 10*(1), 24–32.

Niederman, F. (1997). Facilitating computer-supported meetings: an exploratory comparison of U.S. and Mexican facilitators. *Journal of Global Information Management, 5*(1), 17–26.

Poole, M. S., Seibold, D. R., & McPhee, R. D. (1985). Group decision-making as a structural process. *The Quarterly Journal of Speech, 71*, 74–102. doi:10.1080/00335638509383719

Pruitt, D. G. (1971). Choice shifts in group discussion: an introductory review. *Journal of Personality and Social Psychology, 20*, 339–360. doi:10.1037/h0031922

Quaddus, M. A., & Tung, L. L. (2002). Explaining cultural differences in decision conferencing. *Communications of the ACM, 45*(8), 93–98. doi:10.1145/545151.545157

Rahim, M. A. (1983). A measure of styles of handling interpersonal conflict. *Academy of Management Journal*, *26*(2), 368–376. doi:10.2307/255985

Reinig, B. A., & Mejias, R. J. (2003, January 6-9). *An investigation of the influence of national culture and group support systems on group processes and outcomes.* Paper presented at the 36th Annual Hawaii International Conference on System Sciences (HICSS), Big Island, HI.

Ridgeway, C. L., Berger, J., & Smith, L. (1985). Nonverbal cues and status: An expectation states approach. *American Journal of Sociology*, *90*(5), 955–978. doi:10.1086/228172

Robichaux, B. P., & Cooper, R. B. (1998). GSS participation: A cultural examination. *Information & Management*, *33*, 287–300. doi:10.1016/S0378-7206(98)00033-0

Samarah, I., Paul, S., Mykytyn, P., & Seetharaman, P. (2003, January 6-9). *The collaborative conflict management style and cultural diversity in DGSS supported fuzzy tasks: An experimental investigation.* Paper presented at the 36th Annual Hawaii International Conference on System Sciences (HICSS), Big Island, HI.

Short, J., Williams, E., & Christie, B. (1976). *The Social Psychology of Telecommunication*. London, England: John Wiley and Sons.

Souren, P., Priya, S., Imad, S., & Mykytyn, P. P. (2004). Impact of heterogeneity and collaborative conflict management style on the performance of synchronous global virtual teams. *Information & Management*, *41*(3), 303–321. doi:10.1016/S0378-7206(03)00076-4

Staples, S. D., & Zhao, L. (2006). The effects of cultural diversity in virtual teams versus face-to-face teams. *Group Decision and Negotiation*, *15*, 389–406. doi:10.1007/s10726-006-9042-x

Steiner, I. D. (1972). *Group Processes and Productivity*. New York: Academic Press.

Straub, D., Loch, K., Evaristo, R., Karahanna, E., & Srite, M. (2002). Toward a Theory-Based Measurement of Culture. *Journal of Global Information Management*, *10*(1), 13–23.

Tan, B. C. Y., Wei, K.-K., Watson, R. T., Clapper, D. L., & McLean, E. R. (1998). Computer-Mediated Communication and Majority Influence: Assessing the Impact in an Individualistic and a Collectivistic Culture. *Management Science*, *44*(9), 1263–1278. doi:10.1287/mnsc.44.9.1263

Tan, B. C. Y., Wei, K.-K., Watson, R. T., & Walczuch, R. M. (1998). Reducing Status Effects with Computer-Mediated Communication: Evidence from Two Distinct National Cultures. *Journal of Management Information Systems*, *15*(1), 119–142.

Triandis, H. (1972). *An Analysis of Subjective Culture*. New York: John Wiley & Sons.

Triandis, H. C., Hall, E. R., & Ewen, R. B. (1965). Member homogeneity and dyadic creativity. *Human Relations*, *18*, 33–54. doi:10.1177/001872676501800104

Tung, L. L., & Quaddus, M. A. (2002). Cultural differences explaining the differences in results in GSS: Implications for the next decade. *Decision Support Systems*, *33*, 177–199. doi:10.1016/S0167-9236(01)00143-9

Tung, R. (1995). Strategic human resource challenge: Managing diversity. *International Journal of Human Resource Management*, *6*(3), 482–494.

Usunier, J. C. (1998). *International and Cross-Cultural Management Research*. Thousand Oaks, CA: SAGE Publications.

Valacich, J., Wheeler, B., Mennecke, B., & Wachter, R. (1995). The effects of numerical and logical size on computer-mediated idea generation. *Organizational Behavior and Human Decision Processes, 62*(3), 318–329. doi:10.1006/obhd.1995.1053

Vick, R. M. (1998). Perspectives on and problems with computer-mediated teamwork: current groupware issues and assumptions. *Journal of Computer Documentation, 22*(2), 3–22. doi:10.1145/291391.291392

Vogel, D., Davison, R., & Shroff, R. (2001). Sociocultural learning: A perspective on GSS-enabled global education. *Communications of AIS, 7*(9), 1–41.

Vogel, D., Van Genuchten, M., Lou, D., Verveen, S., Van Eekout, M., & Adams, A. (2001). Exploratory research on the role of national and professional cultures in a distributed learning project. *IEEE Transactions on Professional Communication, 44*(2), 114–125. doi:10.1109/47.925514

Walther, J. B. (1997). Group and interpersonal effects in international computer-mediated collaboration. *Human Communication Research, 23*(3), 342–369. doi:10.1111/j.1468-2958.1997.tb00400.x

Watson, R., Ho, T., & Raman, K. (1994). Culture: A fourth dimension of group support systems. *Communications of the ACM, 37*(10), 44–55. doi:10.1145/194313.194320

Watson, R. T. (1987). *A study of group decision support system use in three and four person groups for a preference allocation decision.* Unpublished doctoral dissertation, University of Minnesota, Minneapolis, MN.

Zakour, A. B. (2004, Feb. 27-28). *Cultural differences and information technology acceptance.* Paper presented at the 7th Annual Conference of the Southern Association for Information Systems, Savannah, Georgia.

Zhang, D., & Lowry, P. B. (2008). Issues, Limitations, and Opportunities in Cross-Cultural Research on Collaborative Software in Information Systems. *Journal of Global Information Management, 16*(1), 61–92.

Zhang, D., Lowry, P. B., Fu, X., Zhou, L., Adipat, B., & Ran, T. (2006, January 4-7). *Culture, social presence, and media effects on group decision making under majority influence.* Paper presented at the 39th Annual Hawai'i International Conference on System Sciences (HICSS), Kauai, HI.

Zhang, D., Lowry, P. B., Zhou, L., & Fu, X. (2007). The Impact of Individualism-Collectivism, Social Presence, and Group Diversity on Group Decision Making Under Majority Influence . *Journal of Management Information Systems, 23*(4), 53–80. doi:10.2753/MIS0742-1222230404

Zigurs, I., Poole, M. S., & DeSanctis, G. (1988). A study of influence in computer-mediated group decision making. *MIS Quarterly, 12*(4), 625–644. doi:10.2307/249136

ENDNOTES

1 Not all studies included U.S. participants, but all included non-U.S. participants.

2 A handful of published and unpublished (dissertations) research articles exist that discuss the remaining four task types and study them empirically, but these articles did not include culture as an IV or DV, and were thus excluded from this review.

3 These are business executives receiving part-time doctoral level education at top ranked business schools – thus, they have the knowledge and experience typical students lack. Business schools at Case Western Reserve University and Georgia State University, among others, have EDM programs which take advantage of the demand executives have for higher education.

4 Staples and Zhao (2006) also mention the affect CMC has on status effects, but this is not a focal point of their study.

APPENDIX I

Existing Studies on Culture and Collaborative Software (see Table 4)

Table 4.

Authors	Research Focus	Research Methodology	Task(s) Used	Independent (IV) and Dependent (DV) Variables	Cultures Involved and Group Size	Underlying Theory or Model	Major Findings
Aiken et al. (1993)	Preliminary study comparing North American and Malaysian groups using GSS; had Malaysian groups switch between English and Malay.	Laboratory experiment	Creativity task	(IV) language; (DV) production blocking, evaluation apprehension, satisfaction	9 Malaysians speaking Malay; 9 Malaysians speaking English; 16 North Americans speaking English	Not specified	Found no differences between all-North American groups and all-Malaysian groups using GSS in terms of production blocking (all low), evaluation apprehension (all low), and satisfaction (all high).
Aiken et al. (1995)	Compares the perceived effectiveness and satisfaction of users who use English and Korean versions of the same GSS.	Laboratory experiment	Creativity tasks	(IV) language (Korean vs. English); (DV) production blocking, evaluation apprehension, process satisfaction	12 Korean students at University of Mississippi (1 group)	Confucian philosophy in Korean society	No significant differences found between English and Korean versions of systems in terms of ratings of evaluation apprehension, production blocking, and process satisfaction. GSS reduced negative effects of verbal meetings conducted in Korea.
Anderson & Hiltz (2001)	Compares groups from the same cultural background with groups from varied cultural backgrounds when they use two different communication media systems.	Laboratory experiment	A value-based cognitive conflict (negotiation) task	(IV) communication mode (Manual F2F and asynchronous distributed) and group composition (culturally homogeneous and heterogeneous); (DV) adaptation factors and outcome factors	A total of 46 groups; 20 homogeneous (U.S.) manual F2F groups and distributed groups; 26 heterogeneous groups consisting of members from non-U.S. countries	Hofstede's cultural dimensions	FtF culturally heterogeneous (mixed) groups had the highest level of post-meeting consensus, while asynchronous culturally homogeneous (U.S.) groups had the lowest level; no significant differences were found based on cultural composition of the groups.
Atkinson & Pervan (1998)	Exploratory study compares productivity of groups from four national cultures using GroupSystems.	Exploratory laboratory experiment (4*2 repeated measure design)	Creativity task (idea generation)	(IV) anonymity and culture; (DV) group productivity	Australia (3 groups), Singapore (1 group), Malaysia (1 group), Indonesia (1 group); most groups included 10 participants	Hofstede's model	Exploratory, low sample study indicates higher power-distance cultures may derive greater productivity from anonymity; all groups from different cultures perceive anonymity as an advantage.
Calhoun, Teng, & Cheon (2002)	Exploratory survey study that examines the use of IT for organizational decision making in Korea and U.S.	Survey	Respondents were asked to consider the use of CMC to send and receive info in decision making	(IV) intensity of IT use for decision making; (DV) 17 decision attributes	65 Korean participants; 77 U.S. participants; all were employees	Hofstede's model	Exploratory results show that decision makers in Korea and U.S. had different perceptions of the IT use that impacted their decision-making activities.

Authors	Research Focus	Research Methodology	Task(s) Used	Independent (IV) and Dependent (DV) Variables	Cultures Involved and Group Size	Underlying Theory or Model	Major Findings
Clear and Kassabova (2005)	Exploratory review of cross-cultural collaborative experiences of students from Sweden and New Zealand. The intent is to understand motivation to participate and learn in global virtual teams.	Interviews, field observations, questionnaires, and analysis of written reports	Preference and cognitive-conflict task	Not specified, but implied: (IV) cultural barriers and task type; (DV) motivation to learn and motivation to participate	332 students from Sweden and New Zealand (not stated how many in each group)	transformative model of pedagogy (D. Leidner & Jarvenpaa, 1995)	Motivation to perform tasks may vary depending on culture (the Chinese speaking individuals reported largely that they remained committed despite disliking the experience, whereas other students remained committed because they enjoyed the experience, and others commitment depended on the perceived commitment level of the other group members.
Daily et al. (1996) Daily & Steiner (1998)	Examines the influence of a GSS on contribution and commitment levels in culturally homogeneous and CC (cross-cultural) decision-making groups. Two papers report on the same study's data.	Laboratory experiment (with 2 * 2 factorial design)	Three creativity tasks	(IV) GSS support (w/ and w/o GSS), cultural diversity; (DV) perceived contribution, number of unique ideas generated, solution quality, commitment, personal influence	Hispanic, Anglo, and others; 12 groups: 6 heterogeneous and 6 homogeneous groups (4 to 5 members per group)	Not specified	Culturally diverse groups outperformed culturally homogeneous groups on the number of ideas generated, but no significant effect on the solution quality. None of the effects of perceived contribution, commitment or personal influence were found to be significant.
De Vreede, Jones, & Mgaya (1999)	Explores the effective use and acceptance of GSS in a CC context.	Field study	Multiple tasks, including preference task and creativity task	(IV) culture; (DV) the use of GSS for decision making	3 countries: Tanzania, Malawi, and Zimbabwe; group sizes varied from 5 to 120 in each project	Hofstede's model and Technology Acceptance Model (TAM)	GSS could lead to significant differences in technology acceptance, use, and diffusion, as well as user satisfaction.
El-Shinnawy & Vinze (1997)	Examines the impact of GSS and culture on the process and outcomes of group decision making (polarization).	Laboratory experiment (2 * 2 repeated factorial design)	Preference task (the Pentium problem)	(IV) medium (FtF vs. CMC) and culture; (DV) polarization, persuasive arguments, novelty, validity	U.S. (24 groups) vs. Singapore (24 groups); 6 members per group	Hofstede's model; Persuasive Arguments Theory (PAT)	Culture and communication medium had significant effects on polarization; neither medium nor culture had main effects on persuasive arguments; GSS medium had higher impact on groups in the U.S. than on groups in Singapore.
Griffith (1998)	A cognitive model of CC implementation is tested using GroupSystems and Bulgarian and U.S. students.	Laboratory experiment	Preference task(lunar survival problem)	(IV) culture; (DV) innovation, critique, satisfaction	U.S.(16 students) vs. Bulgaria (15 students); data analysis on individual level	Hofstede's model (power distance)	Showed that Bulgarian students may be more likely to challenge authority than their U.S. counterparts. Power distance mediates some effects between culture and satisfaction with GSS.

Authors	Research Focus	Research Methodology	Task(s) Used	Independent (IV) and Dependent (DV) Variables	Cultures Involved and Group Size	Underlying Theory or Model	Major Findings
Hardin et al. (2007)	A virtual team study that tests differences between U.S. and Hong Kong with regards to self-efficacy in different contexts.	Three surveys administered during a series of virtual team projects	Preference tasks	(IV) Cultural diversity and communication medium (CMC vs. FtF) ; (DV) Computer Self-Efficacy (CSE) Group Self-Efficacy (GSE) Virtual Team Self-Efficacy (VTSE) Computer Collective Efficacy (CCE) Group Potency (GP) Virtual Team Efficacy (VTE)	U.S. (119) vs. Hong Kong (124)	Hofstede's individualism-collectivism dimension	Students are more comfortable working face to face than in virtual teams regardless of cultural background, but overall, individualist cultures report higher self-efficacy than collectivist cultures (FtF or CMC).
Ho, Raman, & Watson (1989)	A GSS study (using SAMM) in Singapore that explores the cultural differences between U.S. and Singapore.	Laboratory experiment	Preference task (allocation of funds to 6 projects)	(IV) level of support (3 levels); (DV) post meeting consensus, influence equality	Singapore: 48 5-person groups results were compared with the findings in a similar U.S. study (R. T. Watson, 1987)	Hofstede's individualism-collectivism dimension	Singaporean groups were indirect in the communication and seldom expressed disagreement in an open manner; the anonymity feature led to lower influence equality in Singapore.
Kunene (2005)	A field experiment done in South Africa on the effect of task decomposition on the quality and quantity of decisions in a group support environment.	Field experiment	Creativity task (brainstorming – idea generating)	(IV) task decomposition; (DV) number and quality of ideas	South Africa (12 split into 2 six person groups). No U.S. participants but compared to Dennis et al. (1999) results in order to show cultural effect.	Not stated, but it seems to be GSS group performance (A.R. Dennis & Wixon, 2001)	"Task decomposition resulted in 40% more ideas than no decomposition; the effect on decision quality is statistically significant only when decision quality is measured as the number of good ideas" (p. 13).
Lin et al. (2008)	A multi method design to discover what factors affect the effectiveness of virtual teams	meta analysis of the literature, a field experiment, and survey	Cognitive-conflict	(IV) communication, coordination, cohesion, relationship building, and trust; (DV) performance and satisfaction	Australia (200 students) No U.S. participants	No single underlying model or theory	"Social dimensional factors need to be considered early on in the virtual team creation process and are critical to the effectiveness of the team" (p. 1031).
Mejias, Shepherd, et al. (1997)	Examines the effect of culture on productivity, consensus level, and participation equity during the use of GSS.	Field study with 2*2 within-subjects design	Creativity task	(IV) GSS support, anonymity, national culture; (DV) number of ideas and unique ideas, participation equity, consensus level, satisfaction with decision	U.S. (22 groups) vs. Mexico (20 groups); all were divided into 3 treatments	Hofstede's model (first 4 dimensions)	Found significant differences in the number of ideas generated, consensus levels, and relative levels of user satisfaction across cultures.
Morales, Moreira, & Vogel (1995)	Explores the application of GroupSystems in regional development in Mexico and compares with findings from U.S.	Field study	Preference task (regional development)	Not specified	293 Mexican participants from actual organizations	Hofstede's model	Participants agreed that communication within the group was more effective with the use of the GSS; disagreement as to whether FtF communication would be more effective than the use of GSS.

Authors	Research Focus	Research Methodology	Task(s) Used	Independent (IV) and Dependent (DV) Variables	Cultures Involved and Group Size	Underlying Theory or Model	Major Findings
Niederman (1997)	Exploratory and atheoretical study compares Mexican and U.S. group facilitators using key elements of meeting success and selection of GSS tools.	Interview and tape recordings	Not specified	Not specified	U.S. vs. Mexico 7 Mexican group facilitators; 37 U.S. facilitators	Hofstede's model	Results found no compelling differences between what Mexican and U.S. facilitators consider important measures of meeting success, expected benefits and concerns, tool selection, and so forth.
Quaddus & Tung (2002)	Compares two cultures in the context of group conflict generation and management via a non-networked GSS.	Laboratory experiment (2 * 2 factorial design)	Preference and creativity tasks: (1) resource allocation, (2) strategic planning	(IV) technical support and task; (DV) amount and type of conflict, conflict resolution strategies, productivity	5 groups for both Australia and Singapore (3 or 4 members per group)	Hofstede's model	Higher levels of conflict were generated in Australia than in Singapore; Australians tended to use fewer avoidance strategies and report more productivity than the Singaporeans.
Reinig & Mejias (2003)	Examines the influence of GSS and national culture on group processes, meeting satisfaction, and group outcomes.	Laboratory experiment (2*2 factorial design)	Preference task	(IV) GSS support and national culture; (DV) levels of consensus, production blocking, dominance, satisfaction, participation equality	U.S.: 22 groups (11 GSS and 11 FtF groups, with 7 to 8 members per group); Hong Kong: 18 groups (9 GSS and 9 FtF groups, with 7 to 8 members per group)	Hofstede's model and Social Information Processing (SIP) theory	Find no substantial differences between cultures: GSS users reported less production blocking and dominance and lower levels of consensus and satisfaction than did FTF participants across both U.S. and Hong Kong samples.
Samarah et al. (2003)	Examines the moderating effect of cultural diversity on the relationship between the conflict management style and group performance.	Laboratory experiment	Fuzzy task	(IV) conflict mgt. style; moderator: culture diversity; (DV) degree of agreement, perceived decision quality, participation; moderator: culture	U.S. vs. India: 4 U.S. homogeneous groups; 9 Indian homogeneous groups; 9 heterogeneous groups; 3 to 4 members per group	Hofstede's model	Showed that cultural diversity has a positive moderating effect on the degree of group agreement and perceived decision quality.
Souren et al. (2004)	Investigates the impact of heterogeneity and collaborative conflict management style on the performance of synchronous virtual teams using a Web-based GSS.	Laboratory experiment (4*2 factorial design)	Preference task (selecting one option to recommend to a university about adopting a computer-use fee)	(IV) group heterogeneity vs. heterogeneity and conflict mgt. style; (DV) satisfaction, perceived decision quality, perception of participation, group agreement	U.S. vs. India: 15 4-person groups and one 3-person group. U.S. homogeneous groups.	Mentions Hofstede's model but not to generate hypothesis or interpret results	Collaborative conflict management style positively impacted satisfaction with the decision-making process, perceived decision quality, and perceived participation of virtual teams; weak evidence links a group's heterogeneity to its collaborative conflict management style.
Staples and Zhao (2006)	Investigates whether cultural diversity effects performance outcomes in teams working virtually versus FtF.	Laboratory experiment (2*2 factorial design)	Preference task	(IV) cultural diversity and communication medium; (DV) satisfaction and performance	North America (195), Asia (126) Europe (17) Africa (11) South America (11) Middle East (9) Mexico (8) Central America (2) Australia (1)	Hofstede's model (individualism-collectivism)	"Heterogeneous teams were less satisfied and cohesive and had more conflict than the homogeneous teams, although there were no statistical differences in team performance levels" (p.389).

Authors	Research Focus	Research Methodology	Task(s) Used	Independent (IV) and Dependent (DV) Variables	Cultures Involved and Group Size	Underlying Theory or Model	Major Findings
Tan, Wei, Watson, Clapper, & McLean (1998)	Investigates whether CMC can reduce normative influence from majorities in three decision-making settings.	Laboratory experiment (3*2*2 factorial design)	(1) An intellectual task; (2) a preference task (mock jury)	(IV) national culture, task type and communication medium; (DV) the number of rounds taken by the group to reach consensus	U.S. (8 groups in each treatment) vs. Singapore (11 or 12 groups in each treatment); 4-person groups; 6 treatments	Hofstede's model (individualism-collectivism)	Subjects in the unsupported setting took fewer rounds to reach consensus than those in FtF CMC and dispersed CMC; for both tasks, majority influence did not vary with communication medium.
Tan, Wei, Watson, & Walczuch (1998)	Examines whether CMC can reduce status effects during group communication in two national cultures.	Laboratory experiment (2*2*2 factorial design)	(1) An intellectual task; (2) a preference task	(IV) national culture, task type, and communication medium; (DV) status influence, sustained influence, perceived influence	U.S. (45 groups) vs. Singapore (48 groups); Five-person groups; four treatments, with 10 to 12 groups per treatment	Hofstede's model (individualism-collectivism and power-distance)	Task type and communication medium had significant main effects on status influence; status influence was not significantly stronger in Singapore groups than in U.S. groups; status influence was higher in preference task groups than in intellective task groups, etc.
Tung & Quaddus (2002)	Conducts a comparable study on the use of GSS in two different countries to explain the impact of culture on differences in results.	Laboratory experiment (2 * 2 factorial-repeated measure)	Preference task and creativity task: (1) resource allocation; (2) strategic planning	(IV) task and technical support; (DV) outcome in terms of the "productivity" of the conflicts	Australian: 6 groups (3 to 5 members per group); Singapore: 20 groups (3 or 4 members per group)	Hofstede's model	Revealed differences in the significance of technical support and tasks with productivity in the Singaporean and Australian studies (higher avoidance behaviors in Singaporean groups and higher levels of interpersonal conflict in Australian groups).
Vogel, Davison, & Shroff (2001)	Explores how GroupSystems can facilitate virtual teams in an educational environment.	Field study	7 joint projects (identify the impact of software defects & CSFs) (intellectual task)	Not specified	Netherlands, Greece, and Hong Kong; no between-group comparison; each project consists of one group only, with at least 48 students from 2 different regions	Hofstede's model and Sociocultural Learning theory	Encountered some communication problems; richer interaction led to higher performance; attraction to work with different cultures varied greatly among students; cultural differences emerged in team feelings.
Vogel, Genuchten, et al. (2001)	Reports the cultural difference reflected in group member behavior in a CC course project.	Field study	A 7-week joint project on a specific IT-related subject, resulting in a joint report (intellectual task)	Not specified	32 Hong Kong students and 39 Dutch students; 10 CC groups, with 6 to 10 members per group	Hofstede's model and Sociocultural theory	A cultural effect existed, reflected by different behaviors of members from different cultures (e.g., Hong Kong students tended to resolve issues by discussing them with their local teammates, while Dutch students were more inclined to address teammates from both cultural backgrounds).

Authors	Research Focus	Research Methodology	Task(s) Used	Independent (IV) and Dependent (DV) Variables	Cultures Involved and Group Size	Underlying Theory or Model	Major Findings
Walther (1997)	Examines the interplay of culture with long-term and short-term groups in FtF and distributed CMC conditions.	Laboratory experiment (2*2 factorial design)	Writing a paper summarizing, critiquing, and commenting on five articles	(IV) team duration (long term vs. short term), identity (social vs. individual); (DV) social attractiveness, task attractiveness, physical attractiveness	54 students, in groups of 5 to 6, drawn from U.S. and Britain	Recent interaction theories	Found that distributed groups were just as effective when examining social attractiveness, task attractiveness, and physical attractiveness.
Watson, Ho, & Raman (1994)	Evaluates the cultural effect on change in consensus and influence equality in three different communication settings.	Laboratory experiment (3*2 factorial design)	Preference task: allocation of money to six projects	(IV) type of decision support (CS, manual, baseline), national culture; (DV) change in consensus, influence equality	U.S. vs. Singapore U.S.: 3 to 4 members per group, group sizes for 3 decision support treatments were 27, 26, and 29 Singapore: 5-person groups; group sizes for 3 decision-support treatments were 14, 16, and 15	Hofstede's model and Adaptive Structuration Theory (AST)	Singaporean groups had higher pre-meeting consensus than U.S. groups; all groups in both cultures had the same level of post meeting consensus; change in consensus was greater in U.S. than in Singaporean groups.

APPENDIX II

Evaluation of Five New Studies against the Seven Failures (Table 5)

Table 5.

Authors	Absurdity test	Grouping by Nation	Limited Sampling	Homogeneous groups	Just FtF	Small Groups	Lack Realism
Clear and Kassabova (2005)	"It appears there is a cultural influence on the motivation for this grouping where one perseveres with the task at hand regardless of the negative perception" (p. 54). No further explanation was given. There are no other explanations of possible cultural effects.	Not applicable. This failure is meant to include studies which make inferences or judgments based on a nation as a whole, which this study did not do.	More than 15 teams studied.	Groups were heterogeneous with Swedish students at UU in Sweden and multicultural students at AUT in New Zealand.	Used asynchronous, distributed, virtual teams.	8-15 students per virtual team	All students. Tasks included ice-breaking game and website evaluation. The students did have vested interest in the tasks, as they were part of their grade, but they could opt out at any time.
Hardin et al. (2007)	Provided excellent explanations for cultural effects.	Although they grouped by Collectivist (Hong Kong)/ Individualist (U.S.) cultures, they acknowledge there has been criticism in doing this, and so they performed a manipulation check to ensure that collectively, Hong Kong students were actually more collectivist than U.S. students.	Study was interested in individual statistics; n = 243	Used heterogeneous teams of students from Hong Kong and U.S.	Used asynchronous, distributed, virtual teams.	Not specified.	Students were used, but the projects "had a significant impact on students' grades" (p. 140). Projects were typical of team projects in a work environment, and for all intents and purposes, they were realistic.

Authors	Absurdity test	Grouping by Nation	Limited Sampling	Homogeneous groups	Just FtF	Small Groups	Lack Realism
Kunene (2005)	Stated that culture did not appear to have an effect because their study produced similar results as previous studies performed within other cultures.	Not applicable. Participants were all from South Africa, but no quality statements were made concerning the participants as a whole.	2 six person groups.	Groups consisted of all South African students.	Group members were co-located, but used a CSW to generate ideas.	Six person groups.	Lab experiment with students in a timed setting. A timed brainstorming task.
Lin et al. (2008)	Largely ignored culture since it turned up insignificant in the meta-analysis. No effort was spent to explain why there was no effect from culture. So, N/A.	Not applicable. Participants were all from Australia. No generalizing cultural statements were made about the participants.	25 teams of 8 members each	Groups consisted of all Australian students.	Compared virtual teams to FtF teams.	8 members in each group.	Fictitious case task; restricted virtual team communication to text chat only. All student participants. No effect on grade.
Staples and Zhao (2006)	Provided excellent explanations for cultural effects.	Individualism/Collectivism scores were based on questionnaires, not on country of birth.	79 five person teams	Used both heterogeneous and homogenous groups.	Compared virtual teams to FtF teams.	5 members in each group	All students in voluntary experiment, restricted communication, timed, and no effect on grade.

Chapter 7
Project Quality of Off-Shore Virtual Teams Engaged in Software Requirements Analysis:
An Exploratory Comparative Study

Dhruv Nath
Management Development Institute, India

Varadharajan Sridhar
Management Development Institute, India

Monica Adya
Marquette University, USA

Amit Malik
Management Development Institute, India

ABSTRACT

The off-shore software development companies in countries such as India use a global delivery model in which initial requirement analysis phase of software projects get executed at client locations to leverage frequent and deep interaction between user and developer teams. Subsequent phases such as design, coding and testing are completed at off-shore locations. Emerging trends indicate an increasing interest in off-shoring even requirements analysis phase using computer mediated communication. We conducted an exploratory research study involving students from Management Development Institute (MDI), India and Marquette University (MU), USA to determine quality of such off-shored requirements analysis projects. Our findings suggest that project quality of teams engaged in pure off-shore mode is comparable to that of teams engaged in collocated mode. However, the effect of controls such as user project monitoring on the quality of off-shored projects needs to be studied further.

INTRODUCTION

The past two decades have witnessed significant globalization of the software development process with development rapidly moving away from the traditional collocated model, often called *on-site development*, to the off-shoring model. With the availability of increasingly skilled, flexible, and economical IT workforce in countries such as India, Malaysia, and China, it makes financial sense for United States and European client organizations to execute a significant portion of software projects in these countries. This growing trend towards off-shoring has, in turn, spurred growth in many Asian nations, creating improved economic and IT infrastructure and enhancing the viability of these countries as software service providers. For example, India has emerged as a dominant off-shore software development industry with revenue of about $16.7 billion, which is projected to reach $60 billion by the year 2010 (Carmel, 2006; National Association of Software and Service Companies, 2005).

The Indian off-shore software industry has matured over the years, and process capability has been steadily improving. Coordination and communication problems typically encountered in off-shore development (see Battin, Crocker, Kreidler, & Subramanian, 2001, for an extended discussion), are mitigated by the use of processes such as rational task assignments and liaisoning, and tools such as centralized bug reporting system and software configuration management platforms. A case in point is India's Infosys Technologies, which has significantly leveraged time zone differences with its clients by modifying its organizational culture, processes, and communication technologies (Carmel, 2006).

The typical off-shore development model, followed successfully for over a decade by many Indian software companies such as Infosys, Wipro, TCS, and Satyam, is illustrated in Figure 1.

Requirements analysis refers to that stage of the system development life cycle wherein the information and information processing services needed to support select objectives and functions of the organization are (i) determined and (ii) coherently represented using well-defined artifacts such as entity-relationship diagrams, dataflow diagrams, use cases, and screen prototypes (Hoffer, George, & Valacich, 1999). As suggested in Figure 1, typically this phase is conducted at the client location, since this phase requires frequent and significant interaction between users and developers. Business and systems analysts are physically located at the client site to perform this activity. Global projects consultant teams from off-shore location travel to the user site to gather and analyze requirements in face-to-face meetings (Damian & Zowghi, 2002). The consultants then communicate the requirements to the development staff in the offshore site. Depending on the nature of the project, high-level design is conducted in both on-site and off-shore mode due to comparatively lower interaction needs with the client. Detailed design, coding, and testing are executed at the off-shore site. Off-shore vendors also deploy liaisons who coordinate activities between on-site users and the off-shore development team. These liaisons are critical for effective communication and coordination between users and developers (Battin et al., 2001).

Increasingly, both client and software providers are now considering the possibility of off-shoring the requirements analysis phase, traditionally done on client site, away from the client location. In such a scenario, analysts and developers located at the off-shore location would interact in a virtual mode with the clients situated at their premises to determine and structure the requirements. Such a shift could potentially improve the cost arbitrage of the projects for instance by cutting down travel costs incurred for sending analysts to the client site for face-to-face meetings. In an extreme case, the entire team of analysts and developers could be based in off-shore location such as India while the client could be in Europe or the United States. Requirements gathering would then be

Figure 1. The off-shore software development model

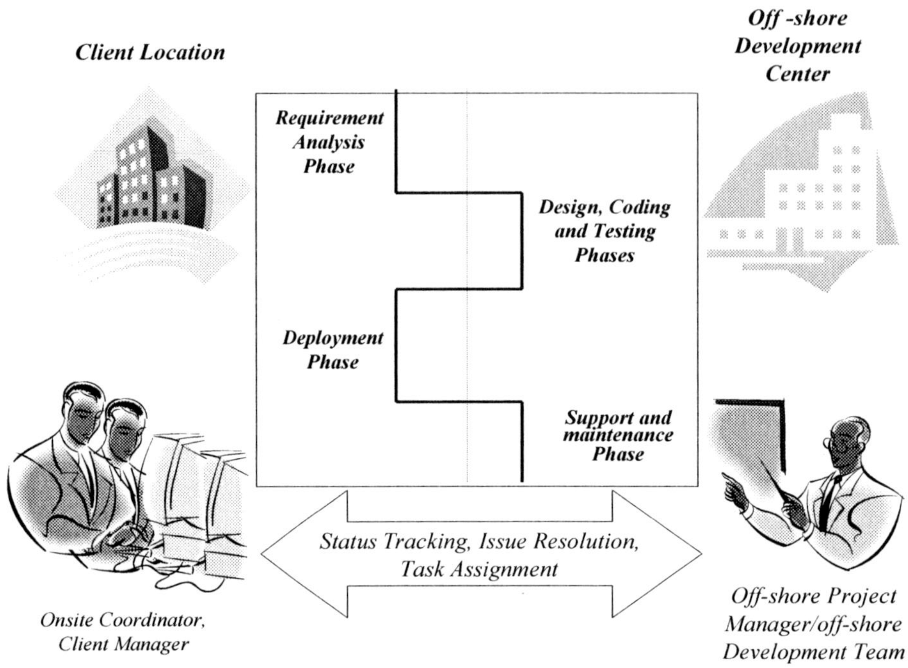

conducted between these virtual teams using existing computer-mediated communications such as chat, e-mail, and video conferencing. The questions of research interest then are:

1. Can requirements analysis conducted by collocated teams using face-to-face communication be comparable or better than those produced by virtual off-shore teams using computer-mediated communication?
2. What forms of control are necessary to facilitate high-quality outcomes from virtual requirements analysis undertakings?

Using theories of social presence, media richness (Burke & Chidambaram, 1999), as well as control theory (Kirsch, 2002), we develop and test hypotheses regarding these questions.

Traditionally, user involvement in IS projects has been an important contributor to project success (Hartwick & Barki, 1994; Foster & Franz ,1999; Lin & Shao, 2000; Sridhar, Nath, & Malik, in press). Lack of user proximity in a virtual setting can potentially limit the quality of requirements elicitation due to limitations of communications media. In order to mitigate these limitations and the absence of analysts and developers at customer premises, user involvement is expected to take the form of close project monitoring and control to ensure that requirements and project goals are met. Control theory provides the required theoretical foundations for analyzing the effect of different types of controls on teams (Crisp, 2003). In this study, we specifically consider user project monitoring as a behavioral control mechanism and examine its impact on project quality during requirements analysis phase of off-shored software projects. Further, we explore the intersection of media richness and control theories to find early answers to the research questions raised earlier.

This study is exploratory in nature. Without loss of generality, we restrict our attention to the requirements analysis phase as defined in the structured systems analysis and design (SSAD) methodology as defined by Hoffer et al. (1999). We define requirements analysis as subsuming the following two phases:

1. Requirements determination: The process by which the analysts determine the requirements of the system from the users through discussions and interviews and exchanging forms, reports, job descriptions and other necessary documents.
2. Requirements structuring: The process by which the analysts coherently represent the information gathered as part of requirements determination using process modeling and logic modeling tools as described in SSAD.

Our interactions with managers in client firms engaged in software development indicate that off-shoring of requirements analysis is still uncommon. Hence it is not practical to analyze this phenomenon of pure off-shoring of requirements in real-life setting. It is also difficult to do in-depth longitudinal or cross-sectional case studies. Given these arguments, an exploratory research study was conducted in an academic setting involving management students enrolled in a graduate-level information systems course at Management Development Institute (MDI), India, and management students enrolled in a graduate level IT Project Management course at Marquette University (MU), United States. MU students role-played as virtual users/project managers while MDI students were software developers for MU teams as well as user clients for collocated MDI teams. Prior to a full description of our undertaking, we first discuss existing literature on virtual teams in software projects. We then describe the theoretical foundations of this study and elaborate on our research design. Next, we discuss our measures and discuss study outcomes. The article concludes with implications for future research in this context.

VIRTUAL TEAMS IN SOFTWARE PROJECTS

In a pure off-shore mode, users at the client location and the developers at the off-shore location never meet face to face and hence operate as virtual teams, primarily linked through technology across national boundaries. It is in this context that we review previous research on such virtual teams, specifically those engaged in software development projects. Virtual teams are becoming the norm in most corporate environments such as consulting firms, technology products, and e-commerce (Lurey & Raisinghani, 2001) and are being increasingly examined in academic literature (see Powell, Piccoli, & Ives, 2005 for a comprehensive survey of virtual teams). Battin et al. (2001) described how Motorola deployed global virtual teams across six different countries for a Third Generation Cellular System product development. Software development in Alcatel was handled by a central group of several thousand engineers distributed throughout the world (Ebert & De Neve, 2001).

Few studies however, have, examined the use of virtual teams for requirements analysis. Edwards and Sridhar (2005) studied the effectiveness of virtual teams in a collaborative requirements analysis practice. In that study virtual teams at near and far locations participated in requirements analysis phase of the project. This typically is applicable in collaborative global product development exercises as described in Battin et al. (2003). In contrast, in this study we look at the requirements analysis phase of off-shored software projects in which the two protagonists are (i) users who specify the requirements, and (ii) developers who determine and document these requirements together constituting a collaborative virtual teams. Damian and Zowghi (2002) studied the interplay between culture and conflict and the impact of distance on the ability to reconcile different viewpoints with respect to "requirements negotiation" processes. They found that lack of a common understanding of requirements, together with reduced awareness of local context, trust level, and ability to share work artifacts significantly challenge effective collaboration among remote stakeholders in negotiating a set of requirements that satisfies geographically dispersed customers. Damian, Eberlein, Shaw, and Gaines (2000) examined the effect of the distribution of various stakeholders in the requirements engineering process. They found that highest group performance occurred when customers were separated from each other and collocated with the facilitator or system analyst. Our study further contributes to the literature on virtual teams engaged in off-shored software requirements analysis.

THEORETICAL FOUNDATIONS AND HYPOTHESES DEVELOPMENT

Social Presence and Media Richness Theories

Social presence is the extent to which one feels the presence of a person with whom one is interacting. Short, Williams, and Christie (1976) suggested that some media convey greater social presence than others. For instance, face-to-face interaction is considered to be high in social presence, primarily because of the capacity of the medium to transmit proximal, facial, and other nonverbal cues relative to other media. In contrast, computer-mediated communication such as e-mail exhibit inherently lower bandwidth than face-to-face interaction, thus permitting transmission of fewer visual and nonverbal cues and restricting socio-emotional communication (Rice & Love, 1987). In addition to differences in social presence, media richness theory proposes that, given their limited cue-carrying capacity, leaner media such as e-mail, will be less effective for groups performing ambiguous tasks which require a variety of cues to be exchanged. However, Burke and Chidambaram (1999) pointed out that despite some support for media characteristics-dependent theories, overall empirical evidence has been mixed.

Quality of Off-Shored Projects vs. Collocated Projects

Teams engaged in pure off-shored projects primarily rely on computer-mediated communications (synchronous such as chat, audio and video conferencing as well as asynchronous such as e-mail) for interaction. However, collocated teams have the luxury of rich face-to-face communication. Based on the social presence and media richness theories, we formulate the following hypothesis:

H1: *Collocated teams using face-to-face communication will produce higher quality project artifacts compared to virtual teams using computer-mediated communication during the requirements analysis phase of software projects.*

In a subsequent section, we define *quality of project artifacts* and how it is measured. To the best of our knowledge, quality of projects and performance of virtual teams engaged in the software requirements analysis has not been studied in the literature thus far. Although several researchers have compared performances of traditional collocated teams with that of virtual teams, the conclusions have been mixed. While one study reported greater effectiveness for virtual teams (Sharda, Barr, & McDonnell 1988), others such as McDonough, Kahn, and Barczak (2001) have found that virtual teams could not outperform traditional teams. Andres (2002) reported that teams working in face-to-face settings experienced greater productivity compared to those supported using videoconferencing. Generally, computer-mediated teams exhibit lower frequency of communication than face-to-face teams, although they tend to exchange more task-oriented messages as a proportion of total communication (Burke & Chidambaram, 1999; Chidambaram,

1996). This enhanced communication leads to comparable or even higher performance of virtual teams as compared to collocated teams (Burke & Chidambaram, 1999). Consistent with these findings, Schmidt et al. (2001) reported that virtual teams are more effective in new product development decisions as compared to face-to-face teams. However, a majority of the early work has detected no difference between the two types of teams (Burke & Aytes, 1998). Other studies have found no significant differences between traditional and virtual teams when examining decision quality (Archer, 1990; Chidambaram & Bostrom, 1993) as well as the number of ideas generated by decision making teams (Archer, 1990; Lind, 1999; Sharda et al., 1988). Walther (2005) further suggested that complex human processes such as negotiation actually improve between physically distributed individuals who communicate using media low in richness. Studies comparing performance of virtual and collocated teams in software requirements analysis phase are even fewer. Damian et al. (2000) found that groups in face-to-face meetings performed no better than the electronically mediated groups in the requirements negotiation phase of the software development life cycle.

Control Theory

Control is defined as the set of mechanisms designed to motivate individuals to work in such a way that desired objectives are achieved (Kirsch, 1996). *Formal controls* rely on mechanisms that influence the controllee's behavior through performance evaluation and rewards (Choudhury & Sabherwal, 2003). Controllers utilize two modes of formal control: behavior and outcome (Kirsch, 2002). In behavior control, appropriate steps and procedures for task performance are defined by controllers, and then controllees' performance is evaluated according to their adherence to the prescribed procedures. In outcome control, controllers define appropriate targets and allow controllees to decide how to meet those output targets. Controllees' performance is evaluated on the extent to which targets were met, and not on the processes used to achieve the targets (Kirsch 2002).

Informal control mechanisms utilize social or people strategies to reduce goal differences between controller and controllee. Self-control, one mode of informal control, occurs when an individual sets up his or her own goals, self-monitors goal achievement, and rewards or sanctions him- or herself accordingly (Kirsch, 2002). *Clan control,* the other type of informal control, is implemented through mechanisms that minimize the differences between controller's and controllee's preferences by "promulgating common values, beliefs and philosophies within a clan, which is defined as a group of individuals who are dependent on one another and who share a set of common goals" (Choudhury & Sabherwal, 2003). Kirch et al (2002) extended the control theory to the role of client liaisons, exercising control of IS project leaders to ensure that IS projects meet their goals. The study examined the conditions under which client liaisons of IS development projects choose various modes of control. In a related work, Choudhury and Sabherwal (2003) examined the evolution of portfolio of controls over the duration of outsourced IS development projects. They conclude that in outsourced software projects outcome controls are exercised at the start of the project. Behavioral controls are added later in the project. Clan controls are used when the client and vendor had shared goals, and when frequent interactions lead to shared values. Both these studies analyzed the evolution and choice of controls in IS projects and not on the effect of these controls on project outcome. In this study we focus on the effect of formal modes of control (both outcome and behavior) on the quality of project artifacts produced by virtual teams engaged in software requirements analysis. Project monitoring provides opportunities for both forms of formal control previously described through tracking, interpretation and transmission of status information (Crisp, 2003). In this study, we define *user control* to include not only monitoring the project plan (a form of behavioral control) but also the evaluation of the formal artifacts produced (a form of outcome control) during the requirements analysis process. Monitoring of costs is excluded as requirements analysis is often part of a large IS outsourcing project. Though cost monitoring is vital, it does not assume much significance when considered for only one phase of the project and hence is excluded. Based on the control theory and literature review of virtual teams, our second hypothesis is as follows:

H2: *Developer teams that are closely monitored by their users in a virtual team mode will produce higher quality of artifacts as compared to developer teams that are not closely monitored by their users.*

RESEARCH DESIGN

To test both the aforementioned hypotheses, we conducted two overlapping quasi experiments involving students at MU and MDI in controlled settings. Such experimental settings have been actively used in distributed software engineering laboratories and business schools to conduct virtual team exercises in their courses (Powell et al., 2005). A controlled experimental approach provides three benefits. Firstly, it makes available several teams that work in parallel, thereby generating rich data for drawing conclusions. Secondly, it permits researchers to experiment with newer approaches, which may not yet have been explored by the industry. Finally, it equips and trains software engineering students to understand and to handle the challenges of working in global software teams (Favela & Pena-Mora, 2001). A survey on virtual team research by Powell et al. (2005) cited 28 academic experiments and only 13 case study research papers. Our experimental setup is illustrated in Figure 2 and described in greater detail next.

Experiment 1—Testing H1: The Impact of Media Richness on Project Quality

For hypothesis 1 (H1), we compared the quality of projects produced by collocated teams with those that were produced by virtual teams. The collocated teams were students of the postgraduate program in management (equivalent to an MBA) who were attending a core course in management information systems (MIS) at MDI. One hundred and twenty-seven students were divided into two roughly equal sections, section *A* and section *B*. Students from section *A* were grouped into 10 teams of 5 or 6 students each. Each team played the role of users for the collocated project. Figure 2(a) shows one such team, referred to as MDI team A1. Students from section *B* were also grouped into 10 teams of 5 or 6 students each. Each of these teams formed developer teams for the collocated project. Figure 2(a) shows one such team, referred to as MDI team B1. Each MDI *A* team was then paired with one of the MDI *B* teams, as shown in Figure 2(a). Thus MDI team A1 served as users to MDI team B1, the developers in the collocated project. Similarly, MDI team A2 was the user for MDI team B2, and so on.

Setting for the Virtual Teams

MU students, enrolled in a graduate elective course in IT project management, assumed the role of virtual users. Twenty-eight students divided into 10 teams (each with a team size of 2-3 members), referred to as *MU Teams*. Figure 2(a) shows one of these MU teams, team 1. Each MU team was paired with one of the MDI B teams. Thus MDI B teams became the off-shore development teams for the associated MU user teams. These teams consisting of users and developers worked in

Figure 2. The experimental set-up

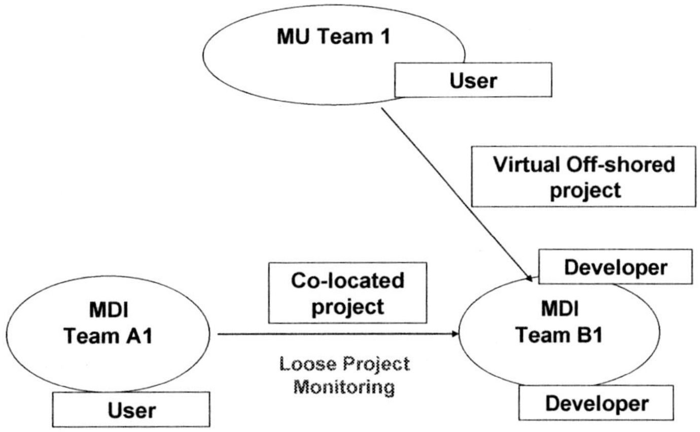

(a) Experiment 1: Collocated vs. Virtual Teams

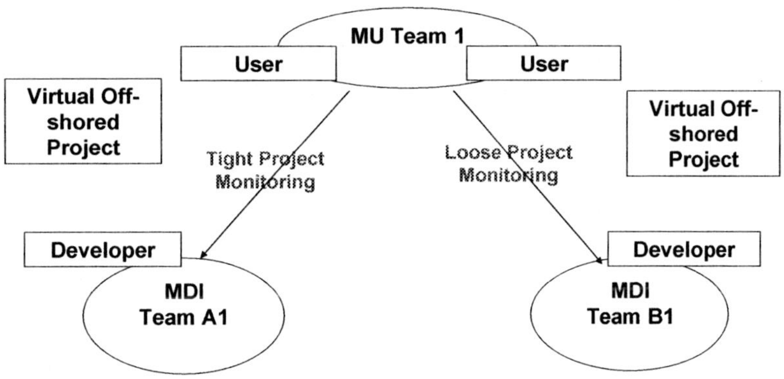

(b) Experiment 2: Virtual Teams Under Tight Project Monitoring vs. Loose Project Monitoring

virtual team mode. In summary, each MDI team *B* was involved in the following two projects: (i) collocated project with MDI user team *A* and (ii) virtual off-shored project with MU user team.

In both projects, the MDI *B* teams were required to submit a project plan at the beginning of the project, detailing various activities and timelines. The final delivery date was predetermined by the instructors based on the course schedule. Project monitoring was voluntary between MDI B and MDI A user teams, so as to minimize the impact of any other variables on the experiment. The MDI B development teams communicated with their corresponding user teams at MU through online means such as e-mail, instant messaging, and voice chats such as Skype and with their MDI A user teams through face-to-face meetings while having face-to-face interactions with their collocated MDI *A* teams. It must be noted that each developer teams (i.e., MDI *B* teams) had 5 or 6 members, thus controlling for the effects of team sizes on the quality of the project.

Experiment —Testing H2: The Impact of Project Monitoring on Project Quality

To test H2, we compared the quality of two sets of virtual teams, one in which the users imposed project monitoring (referred to as *tight* monitor-

Table 1. Experimental set-up

	MU Teams	MDI *A* Teams	MDI *B* Teams	Treatment	Hypothesis Tested
Experiment 1	Users	Users	Developers	MU Users <-> MDI *B* Developers, Virtual Teams MDI *A* Users <-> MDI *B* Developers, Collocated Teams	H1
Experiment 2	Users	Developers	Developers	MU Users <-> MDI *A* Developers, Virtual and tightly controlled Teams MU Users <-> MDI *B* Developers, Virtual and loosely controlled Teams	H2

ing), and the other one in which user project monitoring was voluntary (referred to as *loose* monitoring). For this purpose, we used a portion of the data collected as part of experiment 1. Recall that in experiment 1 we already had a set of virtual teams, namely the teams formed by MU user team and the MDI *B* developer teams, operating in voluntary project monitoring mode. We then formed another set of virtual teams by pairing each MU user team with MDI *A* teams. However, in this experiment MDI *A* teams performed the role of developers for their corresponding MU user teams (compared to the role of users they played in experiment 1). MU user teams were required to tightly monitor their projects with MDI *A* teams. This is illustrated in Figure 2(b), where MU team 1 was the user for MDI team A1, under tight project monitoring, and was also the user for MDI team B1, under loose project monitoring (part of experiment 1). Similarly, the MU team 2 was the user for MDI team A2 and B2, and so on. Once again, each of the developer teams (i.e., MDI *A* and *B* teams) had 5 or 6 members, thus controlling for effects of team size on success of the project.

Tight and loose control was implemented as follows: In the case of virtual teams operating under imposed tight project monitoring (MU and MDI *A* teams), the developers were told to submit weekly project reports to their respective user teams. The user teams were required to review and ask for changes/actions as required, thus implementing behavioral control. In addition, MDI teams were required to conduct requirements analysis in iterative model, returning a set of intermediate artifacts which would also be reviewed and commented on by their users, thus implementing outcome control. This formed the control group in our experiment. In contrast, teams operating under voluntary user project monitoring did not have to submit regular project status reports nor any intermediate artifacts to their users. They received requirements specifications from their users, asked for clarifications where necessary, and submitted the final artifacts at the end of the project. Any communication between these teams and their users was strictly on a need-be basis. This formed the experimental group in our research design. MU teams were graded partly on the communication plans and weekly project status reports they developed for monitoring their MDI *A* teams. This ensured that MU team users spent more time and effort in monitoring their associated MDI *A* teams than MDI *B* teams. This design resulted in the two overlapping experiments 1 and 2 described previously. Table 1 illustrates the roles of MDI and MU teams in these experiments.

All student teams were formed in such a way that the technical background and average work experience of group members were almost the same across groups, thereby controlling team

Table 2. ANOVA comparing means of variables across teams

Variable	*F*	Significance
Work Experience	0.601	0.795
Experience in Programming	1.356	0.213
Experience in Participating in Virtual Teams	0.803	0.614
Experience in Software Project Management	0.973	0.465
Experience in Systems Analysis and Design	0.543	0.841

member heterogeneity. Table 2 provides ANOVA results comparing means of various parameters across teams. Results suggest no significant differences in the means of various parameters across teams confirming their homogeneity. Students had sufficient stake in the virtual team project as up to 30% of the course grade was assigned to the project.

Our research design adopts the quasi experiment approach where the participants are allotted to teams, based on certain criterion, as explained previously, and not randomly. Hence the limitations of quasi experimentation as explained in Campbell and Stanley (1966) applies to our research setting as well.

Tasks

Virtual Team Exercise

The virtual team interactions (in both experiments) were broken down into two phases: (1) *socialization,* which permitted the teams to develop relationships and negotiate communication terms and requirements; and (2) *project execution,* which allowed requirements gathering, clarifications, and exchange of analysis artifacts.

Phase 1: Socialization

It is an increasingly common practice in virtual teams to engage in formal socialization before embarking on virtual projects in order to understand each others' work styles and expectations, negotiate communications strategies and protocols, and build trust for sustained relationships (Jarvenpaa & Leidner, 1999). In our experiment, this was not feasible due to resource and other restrictions, not unlike those faced by organizations new to off-shoring as well as those involved in small, preliminary initiatives. Furthermore, our objective was to draw benchmark conclusions regarding effects of user project monitoring on teams engaged in a fully virtual team environment. Therefore we encouraged the MU and MDI teams to communicate and socialize with each other on-line before initiating actual work on the project. The virtual teams—MU, MDI *A,* and MDI *B*—socialized with each other using on-line media such as e-mail, Internet chat, bulletin boards, and e-groups for a period of 2 weeks. Project details were withheld from all teams till conclusion of the socialization phase in order to ensure that communication was more personalized and oriented towards relationship and trust building (Sarkar & Sahay, 2002) rather than requirements exchange.

Phase 2: Project Execution

Subsequent to socialization, the projects were initiated, and team roles were detailed. Marquette University has a service learning office that obtains information systems projects from nonprofit organizations and small businesses in and around Milwaukee. Such real-life projects were given to MU users. Examples of these projects include a donation management system for a nonprofit organization, a volunteer management system, an alumni website, a tracking system for battered and abused women, and a book inventory management system.

The MDI teams elicited project requirements from MU teams through various on-line media, as described previously. SSAD methodology was used in the experiment. The gathered requirements were structured using process modeling tools such as context analysis diagram (CAD), data flow diagrams (DFDs) and process specifications. MDI teams also modeled the data and associated relationships using entity relationship diagrams (ERDs). MDI teams also created screen-based prototypes as part of the requirements analysis exercise. These artifacts were submitted by the MDI teams to MU user teams as part of the deliverables.

In addition, the MDI A development teams that experienced tightly monitored projects submitted the following additional artifacts to the users:

a. A weekly status report of the project, explaining reasons for delays and plans for overcoming any slippages.
b. Any modifications to the project plan.
c. A draft (intermediate) version of all the above artifacts, midway through the project Based on their requirements, users provided feedback and corrections, which were incorporated by the developers into the final version.

Details of all these deliverables submitted by the different teams for this virtual team exercise are shown in Table 3. The table also shows several artifacts/reports that the MU teams had to submit to the course instructors.

Collocated Exercise

For the collocated team exercises, each MDI *A* team had at least one member who had prior work experience of 2 to 3 years. These individuals were asked to select an information system project they had encountered at work, to ensure realism and familiarity with system features. Each collocated team developed requirements analysis artifacts for these projects. The instructors had discussions with each group and scoped the projects such that the project complexity was almost the same as that of the virtual teams. The MDI *B* teams were asked to submit to MDI team *A* artifacts identical to those submitted to MU teams during the virtual team project (see Table 1). The entire project duration for both virtual and collocated projects was 8 weeks.

OUTCOME MEASURES

Quality of Projects

Quality of MU-MDI projects were determined through (i) expert evaluation of project artifacts produced by developer teams and (ii) user perceptions about the project deliverable quality. Quality of project artifacts was measured on several dimensions—namely, correctness of the artifacts (e.g., whether the data flow diagrams were drawn correctly, whether or not they satisfied user requirements), adherence of the artifacts to user requirements, and consistency of the artifacts with each other.

i. Completeness and Adherence of the Artifacts to User Requirements

Completeness and adherences were analyzed by an external expert who was not part of the MU-MDI teams. This expert had 2 to 3 years of experience in software projects and had taken courses in SSAD. The expert evaluated the completeness and adherence of each of the following artifacts:

1. Context analysis diagram
2. Data flow diagrams (DFDs)

Table 3. Artifacts submitted by the different teams for the virtual team projects

Artifact	MDI *A* Teams for the Virtual Team Projects under tight Project Monitoring	MDI *B* Teams for both the Virtual and Collocated Projects under loose Project Monitoring	MU Teams for the Virtual team Projects (to be submitted to the instructors)
Context Analysis Diagram	✓	✓	
Data Flow Diagrams	✓	✓	
Entity Relationship Diagrams	✓	✓	
Process Specifications	✓	✓	
Screen shots	✓	✓	
An intermediate version of all the above artifacts	✓		
Weekly Development Status Report	✓		
Communication Plans			✓
Risk Assessment			✓
Contingency Plans			✓
Weekly Project Status Report (to the Instructors)			(only with MDI *A* teams)
Project Closure Report			✓
Team *A* and *B* Assessment			✓

3. Process specifications
4. Entity-relationship diagrams (ERDs)
5. Screen shots of the proposed system

The expert analyzed and scored the above artifacts for each project on a 7-point Likert-type scale. Though the expert had only 2 to 3 years of experience, by following a standard evaluation procedure such as the one outlined previously, this individual was able to arrive at an objective assessment of project quality. This evaluation was validated for consistency and accuracy by a second expert who had more than 20 years of SSAD industry experience, thus reducing possible biases in the evaluation process. The average of these scores across all artifacts for each project was taken as a measure of completeness and adherence of project artifacts to user requirements. By making the team assignments to the projects blind to the expert, we minimized subjective bias of the expert during the assessment.

ii. Consistency of the Artifacts

The expert also analyzed the consistency of the screen prototypes submitted by development teams with the DFDs and ERDs submitted. Using a 7-point Likert-type scale, the expert analyzed and scored for each project the consistency across

1. Screen prototypes and DFDs
2. Screen prototypes and ERDs

Table 4. Detailed hypotheses based on different measures

Research Question	Hypotheses
Quality of Projects of Virtual Teams vs. Collocated Teams	**H1a:** Adherence and completeness of the requirements analysis artifacts produced by the collocated teams using face-to-face communication will be better than those produced by the virtual teams using computer-mediated communication. **H1b:** Consistency of the screen shots and requirements analysis artifacts produced by the collocated teams using face-to-face communication will be better than those produced by the virtual teams using computer-mediated communication. **H1c:** The users will perceive the quality of project artifacts produced by collocated teams using face-to-face communication to be better than those produced by the virtual teams using computer-mediated communication.
Impact of User Project Monitoring on of the Quality of Projects	**H2a:** Quality of project artifacts (as defined by the three measures of completeness & adherence, consistency, and user perception) produced by the developer teams that are closely monitored by their associated users in a virtual team mode will be better than those produce by the developer teams that were not closely monitored by their users.. **H2b:** Quality of project artifacts (as defined by the three measures of adherence & completeness, consistency, and user perception) produced by of the developers that perceived higher levels of project monitoring by their users will be better than those produced by the developer teams that perceived lower levels.

Using the same evaluation and validation procedure described in (i), an average score measuring the consistency of the project artifacts was generated.

iii. User-perceived quality

User perceptions about the quality of artifacts submitted by the developer teams were also collected through a survey questionnaire as the third measure of team performance. A 7-point Likert-type scale was used to elicit response from the user team members. Items adapted from Edwards and Sridhar (2005) are detailed in Appendix I. Scores given by all the users to a particular development team were averaged and were treated as measure of user-perceived quality. Therefore, there was one rating/score per user teams. Based on measures of quality already mentioned, hypothesis H1, which was constructed in the previous section, can be refined and are presented in Table 4.

By specifying the two dimensions of completeness and adherence as well as consistency, any errors in the assessment of the quality of the projects was thought to be minimized.

User Project Monitoring

We also measured perceived project-monitoring practices of all users and developers involved in both tight and loosely monitored projects. Responses were elicited on a 7-point Likert-type scale at the end of the project. Items are shown in Appendix I. In order to capture the responses for perceived quality and user project monitoring based on the roles they played (user/developer) and the team (collocated/ virtual) with which they did the projects, different versions of the survey was prepared and administered to students at MDI and at MU. The various versions included same items for each construct but were worded differently, depending on the roles the participants played.

Based on the experimental measure of perceived project management practice, hypothesis H2 can be further articulated as in Table 4.

ANALYSIS, RESULTS, AND DISCUSSIONS

A principal component analysis was performed on the items constructed for the previously mentioned measures with Varimax rotation and Kaiser normalization; the results are given in Table 5. Reliability of all these measures of (i) completeness and adherence of artifacts, (ii) consistency of project artifacts, (iii) user-perceived quality, and (iv) perceived user project monitoring practices are given in Table 6. Cronbach's alpha values of 0.70 and higher indicate construct reliability.

Performance of Collocated vs. Virtual Teams

To test hypothesis **H1,** a one-way ANOVA test was performed on the three measures of project quality, as were previously described, between virtual and collocated teams that participated in Experiment 1. Note that in this case the project artifacts are produced by the same developer teams, and the project complexity of both the virtual and collocated projects were moderated by the instructors to be almost the same. However, due to constraints in conducting the experiment, the user teams could not be the same. User project monitoring was kept loose for both virtual and collocated projects. ANOVA results are represented in Table 7.

Results indicate that all the variations (H1a, H1b and H1c) of hypothesis H1 can be rejected. Although two of the mean quality measures of

Table 5. Principal component analysis of various constructs indicating factor loadings of survey items

Item No	Adherence and Completeness of Project Artifacts	Consistency of Project Artifacts	User-Perceived Quality	Perceived User Project Monitoring
1	.792	.892	.882	0.663
2	.869	.885	.935	0.845
3	.699		.871	0.700
4	.400		.956	0.615
5	.680			0.759
6				0.548
7				0.686

Note. Extraction method: principal component analysis; rotation method: varimax with kaiser normalization

Table 6. Reliability coefficients (Cronbach's Alpha) of constructs

Constructs (Number of items)	Cronbach's Alpha Value
Completeness and Adherence of Project Artifacts (5)	0.70
Consistency of Project Artifacts (2)	0.71
User-Perceived Quality (4)	0.93
Perceived User Project Monitoring (7)	0.73

collocated teams are better than that of virtual teams, they are not significantly different. This is contrary to expectations that the quality of projects that are produced by collocated teams and that benefit from higher social presence, media-rich face-to-face communications is no better than that produced by virtual teams that use lean media. This potentially suggests that the requirements analysis phase of software projects may be successfully off-shored in full and conducted in virtual team mode without significantly affecting the quality of projects.

Effect of User Project Monitoring

To test H2a, we compared mean values of the quality measures between the tightly monitored control group and the loosely monitored experimental group. Results presented in Table 8 indicate that the completeness and adherence of project artifacts produced by the control group were significantly superior to those produced by the experimental group, suggesting that close project monitoring by users had a positive impact on this measure of project quality. However, neither the consistency of project artifacts nor the user-perceived quality differed significantly across the two sets of teams. As expected, participants in the control group perceived that their projects were indeed closely monitored, compared to those in the experimental group.

Mean values of the perceived monitoring of the virtual team were then computed. We categorized those responses that were above the mean value as *high perceived user project monitoring* and those that were below as *low perceived project monitoring*. The performance measured on all the three dimensions were then compared across these two sets, using a one-way ANOVA test. The results as presented in Table 9 indicate that artifacts produced by developers who perceived higher levels of user project monitoring practices

Table 7. ANOVA Results (Collocated vs. Virtual teams)

Construct	Mean (Collocated team)	Mean (Virtual team)	*F*-value (significance)
Completeness and Adherence of Project Artifacts	4.92	4.56	0.551(0.467)
Consistency of Project Artifacts	6.32	6.51	1.025(0.323)
User-Perceived Quality	4.91	4.75	0.616(0.435)

Table 8. ANOVA results (tight vs. loose project monitoring)

Construct	Mean (Control group-imposed tight user project monitoring)	Mean (Experimental group—voluntary loose user project monitoring)	*F*-value (significance)
Completeness and Adherence of Project Artifacts	**5.60**	**4.50**	**4.6(0.044)**
Consistency of Project Artifacts	6.39	6.51	0.314(0.582)
User-Perceived Quality	4.61	4.75	0.076(0.785)
Perceived User Project Monitoring	**5.18**	**4.35**	**37.2 (0.000)**

Table 9. ANOVA results (perceived user project monitoring)

Construct	Mean (Perceived HIGH user project monitoring)	Mean (Perceived LOW user project monitoring)	*F*-value (significance)
Completeness and Adherence of Project Artifacts	**5.30**	**4.73**	**6.18(0.044)**
Consistency of Project Artifacts	6.41	6.49	0.107(0.768)
User-Perceived Quality	**5.01**	**4.17**	**8.91(0.003)**

Table 10. Pair-wise correlations between input and output variables

Construct	Quality of Projects		
	***Completeness and Adherence of Project Artifacts* (p)**	***Consistency of Project Artifacts***	***User-Perceived Quality***
Perceived User Project Monitoring	**0.215 (0.021)**	0.042(0.643)	**0.281(0.002)**

were better on the two dimensions of completeness and adequacy, as well as user-perceived quality, as compared to those who perceived low user monitoring.

A pair-wise correlation was carried out between perceived project monitoring and the three measures of project quality, which further confirmed these findings. (These correlations in presented in table 10.)

It is important to understand the difference between imposed project monitoring as defined in the control and experimental groups and perceived project monitoring. Though ANOVA results in Table 8 indicate that the mean values of perceived project monitoring of the control group were significantly higher compared to that of the experimental group, the mean of the experimental group was significantly higher (4.35) in the Likert scale. We also observed that in the experimental group, some of the MU teams, along with their corresponding MDI *B* teams, had voluntarily adopted closer project monitoring practices. These MDI *B* teams had been submitting their project plans and intermediate artifacts to their MU user teams, thus resulting in higher levels of perceived project monitoring. From an experimental perspective, there was a positive impact of both imposed project monitoring as well as perceived project monitoring on adherence of artifacts. At the same time, there was a positive impact of perceived project monitoring on user-perceived quality, possibly because of the close working relationship adopted by the users and developers. This could have occurred through informal behavioral control mechanisms such as clan control deployed by the MDI *B* teams and their corresponding MU user teams. However this issue warrants further analysis. Table 11 gives a summary of the results.

CONCLUSION

In this article we have described an exploratory study that examines two aspects of virtual teams in off-shored software development projects, specifically in the requirements analysis phase. First, we examine whether the quality of projects produced by virtual teams engaged in pure off-shore mode is at par with that of traditional, collocated teams. Secondly, within the ambit of virtual teams, we examine whether user monitoring of the projects has an impact on the quality of projects.

Table 11. Summary of results of teams engaged in software requirements analysis

	Collocated Teams vs. Virtual Teams in Off-Shore Mode	User Project Monitoring of Off-Shored Projects in Virtual Team Mode	
		Control/ Experimental	Perceived
Completeness and Adherence of Project Artifacts	-	TPM > LPM	HUPM > LUPM
Consistency of Project Artifacts	-	-	-
User-Perceived Quality	-	-	HUPM > LUPM

Note. TPM = tight project monitoring; LPM = loose project monitoring; HUPM = high user project monitoring; LUPM = low user project monitoring

Contributions of the Study

Our study is one of the few to apply social presence, media richness and control theories to develop and test a research model of the antecedents of quality of software requirements analysis projects conducted in off-shore virtual team environment. As client and vendor organizations are increasingly considering off-shoring parts of requirements analysis phases, our early conclusions might enable organizations to design communications and governance structures that might facilitate virtual requirements analysis. Considering the rapid leaps in technological infrastructure globally, technology will become a moot point in this facilitation. From an academic perspective, the introduction of these two theories in an offshore context lays the foundations for extended empirical research.

We find that there is no significant difference in the quality of projects produced by virtual teams that used lean media and that by collocated teams that used rich face-to-face communications. This is similar to findings reported in Burke and Chidambaram (1999) where, despite the persistently lower social presence of leaner media, distributed groups performed better than face-to-face counterparts. Possibly, a more task-focused approach and limited social interaction may have enabled teams to generate higher quality outputs. This could be a potentially important result because it implies that off-shoring, which was so far restricted to the lower level phases of system development (such as low-level design, coding, and testing) could successfully be extended to the requirements analysis phase as well. A key benefit, of course, is that software firms could save significantly on costs by locating their business and systems analysts in off-shore locations and facilitating interactions with users through virtual channels. While this may currently be challenging, our study highlights the need for future research in improving these virtual interactions between users and off-shored development teams.

The effect of user project monitoring (control/experimental) on the quality of off-shored requirements analysis projects is ambiguous. Formal behavioral and outcome control implemented through the experimental set up had a positive effect on one measure of quality. It did not have any effect on the other two measures. Piccoli and Ives (2003) pointed out that behavior control mechanisms, which are typically used in traditional teams, have a significantly negative impact on trust in virtual teams. It was reported that behavior control mechanisms increase vigilance and create instances in which individuals perceive team members failing to uphold their obligations. On the other hand, the perceived user project monitoring had significant positive effect on two dimensions of quality (one assessed and one perceived).

We also infer that, even when project management practices were not enforced, teams might have adopted these practices to improve their performance through clan control. This observation, though anecdotal based on class observations and our analysis of perceived user project monitoring, has important implications. It provides clues that, apart from forced formal controls, informal controls existed between the users and developers when they share common goals (Choudhury & Sabherwal, 2003).

Our findings have important implications for the industry as well. Companies engaged in off-shore software development have produced strong processes around their global delivery model. However, whether the same process and project monitoring discipline will lead to success of projects conducted in pure off-shore mode in virtual team setting during the early stages of system development work has not been explored. Our research indicates that teams engaged in virtual teamwork might develop their own informal control mechanisms and even bypass the forced control mechanisms necessitated by the standard operating procedures while doing their projects. The firms (viz. both the clients and software developers) engaged in off-shore work should develop a conducive climate for team members to develop these informal controls that seem to affect project quality. Apart from this, our study fills the gap in the literature in the area of analysis of quality of projects implemented by virtual teams engaged in off-shore system requirements analysis. Further research is needed to confirm our exploratory findings.

Limitations of the Study: Opportunities for Future Research

Use of Experiments

Literature in the area of virtual teams has mainly followed three research methodologies—case studies, industry surveys, and experiments. Experimental methods make possible the careful observation and precise manipulation of independent variables, allowing for greater certainty with respect to cause and effect, while holding constant other variables that would normally be associated with it in field settings (Damian et al., 2000). They also encourage the investigator to try out novel conditions and strategies in a safe and exploratory environment before implementing them in the real world (McGrath, 1984). The industry is yet to adopt off-shoring of the requirements analysis phase. This precludes the use of case study or industry survey for this research. Hence, we used experiments where we can explore this emerging phenomena.

In our experiment, MDI *A* teams played the roles of both users (in Experiment 1) and developers (in Experiment 2). The dual roles could have created conflicts that might have affected (positively or negatively) their project quality. The same is true with MDI *B* teams, who performed the roles of consultants for both MU teams as well as MDI *A* teams. MU teams also had to manage two projects: one with tight monitoring (with MDI *A* teams) and the other with loose monitoring (with MDI *B* teams). To remove the confounding effects of dual roles played by the teams, it is recommended that a true controlled factorial experiment be conducted to verify our findings.

Use of Students as Surrogates

There are criticisms for the use of students in academic experiments as surrogates. However, MBA students have been used as surrogate users in a range experiments conducted (see, e.g., Briggs, Balthazard, & Dennis, 1996; Hazari, 2005). Even in requirement negotiation phase, students with work experience were taken as users for developing a small system (Damian et al., 2000). Remus (1986) argued that graduate students could be used as surrogates for managers in experiments on business decision making.

Students often represent a typical working professional and organizational member due to the variety of backgrounds and goals (Dipboye & Flanagan, 1979). Studies in industrial organization psychology and organization behavior have found that results obtained from students were similar to those from managers (see, e.g., Locke, 1986). Despite the fact that users and developers in our experiments had 2 to 4 years of work experience, limitations of using students as surrogates are still applicable in our study. As the industry evolves, we suggest the extension of these experiments to business settings.

Complexity of Projects

Requirements analysis is intensive, and hence it is not possible to completely replicate in student experiments. However, our objective was to study the research questions on comparable, relatively well-defined small projects in which complexity of requirements analysis is not high.

Though the experiments were carefully designed, the projects were limited in scope and size compared to large-scale industrial projects. Furthermore, no formal measures of complexity were used in the study so that we could compare the projects used in the experiments with real-world industrial projects. Further research is needed to assess the impact of these findings on large-scale industrial projects with complex requirements.

Future Research Directions

One way of dealing with the lack of realism in laboratory experiments is to use multiple methods (McGrath, 1984) so that strengths of some compensate weaknesses of others. To truly test the predictive ability of the research results, the studies must also involve a multiplicity of research methodologies in order to avoid biases due to the methods used (Jarvenpaa, Knoll, & Leidner, 1988). Simulated laboratory negotiations could be complemented by field studies or validations (whose strength is realism), if the lack of realism is an issue. In our research, internal validity of results was established through conducting experiments in a controlled environment. We expect to conduct external validity through industry survey.

Finally, while we have explored one variable of project control, quality of projects can be affected by other variables such as team motivation, trust, cohesion, coordination, and communication (Chidambaram, 1996; Jarvenpaa et al., 1998; Lurey & Raisinghani, 2001). Hence, a comprehensive model that defines all factors affecting the quality of off-shored software requirements analysis projects must be developed. Further research is required to determine how informal controls develop between the virtual team members. One cause may be the amount of initial online socialization, when the teams familiarize with each other before the start of the project, for the design of such experiments in the future. Since it may not always be feasible to make experimental and control groups adhere to experimental requirements in a classroom setting, a flexible approach is needed in experimental design.

REFERENCES

Andres, P. (2002). A comparison of face-to-face and virtual software development teams. *Team Performance Management, 8*(1/2), 39-48.

Archer, N. P. (1990). A comparison of computer conferences with face-to-face meetings for small group business decisions. *Behavior & Information Technology, 9*(4), 307-317.

Battin, R., Crocker, R., Kreidler, J., & Subramanian, K. (2001). Leveraging Resources in global software development. *IEEE Software, 18*(2), 70-77.

Briggs, R. O., Balthazard, P. A., & Dennis, A. R. (1996). Graduate business students as surrogates in the evaluation of technology. *Journal of End User Computing, 8*(4), 11-17.

Burke, K., & Aytes, K. (1998). A longitudinal analysis of the effects of media richness on cohesion development and process satisfaction in computer-supported workgroups. In *Proceedings of the 31st Hawaii International Conference on Systems Sciences* (pp. 135-144).

Burke, K., & Chidambaram, L. (1996). How much bandwidth is enough? A longitudinal examination of media characteristics and media outcomes. *MIS Quarterly, 23*(4), 557-580.

Campbell, D. T., & Stanley, J. C. (1966). *Experimental and quasi-experimental designs for research.* Chicago: Rand McNally.

Carmel, E. (2006). Building your information systems from the other side of the world: How Infosys manages time zone differences. *MIS Quarterly Executive, 5*(1), 43-53.

Chidambaram, L. (1996). Relational development in computer-supported groups. *MIS Quarterly, 20*(2), 143-163.

Chidambaram, L., & Bostrom, R. (1993). Evolution of group performance over time: A repeated measures study of GDSS effects. *Journal of Organizational Computing, 3*(4), 443-469.

Choudhury, V., & Sabherwal, R. (2003). Portfolios of control in outsourced software development projects. *Information Systems Research, 14*(3), 291-314.

Crisp, C. B. (2003). Control enactment in global virtual teams. *Dissertation Abstracts International.* (UMI No.)

Damian, D. E, Eberlein, A., Shaw, M. L. G., & Gaines, B. R. (2000). Using different communication media in requirements negotiation. *IEEE Software, 17*(3), 28-36.

Damian, D. E., & Zowghi, D. (2003). An insight into interplay between culture, conflict and distance in globally distributed requirement negotiations. In *Proceedings of the 36th Hawaii International Conference on System Sciences.*

Dipboye, R. L., & Flanagan, M. F. (1979). Research setting in industrial and organization psychology: Are findings in the field more generalizable than in laboratory. *American Psychologist, 34*(2), 141-150.

Ebert, C., & De Neve, P. (2001). Surviving global software development. *IEEE Software, 18*(2), 62-69.

Edwards, K., & Sridhar, V. (2005). Analysis of software requirements engineering exercises in a global virtual team setup. *Journal of Global Information Management, 13*(2), 21-41.

Favela, J., & Pena-Mora, F. (2001). An experience in collaborative software engineering education. *IEEE Software, 18*(2), 47-53.

Foster, S., & Franz, C. (1999). User involvement in information systems development: A comparison of analyst and user perceptions of system acceptance. *Journal of Engineering Technology Management, 16*(3-4), 329-348.

Hartwick, J., & Barki, H. (1994). Explaining the role of user participation in information system use. *Management Science, 40*(4), 440-465.

Hazari, S. I. (2005). Perceptions of end-users on the requirements in personal firewall software: An exploratory study. *Journal of Organizational and End User Computing, 17*(3), 47-65.

Hoffer, J., George, J., & Valacich, J. (1999). *Modern systems analysis and design.* Reading, MA: Addison Wesley.

Jarvenpaa, S., Knoll, K., & Leidner, D. (1998). Is anybody out there? Antecedents of trust in global virtual teams. *Journal of Management Information Systems, 14*(4), 29-64.

Jarvenpaa, S., & Leidner, D. (1999). Communication and trust in global virtual teams. *Organization Science, 10*(6), 791-815.

Kircsh, L. J. (1996). The management of complex tasks in organizations: Controlling the systems development process. *Organizational Science, 7*(1), 1-21.

Kircsh, L., Sambamurthy, V., Ko, D., & Purvis, R. (2002). Controlling information systems development projects: The view from the client. *Management Science*, *48*(4), 484-498.

Lin, W., & Shao, B. (2000). A relationship between user participation and system success: A simultaneous contingency approach. *Information & Management, 37*(6), 283-295.

Lind, M. (1999). The gender impact of temporary virtual work groups. *IEEE Transactions on Professional Communication*, *42*(4), 276-285.

Locke, E. A. (1986). *Generalizing from laboratory to field setting: Research finding from industrial organization, organization behavior, and human resource management.* Lexington, MA: Lexington Books.

Lurey, J., & Raisinhgani, M. (2001). An Empirical study of best practices in virtual teams. *Information & Management, 38*(8), 523-544.

McDonough, E., Kahn, K., & Barczak, G. (2001). An investigation of the use of global, virtual, and collocated new product development teams. *The Journal of Product Innovation Management, 18*(2), 110-120.

McGrath, J. (1984). *Groups: Interaction and performanc*e. Upper Saddle River, NJ: Prentice Hall.

National Association of Software and Service Companies. (2005). *Indian IT industry.* Retrieved March 3, 2005, from http://www.nasscom.org/

Piccoli, G., & Ives, B. (2003). Trust and the unintended effects of behavior control in virtual teams. *MIS Quarterly*, *27*(3), 365-395.

Powell, A., Piccoli, G., & Ives, B. (2004). Virtual teams: A review of current literature and directions for future research. *The DATABASE for Advances in Information Systems, 35*(1), 6-36.

Remus, W. E. (1986). An empirical test of the use of graduate students as surrogates for managers in experiments on business decision making. *Journal of Business Research, 14*(1), 19-25.

Rice, R. E., & Love, G. (1987). Electronic emotion: Socio-emotional content in a computer-mediated communication network. *Communication Research*, 14(1), 85-108.

Sharda, R., Barr, S. H., & McDonnell, J. C. (1988). Decision support system effectiveness: A review and an empirical test. *Management Science, 34*(2), 139-157.

Schimdt, J. B., Montoya-Weiss, M. M., & Massey, A. P. (2001). New product development decision-making effectiveness: Comparing individuals, face-to-face teams and virtual teams. *Decisions Sciences*, *32*(4), 575-600.

Sarkar, S., & Sahay, S. (2002). Information systems development by US-Norwegian virtual teams: Implications of time and space. In *Proceedings of the 35th Annual Hawaii International Conference on System Sciences* (pp. 1-10).

Short, J., Williams, E., & Christie, B. (1976). *The social psychology of telecommunications.* London: Wiley.

Sridhar, V., Nath, D., & Malik, A. (in press). Analysis of user involvement and participation on the quality of IS planning projects: An exploratory study. *Journal of Organizational and End User Computing.*

Stevenson, W., & McGrath, E. W. (2004). Differences between on-site and off-site teams: Manager perceptions. *Team Performance Management, 10*(5/6), 127-132.

Townsend, A., DeMarie, A. M., & Hendrickson, A. R. (1998). Virtual teams: Technology and the workplace of the future. *Academy of Management Executive, 12*(3), 17-29.

Walther, J. (1995). Relational aspects of computer-mediated communication: Experimental observations over time. *Organization Science, 6*(2), 186-203.

This work was previously published in the Journal of Global Information Management, Vol. 16, Issue 4, edited by F. Tan, pp. 24-45, copyright 2008 by IGI Publishing (an imprint of IGI Global).

Chapter 8
Culture and Consumer Trust in Online Businesses

Robert Greenberg
Washington State University, USA

Bernard Wong-On-Wing
Southwestern University of Finance and Economics, China and Washington State University, USA

Gladie Lui
Lingnan University, Hong Kong

ABSTRACT

The importance of consumer trust to the success of online businesses is well documented in the literature. Given the global nature of online transactions, an important question is whether trust and trust formation differ across cultures. This study compared Hong Kong and U.S. consumer trust in online businesses. Specifically, the study examined security and privacy risks related to the purchase of products as well as services. The results show that significant differences exist between consumers from the two countries regarding the perceived level of online business risks and the formation of trust via the transference process. These findings reiterate and underscore the significance of including national culture in studies of trust in e-commerce. The results also have potential implications for online businesses as well as third party certification and assurance services.

INTRODUCTION

Concern with the determinants of consumers' willingness to engage in e-commerce has been the focus of numerous studies (e.g., George, 2004; Gefen, Karahanna, & Straub, 2003a, b; Tan & Sutherland, 2004; Jarvenpaa & Tractinsky, 2003; Pavlou, 2003; McKnight, Choudhury, & Kacmar, 2002; McKnight & Chervany, 2001; Jones, Wilikens, Morris, & Masera, 2000). For example, based on the theory of planned behavior, George (2004) finds that trustworthiness is a significant factor in the development of attitudes concerning e-commerce. Similarly, Gefen et al. (2003a, b) used the technology acceptance model (TAM) (Davis, 1989; Davis, Bagozzi, & Warshaw, 1989; Venkatesh & Davis, 2000) to examine the role of trust in consumers' intention to use e-commerce. In a study of repeat customers, Gefen et al. (2003a) find that beliefs about structural assurances such as online seals were significant antecedents of trust, thereby contributing to intended use. In a separate study, Gefen et al. (2003b) found that familiarity and trust primarily determined the purchase intentions of *potential* as opposed to *repeat* customers. They conjecture that in initial encounters with an e-vendor (with its attendant higher uncertainty), potential customers employ the uncertainty reducing constructs of trust and social norms as primary determinants.

Together, the foregoing studies highlight the importance of consumer trust to the success of online businesses. If consumers do not trust the Internet or specific vendors, they are unlikely to engage in online transactions. Individuals may not trust the Internet or online businesses because of various risks related to issues such as privacy violation and inadequate security when completing online transactions. For example, consumers may be worried about the risk that personally identifiable information they submit to a company's Web site may intentionally or inadvertently be used for unintended purposes.

Given the global nature of online transactions, an important question is whether trust issues differ across cultures (Gefen & Heart, 2006; Tan & Sutherland, 2004; Liu, Marchewka, & Ku, 2004; Jarvenpaa & Tractinsky, 2003). Different cultures exhibit differing social norms and propensities to trust (Srite & Karahanna, 2006; Doney, Cannon, & Mullen, 1998). Thus, it is expected that cross-cultural differences may be observed in the propensity to engage in e-commerce. This is relevant since cross-cultural differences may have potentially significant implications for online businesses. For example, the design of electronic storefronts may be improved to create a better sense of trust among customers by taking into account possible cultural differences in disposition to trust. Similarly, cross-cultural differences in trust issues may have potential implications for the marketing of third party certification and assurance services. Elliott and Pallais (1997) note that the first step in identifying a new assurance service is to focus on user needs. Differences between cultures may call for different marketing strategies to better meet online customer needs.

The purpose of this study is to examine the effect of culture on consumers' trust in online businesses. It is motivated by two related findings in previous research. First, Tan and Sutherland (2004) specifically highlight the lack of research that examines the effect of culture on consumers' disposition to trust. They posit that consumers' disposition to trust influences their trust in the Internet (institutional trust) as well as their trust in specific online vendors (interpersonal trust). Thus, to the extent that cultures differ in dispositional trust, differences would be expected in institutional and interpersonal trust. The present study focuses on interpersonal trust. Second, while two studies (Jarvenpaa & Tractinsky, 2003; Liu et al., 2004) that specifically examined consumers' trust in online vendors have failed to provide evidence of a cultural effect, a more recent study by Gefen and Heart (2006) found cross-cultural differences in the effects of familiarity with, and predictability of an online vendor on trust beliefs. The present study re-examines potential cross-cultural differences in consumers' interpersonal trust in online businesses.

The current research has potentially significant implications for both research and practice. From a research standpoint, it contributes to the literature in several ways. First, it provides insights into the apparent inconsistency in findings among the mentioned studies. Specifically, consistent with the propositions by Tan and Sutherland (2003), the present study finds cross-cultural differences in consumer trust in online businesses. This is in contrast to the findings of two earlier studies (Jarvenpaa & Tractinsky, 2003; Liu et al., 2004) which did not find such cross-cultural differences. Second, similar to the study by Gefen and Heart (2006) that examined the *prediction* process as a mode of trust creation, the current research provides evidence of cross-cultural differences in the effectiveness of the *transference* process as a means of building trust, as postulated by Doney et al. (1998). Third, the current study provides evidence of the generalizability of the recent findings of Gefen and Heart (2006), which suggests that online consumer trust models need to take into account the effect of culture. Whereas, that study compared online consumers in the United States (U.S.) and Israel, the present study examined U.S. and Hong Kong consumers. Moreover, unlike prior studies that examined trust in specific online businesses (e.g., Amazon.com), the present research investigates trust related to various types of online transactions.

With respect to practice, the current research provides insights into possible causes of the low rate of online business adoption specifically in Hong Kong where in spite of a high level of Internet use, the success of online businesses has been very limited (Burton, 2002; Ng, 2000). For example, according to a study conducted by the Hong Kong Productivity Council (HKPC, 2003) from January to June 2003, only about 10% of the companies surveyed offer customers the ability to order online. The present study examines the extent to which differences in interpersonal trust between Hong Kong and U.S. consumers may contribute to the observed difference in the rate of online business adoption between the two countries. The results also provide useful insights related to the marketing of third party certification and assurance services in Hong Kong.

The remainder of this article is organized as follows. The next section reviews relevant literature and provides the basis for the study. After the research hypotheses are developed, the survey method is presented followed by a description of the results. The article concludes with a discussion of the findings and their implications.

LITERATURE REVIEW

Online Trust

As noted earlier, the importance of consumer trust to the success of online businesses is well documented in the literature (see Gefen et al., 2003a for an excellent review of trust literature related to e-commerce). Several models (see e.g., Tan & Sutherland, 2004; George, 2004; Pavlou, 2003; McKnight et al., 2002; Jarvenpaa & Tractinsky, 2003) have been suggested for studying online consumer trust. The framework proposed by Tan and Sutherland (2004) recognizes a three-dimensional construct of trust. Specifically, the authors distinguish among dispositional, institutional, and interpersonal trust. Dispositional trust relates to a person's ability and willingness to trust. It is influenced by individuals' upbringing, personality, and cultural values. Institutional trust in the current context refers to trust in the Internet as a whole. It is primarily affected by individuals' beliefs regarding the adequacy of the Internet's regulatory, legal, or technical protection. Interpersonal trust relates to trust in a specific party such as a particular online vendor. It is influenced by individuals' perception of the other party's competence, predictability, benevolence, and integrity. All three dimensions of trust are inter-related and contribute to the overall assessment of trust. Tan and Sutherland (2004) posit that dispositional trust is the primary foundation to the development of trust and the associated outcomes. Their three-dimensional construct of trust is consistent with that proposed by McKnight et al. (2002). The latter similarly postulate that dispositional trust is an antecedent of both institutional trust and interpersonal trust (trusting beliefs). The present study examines consumers' level of interpersonal trust by assessing their perceived risk associated with online businesses. Next, the relationship between trust and risk, and the relevance of third party assurance are discussed.

Trust and Risk

Consumers' level of trust is associated with their perceived risk in that the former moderates the latter (Jarvenpaa & Tractinsky, 2003; Pavlou, 2003). In general, the higher the initial perceived risk, the higher is the level of trust needed to persuade the consumer to engage in an online transaction. Online businesses attempt to mitigate consumers' perceived risk by creating a sense of trust. One way that this can be achieved is by displaying seals of approval by third parties (Kimery & McCord, 2002; Cook & Luo, 2003; Palmer, Bailey, & Faraj, 2003; Zhang, 2004). Such third party seals enhance trust through a transference process. According to Doney et al. (1998), the *transference process* describes the trustor's transfer of trust from a trusted third party "proof source" to an unknown entity with which the trustor has little or no direct experience. The present study focuses on online consumers' perceptions related to such assurance seals since they are specifically intended to enhance online vendors' trustworthiness.

Cook and Luo (2003) provide a survey of available third-party assurance seals and providers. Several organizations offer third party certification or assurances to address the risk concerns that consumers may have regarding online transactions. These include logo or seal programs offered by secure electronic transaction (SET), BBBOnline, TRUSTe and the TruSecure Corporation through its International Computer Security Association (ICSA) labs. SET licenses the use of the SET logo (or SET Mark) to Web sites that utilize technology that has passed its compliance testing. BBBOnline, a wholly owned subsidiary of the Council of the Better Business Bureaus, offers a reliability seal and a privacy seal program. TRUSTe, an independent nonprofit organization, awards a TRUSTe seal to Web sites that adhere to established privacy principles, and agree to comply with ongoing TRUSTe oversight and consumer resolution procedures. TruSecure Corporation provides certification of organizations that meet established requirements necessary to achieve and maintain security. Zhang (2004) finds that some seals are more effective in increasing purchases than others. For example, seals assuring reliability increased sales of both commodity and "look-and-feel" products; assuring the information only increased commodity purchases.

WebTrust, a more comprehensive assurance program is offered by licensed certified public accountants (CPAs). The WebTrust assurance program was jointly created by the American Institute of Certified Public Accountants (AICPA) and the Canadian Institute of Chartered Accountants (CICA). The intended goal is to alleviate concerns that consumers have when transacting online. For example, individuals may be concerned about the privacy of personally identifiable data that they submit to a Web site to complete an online purchase.

In a WebTrust engagement, a licensed practitioner verifies whether an online business complies with principles and criteria regarding matters such as privacy, security, availability, and business practices. If a business meets the WebTrust principles and criteria, it is awarded an electronic seal that can be displayed on the company's Web site. Consumers can click on the seal to view the digital certificate that authenticates the seal. In addition, they can review the report of the public accountant as well as the company's business practices.

WebTrust has recently been introduced in several European and Asian countries including Hong Kong. It is regarded as the catalyst that can help in the development of online businesses. As in the U.S., it is also viewed as a new product with significant potential for CPAs if it is marketed correctly (Pawlyna, 2000). Because of the comprehensiveness of its program, the current research uses the WebTrust framework of principles to examine consumers' interpersonal trust. The present study specifically assesses individuals' risk related to the WebTrust privacy and security principles.

Culture and Trust

The interaction of culture and information systems has been the focus of several streams of research. See Leidner and Kayworth (2006) for a review. In the present context, Tan and Sutherland (2004) note the lack of research that examines the effect of culture on online consumers' disposition to trust. They suggest that cultural values may play a role in influencing individuals' dispositional trust. According to Hofstede (1997), "The core of culture … is formed by values. Values are broad tendencies to prefer certain states of affairs over others." Based on a survey of IBM employees around the world, Hofstede identified four value dimensions of culture: power distance, individualism (versus collectivism), masculinity (versus femininity), and uncertainty avoidance. Power distance refers to the extent to which less powerful members of institutions and organizations within a country expect and accept that power is distributed unequally. Individualism relates to the degree to which individuals emphasize self-interests versus the interests of the group (collectivism). Masculinity pertains to the importance attached to goals such as career and material success whereas femininity relates to the emphasis on social goals such as relationships, helping others, and the physical environment. Uncertainty avoidance refers to the degree to which members of a society feel uncomfortable with uncertainty and ambiguity. Later, a fifth dimension, Confucian dynamism, was identified. It pertains to the extent to which one has a long-term versus a short-term orientation in life.

A number of studies have specifically examined trust across different cultures. Jarvenpaa and Tractinsky (2003) posit that relative to consumers from collectivist cultures, those from individualistic cultures will tend to exhibit higher trust and a lower perception of risk in specific Internet stores. These expected relationships are based on the notion that collectivists are less trusting of outsiders and more risk-averse. In particular, Jarvenpaa and Tractinsky (2003) note "individualists are more likely to trust others until they are given some reason not to trust. By contrast, collectivists are more likely to base their trust on relationships with first-hand knowledge." Peszynski (2003) makes a similar argument in a study of New Zealand Mäori Internet shoppers.

The study by Jarvenpaa and Tractinsky (2003) focused on trust issues related specifically to the purchase of a book and the planning of a holiday trip online. The results showed no support for the hypothesized cultural effects among their samples. Jarvenpaa and Tractinsky (2003) nevertheless caution online businesses against concluding that the same Web site attributes can be used to create a sense of trust among consumers from different cultures. They further note that the lack of findings may be attributable to the relative cultural homogeneity across their samples (consumers from Australia, Israel, and Finland), the use of country as a surrogate measure of culture, or the narrow measurement of trust.

Similarly, Liu et al. (2004) compared American and Taiwanese perceptions of privacy issues related specifically to a fictitious electronic commerce bookstore. They found no evidence of cultural differences related to privacy, trust, and behavioral intention. In general, they note that the lack of difference between American and Taiwanese consumers could be attributable to aspects of the new Internet environment within which individuals' perceptions and behavior may be unaffected by cultural background. Liu et al. (2004) suggest more research to better understand the effect of cultural values in the global marketplace.

Together, the foregoing two studies failed to provide support for Tan and Sutherland's (2004) propositions regarding the effect of culture on trust. More recently, however, Gefen and Heart (2006), found differences in the effectiveness of modes of trust creation between online consumers in the U.S. and Israel. In particular, they observed that familiarity (with an online vendor, i.e., the trustee) has a stronger effect on trusting behavioral intentions in Israel than in the U.S. In contrast, predictability (ability to predict the trustee's behavior) contributed more trust in the U.S. than in Israel. An important implication of the findings of Gefen and Heart (2006) is the need to include national culture in e-commerce trust studies.

In light of the foregoing inconsistent findings, the present study re-examines the effect of culture on consumers' interpersonal trust in online businesses. However, it differs from the research by Jarvenpaa and Tractinsky (2003), Liu et al. (2004), and Gefen and Heart (2006) in several ways. First, whereas these studies examined consumers from Australia, Israel, and Finland, from the U.S. and Taiwan, and from the U.S. and Israel respectively, the present research compares U.S. and Hong Kong consumers' interpersonal trust. Second, unlike the prior studies, the current investigation does not focus on trust related to one specific vendor. Instead, the present study examines consumers' interpersonal trust by assessing their perceived risk across a variety of online transactions. Third, the prior research did not investigate online consumers' trust related to individual WebTrust principles. The current study examines interpersonal trust with respect to the privacy and security principles. The specific research hypotheses are presented in the next section.

RESEARCH HYPOTHESES

The present study compares the interpersonal trust of online consumers from two specific countries: Hong Kong and the United States. While each country has its unique characteristics, it is generally accepted that the two countries reflect cultural values of the East and the West respectively. For example, although they are unique as a result of having been under British rule for more than a century, Hong Kong Chinese share Confucian values with other Chinese societies such as Taiwan and Mainland China. The present study's hypotheses are based primarily on known differences in these deep-rooted cultural values (Hofstede, 1980, 1997, 2001) between the two countries as shown in Table 1. No hypothesis is based on masculinity, given that the U.S. and Hong Kong differ only marginally on that dimension.

Trust and Risk

According to Hofstede (2001), "Individualism stands for a society in which the ties between individuals are loose: Everyone is expected to look after him/herself and her/his immediate family only. Collectivism stands for a society in which people from birth onwards are integrated into strong, cohesive in-groups, which throughout people's lifetime continue to protect them in exchange for unquestioning loyalty." Based on this significant difference in cultural values, it is expected that relative to consumers from collectivist societies, those from individualist cultures will tend to view online businesses as more trustworthy. This is because relative to individualists, collectivists tend to be less trusting of outsiders. Moreover, people from individualist societies are accustomed to opportunistic behavior.

Table 1. Index values of Hofstede's (1980, 1997, 2001) cultural dimensions

	U.S.	Hong Kong	Range
Individualism	91	25	6-91
Long Term Orientation	29	96	0-118
Power Distance	40	68	11-104
Uncertainty Avoidance	46	29	8-112
Masculinity	62	57	5-95

Consequently, they expect and are more tolerant of such behavior than people from collectivist societies (Doney et al., 1998). In collectivist societies, the likelihood of opportunistic behavior is lower because people hold group values and seek collective interests. Collectivists are thus, less tolerant of opportunistic behavior. Based on the foregoing, it is expected that the novelty of, and lack of familiarity with, online vendors are expected to increase the sensitivity to and the perceived likelihood of opportunistic behaviors among consumers from collectivist cultures. Moreover, this effect is anticipated to be less pronounced among consumers from individualist cultures. This expectation is consistent with those postulated by Gefen and Heart (2006), Tan and Sutherland (2004), Jarvenpaa and Tractinsky (2003), and Peszynski (2003).

The long-term orientation dimension is also expected to influence consumers' trust in online businesses. The definitions of individualism and collectivism reflect their close association with the long-term/short-term orientation values. Indeed, long-term orientation has been found to be strongly and negatively associated with affiliation with *outsiders* (Hofstede, 2001). The relationship between long-term/short-term orientation and individualism/collectivism, and their significance to trust can be illustrated using *guanxi*, which is an important concept in Asian business. Guanxi refers to personal connections and acquaintances that are essential in business. The significance of developing relationships reflects the collectivism dimension whereas the importance of maintaining guanxi for a lifetime reflects the long-term orientation dimension (Hofstede, 2001). Thus, in the current context, it can be expected that relative to short-term oriented consumers, long-term oriented consumers are less likely to exhibit interpersonal trust in online businesses. This is because they perceive that developing and maintaining a trusting relationship with a new and unfamiliar online vendor are a long-term endeavor. That view is not likely to be shared by short-term oriented consumers.

Together, the foregoing suggests that people from individualist (collectivist) and short-term oriented (long-term oriented) cultures will exhibit higher (lower) interpersonal trust. Consequently, compared to their Hong Kong counterparts, U.S. consumers can be expected to be less concerned about the WebTrust principles and to perceive a lower risk of violation of the WebTrust principles. Given that Hong Kong is more collectivist and long-term oriented than the U.S., the first two hypotheses are:

H1:*Compared to U.S. consumers, Hong Kong consumers have higher levels of concern about the WebTrust principles.*

H2:*Compared to U.S. consumers, Hong Kong consumers perceive a higher likelihood of violation of the WebTrust principles.*

Transference Process

As noted earlier, trust can be developed through a transference process (Doney et al., 1998). In that process, a trustor (consumer) transfers trust from a known entity (third party assurance provider) to an unknown one (online vendor). Research findings suggest that the transference process is effective in the U.S. For example, studies by Hunton, Benford, Arnold, and Sutton (2000) and Kovar, Burke, and Kovar (2000) find that, overall, U.S. consumers view third party seals to be valuable because it alleviates concerns that they may have about transacting online. Zhang (2004) finds that seals effectively increase online consumers' willingness to buy and are especially effective with inexperienced online consumers.

Whether the transference process is effective in other cultures is unknown. Doney et al. (1998) postulate that trust is more likely to be formed via the transference process, among low power distance than among high power distance cultures.

Presumably, compared to people in high power distance societies, people in low power distance societies feel less threatened by others because equality of rights is valued. Consequently, relative to people in high power distance societies, people in low power distance societies also tend to be more trusting of others. Because people in high power distance societies are less trusting of others (including assurance providers), the transference process is thus less likely to be effective in among consumers from high power distance cultures than among those from low power distance cultures.

Similarly, Doney et al. (1998) postulate that relative to people in low uncertainty avoidance cultures, those in high uncertainty avoidance cultures are more likely to form trust via the transference process. This is because low uncertainty avoidance reflects "high tolerance for behavior and opinions that are different" from one's own and possibly a lower propensity to "judge others to be similar." As a result, identifying a source from which to transfer trust may be difficult.

Together, the foregoing suggests that forming trust via the transference process is less (more) likely to be effective in a high (low) power distance and low (high) uncertainty avoidance culture. Given that power distance is higher and uncertainty avoidance is lower in Hong Kong than in the U.S., the third hypothesis is:

H3: *Compared to U.S. consumers, Hong Kong consumers will perceive the seal of assurance to be less valuable in reducing concerns about the WebTrust principles.*

A key component of the transference process is the identity and trustworthiness of the proof source (assurance seal provider). In the current context, some may prefer CPAs because of their reputation for objectivity and integrity. Others may see an advantage in assurance providers that are perceived to have superior knowledge of specific technical areas. Yet others may prefer a government agency to attend to issues such as privacy, security, and availability. According to Hofstede (2001), people from high (low) collectivism cultures tend to exhibit emotional dependence on (independence from) institutions and organizations. Given their higher collectivism, Hong Kong consumers are likely to view a government agency as the most trusted assurance provider because it is the best-known institution/organization. In contrast, the more individualist U.S. consumers are expected to be less likely to select a government agency as an assurance provider. Given that Hong Kong is more collectivist than the U.S., the fourth hypothesis is:

H4: *Compared to U.S. consumers, Hong Kong consumers are more likely to view a government agency as the most trusted assurance provider for the WebTrust principles.*

METHOD

Subjects

Following other studies of Internet users (e.g., Srite & Karhanna, 2006; Pavlou & Fygensen, 2006; Venkatesh & Ramesh, 2006; Galletta, Henry, McCoy, & Polak, 2006), participants in the present research were undergraduate students from both cultures. According to Kovar et al. (2000), student-subjects provide a reasonable surrogate for online consumers who tend to be younger and more educated than traditional consumers.

In the present study, the Hong Kong participants were 214 undergraduate students enrolled in a managerial accounting principles course at a university in Hong Kong. The U.S. subjects were 217 undergraduate students enrolled in an introductory management information systems course in the U.S. Using students as subjects allowed the samples to be closely matched. The two groups were comparable in that they consisted of students enrolled in a required (accounting or information system) course, and intending to major in different fields in business. Moreover, the two samples did not differ significantly in age (p>0.10).

Table 2 shows Hong Kong and U.S. subjects' experience with the seven online transactions surveyed. The results confirm the continued limited experience of Hong Kong consumers with online transactions relative to U.S. consumers. For example, 90% of the Hong Kong consumers surveyed had never purchased a plane ticket online compared to 35% of the U.S. consumers. In addition, only 27 (12.6%) of the Hong Kong respondents, compared to 113 (52%) of the U.S. subjects, indicated that they had engaged in online transactions other than the seven listed. These included buying gifts, clothing, and concert or movie tickets. Overall, 107 (50%) of the Hong Kong subjects, compared to only 9 U.S. respondents (4.1%), had never completed online transactions of any type.

Procedures

The survey was administered to the subjects during their classes. The time required to complete the questionnaire ranged from 15 to 20 minutes. Subjects received extra credit for their participation.

Questionnaire

As noted earlier, prior studies by Jarvenpaa and Tractinsky (1999) and Liu et al. (2004) did not find any effect of culture on interpersonal trust. This may be due the specificity of the online vendors (bookstores and travel agencies) examined. The current research employed a different approach to examine the potential effect of culture on interpersonal trust. Rather than focusing on a particular vendor, the present study surveyed consumers across a variety of online transactions representing different types of businesses. Although such an approach does not allow the examination of

Table 2. Participants' experience with online transactions (percentages are in parentheses)

	HK/ US	Never	Rarely	Sometimes	Frequently	TOTAL*
Buying plane tickets	H.K.	192 (90.5%)	13 (6.2%)	6 (2.8%)	1 (0.5%)	212 (100%)
	U.S.	76 (35%)	44 (20.3%)	50 (23%)	47 (21.7%)	217 (100%)
Trading stocks	H.K.	202 (95.2%)	5 (2.4%)	5 (2.4%)	0 (0.0%)	212 (100%)
	U.S.	179 (82.5%)	16 (7.4%)	13 (6.0%)	9 (4.1%)	217 (100%)
Banking and paying bills	H.K.	136 (64.2%)	43 (20.3%)	27 (12.7%)	6 (2.8%)	212 (100%)
	U.S.	86 (39.8%)	47 (21.8%)	37 (17.1%)	46 (21.3%)	216 (100%)
Participating in auctions	H.K.	179 (84.5%)	20 (9.4%)	11 (5.2%)	2 (0.9%)	212 (100%)
	U.S.	116 (53.5%)	51 (23.5%)	31 (14.3%)	19 (8.7%)	217 (100%)
Buying books and CDs	H.K.	155 (73.1%)	41 (19.3%)	12 (5.7%)	4 (1.9%)	212 (100%)
	U.S.	62 (28.7%)	57 (26.4%)	65 (30.1%)	32 (14.8%)	216 (100%)
Filing taxes	H.K.	202 (95.3%)	8 (3.8%)	2 (0.9%)	0 (0.0%)	212 (100%)
	U.S.	161 (74.2%)	21 (9.7%)	19 (8.8%)	16 (7.4%)	217 (100%)
Buying computers	H.K.	194 (91.5%)	16 (7.5%)	1 (0.5%)	1 (0.5%)	212 (100%)
	U.S.	131 (60.4%)	41 (18.9%)	35 (16.1%)	10 (4.6%)	217 (100%)

**Differences in TOTAL are due to incomplete responses.*

detailed attributes specific to one individual vendor, it enables the study of consumer interpersonal trust across a wider spectrum of online business types (e.g., service versus product vendors).

Moreover, as previously mentioned, third party assurance seals such as those provided by WebTrust are specifically intended to enhance consumers' trust in individual online vendors. Thus, one way to assess consumers' interpersonal trust in online businesses is to examine their perceptions related to (1) the level of concern about the principles addressed by the assurance seals, (2) the likelihood of violation of the principles, (3) the value of the assurance seals, and (4) the trust in the provider of the assurance seals. The instrument described below was designed to assess these consumer perceptions based on the intended purpose of third party seals, which is to enhance trust in online vendors. It was developed based on the AICPA's description of the WebTrust principles.

The survey assessed participants' perceptions regarding the WebTrust privacy and security principles on separate pages. The order in which the principles appeared was alternated to preclude order effects in the perception assessment. Demographic data including subjects' experience with online transactions were collected on the last page.

The Appendix shows a page of the survey eliciting the subjects' responses with respect to privacy. A description of the WebTrust principle is provided at the top of the page to ensure that subjects understood the nature of the principle. A seven-point Likert scale elicited the extent of the subject's concern about the principle for each of seven types of online transactions. The scale was anchored from "not at all concerned" (1), to "extremely concerned" (7). This "perceived concern" measure is used to test H1.

A seven-point Likert scale was also used to assess the subject's perception of the likelihood that the principle may be violated. The scale was anchored from "extremely unlikely" (1), to "extremely likely" (7). This "likelihood of violation" measure is used to test H2.

In the next part, subjects were provided examples of violations of the principle and a description of the assurance provided by the WebTrust seal for the principle. Description of the assurances included the disclosure of an entity's practices, compliance with the practices, and the maintenance of effective controls. Subjects were then asked to indicate the degree to which an assurance seal would reduce their concern about the principle using a seven-point Likert scale anchored at "not at all" (1), and "to a great extent" (7). This "perceived value" measure is used to test H3.

Finally, subjects were asked to select the independent assurance entity that they would most trust to provide assurance about each principle from the following: the Better Business Bureau, experts in information technology, CPAs, a government-appointed agency, a nonprofit organization, and some other party. This measure is used to test H4.

DATA ANALYSIS AND RESULTS

Concern about WebTrust Principles (H1)

Recall that the subjects' concern scores for the seven types of transactions were measured on separate seven-point scales (see Appendix). Prior to testing H1, the seven concern scores were analyzed using an exploratory factor analysis to determine if some or all of the transactions were related to a common construct. The analysis was undertaken to enable common transactions to be combined, thereby simplifying the data analysis. For each WebTrust principle, subjects' seven concern scores were subjected to a principal-component factor analysis with varimax rotation. In each case, the results yielded two factors with eigenvalues greater than one. The results (see Table 3) show that

Table 3. Factor analyses on concern about privacy and security principles

	Privacy		Security	
	Factor 1 (Services)	Factor 2 (Products)	Factor 1 (Services)	Factor 2 (Products)
Buying plane tickets	.652	.519	.703	.486
Trading stocks	.812	.322	.843	.284
Banking and paying bills	.899	.202	.883	.248
Participating in auctions	.312	.611	.404	.717
Buying books and CDs	.107	.916	.156	.920
Filing taxes	.892	.186	.871	.210
Buying computers	.315	.839	.309	.841
Eigen value	4.15	1.11	4.45	1.06
Variance explained	41.37%	33.78%	43.22%	35.57%
Cronbach alpha	0.89	0.77	0.91	0.85

four transactions (buying plane tickets, trading stocks, banking & paying bills, and filing taxes) load on one factor, which accounts for 41.37 % and 43.22 % of the variance for the privacy and security principles respectively. This first factor is labeled as the "purchase of services" type of transaction. The remaining three transactions (participating in auctions, buying books & CDs, and buying computers) load on a second factor, which accounts for 33.78% and 35.57 % of the variance for the privacy and security principles respectively. This second factor is labeled as the "purchase of products" type of transaction. The Cronbach alphas (see Table 3) for each principle suggest reasonable reliability for the measures.

To test H1, the scores to the four transactions (buying plane tickets, trading stocks, banking & paying bills, and filing taxes) that loaded on the "purchase of services" type of transaction were averaged. Similarly, the scores of the three transactions (participating in auctions, buying books & CDs, and buying computers) that loaded on the "purchase of products" type of transaction were averaged. These two average scores provided the responses for transaction type (service vs. product) which was analyzed as a within-subjects factor.

To test H1, a 2(culture) x 2 (transaction type) x 2 (WebTrust principle) analysis of variance (ANOVA) was performed on the concern scores with the latter two factors as within-subject variables. The results in Panel A of Table 4 show a main effect of culture ($F(1, 429) = 20.64, p < 0.001$). Panel B of Table 4 shows the Hong Kong and U.S. participants' mean level of concern about the privacy and security principles across the two main types of transactions examined. Hong Kong respondents consistently viewed each WebTrust principle as more of a concern than U.S. respondents across both types of transactions ($p < 0.05$). Taken together, these results support H1.

Panel A of Table 4 also shows that the culture main effect is qualified by an interaction effect of culture and principle ($F(1, 429) = 5.54, p=0.019$). Whereas U.S. consumers are apparently less concerned about security (4.39) than they are about privacy (4.56), Hong Kong consumers appear to

Table 4.

Variable	df	SS	MS	F	p
Between Subjects					
Culture (C)	1	140.83	140.83	20.64	0.000
Error	429	2927.19	6.82		
Within Subjects					
Principle (P)	1	1.68	1.68	1.37	0.243
C x P	1	6.82	6.82	5.54	0.019
Error	429	528.25	1.23		
Transaction (T)	1	415.52	415.52	261.38	0.000
C x T	1	3.86	3.86	2.43	0.120
Error	429	681.98	1.59		
P x T	1	0.35	0.35	0.81	0.369
C x P x T	1	0.03	0.03	0.08	0.780
Error	429	186.42	0.43		

Panel A: Culture x principle x transaction ANOVA on concern about privacy and security

	Privacy		**Security**		Aggregate
	H.K.	U.S.	H.K.	U.S.	
Services	5.48 (1.33) n=214	4.93 (1.76) n=217	5.56 (1.24) n=214	4.78 (1.84) n=217	5.21 (1.59) n=431
Products	4.43 (1.41) n=214	4.08 (1.90) n=217	4.47 (1.24) n=214	3.86 (1.77) n=217	4.25 (1.68) n=431
Aggregate	5.03 (1.19) n=214	4.56 (1.65) n=216	5.10 (1.04) n=214	4.39 (1.68) n=216	

Panel B. Concern about privacy and security across types of online transactions (standard deviations are in parentheses)*

* *Subjects were asked to indicate on a seven-point Likert scale the extent to which they were concerned about each principle for each one of the seven online transactions. The scale was labeled from 1 "not at all concerned" to 7 "extremely concerned." Differences in n are due to incomplete responses.*

be similarly concerned about the two principles (5.10 and 5.03 respectively). The results also show a main effect of transaction type ($F(1, 429) = 261.38$, $p < 0.001$). Online consumers from both Hong Kong and the U.S. are significantly more concerned about the purchase of services (5.21) than they are about the purchase of products (4.25).

Table 5.

Variable	df	SS	MS	F	p
Between Subjects					
Culture (C)	1	0.45	0.45	0.13	0.718
Error	427	1357.72	3.18		
Within Subjects					
Principle (P)	1	41.91	41.91	31.72	0.000
C x P	1	29.67	29.67	22.45	0.000
Error	427	564.25	1.32		

*Panel A. Culture x principle ANOVA on perceived likelihood of violation of privacy and security principles**

	H.K.	U.S.	Aggregate
Privacy	4.50 (1.52) n=214	4.83 (1.51) n=217	4.67 (1.52) n=431
Security	4.43 (1.44) n=214	4.02 (1.52) n=215	4.23 (1.50) n=429
Aggregate	4.47 (1.22) n=214	4.33 (1.30) n=215	

Panel B. Perceived likelihood of violation of privacy and security principles (standard deviations are in parentheses)

* *Subjects were asked to indicate on a seven-point Likert scale the likelihood of violation of each principle. The scale was labeled from 1 "extremely unlikely" to 7 "extremely likely." Differences in n are due to incomplete responses.*

Likelihood of Violation of WebTrust Principles (H2)

To test H2, a 2(culture) x 2 (principle) ANOVA was performed on the violation scores with the latter factor as a within-subject variable. The results in Table 5 Panel A show a significant interaction effect of culture and principle ($F(1, 427) = 22.45$, $p<0.001$). Panel B shows that Hong Kong consumers (4.50) perceived a significantly lower likelihood of violation of the Privacy principle than U.S. consumers (4.83). However, Hong Kong consumers (4.43) perceived the likelihood of violation of the security principle to be higher than U.S. consumers (4.02) did. These results partially support H2.

Panel A of Table 5 also shows a significant main effect of principle ($F(1, 427) = 31.72$, $p<0.001$). Consumers from both Hong Kong and the U.S. perceived a higher likelihood of violation of the privacy principle (4.67) than of the security principle (4.23).

Value of Seal of Assurance (H3)

To test H3, a 2 (culture) x 2 (principle) ANOVA was performed on the value scores with the latter factor as a within-subject variable. The results in

Table 6 Panel A show a significant main effect of culture ($F(1, 421) = 13.80$, $p<0.001$). Panel B shows that Hong Kong consumers perceived the privacy (4.47) and the security (4.33) assurance seals to be less valuable than U.S. consumers (4.87 and 4.78 respectively) did in reducing concerns about these principles. These results are consistent with H3.

Relative Trustworthiness of Assurance Providers (H4)

To test H4, the percentage of consumers selecting a government-appointed agency as the most trusted assurance provider was computed for each country for each principle. As shown in Table 7, for both the privacy and the security principles, the percentage is higher among Hong Kong consumers (55.9% and 51.2% respectively) than among U.S. consumers (29.0% and 31.8% respectively). Using a z-test for comparing proportions in two independent populations, the difference is significant for both the privacy ($z=5.44$, $p<0.001$) and the security ($z=4.06$, $p<0.001$) principles. This pattern of results supports H4.

Table 6.

Variable	df	SS	MS	F	p
Between Subjects					
Culture (C)	1	39.65	39.65	13.80	0.000
Error	421	1209.46	2.87		
Within Subjects					
Principle (P)	1	2.59	2.59	3.25	0.072
C x P	1	0.13	0.13	0.16	0.688
Error	421	336.76	0.80		

*Panel A. Culture x principle ANOVA on perceived value of privacy and security seals**

	H.K.	U.S.	Aggregate
Privacy	4.47 (1.21) n=214	4.87 (1.49) n=212	4.67 (1.37) n=426
Security	4.33 (1.30) n=214	4.78 (1.41) n=213	4.55 (1.38) n=427
Aggregate	4.40 (1.08) n=214	4.83 (1.31) n=209	

Panel B. Perceived value of privacy and security seals (standard deviations are in parentheses)

* *Subjects were asked to indicate on a seven-point Likert scale the degree to which an assurance seal would reduce their concern about each principle. The scale was labeled from 1 "not at all" to 7 "to a great extent." Differences in n are due to incomplete responses.*

DISCUSSION

The purpose of this study was to examine the effect of culture on online consumers' interpersonal trust based on Tan and Sutherland's (2004) three-dimensional construct of trust. The present research compared specifically Hong Kong and U.S. consumers' perceptions regarding privacy and security. Cross-cultural differences were predicted based primarily on known differences in Hofstede's (1980, 1997, 2001) value dimensions. The results in general suggest a cross-cultural difference in interpersonal trust between consumers from the two countries. First, compared to U.S. consumers, Hong Kong consumers expressed a higher level of concern regarding both privacy and security. Moreover, the level of concern was higher for Hong Kong respondents for both purchases of services and purchases of products. Second, compared to U.S. consumers, Hong Kong consumers perceived a higher risk of violation of the security principle. In contrast, U.S. consumers perceived a higher risk of violation of the privacy principle than did Hong Kong consumers. Third, relative to U.S. consumers, Hong Kong consumers did not perceive as much value in the assurance seals for privacy and security. Fourth, compared to U.S. consumers, Hong Kong consumers indicated a stronger preference for government-appointed agencies for providing assurance seals. Taken together, the observed pattern of evidence suggests that Hong Kong consumers exhibit lower interpersonal trust than U.S. consumers.

*Table 7. Preference for government-appointed agency as most trusted assurance provider**

	H.K.	U.S.
Privacy	118 55.9%	63 29%
Security	109 51.2%	69 31.8%

* *Subjects were asked to indicate who they trusted the most to be able to independently provide the seal of assurance for each principle.*

The results of the present study have potentially significant implications for both research and practice. From a research standpoint, it contributes to the literature about cross-cultural consumer trust issues regarding online transactions in several ways. First, the results are generally consistent with Tan and Sutherland's (2004) propositions regarding the importance and the effect of culture on their three-dimensional construct of trust. In addition, the findings are consistent with the predictions based on known differences in Hofstede's (1980, 1997, 2001) value dimensions between Hong Kong and the U.S. This is significant since contrary to the findings of research by Jarvenpaa and Tractinsky (1999) and Liu et al. (2004), the present study found cross-cultural differences in interpersonal trust. One possible reason for the divergent findings may be the difference in countries examined between the present research (i.e., Hong Kong and U.S.) and those studied by Jarvenpaa and Tractinsky (2003) (i.e., Australia, Israel, and Finland), and by Liu et al. (2004) (i.e., U.S. and Taiwan). Another possible reason may be the difference in the specificity of the online vendor between the current and the prior research. Whereas the research by Jarvenpaa and Tractinsky (2003) and Liu et al. (2004) focused on interpersonal trust in specific vendors (bookstores and travel agencies), the present study examined trust across different transactions and different principles.

Second, the current results provide support for Doney et al.'s (1998) postulate regarding differences in the effectiveness of the transference process across cultures. Similar to the study by Gefen and Heart (2006) that examined the *prediction* process as a mode of trust creation, the current research provides evidence of cross-cultural differences in the effectiveness of the *transference* process as a means of building trust.

Third, the current study provides evidence of the generalizability of the recent findings of Gefen and Heart (2006), which suggests that online consumer trust models need to take into account the effect of culture. Whereas that study compared online consumers in the United States and Israel, the present study examined U.S. and Hong Kong consumers. Moreover, unlike prior studies that examined trust in specific online businesses (e.g., Amazon.com), the present research investigates trust related to various types of online transactions. The present study together with that by Gefen and Heart (2006) highlight the importance and the need to include national culture as a central issue in studying online trust.

With respect to practice, the findings indicate a lower frequency of online transactions among Hong Kong subjects than among their U.S. counterparts. More importantly, the results provide evidence regarding possible causes of the low rate of online business adoption specifically in Hong Kong. In particular, consumers in Hong Kong appear less trusting than U.S. consumers when it comes to online transactions regarding privacy and security.

Moreover, compared to U.S. consumers, Hong Kong consumers tend to trust their government more than any other third party for the purpose of providing privacy and security assurance seals. This is noteworthy because it suggests that in a collectivist culture such as Hong Kong, third parties such as SET, BBBOnline, TRUSTe, SET, and WebTrust may not be as trusted as the government. Consequently, the effectiveness of the transference process (Doney et al., 1998) in facilitating trust in e-commerce transactions depends on the specific "proof source." The current results tentatively suggest that the partnering between third party assurance services and the government in Hong Kong is a way to provide the necessary trust via the transference process.

The findings of the present study should be interpreted in light of its limitations. First, only one dimension (interpersonal) of trust was examined. Second, trust was not directly assessed. Instead, it was inferred from subjects' responses related to perceptions about the privacy and security principles. Third, subjects were undergraduate students who represent only one segment of the online consumer market. Fourth, the nature of cross-cultural research is such that it is usually impossible to control for all possible extraneous factors and the present study is subject to this limitation.

The results and limitations of the present study suggest several avenues for future research directed at understanding cultural differences in trust. First, research can examine the effect of culture on other dimensions (dispositional and institutional) of trust. Second, future studies can investigate whether these differences are attributable purely to cultural differences or differences in understanding of the nature of Web-based transactions and processes. Hsu (2003) addresses Chinese culture-related issues that have design and content implications for online businesses including trust. Similarly, Cyr et al. (2005) examined cross-cultural differences in preferences of local and foreign Web sites subsequent perceptions of trust, satisfaction, and e-loyalty. Third, the present study was limited to the examination of only two principles and seven types of transactions. Moreover, subjects (young and college-educated consumers) represented only one segment of the potential market. Future research can examine other principles and other types of online transactions within other market segments. Fourth, future studies can identify the specific reasons why non-government organizations are not perceived to be the most trusted assurance providers in Hong Kong. Such findings would guide future efforts at the marketing of third party certification and assurance. Fifth, similar studies can also be conducted in other Asian countries to determine the generalizability of the current findings. Results of the foregoing suggested research can provide insights into cross-cultural trust issues, which in turn may enhance the level of online business adoption and the likelihood of success of third party assurance services globally.

REFERENCES

Burton, S. (2002). Where are all the shoppers? E-tailing lessons for the Asia Pacific. *Quarterly Journal of Electronic Commerce, 3*(4), 331-342.

Cook, D., & Luo, W. (2003). The role of third-party seals in building trust online. *E-Service Journal, 2*(3), 71-84.

Davis, F. D. (1989). Perceived usefulness, perceived ease of use, and user acceptance of information technology. *MIS Quarterly, 13*(3), 319-339.

Bagozzi, R. P., & Warshaw, P. R. (1989). User acceptance of computer technology: a comparison of two theoretical models. *Management Science, 38*(8), 982-1002.

Doney, P. M., Cannon, J. P., & Mullen, M. R. (1998). Understanding the influence of national culture on the development of trust. *Academy of Management Review, 23*(3), 601-620.

Elliott, R. K., & Pallais, D. M. (1997). First: Know your market. *Journal of Accountancy, July*, 56-63.

Fygensen, M. (2006). Understanding and predicting electronic commerce adoption: An extension of the theory of planned behavior. *MIS Quarterly, 30*(1), 115-143.

Galletta, D. F., Henry, R. M., McCoy, S., & Polak, P. (2006). When the wait isn't so bad: The interacting effects of website delay, familiarity, and breadth. *Information Systems Research*, 20-37.

Gefen, D., & Heart, T. (2006). On the need to include national culture as a central issue in e-commerce trust beliefs. *Journal of Global Information Management, 14*(4), 1-30.

Gefen, D., Karahanna, E., & Straub, D. W. (2003a). Trust and TAM in online shopping: An integrated model. *MIS Quarterly, 27*(1), 51-90.

Gefen, D., Karahanna, E., & Straub, D. W. (2003b). Inexperience and experience with online stores: The importance of TAM and trust. *IEEE Transactions on Engineering Management, 50*(3), 307-321.

George, J. F. (2004). The theory of planned behavior and internet purchasing. *Internet Research, 14*(3), 198-212.

HKPC. (2003). *E-business adoption in Hong Kong.* Hong Kong Productivity Council.

Hofstede, G. H. (1980). *Culture's consequences: International differences in work-related values.* Beverly Hills, CA: Sage Publications.

Hofstede, G. H. (1997). *Culture's consequences: Software of the mind.* New York: McGraw-Hill.

Hofstede, G. H. (2001). *Culture's consequences: Comparing values, behaviors, institutions and organizations across nations.* Thousand Oaks, CA: Sage Publications.

Hsu, J. (2003). Chinese cultures and e-commerce. In T. Thanasankit (Ed.), *E-commerce and cultural values* (pp. 268-289). Hershey, PA: Idea Group Publishing.

Hunton, J. E., Benford, T., Arnold, V., & Sutton, S. (2000). The impact of electronic commerce assurance on financial analysts' earnings forecasts and stock price estimates. *Auditing: A Journal of Practice & Theory,* 19 (Supplement), 5-22.

Jarvenpaa, S. L., & Tractinsky, N. (2003). Consumer trust in an Internet store: A cross-cultural validation. In C. Steinfeld (Ed.), *New directions in research on e-commerce* (pp.33-63). West Lafayette, IN: Purdue University Press.

Jones, S., Wilikens, M., Morris, P., & Masera, M. (2000). Trust requirements in e-business. *Communications of the ACM, 43*(12), 80-87.

Kimery, K., & McCord, M. (2002). Third-party assurances: Mapping the road to trust in e-tailing. *Journal of Information Technology Theory and Application, 4*(2), 63-82.

Kovar, S. E., Burke, K. G., & Kovar, B. R. (2000). Consumer responses to the CPA WebTrust assurance. *Journal of Information Systems, 14*(1), 17-35.

Leidner, D. E., & Kayworth, T. (2006). A review of culture in information systems research: Toward a theory of information technology culture conflict. *MIS Quarterly, 30*(2), 357-399.

Liu, C., Marchewka, J. T., & Ku, C. (2004). American and Taiwanese perceptions concerning privacy, trust and behavioral intentions in electronic commerce. *Journal of Global Information Management, 12*(1), 18-40.

McKnight, D., & Chervany, N. (2001). What trust means in e-commerce customer relationships: An interdisciplinary conceptual typology. *International Journal of Electronic Commerce, 6*(2), 35-39.

McKnight, D., Choudhury, V., & Kacmar, C. (2002). Developing and validating trust measures for e-commerce: An integrative typology. *Information Systems Research, 13*(3), 334-359.

Ng, K. (2000). The new e-commerce horizon. *The Hong Kong Accountant, May*, 24-28.

Palmer, J. W., Bailey, J. P., & Faraj, S. (2003). Intermediaries and trust on the Internet: The use and prominence of trusted third parties and privacy statements. In C. Steinfeld (Ed.), *New directions in research on e-commerce* (pp. 128-146). West Lafayette, IN: Purdue University Press.

Pavlou, P. A. (2003). Consumer acceptance of electronic commerce: Integrating trust and risk with the technology acceptance model. *International Journal of Electronic Commerce, 7*(3), 101-134.

Pawlyna, A. (2000). The seal of approval. *The Hong Kong Accountant, May*, 20-23.

Peszynski, K. J. (2003). Trust in B2C e-commerce: the New Zealand Mäori Internet shopper. In T. Thanasankit (Ed.), *E-commerce and cultural values* (pp. 169-198). Hershey, PA: Idea Group Publishing.

Srite, M., & Karahanna, E. (2006). The role of espoused national cultural values in technology acceptance. *MIS Quarterly, 30*(3), 679-704.

Tan, F. B., & Sutherland, P. (2004). Online consumer trust: A multi-dimensional model. *Journal of Electronic Commerce in Organizations, 2*(3), 40-58.

Venkatesh, V., & Davis, F. D. (2000). A theoretical extension of the technology acceptance model: four longitudinal field studies. *Management Science, 46*(2), 186-204.

Venkatesh, V., & Ramesh, V. (2006). Web and wireless site usability: Understanding differences and modeling use. *MIS Quarterly, 30*(1), 181-2006.

Zhang, H. (2004). Trust-promoting seals in electronic markets: Impact on online shopping decisions. *Journal of Information Technology Theory and Application, 6*(4), 29-40.

APPENDIX

PRIVACY

People who are concerned about privacy are worried about how a company will use personally identifiable information that they submit to the company's Web site. Such information may include their name, address, telephone number, e-mail address, and credit card number. Without their consent, the personal data that they input on a Web site may be sold to other companies for a variety of uses. Below, circle a number to indicate how concerned you would be about the **PRIVACY** of personally identifiable data that you submit for each of the following types online transactions:

Buying plane tickets

not at all concerned 1--- 2--- 3--- 4--- 5--- 6--- 7 extremely concerned

Trading stocks

not at all concerned 1--- 2--- 3--- 4--- 5--- 6--- 7 extremely concerned

Banking and Paying bills

not at all concerned 1--- 2--- 3--- 4--- 5--- 6--- 7 extremely concerned

Participating in auctions

not at all concerned 1--- 2--- 3--- 4--- 5--- 6--- 7 extremely concerned

Buying books and CDs

not at all concerned 1--- 2--- 3--- 4--- 5--- 6--- 7 extremely concerned

Filing your taxes

not at all concerned 1--- 2--- 3--- 4--- 5--- 6--- 7 extremely concerned

Buying a computer

not at all concerned 1--- 2--- 3--- 4--- 5--- 6--- 7 extremely concerned

In your opinion, what is the likelihood that in e-commerce, without your consent, information about you maybe disclosed to a third party or used for purposes other than that for which it was originally intended?

Extremely unlikely 1 ------ 2 ------ 3 ------ 4 ------ 5 ------ 6 ------ 7 Extremely likely

Concern over privacy has grown following major privacy policy changes made on some popular Web sites. For example, last September, online retailer **Amazon.com** revised its privacy policy to allow the disclosure of personal customer information to third parties. More recently, online market place **eBay** received complaints after it reversed customers' previously selected preference to not get called by telemarketers.

One possible solution to reduce privacy concerns is to have an **independent party** evaluate and test whether a company (1) discloses its online privacy practices, (2) complies with such privacy practices, and (3) maintains effective controls to provide reasonable assurance that personally identifiable information obtained in e-commerce is protected in conformity with its disclosed privacy practices. To indicate that a company has met the foregoing conditions, a **seal of assurance** would be displayed on the company's Web site. To what extent would such a seal of assurance reduce any concern that you may have about privacy?

not at all 1 ------ 2 ------ 3 ------ 4 ------ 5 ------ 6 ------ 7 to a large extent

In your opinion, which **one** of the following would you **trust the most** to be able to **independently** provide the above seal of assurance? **PLEASE SELECT ONE ONLY.**

___ The Better Business Bureau

___ Certified Public Accountants

___ A Nonprofit Organization

___ Experts in Information Technology

___ A Government-appointed Agency

___ Some other party
(Specify: ____________________)

This work was previously published in the Journal of Global Information Management, Vol. 16, Issue 3, edited by F. Tan, pp. 26-44, copyright 2008 by IGI Publishing (an imprint of IGI Global).

Chapter 9
The Impact of Leadership Style on Knowledge Sharing Intentions in China

Qian Huang
University of Science and Technology of China – City University of Hong Kong Joint Advanced Research Centre, China

Robert M. Davison
City University of Hong Kong, Hong Kong

Hefu Liu
University of Science and Technology of China – City University of Hong Kong Joint Advanced Research Centre, China

Jibao Gu
University of Science and Technology of China, China

ABSTRACT

Knowledge management (KM) is a dominant theme in the behavior of contemporary organizations. While KM has been extensively studied in developed economies, it is much less well understood in developing economies, notably those that are characterized by different social and cultural traditions to the mainstream of Western societies. This is notably the case in China. This chapter develops and tests a theoretical model that explains the impact of leadership style and interpersonal trust on the intention of information and knowledge workers in China to share their knowledge with their peers. All the hypotheses are supported, showing that both initiating structure and consideration have a significant effect on employees' intention to share knowledge through trust building: 28.2% of the variance in employees' intention to share knowledge is explained. The authors discuss the theoretical contributions of the chapter, identify future research opportunities, and highlight the implications for practicing managers.

DOI: 10.4018/978-1-60566-920-5.ch009

INTRODUCTION

It is necessary for companies to organize their knowledge in order to succeed in today's economy (Davenport & Prusak, 1998). This is also consistent with the knowledge based view of companies: knowledge could help a company maintain its competitive advantage (Kearns & Lederer, 2003). However, knowledge is kept in the human b rain, as well as in documents, and it has been suggested that people tend to turn to other people for information rather than documents and intranets (Allen, 1977; Cross & Sproull, 2004). What is more, knowledge sharing is needed when people attempt to solve complicated or unstructured problems (Augier, Shariq & Vendelo, 2001). Thus, knowledge sharing between employees is quite a significant issue considering its potential impact on enhancing the effectiveness of firms (Cummings, 2004). Since it has been suggested that hoarding knowledge is an inherently human characteristic (Davenport & Prusak, 1998), knowledge sharing behavior could only be encouraged rather than mandated. Therefore, much research has focused on how to encourage employees to share knowledge within and across organizations (Tezuka & Niwa, 2004; Voelpel & Han, 2005).

In prior research which investigated how people can be encouraged to share knowledge, researchers have normally taken a variety of viewpoints, considering: managerial factors (Lin & Lee, 2004; Srivastava & Bartol, 2006); organizational factors (Cummings, 2004; Kolekofski & Heminger, 2003; Southon, Todd & Seneque, 2002); cultural factors (Kyriakidou, 2004; Reid, 2003) and so on. Recently, many researchers have recognised realized the importance of leadership in knowledge management (Chen & Barnes, 2006). However, relatively little attention has been paid to the detailed processes by which leadership style would exert an impact on knowledge management activities. In fact, it is believed that leadership has a direct impact on the way companies arrange knowledge management initiatives because leaders could set the example for employees (Bell, Dyer, Hoopes & Harris, 2004). More importantly, much research has recognized that managers could provide a supportive atmosphere and culture which could help to encourage employees to share their knowledge (McDermott, 2000).

Leader attributes and behaviors will be influenced by societal culture (House, Javidan, Hanges & Dorfman, 2002), and it has been further proposed that the cultural dimensions of power distance and collectivism/individualism have an impact on leadership style (Lu & Lee, 2005). Moreover, given the strong power distance (cf. Hofstede, 2001) that prevails in China, with leaders wielding considerable influence over the actions of their subordinates, the values and attitudes of leaders are of critical importance to the intention of employees to share their knowledge (Lin & Lee, 2004). Further, strong power distance could help to form the initiating leadership structure since attitudes towards authority affect leader-follower relationships (Casimir & Li, 2005). In addition, Chinese people are also inclined to strong collectivism and strive to maintain a good relationship with the people around them so as to achieve a harmonious situation (Wong, Wong & Li, 2007). This cultural characteristic is consistent with the consideration leadership style. Consequently, it is worth investigating whether managers' leadership style (consideration and initiating structure) would affect employees' intention to share knowledge in the Chinese context. Identifying and understanding the detailed process through which leadership style influences employees' intentions to share knowledge is an important contribution to our knowledge about knowledge sharing practices in the Chinese context; indeed, it may have significant implications for organizations that plan to engage in knowledge work in China, a phenomenon that is increasingly frequently encountered.

A critical factor that is related to the impact of leadership style on knowledge sharing intention is trust. Lack of trust is often cited when discussing factors that counteract knowledge transfer

(Davenport & Prusak, 1998). Politis (2003) finds that interpersonal trust has a positive effect on communication and problem understanding which results in an enhancement of team performance. Moreover, trust is a typical and necessary factor in a knowledge sharing culture (Kyriakidou, 2004). Considering that managers could help to create a culture which could facilitate knowledge sharing between employees (Zakaria, Amelinckx & Wilemon, 2004), we investigate the potential of trust as a medium linking knowledge sharing and leadership style.

Since China has become an increasingly important player in the global economy, many multinationals have taken the Chinese market as their important strategic target. We conduct this research in the Chinese context. Given different cultural attitudes and values when compared with Western countries (cf. Hofstede, 2001), it is entirely likely that the lessons gained from knowledge management practices in Western countries will not apply directly in the Chinese context. It is important to point out that this is not simply a matter of the technology that enables knowledge sharing. Rather, it concerns the way people choose to share and communicate their knowledge with others, and as such relates to psychological and social factors.

China has its own unique cultural context. Exploring the culture can lend us insights into how Chinese people and organisations function. Yang (2005) proposed four orientations in Chinese social interaction which are relevant to an appreciation of Chinese culture, viz.:

1. **Familial orientation.** People place the whole family's advantage above their own. An individual's benefit is unimportant compared to benefits that can accrue to the collective – i.e. the whole family. This orientation highlights the fact that individuals should conform to the needs of the collective and constitutes the basis of collectivism.
2. **Guanxi orientation.** This is the main operational mode in Chinese social life. People build guanxi with each other through frequent interaction and giving favors to each other. Also, people will choose different ways to treat others because of different guanxi. People place great value on maintaining harmonious relations with others, so as to protect each other's face.
3. **Authority orientation.** Chinese people are sensitive to and dependent on authority. This orientation is associated with power distance (cf. Hofstede, 2001) and also could help explain why Chinese has a relatively high PDI score.
4. **Social orientation with others.** Chinese people pay attention to others' opinions about them; they have a strong sense of the value of social conformity, focusing on their own position in society, their reputation – and so, their face.

Given the unique cultural context prevalent in China, many authors have focused on knowledge sharing topics using a cultural lens, either to define their research questions, or at least to explain their findings (e.g. Chow, Deng & Ho, 2000; Geng, Townley, Huang & Zhang, 2005; Voelpel & Han, 2005; Weir & Hutchings, 2005). For instance, it has been found that, given high levels of willingness of Chinese employees to sacrifice their own interests for their collective in-group (Chow et al., 2000), it is easier to stimulate knowledge sharing within members of the in-group (i.e. those who work in the same group) than with members of out-groups (i.e. those who work in other groups). It has also been found that Chinese people are more ready to share out of a desire to improve their personal reputation (Voelpel & Han, 2005). However, little previous research has taken a leadership style perspective to knowledge sharing in China. Nevertheless, based on the cultural context, we expect that leadership style should also exert a significant impact on knowledge sharing intentions in organizations. Thus, our research linking leadership style to knowledge sharing intention contributes to practice and research. We also expect that our research findings will be of particular value for managers in the Chinese context. Managers themselves should realize that their own leadership style could facilitate or inhibit knowledge sharing behavior.

The layout of this paper is as follows. Following this introduction, we review the relevant literature on leadership style, trust and knowledge sharing. We then present our research methodology and research model, including the hypotheses. Next, we analyze the results and discuss the implications of the findings for research and practice. Finally we conclude and make suggestions for future research.

THEORETICAL BACKGROUND

There are a number of areas of literature that are relevant to this study. These include leadership style, affect-based and cognition-based trust and their antecedents, finally the intention to share knowledge. Each of these literatures is reviewed in turn, before we turn to the research model and development of hypotheses.

Leadership Style

Behavioral theories of leadership offer an important perspective in leadership research. From this perspective, "leadership was viewed as an observable process" (Jago, 1982) and effective leaders are judged by "how they behaved when interacting with followers or potential followers" (Jago, 1982). Since behavioral theories focus on managers' behavior, it has been suggested that a good leader could be developed through appropriate training (Robbins, 1997). A number of distinct leadership styles have been identified, including initiating structure and consideration; transformational and transactional; etc. Some research focuses on initiating structure and consideration: they find the leadership style would affect the subsequent success of any knowledge management system (Lu & Wang, 1997) or attempt to acquire knowledge (Politis, 2001). Politis (2001) finds that consideration plays a relatively unimportant role in knowledge acquisition while initiating structure plays a much more important role. Judge, Piccolo and Ilies (2004) confirm the contribution of consideration and initiating structure in leadership research and ensure the appropriateness of future studies after reporting these two constructs' validity; in addition, the suggestion is made that future research should identify mediating factors that can explain how leadership has an effect on knowledge sharing. Thus, we will focus on the classification of consideration and initiating structure in our research.

Initiating Structure

Initiating structure "refers to the extent to which the leader is likely to define and structure his or her role and those of subordinates in the search for goal attainment. It includes behavior that attempts to organize work, work relationships and goals" (Robbins, 1997 p.322). It has often been observed that managers who are inclined to a high initiating structure are also the subject of satisfaction by their own superiors due to their better performance and effectiveness (Judge et al., 2004). However, it has also been suggested that a high initiating structure is often linked to high employee turnover (Fleishman & Harris, 1962).

Earlier studies have shown that features of Chinese culture, such as high power distance, Confucian values and centralization would lead to a strong initiating structure leadership style. Pye (1985) also suggests that in China, power represents status. Thus, Chinese managers will be more inclined to impress on their employees their position by telling them what should and should not be done. Chinese employees in consequence have relatively less space to make decisions on their own. The essence of Chinese leadership is, to a large extent, based on one's personal position and authority (cf. also Walder, 1995). What is more, even initiating structure is proposed to be linked to satisfaction in the context of eastern culture (Lok & Crawford, 2004). Thus, we find that initiating structure could embody the character of a Chinese leadership style.

Consideration

"Consideration refers to the extent to which a person has job relationships characterized by mutual trust and respect for subordinates' ideas and feelings" (Robbins, 1997). If managers are inclined to high consideration, the work group tends to behave in a more harmonious fashion, with a correspondingly reduced level of employee turnover, when compared to high initiating structure, due to a higher satisfaction level experienced by subordinates (Filley, House & Kerr, 1976). Also, managers with a high consideration characteristic should raise workgroup productivity (Dunteman & Bass, 1963).

Any one individual manager may display characteristics, to a greater or lesser extent, of each of these styles, and indeed the balance of styles will vary according to the specific job, organization and culture where a manager works. Although Blake and Mouton (1969) have proposed that ideally a manager has the potential to perform strongly according to the principles of both styles, this proposition has been the subject of debate in other research that has suggested that "the hi-hi style is often not any better than a style which emphasizes just one aspect of leader behavior" (Schriesheim, 1982).

Chinese business leaders pay attention to more than initiating structure. Since harmony is an important factor in traditional Chinese culture, Chinese leaders tend to focus on relationships between them and their employees. In order to maintain a good relationship with their employees, Chinese leaders pay considerable attention to communication with them. Furthermore, Chinese managers are more inclined to participate in their employees' life: having dinner, visiting their sick family members, attending their wedding, and so on. In other words, Chinese leaders are inclined to make a great effort to establish a good relationship with their employees so as to ensure a harmonious working environment. This demonstrates that Chinese leaders are highly considerate.

The leadership behavior description questionnaire (LBDQ) is used to measure to what extent managers are inclined to consideration and/or initiating structure. It was developed by the staff of the Personnel Research Board of the Ohio State University and is accepted by many management researchers (Fredendall & Emery, 2003). Moreover, some researchers have started to apply it to the studies of knowledge management (Lu & Wang, 1997; Politis, 2001).

Affect and Cognition Based Trust

Trust can be explained as "the extent to which a person is confident in, and willing to act on the basis of, the words, actions, and decisions of another" (McAllister, 1995). In the past few years, the impact of trust was investigated in a variety of fields such as business relationships, e-commerce, interpersonal trust in organizations, buyer-supplier relationships, etc. (Anderson & Narus, 1990; Gefen, Karahanna & Straub, 2003; Korsgaard, Schweiger & Sapienza, 1995; Zaheer, McEvily & Perrone, 1998).

There is also a body of research that investigates the role of trust in knowledge sharing. Abrams, Cross, Lesser and Levin (2003) studied how to promote knowledge sharing by increasing the level of interpersonal trust from a managerial aspect including organizational factors and personal factors. Panteli and Sockalingam (2005) investigated the function of trust in knowledge sharing within virtual inter-organizational alliances showing that the level of trust between persons would affect both relationships and the extent and nature of the knowledge shared. Mooradian, Renzl and Matzler (2006) show that interpersonal trust has a positive effect on knowledge sharing within and across teams. In general, it has been observed that trust has a positive and significant effect on knowledge sharing behaviors: people who trust each other are more willing to provide their knowledge as well as accept others' knowledge (Andrews & Delahaye, 2000; Levin & Cross, 2004; Mayer & Davis, 1995; Zaheer et al., 1998). Since previous research has indicated that trust plays an important role in the process of knowledge sharing, it has been suggested that trust is "at the heart of knowledge exchange" (Davenport & Prusak, 1998). Meanwhile, the level of trust has been found to have a positive relationship with communication effectiveness (Dodgsom, 1993), since trust can improve the quality of knowledge sharing (Argyris, 1982) and reduce the costs involved (Currall & Judge, 1995).

Many researchers agree that trust is a multidimensional concept (Levin & Cross, 2004; Mayer & Davis, 1995; McAllister, 1995; Nahaipet & Ghoshal, 1998). Trust has been classified in many different ways, but interpersonal trust is often observed to have cognitive and affective foundations (Lewis & Weigert, 1985), a characteristic that is accepted by many researchers (Holste & Fields, 2005; McAllister, 1995). Based on McAllister's (1995) research, we find the relevance of this kind of distinction towards our own research since he concentrates on the organizational environment including interactions between managers and professionals. Also, some researchers have adopted affect and cognition based trust into the knowledge sharing research (Chowdhury, 2005; Holste & Fields, 2005). Besides, Ng and Chua (2006) use affect and cognition based trust in their research focusing on group cooperation and find that these two kinds of trust are "meaningful in the Chinese context"; more importantly, they "can enhance the precision of trust research ".

Cognition based trust can be explained as "we cognitively choose whom we will trust in which respects and under which circumstances and we base the choice on what we take to be 'good reasons'" (Lewis & Weigert, 1985). That is to say, cognition based trust is always established through some understanding toward the person we are going to trust. McAllister (1995) identified the antecedents of cognition based trust as reliable role performance, cultural-ethnic similarity and professional credentials. However, Lewis and Weigert (1985) suggested that a cognitive foundation for trust is far from sufficient for a person to trust others. Consequently, they suggested that trust constructed on an emotional base can constitute a kind of complementary foundation which can also explain "why the betrayal of a personal trust arouses a sense of emotional outrage in the betrayed" (Lewis & Weigert, 1985).

McAllister (1995) identified the antecedents of affect-based trust as citizenship and interaction frequency. Each kind of trust can have its use during the interaction among the people, as Lewis and Weigert (1985, p.972) indicated: "if all cognitive content were removed from emotional trust, we would be left with blind faith or fixed hope, the true believer or the pious faithful. On the other hand, if all emotional content were removed from cognitive trust, we would be left with nothing more than a cold blooded prediction or rationally calculated risk".

Antecedents of Affect and Cognition Based Trust

In order to achieve a better understanding of affect-based and cognition-based trust, the antecedents of each kind of trust should be explored in more detail. For the antecedents of affect-based trust, there are two significant factors: citizenship behavior and interaction frequency (McAllister, 1995).

Organizational citizenship behavior (OCB) has been investigated by many researchers since 1993, and such investigations were not only limited to organization behavior (Podsakoff, MacKenzie, Paine & Bachrach, 2000). Organ (1988) first formally defined OCB as "individual behavior that is discretionary, not directly or explicitly recognized by the formal reward system, and that in the aggregate promotes the effective functioning of the organization". After a complete literature review, Podsakoff et al. (2000) summarized seven dimensions of OCB taking into consideration the fact that different researchers had not been consistent in their use of the construct. The seven dimensions are: (1) Helping Behavior, (2) Sportsmanship, (3) Organizational Loyalty, (4) Organizational Compliance, (5) Individual Initiative, (6) Civic Virtue, (7) Self Development. For the purposes of our research, our measurements cover the first and the fifth dimensions, which are the most relevant to our research questions and also most closely accord with the Organ's definitions. Podsakoff et al. (2000) described it as "extra-role only in the sense that it involves engaging in task-related behaviors at a level that is so far beyond minimally required or generally expected levels that it takes on a voluntary flavor". Compared with Organ's definition, the two definitions have two points in common: first, the behavior is voluntary; second, the behavior is more than the basic requirement of the work.

Three antecedents of cognition-based trust can be identified: reliable role performance, cultural-ethnic similarity and professional credentials (McAllister, 1995). Each will be explained in the following paragraphs.

Reliable role performance is related to how a person implements his/her assigned work. McAllister (1995) deemed that in the work place, it is natural for people to consider how well their coworkers have performed their tasks when assessing whether their coworkers were trustworthy or not. Past performance is one of the aspects of a person's competence. Since competence-based trust will let the person be more willing to communicate with the person he trusts (Abrams et al., 2003), so reliable role performance can be considered to have a positive relationship with cognition-based trust.

Cultural-ethnic similarity is a form of social similarity between individuals which can promote the establishment of trust. McAllister (1995) proposed two reasons to support the positive relationship between culture-ethnic similarity and cognition-based trust. First, social similarity can affect levels of trust. Second, we can conclude from self-categorization theory (Turner, 1987) that persons will be more ready to trust a person in the same group rather than a person in a different group.

People with professional credentials are in a position to demonstrate that they are professionally qualified for their work (cf. McAllister, 1995). However, many studies have previously showed that ability is an important antecedent of trust (Cook & Wall, 1980; Sitkin & Roth, 1993). Mayer and Davis (1995) identified ability as a factor in their model of trust. They defined ability as a "group of skills, competencies, and characteristics that enable a party to have influence within some specific domain".

Intention to Share Knowledge

The intention to share knowledge has a direct effect on knowledge sharing behavior. In consequence, the intention to share knowledge has been the focus of many researchers who have employed the Theory of Reasoned Action (Kolekofski & Heminger, 2003) or the Theory of Planned Behavior (Ryu, Ho & Han, 2003). This body of research suggests that factors such as attitudes toward knowledge sharing and subjective norms play an important role in knowledge sharing intentions (Bock, Zmud, Kim & Lee, 2005; Kolekofski & Heminger, 2003; Ryu et al., 2003). Furthermore, Bock et al. (2005) found that organizational climate affects the intention to share knowledge. Moreover, Wang (2005) has proposed that ethical concerns have positive relationship on the intention to share knowledge while self-interest concerns have a negative relationship.

RESEARCH MODEL

Hofstede (1998) has suggested that employees will follow their managers' instructions if they want to be members of the organization, and so "leaders' values become followers' practice". Furthermore, as Yukl (1992) suggests, there is an assumption built into concepts of leadership such that the leader would affect his/her subordinates' task and social behavior. Indeed, different leadership styles as a manifestation of a manager's values are believed to have different effects on employees' behavior. In China, the leader's effect on their employees is especially important. Chinese people always emphasize the power of the example. They believe that leaders have a certain responsibility to set an example to their employees. Generally speaking, one cannot ask others to do something unless one can do it oneself. Moreover, Southon et al. (2002) have proposed that management policy has a direct influence on communication culture within the company, i.e. leadership style affects employees' behavior. Thus, if managers are more inclined to consideration or initiating structure, then the subordinates of these managers will be correspondingly affected to behave in a manner that is oriented towards their managers' style.

When a manager is more inclined to consideration, he will express more concern for his subordinates and attach importance to the relationships among the groups through respecting his subordinates and paying attention to what his subordinates feel and think. This will make for a warm and caring atmosphere in the work group. Employees working in such groups will also be affected to maintain such an atmosphere by concern and care for the colleagues around them; in this way, citizenship behavior and frequency of interaction will be enhanced. Accordingly,

H1a: *The manager's inclination to consideration will have a positive relationship with the colleagues' citizenship behavior towards each other.*

H1b: *The manager's inclination to consideration will have a positive relationship with the frequency of interaction between the colleagues.*

Some researchers have induced the concept of organizational citizenship behavior into knowledge management so as to explain knowledge sharing willingness (Bock & Kim, 2002; Koh & Kim, 2004). Moreover, Smith & McKeen (2002) demonstrated that knowledge sharing culture goes "deeper than superficial individual behaviors and captures the hearts and minds of the people in an organization". This shows that employees in organizations with a knowledge sharing culture should endeavor to share their knowledge imitatively. Citizenship behavior is an important factor which could encourage people to perform their work. The relationship between citizenship behavior and interaction frequency has not been the focus of much research to date. Lai, Liu and Shaffer (2004) have proposed that network members who frequently contact one another may develop stronger citizenship behavior because frequency of interaction will make them more supportive towards each other. Also, it has been found that positive affectivity could constitute an antecedent of citizenship behavior (Organ, 1988) and frequency of interaction could facilitate the development of positive affectivity. Besides, citizenship behavior could be regarded as a critical factor supporting the development of a knowledge sharing atmosphere which could be established by leaders' endeavor. Thus, we propose that

H2: *The frequency of interaction between colleagues will be positively associated with citizenship behavior.*

When a manager is more inclined to initiating structure, he is likely to prefer subordinates to obey a standard set of rules and procedures, stressing the implementation of a task as the most important thing. Such a manager will pay less attention to employees' feelings and thoughts, instead considering employees as the means to carry out a task. Managers with this kind of style will create a serious atmosphere for the work group and pressure their subordinates; as a result, each employee would be affected to take the task as their most important activity. They will also develop a clear plan and prepare thoroughly to ensure that they can complete this assigned task. Interaction facilitation behavior is deemed as one of the important aspects of leadership and this behavior would improve communication among group members (Bowers & Seashore, 1966). Hemphill and Coons (1957) even obtained this factor out of the Ohio State leadership studies. Thus, we believe frequency of interaction could also be influenced by initiating structure. In addition, two levels of communication including content level (information or topical) and relational level are found and has been shown that content level is related more to initiating structure while relational level related to consideration (Penley & Hawkins, 1985). Part of this preparation will involve interaction between employees so as to ensure that they can work effectively. Accordingly,

H3a: *The manager's inclination to initiating structure will have a positive relationship with the frequency of interaction between the colleagues.*

H3b: *The manager's inclination to initiating structure will increase the reliability of colleagues' role performance.*

Following previous research (McAllister, 1995), we hypothesize that citizenship behavior has a positive relationship with affect-based trust. McAllister (1995) suggests that "altruistic behavior may provide an attributional basis for affect-based trust", since altruistic behavior can be embodied by organizational citizenship behavior. What is more, as in previous research, it was found that organizational citizenship behavior would enhance trust between supervisor and subordinates (Deluga, 1995). Our hypothesis H3 was supported in previous research (McAllister, 1995), where citizenship behavior was identified as the antecedent of affect-based trust.

H4: *The level of the colleagues' citizenship behavior directed towards their fellow employees will be positively associated with the level of the affect based trust in one another.*

Since trust functions primarily in a sociological way and the base upon which it is built is also primarily social (Lewis & Weigert, 1985), we cannot ignore the functions of interactions upon which trust is built. It has also been found that interaction constitutes the main antecedents of high level of trust (Nugent & Abolafia, 2006). McAllister (1995) also identified interaction frequency as the other antecedent of affect based trust. In addition, we consider that the establishment of cognition based trust should be mutual and the frequency of interaction will help each party to know the other's ability better. Thus, we develop the following two hypotheses:

H5a: *The frequency of interaction between colleagues will be positively associated with the level of their affect based trust in one another.*

H5b: *The frequency of interaction between colleagues will be positively associated with the level of their cognition based trust in one another.*

McAllister (1995) proposed three antecedents of cognition-based trust, viz.: peer reliable role performance, cultural-ethnic similarity and professional credentials. However, given our focus on leadership style, we believe that only the first of these, peer reliable role performance, is relevant for our purposes. In our target population, cultural-ethnic similarity is expected to be high,

Figure 1. Research model of the influences on an employee's intention to share knowledge

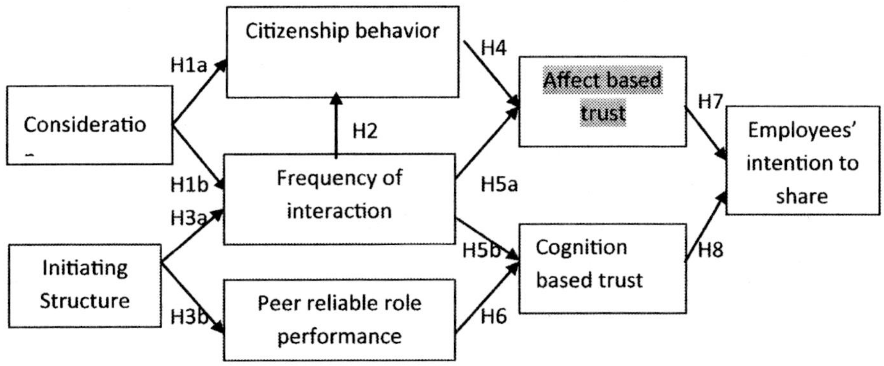

i.e. it is controlled for by the research design that focuses on ethnic Chinese professionals working in the PRC. Likewise, given that the sample is intentionally restricted to current MBA students, all of whom are working full time in organizations, we believe that we can control for the professional credentials of the respondents. It has previously been established (Mayer & Davis, 1995) that ability (defined as the "group of skills, competencies, and characteristics that enable a party to have influence within some specific domain") has an important relationship with trust. Based on this definition of ability, we can find that peer reliable role performance can reflect the ability of respondents' peers. If trust is based on peers' ability, this implies that trustees may only be relied on in the context of their professional responsibility. It also suggests that there is a relationship between ability and reliable role performance in the context of cognition-based trust, which is more related to the tasks that one undertakes. Consequently, we consider that peer reliable role performance is an important factor, and propose:

H6: *The extent to which employees reliably perform their role will be positively associated with the level of the employee's cognition based trust in his colleagues.*

As we discussed in the literature review, many researchers believe that trust is an important precursor of knowledge sharing because people are more inclined to share and accept knowledge when they are in trust relationships with others. Also, research suggests that personal trust could produce cooperation, resource exchange and help employees to ignore competitive messages (Kotlarsky & Oshri, 2005; Parks & Hulbert, 1995; Uzzi, 1997). Previous research (e.g. Chowdhury, 2005; Holste & Fields, 2005) has supported the notion that cognition-based and affect-based trust has a positive relationship with knowledge sharing. Accordingly, we propose:

H7: *The more a person has affect based trust towards his colleagues, the more he will have the intention to share knowledge with them*

H8: *The more a person has cognition based trust towards his colleagues, the more he will have the intention to share knowledge with them.*

RESEARCH METHODOLOGY

Measurement and Data Collection

An English questionnaire was first developed based on previously validated measures. 7-point Likert scales were used to measure all items, ranging from "strongly agree" to "strongly disagree".

The questions in Section A used to measure leadership style were derived from the LBDQ (Halpin, 1957). In Section B, we measured employees' practices: citizenship behavior, frequency of interaction and peer reliable role performance; the questions were adapted from McAllister (1995). The items in Section C were adapted from McAllister (1995) too and were designed to measure the affect and cognition based trust. We used the scales from Ryu et al. (2003) to measure employees' intention to share knowledge in section D. We focused on the intention of knowledge sharing, rather than actual behavior, because "the role of intention as a strong predictor of behavior has been well-established in IS and reference disciplines" (Komiak & Benbasat, 2006). Finally, questions in section E are demographic. Since this survey was conducted in China, we translated the instrument into Chinese firstly and performed a back-translation so as to ensure equivalence of meaning between the English and Chinese versions. The English version of the instrument can be found in Appendix A. The Chinese version is available on request from the authors.

The study population is comprised of MBA students from a university located in Eastern China. All respondents are full time employees working in a variety of organizations and all are Chinese, thus ensuring their unique cultural characteristics. These students were chosen because they met the following sample requirements. First, all of these students have the knowledge background of knowledge sharing because they had taken some knowledge management courses. Second, they were active members in their organizations. A total of 239 individuals were invited to participate in this research (on a voluntary basis). 160 responses were returned, with a response rate of 66.95%. Out of the 160 responses, 9 responses were eliminated due to incomplete information. Thus, the final response rate was 63.18%. The demography of these samples is shown in Table 1. Meanwhile, we used the method suggested by Armstrong and Overton (1977) to test the possible non-response bias in the survey. Assuming that the last 25% of responses received would be indicative of the responses of non-responders, we compared the chi-squares of the responses from the first 25% of the respondents to that of the final 25%. No significant differences between these two groups were indicated by these tests.

Data Analysis

To test the potential common method bias, we adopted Harman's one-factor test (Podsakoff & Organ, 1986). The resulting principal components factor analysis yielded eight constructs with eigenvalues greater than one from all the measures in this study. Meanwhile, numbers listed in table 2 show that these constructs totally accounted for 69% of the variance and each explained roughly equal variance (range = 7-10%). The first construct accounted for 10.32% of the variance. Since no general construct emerged from this analysis and one-construct did not account for the most of the variance, this indicated that common method bias was unlikely to be a major threat in our study.

To validate our research model, a structural equation modeling technique, partial least squares (PLS) was adopted. PLS was used as it supports not only confirmatory research but also exploratory research (Gefen, 2000). Compared with other structural equation modeling techniques, it is more suitable for prediction, especially for a research model that is under development and that has not been tested extensively (Chin, 1998; Guinea, Kelley & Hunter, 2005). Due to the dearth of studies on the relationships between managers' leadership style and employee's knowledge sharing, our research is exploratory in nature. Thus, PLS was suitable compared to other structural equation modeling techniques.

Measurement Model

According to Chin's (1998) recommendations, the measurement model and structural model can

Table 1. Demographic information of respondents

Measure	Items	Frequency	Percent
Age	25 or below	14	9.27%
	26-35	125	82.78%
	36-45	12	7.95%
Position	Employee	44	29.14%
	Manager	51	33.77%
	Director	32	21.19%
	(Vice) President	4	2.65%
	Others	20	13.25%
Org style	Multinational	27	17.88%
	SOE	58	38.41%
	Private Owned	43	28.48%
	Foreign capital	7	4.64%
	Joint Venture	4	2.65%
	Others	12	7.94%
Org size	50 or below	20	13.25%
	51-100	15	9.93%
	101-500	46	30.46%
	501-1000	17	11.26%
	1001 or more	53	35.10%
Number of colleagues	1--10	76	50.33%
	11--20	28	18.54%
	21 or more	47	31.13%

Table 2. Eigenvalues and variances of the rotated factors

	Eigenvalues	Variance (%)	Cumulative variance (%)
1	12.199	10.315	10.315
2	3.240	10.176	20.491
3	2.508	9.810	30.301
4	2.174	9.149	39.451
5	1.799	8.180	47.630
6	1.450	7.267	54.897
7	1.182	7.232	62.129
8	1.109	7.229	69.359
Extraction Method: Principal Component Analysis.			

be examined simultaneously in PLS. In order to validate the measurement model, we assessed content validity, convergent validity and discriminant validity. Normally, if a measure's items were selected and refined through an extensive process based on a literature review, the measure could be

Table 3. Results of confirmatory factor analysis

Measures	Items	Cronbach's Alpha	Composite Reliability	AVE
Consideration (CON)	5	0.849	0.892	0.624
Initiating (INI)	4	0.878	0.917	0.734
Citizenship behavior (CB)	5	0.901	0.926	0.716
Frequency of Interaction (FI)	4	0.850	0.899	0.691
Peer Reliable Role Performance (RRP)	6	0.864	0.898	0.596
Affect based trust (ABT)	5	0.802	0.864	0.560
Cognition based trust (CBT)	5	0.902	0.927	0.718
Employees' Intention to Share Knowledge (ISK)	3	0.837	0.907	0.756
AVE: Average Variance Extracted				

said to possess content validity. As previously discussed, the conventional process of our measures being chosen has proved our instrument's content validity. We used the reliability of items, composite reliability and average variance extracted (AVE) to access convergent validity. In Appendix B, most individual item loadings meet the 0.7 criterion which was suggested by Barclay, Thompson & Higgins (1995). Although three items' loadings are less than 0.7, they were significant at the .001 level. Thus, we keep them in the model. Table 3 below showed the composite reliability values ranged from 0.864 to 0.927 which above the .70 recommended level (Fornell & Larcker, 1981).

To assess discriminant validity, we took the relationship between correlations among constructs and the square root of AVEs and items' cross-loadings into consideration. First, according to Fornell and Larcker's (1981) recommendation, the square root of AVEs should be larger than the correlations among constructs, which implies that all constructs share more variance with their items than with other constructs. Table 4 shows that the square roots of all the AVEs are greater than the correlations among constructs, indicating good discriminnat validity of all the constructs. Second, the test of items' cross-loading also indicates the good discriminant validity of our measurement (Appendix B), because the loadings of the items on their own constructs are higher than their cross-loading on other constructs (Chin, 1998; Gefen, 2000; Gefen et al., 2003). Generally, the loadings per construct are much higher in PLS than in a Principal Components Analysis (PCA) (Gefen & Straub, 2005). Thus, the loadings shown in Appendix A are different to the loadings shown in Appendix B.

Structural Model

After examining the measurement model, we tested the proposed hypotheses with PLS. The results of the analysis are shown in Figure 2. The betas are shown above the arrows and the number of asterisks refers to the significance level of the beta. The t-values are shown below the betas and they were tested with PLS bootstrap. The values of R^2 are shown above/below the boxes. The model explained 14.5% to 34.3% of the variances, and all the paths are significant.

The PLS results show that all the hypotheses are supported. Managers' consideration leadership style can positively impact employees' citizenship behavior (β=0.102, $p<0.1$) and their frequency of interaction (β=0.296, $p<0.01$). Comparably, managers' initiating leadership style can positively influence employees' peer reliable role performance (β=0.380, $p<0.01$) and their frequency of

Table 4. Correlations between constructs

	CON	INI	CB	FI	RRP	ABT	CBT	ISK
CON	0.790							
INI	0.481	0.857						
CB	0.309	0.242	0.846					
FI	0.383	0.323	0.578	0.831				
RRP	0.283	0.380	0.524	0.505	0.772			
ABT	0.374	0.303	0.497	0.486	0.428	0.748		
CBT	0.320	0.354	0.520	0.489	0.519	0.689	0.847	
ISK	0.257	0.195	0.276	0.391	0.351	0.492	0.483	0.869

*The shaded numbers in the diagonal row are square roots of the average variance extracted.

interaction (β=0.180, p<0.05). Employees' citizenship behavior (β=0.319, p<0.01) and frequency of interaction (β=0.304, p<0.01) then increase their affect based trust, and employees' frequency of interaction (β=0.305, p<0.01) and peer reliable role performance (β=0.365, p<0.01) increase employees' cognition based trust. Meanwhile, employees' frequency of interaction can increase their citizenship behavior (β=0.539, p<0.01). Finally, all employees' affect (β=0.310, p<0.01) and cognition (β=0.271, p<0.01) based trust can increase their intention of knowledge sharing.

DISCUSSION, CONTRIBUTION & LIMITATIONS

Discussion of Findings

The purpose of this study is to establish how leadership style would affect employees' intention to share knowledge and to assess to what extent different leadership styles would affect subordinates' work practices in the organizations, how these work practices would in turn lead to the creation of trust between colleagues, and what the impact of this trust is on the intention

Figure 2. Results of PLS analysis

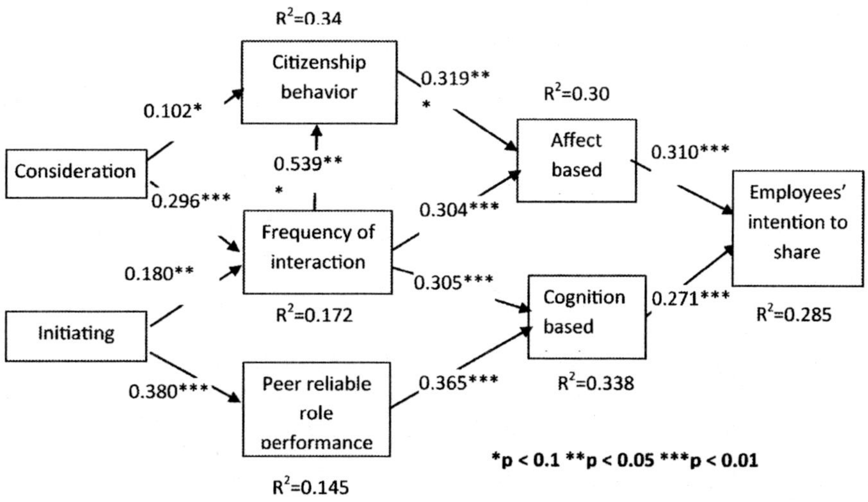

to share knowledge. The present study also tests a western model in the Chinese context to see if it applies or not.

According to the results, citizenship behavior of the employees is influenced positively by managers with a consideration characteristic while peer reliable performance is influenced positively by managers with an initiating characteristic. Besides, both consideration and initiating character have a positive relationship with employees' frequency of interaction. We also find that consideration's influence on frequency of interaction is stronger than on citizenship behavior, while initiating structure's influence on peer reliable role performance is stronger than frequency of interaction. This shows consideration is a more important antecedent of initiating structure. This result could be explained by the character of consideration leadership style: Managers with a high degree of consideration are inclined to create a warm atmosphere in organizations which may serve to encourage more interactions between the employees themselves. What is more, we could see clearly that managers do affect employees' daily practice through their leadership styles. We could also conclude that Chinese leaders do have a certain effect on employees' behavior. In China, people emphasize the function of examples. In other words, being a leader, you should demonstrate the behaviour that you expect from your subordinates, before passing the command to them through both your own action as well as your verbal request. Different leadership styles could be easily identified through leaders' behavior: caring for subordinates, being strict with work standards of the work, framing a role for an employee. Once the leadership style is established and the example has been demonstrated, subordinates will naturally have an idea of what their leaders hope them to be. If subordinates want to continue to be members, they will cooperate and act as necessary according to different leadership styles. In addition, because of a strong authority orientation in China, subordinates are generally quite willing to follow their superiors, which facilitate the influence process.

In addition, we compare the mean of initiating structure (3.133) and consideration (3.461) with a T test. The result shows that leaders' inclination to these leadership styles are significantly different ($t=2.544$, $p<0.05$). This shows that although most managers are inclined both to initiating structure and to consideration, the inclination to consideration is still stronger than to initiating structure. This is consistent with the Chinese way of doing things: a strong emphasis on harmonious relationships and a friendly environment (Westwood, 1997; Yang, 2005). What is more, higher inclination to consideration is also consistent with guanxi orientation, which means that people will respect others' feelings if they want to build guanxi (Fu & Tsui, 2003). We find that these attributes all contribute to the consideration leadership style. Thus, we suggest that the tendency of Chinese culture to emphasize harmony and guanxi could account for high consideration in China.

Our findings for the positive influences of employees' citizenship behavior and interaction frequency on their affect based trust are consistent with previous research (McAllister, 1995). On the other hand, our findings suggest that peer reliable role performance has a positive relationship with cognition based trust which is contrary to previous research (McAllister, 1995). This suggests that peer reliable role performance is one of the important antecedents of cognition based trust. What is more, we also found that frequency of interaction could positively influence citizenship behavior. These results are consistent with our hypothesis, since reliable role performance could fully reflect one's ability which could lead to cognition based trust; frequent interaction could make employees more supportive towards each other, which constitute the antecedents of citizenship behavior.

Both kinds of trust were found to influence employees' intention to share knowledge, though affect based trust has a stronger influence on intention to share knowledge than does cognition based trust. This result confirms previous research findings showing that affective factors of trustworthiness are more salient in a Confucian influenced society (Tan & Chee, 2005). Confucian values are found to be one of the strongest cultural influences in Asia. Confucian values are the basis for what has come to be known as the fifth dimension of culture, first suggested by Bond and his associates (Chinese Culture Connection, 1987) as Confucian Work Dynamism, later modified by Hofstede (2001) to the Long Term Orientation dimension. Tan and Chee (2005) argue that culture will influence both trust building and perceptions of trust. Our research also indicates that affective based trust has a stronger influence than cognition based trust in China. Since China is the cradle of Confucianism, we suggest that affective based trust is relatively more important because harmony and relationships are of great importance in society.

Implications for Theory and Practice

The paper has both theoretical and practical implications. Given the lack of prior studies on the relationship between leadership style and subordinate trust, mediated by subordinate work practices, this study breaks new ground. Furthermore, by considering the development of subordinate trust in organizations in China, we demonstrate that a Western-derived theory, incorporating two types of trust building measures, can be effectively applied in the Chinese context. Finally, we find that leadership styles affect employees' intentions to share knowledge through establishing mutual trust.

Interaction frequency is an important factor mediating leadership style and the establishment of trust. Not only can it be affected by the consideration and initiating styles of leadership, but it can also influence both affect based trust and cognition based trust. Unlike McAllister (1995), we find that interaction frequency both has a greater influence on cognition based trust than on affect based trust, and also has a strong influence on citizenship behavior.

Since it has been found (and we confirm) that affect based trust has a greater influence on the intention to share knowledge than does cognition based trust, people may think that a leadership style of consideration is more effective in facilitating knowledge sharing among employees. In fact, our research suggests that the function of initiating structure is as important as consideration in stimulating knowledge sharing. This is paradoxical because prior research in Western contexts (e.g., Fisher & Edwards, 1988; Fleishman, 1973; Fleishman & Harris, 1962) has found that consideration is a more effective leadership style than initiating structure. However, based on Hofstede (2001), we suggest that high levels of Power Distance (characteristic of the Chinese culture) could result in subordinates displaying a high degree of obedience towards their managers' orders. This may explain why the initiating structure style of leadership has a stronger effect in the Chinese context.

The practical implication of this study is that the sharing of knowledge by employees depends on heightened levels of trust between work-group members. More specifically, this trust can be cultivated by managers encouraging frequent interactions, appropriate citizenship behavior and reliable role performance. Based on our findings, we suggest that managers should adopt a 'high-high' style of leadership so as to encourage knowledge sharing. 'High-high' refers to a leadership style that is high in both consideration and initiating structure. Such a high-high leadership style has the potential to enhance both affect based trust and cognition based trust through citizenship behavior, interaction frequency and reliable role performance, finally leading to strong knowledge sharing intentions. Considering that Chinese managers are currently more inclined to consideration, we suggest that they should pay more attention to initiating structure in order to become more task oriented. This suggestion is consistent with Chinese management culture. It may sound trivial and obvious to recommend that employees engage in regular interactions with one another as a means of stimulating knowledge sharing, but our survey feedback indicates that most respondents do *not* interact with their colleagues on a regular basis (cf. McInerney, 2002; Wang & Guan, 2005). Consequently, while task-based opportunities will provide the context where knowledge sharing is appropriate, incentives from management to share knowledge will be critical as well.

Of course, we can query why employees are not interacting with their colleagues. We have no direct evidence, but based on our familiarity with the research context, we suggest that there is a combination of manager distance and employee apathy, combined with a general reluctance to accept personal responsibility for possibly negative consequences resulting from their contributions (cf. Child, 1991). Employees are apathetic to interact given that information is seen as a personal resource (Child, 1991; Martinsons, 1991), they are neither rewarded, encouraged or otherwise motivated and lack the interpersonal trust to do so (cf. Reader, 1987). In addition, managers, who might be able to exert a useful influence on that intention to share, are perhaps too distant from their subordinates. They need to get down on the 'shop floor' where subordinates work, and encourage them directly with a mix of consideration and initiating structure, i.e. emotional support and authoritative direction.

Limitations

Our study has a number of limitations. We did not integrate Chinese contextual factors into the research model, which may in part explain the low R^2 score. Further, the data about leadership style is based on employees' perceptions. However, each respondent is only one member of a work group, suggesting that other (not surveyed) members' opinions about the same leaders' style may differ. Unfortunately, it was not possible to survey all members of any one work group. Furthermore, this study focuses on the intention to share knowledge among work group members as a whole, not with individual work group members. Clearly, an employee may have a stronger intention to share knowledge with some colleagues, but not others. However, the current research design is not sufficiently sensitive to assess such details. Future research should consider this issue, ideally with an in-depth, qualitative research methodology. What is more, although initiating structure and consideration could describe part of the character of Chinese leaders, there are additional aspects of their character that could be explored in future research. For instance, Li (1998) indicates that guanxi behavior is complementary to the leadership styles of initiating structure and consideration. Thus, it will be necessary for us to explore more aspects of the Chinese character so that we can improve our understanding of this issue in China. The survey conducted in this research only covers two provinces in China (Anhui and Jiangsu provinces) which limits the generalizability of our findings. Finally, this study has paid more attention to general leadership style, without taking into consideration such details as the industry type and the exact position of the respondent.

Given these limitations, we strongly encourage other researchers to undertake more research in this domain. There is a strong need to include more indigenous Chinese elements in future work. It would be useful to conduct a few case studies in organizations so as to understand how different leadership styles facilitate knowledge sharing intentions. We could also usefully learn about the attitudes of the employees themselves towards interaction in general and knowledge sharing in particular. Replicating the study in other cultures would also help to broaden our understanding of the phenomenon. Since, leadership is perceived to be "a reciprocal process between those who choose to lead and those who choose to follow"

(Kouzes & Posner, 1995), future studies could usefully explore how reciprocal processes occur in the knowledge sharing context. Finally, the topic to be studied could also be broadened to actual knowledge sharing, sharing across work groups, with additional Chinese factors included such as guanxi, face and renqing.

REFERENCES

Abrams, L. C., Cross, R., Lesser, E., & Levin, D. Z. (2003). Nurturing interpersonal trust in knowledge sharing networks. *The Academy of Management Executive*, *17*(4), 64–76.

Allen, T. J. (1977). *Managing the Flow of Technology*. Cambridge: MIT Press.

Anderson, J. C., & Narus, J. A. (1990). A model of distributor firm and manufacturer firm working partnerships. *Journal of Marketing*, *54*(1), 42–58. doi:10.2307/1252172

Andrews, K. M., & Delahaye, B. L. (2000). Influences on knowledge processes in organizational learning: The psychosocial filter. *Journal of Management Studies*, *37*(6), 797–810. doi:10.1111/1467-6486.00204

Argyris, C. (1982). *Reasoning, Learning and Action.* San Francisco: Jossey-Bass

Armstrong, J. S., & Overton, T. S. (1977). Estimating nonresponse bias in mail surveys. *JMR, Journal of Marketing Research*, *14*(3), 396–402. doi:10.2307/3150783

Augier, M., Shariq, S. Z., & Vendelo, M. T. (2001). Understanding context: its emergence, transformation and role in tacit knowledge sharing. *Journal of Knowledge Management*, *5*(2), 125–136. doi:10.1108/13673270110393176

Barclay, D., Thompson, R., & Higgins, C. (1995). The partial least squares (PLS) approach to causal modeling: Personal computer adoption and use an illustration. *Technology Studies*, *2*(2), 285–309.

Bell, K., Dyer, G., Hoopes, C., & Harris, S. (2004). Toward a model of effective knowledge management and directions for future research: Culture, leadership, and CKOs. *Journal of Leadership & Organizational Studies*, *10*(4), 26–43. doi:10.1177/107179190401000403

Blake, R. R., & Mouton, J. S. (1969). *Building a Dynamic Corporation through Grid Organization Development* Addison-Wesley Pub Co.

Bock, G. W., & Kim, Y. G. (2002). Breaking the myths of rewards: An exploratory study of attitudes about knowledge sharing. *Information Resources Management Journal*, *15*(2), 14–21.

Bock, G. W., Zmud, R. W., Kim, Y.-G., & Lee, J.-N. (2005). Behavioral intention formation in knowledge sharing: Examining the roles of extrinsic motivators, social-psychological forces, and organizational climate. *MIS Quarterly*, *29*(1), 87–111.

Bowers, D. G., & Seashore, S. E. (1966). Predicting organizational effectiveness with a four-factor theory of leadership. *Administrative Science Quarterly*, *11*(2), 238–263. doi:10.2307/2391247

Casimir, G., & Li, Z. (2005). Combinative aspects of leadership style: A comparison of Australian and Chinese followers. *Asian Business & Management*, *4*, 271–291. doi:10.1057/palgrave.abm.9200132

Chen, L. Y., & Barnes, F. B. (2006). Leadership behaviors and knowledge sharing in professional service firms engaged in strategic alliances. *Journal of Applied Management and Entrepreneurship*, *11*(2), 51–69.

Child, J. (1991). A foreign perspective on the management of people in China. *International Journal of Human Resource Management, 2*(1), 93–107.

Chin, W. W. (1998). The partial least squares approach to structural equation modeling In G. A. Marcoulids (Ed.), *Modern Methods for Business Research*. Mahwah, NJ: Lawrence Erlbaum Associates

Chinese Culture Connection. (1987). Chinese values and the search for culture-free dimensions of culture. *Journal of Cross-Cultural Psychology, 18*(2), 143–164. doi:10.1177/0022002187018002002

Chow, C. W., Deng, F. J., & Ho, J. L. (2000). The openness of knowledge sharing within organizations: A comparative study of the United States and the People's Republic of China. *Journal of Management Accounting Research, 12*, 65–95. doi:10.2308/jmar.2000.12.1.65

Chowdhury, S. (2005). The role of affect-and cognition-based trust in complex knowledge sharing. *Journal of Managerial Issues, 17*(3), 310–326.

Cook, J., & Wall, T. (1980). New work attitude measures of trust, organizational commitment and personal need non-fulfillment. *Journal of Occupational Psychology, 53*(1), 39–52.

Cross, R., & Sproull, L. (2004). More than an answer: Information relationships for actionable knowledge. *Organization Science, 15*(4), 446–462. doi:10.1287/orsc.1040.0075

Cummings, J. N. (2004). Work groups, structural diversity and knowledge sharing in a global organization. *Management Science, 50*(3), 352–364. doi:10.1287/mnsc.1030.0134

Currall, S. C., & Judge, T. A. (1995). Measuring trust between organizational boundary role persons. *Organizational Behavior and Human Decision Processes, 64*(2), 151–170. doi:10.1006/obhd.1995.1097

Davenport, T. H., & Prusak, L. (1998). *Working Knowledge: How Organizations Manage What They Know*: Harvard Business School Press.

Deluga, R. J. (1995). The relation between trust in the supervisor and subordinate organizational citizenship behavior. *Military Psychology, 7*(1), 1–16. doi:10.1207/s15327876mp0701_1

Dodgsom, M. (1993). Learning, trust and technological collaboration. *Human Relations, 46*(1), 77–95. doi:10.1177/001872679304600106

Dunteman, E. A., & Bass, B. M. (1963). Supervisory and engineering success associated with self, interaction, and task orientation scores. *Personnel Psychology, 16*, 13–21. doi:10.1111/j.1744-6570.1963.tb01250.x

Filley, A. C., House, R. J., & Kerr, S. (1976). *Managerial Process and Organizational Behavior*. Glenview. Illinois: Scott, Foresman & Co.

Fisher, B. M. & Edwards, J. E. (1988). Consideration and initiating structure and their relationships with leader effectiveness: A meta-analysis. *Academy of Management Proceedings*, 201-205.

Fleishman, E. A. (1973). *Current Developments in the Study of Leadership*. Carbondale: Southern Illinois University Press.

Fleishman, E. A., & Harris, E. F. (1962). Patterns of leadership behavior related to employee grievances and turnover. *Personnel Psychology, 15*, 43–56. doi:10.1111/j.1744-6570.1962.tb01845.x

Fornell, C., & Larcker, D. F. (1981). Evaluating structural equation models with unobservable variables and measurement error. *JMR, Journal of Marketing Research, 18*(1), 39–50. doi:10.2307/3151312

Fredendall, L. D., & Emery, C. R. (2003). Productivity increases due to the use of teams in service garages. *Journal of Managerial Issues, XV*(2), 221–242.

Fu, P. P., & Tsui, A. S. (2003). Utilizing printed media to understand desired leadership attributes in the People's Republic of China. *Asia Pacific Journal of Management, 20*, 423–446. doi:10.1023/A:1026373124564

Gefen, D. (2000). Structural equation modeling and regression: Guidelines for research practice. *Communications of AIS, 4*(7), 1–77.

Gefen, D., Karahanna, E., & Straub, D. W. (2003). Trust and TAM in online shopping: an integrated model. *MIS Quarterly, 27*(1), 51–90.

Gefen, D., & Straub, D. (2005). A practical guide to factorial validity using PLS-Graph: Tutorial and annotated example. *Communications of the AIS, 16*, 91–109.

Geng, Q., Townley, C., Huang, K., & Zhang, J. (2005). Comparative knowledge management: A pilot study of Chinese and American universities. *Journal of the American Society for Information Science and Technology, 56*(10), 1031–1044. doi:10.1002/asi.20194

Guinea, A. O. d., Kelley, H., & Hunter, M. G. (2005). Information systems effectiveness in small businesses: Extending a Singaporean model in Canada. *Journal of Global Information Management, 13*(3), 55–79.

Halpin, A. W. (1957). *Manual for the Leader Behavior Description Questionnaire*. Columbus, Ohio: The Ohio State University.

Hemphill, J. K., & Coons, A. E. (1957). *Development of the Leader Behavior Description Questionnaire*. Ohio: Bureau of Business Research, Ohio State University.

Hofstede, G. (1998). Attitudes, values and organizational cultures: disentangling the concepts. *Organization Studies, 19*(3), 477–492. doi:10.1177/017084069801900305

Hofstede, G. (2001). *Culture's Consequences*: Sage Publications Newbury Park London

Holste, J. S., & Fields, D. (2005). The relationship of affect and cognition based trust with sharing and use of tacit knowledge. *Academy of Management Best Conference Paper* (MED: B1).

House, R., Javidan, M., Hanges, P., & Dorfman, P. (2002). Understanding cultures and implicit leadership theories across the globe: An introduction to project GLOBE. *Journal of World Business, 37*, 3–10. doi:10.1016/S1090-9516(01)00069-4

Jago, A. G. (1982). Leadership: Perspectives in theory and research. *Management Science, 28*(3), 315–336. doi:10.1287/mnsc.28.3.315

Judge, T. A., Piccolo, R. F., & Ilies, R. (2004). The forgotten ones? The validity of consideration and initiating structure in leadership research. *The Journal of Applied Psychology, 89*(1), 36–51. doi:10.1037/0021-9010.89.1.36

Kearns, G. S., & Lederer, A. L. (2003). A resource-based view of strategic IT alignment: How knowledge sharing creates competitive advantage. *Decision Sciences, 34*(1), 1–29. doi:10.1111/1540-5915.02289

Koh, J., & Kim, Y. G. (2004). Knowledge sharing in virtual communities: an e-business perspective. *Expert Systems with Applications, 26*, 155–166. doi:10.1016/S0957-4174(03)00116-7

Kolekofski, K. E., & Heminger, A. R. (2003). Beliefs and attitudes affecting intentions to share information in an organizational setting. *Information & Management, 40*, 521–532. doi:10.1016/S0378-7206(02)00068-X

Komiak, S. Y. X., & Benbasat, I. (2006). The effects of personalization and familiarity on trust and adoption of recommendation agents. *MIS Quarterly, 30*(4), 941–960.

Korsgaard, M. A., Schweiger, D. M., & Sapienza, H. J. (1995). Building commitment, attachment, and trust in strategic decision-making teams: The role of procedural justice. *Academy of Management Journal, 38*(1), 60–84. doi:10.2307/256728

Kotlarsky, J., & Oshri, L. (2005). Social ties, knowledge sharing and successful collaboration in globally distributed system development projects . *European Journal of Information Systems, 14*, 37–48. doi:10.1057/palgrave.ejis.3000520

Kouzes, J. M., & Posner, B. Z. (1995). *The Leadership Challenge*. San Francisco: CA: Jossey- Bass.

Kyriakidou, O. (2004). Developing a knowledge sharing culture. *Management Services, 48*(6), 22–23.

Lai, C. T. C., Liu, X., & Shaffer, M. A. (2004). Interpersonal citizenship behavior of employees in greater China: A social capital perspective, Business Research Centre Paper on Cross-Cultural Management (Vol. 2004-02,34, pp. http://net2.hkbu.edu.hk/~brc/CCMP200402.PDF)

Levin, D. Z., & Cross, R. (2004). The strength of weak ties you can trust: The mediating role of trust in effective knowledge transfer. *Management Science, 50*(11), 1477–1490. doi:10.1287/mnsc.1030.0136

Lewis, J. D., & Weigert, A. (1985). Trust as a social reality. *Social Forces, 63*(4), 967–985. doi:10.2307/2578601

Li, F. (1998). Same Kentucky Chicken, Different Taste: Cross-cultural Leadership Studies at KFC in Beijing. Unpublished Master Thesis, Blacksburg, Virginia.

Lin, H.-F., & Lee, G.-G. (2004). Perception of senior managers toward knowledge sharing behavior. *Management Decision, 42*(1), 108–125. doi:10.1108/00251740410510181

Lok, P., & Crawford, J. (2004). The effect of organisational culture and leadership style on job satisfaction and organisational commitment A cross-national comparison. *Journal of Management Development, 3*(4), 321–338. doi:10.1108/02621710410529785

Lu, H. P., & Wang, J. Y. (1997). The relationship between management styles, user participation, and system success over MIS growth stages. *Information & Management, 32*, 203–213. doi:10.1016/S0378-7206(97)00021-9

Lu, L. T., & Lee, Y. H. (2005). The effect of culture on the management style and performance of international joint ventures in China: The perspective of foreign parent firms. *International Journal of Management, 22*(3), 452–462.

Martinsons, M. G. (1991). Management philosophy and IT assimilation: the East-West divide. *Journal of Technology Management, 18*(3), 207–218.

Mayer, R. C., & Davis, J. H. (1995). An integrative model of organizational trust. *Academy of Management Review, 20*(3), 709–734. doi:10.2307/258792

McAllister, D. J. (1995). Affect- and cognition-based trust as foundations for interpersonal cooperation in organizations. *Academy of Management Journal, 38*(1), 24–59. doi:10.2307/256727

McDermott, R. (2000). Building a support structure for your communities. *Knowledge Management Review, 3*(3), 5.

McInerney, C. (2002). Knowledge management and the dynamic nature of knowledge. *Journal of the American Society for Information Science and Technology, 53*(12), 1009–1018. doi:10.1002/asi.10109

Mooradian, T., Renzl, B., & Matzler, K. (2006). Who trusts? Personality, trust and knowledge sharing. *Management Learning, 37*(4), 523–540. doi:10.1177/1350507606073424

Nahaipet, J., & Ghoshal, S. (1998). Social capital, intellectual capital, and the organizational advantage. *Academy of Management Review, 23*(2), 242–266. doi:10.2307/259373

Ng, K. Y., & Chua, R. Y. J. (2006). Do I contribute more when I trust more? Different effects of cognition- and affect-based trust. *Management and Organization Review, 2*(1), 43–66. doi:10.1111/j.1740-8784.2006.00028.x

Nugent, P. D., & Abolafia, M. Y. (2006). The creation of trust through interaction and exchange. *Group & Organization Management, 31*(6), 628–650. doi:10.1177/1059601106286968

Organ, D. W. (1988). *Organizational Citizenship Behavior: The Good Soldier Syndrome* Lexington, MA: Lexington Books.

Panteli, N., & Sockalingam, S. (2005). Trust and conflict within virtual inter-organizational alliances: a frame work for facilitating knowledge sharing. *Decision Support Systems, 39*, 599–617. doi:10.1016/j.dss.2004.03.003

Parks, C. D., & Hulbert, L. G. (1995). High and low trusters' responses to fear in a payoff matrix. *The Journal of Conflict Resolution, 39*(4), 718–730. doi:10.1177/0022002795039004006

Penley, L. E., & Hawkins, B. (1985). Studying interpersonal communication in organizations: A leadership application. *Academy of Management Journal, 28*(2), 309–326. doi:10.2307/256203

Podsakoff, P. M., MacKenzie, S. B., Paine, J. B., & Bachrach, D. G. (2000). Organizational citizenship behaviors: A critical review of the theoretical and empirical literature and suggestions for future research. *Journal of Management, 26*(3), 513–563. doi:10.1177/014920630002600307

Podsakoff, P. M., & Organ, D. W. (1986). Self-reports in organizational research: Problems and prospects. *Journal of Management, 12*(4), 531–544. doi:10.1177/014920638601200408

Politis, J. D. (2001). The relationship of various leadership styles to knowledge management. *Leadership and Organization Development Journal, 22*(8), 354–364. doi:10.1108/01437730110410071

Politis, J. D. (2003). The connection between trust and knowledge management: What are its implications for team performance. *Journal of Knowledge Management, 7*(5), 55–66. doi:10.1108/13673270310505386

Pye, L. (1985). *Asian Power and Politics: The Cultural Dimensions of Authority*. Cambridge, MA: Harvard University Press.

Reader, J. A. (1987). Motivating Chinese employees in joint ventures in the PRC: Appalachian State University, April.

Reid, F. (2003). Creating a knowledge-sharing culture among diverse business units. *Employment Relations Today, 30*(3), 43–49. doi:10.1002/ert.10097

Robbins, S. P. (1997). *Organization Behavior* (7th ed.). Prentice-Hall International.

Ryu, S., Ho, S. H., & Han, I. (2003). Knowledge sharing behavior of physicians in hospitals. *Expert Systems with Applications, 25*(1), 113–122. doi:10.1016/S0957-4174(03)00011-3

Schriesheim, C. A. (1982). The great high consideration-high initiating structure leadership myth: evidence on its generalizability. *The Journal of Social Psychology, 116*, 221–228.

Sitkin, S. B., & Roth, N. L. (1993). Explaining the limited effectiveness of legalistic "remedies" for trust/distrust. *Organization Science*, *4*(3), 367–392. doi:10.1287/orsc.4.3.367

Smith, H. A., & McKeen, J. D. (2002). *Instilling a knowledge-sharing culture* (Vol. Learning and Capabilities). Paper presented at the Proceedings of the Third European Conference on Organizational Knowledge, ALBA: Athens, Greece.

Southon, F. C. G., Todd, R. J., & Seneque, M. (2002). Knowledge management in three organizations: An exploratory study. *Journal of the American Society for Information Science and Technology*, *53*(12), 1047–1059. doi:10.1002/asi.10112

Srivastava, A., & Bartol, K. M. (2006). Empowering leadership in management teams: Effects on knowledge sharing, efficacy, and performance. *Academy of Management Journal*, *49*(6), 1239–1251.

Tan, H. H., & Chee, D. (2005). Understanding interpersonal trust in a Confucian-influenced society: An exploratory study. *International Journal of Cross Cultural Management*, *5*(2), 197–212. doi:10.1177/1470595805054493

Tezuka, S., & Niwa, K. (2004). knowledge sharing in inter-organizational intelligence: R&D-based venture alliance community cases in Japan. *International Journal of Technology Management*, *28*(7/8), 714–728. doi:10.1504/IJTM.2004.005779

Turner, J. C. (1987). *Rediscovering the Social Group: A Self-Categorization Theory*. Oxford, UK: B. Blackwell.

Uzzi, B. (1997). Social structure and competition in interfirm networks: The paradox of embeddedness. *Administrative Science Quarterly*, *42*(1), 35–67. doi:10.2307/2393808

Voelpel, S. C., & Han, Z. (2005). Managing knowledge sharing in China: The case of Siemens sharenet. *Journal of Knowledge Management*, *9*(3), 51–63. doi:10.1108/13673270510602764

Walder, A. G. (1995). China's transitional economy: Interpreting its significance. *The China Quarterly*, *144*, 963–979. doi:10.1017/S0305741000004689

Wang, J., & Guan, J. (2005). The analysis and evaluation of knowledge efficiency in research groups. *Journal of the American Society for Information Science and Technology*, *56*(11), 1217–1226. doi:10.1002/asi.20225

Weir, D., & Hutchings, K. (2005). Culture embeddedness and contextual constraints: Knowledge sharing in Chinese and Arab cultures. *Knowledge and Process Management*, *12*(2), 89–98. doi:10.1002/kpm.222

Westwood, R. (1997). Harmony and patriarchy: The cultural basis for 'paternalistic headship' among the overseas Chinese. *Organization Studies*, *18*(3), 445–480. doi:10.1177/017084069701800305

Wong, J., Wong, P. N. K., & Li, H. (2007). An investigation of leadership styles and relationship cultures of Chinese and expatriate managers in multinational construction companies in Hong Kong. *Construction Management and Economics*, *25*, 95–106. doi:10.1080/01446190600632573

Yang, K. (2005). Chinese social orientation: A social interactional approach. In Y. Yang (Ed.), *Chinese Social Psychological Review* (Vol. 1). Beijing: Social Science Academic Press (China).

Yukl, G. (1992). Theory and research on leadership in organizations. *Handbook of Industrial and Organizational Psychology*, 3, 147-198.

Zaheer, A., McEvily, B., & Perrone, V. (1998). Does trust matter? Exploring the effects on inter-organizational and interpersonal trust on performance. *Organization Science, 9*(2), 141–159. doi:10.1287/orsc.9.2.141

Zakaria, N., Amelinckx, A., & Wilemon, D. (2004). Working together apart? Building a knowledge sharing culture for global virtual teams. *Creativity and Innovation Management, 13*(1), 15–29. doi:10.1111/j.1467-8691.2004.00290.x

APPENDIX A

SCALE ITEMS AND DESCRIPTIVE STATISTICS BY CONSTRUCT (Table 5)

Table 5.

Definitions provided to survey respondents		
Colleague in this questionnaire refers to those who share the same rank as you and also share a manager with you .		
Construct	**Item**	**Loadings**
Initiating (INI)	1. He schedules the work to be done.	0.793
	2. He sets goals for the work group.	0.857
	3. He diagnoses group deficiencies.	0.875
	4. He takes remedial action to correct deficiencies.	0.898
	(Halpin, 1957) Mean=3.133 S.D.=1.173	
Consideration (CON)	1. He is friendly and approachable.	0.823
	2. He does little things to make it pleasant to be an employee.	0.869
	3. He puts suggestions made by employees into operation.	0.778
	4. He looks out for the personal welfare of employees.	0.688
	5. He treats all employees as his equal.	0.781
	(Halpin, 1957) Mean=3.461 S.D.=1.083	
Peer Reliable Role Performance (RRP)	1. My colleagues follow standards, rules and regulations when they perform their work	0.692
	2. My colleagues adequately complete assigned duties.	0.809
	3. My colleagues perform all tasks that are expected of them.	0.745
	4. My colleagues fulfill responsibilities specified in their job descriptions.	0.740
	5. My colleagues meet formal performance requirements of the job.	0.856
	6. My colleagues complete their work on time.	0.779
	(McAllister, 1995) Mean=2.741 S.D.=0.786	
Citizenship Behavior (CB)	1. My colleagues will consider the suggestions made by me.	0.833
	2. My colleagues take time to listen to my problems and worries.	0.816
	3. My colleagues willingly help me, even at some cost to personal productivity.	0.859
	4. I have taken a personal interest in my colleagues.	0.868
	5. My colleagues take into consideration my feelings.	0.853
	(McAllister, 1995) Mean=3.121 S.D.=0.930	
Interaction Frequency (FI)	1. I frequently initiate work-related interactions with my colleagues.	0.816
	2. My colleagues frequently initiate work-related interactions with me.	0.869
	3. I frequently interact with my colleagues at work.	0.870
	4. I frequently interact with my colleagues socially at work or informally.	0.765
	(McAllister, 1995) Mean=2.645 S.D.=0.772	

Affect based trust (ABT)	1. I have a sharing relationship with the members of my work team. We can all freely share our ideas.	0.709
	2. I can talk freely with my colleagues about difficulties I am having with my work.	0.730
	3. If one of the members of my colleagues was transferred to work in a different team, I would feel unhappy because I enjoy working with them all.	0.682
	4. If I share my problems with my colleagues, I know that they will respond constructively and caringly.	0.828
	5. I believe that the members of my work team have made considerable emotional investments in our working relationship.	0.783
	(McAllister, 1995) Mean=2.913 S.D.=0.820	
Cognition Based Trust (CBT)	1. My colleagues approach their work with professionalism and dedication.	0.821
	2. I believe that my colleagues are well prepared and competent to do their work.	0.865
	3. I can rely on my colleagues not to make my job more difficult by careless work.	0.823
	4. I trust and respect my colleagues.	0.847
	5. I consider my colleagues to be trustworthy.	0.879
	(McAllister, 1995) Mean=2.839 S.D.=0.9640	
Employees' Intention to Share Knowledge (ISK)	1. I will make an effort to share knowledge with my colleagues.	0.815
	2. I intend to share knowledge with my colleagues when they ask.	0.868
	3. I will share knowledge with my colleagues.	0.922
	(Ryu et al., 2003) Mean=2.20 S.D.=0.872	

APPENDIX B

ITEM LOADINGS AND CROSS-LOADINGS (Table 6)

Table 6.

Items	INI	CON	RRP	CB	FI	ABT	CBT	ISK
INI1	**0.727**	0.139	0.143	0.075	0.054	-0.059	0.235	0.151
INI2	**0.836**	0.089	0.154	0.024	0.051	0.115	0.084	0.047
INI3	**0.833**	0.305	0.025	0.009	0.115	0.138	0.022	-0.038
INI4	**0.838**	0.234	0.116	0.085	0.149	0.086	0.045	0.045
CON1	0.113	**0.749**	0.032	0.078	0.201	0.188	-0.033	0.157
CON2	0.199	**0.811**	-0.011	0.132	0.128	0.162	0.044	0.005
CON3	0.285	**0.679**	0.148	0.040	0.116	0.077	0.118	0.132
CON4	0.206	**0.668**	0.105	0.098	-0.018	-0.015	0.221	-0.031
CON5	0.121	**0.780**	0.003	0.055	0.092	0.072	0.024	0.112
RRP1	0.174	0.028	**0.627**	0.046	0.074	-0.034	0.291	0.154
RRP2	0.103	0.011	**0.802**	0.162	0.074	0.031	0.091	0.178
RRP3	0.081	-0.004	**0.720**	0.214	0.122	0.061	0.115	-0.001
RRP4	0.198	0.070	**0.523**	0.245	0.309	0.208	0.123	0.122
RRP5	0.180	0.089	**0.740**	0.158	0.227	0.156	0.124	0.185

Items	INI	CON	RRP	CB	FI	ABT	CBT	ISK
RRP6	0.051	0.181	**0.719**	0.172	0.156	0.214	0.106	0.018
CB1	0.110	0.061	0.168	**0.701**	0.289	0.120	0.157	0.161
CB2	0.178	0.078	0.248	**0.752**	0.195	0.069	0.107	-0.015
CB3	-0.021	0.133	0.222	**0.752**	0.205	0.145	0.174	0.094
CB4	0.025	0.078	0.140	**0.770**	0.201	0.225	0.253	0.028
CB5	0.027	0.114	0.102	**0.802**	0.168	0.178	0.107	0.128
FI1	0.047	0.016	0.153	0.140	**0.741**	0.017	0.217	0.325
FI2	0.108	0.103	0.136	0.215	**0.795**	0.198	0.122	0.057
FI3	0.167	0.135	0.158	0.174	**0.816**	0.155	0.043	0.107
FI4	0.073	0.235	0.112	0.296	**0.586**	0.156	0.144	0.103
ABT1	0.068	0.196	0.124	0.099	0.120	**0.630**	0.138	0.207
ABT2	0.051	0.222	0.120	0.116	0.191	**0.666**	0.145	0.092
ABT3	0.000	-0.043	0.013	0.106	0.195	**0.612**	0.097	0.322
ABT4	0.166	0.074	0.043	0.209	0.075	**0.675**	0.346	0.163
ABT5	0.126	0.079	0.132	0.176	0.081	**0.594**	0.418	0.120
CBT1	0.117	0.133	0.183	0.081	0.208	0.254	**0.726**	0.096
CBT2	0.122	0.096	0.201	0.153	0.181	0.311	**0.667**	0.249
CBT3	0.117	0.099	0.138	0.244	0.163	0.113	**0.783**	0.072
CBT4	0.171	0.078	0.129	0.159	0.087	0.312	**0.637**	0.361
CBT5	0.096	0.019	0.150	0.214	0.122	0.264	**0.738**	0.228
ISK1	0.068	0.150	0.053	0.077	0.084	0.148	0.199	**0.719**
ISK2	0.064	0.057	0.103	0.031	0.140	0.117	0.127	**0.846**
ISK3	0.011	0.027	0.119	0.055	0.137	0.210	0.068	**0.884**

Chapter 10

Exploring Government Role in Promoting IT Advancement in China:
An Empirical Study on Shanghai Firms' IT Usage[1]

Lili Cui
Shanghai University of Finance & Economics, China

Cheng Zhang
Fudan University, China

ABSTRACT

By analyzing the survey data from 1211 firms across 14 industries and across various ownerships in Shanghai, the study examines factors that influence information technology (IT) usage in Chinese firms applying a technology–organization-environment framework and institutional theory. This study provides an in-depth investigation into the government's role in promoting Chinese firms' IT advancement. The finding suggests distinct paths where government actions affect firms' IT adoption and usage. Although government cannot directly influence firms' IT adoption, it does so by influencing firms' IT infrastructure construction and management respectively. In other words, firms' IT infrastructure development and IT management decision plays as a mediator between different government actions and firms' IT adoption. Furthermore, firms adapt to governmental impact distinguishingly. The findings suggest that e-government approaches and government promotion policies have significant impact on IT usage in manufacturing firms, in local firms and in national-background firms. The study also provides valuable implications to government administrators in China, particularly to those in the modern cities like Shanghai.

INTRODUCTION

With the development of information technology (IT), more and more Chinese firms have invested heavily in IT to catch up with the "new information society paradigm" emerged in the 1990s. However, as a developing country, China is still in the initial period of informatization. Compared with firms in developed countries, Chinese firms' information

DOI: 10.4018/978-1-60566-920-5.ch010

technology usage is far from mature and is uneven across different types and scales of enterprises. A report from Chinalabs (ChinaLabs, 2004) showed that, out of 1000 surveyed firms, only 3.7% of them achieved mature IT usage. A survey hold by Chinese National Informatization Evaluation Center(NIEC, 2008) also shows that top 500 informatization[2] enterprises in China are mostly large manufacturing enterprises, act as the backbone of China's national economy with revenue above 890 billion RMB. Large scale enterprises tend to have better IT usage level. A report from CMP consulting (CMP, 2005) showed that 17.3% of surveyed larger scale enterprises achieved integrated IT application; the same figure for SMEs is only 3.4%. More than half of the surveyed large scale enterprises applied IT into core business, while only 29.3% of the SMEs use IT to support their core business.

In information system research field, factors that affect IT adoption, usage and valuation have long constituted an active research area (Straub, Hoffman, Weber, & Steinfield., 2002). Many researchers and practitioners have sought theoretical models and empirical evidence to explain these factors and to give suggestions regarding firms' IT decision. Most of the research to date has focused on developed countries. However, since developing countries have different markets, legal systems and cultural factors, models from developed countries may not be adaptable to developing countries' environment (Shenkar & Glinow, 1994) and such factors may have different effects. It seems clear that government and culture factors have a greater impact on firms' IT usage in developing countries than in developed countries (Thatcher & Foster, 2003). Research also points out that government regulation plays a more important role in Chinese firms' decision and IT usage (Xu, Zhu, & Gibbs, 2004).

To better understand the factors influence IT adoption and particularly the role government play in promoting IT usage in Chinese firms, we developed a research model based on Technology-Organization-Environment (TOE) framework (Tornatzky & Fleischer, 1990) and focused more on government-related factors. With survey data from 1211 firms across 14 industrial fields, the study provides insightful managerial implications to Chinese firms and valuable practical suggestions to Chinese government by exploring the following research issues: how technological, organizational and environmental factors are important for firms to deploy IT, and whether different industry types, investment property types and ownership types influence firms' IT adoption in Chinese cities like Shanghai.

Focusing on measuring Shanghai's government initiatives can largely reduce the potential interference of different influences on policy execution by various local governments and enhance our observation of the government's role. To make the results generalizable, firms either with headquarter or branches registered in Shanghai were included in the sample.

LITERATURE REVIEW

In management science and information system literature, many studies have explored the factors that drive the business value of IT. The research relevant to this study can be categorized into two streams. One is Technology-Organization-Environment framework (Tornatzky & Fleischer, 1990), which is used to identify technological, organizational and environmental factors that affect IT diffusion in organizations. Here, we concentrate more on external institutional elements as a unique environmental factor. The second research stream is institutional theory perspective, which is used to explore effects of path dependency, governmental intervention, and historical context on the evolution of organizational rules (Zucker, 1987). These streams provide evidence of environment constructs, especially government related factors in the model.

Technology-Organization-Environment Framework (TOE)

Technology-organization-environment (TOE) framework (Tornatzky & Fleischer, 1990) was developed to study the adoption of general technological innovations in organizations. The framework figures three aspects that influence the process of technology diffusion in organizations: technological context, organizational context and environmental context. Technological context refers to technologies that are relevant to firms. Organizational context generally refers to organizational characteristics, such as size, scope and other resources available within a firm. Environmental context is the macro-circumstances in which a firm conducts its business. Environmental factors include industry, competitors, government relations etc. TOE framework is suitable to identify factors shaping innovation adoption (Xu et al., 2004) and provides a reliable theoretical basis for this study.

The impact of technology factors on information system (IS) adoption and business values may be enhanced in the Chinese context; because the overall IT usage in Chinese firms is immature (ChinaLabs, 2004), better IT resources are comparatively rare and probably exert greater influence on firms' IT adoption. A report from National Informatization Evaluation Center (NIEC, 2005) also showed that high IT adoption has successfully helped some large firms to gain competitive advantage and to support the firms' core value realization.

Organizational and management factors also play an important role in firms' IT usage. Research shows that SMEs are more likely to focus on the alignment between IT and business strategy(Levy & Powell, 2003; Tsao, Lin, & Lin, 2004), but tend to lack management support (such as technical consultation), IT management knowledge and business transformation guideline (Yeung, Shim, & Lai, 2003). In China, those obstacles seem to be common. Suffering from an immature IT service market and poor IT management knowledge, most Chinese enterprises have low performance in IT usage and value creation (NIEC, 2004). Therefore, effective IT management has become one of the most critical and urgent problems faced by Chinese enterprises.

External environmental factors, such as trading partners, competitors, government and socio-political conditions, may play an important role in firms' IS/IT adoption and business value generation (Melville, Kraemer, & Gurbaxani, 2004). Due to an immature market, different culture and other reasons, China has environmental characteristics distinct from Western industrial countries (Boisot & Child, 1999). For example, studies find that culture and philosophy have impacts on firms' IT adoption (Davison, 2002; Martinsons & Westwood, 1997). Some researchers (Tan & Ouyang, 2004) examined the diffusion of e-commerce in China and found that the current e-commerce barriers include legal, cultural and governmental issues. Others (Xu et al., 2004) further confirmed that government regulation plays a more important role in China than in the US. As stated above, e-government initiatives and activities, differing from the traditional incentive policies such as legislation and promotion, became a new way through which government could potentially participate in e-business affairs and affect IT diffusion. Government influence can be particularly significant in a government-directed economy or where the private sector is not yet fully developed (Blakeley & Matsuura, 2004).

Overall, the TOE framework provides a theoretical basis for understanding factors that affect firms' IS/IT adoption. In this study, IT infrastructure, IT management and government factors are all investigated.

Institutional Theory

From institutional perspective, organizations can be influenced by varied pressures arising from either external environment or internal organizational factors. The theory emphasizes the importance of institutional environments in shaping organizational structure and actions (W. R. Scott, 1995; W. R. Scott, 2001). Firms become more similar due to isomorphic pressures and pressures for legitimacy by three important legitimization processes: coercive, imitative and normative (DiMaggio & Powell, 1983).

The institutional factors provide a useful research view on IT adoption study. Institutional theory explains IT adoption in terms of pressures exerted on the organization to adopt, pressures that come variously from competitors, trading partners, customers and government. Recent studies have taken an institutional approach to E-commerce diffusion (J. L. Gibbs & Kraemer, 2004; Khalifa & Davison, 2006 ; Teo, Wei, & Benbasat, 2003), which reveals the importance of external pressures, government promotion and legislation in e-commerce adoption and use. Regulatory agencies, such as government and industrial consortium, may create incentives or barriers to adoption and use. On the other hand, firms tend to learn and copy successful IT practices from industry leaders and accept normalized best practice on IT adoption in a fast-changing environment.

From institutional view, firms with strong ties to the public sector are likely to adopt innovations required or supported by government policy (Hinings & Greenwood, 1987; Zucker, 1987). In 2008, the Chinese government has determined "integration of informatization and industrialization" in further promoting its national policy of "informatization-driven industrialization". The Ministry of Information Industry (MII) of China indicates that in future, China will persist in promoting national enterprise informatization plan, led by large scaled backbone enterprises. Given different investment property and ownership, firms' IT adoption may be influenced, differently by government policies and actions. Studies also found that firms' ownership strongly influences their IT implementation, e.g. (Reimers, 2002), and government regulation plays a more important role in Chinese firms' IT decisions and usage than in U.S. (Xu et al., 2004). These environmental factors may play a crucial role on firms' IT adoption in China.

THE RESEARCH MODEL AND HYPOTHESES

With theoretical support by TOE and institutional theory, we developed a research model shown in Figure 1. Our framework is inspired by TOE, while environment factors here are examined by institutional factors of government – e-government, promotion and regulation. Three major factors, i.e. IT infrastructure, IT management, and government factor (Melville et al., 2004; Tan & Ouyang, 2004; Wade & Hulland, 2004; Xu et al., 2004), are proposed in the model, to analyze their impact on IT usage. We also consider the possible relationships between different government factor, firms' IT factors and organizational factors and explore how different government policies may influence firms' IT infrastructure and management decisions, respectively. Furthermore, we sought to determine whether government impacts are diverse across multiple industries, investment properties, and ownerships.

IT infrastructure is a collection of physical technology resources, including shared technology and technology services across the organization (Melville et al., 2004), which facilitate firms' connectivity and operations. Prior research showed that IT infrastructure investment accounted for over 58 percent of firms' IT budget and that percentage is growing at a rate of 11 percent per year (BroadBent & Weill, 1997). The report published by China International Statistical Information Center showed that China's annual informatization level increases at a 30.5% rate between 1999 and 2001, while its IT infrastructure level grew at a rate of 28% (ISIC, 2004). Depending on its use, IT infrastructure can be an important source to influence firms' business value (Kumar, 2004).

Figure 1. The research model

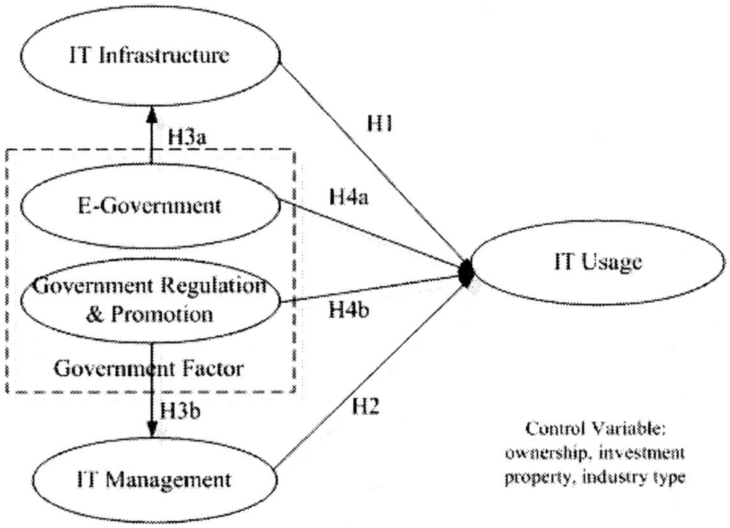

Technology, hardware and software, like computers, networks, database, communication platforms and software, form the core of firms' IT infrastructure (Duncan, 1995). Firms can develop unique capabilities and business value by using their IT infrastructure (Zhu, 2004). Research shows that IT factors, including infrastructure and expertise, play a significant role in IT usage (Zhu, Kraemer, & Xu, 2002). Therefore we propose:

H1: *The greater developed a firm's IT infrastructure, the greater the firm's IT usage.*

Another type of factor is IT management capability (ITMC) in organizations, which denotes firms' technical and managerial knowledge (Byrd & Turner, 2000; Melville et al., 2004) of IT. Compared with physical IT infrastructure, IT management is a set of 'soft' abilities that help firms to deploy IT in an effective manner (Lee, Trauth, & Farwell, 1995; Swanson, 1994). In order to utilize IT physical assets economically, firms need to pursue a fit between IT functionalities and business strategies (Grabowski & Lee, 1993; McLaren & Head, 2004) and manage IT infrastructures to improve organization performance (Markus & Soh, 1993). Therefore we propose:

H2: *The greater a firm's IT management capability, the greater the firm's IT usage*

Considering relatively immature markets and information asymmetry in China, government regulations or promotion policies are likely to have broader impact on China's local firms' behaviours, including their IT decision, management and usage. The government influence is more direct and visible than other environment factors, such as culture or philosophy. Furthermore, Chinese firms are accustoming to adapting government policies, given the history of frequent government interventions in China. Therefore, government regulation affects firms' IT configuration and management.

In detail, governments have various ways to regulate and promote firms' IT usage and further E-commerce by providing funding to companies that are adopting IT, encouraging online tax payment and e-procurement systems, issuing appropriate laws to influence IT usage and security, establishing IT software standards, promoting IT evaluation framework and many other ways. Previous IS research, such as (Tan & Ouyang, 2004; Xu et al., 2004), addresses the importance of government regulation shows that the IT adoption process enabled by governmental policies is still unclear, considering so many different regulatory policies still exist.

According to prior research (Anderson, Bjørn-Anderson, & Dedrick, 2003; Blakeley & Matsuura, 2004), governance activities in IT diffusion can have different influences. One category of government promotion activities are the e-government initiatives to directly influence firms' IT configuration and thus the usage (GDRP), such as transactions with firms in e-government systems, online tax payment and so on. In order to be consistent with these e-government activities, firms are coerced to establish accordant IT infrastructure and IT configuration. In this way, e-government will affect firms' IT plans, especially their IT infrastructure. The other category deals with their regulations and promotion policies (GIRP). These are intended to improve firms' IT related knowledge and to provide a standardized environment, by establishing IT application standards, evaluation frameworks, regulation standards and so on. The government regulations or promotion policies cannot influence firms' IT decision directly, but may shorten firms' learning curve, reduce information asymmetry and improve and accelerate the IT knowledge-diffusion process in the whole market. Firms are motivated to imitate other organizations' IT practice and normalize their IT usage behaviour. Therefore, these regulations or policies can affect firms' IT knowledge and, consequently, their IT management quality. Accordingly, we propose:

H3: *Government IT promotion policies have positive impact on firms' IT infrastructure and IT management*

H3a: *E-government initiatives positively affect firms' IT infrastructure construction*

H3b: *Government regulation and IT promotion policies help firms improve their IT management*

Prior research shows that non-technical environmental factors affect innovation adoption (Kraemer, Gibbs, & Dedrick, 2002; Tornatzky & Fleischer, 1990). While firms in e-commerce survey studies frequently cite environment issues like security, credibility of the system and legal matter as their major concerns, they also point out that incentives provided by the government are key drivers for their new IT and e-Commerce usage (Tan & Ouyang, 2004; Xu et al., 2004). The results denote that government regulation (GRDP) and IT-related promotion policies can affect firms' IT configuration and improve their IT usage. Thus, we propose:

H4: *Government IT-related policies positively affect firms' IT usage*

H4a: *E-Government initiatives help firms' IT usage*

H4b: *Government regulation and IT promotion policies help firms improve their IT usage*

Firms with strong ties to public sector are likely to adopt IT innovations supported by government policy (Hinings & Greenwood, 1987; Zucker, 1987) and to follow up government IT-usage actions. The extent of environmental effect can be defined by firms' ownership, investment property and industry type. Firms with national background are easier to be influenced by government action and regulation. Government may influence firms' IT adoption in diverse ways. With e-government implementation, firms are coercively to adopt their technology infrastructure to align with government's system. With government promotion and regulation on IT standard and practices, firms can imitate other organizations' IT practices and normalize their IT usage behaviour. In this study, we will divide the full sample into sub-sample sets according to firm type and run post-hoc analysis to further explore government's role in firms' IT adoption. In detail, three types of firms by ownership classification: national-owned, private-owned and semi-national (private)-owned, as well as three types of firms by investment property classification: local-invested, joint-invested and foreign-invested. The types indicate different control power by government.

Industry structure is also thought to be a significant factor that cause diversity in IT adoption (J. Gibbs, Kraemer, & Dedrick, 2003). Firms belong to the same industry may have high possibility to imitate, and finally tend to have similar behaviour. On the other hand, some industries are found to be leaders in IT usage, while others lag behind. In this study, we will consider the industry diversity in our data analysis by dividing the sample pool into two sub-sample pools: manufacturing and service industry. The manufacturing industry is one of the most representative industries in China. According to the data from the China Statistic Bureau, in 2003, the added value of the manufacturing industry reached $520 billion US dollars, which accounted for 36.8% of China's GDP. In Shanghai, the figure has accounted for almost half of the city's GDP in recent years. Comparing with manufacturing, service industry receives less attention from the government.

METHODOLOGY

Data and Method

A questionnaire survey method was adopted for the study. The sample frame was enterprises in Shanghai from fourteen industries: machinery manufacturing, transportation services, retail business/wholesale trade, food & beverage and tourism services, food processing, textile, oil and coking processing, pharmaceutical manufacturing, chemical fiber/rubber/plastic products, metal smelt and mangle processing, transport manufacturing, electronic and telecommunication equipment manufacturing, sporting, cultural and educational goods manufacturing, and real estate.

A random sampling process was followed in the selection of the sample enterprises from the list of all enterprises in the 14 vertical industries. The list was provided by the Statistics Bureau of the Shanghai Municipal Government. The sample size is 3735 out from 14234 listed firms. A pre-screening process via telephone was followed to determine the suitability of the representative interviewee for the selected enterprise to answer the survey questionnaire. The key determining factor for the suitability of the representative interviewee in this case was his/her position in the hierarchy of the enterprise that would enable him/her to answer the questionnaire readily and accurately. Overall, qualified interviewees were firms' senior executives who oversaw the company's use of information technology or acted as the head of their IT department. Finally, 1912 firms accepted the survey.

In next 8 calendar weeks, a total of 1,740 questionnaires returned. Among them, 196 firms were lack of PC or lack of use of computers to complete their work, 329 firms did not indicate their ownership and/or investment type information, and 4 firms did not complete the questionnaires correctly. As a result, 1,211 of them were used for this study. Characteristics of the sample are shown in Table 1. Distribution of firms' annual revenue and size shows a suitable portion of small, medium and large firms. The sample also generally covers various ownerships, i.e. national-owned, semi-national owned and private-owed. The consulting firm also assessed the internal processes of setting up the survey and found it satisfactory.

We used the partial least squares (PLS) approach (Haenlein & Kaplan, 2004; Lohmoller, 1989), a structural equation modeling (SEM) technique, to examine the model and hypotheses. PLS assesses the relationships between the research constructs, and between the constructs themselves and their measurement items, so that the error variance is reduced (Ranganathan, Dhaliwal, & Teo, 2004). Furthermore, PLS involves no assumptions about

Table 1. Sample characteristics (N=1211)

Industry	%	Annual Revenue (million)	%
Machinery manufacturing	24	< 1	3
Transportation services	7	1-5	11
Retail business/wholesale trade	7	5-10	9
Food & beverage and tourism services	5	10-50	25
Food processing	4	50-100	9
Textile	8	100-500	13
Oil and coking processing	1	>500	30
Pharmaceutical manufacturing	12	Firm Size (by # of Employees)	%
Chemical fiber / rubber / plastic products	7	<10	3
Metal smelt and mangle processing	2	10-50	23
Transport manufacturing	8	50-100	19
Electronic & telecommunication equipment manufacturing	5	100-500	39
Sporting, cultural & educational goods manufacturing	4	500-1000	9
Real estate	7	1000-5000	5
Total	100	>5000	1

the population or scale of measurement (Fornell & Bookstein, 1982), which means PLS can work on nominal, ordinal, and interval scaled data without distributional assumptions (Haenlein & Kaplan, 2004). Since the questionnaire contained mixed nominal, ordinal and ratio scales, PLS was an appropriate application to test the model. Furthermore, the sample size requirement of PLS is either 10 times the largest measurement number within the same construct or 10 times the largest construct number affecting the same construct (Chin & Newsted, 1999). Our sample size in the study is far greater than the minimum needed to satisfy the criteria. The software used to apply PLS to the model was PLS-Graph (Chin, 2001).

Measures and Validity

Items were either measured by ratio scale, such as IT infrastructure, ordinal scale, such as importance of IT usage, or nominal scale, such as specific promotion policy. The content validity of the measures was examined by pre-tests with professionals and a few IT managers from firms.

Three items, i.e. firms' IT hardware, software, and network status, were used to measure IT infrastructure, which were also used in prior works (Byrd & Turner, 2000; Duncan, 1995). To measure IT management factor, we studied the practice of IT-related planning, evaluation and management activities in firms (Byrd & Turner, 2000).

To measure the government environment, the questions about how government actions, including online procurement requirement, incentives, law and legal protection, would affect firms' IT adoption were adapted from prior research (Tan & Ouyang, 2004; Xu et al., 2004). Other new items, including funding, e-government service, establishing application standards and establishing evaluation framework were added after careful discussion among professionals and were validated in the pre-test. Among these, adopting web-based online e-government services are categorized as e-government, and others are attributed to government regulations and promotion policies.

Finally, IT usage included measures on firms' computer usage and application usage. IT value was measured by firms' IT adoption extent (Sam-

Table 2. Reliability, average variance extracted of Construct and its measures' loading ($p<0.01$)

Construct and Items	Loading
IT Infrastructure (Composite Reliability = 0.79, AVE = 0.57)	
Number of IT hardware (HS, ratio scale)	0.56
Networked status (NS, ordinal scale)	0.84
Number of IT software (SS, ratio scale)	0.84
IT Management (Composite Reliability = 0.83, AVE = 0.62)	
Extent of IT related management systems and policies (MSP, ordinal scale)	0.83
The practice of IT planning (PP, ordinal scale)	0.82
The practice of evaluation of IT investment or competence of using IT (PEI, ordinal scale)	0.70
Government Regulation and Promotion (Composite Reliability = 0.84, AVE = 0.58)	
Providing funding to companies adopting informatization (PF, nominal scale)	0.75
Establishing enterprise application software standards (ASS, nominal scale)	0.85
Establishing evaluation framework for the level of enterprise informatization (IES, nominal scale)	0.74
Promoting large retail chains and its downstream enterprises in adopting web-based e-procurement (PEP, nominal scale)	0.68
E-Government (Composite Reliability = 0.84, AVE = 0.73)	
Adopting web-based online reporting of taxes, annual inspection and etc. (AOR, nominal scale)	0.82
Adopting web-based e-procurement for government procurement activities (AEP, nominal scale)	0.89
IT Usage (Composite Reliability = 0.71, AVE = 0.55)	
PC usage status in workplace (PCUW, ordinal scale)	0.65
Extent of application systems usage in workplace (AUW, ordinal scale)	0.82

bamurthy & Zmud, 1994) and its importance to firms' competitive advantage (Melville et al., 2004; Wade & Hulland, 2004). Two indicators for a construct are the minimum requirement for structural equation mode. Since non-significant results probably caused by fewer indicators will be amended by using a large sample size (this study uses 1211 samples) or more reliable indicators (i.e., loadings higher than 0.70) (Chin, Marcolin, & Newsted, 2003), two indicators here is safe without losing statistic significance. The details of the questionnaire can be found in the appendix.

To validate the instruments, we examined internal consistency, convergent validity, and discriminant validity. Internal consistency was examined using composite reliability. In PLS, composite reliability relies on actual loadings to compute the factor scores and is a better indicator of internal consistency than Cronbach's alpha (Ranganathan et al., 2004). As shown in Table 2, the composite reliability values for the constructs in the model were all above the suggested threshold of 0.7 (Chin, 1998; Straub, 1989) and thus supported the reliability of the measures.

Two tests were used for convergent validity. The first was to examine item reliability by their factor loading on the construct. As shown in Table 2, all items had a loading above the suggested of 0.55 by Falk and Miller (Falk & Miller, 1992). The second test was to examine average variance extracted (AVE) of the construct. In the study, the AVE values for all the constructs were above the limit of 0.50 advised by Fornell and Larcker (Fornell & Larcker, 1981). Furthermore, all estimated standard loadings were significant at the 0.01 level ($p<0.01$), suggesting good convergent validity. In summary, the convergent validity was supported.

Table 3. Constructs' Inter-correlations (The bolded numbers in the diagonal row are square roots of the average variance extracted.)

	ITIF	ITUS	GIRP	GDRP	ITMC
IT Infrastructure (ITIF)	0.753				
IT Usage (ITUS)	0.560	0.742			
Government Regulation & Policy (GIRP)	0.254	0.195	0.760		
e-Government Action (GDRP)	0.189	0.172	0.651	0.854	
IT Management (ITMC)	0.644	0.450	0.246	0.166	0.788

The discriminant validity was examined at both the item and construct level. At item level, no item should load higher on another construct than it does on the one it is intended to measure (Barclay, Higgins, & Thompson, 1995). In every case of testing, the covariance between the item and its outer construct was lower than the item's loading on the construct it was intended to measure. At the construct level, average variance extracted for each construct should be greater than the squared correlation between constructs (Fornell & Larcker, 1981). Table 3 presents the construct inter-correlations. In every case, the squared root of AVE of each construct was higher than correlation coefficient between two constructs.

DATA ANALYSIS

Full Sample Analysis

All hypothesized paths, except the link between government factors and IT usage, were found significant ($p<0.01$), as shown in Table 4. The path coefficient from infrastructure to usage is 0.453, and from IT management to usage is 0.147, which suggests significant impacts of IT infrastructure and management issues on appropriate IT usage in firms. Furthermore, the paths from e-government to the infrastructure and from government regulation & promotion to IT management are also positively significant. The path coefficients are 0.189 and 0.246, respectively. The results suggest a clear influence of governmental effect on firms' IT configuration and management. However, the impact of government factors on firms' IT usage is not significant. This result suggests that government affect firms' IT usage in an indirect manner. The mediate factors are firms' IT infrastructure and IT management.

The result of the structural model is shown in Figure 2. The important dependent construct, i.e. IT usage, have R^2 of 0.331, suggesting a reasonable explanation of data variation in TOE framework. In summary, H1, H2, H3ab are supported, while H4a, H4b are not supported.

To verify the mediate effect of IT management and IT infrastructure on government factors and IT usage, we remove the paths between government factors and IT infrastructure and IT management and re-run the model. Result shows that the paths from government factors to IT usage are not significant, while other paths are still significant. The test demonstrates that government factors affect firms' IT usage indirectly, with IT infrastructure and IT management as mediators.

Sub-Sample Analysis

Industry Difference Analysis

To test for industry differences of the model, we split the full sample set into two sub-samples: one including 988 samples from the manufacturing industry (MI) and 223 samples from the service industry (SI). According to China's na-

*Table 4. Hypotheses and model result (*** $p<0.01$)*

Hypothesis	Path coefficients
IT Infrastructure -> IT Usage	0.453 ***
IT Management -> IT Usage	0.147***
E-Government -> IT Infrastructure	0.189***
Government Regulation & Promotion -> IT Management	0.246***
E-Government -> IT Usage	0.058 (n.s.)
Government Regulation -> IT Usage	0.006 (n.s.)

tional standard of statistics, the service industry includes retail business/whole sale trade, food, beverage and tourism services and real estate. The remaining industries belong to the manufacturing industry. After examining the internal consistency, convergent validity, and discriminant validity of the model with each sub sample set, we then ran PLS analysis.

As shown in Table 5, the path coefficient from infrastructure to usage and from management to usage, respectively, is of the same significance as those in the full-data mode. The result suggests that the model applies across industries. However, the effect of government on firms' IT infrastructure and IT management is only significant in manufacturing industry, suggesting a distinct government impact on firms' IT decision from different industries. Therefore, the process of IT adoption proves to be general across industries, while government's actions and policies influence only the manufacturing industry significantly.

Investment Property and Ownership Difference Analysis

To further explore whether different types of firms have different IT adoption behaviour, we divided firms into several groups according to their investment property and ownership types, as shown in Table 6. With respect to investment property, firms were divided into three groups: local-invested, joint-invested and foreign-invested. In terms of

Figure 2. PLS Structural Model

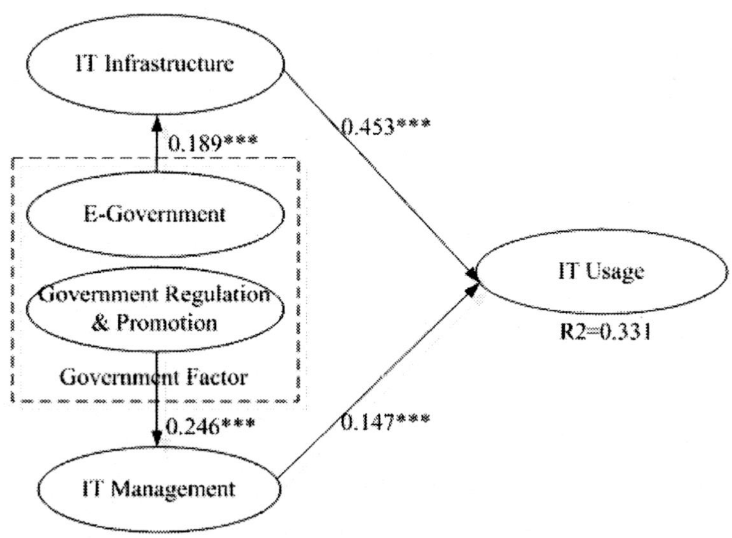

Table 5. Hypotheses and model result ($p<0.01$) with data from manufacturing industry and service industry. MI: data from manufacturing industry; SI: data from service industry

Hypothesis	Path coefficients of MI / SI
IT Infrastructure -> IT Usage	0.467 / 0.355
IT Management -> IT Usage	0.153 / 0.105
E-Government -> IT Infrastructure	0.199 / n.s.
Government Regulation & Promotion -> IT Management	0.242 / n.s.
E-Government -> IT Usage	n.s. / n.s.
Government Regulation -> IT Usage	n.s. / n.s.

ownership, firms were divided into three groups: state-owned, private-owned and semi-national (private)-owned.

Table 7 shows the model result of different investment property firms. The impacts of technological and organizational factors on firms' IT adoption are significant. However, the government influence on firms' IT infrastructure and IT management is only significant in local firms, suggesting a distinct government impact on firms' IT decision from different investment property. Furthermore, IT management, compared with IT infrastructure, plays a more important role in foreign-invested firms than that in local and joint-invested firms, which may suggest different focus on IT strategy among local, joint and foreign firms. Therefore, government's actions and policies influence local firms' IT adoption only.

Table 8 shows the model result of different ownership firms. The impacts of technological and organizational factors on firms' IT adoption are significant across firms' ownership. However, the government influence on firms' IT infrastructure and IT management is not significant in private firms, suggesting a distinct government impact on firms of different ownership. Therefore, government's actions and policies influence national-background firms significantly.

DISCUSSION AND CONCLUSION

Compared to developed countries, developing countries tend to have more government actions in promoting technology advancement. To study the government role in firms' IT adoption and usage in China's strong governmental impact context, we developed a research model and examined the model with empirical data from fourteen selected vertical industries in Shanghai. The empirical analysis reveals several major findings.

- **Finding 1:** Government actions affect firms' IT adoption via different paths. Firms' IT infrastructure development and IT management decisions act as mediators

Table 6. Sample characteristics on investment property and ownership types (N=1211)

Investment Property	# of firm	%	Ownership	# of firm	%
Local-invested	793	65	National-owned	333	28
Joint-invested	289	24	Semi-national-owned	404	33
Foreign-invested	129	11	Private-owned	474	39
Total	1211	100	Total	1211	100

Table 7. Hypotheses and model result (p<0.01) with data from local-, joint- and foreign- invested firms. L: data from local firms; J: data from joint-invested firms; F: data from foreign-invested firms.

Hypothesis	Path Coefficients of L / J / F
IT Infrastructure -> IT Usage	0.451 / 0.479 / 0.298
IT Management -> IT Usage	0.147 / 0.153 / 0.325
E-Government -> IT Infrastructure	0.096 / n.s. / n.s.
Government Regulation & Promotion -> IT Management	0.132 / n.s. / n.s.
E-Government -> IT Usage	n.s. / n.s. / n.s.
Government Regulation -> IT Usage	n.s. / n.s. / n.s.

between different government actions and firms' IT adoption

China, with its booming economy and large population, has been gaining increasing interest from both the business world and the academy. Considering the relatively immature markets, not fully evolved economy structure (Shih, Kraemer, & Dedrick, 2008), information asymmetry and relatively strong tradition of subservience to government authority in China, government actions may have broad impacts on local firms. Although prior research often concluded that government regulation, as an important environmental factor, would significantly influence firms' operation and decisions, exactly how government factors work is not as clear and few empirically examined the role of government in driving the IT adoption in Chinese firms.

In this study, government actions are initially classified into two categories: e-government approach and regulation approach. The data suggests that different government actions promote business IT advancement by affecting firms' IT adoption via different ways. Although government cannot directly push firms to adopt IT, it does so by influencing firms' IT infrastructure construction and management respectively. Further examination of mediating effects proves that IT infrastructure and management are mediators between government factors and IT usage. In other words, firms' IT infrastructure development and IT management decisions act as a mediator between different government actions and firms' IT adoption.

By exploring the government intervention power on firms' IT infrastructure construction and IT application usage, we find that e-government

Table 8. Hypotheses and model result (p<0.01) with data from national-, semi-national (private) - and private-owned firms. N: data from national-owned firms; S: data from semi-national (private)-owned firms; P: data from private-owned firms.

Hypothesis	Path coefficients of N / S / P
IT Infrastructure -> IT Usage	0.412 / 0.498 / 0.454
IT Management -> IT Usage	0.159 / 0.123 / 0.194
E-Government -> IT Infrastructure	0.091 / 0.150 / n.s.
Government Regulation & Promotion -> IT Management	0.108 / 0.106 / n.s.
E-Government -> IT Usage	n.s. / n.s. / n.s.
Government Regulation -> IT Usage	n.s. / n.s. / n.s.

can affect firms' IT adoption by affecting their IT infrastructure construction. The finding seems reasonable. For example, when adopting online tax-payment systems, firms have to configure proper hardware, network connections and software to pay taxes online. Similarly, if firms want to evolve into government e-procedure, they have to be accordant with the e-government systems. Since government regulation and promotion policies can improve firms' IT-related knowledge, the promotion policies interactively act on firm's IT management.

The results also suggest that government's regulation and promotion policies affect firms' IT adoption by influencing their IT management decision. The finding seems reasonable and practical. Because IT adoption is emergent as a technological innovation for most Chinese firms in recent years, firms lack knowledge and experience on how to adopt IT to support their management and business practices. Without theoretical advancement or empirical examination in the context of China, firms cannot receive useful suggestions from the academy either. Given these reasons, government actions (such as establishing case studies and IT adoption evaluation framework, promoting IT learning and firms' IT practice, and adopting web-based tax reporting, inspection and government e-procurement transaction) give firms a great opportunity to learn and act. For example, case studies and IT research can help firms know more about IT, providing an IT adoption evaluation framework that can help firms clarify their direction of IT adoption, while promoting IT practices and e-government systems can directly motivate firms to initialize their IT adoption process.

However, since China is gradually transforming to a market economy, and the economy structure is keeping evolving, the government's impact on firms is decreasing. Although the government's promotion gives firms useful information to configure IT infrastructure and set up management rules, firms are likely to determine their own usage of IT according to their specific conditions and purposes, rather than following exactly what the government has provided. Also because IT usage is a complex process of fitting IT asset with business operations and strategies, government promotion policies cannot influence manufacturing firms' IT usage directly, but do so indirectly by affecting firms' IT infrastructure and management. The observation will help the government assess its IT policies. For example, when considering new regulations, the government may find it more effective to help firms improve their IT management knowledge, rather than to intervene on their IT usage or direct invest.

- **Finding 2:** Firms adapt to governmental impact in distinct ways. Government impacts on firms' IT adoption are most obvious in the manufacturing industry and are different among firms of different investment property and ownership types

The manufacturing industry is one of the most vital industries in China. With fast globalization and industrialization, China is playing an important role in the global production network (Ernst, 2003), and facing more pressure from global competition. Since China has determined the "informatization-driven industrialization" as its national development strategy, the government put more attention on manufacturing firms' IT usage than on service firms. Comparing the manufacturing industry with the service industry provides clear evidence of how local government can influence firms' IT usage.

Firms' investment property types and ownership types indicate different degrees of control by government and probably different IT usage & management style in firms. From the empirical data, it seems clear that government policies show differing impacts on local-, joint- and foreign-invested firms. It is clear that both e-government approaches and promotion policies play a significant role on local firms' IT adoption. In other word, local firms' IT usage is more influenced by government than in the case of firms with foreign investment. Compared to firms with foreign investment, local firms usually have less experience with how western firms operate and mature way of using IT. As a result, local firms are willing to receive support from government when making IT-related decisions. Besides, government influence on local firms is historically strong in a government-directed economy. As market economics in China becomes mature, government influence is weakening, but the empirical data in the study may still suggest a stronger influence on local firms, compared with foreign-invested firms. The result also suggests that government policies and actions in China are critically important factors influencing firms' IT usage.

Government policies show distinct impact on national-, semi-national and private firms. It is clear that firms with a national background are more significantly influenced by government policies. The reason is straightforward: national firms are more used to following government policies than other ownership type firms. On the other hand, national firms constitute the major focus of government regulation in China. Government usually targets national firms when making decisions and policy. Therefore, it is not surprising to see a more significant role of government in such firms' operation and management activities in China.

Overall, e-government approaches and government promotion policies have shown a significant impact on manufacturing firms, on local firms and on national-background firms. The result suggests that environment factors, such as government policies, may have varying impact on different types of firms.

With careful theoretical development and large empirical data examination, this paper contributes to China's research and practice. The study investigates government's effects on firms' IT adoption and use. Although prior research has argued the importance of governmental factors in a developing country, few used empirical data to verify this claim. The result of this study shows that government actions have significant and positive impacts on firms' IT infrastructure construction and management, but does not directly influence their IT usage and performance improvement. Furthermore, different government actions affect firms' IT adoption through different ways. E-government approaches tend to help firms' IT infrastructure construction, while government promotion policies have more effects on firms' IT management affairs. Both actions have strong impact on manufacturing firms, on local firms and on national-background firms. The result helps researchers extend their knowledge on the IT diffusion model, and shed new light on the effect of e-government in improving IT diffusion. Also, the result will give important hint for government administrators in promoting firms' IT advancement in the future.

In the study, the sample firms' location is limited in Shanghai. In the way, we may largely reduce the possible underlying interference of different policy executions by different local governments and focus on exploring governmental impact on firms and industries. The firms with headquarter or branches registered in Shanghai were included to promise the data generality. Furthermore, the model is useful to understand the developed cities and provinces in China with the same level of informatization and industrialization as Shanghai has, such as Beijing, Tianjin, Guandong, Zhejiang, Fujian and Liaoning (according to ISIC's report (ISIC, 2004)). Considering the in-depth emphasis on government impact and the representative of Shanghai, the study provides valuable implications on firms' IT usage in China. An empirical survey that covers more cities in China is desired for future extension.

REFERENCES

Anderson, K. V., Bjørn-Anderson, N., & Dedrick, J. (2003). Governance initiative creating a demand-driven e-commerce approach: The case of Denmark. *The Information Society*, *19*, 95–105. doi:10.1080/01972240309475

Barclay, D., Higgins, C., & Thompson, R. (1995). The partial least squares (PLS) approach to causal modeling: personal computer adoption and use as an illustration. *Technology Studies*, *2*, 285–309.

Blakeley, C. J., & Matsuura, J. H. (2004). The use of e-government to encourage e-commerce development. *International Conference on Information and Communication Technologies: From Theory to Applications*.

Boisot, M., & Child, J. (1999). Organizations as adaptive systems in complex environments: The case of China. *Organization Science*, *10*(3), 237–252. doi:10.1287/orsc.10.3.237

BroadBent, M., & Weill, P. (1997). Management by maxim: How business and IT managers can create IT infrastructures. *Sloan Management Review*, *38*(3), 77–92.

Byrd, T. a., & Turner, D. E. (2000). Measuring the flexibility of information technology infrastructure: Exploratory analysis of a construct. *Journal of Management Information Systems*, *17*(1), 167–208.

CCIDNet. (2006). *Increase rate at industrial informatization investment will reach 20% in 2006*: China Market Information Center. Retrieved from http://industry.ccidnet.com/art/7/20060217/431185_1.html

Chin, W. W. (1998). Issues and opinion on structure equation modeling. *MIS Quarterly*, *22*(1), vii–xvi.

Chin, W. W. (2001). *PLS-graph user's guide*. Soft Modeling Inc.

Chin, W. W., Marcolin, B. L., & Newsted, P. R. (2003). A partial least squares latent variable modeling approach for measuring interaction effects: Results from a Monte Carlo simulation study and an electronic-mail emotion/adoption study. *Information Systems Research*, *14*(2), 189–217. doi:10.1287/isre.14.2.189.16018

Chin, W. W., & Newsted, P. R. (1999). Structural equation modeling analysis with small samples using partial least squares. In R. Hoyle (Ed.), *Statistical strategies for small sample research* (pp. 307-341). Sage Publications.

ChinaLabs. (2004). China informatization report (2004 Q2, Chinese). Retrieved April 30, 2006

CMP. (2005). *Chinese enterprises' IT application demand and market research Report 2004-2005*: CMP Consulting. Retrieved from http://www.cmp.zikoo.com/?item=production&id=22

Davison, R. (2002). Cultural complications of ERP. *Communications of the ACM*, *45*(7), 109–111. doi:10.1145/514236.514267

DiMaggio, P. J., & Powell, W. W. (1983). The iron cage revisited: Institutional isomorphism and collective rationality in organizational fields. *American Sociological Review*, *48*(2), 147–160. doi:10.2307/2095101

Duncan, N. B. (1995). Capturing flexibility of information technology infrastructure: A study of resource characteristics and their measure. *Journal of Management Information Systems*, *12*(2), 37–57.

Ernst, D. (2003). *The new mobility of knowledge: Digital information systems and global flagship networks*. Unpublished manuscript.

Falk, R. F., & Miller, N. B. (1992). *A primer for soft modeling*. OH: University of Akron Press.

Fornell, C., & Bookstein, F. L. (1982). Two structural equation models: LISREL and PLS applied to consumer exit-voice theory. *JMR, Journal of Marketing Research, 19*, 440–452. doi:10.2307/3151718

Fornell, C., & Larcker, D. F. (1981). Evaluating structural models with unobserved variables and measurement errors. *JMR, Journal of Marketing Research, 18*(1), 39–50. doi:10.2307/3151312

Gibbs, J., Kraemer, K. L., & Dedrick, J. (2003). Environment and policy factors shaping global e-commerce diffusion: a cross-country comparison. *The Information Society, 19*(1), 5–18. doi:10.1080/01972240309472

Gibbs, J. L., & Kraemer, K. L. (2004). A cross-country investigation of the determinants of scope of e-commerce use: An institutional approach. *Electronic Markets, 14*(2), 124–137. doi:10.1080/10196780410001675077

Grabowski, M., & Lee, S. (1993). Linking information systems application portfolios and organizational strategy. In R. D. Banker, R. J. Kauffman & M.A. Mahmood (Eds.), *strategic information technology management: Perspectives on organizational growth and competitive advantage* (pp. 33-54). Hershey, PA: Idea Group Publishing.

Haenlein, M., & Kaplan, A. M. (2004). A beginner's guide to partial least squares analysis. *Understanding Statistics, 3*(4), 283–297. doi:10.1207/s15328031us0304_4

Hinings, C. R., & Greenwood, R. (1987). *The normative prescription of organizations*. MA: Ballinger.

ISIC. (2004). The measuring and comparative research of regional imformatization level from 1999 to 2001 of China. *Statistical Research, 3*, 3–11.

ISIC. (2009). Regional differences in informatization development level. Retrieved from http://www.zgxxb.com.cn/news.asp?id=14960

Khalifa, M., & Davison, R. M. (2006). SME adoption: The case of electronic trading systems. *IEEE Transactions on Engineering Management, 53*(2), 275–284. doi:10.1109/TEM.2006.872251

Kraemer, K., Gibbs, J., & Dedrick, J. (2002). *Environment and policy facilitators shaping e-commerce diffusion: A cross-country comparison.* Paper presented at the Proceedings of the Twenty-Third International Conference on Information System, Barcelona, Spain.

Kumar, R. L. (2004). A framework for assessing the business value of information technology infrastructures. *Journal of Management Information Systems, 21*(2), 11–32.

Lee, D. M. S., Trauth, E., & Farwell, D. (1995). Critical skills and knowledge requirements of is professionals: A joint academic/industry investigation. *MIS Quarterly, 19*(3), 313–340. doi:10.2307/249598

Levy, M., & Powell, P. (2003). Exploring SME Internet adoption: Towards A contingent model. *Electronic Markets, 13*(2), 173–181. doi:10.1080/1019678032000067163

Lohmoller, J. B. (1989). *Latent variable path modeling with partial least squares*. New York: Springer-Verlag.

Markus, M. L., & Soh, C. (1993). Banking on information technology: Converting IT spending into firm performance. In R. D. Banker, R. J. Kauffman & M.A. Mahmood (Eds.), *Strategic information technology management: Perspectives on organizational growth and competitive advantage* (pp. 375-403). Hershey, PA: Idea Group Publishing

Martinsons, M. G., & Westwood, R. I. (1997). Management information systems in the Chinese business culture: An explanatory theory. *Information & Management, 32*, 215–228. doi:10.1016/S0378-7206(96)00009-2

McLaren, T., & Head, M. M. (2004). *Strategic fit of supply chain management information systems: A measurement model.* Paper presented at the Twenty-Fifth International Conference on Information Systems.

Melville, N., Kraemer, K., & Gurbaxani, V. (2004). Review: Information technology and organizational performance: An integrative model of IT business value. *MIS Quarterly, 28*(2), 283–322.

NIEC. (2005). *Top500 of Chinese enterprise informatization.* National Informatization Evaluation Center.

NIEC. (2008, 3-24). 2007 Survey report of top 500 informatization enterprises in China. *China Economy Weekly, 11.*

Ranganathan, C., Dhaliwal, J. S., & Teo, T. S. H. (2004). Assimilation and diffusion of Web technologies in supply-chain management: An examination of key drivers and performance impacts. *International Journal of Electronic Commerce, 9*(1), 127–161.

Reimers, K. (2002). *Implementing ERP systems in China.* Paper presented at the Proceedings of the 35th Hawaii International Conference on System Sciences.

Sambamurthy, V., & Zmud, R. W. (1994). *IT management competency assessment: A tool for creating business value through IT.* Morristown, NJ: Financial Executives Research Foundation.

Scott, W. R. (1995). *Institutions and organizations.* London: Sage Publications.

Scott, W. R. (2001). *Institutions and Organizations* (2nd ed.). Thousand Oaks, CA: Sage Publications.

Shenkar, O., & Glinow, M. A. v. (1994). Paradoxes of organizational theory and research: Using the case of China to illustrate national contingency. *Management Science, 40*(1), 56–71. doi:10.1287/mnsc.40.1.56

Shih, E., Kraemer, K. L., & Dedrick, J. (2008). IT diffustion in developing countries. *Communications of the ACM, 51*(2), 43–48. doi:10.1145/1314215.1340913

Straub, D. (1989). Validating instruments in MIS research. *MIS Quarterly, 13*(2), 147–169. doi:10.2307/248922

Straub, D., Hoffman, D., Weber, B., & Steinfield, C. (2002). Toward new metrics for net-enhanced organizations. *Information Systems Research, 13*(3), 227–238. doi:10.1287/isre.13.3.227.80

Swanson, E. B. (1994). Information systems innovation among organizations. *Management Science, 40*(9), 1069–1092. doi:10.1287/mnsc.40.9.1069

Tan, Z., & Ouyang, W. (2004). Diffusion and impacts of the Internet and e-commerce in China. *Electronic Markets, 14*(1), 25–35. doi:10.1080/10196780420001 75270

Teo, H. H., Wei, K. K., & Benbasat, I. (2003). Predicting intention to adopt interorganizational linkages: An institutional perspective. *MIS Quarterly, 27*(1), 19–49.

Thatcher, S. M. B., & Foster, W. (2003). *B2B e-commerce adoption decisions in Taiwan: The interaction of organizational, industrial, governmental and cultural factors.* Paper presented at the Proceedings of the 36th Annual Hawaii International Conference on System Sciences (HICSS'03)

Tornatzky, L. G., & Fleischer, M. (1990). *The processes of technological innovation.* Lexington, MA: Lexington Books.

Tsao, H. Y., Lin, K. H. C., & Lin, C. (2004). An investigation of critical success factors in the adoption of B2BEC by Taiwanese companies. *Journal of American Academy of Business, Cambridge.*

Wade, M., & Hulland, J. (2004). Review: the resource-based view and information systems research: Review, extension, and suggestions for future research. *MIS Quarterly, 28*(1), 75–105.

Xu, S., Zhu, K., & Gibbs, J. (2004). Global technology, local adoption: A cross-country investigation of internet adoption by companies in the United States and China. *Electronic Markets, 14*(1), 13–24. doi:10.1080/1019678042000175261

Yeung, J. H. Y., Shim, J. P., & Lai, A. Y. K. (2003). Current progress of e-commerce adoption: Small and medium enterprises in Hong Kong. *Communications of the ACM, 46*(9ve), 227. doi:10.1145/903893.903941

Zhu, K. (2004). The complementarity of information technology infrastructure and e-commerce capability: A resource-based assessment of their business value. *Journal of Management Information Systems, 21*(1), 167–202.

Zhu, K., Kraemer, K. L., & Xu, S. (2002). *A cross-country study of electronic business adoption using the technology-organization-environment framework.* Paper presented at the Twenty-Third International Conference on Information Systems.

Zucker, L. G. (1987). Institutional theories of organization. *Annual Review of Sociology, 13*, 443–464. doi:10.1146/annurev.so.13.080187.002303

ENDNOTES

[1] This revision is based on "Exploring IT Adoption Process in Shanghai Firms: An Empirical Study" by Cui, Lili, Zhang, Cheng, Zhang, Chenghong, and Huang, Lihua, which is published in Journal of Global Information Management (16:2), 2008, pp 1-17.

[2] Informatization refers to IT usage and adoption in organizations and is a widely accepted concept in China.

APPENDIX: SURVEY QUESTIONNAIRE AND ITEMS

IT Infrastructure (ITIF)

Table 9. Number of IT hardware in workplace (HS)

Desktop PCs;	
Graphic workstations;	
Notebook PCs;	
Mobile PCs;	
Servers;	
Mainframes;	
Stand-alone/ networked data storage systems;	
Dedicated input devices (e.g. scanner)	
Common output devices (e. g. printer or plotters)	

Table 10. Number of IT software in workplace (SS)

System security software (e.g. firewall, anti-virus);	
Data storage management software (e.g. backup, recovery);	
Develop tools (e.g. VFP, Frontpage);	
System management software (network inspect)	

Table 11. Networked status in workplace (NS)

No network	LAN	WAN (regional)	WAN (national-wide)
1	2	3	4

IT Management (ITMC)

Table 12. Extent of IT related management systems and policies (MSP). (Description: IT related management systems and policies include: hardware management, software application management, network and communication management, data/document management, security management, etc.)

Have none				Have all
1	2	3	4	5

Table 13. The practice of IT planning (PP)

No plan	Have plan made by firm itself	Have plan made by firm and 3-party organization together
1	2	3

Table 14. The practice of evaluation of IT investment or competence of using IT (PEI)

No evaluation	Evaluation made by firm itself	Evaluation made by firm and 3-party organization together
1	2	3

Table 15. Governmental Regulation & Promotion Policy (GIRP)

Items	Effectiveness(Y/N)
Establishing evaluation framework for the level of enterprise informatization (IES)	
Providing funding to companies adopting informatization (PF)	
Establishing enterprise application software standards (ASS)	
Promoting large retail chains and its downstream enterprises in adopting web-based e-procurement (PEP)	
Adopting web based online reporting of taxes, annual inspection and etc. (AOR)	
Adopting web-based e-procurement for government procurement activities (AEP)	

IT Usage (ITUS)

Table 16. Extent of PC usage in workplace (PCUW)

0-20%	21-40%	41-60%	61-80%	81-100%
1	2	3	4	5

Table 17. Extent of application systems usage in workplace (AUW)

Application types	No (1)	Using (2)	Advanced using (3)
Finance management			
HR management			
Sales management			
Procurement management			
Production management			
Design management			
Storage management			
Transportation management			
Import and exports management			
Customer service			

IT Value (ITVA)

Table 18. Satisfaction with IT usage to support work (Sat)

Not at all satisfied						Extremely satisfied
1	2	3	4	5	6	7

Table 19. Importance of IT relevance to firm's market competitiveness (Imp)

Not at all Important						Extremely Important
1	2	3	4	5	6	7

Chapter 11
Development of a Scale to Measure Information Technology Capability of Export-Focused SMEs in China

Man Zhang
Bowling Green State University, USA

Suprateek Sarker
Washington State University, USA

Jim McCullough
University of Puget Sound, USA

ABSTRACT

This chapter addresses the conceptual and measurement issues related to the study of information technology capability (ITC) in small to medium businesses that focus on exports. The authors review the concept of ITC and its components and reports on the construction and psychometric assessment of a measure of ITC. The authors develop a multi-dimensional scale showing strong evidence of reliability and validity in samples from export-focused SMEs based in Mainland China. Finally, this chapter demonstrates nomological validity by examining the relationship between ITC and export-focused SMEs' performance.

INTRODUCTION

Contemporary thinking on organizational capability has been profoundly influenced by the resource-based view of the firm (Barney, 1991; Eisenhardt & Schoovenhover, 1996; Peppard & Ward, 2004). The proponents of this view argue that firms possess costly-to-imitate capabilities (i.e., unique configurations of resources) that are regarded as the fundamental drivers of superior performance (Bharadwaj, Sambamurthy, & Zmud, 1999). While firm resources may be copied relatively easily, capabilities are more difficult to replicate because they are often tightly connected to the history, culture, and experience of the firm. Recent writings in the IS literature have examined the role of information

DOI: 10.4018/978-1-60566-920-5.ch011

technology capability (ITC) in enabling superior IT-based innovation and business performance (Wang & Alam, 2007) and have emphasized that "technology itself has no inherent value and IT alone is unlikely to be a source of sustainable competitive advantage"; rather, the "business value derived from IT investments emerges only through business changes and innovations" (Peppard & Ward, 2004, p.169).

While some path-breaking work has been conducted on ITC in recent times, much of this work has focused on large firms. However, business models and assumptions that are appropriate for large businesses do not necessarily apply to small and medium sized enterprises (SMEs). This is because SME managers face different opportunities and constraints than managers of large businesses (Hunter, 2004). They typically have fewer financial resources, lower technical expertise and poor management skills. Due to these limited resources, SMEs have started to use IT only recently (Caldeira & Ward, 2002).

As investments in information technology (IT) continue to grow, SMEs managers' awareness of the need to derive the value of IT is also increasing (Love, et al., 2005; Bruque & Moyano, 2007;). Indeed, Abouzeedan and Busler (2002) argue that information technology is having a profound effect on SMEs' management. Using IT tools, time-consuming and labor-intensive activities often takes less time and effort. Thus, SME managers are increasingly adopting new IT technologies in all aspects of business activities (Abouzeedan & Busler, 2006; Kim & Jee, 2007). Moreover, efficient and effective management of IT resources is critical for SMEs, not only for competitive advantage but also for mere survival (Montazemi, 2006). Reasons, which were alluded to earlier, include: (a) SMEs tend to generalists rather than specialists, which in turn results in a lack of in-depth IT/IS knowledge and technical skills within the organization; (b) SMEs typically lack the financial resources to develop and maintain a sophisticated IT infrastructure and to train their IT users; and (c) SMEs simply do not have necessary management and financial resources to correct situations arising from an unwise/unsuccessful IT investment.

Recently, a specific type of SME (i.e., export-focused SME) has been recognized as significant business entities, playing an important role in economies of various countries (e.g., Moen and Servais, 2002; Rennie, 1993). The issue of ITC is particularly important to such firms, which often expand abroad while they are still in their infancy, facing dual liabilities of being both new and foreign. The value-adding processes of these firms are often based on the creation and exploitation of knowledge and knowledge-intensive services. Also, the attention of these firms is typically focused on information acquisition, accumulation, and integration (Knight & Cavusgil, 2004; Nonaka & Takeuchi, 1995), all of which require strong ITC (e.g., Feeny & Willcocks, 1998 a, b). Moreover, these firms need to operate in geographically dispersed uncertain environments, requiring the support of ITC for communication/coordination as well as for information processing (Galbraith 1973; Saunders 2000). The ability to effectively harness IT resources enables these firms to reduce costs, improve customer service, create links with suppliers, differentiate product/services, develop innovations, and thus increase overall firm performance (Kyobe, 2004; Kim & Jee, 2007). There is thus a clear need to study the topic of ITC in the context of export-focused SMEs.

Although such SMEs are found worldwide, they are particularly appealing in developing countries, such as China, where a generation of improved higher education has placed many skilled people into the workforce, but where a large percentage of national income still depends on export sales. In particular, newly-minted SMEs in developing countries tend leverage the Internet and other ICTs to gain regional or global exports. And this means that developing nations might be able to leapfrog the initial stages of internationalization traditionally ascribed to businesses. This would speed export centered development and permit these countries to become competitive more quickly, more broadly, and less expensively than ever before (Kundu & Katz, 2003). SMEs have grown exponentially in China over the last several years due to the country's rapid economic growth, its entry into the World Trade Organization (WTO), and abundance of suitable labor (Zhang & Tang, 2002). Reports indicate that SMEs contribute somewhere in the range of 30 to 60 per cent of the GDP of China (e.g., Harvie & Lee, 2003). In fact, Wang and Yao (2002) have described SMEs as the "backbone of China's economic growth" (p. 199). An increasing proportion of Chinese SMEs are characterized as *young* and *internationalized* – that is, they focus on exports and operate on an international scale soon after they are founded (e.g., Cavusgil, 1994). Indeed, it is estimated that in China such SMEs contribute directly to at least 35% of the country's exports, with the growth rate of SME exports being much higher than that of the overall exports (Harvie & Lee, 2003). It must however be acknowledged that, in order to compete with larger firms in the international market, such SMEs need to get quick and broad access to resources to build volume quickly, make functionally-specialized investments abroad, and create a tightly networked organization. All of these goals aren't easy to achieve without significant use of information technology, and indeed, some scholars have pointed to "technological capability" as a key enabler of their global competitiveness (Dhungana 2003, p.7; Johnson, 2004).

Unfortunately, despite the featured successes of many of these export-focused SMEs, they face several challenges in growing their exports, and realizing high firm performance. Often, a barrier to success of these SMEs in China is that they are constantly faced with "resource poverty," especially with respect to financial resources; this lack of financial resources partly arises due to governmental regulatory policies, which allow SMEs limited "access to formal financial markets" (Wang & Yao, 2002). Further, it has been reported that SMEs in China lack adequate information regarding markets, competitors, scope, etc., making it difficult for them to assess market trends and make accurate forecasts, and thus compete effectively in the international market (Wang & Yao, 2002). This might explain why, despite the advantages SMEs enjoy, such as their flexibility, many are unable to thrive or even survive (Hollenstein, 2005; Wang & Yao 2002).

It is thus important to examine and understand the specific capabilities that enable strong performance of export-focused SMEs in China. Prior research, though not specifically in the Chinese context, has attempted to explore the role of several drivers and impediments to SME effectiveness (e.g., Madsen et al., 2000; Oviatt & McDougall, 1999), with some scholars pointing to "technological capability" as an enabler of global competitiveness (Dhungana 2003, p. 7; Johnson, 2004). Given the increased recognition of the strategic role of IT in contemporary organizations, it is imperative to gain a deeper understanding of the factors that govern a firm's ITC. Yet, there is a lack of understanding as to what constitutes a firm's ITC and how it could be measured (Bharadwaj, 2000; Santhanam & Hartono, 2003).

Thus, the primary objective of this study is to identify the dimensions of ITC and to develop and validate an instrument for measuring this construct in the context of export-focused SMEs, specifically in developing countries such as China, where such organizations play an important role in the economy. The secondary objective is to examine the effect of ITC on the firms' global performance so as to demonstrate nomological validity of ITC as defined in this study.

THEORETICAL FOUNDATION OF THE STUDY

Prior Research on ITC

The concept of ITC draws on a number of theoretical perspectives (e.g., work design, power relationships, process transformation), and there is very little consensus on the dimensions of ITC or how it should be measured (Mulligan, 2002).

Table 1 presents definitions of ITC in the existing literature. Our review of the literature suggests that, in the past, ITC has been conceptualized primarily in terms of managerial capabilities (e.g., Sambamurthy & Zmud, 1992; Ross, Beath, & Goodhue, 1996; Prasad, Ramamurthy, & Naidu, 2001) or technological capabilities (e.g., Sabherwal & Kirs, 1994; Teo & King, 1997; Clark, Cavanaugh, Brown, & Sambamurthy, 1997; Sabherwal, 1999; Byrd & Turner, 2000). Recently, however there have been attempts to adopt a more inclusive view of ITC which takes into account both the technological and managerial aspects. For example, Ray, Muhanna, and Barney (2005) view ITC as being composed of two categories of resources: the first consists of raw IT spending, the technical skills and generic information technologies within the firm (i.e., the technology components), and the second consists of more managerial capabilities that "influence how the first [category] of resource is used" (p. 628). Bhatt and Grover (2005) view ITC as being composed of the value or technological capabilities (e.g., IT infrastructure), and more managerial capabilities such as competitive capabilities (e.g., IT business experience, relationship infrastructure), and dynamic capabilities (e.g., intensity of organizational learning).

Taking a similar integrative approach, and drawing on the resource-based view of the firm, Bharadwaj (2000), provides a rich conceptualization of ITC and views it as a set of resources that enable an organization to gain (and maintain) competitive advantage (Song, Nason & Di Benedetto, 2008). Supporting this perspective, Wade and Hulland (2004) suggest that a resource-based view of ITC is appropriate, since such a perspective enables researchers to understand how ITC affects a firm's financial and strategic performance. In this study, we thus draw on the integrative view of ITC and the proponents of the resource-based view, and define ITC as: *a firm's ability to acquire, deploy, and leverage its IT related resources in combination with other resources in order to achieve business objectives through IT implementation.* It is important to note that in the prior literature, ITC and IT resources have often been used interchangeably (e.g., Santhanam & Hartono, 2003; Bhatt & Grover, 2005). This is not surprising given that much of the research on ITC has been informed by the resource-based view of the firm, where the ITC of the firm has been argued to be "valuable," "heterogeneously distributed," "imperfectly mobile," and therefore a source of sustained competitive advantage for the firm. However, Bharadwaj (2000) have attempted to create a distinction between the term "IT resources," and "ITC." According to Bharadwaj (2000, p. 176), the individual components such as IT infrastructure, IT human skills, etc. are "firm-specific resources, which in combination create a firm-wide ITC" (emphasis added). Following Bharadwaj's suggestions (2000), in this study, we view ITC as a holistic combination of IT-related resources that enable a firm to gain (and sustain) competitive advantage.

Even though past studies do not unequivocally validate the proposed positive relationship between ITC and firm performance (Love & Irani, 2004), fragmented literature does suggest that SMEs are likely to benefit from enhanced ITC. For example, Levy et al. (2003) argue that IT enables SMEs to better manage their customer bases, keep information about customers in a more organized manner, and also share knowledge within the organization more efficiently. Likewise, Arenius, Sasi, and Gabrielsson (2006) suggest that export-focused SMEs can realize superior

Table 1. Definitions of ITC in existing literature

Authors	Conceptual Definition
ITC conceptualized as managerial capabilities	
Sambamurthy & Zmud (1992)	The internal capabilities on which its competitive strategies are based…it also refers to the managerial capabilities required for a firm to productively acquire, deploy and leverage its IT investments.
Prasad, Ramamurthy, & Naidu (2001)	A firm's ability to use IT to support and enhance its distinctive competencies and skills in other business functions.
Ross, Beath, & Goodhue (1996)	The ability to control IT-related costs, deliver systems when needed, and affect business objectives through IT implementations.
ITC conceptualized as technological capabilities	
Teo & King (1997)	The capabilities of the IS function…can be operationalized in terms of general technical expertise and technological leadership in the industry…
Byrd & Turner (2000)	The ability to easily and readily diffuse or support a wide variety of hardware, software, compunctions technologies, data, core applications, skills and competencies, commitments and values within the technical physical base and the human component of the existing IT infrastructure.
Clark, Cavanaugh, Brown, & Sambamurthy (1997)	The ability to enhance competitive agility by delivering IT-based products, services and business applications within short development cycle times; build a highly skilled, empowered, and energized IS workforce with an entrepreneurial orientation toward leveraging technological knowledge into business applications.
Sabherwal & Kirs, (1994) Sabherwal (1999)	The extent to which the technologies needed for manipulation, storage and communication of information are available within the organization.
ITC conceptualized as a combination of both managerial and technological capabilities	
Ray, Muhanna & Barney (2005)	It is composed of two categories of resources: the first consists of raw IT spending, the technical skills and generic information technologies within the firm (i.e., the technology components), and the second consists of more managerial resources that "influence how the first [category] of resource is used" (p. 628).
Bhatt & Grover (2005)	It is composed of value capabilities, competitive capabilities, and dynamic capabilities.
Feeny & Willcocks (1998 a, b)	The pursuit of high-value-added applications of IT, and to capitalize on the external market's ability to deliver cost-effective IT services.
Bharadwaj (2000)	The ability to mobilize, and deploy IT-based resources in combination with other resources and capabilities.
Wade & Hulland (2005)	The capability can be sorted into inside-out, outside-in and spanning capabilities

international performance by developing greater IT capability. They contend that such firms suffer from the "*liability of foreignness*" (arising from the costs associated with travel and transportation to foreign markets, and the lack of familiarity with the foreign nation's business environment), and from human and financial *resource scarcity*. Such challenges are often mitigated by IT, enabling SMEs to ultimately realize superior performance.

Evidence of multidimensionality of ITC is evident in the work of earlier researchers. However, there is no widely accepted reconciliation/integration of this body of work, where scholars offer varying perspectives. For example, Sabherwal and Kirs (1994) argue that ITC has four dimensions, Ross, Beath, and Goodhue (1996) identify yet another set of four dimensions, Feeny and Willcocks (1998a, b) discuss eight different

Table 2. Mapping existing research to ITC dimensions

Information Technology Capability Dimensions	Sabherwal & Kirs, (1994, 1999)	Ross, Beath, & Goodhue (1996)	Feeny & Willcocks (1998 a, b)	Bharadwaj (2000)
IT architecture	Information retrieval		Designing technical architecture IS/IT governance	Systematic data and application design
IT infrastructure	Computing facilities Electronic communication technologies	Technology asset		Hardware and Software assets
IT human resource	Computer related education	Human asset	Business systems thinking Making technology work	IT Personnel skills
IT relationship resource		Relationship asset	Relationship building Informed buying Contract facilitation Contract monitoring Vendor development	Intangible IT-enabled resources

aspects, and finally, Bharadwaj (2000) categorizes various aspects of ITC within four dimensions. It is useful to observe that there are varying degrees of overlap amongst the existing perspectives on ITC (See table 2 for more details of the dimensions). Based on these and other studies, we have combined the similar elements of ITC and derived a more integrative set of underlying dimensions of the construct: (1) IT infrastructure, (2) IT architecture, (3) IT human resource, and (4) IT relationship resource. Table 2 shows how existing research maps on to the facets of ITC. We note that a majority of these studies do not address all four dimensions mentioned above.

The IT architecture dimension is primarily comprised of *information retrieval* from Sabherwal and Kirs (1994, 1999), designing *technical architecture and IS/IT governance* from Feeny and Willcocks (1998 a, b), and *systematic data and application design* from Bhaladwaj (2000). *Computing facilities and electronic communication technologies* from Sabherwal and Kirs (1994, 1999), *technology assets* from Ross, Beath, and Goodhue, (1996), and *hardware and software assets* from Bharadwaj (2000) are integrated into IT infrastructure. *Computer related education* from Sabherwal and Kirs (1994, 1999), *human assets* from Ross, Beath, and Goodhue (1996), *business systems thinking* and *making technology work* from Feeny and Willcocks (1998a, b), and *IT personnel skills* from Bharadwaj (2000) are combined into the IT human resource. Our last dimension of IT relationship resource comes from Ross, Beath, and Goodhue 's (1996) *relationship assets,* Feeny and Willcocks' (1998a,b) *relationship building, informed buying, contract facilitation, contract monitoring, vendor development* and Bharadwaj's (2000)*intangible IT-related resources*. Below, we describe each of these dimensions.

IT Architecture

The definition of IT architecture has emerged slowly over time (Sullivan, 1982) with researchers usually focusing on different components of information systems, such as data storage, communications, or applications. For example, Spencer (1985) and Inmon (1989) focused on the data architecture; in contrast, Barrett and Konsynski (1982) emphasized communications in their definition of architecture, while Venkatraman (1991) and Keen (1991) defined the architecture in terms of applications. Gibson (1994) adopted a more integrative approach and viewed architecture as being composed of four physical elements: computing compatibility, data organization, communications connectivity, and applications functionality. Following Gibson's (1994) approach, IT architecture may be defined as a high-level map of information and technology requirements of the entire firm in this study. It provides a vision for how a firm will select and deploy its corporate IT resources to derive business value. Well- designed and well-planned IT architectures deliver significant benefits to a firm, by lowering IT cost through technology standardization, and by enabling agility in the organization (Bhatt, 2000; Sambamurthy, Bharadwaj & Grover 2003).

IT Infrastructure

The value of IT infrastructure, often defined as a shared information delivery base relying on hardware, software, and networks, is growing rapidly in today's organizations (Byrd & Turner, 2000). Many companies have placed the development of an effective IT infrastructure among the top concerns of their overall IT management (Chanopas, Krairit, & Khang, 2006). An IT infrastructure provides a shared foundation of ITC for building business applications and training employees, and is usually managed by the information systems group. It is comprised of the computer and communication technologies and the shareable technical platforms, providing consistent and quick information support by enabling access to relevant databases throughout the organization (Ross, Beath, & Goodhue, 1996; Weill, Broadbent, & Butler, 1996). This IT infrastructure may thus be seen as a key source for attaining long-term competitive advantage (Keen, 1991; McKenney, 1995; Fink & Neumann, 2007), serving as an enabler for future applications, and helping the organization cope with the uncertainty of future needs (Grossman & Packer, 1989; Sawy & Pavlou, 2008).

It is useful to note that there is some conceptual overlap between IT architecture and IT infrastructure, at least as represented in the earlier literature. The difference between the two dimensions lies in their respective foci. While *IT infrastructure focuses on the presence or absence of relevant technologies, IT architecture is concerned with the degree to which the technologies and data are systematically planned, and are harnessed in a consistent and flexible form.*

IT Human Resource

As the importance of IT has risen in modern organizations, the role of IT personnel has also become an increasingly critical aspect of ITC. IT staff that consistently solves business problems and addresses opportunities through information technology is a valuable human asset. Insightful IT leaders recognize that the greatest impediments to success are often related to people rather than to information, technology, and systems. Thus, along with technical skills, managerial, business, and interpersonal skills have been increasingly cited as mandatory for these technical employees (Roepke, Agarwal, & Ferratt, 2000). Bharadwaj (2000) argues that these two kinds of skills, namely the technical skills and managerial skills, are the two critical dimensions of Human IT resources. Based on existing literature, technical skills include the ability to evaluate and control IS projects, IT skill base, and IT systems development practices; managerial skills include abilities such as the effective management practice, and planning capability and effectiveness (Capon & Glazer, 1987; Copeland & McKenney, 1988). Research has suggested that those softer skills are crucial to programmers, systems analysts, database administrators, and other IT personnel in modern organizations (Rockart, Earl, & Ross, 1996; Ross, Beath, & Goodhue, 1996).

Recent research and practitioner literature has stressed the value of a broad range of skills for IT professionals in meeting the operational requirements of modern organizations. To add value, IT professionals are called on to blend technical skills with managerial skills and a deep understanding of the business. Drawing from the existing literature, in this study, IT human resource is defined as organizational staff that is capable of addressing; a) IT-related problems/opportunities, and b) business problems/opportunities associated with IT.

IT Relationship Resource

In order to effectively apply IT in the firm, IT management and business units need to share the risk and responsibility. This sharing requires trust and mutual respect, and an ability to communicate, coordinate or negotiate quickly and effectively.

IT relationship resource includes the establishment of IT priorities with the active involvement of relevant stakeholders. To do so, a number of firms have established committees of senior managers, with understanding of the organizational/business needs, to participate as members of IT steering committees. To some degree, this helps ensure a) the wise investment of limited organizational resources, and b) the selected projects have strong support and sponsorship of business managers (Ross, Beath, & Goodhue, 1996). The committees also articulate organizational strategies and specify how IT should support them. The more IT staff people and individuals representing different organizational functions communicate, coordinate, negotiate, and work together, the stronger the partnership becomes, and the more effective the process of planning, risk-taking, and experimentation, which in turn, leads to the development of new applications (Powell & Dent-Micallef, 1997).

IT relationship resource also includes the social capital developed through relationship building. Specifically, it involves developing users' understanding of IT's potential, and boosting users' feelings of ownership and satisfaction. It plays an important role in fostering mutual confidence, harmony of purpose, and enabling successful communication among those focused on the business and technical agendas (Feeny & Willcocks, 1998 b). A strong IT relationship is characterized by high levels of respect and goodwill between IT personnel and clients, which results in excellence in bi-directional communication without significant distortion of meaning and collaboration across both sides of the relationship. This in turn enables mutual knowledge sharing and appreciation of the capabilities of information technology and the needs of the business. An important element of IT relationship is that it enables convenient IT-based linkages with the organization's customers as well as suppliers, and indeed such connectivity can often be transformed to valuable inter-organizational collaborations, leading to: the creation of joint designs, reduction of transaction costs, better management of inventory, greater agility of the relationship, etc. (Grewal, Johnson, & Sarker, 2007; Turban, Leidner, McLean, & Wetherbe, 2006).

Based on the literature, IT Relationship Resource is defined as the nature of relationship the IT group has with management and other business units/stakeholders within the organization. In addition, IT relationship resource includes the technology-based linkages between the firm and its key business partners, including customers, suppliers, and external collaborators.

RESEARCH METHOD

Instrument Design and Validation

As mentioned earlier, the broad purpose of this study is to develop a scale to measure ITC in export-focused SMEs. We undertake the study in the national context of China, a country where export-focused SMEs have been recognized as having significant contribution to the economy (Wang & Yao, 2002; Harvie & Lee, 2003). According to the existing literature, there are three ways of obtaining the measures of a construct (Torgerson, 1967): (1) fundamental measurement, where numbers are assigned according to natural laws to represent the construct (e.g., the measurement of volume or length); (2) derived measurement, in which a construct is measured by relating it through laws to other constructs (e.g., density is measured by a ratio of mass to volume); and (3) measurement by fiat, where a construct is measured by arbitrary definition. Measurement by fiat is undertaken when there exists a common-sense concept that on a priori grounds seems to be important but for which there are no direct measures. Most constructs in social and behavioral sciences and in information system involve measurement by fiat (Sethi & King, 1991). In measurement by fiat, one or more observable construct properties are selected and their simple/weighted sum is taken as a measure of the construct. The difficulty with this process is that construct measures may be defined in a multitude of ways. To develop a measure that has desirable reliability and validity properties, Churchill (1979) recommended an eight-step procedure, which has been simplified by Sarker, Valacich and Sarker (2003), among others, to five sequential steps. The steps are as follows:

a. Specification of the domain of construct (i.e., conceptualization of the constructs)
b. Generation of the sample of items and establishment of content validity
c. Collection of data
d. Purification of measures (i.e., calculation of the coefficient alpha for assessing reliability) and assessment of discriminant validity
e. Assessment of convergent validity and the unidimensionality of the measurement items.

In this study, we have followed the above-mentioned steps in assessing the validity of our instrument. We discuss these steps in further detail below:

Specification of the Domain of Construct

According to the guidelines, researchers should conduct a thorough literature review to understand the definitions of the constructs of interest, and to make sure that an exhaustive list of factors has been identified. Our literature review was performed in this study wherein the definition of ITC was clarified. Further, it was identified that ITC is multidimensional (e.g., Bharadwaj, 2000; Sabherwal & Kirs, 1994) and in order to build a comprehensive instrument of ITC, it is important to include the constructs of IT architecture, IT human resource, IT infrastructure, and IT relationship resource. The operational definitions and scale sources are provided in Table 3.

Generation of the Sample of Items and Establishment of Content Validity

Light, Singer, and Willett (1990, pp. 151-152) argue that an instrument has content validity "if its individual items, as a group, cover all the different domains you want to measure." They further argue that content validity can be of two types: 1) face validity, and 2) sampling-content validity. Face validity is ensured by "having 'experts' examine the measure and agree that it does assess what it is supposed to assess." Face validity is considered to be a "weaker" form of content validity, since "it is in the eye of the beholder." Thus, Light et al. (1990) suggest that researchers developing new instruments should also ensure the sampling-content validity, in addition to its face validity. In this study, in ensuring the content validity of our measures, we followed Light et al.'s (1990) guidelines.

Sampling-content validity can be established by "identifying all the specific domains of interest," and by ensuring that all of the items taken together cover these domains of interest. To ensure the sampling-content validity of our instrument,

Table 3. Construct operationalization and scale sources

Construct	Conceptual Definition	Operational Definition	Theoretical Underpinnings
IT Architecture	A high-level map of information and technology requirements of the entire firm.	Degree to which a firm can effectively select and organize its corporate IT resources, such as data and applications	Based on Fertuck (1992); Sullivan (1982); Gibson (1994)
IT Infrastructure	A shared information delivery base relying on hardware, software, and networks	Information and Communication technologies that support the access and use of data/applications.	Based on Sabherwal & Kirs (1994); Bharadwaj et al. (1999); Ross, Beath, & Goodhue (1996)
IT Human Resource	Organizational staff that is capable of addressing: a) IT-related problems/opportunities, and b) business problems/opportunities associated with IT.	Level of organizational staff's technical skills, business understanding, and problem-solving orientation.	Based on Ross, Beath, and Goodhue (1996); Bharadwaj et al. (1999)
IT Relationship Resource	The relationship between the IT group and other business units/stakeholders.	Level of linkages/collaboration between the IT group and relevant stakeholders.	Based on Feeny & Willcocks, (1998 a, b), Bharadwaj et al. (1999), Ross, Beath, & Goodhue, (1996)

an extensive review of the past research was conducted, and a synthesized definition of ITC was developed. Using this definition, prior empirical research on ITC was consulted for developing the initial set of items. Drawing on the work of Bharadwaj et al. (1999); Ross, Beath, & Goodhue, (1996); Sabherwal & Kirs (1994); Sabherwal (1999); Heijden (2000) & Grewal, Comer, & Mehta (2001), a pool of 88 items (modified to an export-focused SME context) was developed. This helped ensure the sampling-content validity of the measures.

To ensure the face-validity of the items, four rounds of "reviews" were conducted. The initial set of items were distributed to three IS academicians, and three groups of about ten IT professionals familiar with the topic, for review. Each round of review resulted in some modifications to the scale, in terms of addition or deletion of items, rephrasing of items, and so on. The proposed model and measures are shown in Table 4. The several rounds of review resulted in the pool of items being dropped from 88 to 22, removing redundancies. We believe that the intense rounds of review of the instrument by several experts helped ensure the face validity of the instrument (Light et al. 1990)

In addition to the sampling-content and the face validities, we also pilot tested the questionnaire with 20 small manufacturing firms from China. Data from the pilot test was used for calculating the Cronbach's alpha for each of the dimensions of ITC, and therefore, enabled us to assess their reliability (Cronbach, 1970). Nunnally (1978) suggests that in the early stages of research, reliabilities of 0.50 to 0.60 should be considered satisfactory. As a result, for the pilot study, the minimum reliability was set at 0.50. Once the reliabilities of the items were ensured to be over .50, the instrument was considered to be ready for use in the actual study.

Data Collection

A survey methodology was used for the study. The survey was administered to SMEs in China

Table 4. Hypothesized dimensions of ITC and their proposed measures

IT Architecture	
	To what extent do you agree/disagree with the following statements:
ITA1	There is consistency in IT policies throughout the enterprise.
ITA2*	There is appropriateness of data architecture.
ITA3*	There is adequacy of architecture flexibility.
ITA4	There is consistency in IT application portfolios, which is a set of different types of IT applications, with business processes.
ITA5	There is clarity of vision regarding how IT contributes to business value.
IT Infrastructure	
	To what extent are the following found in your organization:
ITINF1	Communication devices for access of remote database.
ITINF2	Computer facilities for IT projects.
ITINF3	Computer labs for employee instruction.
IT Human Resource	
	To what extent are the following found in your organization:
ITHR1	IT evaluation and control systems.
ITHR2	IT skill base.
ITHR3	IT project management practice.
ITHR4	IT planning capabilities
ITHR5	IT planning effectiveness
ITHR6	IT systems development practices
IT Relationship Resource	
	To what extent do you agree/disagree with the following statements:
ITRR1*	The IT department of our organization maintains close relationship with business management.
ITRR2	We use IT based entrepreneurial collaborations with external partners.
ITRR 3*	We have good relationship between line management and IT service providers.
ITRR4*	We have good line management sponsorship of IT initiatives.
ITRR5*	We have a climate that encouraging risk taking and experimentation with IT
ITRR6	We have technology-based links with customers.
ITRR7	We have technology-based links with suppliers.
ITRR8*	We have multi-disciplinary teams to blend business and technology expertise.

Notes:* Indicates item with factor loadings less than 0.70 was dropped in the scale purification process.

that were export-focused from their inception. We focused on these specific types of export-focused SMEs since they are a growing breed of SMEs in China, and are seen to have immense potential (McKinsey & Co, 1993). To overcome potential problems arising from postal systems and the lack of reliable archival data (Li & Atuahane-Gima, 2001), instead of the "mail survey" approach, we used the alternate "key informant technique" that is recommended for such contexts (e.g., Lambe et al., 2002). Consistent with this approach, members of top management were first contacted to make sure that they were willing to participate in the study. Data was collected using an on-site interview, whereby a trained interviewer completed the questionnaire based on the responses of a designated key informant in the organization (Bhatt & Grover 2005; Li & Atuahane-Gima 2001).

Firm performance, especially of large and multinational organizations is often measured using objective financial indicators. However, objective financial measures are difficult to obtain in the case of Chinese SMEs, since such firms prefer to maintain a high-level of secrecy regarding the specifics of their business operations and are "sensitive" to the public disclosure of financial data (Siu, Fang, & Lin 2004). Thus, studies involving Chinese SMEs typically use self-assessed measures of performance (Siu et al., 2004). Given that our study is focused on Chinese export-focused SMEs, and prior research has demonstrated that self-reported measures of performance are appropriate, we used self-assessed measures of international performance. Specifically, we drew on a scale developed by Zou, Taylor, & Osmond (1998) to measure international performance of firms in Asia, which has also been utilized extensively in prior authoritative work in international business (e.g., Dow, 2006; Morgan, Kaleka, & Katsikeas, 2000). The scale incorporates prior conceptualizations of export performance (e.g., financial and strategic), and also takes into consideration the firm's performance *relative* to its competitors, which has been viewed as a superior approach for assessing performance (Wade & Hulland 2004).

All the instruments were professionally translated to Chinese and the Chinese version of the questionnaires were administered to the respondents. Prior to its administration, the instruments were back-translated, and refinements were undertaken by two independent bilinguals, as suggested by Douglas and Craig (1983). Unless otherwise stated, items were measured on a scale of 1 (Strongly disagree) to 7 (Strongly agree). Confidentiality was assured to all respondents to encourage candid responses. Top management of 180 of the 240 firms contacted agreed to participate in the study. Our data collection efforts finally yielded 136 completed questionnaires, all from manufacturing firms. Missing data and listwise deletion further reduced the current analytic sample to 99, for an effective response rate of 55%. Table 2 presents descriptive statistics of the responding firms.

Purification of Measures and Assessment of Discriminant Validity

This step involves the calculation of the coefficient alpha to assess the reliability of the construct items (Cronbach, 1951), and also the assessment of the discriminant validity of the instrument through an exploratory factor analysis (Bagozzi et al. 1979). Consistent with this step, in this study we calculated the coefficient alpha for each of the factors, and also conducted an exploratory factor analysis. In conducting the exploratory factor analysis, we adopted the Kaiser-Guttman rule (which states that factors with Eigen values >1 should be accepted) to identify the underlying factors and their constitution based on an analysis of the data. In the next few paragraphs, the process of factor acceptance and labeling will be described.

Three items loaded above 0.70 on factor one with a reliability coefficient of 0.835. Each of these items is related to how firms plan and deploy IT related resources. Specifically, the items address issues such as policies for managing IT. We thus labeled this construct as "IT architecture." Three items loaded above 0.70 on the second factor with a reliability coefficient of 0.842. Each of these items is related to the infrastructure of the firm's IT resources, thus this factor was labeled as "IT

Table 5. Scale items, reliabilities and confirmatory factor analysis results

Scale Items	Component				Coefficient α
	1	2	3	4	
Information Technology Architecture (ITA)					
There is consistency in IT policies throughout the enterprise.	.215	.137	**.845**	.031	**0.835**
There is consistency in IT application portfolios.	.146	.075	**.834**	.165	
There is clarity of vision regarding how IT contributes to business value.	.139	.328	**.777**	.160	
Information Technology Infrastructure (ITINF)					
Communication devices for access of remote database.	.256	.158	.255	**.760**	**0.842**
Computer facilities for IT projects.	.381	.012	.126	**.816**	
Computer labs for employee instructions.	.354	.113	.026	**.779**	
Information Human Recourse (ITHR)					
IT evaluation and control systems.	**.863**	.116	.125	.217	**0.947**
IT skill base.	**.864**	.039	.145	.186	
IT project management practice.	**.826**	.156	.229	.230	
IT planning capabilities.	**.815**	.210	.202	.267	
IT planning effectiveness.	**.804**	.273	.136	.279	
IT systems development practices.	**.768**	.206	.077	.295	
Information Technology Relationship Resource (ITRR)					
We have technology based links with customers.	.112	**.804**	.149	.094	**0.813**
We have technology based links with suppliers.	.162	**.846**	.128	.102	
We use IT based entrepreneurial collaborations with external partners.	.234	**.792**	.175	.043	

Note: Each item is measured on a seven-point scale ranging from "7=strongly agree" to "1=strongly disagree". All loadings are significant at 0.01 level.

infrastructure." Six items loaded above 0.70 on the third factor with a reliability coefficient of 0.947. Each of these items addressed the issues of IT technical skills or managerial skills of the firm, and was thus labeled as "IT human resource." The last three items loaded above 0.70 on the fourth factor with a reliability coefficient of 0.813. This construct was labeled as "IT relationship resource," since the items addressed issues such as the relationship between the technology-provides and the technology-users (See table 5).

Overall, the exploratory factor analysis helped establish the multidimensionality of the construct of ITC. Specifically, it showed that ITC in export-focused SMEs has distinct dimensions and can be broken down to the constructs of IT architecture, IT infrastructure, IT human resource, and IT relationship resource, as identified in prior literature.

Discriminant validity is inferred when measures of each factor converge on their respective score that are unique from the scores of other factors. Following Bagozzi et al. (1991) and Venkatraman (1989), discriminant validity for the factors of the ITC construct is also assessed by testing whether correlations between pairs of factors in each component set were significantly different from unity. The evidence for this comparison can be obtained from the estimates of an unconstrained model that free the correlation between the factor pair and a constrained model that sets this correlation to unity. The difference between the chi-square values with degree free-

Table 6. Results of discriminant validity tests

			Chi-square (d.f.)		
Test	ML Estimate	t-value	Constrained Chi-square	Unconstrained Chi-square	Chi-square difference
IT architecture with					
IT infrastructure	0.56	3.16	21.8 (9)	17.8 (8)	4.0**
IT human resource	0.63	3.66	63.0 (27)	59.6 (26)	3.4*
IT relationship resource	0.40	3.51	20.0 (9)	7.5 (8)	12.5***
IT infrastructure					
IT human resource	0.71	4.65	50.8 (27)	43.6 (26)	7.2***
IT relationship resource	0.36	2.54	15.1 (9)	5.3 (8)	9.8***
IT human resource					
IT relationship resource	0.51	3.48	69.5 (27)	62.9 (26)	6.6***

Note: Significant at the *p<0.10; **p<0.05;***p<0.01;****p<0.001 level.

dom equal to one is also a chi-square variate. A significant difference in this chi-square variate indicates that the unconstrained model is a better fit than the constrained model. Such results imply that presence of discriminant validity between the pair of factors (Byrd and Turner 2000). This test was performed on all possible pairs of factors. Table 6 reports the results of the six pair wise tests of the factors for ITC. All results are significant. This evidence helps establish the discriminant validity of the scale.

Convergent Validity and Unidimensionality

Convergent validity can be assessed through a confirmatory factor analysis (CFA) using the structural equation modeling (SEM) technique, which provides researchers with a chi-squared goodness-of-fit test for the measurement model. This method also helps in establishing the one-dimensionality of the indicators (Anderson and Gerbing, 1982), meaning a set of items measure only a single construct.

This study follows the guidelines of Anderson and Gerbing (1982) and Bagozzi et al. (1979) to test the convergent validity of the construct. The hypothesized model (ITC) was assessed with a confirmatory factor analytic model using AMOS 4.0 (Arbuckle & Wothke, 1999).

While the objective in the EFA was to obtain an overview of the structure of our instrument and identify the "latent sources of variation and covariation" in the original instrument (Jöreskog & Sörbom, 1988). The objective in the CFA was to understand how well our final set of items (generated from the EFA) fit our dataset. The focus was on the creation of the measurement model in AMOS, which specified how the "latent variables or hypothesized constructs" were measured in terms of the observed variables (Jöreskog & Sörbom, 1988). After the creation of the models, the fit of the models was analyzed using the maximum likelihood (ML) method which assumes that the "observed variables have a multi-normal distribution" (Jöreskog & Sörbom, 1988, p. 21). Table 5 shows the measures, grouped into four dimensions that satisfied the one-dimensionality and convergent validity criteria and Figure 1 shows the conceptual model and the standardized coefficients of the items.

All the path coefficients for the model are significant at the alpha level of 0.01. In addition to the ML estimates, an important way in which the

Figure 1. The Confirmatory Model for ITC: Standardized Coefficient of the Model[1]. Note: a) ITA=Information technology architecture, ITINF=Information technology infrastructure, ITHR=Information technology human resource, ITRR=Information technology relationship resource. b) Model fit statistics: χ^2 =132.0, d.f. =84, CFI=0.951, TLI=0.930, IFI=0.953, RMSEA=0.07.

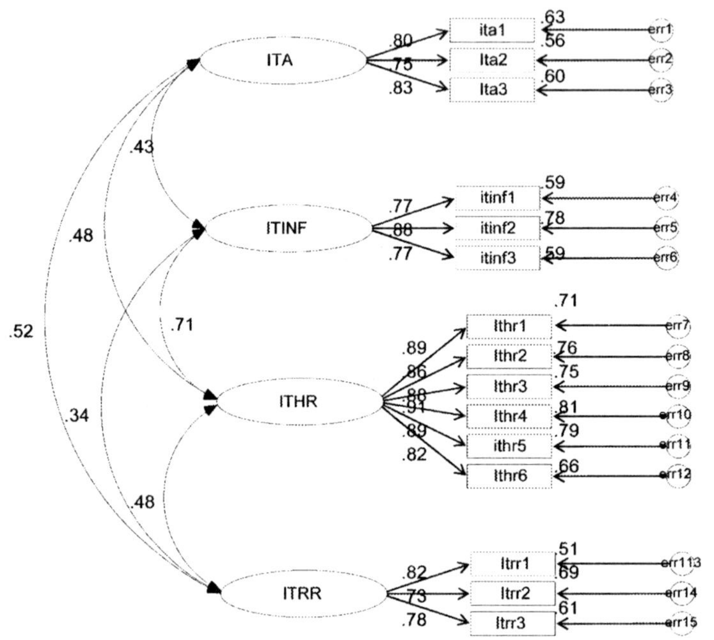

fit of a model can be assessed in SEM is by using the overall fit criteria such as the comparative fit index (CFI) (Bentler, 1990), the Tucker-Lewis index (TLI) (Tucker & Lewis, 1973), Incremental index of fit (IFI) (Bollen, 1989b), and the root mean square error of approximation (RMSEA) (Jöreskog & Sörbom, 1988). To do so, we use AMOS 4.0 (Arbuckle & Wothke, 1999). We report the fit statistics in Table 6.

Results in Figure 1 show that all the criteria were satisfied. According to Hair et al. (1998), the chi-square should be non-significant and its ratio to degrees of freedom should not be more than 3. The results in our study show that the chi-square is non-significant and its ratio to degrees of freedom is 1.51, which falls in between 1 to 2 or 3. All the other fit indices are above 0.90; the CFI is 0.951, the TLI is 0.930, the IFI is 0.953, and RMSEA is 0.07[2]. To summarize, the study scales were found to be both reliable and valid.

Figure 2 provides a partial nomological network and the results of additional analysis to address nomological validity issues. The literature suggests that ITC has a direct influence on firm's performance (Wade & Hulland, 2004). In this study, we argue that ITC has positive influence on the export focused small and medium sized firms' global market performance. A firm's global market performance is seen as having both a strategic and financial dimension, and is assessed on a worldwide basis that includes the domestic market. In this study, strategic performance refers to a firm's global market share and competitive position relative to major rivals. And financial performance refers to a firm's efficiency of generating high volume sales, sales growth, and profitability in the global market. Although financial performance is the ultimate goal for many firms, strategic performance is a vital intermediary gauge because it can lead to enhanced financial performance (Zou & Cavusgil 2002). Thus, using this simple nomoligical network, we tested a structural model with the four composite dimension scores as indicators of ITC. The results in Figure 2 show that the model fits the data very well (χ^2 =79.2, d.f.=32, CFI=0.926, IFI=0.929, RMSEA=0.10), and the standardized regression coefficients from: (1) ITC to strategic performance ($\gamma1$=0.55, t=4.18); (2) strategic performance to financial performance ($\gamma2$=0.84, t=7.94) are both statistically significant. Yet, the coefficients from ITC to financial performance (3) is not significant at 0.05 level ($\gamma3$=0.11, t=1.28).

DISCUSSION AND IMPLICATIONS

This paper reports on the development and validation of a measure of ITC for export-focused SMEs. The ITC scale was found to demonstrate adequate reliability and validity within the Chinese context[4]. Despite an increasing attention being paid to the concept of ITC in the area of IS research, till date, there has been no known work that has attempted to provide a conceptualization of *ITC of export-focused SMEs* which are important contributors to the global economy today. Whatever limited empirical work has been done in this area (e.g., Bharadwaj 2000), has been undertaken on larger firms in North America, and may not be directly applicable to export-focused SMEs for the following reasons: First of all, unlike larger firms, export-focused SMEs are constantly faced with "resource poverty" (Wang & Yao, 2002). Secondly, unlike many other large firms, these firms suffer from the "liability of foreignness" (arising from the costs associated with travel, transportation, etc. to foreign markets, and lack of familiarity with the foreign nation's business environment). We believe that the two above-mentioned differences of export-focused SMEs from larger firms will likely lead to the criticality of a different set

Figure 2. ITC and firm performance[3]. Note: Model fit: χ^2 =76.6, d.f. =32, CFI=0.946, TLI=0.907, IFI=0.948, NFI=0.913, RMSEA=0.10.

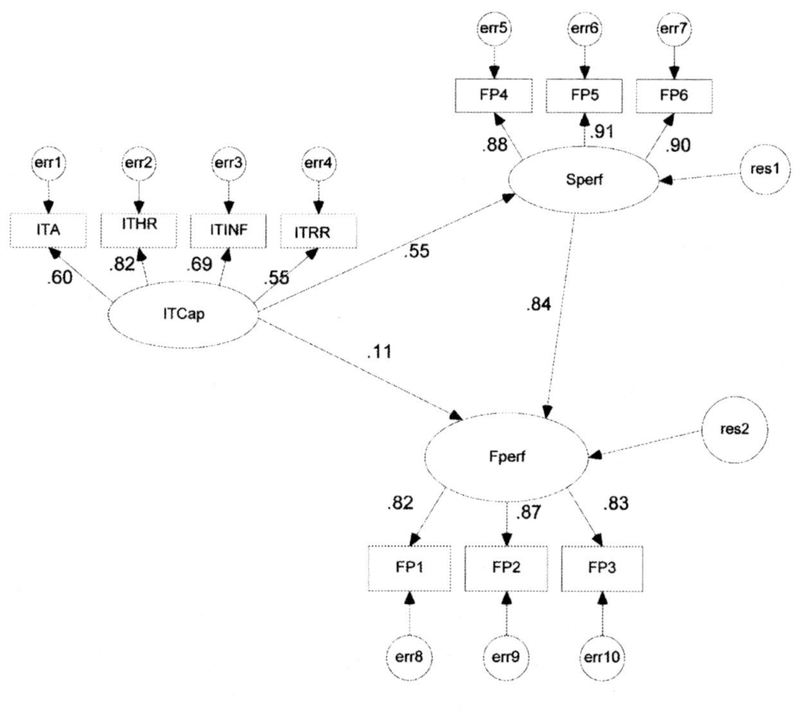

of ITC in such firms, and therefore warrant new empirical examination. Thus, this study attempts to fill this void. Our empirical examination also confirms that components of ITC relevant for large US firms may not be altogether relevant for export-focused SMEs in the developing world. For example, if we refer back to Table 4, we see that data architecture and architecture flexibility was found to be beyond the scope of IT architectural considerations of Chinese export-focused SMEs. Given their resource scarcity, and relatively smaller size, such organizations do not really invest time and money into formal integrative data architectures (e.g., Dhungana 2003); moreover, the architecture used is relatively simple, and thus inherently changeable, unlike in large organizations, where through the process of institutionalization, certain architectures may become linked to work practices in parts of the organization, making it difficult to modify.

The present study makes both academic and practical contributions and provides several implications for future research. The current study advances current literature on ITC in the following ways: First, it helps in understanding the multidimensionality of ITC, by unearthing the four components of ITC, namely, IT architecture, IT infrastructure, IT human resource and IT relationship resource. While some of the ideas and dimensions of ITC expressed in this paper may have been familiar to prior researchers, the value of this current study lies in the integration of these dimensions, and in the development of a more comprehensive model of ITC. Second, the study develops and empirically validates an instrument for measuring the four dimensions of ITC in the context of export-focused SMEs in China, and therefore provides a useful foundation for future researchers.

The proposed scale can also be used by practitioners, such as born global managers as a diagnostic tool to identify areas where specific improvements are needed, and to pinpoint aspects of the firm's ITC that require work. In addition to aiding in the diagnostic process, the components of ITC (especially, IT human resource) can also serve as training tools by helping human resource managers to develop appropriate training programs that can help in developing ITC.

Another significant finding of this study is that the ITC of export-focused SMEs has a positive and significant effect on a firm's global market performance. Specifically, ITC was found to influence a firm's strategic performance positively. However, the relationship between ITC and financial performance was not found to be significant. In this regard, Clemons and Row (1991) suggest that the 'benefits resulting from an innovative application of information technology can be more readily defended if the system exploits unique resources of the innovating firm so that competitors do not fully benefit from imitation.' Other researchers suggest that the effect of IT on a firm's financial performance cannot be measured directly, but can only be quantified by examining the indirect effect on some intervening firm capability such as organizational learning (Tippins & Sohi, 2003). We believe that the above discussion provides an explanation as to why ITC in this study, while positively affecting strategic performance, was not found to significantly impact born global firms' financial performance.

In summary, ITC is not as much a specific set of sophisticated technological functions as it is an enterprise-wide capability to leverage technology to differentiate from competition (Henderson & Venkatraman, 1993). To be able to accomplish this, a firm is required to have a clear understanding of the critical components of ITC and their role in supporting and shaping business strategy. This study represents a step toward a better understanding of the ITC construct and its dimensions. It also offers managers a comprehensive inventory of IT-related sources and activities, which can be used to identify areas of strength as well as areas in need of improvement.

LIMITATIONS AND FUTURE RESEARCH

A question that we see as important to address is: What is our generalizability claim with respect to the validated instrument? (See Table 5) We believe that while the underlying dimensions may remain the same across different types of organizations (export-focused SMEs or not) and across different cultures (Chinese or not), different items are likely to become relevant in different contexts. For example, the conception of information as personal resource rather than organizational resource, the informal nature of information use, and managerial decision-making based on personal experience and intuition within Chinese organizations (Wang et al. 2005; Martinson & Westwood, 1997), particularly those that are small and medium-sized, reduce the need for integrative data architectures (e.g., He, 2004). Data architectures often become inflexible in adapting to change in such contexts, because of the intricate set of dependencies that develop over time. This makes items ITA2 and ITA3 less relevant in this context. Moreover the hierarchical social structuring, leading to decision-making power residing solely with management, the informal nature of communication and information gathering, and the collectivist culture associated with the Chinese makes items ITRR1, 3, 4, and 8 unnecessary. Another possible reason is the small size and low age of these organizations, leading to relatively low level of hardened role differentiation and cross-functional barriers. Further, the question of good relationship with and sponsorship by management of IT efforts does not arise within the Chinese export-focused SME context, since without the sponsorship of management, there would be no IT group or IT projects in these organizations! With respect to ITRR5, given the "resource poverty" of the export-focused SMEs in China, it is not surprising that risk taking and experimentation with IT is not seen to contribute to IT relationship resource. It is altogether possible that, in larger more resourceful organizations in China or elsewhere, freedom to take risks and experiment with IT given to the IT group would be an important aspect of ITC arising from the relationship with management.

One possible limitation, then, is that the instrument is not necessarily generalizable across all types of organizations and cultures; however, as Lee and Baskerville (2003, p. 237) point out that the only way to legitimately claim generalizability for the instrument would be for it "to be actually tested and confirmed in the new setting." We submit, however, that export-focused SMEs, which need to survive in the global marketplace, do have many common characteristics and priorities, irrespective of their countries of origin. Thus, the items identified in Table 4, with some customization to specific contexts, should have relevance across the world, beyond China.

Another limitation of this study is the fact that we used the same dataset for both the exploratory and the confirmatory factor analyses (i.e., the tests for discriminant and convergent validity of the instruments), as opposed to using different data sets, which has been recommended in some prior studies. However, more recent literature argues that application of the EFA and CFA techniques to two different datasets could lead to problems in accurately interpreting the results, especially when there is a lack of correspondence between the results of the EFA and the CFA (Prooijen & Kloot, 2001). As a result, some researchers suggest that the EFA and the CFA should be conducted on the same data to start with (e.g., Van de Vijver & Leung, 1997; Prooijen and Kloot, 2001). The argument behind this is that it is important to know whether there is a fit of the CFA model and the data from which the factor structure was originally derived (i.e., the set of factors that were drawn from the EFA). If the CFA cannot confirm the results of the EFA on the same data, one cannot expect it to confirm the results of EFA in a different sample or population. We thus believe that given the paucity of instruments measuring ITC of export-focused SMEs in China, the use of the same dataset for both the EFA and the CFA could be justified at this point.

Yet another limitation of the study arises from the apparently mixed results of tests for nomological validity. While ITC was indeed found to have an effect on the strategic performance of export-focused firms (as per theoretical expectations, thereby indicating nomological validity), the lack of a significant effect of ITC on financial performance could potentially cast doubt on the nomological validity of the ITC construct. However, as discussed earlier, we do not believe that this poses a serious challenge, since prior literature indicates that in small-medium enterprises, ITC affects financial performance only indirectly through other factors such as organizational learning (e.g., Tippins & Sohi, 2003).

Finally, we must acknowledge that while we believe that we have comprehensively covered key aspects of ITC indicated in the literature, there are subtle aspects we and other researchers may have missed, or there may be other aspects of ITC that may become more (or less) salient as different technologies (e.g., web services, mobile collaboration) come to be increasingly utilized by SMEs.

CONCLUSION

This paper has sought to advance the existing body of knowledge on ITC in export-focused SMEs and are important players in the global business arena. In this paper, the definition of ITC has been clarified and its core components have been unearthed. Further, an instrument for measuring ITC in export-focused SMEs has been developed and empirically validated within the national context of China. While researchers may use the instrument provided in this paper with confidence, there is need for revisiting and re-validating the instruments for other cultures and contexts.

The validated instrument should also open other avenues for research. Since ITC has a strong influence on business performance in global market, it is essential to uncover the key antecedents of such capability. For example, how do different firm-level factors relevant to born-globals (e.g., international entrepreneurship orientation) and environmental factors (e.g., information intensity) impact the level and nature of ITC development? Moreover, a firm that pursues a given strategy develops certain capabilities that help it implement that strategy, thus increasing the likelihood that it will continue to use that same strategy in response to future environmental shifts. Yet, there is no known study on how ITC help implement firm strategies. Thus, future research could examine how firm level strategies are affected by ITC. Finally, given that capabilities are often created dynamically, future research could also investigate longitudinally how ITC is formed, strengthened, and redefined over time in the export-focused SMEs.

There is much to learn about export-focused companies and the role of ITC in determining their fates. We are hopeful that this study will prompt future researchers to further explore issues surrounding this important construct of ITC in "born globals" as well as other types of SMEs across the globe.

REFERENCES

Abouzeedan, A., & Busler, M. (2002). Information technology (IT) impact on performance of small and medium-size enterprises (SMEs). In *Proceedings of RENT XVI, Research in Entrepreneurship and Small business, 16th Workshop 2* (pp. 127-156).

Abouzeedan, A., & Busler, M. (2006). Information technology (IT) and small and medium-sized enterprises (SMEs) management: The concept of firm impact sphere. *Global Business Review*, *7*(2), 243–257. doi:10.1177/097215090600700204

Anderson, J. C., & Gerbing, D. W. (1982). Some methods for respecifying measurement models to obtain unidimensional construct measurement. *JMR, Journal of Marketing Research, 19*(4), 453–461. doi:10.2307/3151719

Arbuckle, J. L., & Wothke, W. (1999). AMOS 4.0 [Computer software]. Chicago: Smallwasters.

Arenius, P., Sasi, V., & Gabrielsson, M. (2006). Rapid internationalization enabled by the Internet: the case of a knowledge intensive company. *Journal of International Enterprise, 3*(4), 279–290. doi:10.1007/s10843-006-7856-x

Bagozzi, R.P., Tybout, A.M., Craig, S., & Sternthal, B.(1979). The construct validity of the tripartite classification of attitudes. *Journal of Marketing Research* (pre-1986), *16*(1), 88-96.

Bagozzi, R. P., Yi, Y., & Surrendra, S. (1991). On the use of structural equation models in experimental designs: Two extensions. *International Journal of Research in Marketing, 8*(2), 125–140. doi:10.1016/0167-8116(91)90020-8

Barney, J. B. (1991). Firm resources and sustained competitive advantage. *Journal of Management, 17*(1), 99–120. doi:10.1177/014920639101700108

Barrett, S., & Konsynski, B. (1982). Inter-organization information sharing systems. *MIS Quarterly*, (Special Issue), 93–105. doi:10.2307/248993

Bentle, P. M. (1990). Comparative fit indexes in structural models. *Psychological Bulletin, 107*(2), 238–246. doi:10.1037/0033-2909.107.2.238

Bharadwaj, A. S. (2000). A Resource-based perspective on information technology capability and firm performance, an empirical investigation. *MIS Quarterly, 24*(1), 169–196. doi:10.2307/3250983

Bharadwaj, A. S., Sambamurthy, V., & Zmud, R. W. (1999). *IT Capabilities: theoretical perspectives and empirical operationalization.* Paper presented at 20th International Conferences on Information Systems, Charlotte, NC.

Bhatt, G. D. (2000). Exploring the relationship between information technology, infrastructure and business process re-engineering. *Business Process Management Journal, 6*(2), 139–163. doi:10.1108/14637150010324085

Bhatt, G. D., & Grover, V. (2005). Types of information technology capabilities and their role in competitive advantage. *Journal of MIS, 22*(3), 253–277.

Bollen, K.A. (1989b). A new incremental fit index for general structural models. *Social logical Methods & Research, 17*(3), 303-316.

Bruque, S., & Moyano, J. (2007). Organisational determinants of information technology adoption and implementation in SMEs: The case of family and cooperative firms. *Technovation, 27*, 241 253. doi:10.1016/j.technovation.2006.12.003

Byrd, T. A., & Turner, D. E. (2000). Measuring the flexibility of information technology infrastructure, exploratory analysis of a construct. *Journal of Management Information Systems, 17*(1), 167–208.

Caldeira, M. M., & Ward, J. M. (2002). Understanding the successful adoption and use of IS/IT in SMEs: an explanation from Portuguese manufacturing industries. *Information Systems Journal, 12*(2), 121–152. doi:10.1046/j.1365-2575.2002.00119.x

Capon, N., & Glazer, R. (1987). Marketing and technology, a strategic co alignment. *Journal of Marketing, 51*(3), 1–14. doi:10.2307/1251644

Cavusgil, S. T. (1994). A quiet revolution in Australian exporters. *Marketing News, 28*, 18–21.

Chanopas, A., Krairit, D., & Khang, D. B. (2006). Managing information technology infrastructure: a new flexibility framework. *Management Research News*, *29*(10), 632–651. doi:10.1108/01409170610712335

Churchill, G. A. (1979). A Paradigm for developing better measures of marketing constructs. *JMR, Journal of Marketing Research*, *16*, 64–73. doi:10.2307/3150876

Clark, C. E., Cavanaugh, N. C., Brown, C. V., & Sambamurthy, V. (1997). Building change-readiness capabilities in the IS organization: insights from the Bell Atlantic experience. *MIS Quarterly*, *21*(4), 425–456. doi:10.2307/249722

Clemons, E. K., & Row, M. C. (1991). Sustaining IT advantage: the role of structural differences. *MIS Quarterly*, *15*(3), 275–294. doi:10.2307/249639

Copeland, D. G., & McKenney, J. L. (1988). Airline reservations systems, lessons from history. *MIS Quarterly*, *12*(3), 353–371. doi:10.2307/249202

Cronbach, L. J. (1951). Coefficient Alpha and the Internal Structure of Tests. *Psychometrica*, *16*(3), 297–334. doi:10.1007/BF02310555

Cronbach, L. J. (1970). Essentials of psychological testing (3rd ed.). New York: Harper & Row.

Dhungana, B. P. (2003). *Strengthening the competitiveness of small and medium enterprises in the globalization process: prospects and challenges*. Investment Promotion and Enterprise Development Bulletin for Asia and the Pacific.

Douglas, S. P., & Craig, C. S. (1983). *International Marketing Research.* Englewood Cliffs, NJ: Prentice-Hall.

Dow, D. (2006). Adaptation and performance in foreign markets: evidence of systematic under-adaptation. *Journal of International Business Studies*, *37*(2), 212–226. doi:10.1057/palgrave.jibs.8400189

Eisenhartd, K. M., & Schoonboven, C. B. (1996). Resource-based view of strategic alliance formation: strategic and social effects in entrepreneurial firms. *Organization Science*, *7*(2), 136–151. doi:10.1287/orsc.7.2.136

El Sawy, O. A., & Pavlou, P. A. (2008). IT-enabled business capabilities for turbulent environments. *MIS Quarterly Executive*, *7*(3), 139–150.

Feeny, D. F., & Willcocks, L. P. (1998a). Core IS Capabilities for exploiting information technology. *Sloan Management Review*, ▪▪▪, 9–21.

Feeny, D. F., & Willcocks, L. P. (1998b). Redesigning the IS function around core capabilities. *Long Range Planning*, *31*(3), 354–367. doi:10.1016/S0024-6301(98)80003-4

Fertuck, L. (1992). *Systems Analysis and Design with CASE Tools*. Wm. C. Dubuque, Iowa: Brown Communications Inc.

Fink, L., & Neumann, S. (2007). Gaining agility through IT personnel capabilities: the mediating role of IT infrastructure capabilities. *Journal of the Assocation for Information Systems*, *8*(8), 440–462.

Galbraith, J. (1973). *Designing Complex Organizations.* Reading, MA: Addison-Wesley Publishing Co.

Gibson, R. (1994). Global information technology architectures. *Journal of Global Information Management*, *2*(1), 28–39.

Grewal, R., Comer, & J.M., Mehta, R. (2001). An investigation into the antecedents of organizational participation in business-to-business electronic markets. *Journal of Marketing*, *65*(3), 17–34. doi:10.1509/jmkg.65.3.17.18331

Grewal, R., Johnson, J., & Sarker, S.(2007). Crises in Business Markets: Implications for Interfirm Linkages. *Journal of the Academy of Marketing Science*.

Grossman, R. B., & Packer, M. B. (1989). Betting the business, strategic programs to rebuild core information systems. *Information Technology & People*, *5*(4), 235–244. doi:10.1108/EUM0000000003537

Hair, J. F., Anderson, R. E., Tatham, R. L., & Black, W. C. (1998). *Multivariate Data Analysis*. Upper Saddle River, NJ: Prentice-Hall.

Harvie, C., & Lee, H. H. (2003). Export-led industrialization and growth: Korea's economic miracle, 1962-1989. *Australian Economic History Review*, *43*(3), 256–286. doi:10.1046/j.1467-8446.2003.00054.x

He, X. (2004). The ERP challenge in China: a resource-based perspective. *Information Systems Journal*, *14*(2), 153–167. doi:10.1111/j.1365-2575.2004.00168.x

Heijden, H. V. D. (2000). Measuring IT core capabilities for electronic commerce, results from a confirmatory factor analysis. *Proceedings of the 21st ICIS, December*.

Henderson, J. C., & Venkatraman, N. (1993). Strategic alignment, Leveraging information technology for transforming organizations. *IBM Systems Journal*, *32*(1), 40–64.

Hollenstein, H. (2005). Determinants of international activities: are SMEs different? *Small Business Economics*, *24*(5), 431–450. doi:10.1007/s11187-005-6455-x

Hunter, M.G. (2004). Information system and small business: research issues. *Journal of Global Information Management,* Oct-Dec, *12*(4), 1-6.

Inmon, W. H. (1989). *Data architecture, The information paradigm*. Wellesley, MA, QED Information Sciences.

Johnson, J. E. (2004). Factors influencing the early internationalization of high technology start-ups: U.S. and U.K. evidence. *Journal of International Entrepreneurship*, *2*(2), 139–152. doi:10.1023/B:JIEN.0000026910.87323.4e

Jöreskog, K. G., & Sörbom, D. (1988). *LISREL 7, A Guide to the program and applications.* Chicago, IL: SPSS Inc.

Keen, P. G. W. (1991). *Shaping the future, business design through information technology.* Boston: Harvard Business School Press.

Kim, M. K., & Jee, K. Y. (2007). Factors influencing strategic use of informationt technology and its impact on business performance of SMEs. *ETRI Journal*, *29*(4), 497–506. doi:10.4218/etrij.07.0106.0303

Knight, G. A., & Cavusgil, S. T. (2004). Innovation, organizational capabilities, and the born-global firms. *Journal of International Business Studies*, *35*(2), 124–141. doi:10.1057/palgrave.jibs.8400071

Kundu, S. K., & Katz, J. A. (2003). Born-International SMEs: BI-level impacts of resources and intenstions. *Small Business Economics*, *20*(1), 25–48. doi:10.1023/A:1020292320170

Kyobe, M. E. (2004). Investigating the strategic utilization of it resources in the small and medium-sized firms of the eastern free state province. *International Small Business Journal*, *22*(2), 131–158. doi:10.1177/0266242604041311

Lambe, C. J., Spekman, R. E., & Hunt, S. D. (2002). Alliance competence, resources, and alliance success: conceptualization, measurement, and initial test. *Journal of the Academy of Marketing Science*, *30*(2), 141–158. doi:10.1177/03079459994399

Lee, A. S., & Baskerville, R. L. (2003). Generalizing generalizability in information systems research. *Information Systems Research*, *14*(3), 221–243. doi:10.1287/isre.14.3.221.16560

Levy, M., Loebbecke, C., & Powell, P. (2003). SMEs, co-opetition and knowledge sharing: the role of information systems. *European Journal of Information Systems, 12*(1), 3–17. doi:10.1057/palgrave.ejis.3000439

Li, H., & Atuahene-Gima, K. (2001). Production innovation strategy and the performance of new technology ventures in China. *Academy of Management Journal, 44*(6), 1123–1134. doi:10.2307/3069392

Light, R. J., Singer, J. D., & Willett, J. B. (1990). *By Design: Planning Research on Higher Education*, Cambridge, MA: Harvard University Press.

Love, Peter, E.D., & Irani, Z. (2004). An exploratory study of information technology evaluative and benefits management practices of SMEs in the construction industry. *Information & Management, 42*(1), 227–242.

Love, P. E. D., Irani, Z., Standing, C., Lin, C., & Burn, J. M. (2005). The enigma of evaluation: benefits, costs and risks of IT in Australian small-medium-sized enterprises. *Information & Management, 42*(7), 947–964. doi:10.1016/j.im.2004.10.004

Madsen, T. K., Rasmussen, E., & Servais, P. (2000). Differences and similarities between born globals and other types of exporters. *Advances in International Marketing, 10*(2), 247–265. doi:10.1016/S1474-7979(00)10013-4

Martinsons, M. G., & Westwood, R. I. (1997). Management information systems in the Chinese business culture: An explanatory theory. *Information & Management, 32*(5), 215–228. doi:10.1016/S0378-7206(96)00009-2

McKenney, J. L. (1995). *Waves of Change, Business Evolution through information technology.* Cambridge, MA: Harvard Business School Press.

McKinsey & Company. (1993) *Emerging exporters: Australia's high value-added manufacturing exporters*. Melbourne: McKinsey and Company and the Australian manufacturing council.

Moen, O., & Servais, P. (2002). Born Global or Gradual Global? Examining the export behavior of small and medium-sized enterprises. *Journal of International Marketing, 10*(3), 49–72. doi:10.1509/jimk.10.3.49.19540

Montazemi, A. R. (2006). How they manage IT: SMEs in Canada and the U.S. *Communications of the ACM, 49*(12), 109–112. doi:10.1145/1183236.1183240

Morgan, N. A., Kaleka, A., & Katsikeas, C. S. (2000). Antecedents of export venture performance: a theoretical model and empirical assessment. *Journal of Marketing, 68*(1), 90–108. doi:10.1509/jmkg.68.1.90.24028

Mulligan, P. (2002). Specification of a capability-based IT classification framework. *Information & Management, 39*(8), 647. doi:10.1016/S0378-7206(01)00117-3

Nonaka, I., & Takeuchi, H. (1995). *The knowledge-creating company, how Japanese companies create the dynamics of innovation.* New York: Oxford University Press.

Nunnally, J. C. (1978). *Psychometric Theory.* New York: McGraw Hill, Inc.

Oviatt, B. M., & McDougall, P. P. (1994). Toward a theory of international new ventures. *Journal of International Business Studies, 25*(1), 45–64. doi:10.1057/palgrave.jibs.8490193

Oviatt, B. M., & McDougall, P. P. (1999). Challenges for internationalization process theory: the case of international new ventures. *Management International Review, 37*(1), 85–99.

Peppard, J., & Ward, J. (2004). Beyond strategic information systems: towards an IS capability. *The Journal of Strategic Information Systems, 13*(2), 167–194. doi:10.1016/j.jsis.2004.02.002

Powell, T. C., & Dent-Micallef, A. (1997). Information technology as competitive advantage, The role of human, business, and technology resources. *Strategic Management Journal, 18*(5), 375–405. doi:10.1002/(SICI)1097-0266(199705)18:5<375::AID-SMJ876>3.0.CO;2-7

Prasad, V. K., Ramamurthy, K., & Naidu, G. M. (2001). The influence of Internet-marketing integration on marketing competencies and export performance. *Journal of International Marketing, 9*(4), 82–111. doi:10.1509/jimk.9.4.82.19944

Prooijen, J. W. V., & Kloot, V. D. (2001). Confirmatory analysis of explanatively obtained factor structures. *Educational and Psychological Measurement, 61*(5), 777–792. doi:10.1177/00131640121971518

Ray, G., Muhanna, W. A., & Barney, J. B. (2005). Information technology and the performance of the customer service process: A resource-based analysis. *MIS Quarterly, 29*, 625–652.

Rennie, M. W. (1993). Global competitiveness, Born Global. *The McKinsey Quarterly* Number 4, 45-52.

Rockart, J. F., Earl, M. J., & Ross, J. W. (1996). Eight imperatives for the new IT organization. *Sloan Management Review, 38*(1), 43–56.

Roepke, R., Agarwal, R., & Ferratt, T. W. (2000). Aligning the IT human resource with business vision: the leadership initiative at 3M. *MIS Quarterly, 24*(2), 327–353. doi:10.2307/3250941

Ross, J. W., Beath, C. M., & Goodhue, D. L. (1996). Develop long-term competitiveness through IT assets. *Sloan Management Review, 38*(1), 31–33.

Sabherwal, R. (1999). The relationship between information system planning sophistication and information system success, An empirical assessment. *Decision Sciences, 30*(1), 137–168. doi:10.1111/j.1540-5915.1999.tb01604.x

Sabherwal, R., & Kirs, P. (1994). The alignment between organizational critical success factors and information technology capability in academic institutions. *Decision Sciences, 25*(2), 301–331. doi:10.1111/j.1540-5915.1994.tb01844.x

Sambamurthy, V., Bharadwaj, A., & Grover, V. (2003). Shaping agility through digital options: Reconceptualizing the role of information technology in contemporary firms. *MIS Quarterly, 27*(2), 237–263.

Sambamurthy, V., & Zmud, R. W. (1992). *Managing IT for success, The empowering business partnership*. Morristown, NJ: Financial Executives Research Foundation.

Santhanam, R., & Hartono, E. (2003). Issues in linking information technology capability to firm performance. *MIS Quarterly, 27*(1), 125–153.

Sarker, S., Valacich, J., & Sarker, S. (2003). Virtual team trust: instrument development and validation in an IS educational environment. *Information Resources Management Journal, 16*(2), 35–55.

Saunders, C. S. (2000). *Virtual Teams: Piecing Together the Puzzle.* In R.W. Zmud (Ed.), *Framing the Domains of IT Management: Projecting the Future through the Past.* Cincinnati, OH: Pinnaflex.

Sethi, V., & King, W. R. (1991). Construct measurement in Information systems research, An illustration in strategic systems. *Decision Sciences, 22*(3), 455–472. doi:10.1111/j.1540-5915.1991.tb01274.x

Siu, W., Fang, W., & Lin, T. (2004). Strategic marketing practices and the performance of Chinese small and medium-sized enterprises Taiwan. *Entrepreneurship and Regional Development, 16*(2), 161–178. doi:10.1080/08985620410001677862

Song, M., Nason, R. W., & Di Benedetto, C. A. (2008). Distinctive marketing and information technology capabilities and strategic types: A cross-national investigation. *Journal of International Marketing, 16*(1), 4–38. doi:10.1509/jimk.16.1.4

Spencer, R. A. (1985). Information Architecture. *Journal of Systems Management, 36*(11), 34–42.

Sullivan, C. H., Jr. (1982). Rethinking computer systems architecture. *Computerworld extra,* XVI, 5-10.

Teo, T. S. H., & King, W. R. (1997). An assessment of perceptual differences between informants in information systems research. *Omega, 25*(5), 557–566. doi:10.1016/S0305-0483(97)00031-5

Tippins, M. J., & Sohi, R. S. (2003). IT competency and firm performance: Is organizational learning a missing link? *Strategic Management Journal, 24*(8), 745–761. doi:10.1002/smj.337

Torgerson, W. S. (1967). *Theory and methods of scaling*. New York: Wiley.

Tucker, L. R., & Lewis, C. (1973). A reliability coefficient for maximum likelihood factor analysis. *Psychometrika, 38*(1), 1–10. doi:10.1007/BF02291170

Turban, E., Leidner, D., McLean, E., & Wetherbe, J. (2006). *Information Technology For Management* (5th Ed.). NJ: John Wiley & Sons.

Van de Vijver, F., & Leung, K. (1997). *Methods and data analysis for cross-cultural research.* Thousand Oaks, CA: Sage.

Venkatraman, N. (1989). Strategic orientation of business enterprises: The construct, dimensionality, and measurement. *Management Science, 35*(8), 942–962. doi:10.1287/mnsc.35.8.942

Venkatraman, N. (1991). *IT-related business reconfiguration*. New York: Oxford University Press.

Wade, M., & Hulland, J. (2004). Review: The resource-based view and information systems research: Review, extension, and suggestions for future research. *MIS Quarterly, 28*(1), 107–143.

Wang, C., Xu, L., Liu, X., & Qins, X. (2005). ERP research, development and implementation in China: an overview. *International Journal of Production Research, 43*(18), 3915–3932. doi:10.1080/13629390500124556

Wang, Li., & Alam, P. (2007). Information technology capability: firm valuation, earnings uncertainty, and forecast accuracy. *Journal of Information Systems, 21*(2), 27–48. doi:10.2308/jis.2007.21.2.27

Wang, Y., & Yao, Y. (2002). Market reforms, technological capabilities and the performance of small enterprises in China. *Small Business Economics, 18*(2), 197–211.

Weill, P., Broadbent, M., & Butler, C. (1996). Exploring how firms view IT infrastructure. Working Paper.

Zhang, Y., & Tang, Y. (2002). Challenges facing SMEs in China: A preliminary analysis. In Shaw, R., Adam, S., McDonald H. (Eds), *Proceedings of the Australia New Zealand Marketing Academy Conference.*

Zou, S. M., & Cavusgil, S. T. (2002). The GMS: A broad conceptualization of global marketing strategy and its effect on firm performance. *Journal of Marketing, 66*(Oct), 40–56. doi:10.1509/jmkg.66.4.40.18519

Zou, S. M., Taylor, C. R., & Osland, G. E. (1998). The EXPERF Scale: A cross-national generalized export performance measure. *Journal of International Marketing*, *6*(3), 37–58.

ENDNOTES

1 Latent constructs are shown in ellipses, and observed variables are shown in rectangles. All coefficients are significant at $p<0.001$.

2 Suggested values for CFI, TLI, IFI are greater than 0.90, and the suggested value for RMSEA is less than 0.08 (Hair, et al., 1998)

3 Latent constructs are shown in ellipses, and observed variables are shown in rectangles.

4 In developing our study, we had two choices: (1) to develop measurement items initially that were customized closely to fit the context of Chinese export-focused SMEs that relied on exports soon after inception; or (2) to develop, through a thorough review of the ITC literature, a set of items within the four dimensions of ITC that appeared relevant to SMEs in general, and then to empirically determine (deductively) which of them turned out to be relevant in the Chinese export-focused SMEs context. We chose the latter. Indeed, through the scale validation process, only those items that were relevant to the Chinese export-focused firms survived, and in that sense, the scale we present can be directly utilized by researchers interested in Chinese SMEs. There was an additional advantage of using the second approach. Because we started with a set of items potentially suitable for a broader set of organizations (not just Chinese export-focused firms), future researchers investigating ITC is different contexts (e.g., export-focused firms in say Australia) may choose to use our initial set of items and then empirically determine which of those items are applicable to their context of interest.

Chapter 12
Internet-Based E-Commerce in Small Chinese Firms in New Zealand

Jihong Chen
University of Waikato, New Zealand

Robert J. McQueen
University of Waikato, New Zealand

ABSTRACT

This chapter investigates an e-commerce "stages of growth" model in a cross-cultural business context for small firms operated by Chinese-born owners in New Zealand. Research findings from fourteen case studies show that the Chinese owners/managers of these small firms have a high power distance, and their attitude toward e-commerce technology directly influences their firms' e-commerce growth process. It was found that the higher the stage of e-commerce adoption, the greater the need for owners having a more positive attitude toward e-commerce, more innovativeness and enthusiasm, and more technology literacy. The stronger the uncertainty avoidance and the higher the risk-taking propensity, the higher the stage of e-commerce adoption achieved. In addition, firms at lower growth stages of e-commerce adoption are highly rated on individualism, while those firms at higher growth stage of commerce adoption are highly rated on collectivism. The research has implications for small business managers operating in a cross-cultural business context as they move through the different stage of e-commerce adoption.

INTRODUCTION

Electronic commerce (e-commerce) refers to the use of the Internet for buying and selling activities (Rodgers, Yen, & Chou, 2002). It covers processes that touch customers, suppliers and external partners, including sales, marketing, order taking, delivery, customer service, purchasing of raw materials and supplies for production and procurement of indirect operating-expense items, such as office supplies (Bartels, 2000). Driven by the Internet and economic globalization, e-commerce is becoming important in many organizations, both large and small. There is a growing body of literature dedicated to the analysis of factors affecting e-commerce adoption (e.g., Bakker, Zheng, Knight, & Harland, 2008; Hong & Zhu, 2006; To & Ngai, 2006).

DOI: 10.4018/978-1-60566-920-5.ch012

In recent years, Asian immigration has increased dramatically in New Zealand. Statistics New Zealand (2003) forecast that New Zealand's Asian population would reach 667,000 in 2021, more than double the estimated resident population of 272,000 at 30 June 2001. Within the Asian migrant group, the Chinese ethnic group has grown quickly. Statistics New Zealand (2001) indicates that the overseas-born Chinese ethnic group experienced the largest increase in population between 1991 and 2001. In 1991, 28,401 Chinese people moved to New Zealand but this number increased dramatically to 78,519 in 2001 with 5508 of these new immigrants working in the retail trade industry. For the 2003/2004 year the top four groups of migrants, were Britain(20.8%), China (16.6%), Australia (14%), and India (6.6%) (NZIS, 2004). Many of the Asian immigrants have invested and established their business in New Zealand. The direct Asian investment to New Zealand has grown from US$70 billion in 1985 to US$1,785 billion in 2006. Over the last 20 years, about US$28 billion – slightly more than 1.5% of the total additional investment growth (NZIER, 2008). Large Asian investors in Auckland have been estimated to each have between $20-30 million invested in the region (McMillan, 2002). According to Statistics New Zealand reports, from year 2001 to year 2003, there has been a great increase in the number of small Chinese firms being founded in New Zealand (Statistics New Zealand, 2003) and adopting e-commerce in their businesses. The increase in Chinese companies will play an important role in the New Zealand economy.

However, there has been little research published on the influence factors of e-commerce adoption in small firms in a cross-cultural business context. This research will explore the adoption of Internet-based e-commerce technology in small Chinese firms with a cross-cultural business context, ranging from the use of e-mail to the development of advanced online transaction websites. At each stage of the evolution, this study will investigate what adoption motivators and adoption inhibitors influence the evolution. This study will analyze what factors affect the decisions that small business executives make as they move through the different stages or levels of Internet-based e-commerce adoption. Mirchandani and Motwani (2001) argue that some inhibitors could be present at all levels and some ones could only be present at certain levels and disappear at other levels. This study will identify inhibitors and motivators linked to adoption stages. In addition, this study will investigate whether the Chinese cultural profile still applies when these owners consider adoption of e-commerce in the New Zealand business context.

The Australian Bureau of Statistics defines a small firm as any business employing less than 20 people, which is closely controlled by the owner/managers who contribute most of the operating capital. The principal decision making rests with the owner/managers (Australian Bureau of Statistics, 2004). In this study, small Chinese firms in New Zealand are defined here as the small firms with fewer than 20 employees established by Chinese immigrants in New Zealand.

The remainder of the paper is structured as follows. Section two briefly examines the literature on e-commerce growth models, influence factors on e-commerce adoption, and business culture differences between New Zealand and Chinese; section three describes the research methodology; section four presents the research findings and discussions; and section five draws conclusions from the research, points out limitations and provides managerial implications of this work.

LITERATURE REVIEW

Small Firms' E-Commerce Growth Model

A review of the literature relating to e-commerce adoption in small firms reveals that the adoption of e-commerce typically proceeds in a set

Table 1. Daniel Model

Stage	Main E-commerce Activities
Stage one (Developers)	1.Search information 2.Using on-line services 3.Using e-mail to communicate with customers and suppliers;
Stage two (communicators)	Development of websites to provide company or product and service information Extensive use of email to communicate with customers and suppliers Electronically exchanging documents and designs with customers, suppliers and employees 4.Email ordering
Stage three (web presence)	1.Websites that have information about their company, and its products and services 2. Taking of orders and receiving orders online 3. Having shopping cart on the website
Stage four (Transactors)	1. Receiving on-line credit card payments 2. Providing after-sales service or contact 3. Ordering and payment of inventory purchasing

of sequential stages (Allcock S, Webber S, & Yeates, 1999; Daniel, Wilson, & Myers, 2002; Department of Trade and Industry, 2000; Nolan, 1979; PriceWaterhouseCoopers, 1999; Rao, Metts, & Monge, 2003). Staged models have been criticized in the literature for being too simplistic, and because many small businesses never get to advanced stages (Levy & Powell, 2003; Mendo & Fitzgerald, 2005). In spite of these concerns, substantial research has been undertaken using these models, and the most prominent of these e-commerce adoption sequential models are summarized as follows.

Nolan Model

Nolan (1979) states that there are six stages of growth in a company's data process function from the inception of the computer into the organization to mature management of data resources. The six stages include stage I initiation, stage II contagion, stage III control, stage IV integration, Stage V data administration and stage VI maturity.

Daniel Model

Daniel, Wilson and Myers (2002) point out four distinct stages in e-commerce adoption. These are developer, communicator, web presenter and transactors. The four distinct stages in e-commerce adoption are classified in Table 1.

DTI Model

The Department of Trade and Industry (DTI) (2000) developed a six-step e-commerce adoption ladder, which includes messaging, online marketing, online ordering, online payment, order sales support and e-business. The six-step e-commerce adoption ladder is summarized in Table 2 (Department of Trade and Industry, 2000).

PriceWaterhouseCoopers Model

PriceWaterhouseCoopers (1999) points out four levels of e-commerce adoption by SMEs. The four levels suggest a development process consists of having basic online capabilities, developing a home page with online catalogue, having online ordering, and having the ability to make online payments. The four levels of e-commerce development are summarized in Table 3.

Allcock Model

Allcock et al. (1999) constructed a 4-step 'staircase of Internet engagement' approach. The approach points out the steps of Internet adoption from only

Table 2.DTI's Model

Step	Main E-commerce Activities
Messaging	Use of e-mail to send text messages
Online marketing	Creation of a website or e-mail to publish information about products and services
Online ordering	Online interaction between a business and its customers, or a business and its suppliers, for the placement of an order.
Online payment	An invoice can be issued or received, and the transaction online can be completed by an electronic payment. This can be undertaken through the use of debit and credit cards, electronic cash, electronic funds transfer, or through an EDI service.
Order progress/online sales support	The use of e-commerce to support the business relationship between a customer and a supplier
E-business	An integration of all these activities with the internal processes of a business through ICT.

Table 3. PriceWaterhouseCoopers Model

Level	Main E-commerce Activities
Level 1	Having a very basic or no online capabilities
Level 2	Having a web site, but no advanced capabilities
Level 3	Having the ability to take orders and provide customer service on their web site;
Level 4	Having the ability to make complete transactions and receive payment on their web site

having a computer, to connecting with the Internet, having static website, or having an interactive website (Allcock S, Webber S, & Yeates, 1999). The staircase of Internet engagement staged approach is summarized in Table 4.

Rao Model

Rao, Metts and Monge (2003) proposed an E-commerce stage growth model. The model includes four stages: presence, portals, transactions integration and enterprises integration. The four-stage e-commerce growth model is summarized in Table 5.

Synthesis of a Small Firm E-Commerce Growth Model

In this paper, these approaches are synthesised and integrated within the following model for stages of evolution of e-commerce adoption (see Table 6). This model provides a basis on which to understand how businesses progress from relatively simple to more complex e-commerce activities.

Table .4. Allcock Model

Steps	Main E-commerce Activities
1. Threshold	Having computers, but without connecting to Internet
2. Beginner	Connected to Internet, but without website
3. Intermediate	Having a static website, and email to suppliers, but without e-commerce development strategy
4. Advanced	Having interactive website, high ICT skills, strong ICT strategy, being networked.

Table 5. Rao Model

Steps	Main E-commerce Activities
1. Presence	Involving the initial steps that organizations gets involved in a digital environment and having a "window to the Web"
2. Portals	Introducing a two-way communication, customer or supplier order placing, the use of profiles and cookies, but without financial transactions.
3. Transactions Integration	Presenting financial transactions between partners, including the participation in virtual communities and allow participants to share information around an area of common interest, electronic auctions and third party e-marketplaces.
4. Enterprises integration	Completing integration of business processes. The level of integration involves high levels of collaboration between customers and suppliers. Enterprises integration includes full integration of B2B and B2C business including value chain integration (i.e E-commerce + CRM + SCM).

The four stages of this synthesised model are presented in Table 6.

If all four stages are completed, the firm will move from simple e-commerce into full e-business. This article will focus mainly on the first three stages, because the fourth and final stage, e-business, is relatively uncommon in small businesses, perhaps because such capabilities are expensive for many small firms at this point in time.

Influence Factors on E-commerce Adoption by Small Firms

Motivators of E-Commerce Adoption in Small Firms

Much e-commerce literature is devoted to descriptions of the motivators to e-commerce adoption in small firms. There are numerous motivators that have been suggested, so they are summarized in Table 7. With the increasing awareness and

Table 6. Four-stage Adoption Model

Stage	Main E-commerce Activities
Stage one (Messaging)	1.Searching information; 2.Using on-line services; 3.Using e-mail to communicate with customers and suppliers;
Stage two (Online marketing)	1. Having static website and an on-line version of a paper-based catalogue; 2.Extensive use of email to communicate and exchange documents and orders with customers, suppliers and employees; 3.Email ordering;
Stage three (Online ordering)	1. Having two-way information interactive websites that provide topics search, company information query; 2. Using shopping cart software to place an order on the website; 3. Payment can be fulfilled manually by bank deposit, bank cheque or internet banking; 4. Expanding the potential market nationally;
Stage four (Online transaction)	1. Online order fulfilment can be accomplished automatically, i.e. an order can be received or confirmed, and an invoice can be issued or received online; 2. Online payment can be undertaken through debit and credit cards, electronic cash, electronic funds transfer, or through an EDI service; 3. Integrating online front-end and back-end system; 4. Expanding the potential market internationally;
E-business	Integrating all these activities with the internal processes of a business through ICT

Table 7. Summary of previous literature on adoption motivators of e-commerce in small firms

Component	Motivators	Source
Owner's Characteristics	Strongly leadership-oriented in computerization	(Bridge, O'Neill, & Cromie, 2003; Moran, 1998)
	Tolerance for ambiguity	(Moran, 1998; Sexton & Bowman, 1984)
	Risk-taking propensity	(Begley & Boyd, 1986; Brockhaus, 1980; Moran, 1998)
	Innovativeness	(Gengatharen & Standing, 2005; Kirton, 1976,, 1984; Thong, 1999)
	Enthusiasm toward e-commerce	(Elliott & Boshoff, 2007; Mirchandani & Motwani, 2001)
Owner's Knowledge	Knowledge of e-commerce	(Ettlie, 1990; Gable & Raman, 1992; Hong & Zhu, 2006; Thong, 1999)
Increasing the performance of the business	Increasing efficiency	(Bowden et al., 2001; Malone, 2002; NOIE & Young, 2001; Rao, Metts, & Monge, 2003; Robeiro & Love, 2003; Rodgers, Yen, & Chou, 2002; SETEL, 1999)
	Increasing productivity	(Abell & Black, 1997; Chong, 2001; Cloete, Courtney, & Fintz, 2002; Cowles, Kiecker, & Little, 2002; Malone, 2002; Rodgers, Yen, & Chou, 2002)
	Increasing sales and revenue	(Nancy, Michael, & Andrew, 2004; PriceWaterhouseCoopers, 1999)
	Improving competitive position, increasing market share of products/services	(Amor, 2000; Cloete, Courtney, & Fintz, 2002; Nancy, Michael, & Andrew, 2004; PriceWaterhouseCoopers, 1999; Rao, Metts, & Monge, 2003)
Market promotion	Direct and indirect advertising	(Amor, 2000; Chong, 2001; Cloete, Courtney, & Fintz, 2002; Cowles, Kiecker, & Little, 2002; Elliott & Boshoff, 2007; Hornby, Goulding, & Poon, 2002; Mehrtens, Cragg, & Mills, 2001)
Improving CRM	Improving customer relations	(Bowden et al., 2001; Cloete, Courtney, & Fintz, 2002; Malone, 2002; Nancy, Michael, & Andrew, 2004; Scupola, 2002)
	Improving customer service	(Amor, 2000; Bowden et al., 2001; Malone, 2002; NOIE & Young, 2001; Rodgers, Yen, & Chou, 2002; SETEL, 1999)
	Improving communication with customers	(Amor, 2000; Bowden et al., 2001; Cowles, Kiecker, & Little, 2002; Mehrtens, Cragg, & Mills, 2001; Riquelme, 2002; Scupola, 2002; SETEL, 1999)
	Increasing customer satisfaction	(Abell & Black, 1997; Malone, 2002)
	Expanding customer base	(Amor, 2000; Cowles, Kiecker, & Little, 2002; Hornby, Goulding, & Poon, 2002; Malone, 2002; Riquelme, 2002)
	Track customers' tastes and preferences	(Riquelme, 2002; SETEL, 1999)
Enhancing supply chain collaboration and coordination	Improving relationships with suppliers	(Bakker, Zheng, Knight, & Harland, 2008; Chong, 2001; Malone, 2002; NOIE & Young, 2001)
	Improving coordination with suppliers (Better service and support from suppliers)	(Abell & Black, 1997; Malone, 2002; Rao, Metts, & Monge, 2003)
	Speed of fulfilling orders	(Malone, 2002; Rodgers, Yen, & Chou, 2002; SETEL, 1999)
	Improving inventory management	(Chong, 2001; Hong & Zhu, 2006; Malone, 2002)
	Greater approximation to a just-in-time inventory scheme	(Rodgers, Yen, & Chou, 2002)

Table 7. continued

Component	Motivators	Source
Savings in time and costs	Speedy and timely access to information from Websites	(Abell & Black, 1997; Anumba & Ruikar, 2002; Chong, 2001; Hornby, Goulding, & Poon, 2002; Malone, 2002; Mehrtens, Cragg, & Mills, 2001; SETEL, 1999)
	Savings in communication costs	(Chong, 2001; Cloete, Courtney, & Fintz, 2002; Hornby, Goulding, & Poon, 2002; Malone, 2002; Mehrtens, Cragg, & Mills, 2001; Robeiro & Love, 2003; SETEL, 1999)
	Disintermediation & quicker product comparison in term of price & quality	(Anumba & Ruikar, 2002)
New business models	New sales channels, reach new markets	(Abell & Black, 1997; Chong, 2001; Cloete, Courtney, & Fintz, 2002; Malone, 2002; SETEL, 1999)
	Simplified, flexible way of doing business	(Anumba & Ruikar, 2002; SETEL, 1999)
External pressure	Pressure from trading partners	(Bakker, Zheng, Knight, & Harland, 2008; Beatty, 1998; Hong & Zhu, 2006; Iacovou, Benbasat, & Dexter, 1995; Premkumar & Ramamurthy, 1995; Saffu, Walker, & Hinson, 2008; To & Ngai, 2006)
	More competitors adopt e-commerce	(Crum, Premkumar, & Ramamurthy, 1996; Gatignon & Robertson, 1989; Iacovou, Benbasat, & Dexter, 1995; Thatcher, Foster, & Zhu, 2006; To & Ngai, 2006)
ICT infrastructure	Telecommunications infrastructure	(European Commission, 1999; Hawk, 2004; Tang, Powell, Worlock, & Bingham, 2000; WSIS, 2003)
	Internet infrastructure service	(Thatcher, Foster, & Zhu, 2006; To & Ngai, 2006)
	Availability of wide-diffused computer hardware and software	(Cloete, Courtney, & Fintz, 2002; Dedrick & Kraemer, 2001; Thatcher, Foster, & Zhu, 2006)
Government policy	A stable legal and regulatory framework	(Castells, 2000; New Zealand Ministry of Economic Development, 2000)
	Government fund adoption initiatives	(Tang, Powell, Worlock, & Bingham, 2000; WSIS, 2003)
	Expertise directory	(Tang, Powell, Worlock, & Bingham, 2000; UK online for busienss, 2003)

understanding of the advantages of e-commerce, small firms may be more interested in adopting e-business technology in their businesses.

Inhibitors of E-Commerce Adoption in Small Firms

Studying the inhibitors of e-commerce adoption is useful in determining the reason why a small firm is at a certain level. Much e-commerce literature is devoted to descriptions the inhibitors to e-commerce adoption in small firms, and is summarized in Table 8.

Another aspect of e-commerce adoption by small firms that was of interest to the research was the impact of cultural issues, when a set of small business managers with a common cultural background had set up and were running their businesses in a country with a different culture.

Chinese Business Culture and New Zealand Business Culture

Hofstede (1997) provides empirical support for the proposition that there is a fundamental difference between New Zealand and Chinese business

Table 8. Summary of previous literature on adoption inhibitors of e-commerce in small firms

Component	Inhibitors	Source
Owner's attitude toward e-business	Owner's attitudes	(Chen, Chen, & Shao, 2003; David, 2004; Elliott & Boshoff, 2007; Heung, 2003; Matti & Andrew, 2004; Mehrtens, Cragg, & Mills, 2001; Mirchandani & Motwani, 2001; OECD, 1998; USHER, 2003)
	General awareness & education	(Chong, 2001; Cloete, Courtney, & Fintz, 2002; Damaskopoulos & Evgeniou, 2003; Heung, 2003; Matti & Andrew, 2004; USHER, 2003)
Internal Business Process Issues	Difficulty integrating e-commerce new process with existing business process	(Chong, 2001; Mirchandani & Motwani, 2001; Sabo, 2003; Willcocks L. et al., 2000)
	Fear of opening up corporate systems to business partners	(WITSA, 2001)
People issues	Lack of skilled, talented workers	(Chong, 2001; Clark, Bowden, & Corner, 2002; Cloete, Courtney, & Fintz, 2002; Heung, 2003; Matti & Andrew, 2004; May, 2000; Rao, Metts, & Monge, 2003; Riquelme, 2002; Sabo, 2003; Tang, Powell, Worlock, & Bingham, 2000; WITSA, 2001; WSIS, 2003)
Costs & Finance issues	Initial implementation costs	(Accounting, 1999; Chen, Chen, & Shao, 2003; Chong, 2001; Clark, Bowden, & Corner, 2002; Cloete, Courtney, & Fintz, 2002; Heung, 2003; Mallett, 2000; OECD, 1998; Rao, Metts, & Monge, 2003; Riquelme, 2002; Rodgers, Yen, & Chou, 2002; Tang, Powell, Worlock, & Bingham, 2000; USHER, 2003; WITSA, 2001)
	On-going operational costs	(Chong, 2001; Heung, 2003; Matti & Andrew, 2004; Mirchandani & Motwani, 2001; Purao & Campbell, 1998; Sabo, 2003; Tang, Powell, Worlock, & Bingham, 2000; USHER, 2003)
	Return on investment (ROI) Uncertainty of financial benefits	(Clark, Bowden, & Corner, 2002; Matti & Andrew, 2004; USHER, 2003)
	External support	(Tang, Powell, Worlock, & Bingham, 2000; USHER, 2003)
Technical issues	Compatibility with other trading partners	(Heung, 2003; Mirchandani & Motwani, 2001; USHER, 2003)
	Difficulty of standardising trading partners frameworks	(Chong, 2001; Rodgers, Yen, & Chou, 2002; Sabo, 2003; USHER, 2003)
Internet users issues	Insufficiency of Customers' access to Internet	(Abell & Black, 1997; Chong, 2001; Clark, Bowden, & Corner, 2002; Cloete, Courtney, & Fintz, 2002; David, 2004; Heung, 2003; Javidan, Stahl, Brodbeck, & Wilderom, 2005; Mallett, 2000; Matti & Andrew, 2004; Mirchandani & Motwani, 2001; Tang, Powell, Worlock, & Bingham, 2000; USHER, 2003; WSIS, 2003)
	Customers Resistance & Inventory-related issues	(Burke, 2005; Chen, Chen, & Shao, 2003; Heung, 2003)
Business partners issues	Business partners not ready	(Clark, Bowden, & Corner, 2002)
	Low supplier use of E-commerce	(Clark, Bowden, & Corner, 2002)
E-commerce infrastructure in a country	Trust issues	(Boulle, 1996; Cowles, Kiecker, & Little, 2002; Damaskopoulos & Evgeniou, 2003; Sabo, 2003; Tunzelana & Technikon, 2003; WITSA, 2001)
	Security: unauthorized attacks	(Boulle, 1996; Chong, 2001; Cloete, Courtney, & Fintz, 2002; David, 2004; Heung, 2003; Javidan, Stahl, Brodbeck, & Wilderom, 2005; Mallett, 2000; Matti & Andrew, 2004; Nancy, Michael, & Andrew, 2004; Purao & Campbell, 1998; Rodgers, Yen, & Chou, 2002; Sabo, 2003; USHER, 2003; WSIS, 2003)
	Security of the transaction	(Boulle, 1996; Clark, Bowden, & Corner, 2002; Damaskopoulos & Evgeniou, 2003; Nancy, Michael, & Andrew, 2004)
	Authentication: unsure of the true identity and credentials of communicating parties	(Damaskopoulos & Evgeniou, 2003; Sabo, 2003)
	Legal issues	(Boulle, 1996; Chong, 2001; Cloete, Courtney, & Fintz, 2002; Damaskopoulos & Evgeniou, 2003; Heung, 2003; Kittikanya, 2000; Matti & Andrew, 2004; Nancy, Michael, & Andrew, 2004; OECD, 1998; Rao, Metts, & Monge, 2003; Sabo, 2003; USHER, 2003)

Table 9. Contrasting New Zealander and Chinese cultural values

Cultural element	New Zealand perspective	Chinese perspective
Power distance	Small	Large
Uncertainty avoidance	Strong (problem-solving orientation)	Weak (Situation-accepting orientation)
Individualism-Collectivism	Individual	Collective

Source: Hofstede (1997)

cultures. Hofstede (1997) suggests that culture can be scaled or ranked by dimensions, and the scores can be used to predict cultural differences. The classification of cultural dimensions presents a theoretical foundation that has been frequently used for exploring the impact of cultural differences on the adoption and use of information technology. There are four cultural dimensions: (1) power distance: the extent to which the members of a society accept inequality in an organizations. It reflects the non-symmetrical nature of relationships that may exist between knowledge provider and recipient. (2) individualism/collectivism: the extent to which a person sees himself or herself as an individual rather than part of a group. In individualistic cultures, ties among individuals are very loose. Everyone is expected to look after himself or herself. Collectivist societies reinforce the notion of group. Such cultures are generally driven by group rather than by self-interest interest. (3) uncertainty avoidance: the degree to which the member of a society feel uncomfortable with uncertainty and ambiguity. (4) masculinity/femininity is the willingness to promote societal values. In masculine cultures, emotional gender roles are clearly distinct: men are supposed to be assertive, tough, and focused on material success, whereas woman are supposed to be more modest, tender, and concerned with the quality of life. In feminine cultures, emotional gender roles overlap: both men and women are supposed to be modest, tender, and concerned with the quality of life. In this study, the research only focuses on power distance, the level of uncertainty avoidance and individualism-collectivism (see Table 9).

In terms of power distance, the scores on power distance for New Zealand society is lower (22) than China's (80) (Hofstede & Hofstede, 2005) New Zealand employees like to have a voice in their organization's decision making and prefer their company to have an open and accessible communication system. In contrast, the culture of China is predominantly that of a high power distance. Inequality in power is accepted as appropriate and legitimate. Chinese employees seldom involve themselves in the organizational decision making process (Redding & Richardson, 1986). In terms of uncertainty avoidance, Hofstede and Hofstede (2005) points out that New Zealanders have stronger of uncertainty avoidance (49) than that of Chinese, where score relatively low on uncertainty avoidance (30), which means New Zealander feel high level anxiety to uncertain or unknown situations than Chinese does. They look for a structure in their organizations to make events clearly interpretable and predictable. They have a greater willingness to take risks to reduce ambiguity than Chinese does (Hofstede & Hofstede, 2005). In terms of individualism New Zealand ranks highly. In a high individualism culture, people are concerned about themselves and their own self-interest. The individuals have the personal freedom and autonomy to pursue their own goals. In New Zealand, people are encouraged to pursue self-interest. This contrasts with Chinese culture, which tends to be collectivist. People consider themselves primarily as members of a group and tend to look after one another. Moreover, organizational coordination and control are achieved using informal, relational and implicit means (Ko, 1995) rather than the formal, transactional and explicit approaches common to New Zealand's corporate settings

When small Chinese firms run their businesses in the New Zealand business context, they may face a cross-cultural difficulty in e-commerce implementation. Burnson (1989) points out that cultural difference is a major obstacle in global Internet technology development, which will result in these types of organisations unavoidably encountering some cross-cultural difficulties in information and communications technology (ICT) application. The literature suggests that the varying cross-cultural environments across countries in terms of the legal, political and cultural variables have resulted in business people having different attitudes towards e-commerce (Jiang & Prater, 2002). Because China differs from New Zealand in the state of economic development as well as in national and business culture, when these small Chinese firms implement e-commerce outside of the Chinese economy they cannot use their Chinese experience directly. These factors are a great challenge for them in adopting e-commerce in the New Zealand business context.

Cultural Dimension Impacts on E-Commerce Growth Stages

A review of literature shows that e-commerce technology adoption by the native people in different countries reflects local cultural values, and these patterns are consistent with Hofstede's evaluation of these cultures (Kambayashi & Scarbrough, 2001; O'Kane & Hargie, 2004; Singh, Kumar, & Baack, 2004). For instance, Kambayashi and Scarbrough (2001) discovered significant national cultural differences between individualistic and control oriented IT use in British and Japanese firms. These studies confirmed the national culture differences, and are consistent with Hofstede's evaluation of these cultures. The following sections will discuss how national culture influences e-commerce adoption over the four growth stages.

Stage One: Messaging

From a basic website communication perspective, a few studies were found that focus on the cultural factors that influence e-commerce acceptance in different national cultures. O'Kane and Hargie (2004) investigate the similarities and differences in attitudes towards communication technology (i.e. e-mail and intranet) between the United Kingdom (UK) and Norway. Results indicated that significant differences in attitude towards communication technology exist between the two cultures. In relation to Hofstede's cultural framework, communication technology was found to encourage higher levels of individualism within the Norwegian company, and femininity within the UK one. Employees in the UK Company exhibited a more positive overall attitude towards the use of communication technology.

Huang, Lu and Wong (2003) examined the influence of power distance on email acceptance in China based on the technology acceptance model. They found that for a person who has higher power distance, "the power distance reinforcing effect in increasing the influence of subjective norms on perceived usefulness is more likely to be offset by the inappropriateness of using email due to its levelling effect on power and hierarchy manifestation (Huang, Lu, & Wong, 2003, p. 98).

Stage Two: Online Marketing:

From website design and website marketing perspective, several studies point out that web site advertising and communication show local cultural values (Cyr, Bonanni, Bowes, & Ilsever, 2005; Guan, Tan, & Hua, 2004; Singh, Kumar, & Baack, 2004). Singh et al. (2004) analyzed the cultural values depicted on the web pages of US, French and German web sites. The finding results show significant differences in the depiction of cultural values on local American, French and German web sites. The cultural values presented in the local web sites of the three courtiers are linked to Hofstede's theoretical work regarding cultural differences between the countries.

With regard to localization or internationalization of web sites, Guan, Tan and Hua (2004) suggest that many problems in the visual design of B2C web pages have general solutions even in terms of international use. The comparison of the evaluation of impressions based on Japanese, Chinese and UK groups of subjects shows that some design factors have special culture-dependent characteristics. For this kind of design factor, the optimal design or improvement of B2C web pages must take into consideration the localization of the visual design. Cyr, Bonanni, Bowes, and Ilsever (2005) compare between cultures for design preferences of local and foreign Web sites and subsequent participant perceptions of trust, satisfaction, and e-loyalty in four groups of Americans, Canadians, Japanese and Germans. The findings show that design preferences were most similar for Americans and Canadians, moderately similar for Canadians and Americans with Germans, and most dissimilar among these three countries with the Japanese. Okazaki (2004) examined whether Japanese companies' Web communication strategies were standardised or localised for their cross-cultural target markets. The results confirmed that companies need to localise their Web sites to meet the target market culture through tailoring content and creative strategies.

Stage Three: Online Ordering and Stage Four: Online Transactions

Surprisingly, only a few studies have provided insights into the impact of culture on online ordering and online transactions in the third and fourth stages of e-commerce growth. Thatcher, Foster and Zhu (2006) investigated the cultural factors influence B2B e-commerce adoption decisions in Taiwan. The result findings showed that Taiwanese culture might hold back an organisation to adopt e-commerce, because Taiwanese believe that "there is much more meaning to a relationship than is coded in a particular transaction" (p. 101). They preferred "looking their suppliers in the eyes" (p. 101) when asking for a quote rather than automating their process, as they thought that automatic transaction may not be effective since they were unable to take advantage of the personal relationships that have been nurtured over a period of years (Thatcher, Foster, & Zhu, 2006).

Previous studies have investigated the small firms' e-commerce growth model and general adoption motivations and inhibitors in overall e-commerce adoption. However, little research has identified the adoption motivators and inhibitors at the different stages of e-commerce growth in a cross-cultural environment. Also little research has identified how culture factors influence the progress through the stages of e-commerce growth and how local culture impacts on e-commerce technology adoption by a person who moved from his or her home country to a new country and whether his or her home cultural dimensions still apply. This study tries to develop a framework for explaining how culture in relation to Hofstede's cultural dimensions impact the transitions through e-commerce stages of growth by small firms in a cross-cultural business context.

RESEARCH METHOD AND FIELD RESEARCH DATA COLLECTION

Research Method

This research was conducted as an interpretive case study. One of the main strengths attributed to case research is that this method is an appropriate research strategy where a contemporary phenomenon is to be studied in its natural context (Yin, 1989). Cavaye (1996) states that case study research is considered to be particularly appropri-

Table 10. Summary of the case study participants

Stage of E-commerce adoption	Firm	Number of employees	Interviewee	Age range	Years of residence in NZ	Years of trading in NZ	Years of e-commerce adoption in NZ
Stage O	O	1	owner	>50	20	16 years	0 years
Stage one	A	1	owner	40~45	7	5 years +	1 year
	B	1	owner	35~40	4	1.5 year	1.5 year
Stage two	C	5	Owner, Technician	>50 <30	9 2	6 years +	5 years +
	D	7	Owner, Technician	45~50 30~35	12 4	9 years +	5 years +
	E	3	Owner	45~50	6	3 years +	1.5 years
	F	3	Owner	30~35	2	1 year+	1 year+
	G	2	Owner	<30	4	2 years+	2 years+
Stage three	H	7	Owner	45~50	8	5 years +	2 year +
	I	<20	Owner, IS manager	35~40 35~40	5 4	4 years	4 years
	J	3	Owner	35~40	3	2 years	2 years
	K	4	Owner	30~35	2	1 year+	1 year+
	L	10	Owner, IS manager, Technician	35~40 35~40 <30	5 2 3	4 years	4 years
Stage four	M	5	Owner	30~35	22	7 years	7 years
	N	7	Owner, IS manager	30~35 <30	17 3	6years +	4 years +

ate when theoretical knowledge on a phenomenon is limited or when the need for capturing context is important. The research attempts to identify what adoption motivators and inhibitors influence the e-commerce evolution in small Chinese firms in New Zealand. There is little research in this field so case study research is particularly appropriate. Second, the research method has the potential to provide a more detailed understanding of what factors affect subsequent decisions small business executives make as they move through the different stages or levels of e-commerce adoption and the reasons why the factors affect small business owners' decision than the quantitative surveys that have been more frequently employed in this field research (e.g. Abell & Black, 1997).

Research Participants

Bonoma (1985) recommended selecting firms from the same industry, so small Chinese firms in the computer retailing industry in Auckland and Hamilton, New Zealand were identified through Yellow Pages and personal contacts as potential participants. These firms were then contacted and asked if they would be willing to participate in the study by giving time for an interview. Fifteen firms agreed to participate in the research. The computer retail industry appears to be a suitable place to examine e-commerce adoption by small Chinese firms, because the computer retailing industry is at the forefront of e-commerce implementation so it is straightforward to collect significant data about e-commerce adoption in small Chinese firms. The sample also needs to reflect different stages of e-commerce growth, because firms that are at different stages of e-commerce development could experience different motivators and encounter different inhibitors.

The participants were selected based on the following criteria.

- The organization should be small Chinese firms in the computer retail industry in New Zealand
- The organization has considered some form of e-commerce technology in its business
- The organization is willing to participate in the study.

Based on the site selection criteria, 25 firms were contacted initially for this study and 15 firms agreed to participate the research. In each firm, the owner-managers were the main interviewees, although in some cases other key staff were also interviewed. The case study participants (see Appendix 1) are classified according to the "four-stage adoption ladder" model developed in this study, as shown in Table 10. One firm is at Stage 0, two at Stage one, five at Stage two, five at Stage three and two at Stage four.

The major method of data collection was through semi-structured interviews with owner-managers and other key staff. The interviews were conducted personally at the firm's site and lasted between 30 and 45 minutes each. Eleven interviews were audio taped and subsequently transcribed. Four interviews were not recorded so notes were recorded immediately after the interview.

Before the main research began, Firm I was chosen for a pilot study to test whether the research method and research questions could achieve the research objectives (Since the interview schedule was changed following the pilot study, Firm I was excluded from the sample set). Ambiguous questions were revised as a result of the pilot study. Triangulation of evidence was achieved by examining each web site and asking the participants the same questions in different ways and at different times to confirm their opinions.

Data Analysis

With regard to data analysis, Eisenhardt (1989) claims that multiple-case data analysis can be divided into two steps: within-case analysis and analysis of cross-case patterns. At the within-case analysis step in this study, Yin's (1989) pattern-matching techniques were used to generate patterns for each case, to match the real adoption motivators and inhibitors that were faced by each small Chinese firm with the motivators and inhibitors categories that were developed in the literature review part and to see whether each motivator and inhibitor can be proven by each case. At the cross-case patterns step, the investigator classified cases into groups based on the stage of e-commerce development, and then the groups were compared in terms of the similarities and differences within the case group and outside of the case group.

RESEARCH FINDINGS AND DISCUSSION OF CASE STUDIES

The research examined factors affecting e-commerce stages of growth in the context of Hofstede's cultural framework. The study findings from the fourteen case studies provide some interesting insights into the e-commerce evolution process of e-commerce.

Adoption Motivators

Table 11 identifies the areas of the motivating factors influencing firms on advancing in overall e-commerce adoption process that fall within each of the Hofstede's cultural dimensions: power distance, uncertainty avoidance, individualism and collectivism. In the table, "0→1" stands for the stage moving forward from non-adoption stage

Table 11. Hofstede's dimensions and motivating factors influencing firms on advancing in overall e-commerce adoption process

Stage transition Motivators		0→1		1→2					2→3				3→4	
		A	B	C	D	E	F	G	H	J	K	L	M	N
Power distance														
Owner's Characteristics	Strongly leadership-oriented in computerization								√	√			√	√
	Innovativeness									√			√	√
	Enthusiasm toward e-commerce				√		√	√	√	√	√	√	√	√
Owner's Knowledge	Knowledge of e-commerce	√	√	√	√	√	√	√	√	√	√	√	√	√
Individualism														
Increasing the performance of the business				√	√	√	√	√	√	√	√	√	√	√
Direct and indirect market promotion				√	√	√	√	√						
Improving CRM	Improving customer relations								√	√	√	√		
	Improving communication with customers		√		√	√			√	√	√	√		
	Increasing customer satisfaction								√			√		
	Expanding customer base			√	√	√	√	√	√	√	√	√		
	Track customers' tastes and preferences												√	
Savings in time and costs	Savings in time in searching for information	√	√		√	√								
	Savings in communication costs			√								√		
New business models	Speedy and timely access to information from Websites			√	√	√	√	√	√	√	√	√		
	New sales channels, reach new markets								√	√	√	√		
	Simplified, flexible way of doing business								√				√	√
Collectivism														
External pressure	Pressure from trading partners	√	√		√	√	√	√	√	√		√		
	More competitors adopt e-commerce			√		√	√	√	√		√	√		
Relationships-lateral communication	Improving coordination with suppliers (Better service and support from suppliers)												√	√
	Enhancing shared supply chain processes												√	√
	Improving inventory management								√	√			√	√
	Reducing inventory levels								√				√	√
Uncertainty avoidance														
Owner's Characteristics	uncertainty avoidance												√	√
	Risk-taking propensity												√	√

to stage 1, with the current stage being stage 1, and in a similar fashion for the other stages. In Hofstede's framework, individualism and collectivism are presented as a bipolar dimension, while for this study they are used as independent measures. This is based on research (e.g., Cho, Kwon, Gentry, Jun, & Kropp, 1999; Singh, Kumar, & Baack, 2004) showing that individualist and collectivist tendencies can co-exist in societies, and that it is more appropriate to treat them as separate dimensions.

Power Distance

In terms of the power distance dimension, this research found that Chinese owners transferred their home cultural dimensions and applied them in the New Zealand business environment. They have high power authority in their companies. Since the owner has high power and is the main decision maker, the characteristics of the owner are especially important in determining the technology adoption attitude of the small business (Hyvarinen, 1990; Rizzoni, 1991). This finding also fits with the literature that an individual's perception of power distance in workplaces may render him or her to think that the use of e-commerce is desirable for e-commerce may increase reverence to superiors or make superiors feel more authoritative (Huang, Lu, & Wong, 2003). Table 10 shows that owner's knowledge is one of the most important motivators that is present at all stages of e-commerce adoption. It seems that once owners have knowledge about the techniques of each stage of e-commerce adoption, the firm is likely to move forward. For example, the owners of firms M and N have some knowledge about Stage four of e-commerce adoption techniques, thus they can move to Stage four. This aligns with Cloete (2002) who found that if an owner has a high level of computer literacy and knowledge on how to use the technology, the business is more likely to adopt e-commerce. In addition, the managerial enthusiasm toward e-commerce is another important motivating factor that presents at Stage "1→2", Stage "2→3" and Stage "3→4". For instance, the owners of the firms D, F and G are enthusiastic to Stage two of e-commerce adoption. This is because they have some knowledge about this stage of e-commerce development and know what benefits they could gain from implementing this stage. The owner of Firm D said:

We are computer retail and service company. We have some knowledge about e-commerce. It is not hard for us to develop and update a static website by ourselves. So there are little initial implementation costs and on-going operational costs we need to pay. Also there is not too much security risk at Stage one and Stage two. It is very easy for us to adopt these two stages. Why not adopt it?

In addition, the owners of Firm M and Firm N have a positive attitude toward e-commerce, and are closely involved in e-commerce implementation, so their firms can move to Stage four and stand at the leading position in the computer retail industry. It seems that the higher the level of e-commerce adoption the greater the need for owner's support. The owner from Firm N stated:

At Stage three, although customers can make an order online, after the customer makes an order, they still need to confirm the order via e-mail, and make payment through a direct bank transfer. These traditional methods still cannot provide more satisfactory service to customers. We decided to improve customer service and move to Stage four when we had more and more customers placing orders online because at that stage, the online order can be fulfilled automatically.

Moreover, owners' innovativeness and owners' strong leadership in computerization play vital roles in a firm's decision of moving to Stage three and Stage four. It has been shown in this study that the innovative owner and the owner who has a strong level of uncertainty avoidance and risk-taking propensity, is closely involved in e-commerce implementation, and would be more willing to adopt e-commerce at high level. The findings show that if the owner has a high power distance, the power distance reinforces the effect by increasing the influence of their subjective norm on perceived usefulness of e-commerce technology (Huang, Lu, & Wong, 2003). The results confirm similar findings from studies conducted by Moran (1998). Also, the findings show that small Chinese owners did not change their cultural dimensions in terms of power distance when they run business in New Zealand.

Individualism

In terms of the individualism dimension, it can be seen that "increasing the performance of the business" is a prominent facilitator across stages "1→2", "2→3" and "3→4" of the e-commerce growth process. It drives the firm moving from the earlier stage to the advanced stage. Most of the firms' (Firm C, D, E, F, G) owners stated that advertising their companies and products on their websites enabled more potential customers to know about their firms. It can increase in-store customer traffic, increases sales and revenues. The owners of firms (H, J, M, N) at Stage three and Stage four claimed that online sales was a new sales channel, which can reach new markets and increase sales and revenues.

Second, it was found that some adoption motivators are present only at certain stages. It seems that the firms at the different stages have different goals or benefits they want to achieve. For example, firms A and B who are at Stage one of e-commerce adoption want to achieve the benefit of saving time in searching for information. Firms C, D, E, F and G at Stage two expect to achieve the benefits of advertising their firms and their products through their websites, thereby expanding their customer bases. At Stage three, firms H, J, K and L want to gain the benefits of improving customer relationship management and exploring a new sales channel.

Surprisingly, none of the firms expected to achieve the benefits of saving costs from e-commerce implementation. Most (such as firms J, H, K and M) stated that they would not really save communication costs by implementing e-commerce. For example, if a firm adopts e-commerce, it could save costs in postage, but they spend more paying Internet connection fees and telephone bills. In addition, the Chinese preference for face-to-face negotiations and personal relationships extends to the Internet and affects the negotiation of deals (Haley, 2002). Even if a Chinese firm connect Internet, they still need more information-rich media such as face-to-face communication and telephone communication. Thus saving communication costs is not the main factor that affects small business owners' decisions.

Collectivism

In terms of the collectivism dimension, it was found that 'pressure from trading partners' is the most significant adoption motivator that is present at Stage "0→1", Stage "1→2" and Stage "2→3". Most of the firms' (Firms A, B, E, G, J, and L) owners claimed that catching up with their trading partners was the motivator that encouraging them to go online. For example, firms' (A and B) owners stated that trading partners exchanged documents and data through the Internet, so they needed to keep up with this trend. In addition, the 'more competitors adopt e-commerce' is another motivator affecting subsequent decisions made by the owners of firms at Stage two and Stage three. This finding is also in line with the study of Iacovou et al. (1995) that small firms were more likely to adopt e-commerce in order to maintain their own competitive position as more competitors adopted e-commerce. However, the owners of firms (M and N) at Stage four were not affected by the "external pressure". The decision to move to Stage four was influenced by their proactive attitude toward e-commerce. Therefore, the firms at Stage one, two, three of e-commerce adoption who were driven by "external pressure" to adopt e-commerce can be defined as "reactive". However, firms N and M at Stage four who were driven by an attitude toward business development can be defined as "active". This implies that these firms have 'active' motivation for developing their e-commerce activities and seek new business ideas to crowd-out their strongest rivals.

Interestingly, only firms M and N who at Stage four expect to improve relationships-lateral communication and enhance supply chain collaboration and coordination, and to do business in a simplified and flexible way.

Uncertainty Avoidance

It was found that the reason why not many small Chinese firms in New Zealand accept credit cards (due to online fraud) and move to Stage four was that the perception of risk by Chinese business people about online selling was high. Chinese have a very weak uncertainty avoidance culture (Yau, 1988), and therefore they would like to sit back and wait and see when faced with the threat of uncertainty and ambiguity. Therefore, few Chinese Internet vendors like to take the risk of accepting credit card payments online. It is found that most small Chinese owners in New Zealand held their Chinese cultural profile in terms of uncertainty avoidance. This attitude toward the payment method loses them some New Zealand customers who are used to paying by credit card on New Zealand companies' websites. That is the reason why only a few firms (firms M and N) have adopted Stage four of e-commerce. The owners of firms M and N also have a strong level of uncertainty avoidance and risk-taking propensity as there were a few firms adopting Stage four of e-commerce. These characteristics of the owners encourage the firms adopt Stage four of e-commerce. The owner of firm M explained:

Currently, there were not many firms who have moved to Stage four. We thought if we could implement this stage early, we could improve our company image and increase our market share. We have planned to move to Stage four of e-commerce adoption for a long time. Initially, it was very hard for us to get the information about how to implement Stage four. We contacted many e-commerce development companies and compared their feasibility and prices. You know, some consultant companies ask thousands of dollars to implement Stage four. The high initial implementation cost must have hindered many firms from implementing Stage four. Due to our enthusiasm, we never gave up the dream of moving to Stage four. Recently, we found the best and most economical way to implement it.

It can be seen that the owners of firms M and N have aligned with the New Zealander cultural dimension and have adopted a strong uncertainty avoidance culture. It is found that they are having stayed in New Zealand more than 15 years and they immigrate to New Zealand without previous working experience in China.

Adoption Inhibitors

This research studied the relation of inhibitor factors and Hofstede's cultural framework. Table 12 identifies the areas of the inhibiting factors that fall within Hofstede's cultural dimensions: power distance,individualism, collectivism and uncertainty avoidance. In this table, "0→1" stands for the stage moving forward from non-adoption stage (do not adopt any online activity) to stage 1, with the current stage being the non-adoption stage (and in a similar way for the other stages).

Power Distance

In terms of the power distance dimension, since Chinese owners have powerful authority in their companies, the owner's negative attitudes towards e-commerce plays a vital role in hindering e-commerce from making progress at all stages of e-commerce adoption. This finding fits with the literature that if an owner is not interested in e-commerce adoption it could be a big barrier to e-commerce adoption (Chen, Chen, & Shao, 2003). This adoption inhibitor increases in inten-

Table 12. Hofstede's dimensions and inhibiting factors for firms advancing in overall e-commerce adoption process

Stage transition Inhibitors		**0→1**	**1→2**		**2→3**					**3→4**				**4→ e-business**	
		O	**A**	**B**	**C**	**D**	**E**	**F**	**G**	**H**	**J**	**K**	**L**	**M**	**N**
Power distance															
Owner's attitude toward e-business	Owner's negative attitudes	√	√		√		√		√	√		√	√	√	√
	General awareness & education	√													
Individualism															
Internal Business Process Issues	Preference for information-rich media negotiations	√	√	√	√	√	√	√	√	√	√	√	√	√	√
	Difficulty integrating new e-commerce products with existing systems													√	√
	Fear of opening up corporate systems to business partners										√		√		
People issues	Lack of skilled, talented workers				√		√	√	√	√		√	√		
Collectivism															
Technical issues	Compatibility with other trading partners									√	√	√	√	√	√
	Difficulty of standardising trading partners frameworks									√	√	√	√	√	√
Business partners issues	Business partners not ready									√	√		√	√	√
	Low supplier use of E-commerce								√						
	B2B Trust issues		√	√	√	√		√	√			√	√	√	√
Uncertainty avoidance															
Costs and Finance issues	Initial implementation costs				√		√	√	√	√	√		√		
	On-going operational costs					√			√	√				√	
	Return of Investment Uncertainty of financial benefits									√	√	√	√	√	√
	External support					√			√						
Internet users issues	Insufficiency of Customers' access to Internet		√	√	√		√	√	√	√	√	√	√		
	Customers Resistance & Inventory-related issues		√	√	√				√						
E-commerce infrastructure in a country	Security: unauthorized attacks					√			√	√				√	√
	Security of the transaction									√		√	√		
	Authentication: unsure of the true identity and credentials of communicating parties							√					√		

sity at the Stage "3→4" and "4→e-business". In addition, the owner of firm O lacks e-commerce "savvy" and has a negative and indifferent attitude toward e-commerce adoption. In explaining his view, the owner said:

I think the purpose of most companies advertising their products and services on their websites is using the low price to attract customers' attention. The price of my products does not have an advantage over these companies. I depend on the excellent personal service provided to attract more customers. The service cannot be weighed by price. It is hard for customers to evaluate which company provides sound service through browsing the website. So, even if I established a website it still cannot attract more customers. And also the cost will increase, so I think I'd better give up the Internet.

In addition, the owner has probably not perceived the usefulness of e-commerce and understood its potential benefits. He stated:

I don't think I am slower in getting new information. I also can get useful information from my suppliers, and they often introduce some new products to me by post. Probably, Internet is quicker than post, but I don't think the small difference in speed would make a difference to my business

Individualism

In terms of individualism, it is found that at the initial stages of e-commerce adoption, ties between individual companies and their trading partners are loose, personal freedom is valued and individual decision-making is encouraged. At these initial stages, small Chinese firms focus on internal e-commerce implementation, and they experience some difficulties. Firstly, 'lack of skilled, talented workers' and 'initial implementation costs' are prominent barriers across Stage "2→3" and Stage "3→4". It is noted that the need for high-skilled computer staff increases as small firms shift from simple to more complex e-commerce adoption paths. Unfortunately, firms at stages "2→3" and "3→4" lack highly-skilled computer staff, so they cannot implement e-commerce in house. This is the factor that hinders the firms from moving to the next stage. In addition, due to the lack of initial implementation costs, they are also reluctant to outsource the e-commerce implementation project to an external company. Therefore, financial issues and a lack of highly-skilled people affect subsequent decisions small business executives make as they move moving to next stage of e-commerce development.

Furthermore, the "difficulty integrating new e-commerce products with existing systems" is another main issue presenting at Stage "4→ e-business". The firms' (firm M and N) owners stated that although they have moved to Stage four, they have not integrated the new e-commerce processes into the existing business processes. This is consistent with a study by Willcocks, et al. (2000) that found that the real challenge of integration is in transforming the organizational culture and infrastructure.

Regarding the selection and the use of communication channels between business partners, the Chinese preference is for information-rich media negotiations (Haley, 2002). The owner from firm M said that the most frequent communication method they used to contact suppliers and customers was the telephone. He claims that the Internet is static while people are more flexible, and he needs to negotiate the price with suppliers by telephone or face-to-face communication. If he orders many products, he perceives he can get cheaper prices this way. Therefore, he only uses the Internet as a tool, to get product information and the status of stock. For the negotiation of deals, he needs more interactive and information-rich media channels such as face-to-face communication and telephone communication. This is the reason why

Chinese small firms do not perceive that they can save communication costs by implementing e-commerce.

Collectivism

In terms of collectivism, it was found that collectivism characteristics mostly are visible at the higher stages of e-commerce adoption. At these higher stages, ties between individual companies and their trading partners are close and strong, societal norms are valued, and group decision-making is encouraged. The most important issue arising for trading partner cooperation and coordination at the higher stages of e-commerce adoption in small Chinese firms is "Business-to-Business trust issues". Firstly, the owners of small Chinese firms usually only trust personal relationships. They cannot gain new suppliers just from Internet interaction. In fact, they often gain new suppliers through friends' introductions. This is the typical way Chinese businessmen operate. In China, personal relationships are very important for doing business. It is hard for Chinese businessmen to establish a partnership with New Zealand suppliers via Internet without an introduction from a friend. This is another finding which demonstrates that small Chinese owners tend to hold their home cultural profile when they operate business in the New Zealand business cultural context. Secondly, small Chinese firms usually do not trust outsiders (such as its suppliers). They cannot ask suppliers to deliver products to the customer directly, and they worry that they could lose customers because they do not know whether the customer is bypassing them in ordering products by contacting the supplier directly. They could lose the customer. Therefore, at present, they always ask suppliers to deliver products to them, and then they deliver products to the ultimate customer with their own staff or by courier. Additionally, because small Chinese firms usually do not accept credit card payments online, they still use cash payment on delivery method for local customers. In this way, they need their staff to collect money when they deliver the product. The distrust of customers and suppliers and poor payment and delivery methods lead to delays in the delivery time. Furthermore, it is noted that Chinese firms refuse to integrate inter-organisational systems with their trading partners. Some small Chinese firms (firm J and L) feared opening up corporate information to their business partners. This is caused by the small Chinese firms' distrust of the trading partners. They believe that there should be some confidential information that should not be shared with their trading partners such as inventory and price.

As far as business partners issues are concerned, 'business partners not ready' is present at Stage "3→4" and Stage "4→e-business". At these stages, most of the firms faced the barrier of their business partners refusing to open their internal information system to them. If business trading partners (such as suppliers) are not willing to open their inventory information to their retailers, retailers cannot really gain the benefits (enhancing supply chain collaboration and coordination) from Stage four of e-commerce adoption. This inhibitor is the significant factor influencing the decision small firm owners make.

The factors "technical issues", "Compatibility with other trading partners" and "difficulty of standardizing trading partners' frameworks", are present at Stage "3→4" and Stage "4→e-business". At these stages, firms should try to link their company's website to their suppliers' database and let their customers check product information on their suppliers' database. However, currently, the trading partners of the small Chinese firms in this study use a variety of different standards, different data definitions and different e-commerce applications. These variations across different organizations result in incompatibility in e-commerce applications and thus it is difficult to link a firm's suppliers' into a single database driving a website. These are the factors that impede the firms at Stage three and Stage four from moving to the advanced stage.

Uncertainty Avoidance

In terms of uncertainty avoidance, the research results show that small Chinese firms are weak on the avoidance of uncertainty, and have a stronger tolerance for ambiguity situations. These characteristics are indicated by their worry about poor return on investment (ROI), insufficiency of customers' access to internet and unauthorized attacks by viruses or hackers.

In terms of return on investment, it is present at Stage "3→4" and Stage "4→e-business". At these two stages, because initial implementation costs get higher and higher, small firms have to spend large amounts of money in implementing e-commerce. However, the size of New Zealand market is small. In the computer retail industry, New Zealand is an import country, rather than an export country. So there is only a small domestic market in this industry. The smaller market and insufficient customers online would result in lower ROI. This is an important inhibiting factor affecting a small business owners' subsequent investment into e-commerce development.

As far as Internet user issues are concerned, "insufficiency of customers' access to internet" is present at Stage "1→2", Stage "2→3" and Stage "3→4". Most of the firms (B, D, E, F, G, H, K, and L) stated that they did not want to move forward with e-commerce development because the volume of email contact, email order and online order was not high enough to make the effort worthwhile. This finding is similar to Amor (2000) who found that if a firm has very low order volume, there is no need for a complex shopping system. If the order volume or the number of products increases, it is fairly easy to extend the system to process the orders automatically. Therefore, the volume of customers' online contacts is a crucial factor that the small firm owner takes into account as they move through the different stages of e-commerce adoption. Additionally, "Customers Resistance & Inventory-related issues" is another issue that is present at Stage "1→2" and Stage "2→3". Nambisan and Wang (1999) point out that the initiative of customers adopting Internet shopping is to gain the benefits of cheaper price and quick service. However, most firms at Stage one and Stage two cannot provide a very cheap price for on line customers because they cannot reduce their operating cost. In addition, a number of inventory-related issues makes it more difficult for consumers to shop via the Internet compared to a conventional retail store: customers cannot touch and feel the products, have to pay delivery costs, and worry about after sales service.

The risk of "unauthorized attacks' is present at Stage "2→3", Stage "3→4" and Stage "4→e-business". With the higher stage of e-commerce adoption, a higher level of security risk will be faced by firms. This is another factor that affects a small business owner's decision. "Security of e-financial transaction issues" is present at Stage "3→4". All firms at Stage three of e-commerce adoption were using traditional financial transaction methods (i.e. cash, cheques and direct deposit) because they were worrying about online fraud.

The Prominent Adoption Motivators and Inhibitors of the E-commerce Growth Process

Following the above research discussion, a growth model is presented in Table 13. This model is based on prior literature of e-commerce adoption sequential models and on the findings of this study of the adoption motivators and inhibitors on the e-commerce growth process at small Chinese firm in New Zealand business context. They are categorized into the four cultural dimensions derived from Hofstede: power distance, individualism, collectivism and uncertainty avoidance. This model may be suitable for other small firms who are adopting e-commerce in a cross-cultural business context.

The growth model is divided into four stages, chronologically ordered. From this table, it was found that the leaders of small Chinese firm in

Table 13. Prominent adoption motivators and inhibitors for the growth stages of e-commerce for small chinese firms in New Zealand

Stage		Power distance	Individualism	Collectivism	Uncertainty avoidance
Stage 0→1	Inhibitors	Owner's attitude Owner's awareness			
	Motivators	Owner's knowledge	Savings in time in searching for information	Pressure from trading partners	
Stage 1→2	Inhibitors	Owner' attitude	Trust issues		Customers' access to Internet is insufficient (email contact <2%);
	Motivators	Owner's knowledge Owner's enthusiasm	Benefits of increasing business performance & market promotion;;	External pressure	
Stage 2→3	Inhibitors	Owner' attitude;	Lack of skilled, talented workers; Initial implementation costs;		Customers' access to Internet is insufficient (email order<10%); Trust issues
	Motivators	Owner's knowledge, Owner's enthusiasm, Strongly leadership-oriented in computerization	Benefits of increasing business performance & improving CRM		External pressure
Stage 3→4	Inhibitors	Owner' attitude;	Lack of skilled, talented workers; Initial implementation costs;	Trust issues; Technical issues; Business partners not ready;	Return On Investment Customers' access to Internet is insufficient (email contact <20%); Security of the transaction
	Motivators	Owner's knowledge, enthusiasm toward e-commerce, innovativen-ess	Benefits of increasing business performance	Enhancing supply chain coordination	Hihg uncertainty avoidance and Risk-taking propensity

New Zealand tended to adopt their birth country cultural dimensions and apply them in the New Zealand business environment. It was shown that these firms have high levels of power distance features. The owners' attitude and knowledge about e-commerce are direct influences on which stage of e-commerce adoption is achieved. It is noted that those owners who are enthusiastic towards e-commerce and show strong leadership in computerization will drive firms to move to higher stages of e-commerce adoption. At the same time, those owners who have negative attitudes towards e-commerce and are not aware of the usefulness of the e-commerce technology, will inhibit firms from moving to higher stages of e-commerce adoption.

In terms of individualism-collectivism, it was found that firms at a lower growth stage of e-commerce adoption are more highly focussed on individualism. These firms focus on individuals' benefits as a driver for their firms' development. In contrast, those firms at higher growth stage of e-commerce adoption are highly focussed on collectivism. They have high levels of communication via Internet, more group decision-making, and are willing to share information via the Internet.

Better supply chain collaboration and coordination motivate firms to move to a higher growth stage, while difficulty of standardising trading partners' frameworks and compatibility with other trading partners are obstacles preventing firms moving forward.

In terms of uncertainty avoidance, it was found that firms at higher growth stages of e-commerce adoption have stronger uncertainty avoidance, and their people are relatively more risk takers, and have a less tolerance for uncertainty. It was also noted that the cultural dimensions of the person will transfer as they were from their home country, and not be unduly influenced by the environment of the new country in the first few years after they arrive. However, if a person immigrates to New Zealand at an early age without previous working experience in China, and stays in New Zealand more than 15 years, the new country cultural dimension will apply.

CONCLUSION, LIMITATIONS, AND IMPLICATIONS

This study views e-commerce growth as a process in small Chinese firms, with different types of adoption motivators and inhibitors taking place, influenced by Hofstede's three cultural dimensions: power distance, individualism-collectivism and uncertainty avoidance.

This study uncovered some of the reasons why the small Chinese firms in this study, who are in a similar business context and have similar business backgrounds, are at different stages of e-commerce adoption. It was found that when small firms' owners have a high power distance, their attitude toward e-commerce technology directly influences their firms' e-commerce growth process. It was found that for firms at higher stages of e-commerce adoption, there was a greater likelihood of the presence of a more positive attitude toward e-commerce, more innovativeness and enthusiasm, more uncertainty avoidance and risk-taking propensity, and more technology literacy for owners. It was also found that the stronger the uncertainty avoidance and the higher the risk-taking propensity present in the owner's attitudes, the higher the stage of e-commerce adoption that was achieved. As well, the amount of financial resources and the number of high-skilled e-commerce staff in a small Chinese firm also affected the adoption of advanced stages. In addition, this study identified that firms at a lower growth stage of e-commerce adoption are highly ranked on individualism, while those firms at higher growth stage of commerce adoption are highly ranked on collectivism.

Despite conducting interviews in fourteen firms and attempting to gain the best possible quality of information, there are still a number of limitations of this study:

- The research was limited in the firms in one industry (the computer retail industry) in two cities (Auckland and Hamilton) and in one country (New Zealand).
- The firms and owner/managers which participated in this study were those who were willing to state their views or opinions.
- Much of the evidence was collected using interviews and interpreted by the investigator. The data analysis may have been influenced by investigator subjectivity.
- Many adoption motivators and inhibitors are encountered in this investigation that may be unique to the organizations in the case studies. In particular, only one non-adopter firm was interviewed. Although the models developed in this investigation are intended to be useful as a starting point in understanding e-commerce adoption in any small firm in a cross cultural context, the results are limited to the specific case studies undertaken.

This research has implications beyond just the subject Chinese firms in New Zealand. It raises the important issue about whether national culture is "sticky" to individuals, and how much people who have been born, raised, and started a business career in one culture will tend to continue to use their home country culture when starting and operating businesses in a new country with significant differences in cultural dimensions.

It is hoped that the findings of this study will be helpful for the owner/managers of small firms to help them understand their environment as they move through the different stages of e-commerce adoption in a cross-cultural business context, particularly when that owner/manager has come from a different cultural background to the country in which the business is operating. The findings also provide important information about what kind of support and understanding small Chinese firms may need from government assistance agencies, their suppliers and customers, and their e-commerce consulting partner firms in order to develop better e-commerce business relationships in a cross-cultural environment.

REFERENCES

Abell, W., & Black, S. (1997). Business use of the internet in New Zealnad: a follow-up study. Retrieved June, 27, 2003, from http://www.lincoln.ac.nz/amac/publish/acms/followup.htm

Accounting, M. (1999). Top management complacent or uncertain about the implications of e-business? *Management Accounting*, *77*(11), 4–5.

Allcock S, Webber S, & Yeates, R. (1999). *Business Information and the Internet: use of the Internet as an information resource for SMEs.*

Amor, D. (2000). *The e-business (R)evolution: living and working in an interconnected world / Daniel Amor.* London: Upper Saddle River, NJ: Prentice Hall PTR.

Anumba, C. J., & Ruikar, K. (2002). Electronic commerce in construction--trends and prospects. *Automation in Construction*, *11*(3), 265–275. doi:10.1016/S0926-5805(01)00087-5

Australian Bureau of Statistics. (2004). Glossary. Retrieved July 9, 2004, from http://www.abc.net.au/eightdays/glossary/default.htm

Bakker, E., Zheng, J., Knight, L., & Harland, C. (2008). Putting e-commerce adoption in a supply chain context. *International Journal of Operations & Production Management*, *28*(4), 313–330. doi:10.1108/01443570810861543

Bartels, A. (2000). The difference between e-business and e-commerce. *Computerworld*, *34*(44), 41.

Beatty, R. (1998). *An empirical investigation into the salient factors used by organisations in the adoption of Web site technology*: Mississippi State University, DBA.

Begley, T. M., & Boyd, D. Y. (1986). Psychological Characteristics Associated with Entrepreneurial Performance. In R. Ronstadt (Ed.), *Frontiers of Entrepreneurship Research.*

Bonoma, T. V. (1985). Case research in marketing: opportunities, problems, and a process. *JMR, Journal of Marketing Research*, *22*(3), 199–208. doi:10.2307/3151365

Boulle, C. (1996). HLSG report No. 2 barriers to electronic commerce in support of SMEs. Retrieved June, 23, 2003, from http://www.ict.etsi.fr/Activities/Documents/HLSG_Report2.pdf

Bowden, S., Clark, D., Patricia, C., Gibb, J., Kearins, K., & Pavolich, K. (2001). *Adoption and implementation of e-business in New Zealand: Preliminary results.* Paper presented at the 9th Annual Conference of the New Zealand Strategic Management Society.

Bridge, S., O'Neill, K., & Cromie, S. (2003). *Understanding Enterprise, Entrepreneurship and small Business*. London: MacMillan Business.

Brockhaus, R. H. (1980). Risk Taking Propensity of Entrepreneurs. *Academy of Management Journal, 23*, 509–520. doi:10.2307/255515

Burke, K. (2005). The Impact of Firm Size on Internet Use in Small Businesses. *Electronic Markets, 15*(2), 79–93. doi:10.1080/10196780500083738

Burnson, A. (1989). The perils of going global. *InfoWorld*, (August): 14, 39–40.

Castells, M. (2000). *The Information Age I-III*. Oxford: Oxford University Press.

Cavaye, A. L. M. (1996). Case study research: a multi-faceted research approach for IS. *Information Systems Journal, 6*, 227–242. doi:10.1111/j.1365-2575.1996.tb00015.x

Chen, M., Chen, A. N. K., & Shao, B. B. M. (2003). The Implications and Impacts of Web Services to Electronic Commerce Research and Practices. *Journal of Electronic Commerce Research, 4*(4), 128–139.

Cho, B., Kwon, U., Gentry, J. W., Jun, S., & Kropp, F. (1999). Cultural values reflected in theme and execution: a comparative study of US and Korean television. *Journal of Advertising, 28*(4), 59–73.

Chong, S. (2001). *Electronic Commerce Adoption by Small- and Medium-sized Enterprises in Australia and Singapore*. Curtin University of Technology.

Clark, D. N., Bowden, S., & Corner, P. (2002). *Adoption and implementation of E-Business in New Zealand: Comparative empirical results, 2001 and 2002*. University of Waikato Management School Research Report.

Cloete, E., Courtney, S., & Fintz, J. (2002). Small Businesses' Acceptance and Adoption of E-Commerce in the Western-Cape Province of South-Africa. *Electronic Journal on Information Systems in Developing Countries, 10*(4), 1–13.

Collin, S. (1999). *Doing business on the Internet*. London: Kogan Page.

Cowles, D. L., Kiecker, P., & Little, M. W. (2002). Using key informant insights as a foundation for e-retailing theory development. *Journal of Business Research, 55*(8), 629–636. doi:10.1016/S0148-2963(00)00203-4

Crum, M., Premkumar, G., & Ramamurthy, K. (1996). An assessment of motor carrier adoption, use, and satisfaction with EDI. *Transportation Journal, Summer*.

Cyr, D., Bonanni, C., Bowes, J., & Ilsever, J. (2005). Beyond Trust: Web Site Design Preferences Across Cultures1. *Journal of Global Information Management, 13*(4), 25.

Damaskopoulos, P., & Evgeniou, T. (2003). Adoption of New Economy Practices by SMEs in Eastern Europe. *European Management Journal, 21*(2), 133–145. doi:10.1016/S0263-2373(03)00009-4

Daniel, E., Wilson, H., & Myers, A. (2002). Adoption of e-commerce by SMEs in the UK. *International Small Business Journal, 20*(3), 253. doi:10.1177/0266242602203002

David, H. B. N. L. (2004). Potential of critical e-applications for engaging SMEs in e-business: a provider perspective. *European Journal of Information Systems, 13*(1), 21. doi:10.1057/palgrave.ejis.3000480

Dedrick, J., & Kraemer, K. L. (2001). China IT Report. *Electronic Journal on Information Systems in Developing Countries, 6*(2), 1–10.

Department of Trade and Industry. (2000). Business in the information age: international benchmarking study 2000. Retrieved June 24, 2004, from http://www.idgl.lu/library/pdf-files/DTI-ecommerce-bench-Oct2000.pdf

Eduard, T. (2001). Adding clicks to bricks. *Consulting to Management*, *12*(4), 10.

Eisenhardt, K. M. (1989). Building Theories From Case Study Research. *Academy of Management Review*, *14*(4), 532–551. doi:10.2307/258557

Elliott, R., & Boshoff, C. (2007). The influence of the owner-manager of small tourism businesses on the success of internet marketing. *South African Journal of Business Management*, *38*(3), 15–27.

Ettlie, J. E. (1990). What makes a manufacturing firm innovative? *Academy of Management Executive*, *4*(4), 7–20.

European Commission. (1999). *The Wider Picture: Enlargement and Cohesion in Europe*. Seville, Spain.

Gable, G. G., & Raman, K. S. (1992). Government initiatives for IT adoption in small businesses: experiences of the Singapore Small Enterprise Computerization Programme. *International Information Systems*, *1*(1), 68–93.

Gatignon, H., & Robertson, T. S. (1989). Technology diffusion: an empirical test of competitive effects. *Journal of Marketing*, *53*(1), 35–49. doi:10.2307/1251523

Gengatharen, D. E., & Standing, C. (2005). A framework to assess the factors affecting success or failure of the implementation of government-supported regional e-marketplaces for SMEs. *European Journal of Information Systems*, *14*(4), 417–433. doi:10.1057/palgrave.ejis.3000551

Guan, S. U., Tan, S. L., & Hua, F. (2004). A modularized electronic payment system for agent-based e-commerce. *Journal of Research and Practice in Information Technology*, *36*(2), 67–87.

Haley, G. (2002). E-commerce in China: changing business as we know it. *Industrial Marketing Management*, *31*(2), 119–124. doi:10.1016/S0019-8501(01)00183-3

Hawk, S. (2004). A Comparison of B2C E-Commerce in Developing Countries. *Electronic Commerce Research*, *4*(3), 181. doi:10.1023/B:ELEC.0000027979.91972.36

Heung, V. C. S. (2003). Barriers to implementing E-commerce in the travel industry: a practical perspective. *International Journal of Hospitality Management*, *22*(1), 111–118. doi:10.1016/S0278-4319(02)00075-0

Hofstede, G. H. (1984). *Culture's consequences: international differences in work-related values*. Beverly Hills: Sage Publications.

Hofstede, G. H. (1997). *Cultures and organizations: software of the mind.* New York: McGraw-Hill.

Hofstede, G. H., & Hofstede, G. J. (2005). *Cultures and organizations: software of the mind.* New York: McGraw-Hill.

Hong, W. Y., & Zhu, K. (2006). Migrating to internet-based e-commerce: Factors affecting e-commerce adoption and migration at the firm level. *Information & Management*, *43*(2), 204–221. doi:10.1016/j.im.2005.06.003

Hornby, G., Goulding, P., & Poon, S. (2002). Perceptions of Export Barriers and Cultural Issues: The SME E-Commerce Experience. *Journal of Electronic Commerce Research*, *3*(4), 213–226.

Huang, L., Lu, M.-T., & Wong, B. K. (2003). The impact of power distance on email acceptance: Evidence from The PRC. *Journal of Computer Information Systems*, (Fall): 93–101.

Hyvarinen, L. (1990). Innovativeness and Its Indicators in Small and Medium-sized Industrial Enterprises. *International Small Business Journal, 9*(1), 65–79.

Iacovou, C. L., Benbasat, I., & Dexter, A. S. (1995). Electronic data interchange and small organisations: Adoption and impact of technology. *MIS Quarterly, 19*(4), 465–485. doi:10.2307/249629

Javidan, M., Stahl, G. K., Brodbeck, F., & Wilderom, C. P. M. (2005). Cross-border transfer of knowledge: Cultural lessons from project GLOBE. *The Academy of Management Executive, 19*(2), 59–76.

Jiang, B., & Prater, E. (2002). Distribution and logistics development in China: The revolution has begun. *International Journal of Physical Distribution & Logistics Management, 32*(9), 783–798. doi:10.1108/09600030210452459

Kambayashi, N., & Scarbrough, H. (2001). Cultural influences on IT use amongst factory mangers: a UK-Japanese comparison. *Journal of Information Technology Cases and Applications, 16*, 221–236.

Kirk, A. R. (2000). *E-commerce for the individual or small business owner*. Wellington, New Zealand: Capital Letters Pub.

Kirton, M. J. (1976). Adaptors and innovators: a description and measure. *The Journal of Applied Psychology, 61*(5), 622–629. doi:10.1037/0021-9010.61.5.622

Kirton, M. J. (1984). Adaptors and innovators-why new initiatives get blocked. *Long Range Planning, 17*(2), 137–143. doi:10.1016/0024-6301(84)90145-6

Kittikanya, C. (2000). E-commerce: Internet slow to make inroads. In P. Chantranontwong (Ed.), *Bangkok post: 2000 Mid-year economic review* (pp. 32-35).

Ko, A. (1995). Towards an understanding of Overseas Chinese management. *Journal of Management systems, 7*(1), 13-28.

Levy, M., & Powell, P. (2003). Exploring SME Internet Adoption: Towards a Contingent Model. *Electronic Markets, 13*(2), 173–181. doi:10.1080/1019678032000067163

Mallett, T. (2000). *E-business update: internet use among small and medium-sized firms*.

Malone, P. (2002). The Benefits of Doing Business Electronically - eBusiness. Retrieved September, 2, 2003, from http://www.noie.gov.au/projects/ebusiness/Advancing/benefits/index.htm

Matti, K., & Andrew, U. (2004). The relationship between quality of service perceived and delivered in mobile Internet communications. *Information Systems and eBusiness Management, 2*(4), 309.

May, P. (2000). *The Business of E-Commerce From Corporate Strategy To Technology* (1st ed.). London: Cambridge University Press.

McMillan, V. (2002, September 4). Little Asia. *The Independent*.

Mehrtens, J., Cragg, P. B., & Mills, A. M. (2001). A model of Internet adoption by SMEs. *Information & Management, 39*(3), 165–176. doi:10.1016/S0378-7206(01)00086-6

Mendo, F., & Fitzgerald, G. (2005). A multidimensional framework for SME e-business progression. *Journal of Enterprise Information Management, 18*(6), 678–696. doi:10.1108/17410390510628382

Ministry of Economic Development. (2000). *E-commerce: a guide for New Zealand business*. Wellington, N.Z.: Ministry of Economic Development.

Mirchandani, A. A., & Motwani, J. (2001). Understanding small business electronic commerce adoption: an empirical analysis. *Journal of Computer Information Systems*, (Spring): 70–73.

Moran, P. (1998). Personality characteristics and growth-orientation of the small business owner-manager. *International Small Business Journal*, *16*(3), 17. doi:10.1177/0266242698163001

Nambisan, S., & Wang, Y.-M. (1999). Roadblocks to Web technology adoption? *Association for Computing Machinery. Communications of the ACM*, *42*(1), 98. doi:10.1145/291469.291482

MacKay, N., Parent, M., & Gemino, A. (2004). A model of electronic commerce adoption by small voluntary organizations. *European Journal of Information Systems*, *13*(2), 147. doi:10.1057/palgrave.ejis.3000491

New Zealand Ministry of Economic Development. (2000). *E-commerce: building the strategy for New Zealand.*

NOIE, & Young, E. (2001). Advancing with e-commerce: a summary of 34 case studies of small business e-commerce ventures. Retrieved September, 3, 2003, from http://www.noie.gov.au/projects/CaseStudies/Ecommerce/SummaryReport/index.htm

Nolan, R. L. (1979). Managing the crises in data processing. *Harvard Business Review*, (March-April): 115–126.

NZIER. (2008). Asian Investment in New Zealand. Retrieved November, 28, 2008, from http://www.asianz.org.nz/our-work/knowledge-research/research-reports/business-research#businessresearch

NZIS. (2004). Statistics of residence decisions by financial year. Retrieved July, 2004, from http://www.immigration.govt.nz/NR/rdonlyres/EC-5C8D0E-BCB7-4382-A35C-44CE16EE38DC/0/R1.xls

O'Kane, P., & Hargie, O. (2004). Technology Travels: Can national culture impact upon attitudes toward communication-technology? *Journal of Intercultural Communication Research*, *33*(1), 49–62.

OECD. O. f. E. C.-o. a. D. (1998). *Small and medium-sized enterprises and electronic commerce.* Paper presented at the Ministerial Conference on Electronic Commerce, Ottawa, Canada.

Okazaki, S. (2004). Do multinationals standardise or localise? The cross-cultural dimensionality of product-based Web sites. *Internet Research*, *14*(1), 81–94. doi:10.1108/10662240410516336

Premkumar, G., & Ramamurthy, K. (1995). The role of interorganizational and organizational factors on the decision mode for adoption of interorganizational systems. *Decision Sciences*, *26*(3), 303–336. doi:10.1111/j.1540-5915.1995.tb01431.x

PriceWaterhouseCoopers. (1999). *SME Electronic Commerce Study.* Paper presented at the Asia Pacific Economic Cooperation (APEC) Telecommunications Working Group.

Purao, S., & Campbell, B. (1998). Critical concerns for small business electronic commerce: some reflections based on interviews of small business owners. In *Proceedings of the Association for Information Systems Americas Conference* (pp. 325-327).

Rao, S. S., Metts, G., & Monge, C. A. M. (2003). Electronic commerce development in small and medium sized enterprises: A stage model and its implications. *Business Process Management*, *9*(1), 11–32. doi:10.1108/14637150310461378

Redding, S. G., & Richardson, S. (1986). Participative management and its varying relevance in Hong Kong and singapore. *Asia Pacific Journal of Management*, *3*(2), 76–98. doi:10.1007/BF01733215

Riquelme, H. (2002). Commercial Internet adoption in China: comparing the experience of small, medium and large businesses. *Internet Research: Electronic Networking Applications and Policy*, *12*(3), 276–286. doi:10.1108/10662240210430946

Rizzoni, A. (1991). Technological innovation and small firms: a taxonomy. *International Small Business Journal*, *9*(3), 31–42. doi:10.1177/026624269100900302

Robeiro, F. L., & Love, P. E. D. (2003). Value creation through an e-business strategy: implication for SMEs in construction. *Construction Innovation*, *3*(1), 3–14.

Rodgers, J., Yen, D., & Chou, D. (2002). Developing e-busienss: a strategic approach. *Information Management & Computer Security*, *10*(4), 184–192. doi:10.1108/09685220210436985

Sabo, D. (2003). Electronic Commerce barriers survey results. Retrieved September, 18, 2003, from http://www.itaa.org/software/research/indpulse/bartext.htm

Saffu, K., Walker, J. H., & Hinson, R. (2008). Strategic value and electronic commerce adoption among small and medium-sized enterprises in a transitional economy. *Journal of Business and Industrial Marketing*, *23*(6), 395–404. doi:10.1108/08858620810894445

Scupola, A. (2002). *Adoption Issues of Business-to-Business Internet Commerce in European SMEs.* Paper presented at the 35th Hawaii International Conference on System Sciences, Hawaii, USA.

SETEL. (1999). Pathways to Electronic Commerce: Getting Australian Small Business Online. Retrieved September 4, 2003, from http://www.smallbusiness.org.au/sbc/pathways/

Sexton, D. L., & Bowman, N. B. (1984). *The Effects of Pre-Existing Psychological Characteristics on New Venture Initiations.* Paper presented at the annual meeting of the Academy of Management, Boston.

Singh, N., Kumar, V., & Baack, D. (2004). Adaptation of cultural content: evidence from B2C e-commerce firms. *European Journal of Marketing*, *39*(1/2), 71–86. doi:10.1108/03090560510572025

Statistics New Zealand. (2001). Information Technology Use in New Zealand: 2001. Retrieved Oct. 26, 2003

Statistics New Zealand. (2003). National Asian Population Projections (2001(base) - 2021) - Media Release. Retrieved July 10, 2004, from http://www.stats.govt.nz/domino/external/pasfull/pasfull.nsf/web/Media+Release+National+Asian+Population+Projections+2001(base)+-+2021?open

Tang, P., Powell, D., Worlock, K., & Bingham, J. (2000). *The impact of electronic commerce on the competitiveness of SMEs in the EU*: The STOA Programme.

Thatcher, S. M. B., Foster, W., & Zhu, L. (2006). B2B e-commerce adoption decisions in Taiwan: The interaction of cultural and other institutional factors. *Electronic Commerce Research and Applications*, *5*(2), 92–104. doi:10.1016/j.elerap.2005.10.005

Thong, J. Y. L. (1999). An integrated model of information systems adoption in small businesses. *Journal of Management Information Systems*, *15*(4), 187.

To, M. L., & Ngai, E. W. T. (2006). Predicting the organisational adoption of B2C e-commerce: an empirical study. *Industrial Management & Data Systems*, *106*(8), 1133–1147. doi:10.1108/02635570610710791

Tunzelana, S., & Technikon, C. (2003). *Obstacles for e-business implementation for SMEs*. South Africa. UK online for busienss. (2003). what is UK online for business. Retrieved Oct.12, 2003, from http://www.ukonlineforbusiness.gov.uk/cms/template/popup-content2.jsp?id=310478

USHER. (2003). The current and future barriers to SMe-volution. Retrieved September,18, 2003, from http://www.usherproject.org.uk/support/scenarios/barriers.pdf

Willcocks, L., Sauer, C., Feeny, D., Basu, K., Moore, K., Ruddle, K., et al. (2000). *Moving to E-Business, the ultimate practical guide to effective e-business*. London: Random House Business Books.

WITSA. (2001). International Survey of Electronic Commerce - 2000: World Information Technology and Services Alliance. Retrieved July 16, 2004, from http://www.witsa.org/papers/EComSurv.pdf

WSIS. (2003). Benchmarking e-business policies for SMEs: The approach. Retrieved September, 18, 2003, from http://www.cio.gv.at/WSIS/events/austria/perspectives/wg2/Beitrag_Technopolis.pdf

Yau, O. H. M. (1988). Chinese cultural values: their dimensions and marketing implications. *European Journal of Marketing, 22*(5), 44–57. doi:10.1108/EUM0000000005285

Yin, R. K. (1989). *Case study research--design and methods (revised edition)*. Newbury Park: Sage Publications.

APPENDIX 1

Case Study Participants

Stage O:

Firm O is a home business. It founded 16 years ago by the owner. This firm provides a personal consultant service. The service involves giving customers suggestions for the type of computer and software they could use to meet their specific purposes and helping customers purchase their computers. The owner of the firm pays attention to the customer's need and also tries his best to provide a good support service for them. He uses "word of mouth" to advertise his company, and to let people know about his firm. The owner did not believe he could get any benefits from Internet. This is the reason why he has not adopted e-commerce.

Stage 1:

Firm A is a home business. It has been established for 5 years, with only one staff in the firm. The firm did not connect to the Internet until February 2004, because the owner lacked enthusiasm in e-commerce adoption. There are two purposes of this firm getting online. First, they want to search up-to-date information online about the computer retail industry. Second, they want to meet the needs of a few customers and suppliers who like to transfer documents by email. However, from the total of the customer contacts each day, the percentage of email contact is quite low (about 3~5%) in comparison in face to face contact or telephone contact. Therefore, there is no need for complex shopping system development in this firm in the next few years.

Firm B is a home business too. It has been founded for one and a half years; only one staff was in the firm. On the road to this firm adopting e-commerce, originally, he was very interested in implementing e-commerce in his firm. He has even tried to establish an online store without it being based on a physical store. He connected to the Internet and established the firm's website, and adopted e-commerce at Stage one and Stage two in 2003. The strategy of the firm was to make a profit through selling products via its website. However, due to a lack of business experience, website development skills and money in employing a professional business consultant, he could not develop a professional website. He also could not establish trust relationships with his customers. Few customers visit his website or place an order by email. In the end, the firm failed in online selling. It closed its website at the beginning of 2004, and returned to Stage one. Currently, the owner has changed his marketing strategy. He is trying to establish a successful physical store, and establish trust relationships with his customers as well as retain more loyal customers. After that, he will plan to run an online business.

Stage 2:

Firm C has a physical store in Manukau city, with 5 employees. The target market of this firm was local market. In order to advertise the firm and its products, and let customers know more details of its products, the firm went online and set up its online catalogue website in 1999. The strategy of this website was to promote its company and products. As a result of having a highly skilled computer staff in the firm, all aspects of e-commerce, such as web site design, maintenance and monitoring have been done in-house. These skilled people help the firm save money in website development and maintenance. Therefore, there was no financial difficulty with initial implementation cost and on-going operational cost. Unfortunately, there is a lower volume of email order in the firm, thus there is no specialist staff in charge of website. The reason why the firm is stopping at Stage two of e-commerce development for 5 years is that they cannot solve the problem of how to provide satisfactory service to customers based on a low level inventory. They have no plan to move to the next stage of e-commerce development in the near future.

Firm D has been established for 9 years. At first, it had a physical store in Hamilton city with 7 employees. The firm was connected to the Internet via a broadband connection and set up a website with online products catalogue in 1999. The specific goal of the firm having its website was to advertise its store, save customers' time and reduce its staff's workload. This firm has a professional website development team. It helps the firm save the website design and development fees. Because the firm's owner attaches importance to the role of website advertisement, he allocates a specialist staff to take responsibility for the e-mail administration and website maintenance to keep the website up-to-date every day. The owner was an e-commerce enthusiast. He was very interested in adopting e-commerce in his business. He had even contacted an external e-commerce development company to help him to adopt e-commerce at Stage four in 2002. However, the external e-commerce development companies provided a high budget proposal to implement Stage four. This firm cannot afford the high budget, and finally it stopped the e-commerce development plan. In addition, this firm experienced online fraud in 2003. This event also hindered the firm's e-commerce growth. This year, it plans to move to Stage three.

Firm E has had a physical store in Auckland for 3 years with 3 employees. The firm's owner is not very interested in e-commerce development in his firm. Occasionally, this firm went online and developed a firm's website using an e-commerce student who completed a practical in his firm and helped him develop a website in 2003. Although the website plays a very important role in advertising its firm and reducing staff work load such as answering customers' inquiries, the owner has not paid much attention to the website development in the future. He has focused on the physical store development and does not want to spend too much money and time in developing online business. In addition, they currently also have some technical difficulty in e-commerce development, such as a lack of technical staff, a great deal of money and time. Moreover, the rate of e-mail order was relatively low. Therefore, there is no plan to move to the next stage of e-commerce development in the near future.

Firm F set up a physical store and a static online catalogue website in 2003. From the firm owner's point of view, he believes that as a computer company, they should have a website. This owner will plan to move to the next stage of e-commerce development after they have established their physical store brand and retained some loyal customers.

Firm G has had a small physical store in Auckland for 2 years. The firm's owner has a high level of e-commerce literacy; he developed a website to promote his physical store and products when the firm was founded. However, this firm is focused on the local market. The purpose of its website is to provide customers with better information about product characteristics, including product description, prices and availability. After customers browse the products on its website, they will order and pick up products in its physical store. The volume of e-mail order is relatively low in comparison to the whole order. Therefore, the owner does not really want to pour much money, time and staff into e-commerce development.

Stage 3:

Firm H was founded in November 1999. There are six employees in addition to the owner. Their customers were the general public with the occasional small business locally and nationally. The firm connected to Internet and established its website in 2002. In order to make it easier for customers to place an order online and save staff's time in website maintenance, the firm adopted Stage three of e-commerce development in 2004. After adopting e-commerce at Stage three, there is no notable increase in the percentage of online order and e-mail order. They have not gained more benefits from it in comparison to the benefits gained at Stage two of e-commerce adoption. Moreover, taking safety and trust into account, there is no plan to move to Stage four of e-commerce development in the near future.

Firm I was set up in 2000, it employed less than 20 people. The firm got online in 2000. In that year, it accessed to the Internet and had an e-mail address. Also it registered firm's domain name and published its website. The target market of this firm is local home users. With the development of the firm, they found there were some weaknesses on their old website, which was a simple, static website. It only can transfer information from the company to customers in a one-way. In order to provide more convenience for their customers, they established the new website in the June of 2004. On the new website, they provide some new functions for customers, such as shopping cart function, search engine, computer builder function. These functions provide better service for their customers. After established the new website, the firm also assigned a specialist staff to take responsibility for the email and website administration. However, as a result of high risk and high investment at Stage four of e-commerce development, the owner of this firm fellow a "wait-and-see" attitude in the next stage of e-commerce development.

Firm J was founded in 2002, it has a small physical store in Auckland, and it has three staff besides owner. It went online in 2002, and the owner established a static website by himself in the same year. With the firm's development and the various products increasing, the website has been improved year by year. This means the website has become more and more professional. In 2004, the owner developed shopping cart software by himself and added this new function in its website. This new function makes the firm move to Stage three of e-commerce development, and it also makes it easier for customers to make an order online. Although the owner is very interested in developing e-commerce in his firm, he cannot implement e-commerce at Stage four by himself. Because he depends on his knowledge and ability, there are some technical problem and knowledge problem about how to implement online payment. Usually, to move to Stage four, a firm needs to contact a bank, and coordinate with its trading partners. It needs the help of a external e-commerce development company. In this situation, even though this owner has ever contacted a bank to set up a credit card account and asked a professional e-commerce development company to do the project, the high investment, high risk and uncertainty of return on investment have blocked the way in the evolution of e-commerce in this firm.

Firm K has established a physical store and online store for one year. In 2003, the firm went online and adopted e-commerce at Stage three directly. Because there were highly skilled computer staffs in the firm, all aspects of e-commerce, such as web site design, maintenance and monitoring, were done in-house. In view of the firm being focused on the local market, the online store is only the supplement of its physical store. In addition, the firm's owner does not want to take a risk of online fraud; he does not want to move to Stage four of e-commerce development.

Firm L was founded in 2000. It has a big physical store in Manukau city with 10 staffs. It went online and had an e-mail address in 2000. It also registered firm's domain name and published website which was developed by their own staff in the same year. In the May of 2003, with the help of owner's friend, the firm redesigned website, added "shopping cart" and "pc builder" functions on its website, these new functions made the firm move to Stage three of e-commerce development. However, due to online fraud, the owner does not want to take the high risk, there is no plan to adopt Stage four in the near future.

Stage 4:

Firm M established a big physical store in Auckland in 1997. After firm was founded in a half year, the firm applied for an account and email address from an ISP and started to communicate with their customers and suppliers via email. One year later, it built its website with products online catalogue. Four years later, it updated their website and moved to Stage three and added shopping cart function in its website and made it easer for customers to place an order on its website. Given that the owner has a high level of e-commerce literacy and he have seen the trend of e-commerce development in the future, as well as he was not satisfied with the old website and wanted to provide more convenient service for nation-wide customers. Therefore, in 2004, they spent a large amount of money employing a professional company to finish online store development project and move to Stage four.

Firm N was established in the March of 1998. It has a professional team to develop and update website. Initially, the firm only had a static website to introduce its firm and products in 2000. With the development of the firm, there were more and more products being introduced on the website and more and more customers placed their orders via email. In 2002, in order to improve online customer service, the team redesigned the website and added shopping cart on the website. At the new website, customers can make an order online directly. In 2004, with an increase in the number of returning customers, in order to enhance supply chain coordinate and reduce inventory level, and provide cheaper, more convenient and automatic online service for customers, the firm invested a great deal of money into contracting with a professional website development company to redesign and modify its website. It finally moved to Stage four of e-commerce development in the September of 2004.

APPENDIX 2

Interview Question Outline

General questions about the company:

- What does your company do?
- Could you tell me how many employees are in your company?
- When was the company established?

General questions about interviewees

- Computer education background
- Age range, years of residence in New Zealand and years of trading in New Zealand
- Years of e-commerce adoption in New Zealand
- Insight of e-commerce development

Could you have a look at this table--- "**e-commerce growth process in small New Zealand firms**" (see appendix 3), and tell me at what stage your firm is in adopting e-commerce at present.

Questions about the evolution of e-commerce in small Chinese firms over time:

- Could you tell me the story about your company e-commerce adoption history?
  - Which year did your firm adopt e-commerce at Stage 1? Stage 2? Stage 3? And Stage 4?
  - What the efforts, investments, and peoples did involve at each stage of e-commerce adoption?
  - What is your firm's future plan about e-commerce development?

Questions of adoption motivators to move to current stage of e-commerce adoption

- When did you adopt it, what events or people motivate you move to this stage?
- What special applications, equipments, and resource do you think you would need to adopt this stage?
- What were specific goals and objectives to be achieved via the stage of e-commerce adoption?
- How this stage e-commerce development did fits into the firm's overall marketing strategy?
- From total of the customer contacts each day, what percentage is telephone, mail, face to face and email?
- What were the drivers or motivators for your firm to move to this stage?
- What was the key "lesson learned" from this stage?

Questions of adoption inhibitors to move to new stage of e-commerce adoption

- Have you planned to the new stage of e-commerce development?
- What barriers or inhibitors have you met at the new stage development?
- What new business skills, business processes, and other requirements do you think you would need to succeed at the new stage adoption of e-commerce?

Question of culture difficulty:

- Is there any cultural difficulty which influences your firm in adopting e-commerce in the New Zealand business context?

APPENDIX 3

E-Commerce Growth Process in Small New Zealand Firms (Table 14)

Table 14.

Stage	Effort	Investment	Risk Rate	Extra People Need	Activities
Stage One Messaging	Apply for a dial up account from ISP	1. Computer, 2. Modem, 3. Browser software 4. Internet connection fees, about $25/month	Low		1.Searching information; 2.Using on-line services; 3.Using e-mail to communicate with customers and suppliers;

Stage	Effort	Investment	Risk Rate	Extra People Need	Activities
Stage Two Online Marketing	1. Register company's domain name. 2. Design, develop, publish website, Put company's product and information online. 3. Add an on-line catalogue that is an on-line version of a paper-based catalogue in company's website. 4. Update the site, update the on-line catalogue. 5. Contract with courier company for delivery products	1. Website design, development fees about $1600 2. Domain name registration fees, about $100/year 3. Rent web space from an ISP	Low	1.Website designer 2.Website updater 3.Website e-mail administrator	1. Having static website and an on-line version of a paper-based catalogue; 2.Extensive use of email to communicate and exchange documents and orders with customers, suppliers and employees; 3.Email ordering;
Stage Three Online Ordering	1.Redesign website 2. Add 'shopping cart' function to website	1. Consultant fees, and website development fees. 2.Purchasing Shopping cart software about $2000	Middle	1. Specialist website designer, consultant 2. Tracking the orders and dealing with customer queries, 3. Confirmation of delivery arrangements	1. Having two-way information interactive websites that provide topics search, company information query; 2. Using shopping cart software to place an order on the website; 3. Payment can be fulfilled manually by bank deposit, bank cheque or internet banking; 4. Expanding the potential market nationally;
Stage Four Online Transaction	1.Integrate company's website into the banking system 2. Integrate company's online front end with its back-end systems 3. Integrate ordering systems to suppliers systems. 3.Integrate the payment and shipping information	1.Buy BNZ's buyline or ASB Bank's Access On-line 2. Set an account with a specialist clearing agency that can handle real-time credit card clearance. 3. Pay extra monthly fees for using SSL technology to maintain a secure section of company site to allow users to enter credit card details safely. 4. Apply for a certificate of authentication. 5. pay for credit card processing and bank charges	High	1. Specialist website designer, consultant 2. Tracking the orders and deal with customer queries, 3. Confirmation of delivery arrangements	1. Online order fulfilment can be accomplished automatically, i.e. an order can be received or confirmed, and an invoice can be issued or received online; 2. Online payment can be undertaken through debit and credit cards, electronic cash, electronic funds transfer, or through an EDI service; 3. Integrating online front end and back-end system; 4. Expanding the potential market internationally;

Chapter 13
A Model of Intraorganizational Knowledge Sharing:
Development and Initial Test

I-Chieh Hsu
National Changhua University of Education, Taiwan

Yi-Shun Wang
National Changhua University of Education, Taiwan

ABSTRACT

Prior research has reported different knowledge management processes, considering each universally applicable. This article proposes that context influences company knowledge sharing policies and practices and their effectiveness. Through a literature review, a model of intraorganizational knowledge sharing is proposed. Within this model, three organizational antecedents of knowledge sharing policies and practices are included, namely: top management knowledge values, an innovation business strategy, and perceived environmental uncertainty. Further, top management knowledge values and knowledge sharing policies and practices are hypothesized to lead to knowledge sharing effectiveness. The model was constructed by taking into account industrial contexts in Taiwan, and was examined using survey data collected from companies in Taiwan. The results showed that top management knowledge values and innovation business strategy are positively and significantly associated with knowledge sharing policies and practices, which in turn lead to knowledge sharing effectiveness. Finally, this article identifies and discusses implications for international information management.

INTRODUCTION

In a knowledge-based economy, both theory and practice recognize that knowledge is one of the key strategic resources of a firm. It is also argued that the richest resource modern companies have is the knowledge that resides within their employees because unlike other types of resources, the value of knowledge increases as it is shared (Quinn, Anderson, & Finkelstein, 1996). Thus, how to foster knowledge sharing among employees so that companies can leverage their richest resource has become a key managerial issue (Michailova & Husted, 2003). Under this premise, companies increasingly develop a range of knowledge management practices, of which the key objective is to facilitate knowledge sharing among employees (Cabrera & Cabrera, 2002; Carneiro, 2000; Earl, 2001; Grant, 1996a). In addition to these knowledge management practices, researchers also stress the importance of IT-based knowledge management systems, believing them to be an effective vehicle for knowledge sharing (Alavi & Leidner, 2001; Scarbrough, Swan, & Preston, 1999; Sher & Lee, 2004).

However, previous literature tends to propose "best" knowledge sharing policies and practices, considering all of them to be universally applicable (Becerra-Fernandez & Sabherwal, 2001). Contributive antecedents of these "best practices" have not been carefully examined. Without considering these antecedents, organizations cannot effectively establish and implement these knowledge sharing policies and practices (Holsapple & Joshi, 2000; Kalling, 2003; McDermott, 1999). Further, unlike previous literature that argues that organizational antecedents influence employees' knowledge sharing behaviors (Constant, Keisler, & Sproull, 1994; Husted & Michailova, 2002; Jarvenpaa & Staples, 2000, 2001), we emphasize the importance and effectiveness of company knowledge sharing policies and practices, that is, organizational policies and practices that facilitate and motivate the diffusion of learning and knowledge within the organization (Husted & Michailova, 2002), in inducing employees to share knowledge (Ruggles, 1998). Examination of the effectiveness of organizational knowledge sharing policies and practices is necessary, but to date such research has rarely been conducted (Choi & Lee, 2003). Thus, the two important and yet under-researched issues, antecedents and effectiveness of knowledge sharing policies and practices, require investigation so that our understanding regarding these two issues can be enhanced.

In this article, we seek to develop and validate a model of intraorganizational knowledge sharing in business organizations. In this model, organizational antecedents and effectiveness of knowledge sharing policies and practices are examined using survey data collected from companies in Taiwan. In recent years, companies in Taiwan, which once created rapid economic growth that caught the attention of the world, have experienced managerial challenges due to the trend of globalization. With the advent of the knowledge economy, the government in Taiwan has begun promoting the importance of knowledge-based competition to companies. The implementation of policies and practices aimed at facilitating and encouraging employee knowledge sharing has been observed among companies in Taiwan (Hsu, 2006; Sher & Lee, 2004). As will also be seen, top managers in Taiwan often show a paternalistic style of management (Chang, 1985; Redding, 1993) that may facilitate employee knowledge sharing. Thus, this style of management, along with government promotions, may act as facilitating backgrounds for intraorganizational knowledge sharing. However, Taiwan has distinct cultural traits from the west that may impede intraorganizational knowledge sharing such as emphasizing hierarchy (Hofstede, 1997) and the tendency of intimate individuals differentiating themselves from distant others (Triandis, 1989).

Neither the antecedents nor the effectiveness of intraorganizational knowledge sharing policies and practices has been carefully studied within business contexts in Taiwan. Thus, this study builds on theory and practice developed in the west to propose a model of intraorganizational knowledge sharing and tests it in a business context in Taiwan. Findings should have theoretical and practical implications for both local and global perspectives.

This article is structured as follows. First, we present our research framework. Then, a review of existing literature helps to frame and define the constructs of our interest, and to develop hypothesized relationships between them. Next, the research method and results are presented. The method consisted of a questionnaire survey distributed to companies in Taiwan. The subsequent analysis of collected questionnaires is used to examine the proposed hypotheses. Finally, implications of the results are discussed and future directions of research are proposed.

RESEARCH FRAMEWORK AND HYPOTHESES

The research framework is presented in Figure 1. We seek to construct and examine an integrative model of intraorganizational knowledge sharing. Such an examination is necessary as it leads to the development of strategic guidelines for companies to improve their knowledge policies and practices (Lee & Choi, 2003). However, the existing literature does not report a knowledge sharing model that can guide our model building process, although discussions of factors that facilitate knowledge management can be found (e.g., Holsapple & Joshi, 2002). Thus, we build the research framework by integrating the various sources of literature as reported next.

The building of the model starts from identifying antecedents of company knowledge sharing policies and practices that facilitate and motivate the diffusion of learning and knowledge within an organization. Porter's (1980) analytic framework of strategy proposes that a firm's exploitation and development of its knowledge resources should take into account the firm's internal and external factors. The internal factor pertains to the firm's strategy, and the external factor the firm's environments. Also, implicit in Porter (1980) and other researchers (e.g., Eisenhardt & Martin, 2000), in addition to strategy and environmental uncertainty, top management values play important roles in guiding organizational policies, practices, and processes when an organization responds to environmental uncertainty. Hamel and Prahalad (1989) argue that top management values guide the choice of the firm's strategy and dissemination and development of knowledge resources. Thus, a firm's allocation, accumulation, dissemination, and retention of knowledge resources should be guided by top management values, strategy, and environmental uncertainty (Hamel & Prahalad, 1993). Following this logic, in the model of intraorganizational knowledge sharing as a firm's attempt to develop and make use of its knowledge resources, we include strategy, top management values, and environmental uncertainty as our three antecedents.

Although knowledge management literature argues for the importance of knowledge sharing as a way to help organizations gain competitive

Figure 1. Research framework

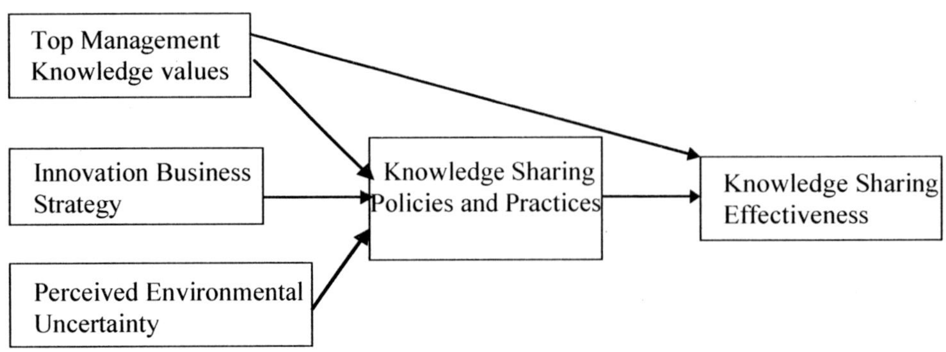

advantage in an environment with increasing uncertainty (Eisenhardt & Santos, 2002; Gold, Malhortra, & Segars, 2001; Quinn et al., 1996), investigation into the relationship between environmental uncertainty and knowledge sharing policies and practices has been lacking (e.g., Argote, McEvily, & Reagans, 2003). Essentially, managers take actions based on how they perceive the nature of organizational environments to be (Daft & Weick, 1984). Thus, understanding the relationship between top management's perceived environmental uncertainty and knowledge sharing policies and practices is necessary. Top management's perceived environmental uncertainty is one of the antecedents included in the model.

Intraorganizational knowledge sharing involves transferring or disseminating knowledge among individuals or groups. It serves as a basis for knowledge utilization to create competitive advantage for the firm (Sabherwal & Sabherwal, 2005). As an important aspect of knowledge activities, it should be guided by the strategy of the firm (Hamel & Prahalad, 1989). However, a systematic attention to the relationship between strategy and knowledge sharing policies and practices is lacking. Thus, another antecedent of knowledge sharing policies and practices should be strategy.

In the model of intraorganizational knowledge sharing, another antecedent should be included: top management knowledge values. This internal factor is included for the following two reasons. First, a firm's strategy requires long-term and steady investments of resources in the implementation stage to fulfill the firm's predetermined goals. Top management values guide such commitments of resources (Hamel & Prahalad, 1989). Second, the greatest challenge faced in intraorganizational knowledge sharing is organizational culture. Top management values have been argued to shape the organizational culture that drives intraorganizational knowledge sharing (Ruggles, 1998). Despite the importance of top management values, few studies have systematically investigated their effect on knowledge related activities including knowledge sharing (Alavi, Kayworth, & Leidner, 2005-2006).

Thus, in the currently proposed model of intraorganizational knowledge sharing, the three antecedents of knowledge sharing policies and practices should be considered in an integrative fashion. These three antecedents are top management values about knowledge as a major source of competitive advantage and support for knowledge sharing (here termed "top management knowledge values"), a business strategy that seeks to differentiate the company from its competitors through product innovation (here termed "innovation business strategy"), and top management's perceived environmental uncertainty. Further, knowledge sharing effectiveness is included to examine the effectiveness of knowledge sharing policies and practices. In this model, we also argue top management knowledge values may directly impact knowledge sharing effectiveness.

The examination of the proposed model is relevant and important for business management in Taiwan. Here, country peculiarities are taken into account. First, top managers in Taiwan typically exhibit a paternalistic style of management that differs from their western counterparts (Chang, 1985; Redding, 1993). Their values are instilled in employees and profoundly affect aspects of organizational life. Second, Taiwan has distinct cultural traits. For example, Taiwanese society emphasizes hierarchy (Hofstede, 1997), and Chinese people tend to differentiate between an in-group (a group of intimate individuals) and distant others (Triandis, 1989). These cultural traits have adverse consequences in intraorganizational knowledge sharing, such as knowledge hoarding by senior employees or by in-groups. Third, in the trend of globalization, companies in Taiwan are facing increasingly uncertain environments. The Taiwan government encourages companies to invest in product/service innovations as a source of competitive advantage and provides funding to support them. Changing environments and the innovation business strategy newly adopted by Taiwan companies should affect knowledge sharing policies and practices, which in turn affect knowledge sharing effectiveness. The study of the proposed model, rarely conducted either in the west or in Taiwan, should lead to theoretical and practical implications. Constructs included in this model and the hypothesized relationships between these constructs are introduced and developed below.

Intraorganizational Knowledge Sharing and Knowledge Sharing Effectiveness

A common definition of organizational knowledge gleaned from previous literature appears in the form of "justified true belief" (Nonaka & Takeuchi, 1995). This belief can be disseminated within organizations as validated information (Liebeskind, 1996), based on which organizational members make inferences and decisions (Tsoukas & Vladimirou, 2001). However, decision-related knowledge may not always be available, as knowledge sharing often does not take place among organizational members. Thus, Grant (1996b) identified knowledge sharing as one major challenge in organizational knowledge management. Should this challenge be overcome, organizational members can absorb new knowledge from their peers and individual knowledge can be leveraged by organizations (Nonaka & Konno, 1998).

The literature suggests that intraorganizational knowledge sharing keeps knowledge and information obtained from various sources up-to-date and serves as a guide for future action (Lukas, Hult, & Ferrell, 1996). As learning in an organization results from an accumulation of individual-level learning (Hedberg, 1981; Shrivastava, 1983), intraorganizational knowledge sharing helps the organization, through the diffusion of individual-level learning, to achieve two major objectives of organizational learning (Dodgson, 1993): improving the efficiency and innovativeness of the organization in facing environmental uncertainty. Thus, the spiral of knowledge proposed by Nonaka (1991) and Nonaka and Takeuchi (1995) depicts four modes of knowledge sharing within a company that create company-specific knowledge, which then leads to sustained competitive advantage for the company. Widen-Wulff and Ginman (2004) further suggest that intraorganizational knowledge sharing enhances an organization's innovativeness and prospects for development, while reducing its transaction costs.

Intraorganizational knowledge sharing involves transferring or disseminating knowledge among individuals or groups. Organizations can initiate sets of policies and practices to facilitate and motivate such sharing so that individual learning can take place (Calantone, Cavusgil, & Zhao, 2002; Grant, 1996b; Moorman & Miner, 1998; Zaltman, Duncan, & Holbek, 1973). Organizational learning takes place as a result of the accumulation of individual learning (Calantone et al., 2002). Previous literature has reported practices that facilitate knowledge sharing, such as IT systems. In such an IT system, rules and norms are applied and individuals can interact and share their knowledge.

Policies also facilitate intraoragnizational knowledge sharing. For example, the use of knowledge sharing mechanisms such as work teams (Lynn, 1998), meetings, manuals, and dialogues (Subramaniam & Youndt, 2005) can facilitate knowledge sharing. Other policies and practices can motivate intraorganizational knowledge sharing. Incentive systems have been widely recognized as a major policy and practice to guide and encourage knowledge sharing (Bartol & Srivastava, 2002; Gupta & Govindarajan, 2000; Hsu, 2006; Quigley, Tesluk, Locke, & Bartol, 2007). With incentive systems, employees are motivated to share knowledge with each other, and knowledge sharing effectiveness can be improved. Based on the foregoing discussion, we propose and define a term, "knowledge sharing policies and practices" as *organizational policies and practices that facilitate and motivate the diffusion of learning and knowledge within an organization* (Husted & Michailova, 2002).

As argued, the benefit of intraorganizational knowledge sharing may be enormous. However, exactly how that contributes to competitive advantage and satisfactory financial performance is neither straight-forward nor very clear (Lee & Choi, 2003). However, previous literature has emphasized more immediate, positive outcomes of knowledge sharing policies and practices, which can be broken down into two categories: employees' exhibition of knowledge sharing behaviors and positive impacts on task performance (Becerra-Fernandez & Sabherwal, 2001; Husted & Michailova, 2002; Sabherwal & Becerra-Fernandez, 2005). For the former category, employee knowledge sharing behaviors are motivated and encouraged and knowledge sharing is expedited. Thus, the efficiency of knowledge sharing processes is improved. For the latter category, employees' task performance can be improved as a result of knowledge sharing policies and practices. We define knowledge sharing effectiveness as *employees' exhibition of knowledge sharing behaviors and positive impacts on task performance*.

In Taiwan, with the strong promotion of the government, companies have started to implement knowledge sharing policies and practices to improve knowledge sharing effectiveness. However, such implementation should take into account Taiwan's national cultural traits, which have been characterized as being hierarchical (Hofstede, 1997). This has been reflected in the managerial style used in local companies (Silin, 1976). Junior employees were often asked to accept company authority and behavioral norms, instead of asking questions and proposing ideas (e.g., Hsu, 2006). Prior literature discusses reasons behind the lack of knowledge sharing among employees. One major reason commonly identified is that knowledge sharers fear the loss of privileges following knowledge sharing (Cabrera & Cabrera, 2002; Husted & Michailova, 2002; Szulanski, 1996). This fear can be worsened by a hierarchical culture of nation because senior people may lose face and privileges if junior employees have improved performance after receiving knowledge from their seniors. Thus, it is not just horizontal but also hierarchical knowledge sharing that is needed in companies in Taiwan. If senior people in companies in Taiwan can take initiative in mentoring junior employees, that will also be a good indicator of knowledge sharing effectiveness. In fact, the use of senior people in mentoring junior personnel has also been stressed in western literature (Lepak & Snell, 1999; Sabherwal & Becerra-Fernandez, 2005). Knowledge sharing policies and practices should encourage such mentoring behavior to take place. Also, companies in Taiwan often emphasize collectivist values, but knowledge is shared among individuals who see each other as together forming an in-group, not with distant others (out-groups) (Hsu, 2006; cf. Lin & Kwok, 2006). Thus, horizontal knowledge sharing is just as important and should be motivated and facilitated.

Based on the discussion that knowledge sharing policies and practices can improve knowledge sharing effectiveness (Becerra-Fernandez & Sabherwal, 2001; Husted & Michailova, 2002; Sabherwal & Becerra-Fernandez, 2005), we believe that in Taiwan, knowledge sharing policies and practices can lead to employees' knowledge sharing behaviors and improved task performance. We thus hypothesize:

H1: *Knowledge sharing policies and practices will lead to knowledge sharing effectiveness in companies in Taiwan.*

Top Management Knowledge Values

Previous literature identifies organizational culture as one of the major factors that facilitate knowledge sharing (Ahmed, Kok, & Loh, 2002; Liebowitz & Chen, 2001). However, values held by top management prescribe how organizational members should behave, how they should conduct business, and what kind of organization they should build. Top management values permeate all aspects of an organization and are the cornerstone of an organization's culture (Collins & Porras, 1996). Thus, we propose that top management values shape organizational culture and have a direct effect on the development of knowledge sharing policies and practices. This direct effect, rarely examined, is included in our study.

Our search of the literature suggests that the development of knowledge management practices should start with top management values that perceive the creation, sharing, and use of knowledge as a source of competitive advantage (Bartlett & Ghoshal, 2002; Grover & Davenport, 2001). Davenport and Prusak (2000) report that when top managers perceive knowledge as the key strategic resource and knowledge sharing as the foundation for value creation, they also support a range of knowledge management practices directed at facilitating knowledge sharing within organizations as the primary objective.

Previous literature suggests that top management knowledge values underlie two dimensions: top management's encouragement of and support for intraorganizational knowledge sharing, and its recognition of the importance of knowledge in creating competitive advantage of the firm (Davenport, De Long, & Beers, 1998; Davenport & Prusak, 2000; Gold et al., 2001). On the surface, the second dimension seems to underlie the first dimension. However, the literature suggests that in reality and theory the two are intertwined and difficult to discern (Gold et al., 2001). Encouraging knowledge sharing is a way to emphasize that knowledge is key to the success of the firm. Emphasizing the importance of knowledge in creating the competitive advantage of the firm also encourages knowledge sharing. Essentially, through the manifestation of values of these two dimensions, top managers set a social norm in the company and knowledge sharing behaviors are exhibited by employees (Alavi et al., 2005-2006). We define top management knowledge values as *top management's recognition of the importance of knowledge in the success of the firm and support for knowledge sharing.*

This is a time for Taiwan's top managers to change their values. In the past they strived to engage in cost-based competition by exploiting low-cost labor. The thriving development of neighboring countries and the trend of globalization have imposed intensified competitive pressures under which companies in Taiwan may be required to change their strategic focus to engage in innovation-based competition (Wong, Maher, Wang, & Long, 2001). To facilitate this change, top managers in Taiwan should equip themselves with knowledge values so that intraorganizational knowledge sharing can be facilitated and knowledge-based competences can be developed for companies in Taiwan. Thus, top managers in Taiwan should recognize the importance of knowledge in the success of the firm and support knowledge sharing. Limited observation has found that top management knowledge values can lead to the implementation of knowledge sharing policies and practices (Hsu, 2006). This merits further investigation. We hypothesize:

H2: *In Taiwan, a company with a top management that values knowledge as important in the company's success and supports knowledge sharing is more likely to establish knowledge sharing policies and practices.*

The importance of top management knowledge values may not just lie in the role of initiating and maintaining knowledge sharing policies and practices. Top management knowledge values may also have the capability to directly affect knowledge sharing behaviors and result in positive knowledge sharing outcomes. The causal mechanisms of this process are rooted in social cognitive theory. First, as argued earlier, top management values are the cornerstone of an organization's culture (Collins & Porras, 1996). Even verbal persuasions from top managers can increase employees' self-evaluations of capabilities (Gist & Mitchell, 1992). Thus, if top managers declare the importance of knowledge sharing and encourage knowledge sharing, employees may develop positive attitudes toward knowledge sharing and may gain confidence in knowledge sharing. New intake may be socialized into knowledge sharers. Second, top managers, when declaring their knowledge values and exhibiting knowledge sharing behavior, portray themselves as role models of knowledge sharing. Behaviors of role models can be imitated, and employees' confidence in knowledge sharing will be developed (Bandura, 1988; Wood & Bandura, 1989). In such a situation, the chance that knowledge sharing behaviors are exhibited is increased.

The effect of top management knowledge values on employee knowledge sharing behaviors and outcomes is very evident in companies in Taiwan. Chinese managers have been reported to exhibit a paternalistic style of management that is distinct from western managers (Chang 1985; Redding, 1993; Sheh, 2001). Under this paternalistic management, the company is a big family with managers as the center of decision authority and employees are part of the family. Thus, Chinese managers tend to look after the personal problems and welfare of their employees. In return, employees are bound by a moral obligation to act according to their superiors' expectations. If top management expects and encourages employees to share knowledge and improve knowledge sharing outcomes, they are obliged to do so even if knowledge sharing is not included in their job descriptions. Although some may argue that the Taiwan society is undergoing changes leading to an increased emphasis on individual needs and autonomy (Wu, 2004). Hsu (2006) observed that senior managers in Taiwan remain heavily involved in the implementation of knowledge sharing policies and practices and personally mentor employee knowledge sharing. This is an extension of the exemplary paternalistic style of management. In time, we should be able to see that top management knowledge values result in employee knowledge sharing behaviors and outcomes. Thus, we hypothesize:

H3: *In Taiwan, a company with a top management that values knowledge as important in the company's success and supports knowledge sharing is more likely to have knowledge sharing effectiveness.*

Innovation Business Strategy

Previous literature argues that strategy is an antecedent of organizational structural design (Chandler, 1962; Miles & Snow, 1978; Mintzberg, 1973). The resource-based view of the firm (e.g., Prahalad & Hamel, 1990), the knowledge-based view of the firm (e.g., Grant, 1996a, b), and the dynamic capabilities perspective (e.g., Teece, 1998; Teece, Pisano, & Shuen, 1997) recognize the importance of strategy in guiding knowledge-related activities to achieve high financial performance and sustained competitiveness of firms. Firms with great innovation capabilities and high innovative performance start with a shared strategic vision that stresses the importance of innovation and that supports organizational knowledge sharing to enhance innovation capabilities (Calantone et al., 2002).

Our literature review further reveals that business strategy is an important factor that affects the implementation of knowledge sharing policies and practices. For example, business strategy concerns an organization's pursuit of competitive advantage through differentiation (Porter, 1980; Prahalad & Hamel, 1990) and this strategy guides the organization's accumulation, dissemination, utilization, and leveraging of knowledge assets (Hamel & Prahalad, 1989, 1993). Noe, Hollenbeck, Gerhart, and Wright (2003, 2004) argue that information sharing practices must be initiated under the framework of an organization's competitive strategy. Grover and Davenport (2001) claim that business strategies can be enhanced and supported through effective use of knowledge. Thus, knowledge management practices should be integrated with business strategy. Knott (2004) further argues that a pursuit of product innovation as a company's strategic posture should lead to knowledge-updating routines that facilitate creation and sharing of knowledge. Bae and his colleagues (Bae & Lawler, 2000; Bae, Chen, Wan, Lawler, & Walumbwa, 2003) argue that a differentiation business strategy leads to the implementation of high performance work systems. Such systems include a variety of practices aiming for information and knowledge sharing. Thus, the focal business strategy that entails *differentiating one company from its competitors through product innovation* (termed "innovation business strategy" for short) will lead to the implementation of knowledge sharing policies and practices.

Companies in Taiwan have faced increased foreign competitions in the last decade, which are imposed from thriving China, and from neighbors such as South Korea (Wong et al., 2001). Taiwan's participation in the WTO has further intensified the competition corporate Taiwan faces. The government has enacted and implemented a series of innovation policies aimed at helping local companies better engage in knowledge-based competition (Shyu & Chiu, 2002; Tsai & Wang, 2004). Companies in Taiwan have experienced a long evolutionary process toward an emphasis on knowledge innovation in terms of products/services in order to maintain their global competitiveness (Ministry of Economic Affairs, Taiwan, 2002, 2003; Mathews, 2001; Wu & Hsu, 2001). However, the link between the strategic posture of innovation and knowledge sharing policies and practices has rarely been investigated in Taiwan. To our knowledge, Hsu's observation (2006) of manufacturing companies in Taiwan suggests that a company that pursues a strategy of product innovation tends to have a greater variety of knowledge sharing policies and practices than one that does not. This merits further investigation. Thus, it can be hypothesized that:

H4: *In Taiwan, a company that pursues an innovation business strategy seeking to differentiate the company from its competitors through product innovation is more likely to establish knowledge sharing policies and practices.*

Top Management's Perceived Environmental Uncertainty

A general theme regarding the nature of business environments has been observed in management literature. This general theme is environmental uncertainty, which addresses the rate of change in the industry and the uncertainty or unpredictability of customers and competitors' moves (Burns & Stalker, 1961; Eisenhardt, 1989; Lawrence & Lorsch, 1967; Miller & Friesen, 1983). To be more specific, environmental uncertainty signifies "the amount and unpredictability of change in customer tastes, production or service technologies, and the modes of competition in the firm's industries" (Miller & Friesen, 1978). Environmental uncertainty has been regarded as the "cutting edge" of organizational analysis and coping with uncertainty is the essence of the management process (Özsomer, Calantone, & Benedetto, 1997; Thompson, 1967). Managers respond to company environments according to how they perceive the nature of the environments (Daft & Weick, 1984).

In a knowledge-based economy, companies are also known to face environments that are becoming increasingly uncertain. The resource-based theory of the firm (Conner & Prahalad, 1996) also recognizes the importance of a company's knowledge assets. Since many resources are relatively easily accessible to all companies, value creation through intangible resources, especially knowledge, is becoming more essential. Thus, the best way to cope with environmental uncertainty is by developing an organization's dynamic capabilities based on knowledge management (Sher & Lee, 2004), in which knowledge sharing is important. Knowledge sharing is also crucial in a highly uncertain business environment as companies require experimentation and iterative processes in strategic decision making, which are facilitated by the diffusion of situation-specific knowledge (Eisenhardt & Martin, 2000). With such dynamic capabilities, organizations can respond to environmental changes with new products and processes (Teece & Pisano, 1994) and business performance is improved (Helfat, 1997). Knowledge sharing promotes the leveraging of individual knowledge and supports knowledge integration for value creation (Hsu, 2005). Evidence also suggests that in a highly uncertain environment, experimentation and the sharing of situation-specific knowledge facilitate organizational learning and improve organizational performance (Brown & Eisenhardt, 1997). Thus, perceived environmental uncertainty should lead to the implementation of knowledge sharing policies and practices.

Further, a good intraorganizational knowledge sharing system supports knowledge and information dissemination and facilitates learning (Moorman & Miner, 1998). When information and knowledge is made available to employees, they are able to make quality decisions and the organization is able to cope with environmental uncertainty (Dodgson, 1993; Tsoukas & Vladimirou, 2001). A knowledge sharing system, as Davenport and Prusak (2000) argue, contains more than just a system built on information technology. It should also contain a set of policies and practices that facilitate sharing and disseminating knowledge. Experience and lessons learned should be disseminated within an organization (Dixon, 1990). Thus, in order to cope with environmental uncertainty, knowledge sharing policies and practices are important and have to be established.

Taiwan's economic growth has depended greatly on international trade, which leaves business operations involved in this economy susceptible to changes in global environments (Ali, Lee, Hsieh, & Krishnan, 2005). Moreover, more than 98% of business entities in Taiwan are small and medium-sized companies (Shyu & Chiu, 2002). They are constantly confronted with increasingly strong competition from across the Taiwan Strait, as well as from neighboring countries (Wong et al., 2001). Increases in costs of production factors and changes in demand conditions further add to the difficulty of doing business, and hence, uncertainty of business environments. It is imperative that we understand how top managers' perceived environmental uncertainty affects the implementation of knowledge sharing policies and practices aimed to enhance the competitive advantage of companies in Taiwan. Such an understanding has not yet been achieved due to a lack of empirical studies on this issue. Our final hypothesis is:

H5: *In Taiwan, companies tend to establish knowledge sharing policies and practices as perceived environmental uncertainty is high.*

RESEARCH METHOD

Sample Target and Procedure

A cross-sectional survey with a convenience sample was employed. Respondents were attendants of a university executive MBA program in Taiwan. Access to high-level managers of companies was obtained through these EMBA students, who came from various industries. A survey using this group of corporate managers allowed us to gain a rich data set, and at the same time avoid any bias toward any single industry.

The survey was administered during the classroom sessions. The lead author explained to the program attendants the purpose of this survey and asked for their cooperation. It was emphasized that respondents should report what they observed, not what they thought their companies should be doing. This was intended to discourage respondents from using their own espoused theories to guide answers. A total of 150 questionnaires were collected. However, respondents working within government agencies were excluded from the analysis. This resulted in 130 usable questionnaires from 130 companies. The 130 respondents averaged 39 years of age and had 15 years of work tenure; the male-to-female ratio was approximately 2.3 to 1. Respondents were 50% senior managers (general managers and board of directors) and 50% functional managers. Industries included information and communication products, electronics and mechatronics, metals and components, petro-chemicals and plastics, vendors of information and communication products, management and financial services, and banking and insurance (Table 1).

Survey Measures and Items

Due to the lack of empirical investigation into organizational knowledge sharing, measures of the pertinent constructs were largely developed from theoretical statements made in the existing literature. The newly proposed research model in this article, along with the proposed measures, suggests the exploratory nature of our study. Seven-point Likert-type scales ranging from "1" (strongly disagree) to "7" (strongly agree) were used throughout the survey. The Appendix lists the survey items used in this empirical research.

The first construct is top management knowledge values. As defined, this construct refers to two dimensions: top management's recognition of the importance of knowledge in the success of the firm and support for knowledge sharing (Davenport & Prusak, 2000). The literature suggests that the two dimensions are intertwined and difficult to discern (Gold et al., 2001). Encouraging knowledge sharing is a way to emphasize that knowledge is key to the success of the firm. Emphasizing the importance of knowledge in creating competitive advantage of the firm also encourages knowledge sharing. Thus, modeling top management knowledge values as a reflective construct is appropriate for capturing the complementarities of the two dimensions of this construct. A formative modeling of top management knowledge values as an alternative approach would not be appropriate because it does not assume any interaction or covariance between the two dimensions of this construct (Chin, 1998). This construct contains a variety of indicators: top management a) emphasizes knowledge sharing within the company, b) believes that its support is key to employee knowledge sharing (Davenport et al., 1998; Davenport & Prusak, 2000), c) regards knowledge sharing policies and practices as contributing to company performance (Hauschild, Licht, & Stein, 2001; Husted & Michailova, 2002), and d) regards firm-specific knowledge as a source of competitive advantage (Cabrera & Cabrera, 2002).

Innovation business strategy measures the degree to which the company seeks to achieve differentiation in the market through product or service innovation. Thus, striving to be different in the market underlies a company's pursuit of its own successful business model. This was included as one of the measurement items. Further, product or service innovation concerns the speed of innovation, the expenditures endowed for the innovation, and sales from new products or services. These three items have also been included in our scale. Overall, these four indicators have been used by Miller (1988) to measure Porter's (1980) innovative differentiation, namely differentiation based on product or service innovation. Again, modeling innovation business strategy as a reflective construct is appropriate for capturing complementarities of its indicators (Chin, 1998), and is done in this study.

Measurement of perceived environmental uncertainty was developed through the following process. According to the works of Miller and Friesen (1978, 1983), Eisenhardt (1989), and Daft (2003), major environmental elements should

Table 1. Surveyed companies' profiles

Characteristics		Frequency	Percentage
Industry Type(Main)	*Industry Type (Sub)*		
Manufacturing	Information and Communications	10	7.7
	Electronics and Mechatronics	13	10
	Metals and Components	19	14.6
	Petrochemicals and Plastics	12	9.2
	Others (textile, medical equipments, pharmaceuticals, etc.)	11	8.5
Service	Information and Communications vendors	14	10.8
	Management and Financial services	14	10.8
	Banking and Insurance	16	12.3
	Others	6	4.6
Not reported		15	11.5
Total		130	100
Number of Employees			
<100		57	43.8
100 to <500		28	21.5
500 to <1000		8	6.2
1000 to < 5000		24	18.5
>= 5000		9	6.9
Not reported		4	3.1
Total		130	100
Annual Sales (in USD)			
< 100000		5	3.8
100000 to < 500000		12	9.2
500000 to < 1 million		9	6.9
1 to < 100 million		52	40
100 to < 500 million		8	6.2
>= 500 million		9	6.9
Not reported		35	26.9
Total		130	100
Capital (in USD)			
< 100000		9	6.9
100000 to < 500000		19	14.6
500000 to < 1 million		14	10.8
1 to < 100 million		42	32.3
100 to < 500 million		8	6.2
>= 500 million		15	11.5
Not reported		23	17.7
Total		130	100

include customers, technology, and competitors. Changes in these environmental elements influence corporate decision-making (Child, 1972). Thus, the survey explored whether changes in these three items affect the company greatly.

Knowledge sharing policies and practices tap into organizational policies and practices that facilitate and motivate the diffusion of learning and knowledge within an organization. Four items were developed to measure this construct. These items include the company: a) analyzing past failure and disseminating the lessons learned among employees (Dixon, 1990), b) investing in IT systems that facilitate knowledge sharing (Lee, Lee, & Kang, 2005; Sher & Lee, 2004), c) developing knowledge sharing mechanisms (Calantone et al., 2002; Guthrie, Spell, & Nyamori, 2002), and d) offering incentives to encourage knowledge sharing (Gupta & Govindarajan, 2000).

Knowledge sharing effectiveness is measured by the perceived employee behaviors and outcomes of intraorganizational knowledge sharing (Becerra-Fernandez & Sabherwal, 2001; Husted & Michailova, 2002). A four-item scale was developed. For example, the items included "employees' knowledge sharing enhances their task performance" and "employees' knowledge sharing behaviors are satisfactory."

Two rounds of survey pre-testing were conducted. In the first round, five high-ranking managers with more than 20 years of work experience were provided with the survey. Ambiguities and sources of confusions in the measures were removed in light of comments and suggestions. The second pretest involved providing the revised measures to a different group of five managers with similar work experience.

Control Variable

Industry was included as a control variable. Previous literature suggests that industry may confront organizations with differing levels of uncertainty (Datta, Guthrie, & Wright, 2005), limit the choice of organizations in their strategies (Porter, 1980), and partially explain performance outcomes of organizations (McGahan & Porter, 1999). Thus, industry may influence how organizational knowledge is managed and the outcome of intraorganizational knowledge sharing. A dummy variable was assigned to two industry categories: manufacturing and service. Of the 130 companies that responded to the questionnaire survey, 115 companies provided their industry information.

RESULTS

Measurement Model

A confirmatory factor analysis using AMOS 4.0 was conducted to test the measurement model. Five model-fit measures were used to assess the model's overall appropriateness of fit: the ratio of chi-square to degrees of freedom (df), adjusted goodness of fit index (AGFI), incremental fit index (IFI), comparative fit index (CFI), and root mean square error of approximation (RMSEA). The reason for using AGFI instead of GFI was due to the adjustment for degrees of freedom (Byrne, 2001). Also, IFI was used to address the issues of parsimony and sample size (Bollen, 1989), while CFI took into account sample size (Bentler, 1990). The model comprising the measurement items showed adequate fit (chi-square/df = 1.32, AGFI = 0.83, IFI = 0.96, CFI = 0.96, RMSEA = 0.05). We next proceeded to evaluate the psychometric properties of the measurement model in terms of reliability, convergent validity, and discriminant validity.

Reliability of our construct scales was estimated through composite reliability. The composite reliability can be calculated as follows: (the square of the summation of the factor loadings)/{(the square of the summation of the factor loadings) + (the summation of item measurement error)}. The composite reliabilities for the five constructs scales suggested acceptable reliability of the scales for further analysis (top management knowledge values: 0.86, innovation business strategy: 0.77, perceived environmental uncertainty: 0.80, knowledge sharing policies and practices: 0.88, and knowledge sharing effectiveness: 0.84). Descriptive statistics and bivariate Pearson correlations for the five scales are presented in Table 2.

Convergent validity was evaluated by examining the factor loadings of the items and their squared multiple correlations (Table 3). Following the recommendation of Hair, Anderson, Tatham, and Black (1998), factor loadings greater than 0.50 were considered to be very significant. All factor loadings reported in Table 3 are greater than 0.50. Consequently, squared multiple correlations between these individual items and their a priori constructs were also high. Thus, all constructs in the measurement model were judged as having adequate convergent validity.

Next, a formal test of discriminant validity was performed. Empirically, such evidence can be obtained through the comparison of an unconstrained model that estimates the correlation between a pair of constructs and a constrained model that fixes the value of the construct correlation to 1.0. A significant difference in chi-square values between these models implies that the unconstrained model is a better fit for the data, thereby supporting the existence of discriminant validity (Anderson, 1987; Bagozzi & Phillips, 1982; Bagozzi, Yi, & Phillips, 1991; Gerbing & Anderson, 1988; Venkatraman, 1989). Table 4 presents the results of the pairwise chi-square difference tests among the five constructs of interest. As shown, all chi-square differences are significant at least at the 0.05 level. This series of tests of discriminant validity was complemented by examining whether the confidence interval around the correlation between any two latent constructs includes one (Anderson & Gerbing, 1988). No confidence interval around the correlation in the measurement model includes one. Thus, discriminant validity was confirmed. Overall, the measurement model demonstrated acceptable reliability, convergent validity, and discriminant validity.

Structural Model

A similar set of fit indices were used to examine the structural model as shown in Figure 2. This model's fit indices showed reasonable fit (chi-square/df = 1.40, AGFI = 0.80, IFI = 0.94, CFI = 0.94, and RMSEA = 0.06). This model helped to explore the predictive power of top management knowledge values, innovation business strategy, and perceived environmental uncertainty on knowledge sharing policies and practices, as well as to explore the influence of top management knowledge values and knowledge sharing policies and practices on knowledge sharing effectiveness. Results of analysis are shown in Figure 2. As AMOS does not estimate a model when the data

Table 2. Descriptive statistics and correlations

Variable	Mean	s.d.	1	2	3	4
1. Top management knowledge values	5.85	1.05				
2. Innovation business strategy	5.10	1.05	0.46***			
3. Perceived environmental uncertainty	4.95	1.12	0.20*	0.07		
4. Knowledge sharing policies and practices	4.63	1.23	0.60***	0.46***	0.25**	
5. Knowledge sharing effectiveness	4.69	1.01	0.46***	0.49***	0.05	0.67***

*N = 130. * $p < 0.05$, ** $p < 0.01$, *** $p < 0.001$ (all two-tailed tests).*

have missing values, we excluded company cases that did not report industry information, reducing our sample size to 115. The results suggested that the industry control variable does not significantly affect knowledge sharing effectiveness.

Hypotheses 2, 4, and 5 investigate the influence of top management knowledge values, innovation business strategy, and perceived environmental uncertainty on knowledge sharing policies and practices. As expected, top management knowledge values (β= 0.39, t-value = 3.16, $p < 0.01$) and innovation business strategy (β= 0.33, t-value = 2.63, $p < 0.01$) showed strong associations with knowledge sharing policies and practices. Hypotheses 2 and 4 were supported. Further, perceived environmental uncertainty (β= 0.15, t-value = 1.64, $p < 0.1$) showed a positive relationship with knowledge sharing policies and practices, and the relationship was not significant. Thus, Hypothesis 5 was not supported. The proposed model explained 47% of the variance in knowledge sharing policies and practices.

Hypothesis 1 examines the path from knowledge sharing policies and practices to knowledge sharing effectiveness. Hypothesis 3 examines the path from top management knowledge values to

Table 3. Factor loadings and squared multiple correlations of items for all constructs

Construct/Items*	Factor Loadings	Squared Multiple Correlations
Top management knowledge values		
TMKV1	0.85	0.72
TMKV2	0.84	0.71
TMKV3	0.79	0.62
TMKV4	0.65	0.42
Innovation business strategy		
IBS1	0.72	0.52
IBS2	0.71	0.50
IBS3	0.65	0.42
IBS4	0.62	0.38
Perceived environmental uncertainty		
PEU1	0.86	0.74
PEU2	0.77	0.59
PEU3	0.62	0.38
Knowledge sharing policies and practices		
KSPP1	0.60	0.36
KSPP2	0.92	0.85
KSPP3	0.90	0.81
KSPP4	0.78	0.61
Knowledge sharing effectiveness		
KSE1	0.60	0.36
KSE2	0.84	0.71
KSE3	0.78	0.61
KSE4	0.79	0.62

* *Item codes correspond to those reported in the Appendix.*

Table 4. Results of discriminant validity tests

Tests[a]	Chi-square Values of Constrained Model	Chi-square Values of Unconstrained Model	Differences in Chi-square Values
TMKV with			
IBS	34.96 (20)[b]	29.13 (19)	5.83*
PEU	32.71 (14)	16.05 (13)	16.66***
KSPP	51.46 (20)	43.23 (19)	8.23**
KSE	26.44 (20)	19.13 (19)	7.31**
IBS with			
PEU	37.67 (14)	10.35 (13)	27.32***
KSPP	51.19 (20)	36.78 (19)	14.41***
KSE	22.98 (20)	18.06 (19)	4.92*
PEU with			
KSPP	44.23 (14)	17.63 (13)	26.60***
KSE	48.97 (14)	17.87 (13)	31.10***
KSPP with			
KSE	53.23 (20)	44.69 (19)	8.54**

a *TMKV: Top management knowledge values, IBS: innovation business strategy, PEU: perceived environmental uncertainty, KSPP: knowledge sharing policies and practices, and KSE: knowledge sharing effectiveness.*

b *Numbers in parentheses: degrees of freedom.*

* $p < 0.05$, ** $p < 0.01$, *** $p < 0.001$

knowledge sharing effectiveness. The analysis suggested that knowledge sharing policies and practices ($\beta = 0.58$, t-value = 4.30, $p < 0.001$) were positively and significantly associated with knowledge sharing effectiveness. Hypothesis 1 was supported. However, no significant relationship was observed between top management knowledge values ($\beta = 0.18$, t-value = 1.56) and knowledge sharing effectiveness. Hypothesis 3 was not supported. The industry control variable does not show a strong association with knowledge sharing effectiveness. The proposed model accounted for 52% of the variance in knowledge sharing effectiveness.

DISCUSSION AND IMPLICATIONS

In this article, we started by developing a model of intraorganizational knowledge sharing based on Porter's (1980) analytical framework and the relevant literature (e.g., Eisenhardt and Martin, 2000; Hamel & Prahalad, 1989, 1993) in order to address two important and yet under-researched issues: important organizational antecedents and effectiveness of knowledge sharing policies and practices. The model was tested in industrial contexts in Taiwan, and thus country peculiarities were taken into account in the development of the model. These peculiarities include cultural traits of Taiwan, paternalistic management distinct in Chinese settings, intensified competition imposed by the trend of globalizations and growth in neighboring countries, and policies of the Taiwan government that encourage innovation business strategy and knowledge sharing. As there was no parallel model of knowledge sharing that could guide our model building process, our study is clearly exploratory in nature. The model of intraorganizational knowledge sharing cannot be said to be fully developed and tested in our study. Future research is needed in order to expand and test the model. However, based on our research findings, the model's theoretical and practical implications are discussed.

Figure 2. Hypothesis testing results

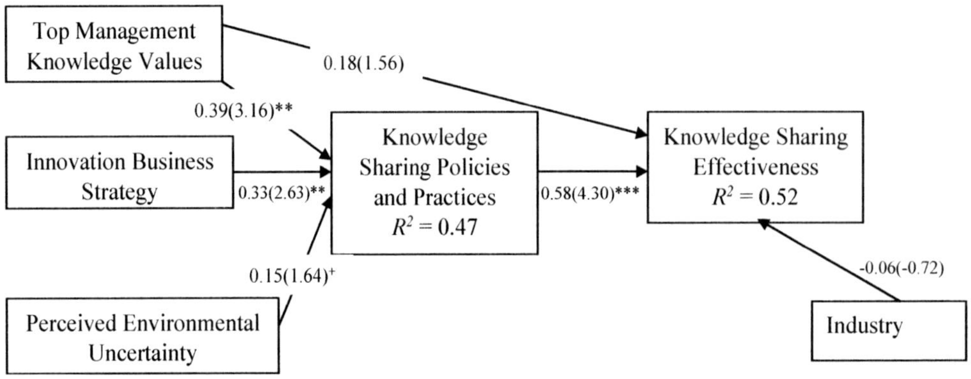

*Notes: +p < 0.10, **p<0.01, ***p < 0.001; t-values for standardized path coefficients are provided in parentheses.*

Implications for Research

Activity-based measures of knowledge sharing policies and practices have been proposed and tested in this article. Existing measures of intraorganizational knowledge sharing have been included in measures of organizational knowledge management (Gold et al., 2001; Lee & Choi, 2003). However, such measures adopt abstract statements instead of referring to specific activities that facilitate knowledge sharing. For example, "Our company stresses exchanging ideas and dialogues" (Lee & Choi, 2003). Exactly how ideas and dialogues can be exchanged was not reported. Our article has discussed how specific policies or practices, couched in terms of knowledge sharing policies and practices, can facilitate and motivate knowledge sharing. Researchers of organizational knowledge sharing can thus be advised as to what these policies and practices actually are. The measurement of knowledge sharing policies and practices reported here can also help practitioners scrutinize the effectiveness of their efforts in implementing these policies and practices (Edvinsson & Malone, 1997). Thus, our measures can be said to be an improvement on existing measures.

Moreover, according to the test results, knowledge sharing policies and practices significantly affect knowledge sharing effectiveness. This finding, although emerging from industrial contexts in Taiwan, supports the U.S. literature that argues for the importance of organizational policies and practices that facilitate and motivate knowledge sharing (Davenport & Prusak, 2000; Gold et al., 2001). The finding is also consistent with the work of Lee and Choi (2003) in South Korea. It appears that the basic tenet that knowledge sharing policies and practices can affect knowledge sharing effectiveness is transnational or transcultural. A longer term goal for us is to observe if the effects of knowledge sharing policies and practices persist so that knowledge sharing enhances employees' skills and capabilities, and the organization achieves competitive advantage, as predicted by western literature (Pfeffer, 1994; Roos, Roos, Edvinsson, & Dragonetti, 1998; Ulrich, 1998; Wright, McMahan, McCormick, & Sherman, 1998). As this finding emerged from industrial contexts differing from the U.S. and supports findings in South Korea, this finding has implications for researchers' quest for a generalizable theory of intraorganizational knowledge sharing.

The following two paths have been for the first time investigated concurrently: the path from top management knowledge values to knowledge sharing effectiveness, and the path starting from top management knowledge values to knowledge sharing policies and practices, and from knowledge sharing policies and practices to knowledge sharing effectiveness. The results do not suggest direct effect of top management knowledge values on knowledge sharing effectiveness. Rather, the evidence suggests that the effect of top management knowledge values on knowledge sharing effectiveness is mediated through knowledge sharing policies and practices. This has at least two theoretical implications:

First, in the building of a country-specific theory of intraorganizational knowledge sharing, this study cautions us about the role of top management knowledge values in improving knowledge sharing effectiveness in Taiwan. Indeed, top management knowledge values can apply under the distinct paternalistic management typically found in Chinese settings. Such managerial style in the context of knowledge sharing will involve encouraging and supporting intraorganizational knowledge sharing. However, researchers should recognize that intraorganizational knowledge sharing involves complex social and interpersonal exchange (e.g., Nonaka, 1994; Wenger & Snyder, 2000). The paternalistic management distinct in Chinese settings is by itself insufficient for improving knowledge sharing effectiveness. Paternalistic management could be important in encouraging knowledge sharing behaviors among employees. However, in Taiwan, knowledge sharing may still be hampered by its hierarchical culture and by employee tendency to distinguish between in-groups and out-groups. The theory of knowledge sharing should not neglect knowledge sharing policies and practices that facilitate social exchange for knowledge sharing. The paternalistic style of knowledge management should guide the implementation of knowledge sharing policies and practices, which will improve knowledge sharing effectiveness.

Second, in the building of a more generalized theory of intraorganizational knowledge sharing, researchers in Taiwan (e.g., Hsu, Ju, Yen, & Chang, 2007) and in Singapore (Kankanhalli, Tan, & Wei, 2005) have sought to root their arguments in social cognitive theory (e.g., Bandura, 1988) and stressed the importance of self-efficacy, an individual's belief about his/her capability in performing a certain task (Bandura, 1988), in predicting knowledge sharing behaviors. Hsu et al.'s (2007) knowledge sharing self-efficacy refers to an individual's self evaluation of his/her capability in performing tasks related to knowledge sharing, while Kankanhalli, Tan, and Wei (2005) addressed the importance of knowledge self-efficacy, which they defined as an individual's belief about potential contributions of his/her shared knowledge in job-related outcomes. Although the construct of self-efficacy was not investigated in our model, we also reviewed the literature on social cognitive theory (e.g., Bandura, 1988; Wood & Bandura, 1989) in forming our hypothesis regarding the relationship between top management knowledge values and knowledge sharing effectiveness. Our study results show social cognitive theory may be of only limited value in predicting how knowledge sharing effectiveness may arise. Our study points to the importance of incentive systems stressed by U.S. researchers in improving knowledge sharing effectiveness (e.g., Gupta & Govindarajan, 2000; Quigley et al., 2007). Incentive systems are included in our construct of knowledge sharing policies and practices. Further, top management knowledge values should guide the implementation of knowledge sharing policies and practices. Knowledge sharing policies and practices can indeed result in satisfactory knowledge sharing behaviors and improved task performance.

Further, among the three organizational antecedents, top management knowledge values have the strongest direct effect on knowledge sharing policies and practices. This finding supports the literature on the importance of top management values in initiating intraorganizational knowledge sharing (Davenport et al., 1998; Leonard-Barton, 1995; Miles, Snow, Mathews, Miles, & Coleman, 1997). However, this article reports the first empirical test of such an effect. In model building efforts for intraorganizational knowledge sharing, top management factors should not be excluded, either in Taiwan or in the west.

Innovation business strategy is the antecedent with the second highest direct effect on knowledge sharing policies and practices. Previous literature has recognized the effect of intraorganizational knowledge sharing on organizational innovativeness (Ahn & Chang, 2004; Widen-Wulff & Ginman, 2004). Although the strategy of the firm should guide knowledge-related activities for competitive advantage of the firm (e.g., Eisenhardt & Martin, 2000; Hamel & Prahalad, 1989), such theoretical claims have not been systematically investigated. This study has presented evidence for the importance of strategy in guiding intraorganizational knowledge sharing that helps companies to exploit and leverage their knowledge assets. A good business strategy results in a set of policies and practices that unify and reconcile employees' knowledge sharing behaviors under clear visions and goals. Such knowledge sharing behavior will in turn support and strengthen the strategic position of the organization. This article reports the first empirical test of the effect of innovation business strategy on knowledge sharing policies and practices. Its findings can inform the current literature of knowledge sharing/management on the causal link between business strategy and intraorganizational knowledge sharing.

This study addresses an issue that has often been neglected in studies of organizational knowledge management. The implementation of innovation business strategy involves new product development/innovation that can be seen as knowledge creation activities (Nonaka, 1994; Nonaka & Takeuchi, 1995), or activities by which new knowledge is generated from existing knowledge (Sabherwal & Sabherwal, 2005). Previously, a stage model of organizational knowledge management proposed that knowledge creation serves as a basis for knowledge sharing (Gold et al., 2001; Sabherwal & Sabherwal, 2005), and this study supports this view. However, prior studies tend to aggregate differing knowledge management activities to form a latent construct to investigate the effect of this construct on organizational performance (e.g., Gold et al., 2001; Sabherwal & Sabherwal, 2005; Tanriverdi, 2005). This statistical approach could be problematic as different knowledge-related activities may have causal links to each other (Gold et al., 2001). This study has suggested a causal relationship between knowledge creation activities and knowledge sharing activities. Based on the results of this study, studies of organizational knowledge management may be able to generate more insight by considering internal causal mechanisms between knowledge-related activities in their model construction.

Bock and Kim (2002) revealed that incentive systems may not necessarily encourage employee knowledge sharing. Our study results can provide an explanation for this finding. Knowledge sharing policies and practices cannot be initiated or transplanted from one organization to another without considering the contexts in which these policies and practices are to be implemented. Knowledge sharing policies and practices should be implemented when the right antecedents are present. That is to say, for knowledge sharing policies and practices to be effective, the company must have top management values that see knowledge as a source of competitive advantage and supports knowledge sharing, and an innovation business strategy that seeks to differentiate the company from competitors through product innovation.

Finally, previous literature argues that the firm should conduct knowledge-related activities to address the challenge imposed from highly uncertain environments (e.g., Eisenhardt & Martin, 2000; Prahalad & Hamel, 1994; Quinn et al., 1996). Although limited evidence suggests that in a highly uncertain environment, the sharing of situation-specific knowledge facilitate organizational learning and improve organizational performance (Brown & Eisenhardt, 1997), a direct test of the relationship between top management's perceived environmental uncertainty and knowledge sharing policies and practices has previously been lacking (e.g., Argote et al., 2003), and was conducted in this study. Our study did not find a significant relationship between perceived environmental uncertainty and knowledge sharing policies and practices. This is not consistent with expectations and with the relevant evidence derived in a U.S. context (Brown & Eisenhardt, 1997). A possible explanation is that managers in Taiwan tend to seek market niches that block competitors and offer protection against technological changes (Chang & Grub, 1992). This strategy is strengthened by establishing and maintaining a reciprocal business network that covers production, distribution, and transportation processes (Wong et al., 2001), and expands horizontally (Redding, 1993; Yu, 2001). Such a network serves information sharing purposes and reduces impacts from environmental changes. Thus, it appears that perceived environmental uncertainty has not been important in influencing managerial decisions to implement knowledge sharing policies and practices.

However, it is worth noting that the non-significant result is consistent with prior studies that generally found internal factors to be more important than external factors, such as in the area of technology adoption (Teo & Tan, 1997-1998) and planning integration (Teo & King, 1997). As suggested in this study, intraorganizational knowledge sharing involves implementing a set of policies and practices, including new technologies and systems. Thus, it appears that in the area of knowledge management/knowledge sharing, internal factors may also be more important than external factors. However, this requires further investigation.

Implications for Practice

Based on our results, we believe that intraorganizational knowledge sharing requires top management capabilities in managing people and technology in such a way that creates synergies for the company. Such a perspective can help managers understand the causal relationships between organizational antecedents, knowledge sharing policies and practices, and organizational performance in an integrative way (Lee & Choi, 2003). The following managerial implications can be drawn from our results for a global perspective.

First, knowledge sharing policies and practices should be implemented to enhance knowledge sharing effectiveness. Such policies and practices should facilitate and motivate both horizontal and hierarchical knowledge sharing. Second, top management support and encouragement can increase employees' willingness to share knowledge and should guide the implementation of knowledge sharing policies and practices. However, knowledge sharing requires complex social interactions, and top management knowledge values alone cannot result in improved knowledge sharing effectiveness. Knowledge sharing policies and practices should be thus implemented for knowledge sharing behaviors to persist and to improve task performance. Third, companies can adopt an innovation business strategy for knowledge creation to drive and to serve as a basis for intraorganizational knowledge sharing. Through knowledge sharing, the company can leverage the new knowledge created in the process of new product development/innovation. Fourth, although the relationship between top management's perceived environmental uncertainty and knowledge sharing policies and practices were not supported, possible explanations have been noted. Corporate managers should still be alert for environmental uncertainty and use intraorganizational knowledge sharing for organizational learning as a source of competitive advantage.

Our findings also offer implications for business practice in Taiwan. First, in Taiwan, if a company seeks to improve knowledge sharing effectiveness, that company should have a top management that sees knowledge as a source of competitive advantage for companies and support knowledge sharing. A multinational company that seeks to enter the market in Taiwan should recruit a chief executive with excellent knowledge values so it can reap the rewards of employee knowledge sharing.

However, equally important is the causal mechanism from top management knowledge values to knowledge sharing effectiveness. Cultural traits of Taiwan may impede knowledge sharing. Thus, knowledge sharing policies and practices should be built to facilitate and motivate knowledge sharing and learning. In a time when Taiwanese companies face increasing competitive pressures from its neighboring countries, top management should adopt knowledge values to drive the implementation of knowledge sharing policies and practices. As shown in this study, knowledge sharing effectiveness would ensue after the implementation of such policies and practices.

Second, innovation business strategy is the second antecedent that leads to knowledge sharing policies and practices. For a Taiwanese company or a multinational company seeking to establish a business in Taiwan, a clear innovation business strategy that guides the implementation of knowledge sharing policies and practices is required. However, as noted earlier, a great majority of companies in Taiwan are small and medium-sized companies. They may gradually learn the importance of having an innovation business strategy. These companies will likely need the support of the Taiwan government in the process of formulating an innovation business strategy and establishing knowledge sharing policies and practices, due to a lack of resources, sources of funding, and managerial capabilities. This support should include knowledge and skills regarding strategic management and funding and skills for implementing knowledge sharing policies and practices. In particular, IT-based systems and technologies, which most small and medium-sized companies do not have, can play an important role in knowledge sharing. Thus, support from the Taiwan government is imperative.

Third, knowledge sharing policies and practices have been demonstrated to be able to improve knowledge sharing effectiveness. Their importance for Taiwanese companies cannot be emphasized too highly. The questionnaire items should provide a hands-on guide for local companies wishing to establish knowledge sharing policies and practices.

Finally, although perceived environmental uncertainty has not been shown to have explanatory power for knowledge sharing policies and practices, managers in Taiwan should still be careful in planning and executing such policies and practices to help monitor changes in the environments. Such monitoring may enable managers to determine new knowledge domains to explore (McKenzie & van Winkelen, 2004). Investing in these knowledge domains can become significant for the company over time as knowledge becomes company-specific and creates value for the company (Lewin & Volberda, 1999). Further, should knowledge sharing policies and practices be extended to facilitate information and knowledge sharing among business networks in Taiwan? The possibility is there and this may offer profitable business opportunities for domestic and global IT/IS companies.

LIMITATIONS AND FUTURE DIRECTIONS

Readers should not over-interpret or over-generalize our results, which have three main limitations. First, the use of a convenience sample includes a risk of sampling bias. At this point in time, we have not been able to determine the representativeness of our respondents due to a lack of systematic records of small-and medium-sized companies in Taiwan, which remain the majority (over 98%) of Taiwan's business entities[1]. Thus, the current study must be viewed within the context of opening a new line of enquiry, rather than presenting any conclusive results.

With this first limitation in mind, we judged the EMBA program as still offering a good set of respondents for the following reasons: First, the considerable work experience and status of the program participants in their respective companies gave them a vantage point to observe the phenomena under study. Second, this particular EMBA program requires that participants complete a research dissertation for their diploma. The training in research methodologies further helped these respondents grasp the meaning and usefulness of our survey items. Third, these EMBA participants were drawn from a diverse range of companies and industries. Based on these reasons, we believe that we have not run the risk of building a "science of the sophomore" by which research findings have no implications for improving managerial practices (Gordon, Slade, & Schmitt, 1986). Although preliminary and exploratory in nature, our findings can be said to be valid and managerial implications can be offered for companies of similar profiles as those reported in this article.

The second limitation of this study pertains to potential common method variance resulting from the use of self-report data. The third limitation is related to potential important factors that may have been excluded in our examination, as is common in social science models (Becerra-Fernandez & Sabherwal, 2001).

Drawing from the limitations reported, we now propose future research directions. The model proposed in this study should be tested in the future in a variety of research contexts in order to establish the generalizability of the research findings. For example, firm size may have an impact on the relationship between knowledge sharing policies and practices and knowledge sharing effectiveness. Future studies should compare between small and medium-sized business samples and large or multinational companies. Future studies should also be applied to industrial contexts with differing national cultural values (Hofstede, 1997) from Taiwan.

Further development and testing of our research framework is necessary. For example, the effectiveness of knowledge sharing policies and practices may not only lie in organizational antecedents, but also in individual-level factors. In future research, these individual-level factors should be included in the model of intraorganizational knowledge sharing. Furthermore, the effect of knowledge sharing policies and practices on organizational adaptability in a highly uncertain environment requires further study. Such a study can address how organizations survive and thrive in a highly uncertain environment.

Future research on intraorganizational knowledge sharing may choose to use the measures developed for this study. Repeated use and modification of our measures will enhance their robustness. Furthermore, in light of the limitations that stem from the use of measurements of perception, the use of objective measures of knowledge sharing effectiveness and company performance would be helpful in this line of enquiry.

Finally, detailed case studies following the line of enquiry reported in this article can be conducted in order to obtain further insights into our research framework. Such studies can enrich the understanding of underlying mechanisms and reveal other antecedents or moderators that may influence the causal relationships reported in this article.

ACKNOWLEDGMENT

The authors would like to thank Professor Clyde Warden, Professor Carol Yeh-Yun Lin, and Professor Shih-Chieh Fang for their helpful comments on this article. They also thank National Science Council, Taiwan for the grants offered for this research (Project No.: NSC92-2416-H-018-006).

REFERENCES

Ahmed, P. K., Kok, L. K., & Loh, A. Y. E. (2002). *Learning through knowledge management*. Woburn, MA: Butterworth-Heinemann.

Ahn, J., & Chang, S. (2004). Assessing the contribution of knowledge to business performance: the KP[3] methodology. *Decision Support Systems, 36*, 403-416.

Alavi, M., Kayworth, T. D., & Leidner, D. E. (2005-2006). An empirical examination of the influence of organizational culture on knowledge management practices. *Journal of Management Information Systems, 22*(3), 191-224.

Alavi, M., & Leidner, D. E. (2001). Review: knowledge management and knowledge management systems: conceptual foundations and research issues. *MIS Quarterly, 25*(1), 107-136.

Ali, A. J., Lee, M., Hsieh, Y.-C., & Krishnan, K. (2005). Individualism and collectivism in Taiwan. *Cross Cultural Management, 12*(4), 3-16.

Anderson, J. C. (1987). An approach for confirmatory measurement and structural equation modeling of organizational properties. *Management Science, 33*(4), 525-541.

Anderson, J. C., & Gerbing, D. W. (1988). Structural equation modeling in practice: a review and recommended two-step approach. *Psychological Bulletin, 103*(3), 411-423.

Argote, L., McEvily, B., & Reagans, R. (2003). Managing knowledge in organizations: An integrative framework and review of emerging themes. *Management Science, 49*(4), 571-582.

Bae, J., Chen, S.-j., Wan, T. W. D., Lawler, J. J., & Walumbwa, F. O. (2003). Human resource strategy and firm performance in Pacific Rim countries. *International Journal of Human Resource Management, 14*(8), 1308-1332.

Bae, J., & Lawler, J. J. (2000). Organizational and HRM strategies in Korea: Impact on firm performance in an emerging economy. *Academy of Management Journal, 43*(3), 502-517.

Bagozzi, R. P., & Phillips, L. W. (1982). Representing and testing organizational theories: A holistic construal. *Administrative Science Quarterly, 27*(3), 459-489.

Bagozzi, R. P., Yi, Y., & Phillips, L. W. (1991). Assessing construct validity in organizational research. *Administrative Science Quarterly, 36*(3), 421-458.

Bandura, A. (1988). Organizational applications of social cognitive theory. *Australian Journal of Management, 13*, 137-164.

Bartlett, C. A., & Ghoshal, S. (2002). Building competitive advantage through people. *Sloan Management Review, 43*(2), 34-41.

Bartol, K. M., & Srivastava, A. (2002). Encouraging knowledge sharing: the role of organizational reward systems. *Journal of Leadership and Organizational Studies, 9*(1), 64-76.

Becerra-Fernandez, I., & Sabherwal, R. (2001). Organizational knowledge management: a contingency perspective. *Journal of Management Information System, 18*(1), 23-55.

Bentler, P. M. (1990). Comparative fit indexes in structural models. *Psychological Bulletin, 107*, 238-246.

Bock, G. W. & Kim, Y.-G. (2002). Breaking the myths of rewards: An exploratory study of attitudes about knowledge sharing. *Information Resources Management Journal, 15*(2), 14-21.

Bollen, K. A. (1989). A new incremental fit index for general structural models. *Sociological Methods & Research, 17*, 303-316.

Brown, S. L., & Eisenhardt, K. M. (1997). The art of continuous change: Linking complexity theory and time-paced evolution in relentlessly shifting organizations. *Administrative Science Quarterly, 42*(1), 1-34.

Burns, T., & Stalker, G. M. (1961). *The management of innovation*. London: Tavistock.

Byrne, B. M. (2001). *Structural equation modeling with AMOS: Basic concepts, applications, and programming*. London: Lawrence Erlbaum Associates.

Cabrera, A., & Cabrera, E. F. (2002). Knowledge-sharing dilemmas. *Organization Studies, 23*(5), 687-710.

Calantone, R. J., Cavusgil, S. T., & Zhao, Y. (2002). Learning orientation, firm innovation capability, and firm performance. *Industrial Marketing Management, 31*, 515-524.

Carneiro, A. (2000). How does knowledge management influence innovation and competitiveness? *Journal of Knowledge Management, 4*(2), 87-92.

Chandler, A. D. (1962). *Strategy and structure*. Cambridge, MA: MIT Press.

Chang, S. K. C. (1985). American and Chinese managers in U.S. companies in Taiwan. *California Management Review, 27*(4), 144-156.

Chang, T., & Grub, P. D. (1992). Competitive strategies of Taiwanese PC firms in their internationalization process. *Journal of Global Marketing, 6*(3), 5-27.

Child, J. (1972). Organizational structure, environment, and performance: The role of strategic choice. *American Journal of Sociology, 60*, 339-342.

Chin, W. W. (1998). Issues and opinion on structural equation modeling. *MIS Quarterly, 22*(1), vii-xvi.

Choi, B., & Lee, H. (2003). An empirical investigation of KM styles and their effect on corporate performance. *Information and Management, 40*, 403-417.

Collins, J. C., & Porras, J. I. (1996). Building your company's vision. *Harvard Business Review, 74*(5), 65-77.

Conner, K. R., & Prahalad, C. K. (1996). A resource-based theory of the firm: Knowledge versus opportunism. *Organization Science, 7*(5), 477-501.

Constant, D., Keisler, S., & Sproull, L. (1994). What's mine is ours, or is it? A study of attitudes about information sharing. *Information Systems Research, 5*(4), 400-421.

Daft, R. L. (2003). *Management* (6th ed.). Mason, Ohio: South-Western.

Daft, R. L., & Weick, K. E. (1984). Toward a model of organizations as interpretation systems. *Academy of Management Review, 9*(2), 284-295.

Datta, D. K., Guthrie, J. P., & Wright, P. M. (2005). Human resource management and labor productivity: Does industry matter? *Academy of Management Journal, 48*(1), 135-145.

Davenport, T. H., De Long, D. W., & Beers, M. C. (1998). Successful knowledge management projects. *Sloan Management Review, 39*(2), 43-57.

Davenport, T. H., & Prusak, L. (2000). *Working knowledge: How organizations manage what they know*. Boston, MA: Harvard Business School Press.

Dixon, N. M. (1990). Organizational learning: A review of the literature with implications for HRD professionals. *Human Resource Development Quarterly, 3*(1), 29-49.

Dodgson, M. (1993). Organizational learning: A review of some literatures. *Organization Studies, 14*(3), 375-394.

Earl, M. (2001). Knowledge management strategies: Toward a taxonomy. *Journal of Management Information System, 18*(1), 215-233.

Edvinsson, L., & Malone, M. S. (1997). *Intellectual capital: Realizing your company's true value by finding its hidden brainpower.* NY: Harper Business.

Eisenhardt, K. M. (1989). Making fast strategic decisions in high-velocity environments. *Academy of Management Journal, 32*(3), 543-576.

Eisenhardt, K. M., & Martin, J. A. (2000). Dynamic capabilities: What are they? *Strategic Management Journal, 21,* 1105-1121.

Eisenhardt, K. M., & Santos, F. M. (2002). Knowledge-based view: A new theory of strategy? In A. Pettigrew, H. Thomas, & R. Whittington (Eds.), *Handbook of strategy and management* (pp. 139-164). London: Sage.

Gerbing, D. W., & Anderson, J. C. (1988). An updated paradigm for scale development incorporating unidimensionality and its assessment. *Journal of Marketing Research, 25*(2), 186-192.

Gist, M. E., & Mitchell, T. R. (1992). Self-efficacy: A theoretical analysis of its determinants and malleability. *Academy of Management Review, 17,* 183-211.

Gold, A. H., Malhortra, A., & Segars, A. H. (2001). Knowledge management: an organizational capabilities perspective. *Journal of Management Information System, 18*(1), 185-214.

Gordon, M., Slade, L., & Schmitt, N. (1986). The "science of the sophomore" revisited: From conjecture to empiricism. *Academy of Management Review, 11,* 91-207.

Grant, R. M. (1996a). Prospering in dynamically-competitive environments: Organizational capability as knowledge integration. *Organization Science, 7*(4), 375-387.

Grant, R. M. (1996b). Toward a knowledge-based theory of the firm. *Strategic Management Journal, 17,* 109-122.

Grover, V., & Davenport, T. H. (2001). General perspectives on knowledge management: fostering a research agenda. *Journal of Management Information Systems, 18*(1), 5-21.

Gupta, A. J., & Govindarajan, V. (2000). Knowledge management's social dimension: Lessons from Nucor Steel. *Sloan Management Review, 42*(1), 71-80.

Guthrie, J. P., Spell, C. S., & Nyamori, R. O. (2002). Correlates and consequences of high involvement work practices: The role of competitive strategy. *International Journal of Human Resource Management, 13*(1), 183-197.

Hair, J. F., Anderson, R. E., Tatham, R. L., & Black, W. C. (1998). *Multivariate data analysis* (5th ed.). Upper Saddle River, NJ: Prentice-Hall.

Hamel, G., & Prahalad, C. K. (1989). Strategic intent. *Harvard Business Review, 67*(3), 63-76.

Hamel, G., & Prahalad, C. K. (1993). Strategy as stretch and leverage. *Harvard Business Review, 71*(2), 75-84.

Hauschild, S., Licht, T., & Stein, W. (2001). Creating a knowledge culture. *The McKinsey Quarterly, 1,* 74-81.

Hedberg, B. (1981). How organizations learn and unlearn. In P. C. Nystrom & W. H. Starbuck (Eds.), *Handbook of organizational design* (pp. 3-27). NY: Oxford University Press.

Helfat, C. E. (1997). Know-how and asset complementarity and dynamic capability accumulation: The case of R&D. *Strategic Management Journal, 18,* 339-360.

Hofstede, G. (1997). *Cultures and organizations: Software of the mind.* NY: McGraw-Hill.

Holsapple, C. W., & Joshi, K. D. (2000). An investigation of factors that influence the management of knowledge in organizations. *Journal of Strategic Information Systems, 9,* 235-261.

Holsapple, C. W., & Joshi, K. D. (2002). Knowledge manipulation studies: results of a Delphi study. *Information and Management, 39*, 477-490.

Hsu, I.-C. (2005, August 5-10). *Developing a model of knowledge management from a human capital perspective—preliminary thoughts.* Paper presented at the 2005 Academy of Management Meeting, Honolulu, Hawaii, U.S.

Hsu, I.-C. (2006). Enhancing employee tendencies to share knowledge—case studies of nine company cases in Taiwan. *International Journal of Information Management, 26*(4), 326-338.

Hsu, M., Ju, T. L., Yen, C., & Chang C. (2007). Knowledge sharing behavior in virtual communities: The relationship between trust, self-efficacy, and outcome expectations. *International Journal of Human-Computer Studies, 65*, 153-169.

Husted, K., & Michailova, S. (2002). Diagnosing and fighting knowledge-sharing hostility. *Organizational Dynamics, 31*(1), 60-73.

Jarvenpaa, S. L., & Staples, D. S. (2000). Thc usc of collaborative electronic media for information sharing: an exploratory study of determinants. *Journal of Strategic Information Systems, 9*, 129-154.

Jarvenpaa, S. L., & Staples, D. S. (2001). Exploring perceptions of organizational ownership of information and expertise. *Journal of Management Information Systems, 18*(1), 151-183.

Kalling, T. (2003). Knowledge management and the occasional links with performance. *Journal of Knowledge Management, 7*(3), 67-81.

Kankanhalli, A., Tan, B. C. Y., & Wei, K.-K. (2005). Contributing knowledge to electronic knowledge repositories: An empirical investigation. *MIS Quarterly, 29*(1), 113-143.

Knott, A. M. (2004). Persistent heterogeneity and sustainable innovation. *Strategic Management Journal, 24*(8), 687-705.

Lawrence, P. R., & Lorsch, J. (1967). *Organization and environment.* Boston: Harvard University.

Lee, H., & Choi, B. (2003). Knowledge management enablers, processes, and organizational performance: an integrative view and empirical examination. *Journal of Management Information Systems, 20*(1), 179-228.

Lee, K. C., Lee, S., & Kang, I. W. (2005). KMPI: measuring knowledge management performance. *Information and Management, 42*, 469-482.

Leonard-Barton, D. (1995). *Wellsprings of knowledge: Building and sustaining the sources of innovation.* Boston: Harvard Business School.

Lepak, D. P., & Snell, S. A. (1999). The human resource architecture: Toward a theory of human capital allocation and development. *Academy of Management Review, 24*(1), 31-48.

Lewin, A., & Volberda, H. (1999). Prologomena on co-evolution: A framework for research on strategy and new organizational forms. *Organization Science, 10*(5), 519-534.

Liebeskind, J. P. (1996). Knowledge, strategy, and the theory of the firm. *Strategic Management Journal, 17*, 93-107.

Liebowitz, J. & Chen, Y. (2001). Developing knowledge-sharing proficiencies: Building a supportive culture for knowledge-sharing. *Knowledge Management Review, 3*(6), 12-15.

Lin, L., & Kwok, L. (2006). Challenges to KM at Hewlett Packard China. *Knowledge Management Review, 9*(1), 20-23.

Lukas, B. A., Hult, G. T. M., & Ferrell, O. C. (1996). A theoretical perspective of the antecedents and consequences of organizational learning in marketing channels. *Journal of Business Research, 36*(3), 233-244.

Lynn, G. S. (1998). New product team learning: developing and profiting from your knowledge capital. *California Management Review, 40*(4), 74-93.

Mathews, J. A. (2001). National systems of economic learning: The case of technology diffusion management in East Asia. *International Journal of Technology Management, 22*(5/6), 455-479.

McDermott, R. (1999). Why information technology inspired but cannot deliver knowledge management. *California Management Review, 41*(4), 103-117.

McGahnan, A. M., & Porter. M. E. (1999). The persistence of shocks to profitability. *The Review of Economics and Statistic, 81*(1), 143-153.

McKenzie, J. & van Winkelen, C. (2004). *Understanding the knowledgeable organization: Nurturing knowledge competence*. London: Thomson Learning.

Michailova, S. & Husted, K. (2003). Knowledge sharing hostility in Russian firms. *California Management Review, 45*(3), 59-77.

Miles, R. E., & Snow, C. C. (1978). *Organizational strategy, structure, and process*. NY: McGraw-Hill.

Miles, R. E., Snow, C. C., Mathews, J. A., Miles, G., & Coleman, H. J., Jr. (1997). Organizing in the knowledge age: Anticipating the cellular form. *Academy of Management Executive, 11*(4), 7-20.

Miller, D. (1988). Relating Porter's business strategies to environments and structure: Analysis and performance implications. *Academy of Management Journal, 31*(2), 280-308.

Miller, D., & Friesen, P. H. (1978). Archetypes of strategy formulation. *Management Science, 24*, 921-933.

Miller, D., & Friesen, P. H. (1983). Strategy-making and environment: The third link. *Strategic Management Journal, 4*, 221-235.

Ministry of Economic Affairs. (2002). *White paper on small and medium enterprises in Taiwan*. Ministry of Economic Affairs, Taiwan: Small and Medium Enterprise Administration.

Ministry of Economic Affairs. (2003). *White paper on small and medium enterprises in Taiwan*. Ministry of Economic Affairs, Taiwan: Small and Medium Enterprise Administration.

Mintzberg, H. (1973). Strategy making in three modes. *California Management Review, 16*, 44-58.

Moorman, C., & Miner, A. S. (1998). Organizational improvisation and organizational memory. *Academy of Management Review, 23*(4), 132-142.

Noe, R. A., Hollenbeck, J. R., Gerhart, B., & Wright, P. M. (2003). *Human resource management: Gaining a competitive advantage* (4th ed.). Boston: McGraw-Hill.

Noe, R. A., Hollenbeck, J. R., Gerhart, B., & Wright, P. M. (2004). *Fundamentals of human resource management*. Boston: Irwin.

Nonaka, I. (1991). The knowledge creating company. *Harvard Business Review, 69*(6), 96-104.

Nonaka, I. (1994). A dynamic theory of organizational knowledge creation. *Organization Science, 5*(1), 14–37.

Nonaka, I., & Konno, N. (1998). The concept of 'Ba': Building a foundation for knowledge creation. *California Management Review, 40*(3), 40-54.

Nonaka, I., & Takeuchi, H. (1995). *The knowledge creating company*. NY: Oxford University Press.

Özsomer, A., Calantone, R. J., & Benedetto, A. D. (1997). What makes firms more innovative? A look at organizational and environmental factors. *Journal of Business and Industrial Marketing, 12*(6), 400-416.

Pfeffer, J. (1994). *Competitive advantage through people: Unleashing the power of the workforce*. Boston: Harvard Business School.

Porter, M. E. (1980). *Competitive advantage: Techniques for analyzing industries and competitors*. NY: Free Press.

Prahalad, C. K., & Hamel, G. (1990). The core competence of the corporation. *Harvard Business Review, 68*(3), 79-91.

Prahalad, C. K., & Hamel, G. (1994). Strategy as a field of study: Why search for a new paradigm? *Strategic Management Journal, 15*, 5-16.

Quigley, N. R., Tesluk, P. E., Locke, E. A., & Bartol, K. M. (2007). A multilevel investigation of the motivational mechanisms underlying knowledge sharing and performance. *Organization Science, 18*(1), 71-88.

Quinn, J. B., Anderson, P., & Finkelstein, S. (1996). Leveraging intellect. *Academy of Management Executive, 10*(3), 7-26.

Redding, S. G. (1993). *The spirit of Chinese capitalism*. Berlin: Walter de Gruyter.

Roos, J., Roos, G., Edvinsson, L., & Dragonetti, N. C. (1998). *Intellectual capital: Navigating in the new business landscape*. NY: New York University Press.

Ruggles, R. (1998). The state of notion: Knowledge management in practice. *California Management Review, 40*(3), 80-89.

Sabherwal, R., & Becerra-Fernandez, I. (2005). Integrating specific knowledge: Insights from the Kennedy Space Center. *IEEE Transactions on Engineering Management, 52*(3), 301-315.

Sabherwal, R., & Sabherwal, S. (2005). Knowledge management using information technology: Determinants of short-term impact on firm value. *Decision Sciences, 36*(4), 531-566.

Scarbrough, H., Swan, J., & Preston, J. (1999). *Knowledge management and the learning organization*. London: IPD.

Sheh, S. W. (2001). Chinese cultural values and their implication to Chinese management. *Singapore Management Review, 23*(2), 75-83.

Sher, P. J., & Lee, V. C. (2004). Information technology as a facilitator for enhancing dynamic capabilities through knowledge management. *Information and Management, 41*, 933-945.

Shrivastava, P. (1983). A typology of organizational learning systems. *Journal of Management Studies, 20*(1), 7-28.

Shyu, J. Z., & Chiu, Y.-C. (2002). Innovation policy for developing Taiwan's competitive advantages. *R&D Management, 32*(4), 369-374.

Silin, R. (1976). *Leadership and values*. Cambridge, MA: Harvard University Press.

Subramaniam, M., & Youndt, M. A. (2005). The influence of intellectual capital on the types of innovative capabilities. *Academy of Management Journal, 48*(3), 450-463.

Szulanski, G. (1996). Exploring internal stickiness: Impediments to the transfer of best practice within the firm. *Strategic Management Journal, 17*, 27-43.

Tanriverdi, H. (2005). Information technology relatedness, knowledge management capability, and performance of multibusiness firms. *MIS Quarterly, 29*(2), 311-334.

Teece, D. J. (1998). Capturing value from knowledge assets: the new economy, markets for know-how, and intangible assets. *California Management Review, 40*(3), 55-79.

Teo, T. S. H., & King, W. R. (1997). Integration between business planning and information systems planning: An evolutionary-contingency perspective. *Journal of Management Information Systems, 14*(1), 185-214.

Teece, D. J., & Pisano, G. (1994). The dynamic capabilities of firms: an introduction. *Industrial and Corporate Change, 3*, 537-556.

Teece, D. J., Pisano, G., & Shuen, A. (1997). Dynamic capabilities and strategic management. *Strategic Management Journal, 18*, 509-533.

Teo, T. S. H. & Tan, M. (1997-1998). A contingency model of Internet adoption in Singapore. *International Journal of Electronic Commerce, 2*(2), 95-118.

Thompson, J. D. (1967). *Organization in action*. NY: McGraw Hill.

Triandis, H. C. (1989). The self and social behavior in differing culture contexts. *Psychological Review, 96*(3), 506-520.

Tsai, K., & Wang, J. (2004). The innovation policy and performance of innovation in Taiwan's technology-intensive industries. *Problems and Perspectives in Management, 1*, 62-75.

Tsoukas, H., & Vladimirou, E. (2001). What is organizational Knowledge? *Journal of Management Studies, 38*(7), 973-993.

Ulrich, D. (1998). Intellectual capital = competence x commitment. *Sloan Management Review, 39*(2), 15-26.

Venkatraman, N. (1989). Strategic orientation of business enterprises: the construct, dimensionality, and measurement. *Management Science, 35*(8), 942-962.

Wenger, E. C., & Snyder, W. M. (2000). Communities of practice: The organizational frontier. *Harvard Business Review, 78*(1), 139-145.

Widen-Wulff, G., & Ginman, M. (2004). Explaining knowledge sharing in organizations through the dimensions of social capital. *Journal of Information Science, 30*(5), 448-458.

Wong, Y., Maher, T. E., Wang, J. L., & Long, F. (2001). Exploring Taiwan's competitive advantages: Present and future. *Management Research News, 24*(6/7), 17-24.

Wood, R., & Bandura, A. (1989). Social cognitive theory of organizational management. *Academy of Management Review, 14*(3), 361-384.

Wright, P. M., McMahan, G. C., McCormick, B., & Sherman, W. S. (1998). Strategy, core competence and HR involvement as determinants of HR effectiveness and refinery performance. *Human Resource Management, 37*(1), 17-29.

Wu, P. (2004) HRM in Taiwan. In P. Budhwar (Ed.), *Managing human resources in Asia-Pacific* (pp. 93-112). London: Routledge.

Wu, S., & Hsu, F. B.-M. (2001). Toward a knowledge-based view of OEM relationship building—sharing of industrial experiences in Taiwan. *International Journal of Technology Management, 22*(5/6), 203-223.

Yu, T. F.-L. (2001). The Chinese family business as a strategic system: An evolutionary perspective. *International Journal of Entrepreneurial Behaviour and Research, 7*(1), 22-40.

Zaltman, G., Duncan, R., & Holbek, J. (1973). *Innovations and organizations*. NY: Wiley.

ENDNOTE

1. We also discovered that mailing questionnaires to companies for the survey would include potential sampling bias due to the lack of systematic records of companies in Taiwan. The sampling frame thus can not be determined with any certainty.

APPENDIX. SURVEY ITEMS

Top Management Knowledge Values

TMKV1. Top management emphasizes knowledge sharing within the company.

TMKV2. Top management believes that its support is key to employee knowledge sharing.

TMKV3. Top management regards knowledge sharing policies and practices as contributing to company performance.

TMKV4. Top management regards firm-specific knowledge (patents, management systems, etc.) as a source of competitive advantage.

Innovation Business Strategy

IBS1. The company is one step ahead of its major competitors in introducing its products or services to the market.

IBS2. The company pursues its own successful business model.

IBS3. In the past 3 years, the company has higher R&D expenses as a percentage of sales than its major competitors.

IBS4. In the company, products or services introduced to the market within the last 3 years have higher sales than other products or services.

Perceived Environmental Uncertainty

PEU1. Major competitors' changes of their market strategy will influence this company greatly.

PEU2. Changes of product or process technologies in this industry will influence this company greatly.

PEU3. The company's operations are influenced greatly by its major clients.

Knowledge Sharing Policies and Practices

KSPP1. The company analyzes its past failure and disseminates the lessons learned among its employees.

KSPP2. The company invests in IT systems that facilitate knowledge sharing.

KSPP3. The company develops knowledge sharing mechanisms.

KSPP4. The company offers incentives to encourage knowledge sharing.

Knowledge Sharing Effectiveness

KSE1. Senior personnel in the company take initiative in mentoring junior personnel.

KSE2. Company-provided knowledge enhances employees' task performance.

KSE3. Employees' knowledge sharing behaviors are satisfactory.

KSE4. Employees' knowledge sharing enhances their task performance.

This work was previously published in the Journal of Global Information Management, Vol. 16, Issue 3, edited by F. Tan, pp. 45-73, copyright 2008 by IGI Publishing (an imprint of IGI Global).

Chapter 14
An Empirical Study of Factors Affecting RFID's Adoption in Taiwan

Dong-Her Shih
National Yunlin University of Science & Technology, Taiwan

Yuh-Wen Chiu
National Yunlin University of Science & Technology, Taiwan

She-I Chang
National Chung Cheng University, Taiwan

David C. Yen
Miami University, USA

ABSTRACT

RFID technologies represent a common standard for data storage and retrieval that could improve collaboration and data sharing between non-competing organizations. With the advent of RFID (radio frequency identification), organizations have the opportunity to rethink how their organization will be. Unlike companies in the United States and Europe which are mandated by large retailers or government departments, most Taiwan companies are investing in RFID without pressure. The article explores the factor affecting radio frequency identification adoption applications in Taiwan. Its objective is to summarize the ways in which organizations are thinking about their possible uses in a wide variety of companies and industries. An empirical investigation (n=134) found seven factors affecting RFID adoption within Taiwan. They are operation efficiency, manufacturing efficiency and supply chain efficiency, organization context, investment cost, market environment, and technology characteristic. By providing insight into these important factors, this article can help further understanding of their role in the adoption and use of RFID. The theoretical and practical implications of these results are discussed.

INTRODUCTION

RFID (radio frequency identification) is an automatic identification and data capture technology that has been around for decades and could be evolved from World War II. It is a promising and already rapidly emerging technology and gained attention in recent years as a means of enhancing data handling processes, which offers greater precision, flexibility, and potential cost savings and has attracted the interest of businesses and public entities (Davis & Luehlfing, 2004; Roberts, 2006).

Keen and Mackintosh (2001) assert RFID technologies as part of "universal infrastructure" that will support mobile commerce. The applications of RFID are wide-ranging and include radio tracking of wild and agricultural animals (Kern, 1999), manufacturing and distribution of physical goods such as automobiles and transmission assembly (Mintchell, 2002), shipping and port operations (D'Amico, 2002; Dornheim, 2002), and pharmaceutical packaging (Forcinio, 2002), among others. Also, RFID systems are used for building access control, like "smart cards" for identification at doors (Finkenzeller, 2003) and "Easy-Pass" for toll motorways and bridges, like EASYCARD, the first 'touch and go' IC card for mass transport in Taiwan (Taipei Rapid Transit Corporation Annual Report, 2003)

Another survey from the RFID case studies in the IDTechEx knowledgebase categorized into 13 different application areas. The applications areas including airlines and airports, animals and farming, financial and security, healthcare, land and sea logistics, laundry, leisure, libraries and archiving, manufacturing, military, other, passenger transport and retail/CPG (IDTechEx, 2005).

Announcements made in 2003 by Wal-Mart Corporation, UK-based retailer Tesco, and the U.S. Department of Defense (DoD) indicating that they will require suppliers to put passive RFID tags on equipment at the pallet, case, and part level by 2005 promise to make these marketing estimates a reality (Application Development Trends, 2003; ABI Research, 2003). Up to today, the expected rapid industry adoption of RFID has, however, not taken place. It was not until now that Wal-Mart is still working hard with its suppliers to expand RFID tagging requirements. According to Wal-Mart, "By January, 500 more of its 3,900 stores will be using RFID technology to track the goods entering their premises, bringing the total number of stores using RFID technology to 1,000" (Swedberg, 2006).

According to IDTechEx's research, global market for RFID including tags, systems, and services is $1.94 in 2005 is $1.94 billion but it will be driven by demand and new laws to $24.50 billion in 2015 (Peter & Raghu, 2005). In 2006, almost three times the volume of RFID tags will be sold than over the previous 60 years since their invention. This exponential growth will continue and, by 2015, the value of sales of RFID tags will have increased by 13 times over the figure for 2005. In addition, IDTechEx assert that the market for RFID interrogators is analyzed—reaching $1.14 billion in 2008 for EPC interrogators and $0.75 billion in the same year for other interrogators, such as Near Field Communication interrogators. Forecasts by territorial region show that by 2010, 48% of RFID tags by numbers will be sold in East Asia, followed by 32% to North America.

East Asia, including Taiwan, all has a track record of quickly adopting and improving upon technology to create high performance business capabilities. With the advent of radio frequency identification technology, East Asia has an opportunity to make improvements in retailing and manufacturing.

After the trend moved toward e-readiness, the Taiwanese government has made a joint effort with the private sectors for the implementation and application of enterprises' mobilization in recent years. The Taiwanese government had launching of a new industrial promotion project in 2005, which was intended to make the implementation of RFID to be a foundation for another new technological and economic miracle. With a "U" to represent "ubiquitous," the project is called U Taiwan because of the capability of RFID to link the various information technologies and telecommunications devices in the modern world. In addition, the government provides guidance and subsidies to businesses and research organizations in Taiwan that develop/implement this valuable new technology (Taiwan Investment Biweekly, 2005).

The "Ubiquitous Taiwan" program will be one of the most important Taiwanese information policies, and RFID is considered as one of the most important enabling technologies to ensure the success to implement this aforementioned program. The Department of Industrial Technology (Ministry of Economic Affairs) indicated that in 2005 the funding provided to support private-sector's R&D in RFID-related fields rose to NT$67 million (approximately U.S. $2.15 million), and will be increased to over NT$100 million (approximately U.S. $3.18 million) in 2006 (Mobile Internet in Taiwan, 2005).

This article conducted a survey to examine a set of factors that effect the adoption of the RFID system in Taiwan. The remainder of this article is organized as follows: The next section provides a brief literature review regarding the RFID technology. Then the methodology and procedure of the study is presented in the third section and the fourth section described the survey result. Finally, conclusion and research trends are discussed.

RFID TECHNOLOGY

RFID is a generic technology concept that refers to the use of radio waves to identify objects (Auto-ID Center, 2002). It is considered a significant improvement over the traditional barcode, which needs to be read by scanners in "line-of-sight" fashion and can be stripped away if the paper product label ripped or damaged. In this section, the literature about RFID technology, including components of RFID system, key attributes, applications, and barriers to implement are reviewed.

The Component of RFID System

The primary function of the RFID technology is the automated identification of objects with electromagnetic fields. RFID uses radio frequency chips to track pallets, cartons, and individual items in warehouses, stores, trunk, and other locations. An RFID system basically consists of four major components (Agarwal, 2001):

1. **E-tags:** Electronic radio frequency tags are tiny, lightweight, cheap (predicted to eventually be less than five cents for a basic tag), and versatile, enabling them to be easily and invisibly embedded in most product packaging, clothing, or parts. Tag readers, based on cellular technology, can scan products as needed so that a system can identify what products are located in a particular physical space. Unlike barcode scanning, RFID does not require line-of sight to read the tag information and readers can deal with hundreds of tags at the same time. It is estimated that 100 billion e-tags will be needed to identify the global supply chain.
2. **Electronic product code (EPC):** EPC is a new universal standard, which are being developed to identify individual product items. These standards will create a unique identifier for an individual item. The new cording scheme is based on a 96-bit code; enable the identification of 1.5 quintillion objects. The EPC will be the minimal information carried on an e-tag. Most other data will reside on a server accessed via the EPC.
3. **Object name service (ONS):** Based on its EPC, an object can be identified by one or

more networks either on the Internet or a virtual private network where information about it resides. The ONS sits on local server and matches e-tag EPC information with other information about the item, including location.

4. **Physical markup language (PML):** The goal of the physical markup language (PML) is to provide a standard vocabulary to represent and distribute information about Auto-ID enabled objects. It aims to standardize the interface between the auto-ID infrastructure (such as RFID readers) and other existing information systems such as ERP and SCM systems.

RFID Advantages over Bar Codes

Bar coding and RFID both are intended to provide rapid and reliable item identification and tracking information. The primary difference is that bar coding scans a printed label with either optical laser or imaging technology, while RFID scans, or interrogates, a semiconductor tag using radio frequency (wireless) technology.

Reik, Patrick, Snell, and Timothy (2004) argued the key attributes to consider when comparing RFID and bar coding center around reading capability, reading speed, tag or label durability, amount of information, flexibility of information, cost, and standards. Summary and compare RFID and bar coding with respect to each of these characteristics from and shown in Table 1.

As unnecessary in unobstructed path between tag and reader, labor is reduced when low-frequency RFID tags are applied to goods. Tags can be read at great distances without anyone running a scanner over the tag as is necessary with bar codes. This makes it possible to instantly take the inventory of a carton without unpacking it and particularly advantageous in warehouse receiving operations and in operations where information needs to be collected from items that may have an inconsistent orientation, such as distribution center sorting applications (Saar & Thomas, 2003; Reik et al., 2004).

Table 1. Important attribute of RFID and bar coding (Source: Reik, Patrick, Snell, & Timothy, 2004)

Characteristics	RFID	Bar Coding
Reading capability	Wireless—line of sight not necessary (some environmental exceptions).	Optical-line of sight required.
Reading speed	RFID can read multiple tags in a single pass.	Bar coding can read a single label per scan.
Durability	RFID tags are capable of storing several thousand characters, or several kilobytes, of information.	Labels tend to be damaged in harsh processes. Etching directly onto part has increased durability.
Amount of information	RFID tags are capable of storing several thousand characters or several kilobytes of information.	A 1D bar code can store 20 alphanumeric characters, while a 2D bar code can store roughly 2,000 characters.
Flexibility of information	To update information, many RFID tags can have their memories updated with new information through wireless communication.	To update information, a bar code label must be replaced with a new bar code label.
Security	RFID tags have manufacturer installed identification codes that cannot be changed, thus making counterfeiting difficult.	2D bar codes provide encryption capability.
Cost per label or tag	RFID tags cost from $0.25-$0.50, up to $250.	Bar code labels typically cost less than $0.01.
Standards	RFID lacks complete standardization, especially in the global environment	Bar coding is standardized and widely accepted.
State of infrastructure	RFID is minimal. Users would have to invest in additional equipment to support RFID.	The infrastructure to support bar codes is in wide existence.

In terms of speed, RFID readers are capable of interpreting over 250 tags per second, far more rapidly than a bar code label can be. The reading speed of RFID has great value in high-volume receiving and shipping applications where a large number of items need to be accounted for quickly. Thus the process of collecting information is automated and occurs more rapidly, then requiring less labor and providing greater inventory visibility (Karkkainen, 2003).

RFID tags can be encased in hardened plastic substrates or other materials, so they are significantly more durable than bar code labels, which are typically paper based. The added durability of an RFID tag allows for item tracking through harsh production processes (Karkkainen, 2003).

High-end RFID tags may contain several kilobytes of memory, more than the traditional 1D or 2D bar code could store. This increased information storage capability creates a portable database of information, allowing a greater number of product attributes to be tracked, such as date of manufacture, time spent in transit, location of distribution center holding the item, expiration date, or last date of service (Reik et al., 2004).

With respect to information dynamics, RFID tags are able to support read/write operations, enabling real-time information updates as an item moves throughout the supply chain. This feature can be of critical importance as production schedules, delivery dates and locations, and shipment contents can change on a regular basis. Bar codes, by contrast, contain static information and, therefore must be replaced with a new label in order to update information (Karkkainen, 2003; Reik et al., 2004).

Applications of RFID

Radio frequency identification is an emerging technology that has caught more attention as it has moved from consideration for niche applications in recent years. Although RFID is still emerging, governments and companies are already exploring a number proof-of-concept application.

Smith and Konsynski (2003) have identified several generic classes of applications that could emerge in the near to medium term, as RFID technology becomes less expensive. These applications are summarized in Table 2.

According the survey result from Accenture, they find the similar perspective. Accenture proposed that to adopt RFID, companies could with capabilities that include finished goods inventory visibility, production visibility, asset visibility, safe and secure supply chain, and supply chain planning (Accenture, 2004b). These capabilities are summarized in Table 3.

Another survey from the RFID case studies in the IDTechEx knowledgebase is categorized into 13 different application areas by industry, which contains 1592 RFID case studies until November 2005. The applications areas including airlines and airports, animals and farming, financial and security, healthcare, land and sea logistics, laundry, leisure, libraries and archiving, manufacturing, military, other, passenger transport, retail, and consumer goods (IDTechEx, 2005). In this knowledgebase, there are 350 cases (22.0%) which belong to the application of retail and consumer goods and give the evidence to examine the perspective: RFID technology is of particular interest to manufacturers and retailers.

Barrier to Implement RFID

Although RFID is a promising and already rapidly emerging technology, its use raises many societal issues and questions, as well as a number of technical barriers that must be solved before it can succeed in becoming a truly pervasive and ubiquitous technology. The study of Wu, Nystrom, Lin, and Yu (2006) explored the existing challenges and obstacles to facilitate RFID's quick adoption. These challenges can be grouped into the following categories, such as technology challenges, standard challenges, patent challenges,

Table 2. Potential classes of RFID applications

Application class	
Perpetual inventory management	With RFID, every item can be tracked regardless of where it is. RFID also enables companies to know what inventory is coming to them. Finally, it helps retailers keep perpetual inventories at the store level. Thus, real time inventory will be possible throughout the supply chain and these data could enable improved replenishment, reduced order cycle times, in-transit tracking of items, better forecast accuracy, increased flexibility in responding to unexpected demands, improved item locating, and easier recalls (Albright, 2002; Alexander et al., 2002).
Automatic scanning.	RFID could reduce the costs involved in these functions by scanning shipments automatically and rapidly, reducing time and effort in the warehouse. All items in a shopping cart could be scanned automatically when a customer leaves the store (Brock, Milne, Kang, & Lewis, 2002).
Product/asset identification	RFID will help companies identify a variety of assets, from items in a shipment to equipment in a hospital. It can also be used to track component parts in finished goods.
Logistics and transportation applications.	Logistics providers can use RFID to track specialized containers and trace reusable containers. It will be possible for postal services and package delivery companies to track small parcels in this manner (Alexander et al., 2002).
Customer service applications	Companies that handle products owned by customers could use e-tags to log the receipt of goods, track their progress, and prevent lost items—all electronically. E-tags could also effectively act as proof of purchase and include warranty and service history information (Brock et al., 2002).
Theft and waste prevention applications	E-tags on products will be able to report when products are stolen, as well as serve as a homing device to report their exact location. Tags could also be used to report when products are reaching their sell-by date, so that they can be quickly sold or returned to the manufacturer (Agarwal, 2001).
Personal and asset status applications	Some companies are considering adding two-way tags to their ID cards. Then, if an employee feels unsafe or needs help, pressing this button will instantly report his or her location and bring assistance. This feature could also be used in hospitals and other facilities that are open to the public (Werbe & Sereiko, 2002).

Table 3. Capabilities delivered through RFID applications

Capabilities	Description
Finished goods inventory visibility	Better performance levels in shipping and receiving labor productivity, order accuracy, and returns processing
Production visibility	Improvements in raw material receipts accuracy, work-in-process inventory management, and receiving labor productivity
Asset visibility	Better asset utilization through better tracking of vehicles, reusable containers, and other high value assets
Safe and secure supply chain	Improvements in recall management, lot track and trace, expiration date management, and improvements in shrink
Supply chain planning	Reduction in inventory and working capital, improved revenue through reduction in out-of-stocks, reduced expediting costs

costs challenges, infrastructure challenges, return on investment (ROI) challenges, and barcode to RFID migration challenges.

The factors discussed in the subsections prove to be the key barriers that have kept RFID from becoming a more widespread implementation (David, 2003; Mario et al., 2002; Reik et al., 2004; Tom, 2003; Shih, Sun, & Chiu, 2004).

Technical Barrier

The first factor is technology aspect. Extensive RFID implementations will generate massive amounts of data that needs to be stored, made available on a real-time basis, and managed. RFID systems will therefore need to integrate well with existing databases, data warehouses, and enterprise applications that address everything

Table 4. Technical barrier to implement RFID

Component	Description
Lack of standards	Standards used to define RFID systems are varied in their levels of acceptance globally. An open standardized system that would heavily accelerate RFID adaptation and the concern of a standardized RFID system is even more important from a global aspect.
Interoperability	Without interoperability between different RFID systems, the availability of many functions of RFID tags cannot be fully utilized.
Read range	RFID read-ranges may sometimes be adversely affected by high electromagnetic noise levels in the vicinity of the tag. Large quantities of metal or heavy-duty power supplies in close proximity to a particular tag or reader can reduce the read-range. By carefully selecting the proper equipment and installation site, many of these adverse influences can be effectively mitigated.
Read quality (accuracy)	RFID read rates are approximately 80% currently, it is expected that end users will require read rates approaching 100% before considering a significant implementation of RFID.
Hardware jamming of RFID	A portion of the high failure rate can be attributed to environment, such as the presence of metals, liquids (UHF products have difficulty reading through liquids), or other RF energy.
Security	Sensitive data protection
To integrate with existing system	The integrity of the RFID device and the system as a whole is a much larger and complex problem.
Volume of data	The data volume generated by RFID could be sizable since RFID tags can carry orders of magnitude with more data than a typical bar code. It is believed that the corporate computer systems in use today are not well suited to handle this level of volume. In addition to volume, the item files in these corporate systems are not currently capable of handling RFID data structures.

from inventory management to order processing systems. The demand for storage systems and network and systems bandwidth will grow to meet the needs of RFID implementations. All of this not only complicates the already difficult integration task that many enterprises already face, but amplifies the cost constraints in a major way (David, 2003; Mario, et al., 2002; Reik et al., 2004; Tom, 2003; Shih et al., 2004).

Technology barriers included lack of standard, interoperability, technology hurdles about read range, read quality (accuracy) and Hardware jamming of RFID, security, to integrate with existing system, and huge volume of data are described in Table 4.

Cultural Barrier

Undoubtedly, RFID solutions that solve current technology shortcomings will develop over time; the more important barriers to adoption are cultural. People may take a long time to understand and trust the technology because it is relatively new to them (Ngai,Cheng, Auc, & Lai, 2007).

Privacy concerns could significantly delay the acceleration of item level tagging, for example. The public fears live tags will remain on items after purchase and that unauthorized readers could therefore scan an individual and know the specific items on their person. Technology companies and standards organizations are aggressively trying to prove that RFID solutions can honor a person's privacy. It would be prudent you're your company to draft and evolve a privacy policy now (David, 2003; Mario et al., 2002; Reik et al., 2004; Tom, 2003; Shih et al., 2004).

The other cultural barrier to RFID adoption involves the relationship between retailers and suppliers. Neither culture readily shares information about the movement of its products or the activities of its customers. This kind of information exchange, however, is intrinsic to auto-ID and the intelligent e-PC network. Until retailers and suppliers can synchronize inter-company processes based on the movement of e-PC data, two things will likely occur (David, 2003; Mario et al., 2002; Reik et al., 2004; Tom, 2003; Shih et al., 2004):

1. Suppliers will receive less value from case- and pallet-level tagging, which will slow their compliance with retail mandates. Case- and pallet-level tagging efforts will remain internally focused.
2. Without the benefit of consistent store-level information, suppliers will resist moving to item level tagging except for internally focused initiatives.

Table 5 describes an overview of cultural barriers to widespread use of RFID. These barriers include privacy concerns, the relationship between retailers and suppliers, environmental constraints, and lack of education.

Financial Barrier

The third barrier to item-level tagging is purely financial: companies will be faced with staggering implementation costs. AMR Research, Inc. estimates that to implement RFID tagging at item level, companies will spend an amount comparable to that spent on Y2K. Most of the cost will be in upgrading, integrating, and replacing applications. As a result, because most retailers and suppliers expect to receive 70 to 80% of RFID's value from case- and pallet-level initiatives, some companies will likely postpone item-level tagging. Exceptions will be opportunistic and largely internally focused, such as item-level initiatives launched to control theft, manage production, and track dated goods (David, 2003; Mario et al., 2002; Reik et al., 2004; Tom, 2003; Shih et al., 2004).

On the other hand, if you select an RFID model that is supported by your network infrastructure, you should significantly decrease implementation costs—especially if you have hundreds or thousands of distributed sites to outfit. In a network model, for example, e-IS functionality is a shared effort involving the edge appliances or mini B2B gateway supplying intelligence, the network access points, whether wired or wireless supporting reader management, and also the routing and switching devices already in your network (David, 2003; Mario et al., 2002; Reik et al., 2004; Tom, 2003; Shih et al., 2004). Table 6 describes an overview of financial barriers to widespread use of RFID.

Table 5. Cultural barrier of RFID

Component	Description
Privacy concerns	Privacy groups have expressed a concern that RFID, due to its small form factor and RF attributes, will allow monitoring of individuals' behavior without their knowledge. It is believed that proponents of the technology will have to alleviate these concerns through technological innovation and proactive education.
The relationship between retailers and suppliers	Neither culture readily shares information about the movement of its products or the activities of its customers. This kind of information exchange, however, is intrinsic to auto-ID and the intelligent e-PC network.
Environmental constraints	RFID is of course subject to the physical laws that affect all RF transmissions. Noise, interference, and distortion must be guarded against, and reader performance must be improved to compensate.
Lack of Education	It is believed that the majority of potential RFID users lack a clear understanding of the potential RFID benefits, instead they remain weary of RFID's relatively high cost. In addition, many end users view implementation of a new technology as a daunting task. It is believed that penetration will increase as users, vendors, value-added resellers, and system integrators create and deploy RFID applications that offer easy system integration and strong returns on investment.

Organizational Barrier

Equally surprising is that RFID is not new, it has been around for well over 10 years, and is already in use in applications like access control and transport, but the widespread use of RFID is new to many organizations. As a result, some organizations are struggling with how to learn about and prepare to leverage this technology and to face the funding issues and business process changes it will bring. If managers do not begin to explore RFID and work with technology partners to define an appropriate solution for business, businesses may end up with the wrong RFID business model as well as staggering implementation costs as managers update RFID infrastructure accordingly; effectively managing organizational change to avoid technology implementation failure (David, 2003; Mario et al., 2002; Reik et al., 2004; Tom, 2003; Shih et al., 2004).

Table 7 describes an overview of organizational barriers to widespread use of RFID. These barriers include redesigning processes and manageability.

THEORETICAL BACKGROUND

Diffusion Research

To date, many popular diffusion models have been introduced to cover the general themes and frameworks related to adopting, diffusing, or infusing information technology into organizational environment. Out of these diffusion models, TAM (Davis, 1989) model which was based on Azjen and Fishbein's TRA, 1975 (Ajzen , 1991), Moore and Benbasat's DOI (1991, 1996) model which was mainly based on Roger's DOI work which could be dated back to 1962 (Rogers,1962, 2003), TPB (Taylor & Todd, 1995; Mathieson, 1991) model which was based on Ajzen's 1985 TPB work (Ajzen & Madden, 1986; Ajzen, 1991), and Goodhue and Thompson's 1995 TTF model are several good examples. Although many of these models may differ in their theoretical structures, constructs, and/or relationships posited, all of them virtually address the use of technology (Chin & Marcolin, 2001). Table 8 summarizes these popular models/ theories in the IT diffusion field.

Prior studies on the adoption of IT innovations have been well documented. In particular, the innovation diffusion theory (IDT) articulated by Rogers (2003) provided a viable framework for studying IT innovation diffusion. IDT has been widely used to predict and explain the adoption of innovation in various domains (Rogers, 2003; Chin & Marcolin, 2001).

Rather than a limited notion referring to the initial application of a new technology or service, innovation like RFID is increasingly considered as a process; which is to say, a process of diffusion (of innovation) that helps understand the process of adoption of a new product or service

Table 6. Financial barrier of RFID

Component	Description
Relatively high cost / infrastructure	RFID's robust functionality can easily lead to significant improvements in supply chain operations; however, it is believed that overall system cost is a key reason why this enhanced functionality remains under-used. A low-end passive RFID tag costs approximately \$0.25-\$0.50, with high-end active tags reaching up to \$250 each. And RFID requires new infrastructure, where RFID readers can cost \$1,200-\$3,500 each. Further, RFID solutions often involve a challenging front-end integration process. As a result, many end users have found it difficult to justify the cost of an RFID system despite the apparent incremental benefits.

Table 7. Organizational barrier to implement RFID

Component	Description
Redesigning processes	While RFID can be used in lieu of bar codes, many potential efficiency and accuracy gains will only be obtained by using it in a different manner than bar code-based systems. The main advantage of RFID over bar codes is that it allows object identification in a non-intrusive manner. However, many existing supply chain applications require direct capture of bar codes through user-initiated scans. A truly scan free warehouse will require different processes than one that relies on bar codes. RFID receiving may be an extremely attractive prospect for many distribution operations. But real productivity gains will probably come more from making it a more flow-through process than by merely substituting a RFID read for a bar code scan. Implementing a flow through receiving process may require changes in an operation's shipment check-in, quality, verification, special handling, and vendor performance monitoring procedures.
Manageability	The amount of information that will one day reside in and be accessed through an EPC network will be staggering. Successful RFID models will need to be scalable and flexible to store, route, monitor, and manage the expected traffic.

among consumers. Innovation, viewed as a diffusion process, may be equated with the process of a specific temporal duration, through which an innovative technology or service enters a social system via different communication channels to circulate within it (Mahler & Rogers, 1999).

The key concept of innovation can be described as "the process in which an innovation is communicated through certain channels, over time, among the members of a social system" (Rogers, 2003). IDT includes five significant innovation characteristics and they are relative advantage, compatibility, complexity, trial ability, and observables. These aforementioned characteristics are typically used to explain the users' adoption and the associated decision making process (Rogers, 2003; Wu & Wang, 2005).

However, prior research have only suggested that such factors including compatibility, complexity, and relative advantages are consistently important during the process to make an adoption decision (Tornatzky & Klein, 1982; Agarwal & Psasa, 1998). Nevertheless, some other researchers to study complex IS argued that classical diffusion variables by themselves are unlikely to be the strong predictors for complex IT adoption and diffusion (Fichman, 1992). Prescott and Conger (1995) further concluded, "IDT factors are not as appropriate for inter-organizational information technologies as they are for others."

Zmud (1984) suggested using the 'technology-push' (TP) and need-pull (NP) concepts to explain the behavior in the adoption of new technology. Chau and Tam (2000) applied the TP-NP theory to explain the adoption of an open system and support for the usefulness of applying TP-NP theory to provide an adequate explanation for the diffusion of complex organizational technologies.

Technology-Push and Need-Pull Concepts

The concepts of technology-push and need-pull were borrowed from the engineering/R&D management discipline to study the underlying motivation and/or driving forces behind the innovation of a new technology (Schon, 1967). The TP force stems from the recognition of a new technological means to enhance/improve the performance. The NP school on the other hand, argues that user's needs are the key drivers for adoption. Still, some researchers proposed that

Table 8. Models/theories in the IT diffusion field

Theory	Author	Major Concepts
Technology acceptance model	Davis (1986)	TAM posits that perceived usefulness and perceived ease of use determine an individual's intention to use a system with an intention to use serving as a mediator for actual system use. Perceived usefulness is also viewed as being directly impacted by perceived ease of use.
Innovation diffusion theory	Moore and Benbasat (1991); Rogers (1962)	Moore and Benbasat (1991) expanded upon the five factors impacting the adoption of innovations presented by Rogers. It includes the following eight factors such as voluntariness, relative advantage, compatibility, image, ease of use, result demonstrability, visibility, and trialability that will impact the adoption of IT.
Theory of planned behavior	Ajzen (1985); Ajzen (1991)	Individual behavior is driven by behavioral intentions where behavioral intentions are a function of an individual's attitude toward the behavior, the subjective norms surrounding the performance of the behavior, and the individual's perception of the ease with which the behavior can be performed (behavioral control).
Task technology fit	Goodhue (1995); Goodhue and Thompson (1995)	IT is more likely to have a positive impact on individual performance and hence it can be used if the capabilities of the IT match with the tasks that the user must perform. A measure of task-technology fit was developed and it consists of eight factors. These eight factors include: quality, locatability, authorization, and compatibility, ease of use/training, production timeliness, systems reliability, and relationship with users.

both TP and NP models may co-exist, but that NP model was generally more prevalent (Zmud, 1984; Langrish, 1972). Munro and Noori (1988) suggested that the integration of both models could eventually contribute to more innovativeness.

Gauvin and Sinha (1993) suggested two types of opportunities for adopting a new technology and they are opportunities from productivity gains and from expansion of resulting demand. The study of Chau and Tam (2000) proposed four factors to examine the adoption of an open system. These four factors to explain TP/NP concept include: benefit of adopting, migration cost, satisfaction level with existing systems, and market uncertainty.

Based on these aforementioned arguments, this proposed study uses the TP/NP concept to examine the adoption of RFID system in Taiwan. Consequently, two constructs are proposed and they are (1) perceive benefits obtained from adopting the RFID system and (2) perceive barriers about implementation this technology in an organization. These factors are assumed in this study to influence the adoption decision of a RFID system. The conceptual is shown in Figure 1.

Innovation-decision process usually begins with the knowledge stage, when an individual (or organization) is exposed to an innovation's existence and then gains some understanding of innovation. The main outcome of the following persuasion stage can be either a favorable or unfavorable attitude toward the innovation. It is further assumed that such persuasion will lead to a subsequent change including later adoption or rejection. But in many cases, attitudes and actions are quite disparate, which is called "KAP-gap" (Rogers, 2003).

It is believed that the RFID system still remains in the early stage of the innovation-decision process in Taiwan. In other words, RFID technology is becoming more mature in the future and the current industry is still a young one. As a result, its full impact is not yet foreseeable and there is still much promise in the near future. Based on these aforementioned arguments, this article explores what the users' perceive about the RFID system in the knowledge and persuasion stages instead of studying the adoption in the decision stage.

TP/NP Factors: Perceived Benefit and Perceived Barrier

Two TP/NP factors are perceived benefits and perceived barriers to adopt the RFID system. Perceived benefits of adopting RFID systems mean the extent of perception of benefits to be gained by adopting RFID systems. The item proposed by Accenture (2004a) was adapted to operationalize the construct. Respondents were asked to give their level of agreement or disagreements with the following 16 perceive benefits of going to an RFID system. The 16 items are presented in Appendix A.

Another major category of factors proposed in this article is the perceived barriers of adopting RFID systems. Higher cost for an innovation is negatively associated with its adoption (Premkumar & Potter, 1995). In RFID systems, the costs of adoption may also include technical or market uncertainty. The second factor means the extent of migration costs associated with the adoption RFID system (Accenture, 2004a). The item proposed by Accenture (2004a) was adapted to operationalize the construct. Respondents were asked to give their level of agreement or disagreements with the following 13 perceive barriers to implement an RFID system. The 13 items are presented in Appendix A.

Figure 1.Conceptual model of RFID system adoption

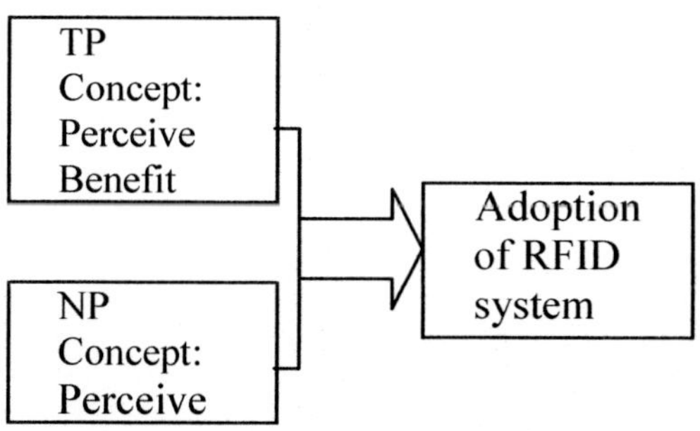

RESEARCH DESIGN AND DATA COLLECTION PROCEDURE

The growing popularity of RFID has made it important to understand the key determinants to affect the RFID system's adoption. To examine the RFID progress in Taiwan, a field study technique was employed. The sampling and instrument development and validation process are described next. An instrument was administered to IT personnel, asking them the situation of RFID technology in their organization and the opinions of RFID technology to determine the critical factors that affect the adoption of RFID technology.

The Instrument

Since there were very few theoretical or empirical studies in existence, the basis of the questionnaire items contained in this research was primarily based on findings from relevant prior research. The basis of the questionnaire items contained in this research was primarily based on findings from relevant prior research including IT periodicals and trade journals. The questionnaire was tested on three doctoral students, they were asked to evaluate and critique each item on the questionnaire. The necessary corrections were made before the instrument was administered to the participants. Based on the feedback from three evaluators, we generate 38 items to measure RFID perceive of IT personnel, included benefits delivered through RFID, and barrier to RFID.

All items were measured using a seven-point Likert-type scale, with "strongly agree" at one end and "strongly disagree" at the other. The purpose of the survey was described, and respondents were asked to answer demographic questions about their organization and personnel, including gender, age, levels of formal education, and years of experience with the business.

Data Collection

Data used in this survey were collected via a convenience sampling method to choose the respondents. The sample for the study was taken from 10 class sections of EMBA of a major university in middle Taiwan. All had considerable work experiences before, and most of them are mid-management in business domain or IT domain now. A total of 500 surveys were distributed and 134 valid responses were returned for a 26.8% response rate, which appears to be consistent with other mail surveys (Rai et al., 2002). The demographic information of the respondents is provided in Table 9-10.

Slightly less than three-quarters (71.6%) of the respondents were male, which outnumbered the female by almost three-to-one. The respondents were mostly 30-40 years old (67.1%), and four-fifths of respondents had worked more than 6 years and almost one-third (31.1%) had worked more than 11 years. In terms of the education background, almost one-half of the respondents were bachelors (50.7%) and more than one-third were graduates (38.8%).

Only 8.2% of respondents said that they were under mandate to implement RFID technology, which is far beyond the survey results from the United States and Europe; one-half and 22% (Accenture, 2004a). But it was similar to another RFID survey in Asia Pacific (Accenture, 2004c). A possible explanation of this may be explained by the marketplace dynamics. In the United States and Europe, mandates from large retails like Wal-Mart and Metro are clear and much of the activity about RFID was prompted by governmental agencies. But in Asia Pacific, very few organizations impacted with corporate or government mandates today, so was in Taiwan.

ANALYSES AND RESULT

Based on TP/NP concept, this study examination two aspects of decision, perceived benefits and perceive barriers about RFID technology. Analysis of the survey data began with an item

Table 9. Demographic data of participants (n = 134)

Characteristic		Frequency	Percent
Gender	Male	96	71.6
	Female	38	28.4
Age	Less than 30	25	18.7
	30-40	90	67.1
	40-50	18	13.2
	50 or more	1	0.7
Education background	High school	1	0.7
	College	13	9.7
	University (Bachelor)	68	50.7
	Graduate	52	38.8
Work years	Less than 2	2	1.5
	3-5	27	20.1
	6-8	38	28.4
	9-11	25	18.7
	11 or more	42	31.3

Table 10. Company profiles of participants (n = 134)

Characteristic		Frequency	Percent
	Less than 100	32	23.9
	101-250	26	19.4
Number of employees	251-500	18	13.4
	501-1000	28	20.9
	1000 or more	30	22.4
	Observe stage	78	58.2
	Piloting the technology	35	26.1
Current state of RFID implementation	Developing some stage of an RFID business case	18	13.4
	Rolling out an RFID/EPC implementation.	0	0
	Others	3	2.2
Under mandate	Yes	11	8.2
	No	123	91.8

factor analysis, using a principal component approach. Returns were adequate to support this form of analysis. The ratio of sample size to item in the current study was 134/29 or around 4.62. This approaches the 5:1 ratio recommended for exploratory work (Comrey, 1991).

Factor Affecting RFID Adoption

There are two ways to determine the factorability of an inter-correlation matrix, Bartlett's test of sphericity and Kaiser-Meyer-Olkin measure of sampling adequacy (KMO). The Kaiser-Meyer-Olkin measure of sampling adequacy tests whether the partial correlations among items are small. Bartlett's test of sphericity tests whether the correlation matrix is an identity matrix, which would indicate that the factor model is inappropriate.

In this study, two bartlett's test of sphericity (p-value=0.000) indicate that the statistical probability that the correlation matrix has significant correlation among at least some of the variables, and the Kaiser-Meyer-Olkin measure of sampling adequacy (0.865 &0.778) show middling to meritorious sampling adequacy (Hair, Anderson, Tatham, & Black, 1998).

Principle components method and Varimax rotation were used to extract factors from an inter-correlation matrix. The rotated pattern matrix was examined for sizable coefficients, that is, coefficients running about 0.45 in absolute value and larger. Including items with cross loading on other (non-primary) factors blurs the distinction between factors. Accordingly, item loading principally on a single factor were favored for the measure. As shown in Figure 2, three factors emerged from perceive benefits construct and four factors from perceive barriers construct. These factors accounted for 60.76 and 64.24% of the total variance. Computing Cronbach's alpha assessed internal consistency, the values range form 0.6163 to 0.8448 with seven factors.

Factors of Perceive Benefit Construct

Three factors were extracted from perceive benefits construct, named operation efficiency, manufacturing efficiency, and supply chain efficiency.

Operation efficiency included better asset use (λ=0.761), shipping and receiving productivity (λ=0.596), returns processing (λ=0.617) and improvement shrink (λ=0.705), lot track and trace improvement (λ=0.703), recall management (λ=0.617), and visibility of other high-value assets (λ=0.501).

Manufacturing efficiency composed of better order accuracy (λ=0.673), raw materials receipts accuracy (λ=0.818), and WIP inventory management (λ=0.829), receiving labor productivity (λ=0.653). Supply chain efficiency formed with reusable containers (λ=0.491), better expiration date management (λ=0.484), reduction in inventory and working capital (λ=0.836), expediting costs and improved revenue through reduction in out-of-stocks (λ=0.633).

RFID had the potential to liberate considerable human labor from certain workflows and facilitate the possibility of making information visible to all participants throughout the value chain (Angeles, 2005). These specific RFID-enabled capabilities were founded in factors extracted from perceive benefits construct. Table 11 gives the items, mean, standard deviation, factor loadings, and the Cronbach's alpha for each factor.

Factors of Perceive Barrier Construct

The results of the survey reveal that companies in Taiwan have embraced RFID, but the majority reported that they would not implement RFID until 2008 or later. Four factors are extracted, market environment, investment cost, technology characteristic, and organization context. The four factors retained represented 64.245% of the variance of the 13 variables. Market environment issues were identified as the leading challenges, including lack of executive sponsorship (λ=0.538), consumer perceptions/privacy concerns (λ=0.540), intellectual property rights/grey market issues (λ=0.818), legislation/government policy (λ=0.852), and data synchronization (λ=0.644).

Figure 2. Factor analysis of RFID system adoption model

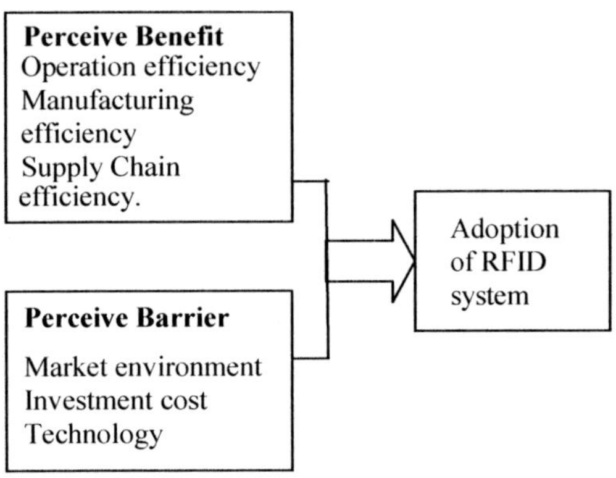

Substantial concerns over investment costs were also cited, including cost of RFID tags and readers (λ=0.635), overall cost of implementation (λ=0.827), and high investment in current solutions (λ=0.746). Market stability (λ=0.792) and standards (λ=0.769) were other significant barriers to implementation. The fourth barrier: organization context composed of complexity of integration with existing systems (λ=0.410); competing business priorities (λ=0.615) and initial decrease in productivity (λ=0.799). Item 17 with loading 0.410 lower than 0.45, but greater than 0.4. Hair et al. (1988) argued that factor loadings greater than 0.4 are considered important in practical significance and the practical significance is an important criterion. Then item 17 is retained to interpreting the factor.

Market issue is the leading challenge in Taiwan, especially grey market issues and government policy. This high ranking could be explained by the status of organizations in Taiwan. For most companies in Taiwan, RFID technology is a "when" and not an "if" question like in the U.S. or in Europe (Accenture, 2004c). Companies in this group are not supplying retailers who are mandating compliance, nor are they facing government regulations. This allows the time to wait and evaluate benefits (Accenture, 2004b).

Cost issue is another important barrier, though RFID tags cost less than half of what they did 5 years ago and prices are continuing to drop. This technology is therefore still substantially more expensive than barcodes and barcode readers.

Table 11. Factors analysis result of perceive benefit construct

Factor	Mean	S.D.	Factor loadings
Operation efficiency (Cronbach's alpha =0.8448)			
Better shipping and receiving productivity (v1)	5.54	1.15	0.596
Better returns processing (v3)	5.29	1.34	0.617
Better asset use through tracking of vehicles (v7)	5.71	1.09	0.761
Visibility of other high-value assets (v9)	5.17	1.31	0.501
Improved recall management (v10)	5.37	1.18	0.617
Improved lot track and trace (v11)	5.89	.98	0.703
Improvements in shrink (v13)	5.48	1.11	0.705
Eigenvalue			6.470
Percentage of variance accumulated			22.006
Manufacturing efficiency (Cronbach's alpha =0.8023)			
Increased order accuracy (v2)	5.48	1.34	0.673
Improved raw materials receipts accuracy (v4)	5.37	1.31	0.818
Better WIP inventory management (v5)	5.51	1.21	0.829
Better receiving labor productivity (v6)	4.66	1.46	0.653
Eigenvalue			1.827
Percentage of variance accumulated			41.752
Supply chain efficiency (Cronbach's alpha =0.7936)			
Reusable containers (v8)	5.00	1.37	0.491
Better expiration date management (v12)	5.59	1.14	0.484
Reduction in inventory and working capital (v14)	5.38	1.23	0.836
Improved revenue through reduction in out-of-stocks (v15)			0.828
Reduced expediting costs (v16)			0.633
Eigenvalue	5.55	1.08	1.425
Percentage of variance accumulated	5.25	1.23	60.766

Substantial concern over standards and stability were identified. Open standards for codes and readers will likely promote lower prices, thus the timeline for implementation may be sooner than respondents anticipate. However, important vendors have subsequently responded and the EAN international and UCC have joined forces to support and maintain EPC global, the international standard for the use of the EPC network. These initiatives have set into motion the widespread diffusion of the RFID technology adoption. Table 12 gives the items, mean, standard deviation, the factor loadings, and the Cronbach's alpha for each factor.

DISCUSSION AND CONCLUSION

While RFID has been a topic of discussion among academic experts and practitioners, little empirical knowledge exists of the RFID practices is followed by industry and few real RFID-based applications have been reported, especially in Asia. This article provided an initial step toward understanding the RFID practices in Taiwan. Based on TP/NP concept, a conceptual model to understand the factors that affect the adoption of the RFID system was proposed. The results of factor analysis point to the strength of contribution of each factor to users perceive.

TP Concept: Perceive Benefit

Operation efficiency contributes the most among users' perceive benefits, especially in finished goods and asset management. Next is manufacturing efficiency and supply chain efficiency. The first two factors reveal that RFID technology holds the promise of closing some of the information gaps in the supply chain, especially in retailing and logistics (Angeles, 2005). The third factor, supply chain efficiency, focuses on supply chain planning and management which represent long-term benefits of the RFID system.

The finding is similar to the results in Europe and the USA. The top-rated benefits include improve track and trace, better recall management, better shipping and receiving and better return processing, which items all related to operation efficiency (Accenture, 2004a). It seems strange but is reasonable. Angeles (2005) argued that first managerial guideline for RFID deployment is making the ROI case for RFID. The opportunity to focus on operation efficiency and manufacturing efficiency will allow companies to build capability internally first without major investment. Compare other countries in Asia Pacific, manufacturing efficiency and operation efficiency also scored high in South Korea, Japan, and Australia (Accenture, 2004c).

NP Concept: Perceive Barrier

Although cost issues received a great deal of attention, the participants in the survey did not see the issue as the most significant barriers to implement the RFID system. Instead, market environment topic was identified as the most significant factor in importance. RFID/EPC strategy matrix argues that if companies are not faced with regulatory or compliancy, the best strategy might be to wait (Accenture, 2004b). Few organizations in Taiwan are impacted with corporate or government mandates and they do not need to build the capability now. Instead, they can take advantage of slow start to wait and learn until more maturing solutions and declining tag and infrastructure costs. Even though, investment costs are still important, including overall cost of implementation, tags, and readers price. The last two factors are technology characteristic and organization context.

Accenture's Asia Pacific survey revealed overall cost of implementation is the following barriers to implementing RFID (Accenture, 2004c). An earlier survey conducted in the United States and Europe concluded cost issues and the stability of RFID were identified as the leading challenges (Accenture, 2004a).

Most companies in Taiwan have embraced RFID, like Asia Pacific countries, but the majority reported that they would not implement RFID until 2008 or later. With the changing environment, Taiwan firms are trying various approaches to improve their performance. The great challenges—issues surrounding market standard and cost—are diminishing and it is believed that when the benefits of these efforts become evident, RFID technology are likely to gain prominence in the next decade in Taiwan

The purpose of this study was to explore the factors affecting RFID adoption. Even though the findings seem to be comparable to past research literature, the dynamic nature of IT could change the order of importance in the future. Much more rigorous studies must be complete to ascertain the importance and relationship of these constructs. And a number of issues remain to be addressed. First, the investigation of RFID adoption is relatively new to IS researchers. The discussed findings and their implications were obtained from one single study that examined a particular technology and targeted a specific user group in

Table 12. Factor analysis result of perceive barrier construct

Factor	Mean	S.D.	Factor loadings
Market environment (Cronbach's alpha =0.7881)			
Lack of executive sponsorship (v23)	5.13	1.48	0.538
Consumer perceptions/privacy concerns (v24)	4.91	1.46	0.540
Intellectual property rights/grey market issues (v25)	4.81	1.40	0.818
Legislation/government policy (v26)	4.82	1.43	0.852
Data synchronization (v27)	5.31	1.25	0.644
Eigenvalue			4.185
Percentage of variance accumulated			19.940
Investment cost (Cronbach's alpha =0.7028)			
Cost of RFID tags and readers (v18)	5.81	1.20	0.635
Overall cost of implementation (v19)	6.04	1.00	0.827
High investment in current solutions (v21)	5.84	1.14	0.746
Eigenvalue			1.794
Percentage of variance accumulated			37.685
Technology characteristic (Cronbach's alpha =0.6614)			
Lack of standards (v28)	5.27	1.44	0.769
Market not stable/too early (v29)	5.21	1.44	0.792
Eigenvalue			1.238
Percentage of variance accumulated			51.065
Organization context (Cronbach's alpha =0.6163)			
Complexity of integration with existing systems (v17)	5.67	1.38	0.410
Competing business priorities (v20)	5.25	1.31	0.615
Initial decrease in productivity (v22)	4.66	1.35	0.799
Eigenvalue			1.135
Percentage of variance accumulated			64.245

Taiwan. Thus, continued research is needed to generalize the findings and discussion to include other groups. Second, there is a need to search for additional variables to improve the ability to predict the adoption of RFID technology. It would be reasonable to add adoption intention or usage to explore the relationship between the factors and adoption intention or usage. Third, the model is cross-sectional; that is, it measures perceptions at a single point at time. However, perceptions changes over time as individuals gain experience. The changes have implications for researchers and practitioners interested in predicted RFID adoption over time.

ACKNOWLEDGMENT

The author thanks to the National Science Council of Taiwan for Grants NSC 94-2213-E-224-036 and NSC 95-2221-E-224-049-MY2 to part of this research.

REFERENCES

ABI Research. (2003). *Not all RFID vendors ready for the Wal-Mart challenge*. Retrieved July 7, 2004, from http://www.abiresearch.com/abiprdisplay2.jsp?pressid=208

Accenture. (2004a). *High performance enabled through radio frequency identification accenture research on manufacturer perspectives*. Retrieved December 15, 2004, from http://www.accenture.com/xd/xd.asp?it=enweb&xd=services\rfid\insights

Accenture. (2004b). *High performance delivered from compliance to competitive impact through radio frequency identification*. Retrieved January 10, 2005, from http://www.accenture.com/xd/xd.asp?it=enweb&xd=services\rfid\insights

Accenture. (2004c). *High performance enabled through radio frequency identification-accenture research on Asia Pacific perspectives*. Retrieved January 2, 2005, from http://www.accenture.com/xd/xd.asp?it=enweb&xd=services\rfid\insights

Agarwal, R., & Prasa, J. (1998). A conceptual and operational definition of personal innovativeness in the domain of information technology. *Information Systems Research, 9*(2), 204-301.

Agarwal, V. (2001). *Assessing the benefits of auto-ID technology in the consumer industry* (MIT Auto-ID Center White Paper WH-003). Retrieved October 8, 2004, from http://www.autoidlabs.org/whitepapers/CAM-WH-003.pdf

Ajzen, I. (1985). From intentions to actions: A theory of planned behavior. In J. Kuhl & J. Beckmann (Eds.), *Springer series in social psychology* (pp. 11-39). Berlin: Springer.

Ajzen, I. (1991). The theory of planned behavior. *Organizational Behavior and Human Decision Processes, 50*(2), 179-211.

Ajzen, I., & Madden, T. J. (1986). Prediction of goal directed behaviour: Attitudes, attitudes, and perceived behavioral control. *Journal of Experimental Social Psychology, 22*, 453-474.

Albright, B. (2002).Will RFID be the answer people want it to be?. *Frontline Solutions, 12*(3), 8.

Alexander, K., Birkhofer, G., Gramling, K., Kleinberger, H., Leng, S., Moogimane, D., & Woods, M. (2002). *Focus on retail: Applying auto-ID to improve product availability at the retail shelf* (MIT Auto-ID Center White Paper BC-001). Retrieved July 8, 2003, from http://www.autoidcenter.org/publishedresearch

Angeles, R. (2005). RFID technologies: Supply-chain applications and implementation issues. *Information Systems Management, 22*(1), 51-65.

Application Development Trends. (2003). *DoD. Wal-Mart pushes RFID*. Retrieved July 25, 2004, from http://www.adtmag.com/article.asp?id=8542

Auto-ID Center. (2002). *Technology guide*. Retrieved July 12, 2004, from http://www.autoidcenter.org

Brock, D. L., Milne, T. P., Kang, Y. Y., & Lewis, B.(2002). *The physical markup language core components: Time and place* (MIT Auto-ID Center White Paper WH-005). Retrieved July 23, 2003, from http://www.autoidcenter.org/publishedresearch

Chau, P. Y. K., & Tam, K. Y. (2000). Organizational adoption of open systems: a `technology-push, need-pull' perspective. *Information and Management, 37*(5), 229-239.

Chin, W. W., & Marcolin, B. L. (2001). Special issue on adoption, diffusion & infusion of IT. *The DATA BASE for Advances in Information Systems, 32*(3), 7-12.

Comrey, A. L., & Lee, H. B. (1992). *A first course in factor analysis* (2nd ed.). Hillsdale, NJ: Lawrence Erlbaum Associates.

D'Amico, E. (2002). Steering clear of new costs. *Chemical Week, 164*(36), 30-32.

David, M. (2003). Networks to unlock the value of RFID: Speeding the adoption & lowering the costs of RFID in the retail supply chain. *Cisco Systems, Important Notices & Privacy Statement*, 1-7.

Davis, E. D., Bagozzi, R. R, & Warshaw, R. R. (1989). User acceptance of computer technology: A comparison of two theoretical models. *Management Science, 35*(8), 982-1003.

Davis, F. D. (1986). *A technology acceptance model for empirically testing new end-user information system: Theory and results.* Unpublished doctoral dissertation, Sloan School of Management, Massachusetts Institute of Technology, Cambridge, MA.

Davis, H. E., & Luehlging, M. H. (2004). Radio frequency identification: The wave of the future. *Journal of Accountancy*; *198*(5), 43-49.

Dornheim, M. A. (2002). Port security. *Aviation Week & Space Technology, 157*(7), 17.

Fichman, R. G. (1992, December). Information technology diffusion: a review of empirical research. In *Proceedings of the Thirteenth International Conference on Information Systems (ICIS)* (pp. 195-206). Dallas

Finkenzeller, K. (2003). *RFID-Handbook: Fundamentals and applications in contact-less smart cards and identification* (2nd ed.). New York: John Wiley &Sons.

Forcinio, H. (2002). Packaging advances showcases. *Pharmaceutical Technology North America, 26*(8), 22-30.

Gauvin, S., & Sinha, R. K. (1993). Innovativeness in industrial organizations: a two-stage model of adoption. *International Journal of Research in Marketing, 10*,165-183.

Goodhue, D. L. (1995). Understanding user evaluations of information systems. *Management Science, 41*(12), 1827-1844.

Goodhue, D. L., & Thompson, R. L. (1995).Task-technology fit and individual performance. *MIS Quarterly, 19*(2), 213-236.

Hair, J. F., Anderson, R. E., Tatham, R. L., & Black, W. C. (1998). *Multivariate data analysis* (5th ed.). New Jersey: Prentice Hall Inc.

IDTechEx. (2005). *RFID case study analysis.* Retrieved December 25, 2005, from http://www.idtechex.com/knowledgebase/en/breakdown.asp

Keen, P., & Mackintosh, R. (2001). *The freedom economy: Gaining the m-commerce edge in the era of the wireless Internet.* New York: McGraw-Hill.

Kern, C. (1999). RFID-technology- recent development and future requirements. In *Proceedings of the European Conference on Circuit Theory & Design ECCTD99* (pp. 25-28). Stresa

Langrish, J. (1972). *Wealth from knowledge: Studies of innovation in industry.* London: Macmillan.

Mahler, V., & Rogers, E. M. (1999). The diffusion of interactive communication innovations and the critical mass: the adoption of telecommunications services by German banks. *Telecommunication Policy, 23*(10-11), 719-740.

Mario, C., Ryan, G., Franziska, H., Kim, M., Chris, N., Natasha, S. et al. (2002). *RFID a week long survey on the technology and its potential.* Retrieved November 12, 2004, from http://www.interaction-ivrea.it/

Mathieson, K. (1991). Predicting user intentions: Comparing the technology acceptance model with the theory of planned behavior. *Information Systems Research, 2*(3), 173-191.

Mintchell, G. (2002). It's automatic: automation shifts transmission assembly into high gear. *Control Engineering, 49*(6), 12.

Mobile Internet in Taiwan. (2005). *RFID leads the way for the implementation of U-Taiwan*. Retrieved November 1, 2005, from http://www.find.org.tw/mit/200506/200506e/200506-008.htm

Moore, G. C., & Benbasat, I. (1991). Development of an instrument to measure the perceptions of adopting an information technology innovation. *Information Systems Research, 2*(3), 192-222.

Moore, G. C., & Benbasat, I. (1996). Integrating diffusion of innovations & theory of reasoned action models to predict utilization of information technology by end- users. In K. Kautz & J. Pries-Heje (Eds.), *Diffusion & adoption of information technology* (pp.132-146). London: Chapman & Hall.

Munro, H., & Noori, H. (1988). Measuring commitment to new manufacturing technology: integrating technological push and marketing pull concepts. *IEEE Transactions on Engineering Management, 35*(2), 63-70.

Ngai, E. W. T., Cheng, T. C. E., Au, S., & Lai, K. H. (2007). Mobile commerce integrated with RFID technology in a container depot. *Decision Support Systems, 43*, 62-76.

Peter, H., & Raghu, D. (2005). *RFID forecasts, players & opportunities 2005-2015*. IDTechEx.

Premkumar, G., & Potter, M. (1995). Adoption of computer aided software engineering (CASE) technology: an innovation adoption perspective. *DATA BASE, 26*(2&3), 105-124.

Prescott, M. B., & Conger, S. A. (1995). Information technology innovations: a classification by IT locus of impact & research approach. *DATA BASE, 26*(2&3), 20-41.

Rai, A. S., Lang, S., & Welker, R. B. (2002). Assessing the validity of IS success models: An empirical test & theoretical analysis. *Information Systems Research, 13*(1), 50-69.

Reik, W. R., Patrick, A., Snell, C. F. A., & Timothy, P. B. (2004). *RFID explained*. Robert W, Baird & Co. Incorporated, 12-13.

Roberts, C. M. (2006). Radio frequency identification (RFID). *Computers and Security, 25*, 18-26.

Rogers, E. M. (1962). *Diffusion of innovations*. New York: Free Press.

Rogers, E. M. (2003). *Diffusion of innovations* (5th ed.). New York: Free Press.

Saar, S., & Thomas, V. (2003). Toward trash that thinks product tags for environmental management. *Journal of Industrial Ecology, 6*(2), 133-146.

Schon, D. (1967). *Technology & social change*. New York: Delacorte.

Shih, D. H., Sun, P. L., & Chiu, Y. W. (2004, October). Barriers to radio frequency identifier. In *Proceedings of the 1st Conference of Service Management and Innovation,* Taiwan.

Smith, H. A., & Konsynski, B. (2003). Developments in practice X: radio frequency identification (RFID)—an Internet for physical objects. *Communications of the Association for Information Systems, 12*, 301-311.

Swedberg, C. (2006, September 12). Wal-Mart's on track to hit target. *RFID Journal*. Retrieved September 30, 2006, from http://www.rfidjournal.com/article/articleview/2649/

Taipei Rapid Transit Corporation Annual Report. (2003). *Corporate overviews*. Retrieved September 30, 2004, from http://www.trtc.com.tw/img/all/A61/report2002-2003.pdf

Taiwan Investment Biweekly. (2005). *U Taiwan: RFID called second IT revolution*. Retrieved October 15, 2006, from http://investintaiwan.nat.gov.tw/en/news/200504/2005042902.html

Taylor, S., & Todd, R. A. (1995). Understanding information technology usage: A test of competing models. *Information Systems Research, 6*(2), 144-176.

Tom, S. (2003). *Understanding RFID: A practical guide for supply chain professionals.* Retrieved September 10, 2004, http://www.tompkinsinc.com, 6-7.

Tornatzky, L.G., & Klein, R. J. (1982). Innovation characteristics & innovation adoption-implementation: a meta-analysis of findings. *IEEE Transactions on Engineering Management, 29*, 28-45.

Werb, J., & Sereiko, P. (2002). More than just tracking. *Frontline Solutions, 3*(11), 42.

Wu, J. H., & Wang, S. C. (2005). What drives mobile commerce? An empirical evaluation of the revised technology acceptance model. *Information & Management, 42*(5), 719-729.

Wu, N. C., Nystrom, M. A., Lin, T. R., & Yu, H. C. (2006). Challenges to global RFID adoption. *Technovation, 26*, 1317-1323.

Zmud, R. W. (1984). An examination of push-pull theory applied to process innovation in knowledge work. *Management Science, 30*(6), 727-738.

Karkkainen, M.(2003). Increasing efficiency in the supply chain for short shelf life goods using RFID tagging. *International Journal of Retail & Distribution Management, 31*(10), 529-536.

APPENDIX A

Survey measures of perceive benefit of adoption RFID system

1...... Better shipping and receiving productivity
2...... Increased order accuracy
3...... Better returns processing
4...... Improved raw materials receipts accuracy
5...... Better WIP inventory management
6...... Better receiving labor productivity
7...... Better asset use through tracking of vehicles
8...... Reusable containers
9...... Visibility of other high-value assets
10...... Improved recall management
11...... Improved lot track and trace
12...... Better expiration date management
13...... Improvements in shrink
14...... Reduction in inventory and working capital
15...... Improved revenue through reduction in out-of-stocks
16...... Reduced expediting costs

Survey measures of perceive barrier to implement RFID system

1...... Complexity of integration with existing systems
2...... Cost of RFID tags and readers
3...... Overall cost of implementation
4...... Competing business priorities
5...... High investment in current solutions
6...... Initial decrease in productivity
7...... Lack of executive sponsorship
8...... Consumer perceptions/privacy concerns
9...... Intellectual property rights/grey market issues
10...... Legislation/government policy
11...... Data synchronization
12...... Lack of standards
13...... Market not stable/too early

This work was previously published in Ubiquitous and Pervasive Computing: Concepts, Methodologies, Tools, and Applications, edited by J. Symonds, pp. 1122-1143, copyright 2010 by Information Science Reference (an imprint of IGI Global).

Chapter 15
Within-Culture Variation and Information Technology:
An Empirical Assessment

Jennifer E. Gerow
Clemson University, USA

Edith Galy
University of Texas at Brownsville, USA

Jason Bennett Thatcher
Clemson University, USA

Mark Srite
University of Wisconsin-Milwaukee, USA

ABSTRACT

This study examines within-culture variance in the influence of values on perceptions and use of information technology (IT). Based on cross-cultural research, the authors suggest cultural values influence technology acceptance and use. Specifically, this chapter argues masculinity/femininity and individualism/collectivism directly influence personal innovativeness with IT, computer anxiety, and computer self-efficacy and have a mediated effect on perceived usefulness, perceived ease of use, and use of IT. Overall, analysis provides support for the research model. Results suggest masculinity/femininity influences computer self-efficacy, computer anxiety, and personal innovativeness with IT. The authors also offer implications for research and practice.

INTRODUCTION

Because migration has resulted in increasingly diverse nation states, information technology (IT) managers have had to develop IT implementation strategies that accommodate diverse cultural values in organizations. Within the existing cross-cultural MIS literature, researchers have examined national culture's influence on IT use in organizations. In general, culture has been synonymous with national boundaries, but a nation could be composed of people of various cultures, and these cultures could also be present in more than one country (Straub et al., 2002).

DOI: 10.4018/978-1-60566-920-5.ch015

Despite challenges posed by globalization for IT managers, limited management information systems (MIS) research has examined the cultural implications of values for IT in organizations (Gallupe & Tan, 1999) (notable exceptions including Cyr et al.'s. (2005), Segev et al.'s (2007), and Cyr's (2008) studies of the impact of within and between culture preferences on web design elements and Zahedi, et al.'s (2006) study of cultural signifiers of masculinity/femininity in websites). Within-culture differences refers to examining the relationship between cultural values and beliefs, attitudes, or behaviors of individuals within a single nation-state (Berry, 1979). Examining within-culture differences is important because cultural psychologists generally agree that indicators such as citizenship or location are weak proxies for individuals' value systems (Fiske, 2002). Research has found that variations in cultural values within nation-states influence individuals' situation specific behavior and beliefs (Oysterman et al., 2002). When extended to the domain of IT, this suggests cultural values may predispose individuals to respond differently to information technologies (Karahanna et al., 2005). Hence, this study examines the following question: does within-culture variation influence information technology acceptance and use?

The paper unfolds as follows; first, cultural values and their relationship to situation-specific traits are reviewed. The research model is then developed. The next section empirically examines the hypothesized relationships. The paper concludes with a discussion of findings, limitations, implications for research and practice, and future directions.

LITERATURE REVIEW

Culture refers to values, traits, beliefs, and behavioral patterns that may characterize a group of people. Hofstede (1991) suggests that culture reflects a composite of human nature (i.e., inherited predispositions shared by all human beings) and personality (i.e., values and more malleable traits inherited or learned by individuals). Although human nature is intransigent, values and traits are shaped by individuals' life experiences (Hofstede, 1991). Values are acquired early in life, mainly through the family, the neighborhood, and later through school (while traits are learned later).

Within countries, individuals' values vary with their participation in groups based on, for example, nationality, religion, and ethnicity. As a result, Straub et al. (2002) suggest that an individual's cultural values "represents that amalgamation of cultures across boundaries (national, organizational, professional, etc.) which fuse together to create one's overall culture. This combination is unique to each individual" (p. 4). Because values are enduring and relatively stable, they may influence the development of more malleable traits that influence individuals' behavior. Traits (also termed practices) are learned later, through socialization at the workplace, after an individual's values are firmly in place. In this study we look at two particular measures of cultural values (masculinity/femininity and individualism/collectivism) and how these values influence three traits (personal innovativeness with IT, computer anxiety, and computer self-efficacy). In turn we examine how these traits affect beliefs of usefulness and ease of use and, ultimately, IT usage.

Traits refer to predispositions to respond to stimuli. Individual traits can be viewed on a continuum from stable to malleable (Ghiselli et al., 1981). Not unlike values, stable traits influence individual behavior across situations. However, some traits are considered to be more malleable, such as computer anxiety and computer self-efficacy (as examined in this study) (Chen et al., 2000). Unlike stable traits, malleable, situation-specific traits may vary with the stimuli and may be changed through interventions, such as training. For example, where the general trait of anxiety exerts an influence across multiple stimuli, computer anxiety is a response linked to a specific stimulus (i.e., computers or IT) that may be reduced through training or experience. Research suggests that values may predispose individuals to express malleable, situation-specific traits. (Bandura et al., 1977; Draguns, 1979; Steenkamp et al., 1999). Hence, while organizational interventions may evoke changes in malleable traits, cultural values may predispose individuals to express malleable traits such as computer anxiety or innovativeness over time.

Within the cross-cultural psychology literature, a growing body of research suggests that examining links between values and malleable traits should extend understanding of how to manage increasingly multi-ethnic workforces (Pineda & Whitehead, 1997; Oysterman et al., 2002). Until recently, MIS researchers have left unexamined the influence of within-culture differences on individuals' IT-specific traits and related beliefs or behaviors (see Crump et al., 2007; Trauth et al., 2008). In general, MIS studies assume individuals possess the cultural values associated with their country of residence (Straub et al., 2002; Gallivan & Srite, 2005). In reality, there might be a great deal of cultural variation within a multi-ethnic nation with several dominant languages and religions (e.g. India or Israel (Enoch and Soker 2006)).

To extend our understanding of within-culture differences' influence on IT acceptance and use, this study examines the relationship between cultural values and malleable traits that lead to IT-focused beliefs and behaviors. We suggest broad cultural values directly affect individuals' malleable, IT-specific traits. In turn, individuals' IT-specific traits influence beliefs about IT. Through gaining a deeper understanding of the influence of values on IT-specific traits and consequently their relationship to beliefs, we contend research may inform how to develop IT implementation strategies and training programs that encourage IT use in culturally diverse environments. The next section of the study develops hypotheses that link variance in cultural values to individuals' usage of information technology.

RESEARCH MODEL

Technology Acceptance

The research model (see Figure 1) uses the Technology Acceptance Model (TAM) as a starting point. Rooted in the Theory of Reasoned Action (TRA), TAM (Davis, 1989) posits that two beliefs, perceived usefulness (PU) and perceived ease of use (PEOU), are important predictors of IT use. In the model, perceived ease of use influences perceived usefulness and, in turn, both beliefs influence behavioral intention to use (BIU) which is a measure of the strength of a person's intention to use an IT (Ajzen & Fishbein, 1980).

Numerous studies have provided empirical support for TAM (Davis, 1989; Davis, 1993; Szajna, 1994; Keil et al., 1995; Taylor & Todd, 1995; Morris & Venkatesh, 2000; Venkatesh & Davis, 2000; Venkatesh & Morris, 2000; Venkatesh et al., 2003). It should be noted however, that a few studies have found non-significant (Jackson et al., 1997) or marginally significant (Chan & Lu, 2004; Elbeltagi et al., 2005) relationships between perceptions of usefulness and behavioral intentions to use/IT use. Elbeltagi, McBride et al. (2005) also found a negative relationship between perceptions of usefulness and usage. Additionally, the relationship between perceptions of ease of use and intentions/use has also been found non-significant in some studies (Adams et al., 1992; Bagozzi et al., 1992; Igbaria et al., 1995; Hu et al., 1999). Furthermore, early TAM studies (Davis, 1989; Mathieson, 1991) incorporated attitudes toward the technology and/or behavioral intention to use as a mediating variable. Attitudes were subsequently dropped from the model, and BIU was modeled as a direct function of PU and PEOU (Taylor & Todd, 1995; Szajna, 1996). Since then, a number of studies have also posited a direct relationship from perceived usefulness and ease of use to self-reported IT use (Szajna, 1994; Straub et al., 1995; Gefen & Straub, 1997; Karahanna & Straub, 1999). This study will utilize the simpler

Figure 1. Research model

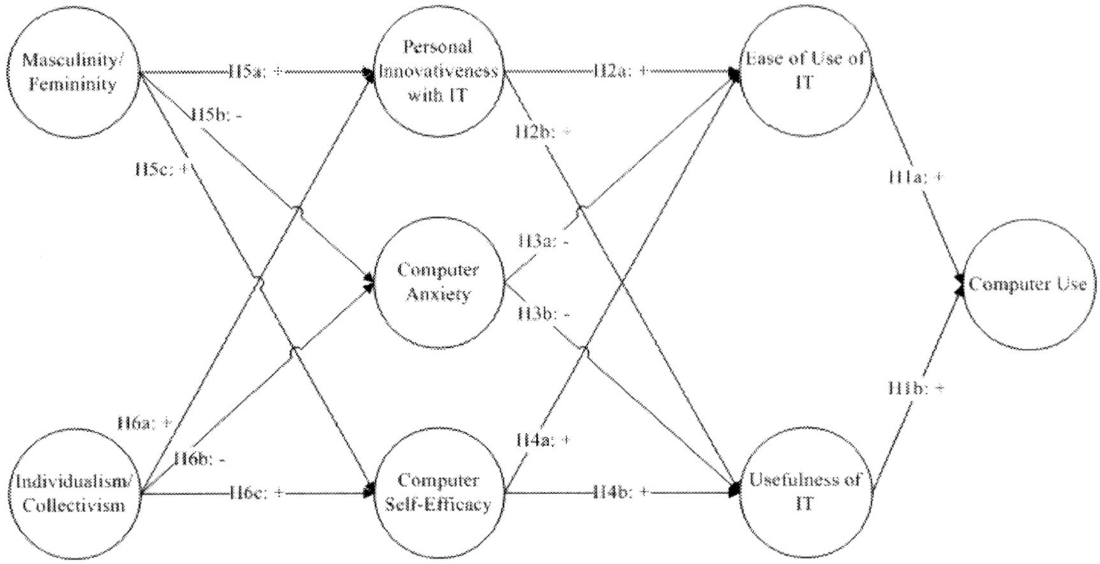

configuration of TAM, which has perceptions of usefulness and ease of use directly influencing IT use. Hence:

H1a: *Perceived usefulness will have a positive effect on IT use.*
H1b: *Perceived ease of use will have a positive effect on IT use.*

Antecedents to Perceived Ease of Use and Perceived Usefulness of IT

Prior research suggests that malleable IT-specific traits may influence the development of PU and PEOU(Agarwal & Karahanna, 2000; Venkatesh, 2000). As noted by Davis (1989), external variables such as attitudes and values are antecedents to perceived usefulness and perceived ease of use.

This study examines three antecedents: personal innovativeness with IT, computer anxiety, and computer self-efficacy. These antecedents were chosen over other antecedents for two reasons. First, our interest in this study is in integrating within-culture variance of values with the existing literature on technology acceptance. Since the 1980s, computer anxiety and computer self-efficacy have been extensively examined in the MIS literature (Marakas et al., 1998). Although introduced relatively recently, personal innovativeness with information technology has received substantial attention in the top management information systems journals (please see (Agarwal & Karahanna, 2000; Thatcher & Perrewe, 2002)). In order to extend the nomological net surrounding IT acceptance and use, we felt it important to theoretically and empirically link values to well-established antecedents to IT use. Second, as noted by Hofstede (1984), culture is composed of the enduring ways of thinking of a group. If cultural values exert a pervasive influence on the formation of individual traits and beliefs, theory suggests that cultural values should influence malleable traits/practices such as innovativeness, computer anxiety, and computer self-efficacy (Straub et al., 2002). Additionally, it was felt that more malleable traits/practices such as innovativeness, computer anxiety, and computer self-efficacy would be more likely to be homogenous within specific cultures and yet vary across cultures than would more quantifiable variables such as level of prior experience. Each antecedent will be discussed in detail in the sections that follow.

Personal Innovativeness with IT. Personal innovativeness with IT refers to "the willingness of an individual to try out any new IT"(Agarwal & Prasad, 1998, p. 205). Agarwal and Prasad (1998) proposed a dual role for personal innovativeness in relation to technology acceptance. They posited that personal innovativeness moderates both the relationship between information about a new IT from alternative channels and perceptions about a new IT (such as perceived usefulness) and the relationship between perceptions about a new IT and intentions to use a new IT. Ndubisi et. al (2005) also proposed and tested innovation as a moderating relationship. Other research has modeled personal innovativeness as a direct antecedent to IT-related beliefs. Karahanna et al. (1999), drawing on the same definition of personal innovativeness, found that personal innovativeness had a direct effect on perceived usefulness and perceived ease of use, as did Mao et. al. (2005). Consequently, instead of looking at personal innovativeness as a moderator, it will be posited as a direct antecedent of perceived usefulness and perceived ease of use. It can be argued that an individual who is more innovative will be better able to see alternative ways of using a technology and be better able to identify useful applications of a technology. Hence:

H2a:*Personal innovativeness with IT will have a positive effect on perceptions of usefulness of IT.*

H2b:*Personal innovativeness with IT will have a positive effect on perceptions of ease of use of IT.*

Computer Anxiety. Anxiety refers to an unpleasant emotional state or condition characterized by feelings of tension or worry (Spielberger et al., 1970). Anxious people frequently avoid the threat posed by a situation and avoid stimuli likely to generate feelings of anxiety (Tellegen, 1985). Computer anxiety (CA) refers to "fear of impending interaction with a computer that is disproportionate to the actual threat presented by the computer" (Howard et al., 1986). Computer anxiety has been conceptualized as a malleable trait that reflects responses to the environment and stable, broadly defined traits or values (Thatcher & Perrewe, 2002). Research has consistently found a direct link from CA to computer attitudes and computer use (Igbaria et al., 1996; Brosnan, 1999). People who report high levels of computer anxiety frequently choose not to use information technology (Igbaria et al., 1989) and report less positive attitudes towards information technology (Igbaria & Chakrabarti, 1990). For example, Brown, Fuller, and Vician (2004) found that CA had a positive effect on computer mediated communication anxiety and a mediated effect on attitude towards IT use and actual usage behavior. Consistent with prior MIS research (Venkatesh, 2000; Venkatesh & Davis, 2000; Venkatesh & Morris, 2000), we propose that computer anxiety negatively affects beliefs leading to IT use. Hence:

H3a:*Computer anxiety will have a negative effect on the perceived usefulness of IT.*

H3b:*Computer anxiety will have a negative effect on the perceived ease of use of IT.*

Computer Self-Efficacy. The construct of self-efficacy, as opposed to computer self-efficacy, has been extensively studied in the field of social psychology (Bandura, 1977; Brown & Inouye, 1978; Barling & Beattie, 1983; Wood & Bandura, 1989). General self-efficacy can be defined as an individual's belief that he/she has the ability to perform a particular behavior (Compeau & Higgins, 1995a). Self-efficacy has also been examined with respect to a number of management situations (Betz & Hackett, 1981; Taylor et al., 1984; Jones, 1986; Frayne & Latham, 1987; Latham & Frayne, 1989).

Computer self-efficacy (CSE), a situation-specific form of efficacy, refers to individuals' judgment of their capabilities to use computers (Compeau et al., 1999). Evidence has been found that supports a relationship between CSE and a number of computer-related behaviors (Hill et al., 1986; Hill et al., 1987; Gist, 1989; Burkhardt & Brass, 1990; Webster & Martocchio, 1992; Webster & Martocchio, 1993). Research has also suggested that those individuals who have high CSE beliefs are more likely to report higher perceptions of usefulness and perceptions of ease of use (Marakas et al., 1998). Prior research supports the notion that computer self-efficacy positively influences beliefs about diverse information technologies (Marakas et al., 1998). Hence:

H4a: *Computer self-efficacy will have a positive effect on the perceived usefulness of IT.*
H4b: *Computer self-efficacy will have a positive effect on the perceived ease of use of IT.*

Culture

The final series of hypotheses link cultural values to personal innovativeness, computer anxiety, and computer self-efficacy. Cross-cultural researchers have identified an array of cultural values such as masculinity/femininity, individualism/collectivism, power distance, time orientation and uncertainty avoidance (Hofstede, 1991). Please see Straub et. al. (2002) for a more complete listing of cultural dimensions. Although each value may influence IT use, due to space limitations we focus on two frequently researched values in this study, masculinity/femininity and individualism/collectivism. Although numerous other dimensions of culture exist and could be seen as potential candidates for this study, particularly uncertainty avoidance, power distance, and long-term orientation, we chose to narrow the focus of our study to the two chosen dimensions for three reasons. First, our subjects had a limited time to complete the survey and, as we wanted to examine the participants' actual cultural values, the addition of additional dimensions would have made the survey considerably longer. Second, given the complexity of our model, the addition of more paths could have led to issues of validity and reliability. Third, we feel masculinity/femininity and individualism/collectivism are the more salient dimensions with respect to the other constructs of the study. To some extent, uncertainty avoidance, which focuses on risk, is already in the model as personal innovativeness incorporates the idea of risk. Power distance, we also feel, was less applicable in that the technology (that of PC use) was volitional, whereas power distance would seem to relate to more mandatory technology use situations. However, we also feel the influence of other dimensions of culture on our research model would be a valid area for future research.

There have been a number of criticisms of Hofstede's measures and method as well as his country-level scores being reused by later researchers studying different populations (Erez & Early, 1993; Tayeb, 1994; Myers & Tan, 2002; Gallivan & Srite, 2005). In spite of these issues, his dimensions have been well received by both practicing managers and academics. These limitations are less of an issue in this study as we are directly measuring the two cultural dimensions in question with revised and updated scales.

Masculinity/Femininity. Masculinity/femininity refers to the beliefs of individuals about gender roles. Masculine cultures tend to have distinct gender roles that expect men to emphasize work goals such as earnings, advancement, and assertiveness. Feminine cultures tend to emphasize good communication skills, flexibility (Crump et al., 2007), and personal goals such as maintaining a friendly atmosphere, getting along with coworkers (Hoecklin, 1995; Crump et al., 2007), and having a comfortable work environment (Hoecklin, 1995). At the individual level of analysis, masculinity and femininity are rooted in a person's socialization rather than biological sex (Stets & Burke, 2000). The economic and cultural influences of society provide cues on appropriate gender roles (Trauth et al., 2008), and males frequently assume more masculine roles while females assume more feminine roles. However, because the gender roles are socially defined, it is possible for individuals to be biologically one sex and perceive themselves in the opposite sex's gender role.

Masculinity/femininity may influence traits and beliefs that lead to IT use. Cultural values embedded in gender roles may send signals about appropriate responses to and uses of IT (Gefen, 2000). For example, when compared to girls, boys receive more encouragement to use computers and participate in computer training programs (Ahuja, 2002); consequently, men typically hold more technical positions while women are more likely to work with the "softer side" of IT (Crump et al., 2007). In addition, research suggests that women and men demonstrate distinct electronic communication styles (Stowers, 1995) and report different reasons for accepting new ITs (Gefen & Straub, 1997). Research (Trauth, 2002) has also examined gender differences, particularly women's interactions with IT, and found disparity in computer conferencing and communications styles between women and men. Taken together, this research suggests that one's perceptions of what is appropriate or inappropriate behavior may vary with one's conception of masculinity and femininity (Trauth, 1999; Kase & Trauth, 2003).

Even though masculinity/femininity reflect socialization, MIS researchers frequently use biological sex, not individuals' values, as a proxy for individuals' beliefs about gender roles and associated responses to IT (Venkatesh & Morris, 2000). Within the domain of MIS, studies have found that biological sex influences malleable traits such as computer anxiety, self-efficacy, or innovativeness (Ahuja, 2002) as well as technology acceptance decisions (Gefen & Straub, 1997). Using biological sex as a proxy for masculinity/femininity is problematic because it frequently does not necessarily map to beliefs about gender roles (Ashmore et al., 1986). As a result, we extend prior research by examining whether variance in masculinity/femininity influences individuals' predispositions towards IT use. Due to differences in socialization, we hypothesize that individuals from more masculine cultures will express greater computer self-efficacy, report less computer anxiety, and are more willing to explore new uses of IT. Hence:

H5a: *Masculinity/Femininity will have an effect on personal innovativeness with IT such that individuals high in masculinity will be more innovative.*

H5b: *Masculinity/Femininity will have an effect on computer anxiety such that individuals high in masculinity will report less computer anxiety.*

H5c: *Masculinity/Femininity will have an effect on computer self-efficacy such that individuals high in masculinity will report greater computer self-efficacy.*

Individualism/Collectivism. Individualism/collectivism refers to the extent to which individuals' emphasis and identity is centered on the self or the group. People who are high on individualism tend to think of themselves as "I," classify themselves by their individual characteristics, and prefer independent action. On the other hand, people high on collectivism tend to focus on the needs of the group over their personal needs (Hoecklin, 1995). Societies differ in their emphasis on individual rights and obligation to society. Individualism describes societies in which the ties between individuals are loose and people are expected to look after themselves. Collectivism is the other extreme where people are integrated into strong, cohesive groups that protect an individual. Within the cross-cultural psychology literature, individualism/collectivism is perhaps the most frequently researched cultural dimension (Oysterman et al., 2002). Within the MIS literature, researchers have found that people from nations characterized by higher individualism are more likely to accept ITs (Gefen & Straub, 1997).

Individualism/collectivism may influence personal innovativeness with information technology. Theorists suggest that people who are high on individualism are likely to be more inventive and non-conformist when compared to their more collectivist peers. When high on individualism, people are less susceptible to social pressure to conform with accepted practices and consequently more likely to be inventive (Hampden-Turner & Trompenaars, 1993) or independent in their search for personal fulfillment (Redding & Baldwin, 1991). Empirical research supports the notion that individualism/collectivism influences innovativeness within specific domains. For example, Steenkamp et al. (1999) found that people from more individualistic cultures were likely to express more personally innovative consumption patterns. When using IT, highly individualistic people's non-conformist values should pre-dispose them to express higher levels of personal innovativeness with IT. The opposite should hold true for people with highly collectivistic values; their desire to conform to societal norms should lower their personal innovativeness with IT.

Not unlike personal innovativeness with IT, individualism/collectivism may influence computer anxiety and computer-self efficacy. Highly individualistic people value independent initiative, capability, and achievement. People in individualistic cultures are more likely to stay current in terms of management ideas and hence be more receptive to, and less anxious regarding, new technologies (Hofstede, 1984). Because individual initiative and achievement may lead to a strong sense of personal capability and lower anxiety, higher levels of individualism may negatively influence a person's computer anxiety and positively influence a person's judgment of their capabilities to use computers in diverse situations (i.e., result in higher self-efficacy) (Bandura, 1997). Because people from individualistic cultures may have a higher sense of their capability, we posit that they will express less computer anxiety and greater computer self-efficacy. Hence:

H6a: *Individualism/Collectivism will have an effect on personal innovativeness with IT such that individuals who are high in individualism will be more innovative.*

H6b: *Individualism/Collectivism will have an effect on computer anxiety such that individuals who are high in individualism will express less computer anxiety.*

H6c: *Individualism/Collectivism will have an effect on computer self-efficacy such that individuals who are high in individualism will express greater computer self-efficacy.*

METHOD

Subjects and Measures

A survey was administered to 350 students enrolled in business classes at three public universities in the United States. Table 1 presents sample characteristics. Although data were collected at US schools, recent research suggests American students possess more heterogeneous value systems when compared to peers in more culturally homogenous countries such as Japan or Korea (Oysterman et al., 2002). To test the heterogeneity of American students, they were asked a series of Likert type items about their views on two of the four cultural dimensions identified by Hofstede (1984). Our inspection of means and standard deviations suggested there was substantial variance in cultural values within our sample (see Table 2).

Measures were drawn from the management of information systems and cultural literatures and were distributed throughout a larger questionnaire examining beliefs, perceptions, and use of information technology. Items and their sources may be found in the Appendix. All items were anchored with 1 = strongly disagree and 7 = strongly agree. To measure use, respondents were asked to

Table 1. Sample characteristics

		Number	
Total		350	
Sex	Male	172	
	Female	168	
Ethnicity	African-American	50	
	Hispanic-American	123	
	White	145	
	Asian-American	8	
	Multiple Responses	6	
	Other	18	
		Mean	**Standard Deviation**
Age		23.4	4.8
Years of College		3.5	1.5
Years of Computer Use		7.9	3.9
Number of Computer Courses		3.6	2.6
Hours of Computer Use Per Week			
	School	6.0	5.4
	Work	7.1	8.3
	Other	6.2	5.9

identify how many hours they used computers for school, work, and other activities each week. The responses were summed and used as a single item in the data analysis. Table 2 presents construct

Table 2. Descriptive statistics and covariance of latent constructs

	Construct	Items	Mean	S.D.	Covariance of Latent Constructs[a]							
					(1)	(2)	(3)	(4)	(5)	(6)	(7)	(8)
(1)	Individualism/Collectivism	5	3.85	1.13	**0.78**							
(2)	Masculinity/Femininity	5	2.71	1.38	.38	**0.84**						
(3)	Computer Anxiety	4	2.58	1.20	.07	.26	**0.81**					
(4)	Computer Self-Efficacy	10	6.50	2.10	.02	.11	-.03	**0.88**				
(5)	Personal Innovativeness with Information Technology	3	4.94	1.43	.03	.13	-.04	.02	**0.83**			
(6)	Perceived Ease of Use of IT	4	5.24	1.11	.02	-.22	-.53	.12	.60	**0.93**		
(7)	Perceived Usefulness of IT	4	5.85	1.00	.00	.14	-.25	.11	.52	.44	**0.92**	
(8)	Hours of Computer Use	1	19.31	14.6	.00	.00	-.17	.04	.21	.19	.32	**n.a.**

[a] Diagonal element of the correlation of constructs is the Cronbach's □.

means, standard deviations, and reliabilities. Data were analyzed for outliers and normality, and, in fact the data displayed a normal distribution curve and no significant outliers were discovered. We elected to survey our participants as to their perceptions regarding general computer usefulness and ease of use as opposed to perceptions of a specific system to ensure familiarity with the technology as well as having well-formed beliefs regarding the technology. Although there might be some issues of habitual use with our selection, we feel these general perceptions are appropriate to tie into our dependent variable of actual general computer use.

Analysis

The model was tested using LISREL 8.54 (Joreskog & Sorbom, 2003). Analysis was patterned after Andersen and Gerbing's (1988) two-step structural equation modeling procedure. In the first step, the fit of the measurement model was assessed. In the second step, the full structural model was tested.

RESULTS

Step One: Measurement Model

The measurement model examines the relationships of the observed variables to the underlying latent constructs. In this study, 36 observed variables (items) were used to predict eight latent constructs. With a ratio of observations (n = 350) to observed variables (n = 35) or latent constructs (n = 8) greater than 5:1, our sample size was sufficient to evaluate the measurement model (Bentler & Chou, 1987).

To demonstrate unidimensionality of the constructs, a confirmatory factor analysis was performed. A correlation matrix of the 36 items was entered into LISREL. Each item was mapped to the appropriate latent construct. Results from this analysis (CFI = .96, PNFI = .77, RMSEA = .04) indicated a strong fit of the overall measurement model. Inspection of standardized path loadings revealed that they were significant and ranged from 1.15 to .26. These results suggest that the observed variables uniquely represent the latent constructs.

Having established unidimensionality, convergent and discriminant validity were examined. Convergent validity was established by comparing the coefficient for the indicators with their standard errors (Anderson & Gerbing, 1988). To be convergent, the standardized path loading for the indicators of a construct must be at least twice its standard error (Anderson & Gerbing, 1988). Because all of the standardized path loadings (.89 to .96) were greater than twice their standard errors (.04 to .20), convergent validity was demonstrated for this study. Discriminant validity was tested by constraining the estimated correlation parameter between two scales to 1.00 and comparing the resulting chi-square (X^2) to the X^2 obtained from the measurement model (Anderson & Gerbing, 1988). If the chi-square of the measurement model is significantly lower than when the correlation is set to 1.00, discriminant validity is shown. This test required calculating 25 chi-square different tests for each pair of latent constructs. Results showed that all chi-square difference tests were significant, thus indicating discriminant validity. Because the measurement model demonstrated overall fit, and requirements for convergent and discriminant validity were satisfied, the next step tested the structural model.

Step Two: Structural Model

To rigorously assess the measurement model, Anderson and Gerbing (1988) suggest conducting a series of nested model comparisons (see Table 3). Each model represents a competing explanation for the relationships found in the data. Support

Table 3. Structural model and overall goodness of fit indices [abcdef]

Model	d.f.	X^2	X^2/d.f.	GFI	AGFI	CFI	PNFI	RMSEA
Model 1 - Structural Null Model	583	894.22	1.53	0.88	0.85	0.96	0.77	0.04
Model 2 - Research Model	596	1020.44	1.71	0.86	0.84	0.94	0.78	0.04
Model 3 - Partial Mediation Model A	593	1011.3	1.71	0.87	0.84	0.94	0.77	0.04
Model 4 - Partial Mediation Model B	592	1016.6	1.72	0.87	0.84	0.94	0.77	0.05
Model 5 - Nearly Saturated Model	591	993.68	1.68	0.87	0.84	0.94	0.77	0.04

[a] X^2/d.f. - To show good fit, Gefen et al (2000) suggest that this ratio needs to be between 1 and 2.

[b] GFI (Goodness of fit index) indicates how well the covariance matrix estimated by the hypothesized model reproduces the observed covariance matrix. Values greater than .90 indicate good fit.

[c] AGFI (Adjusted Goodness of Fit Index) adjusts the GFI by the degrees of freedom to take into consideration the sample size and reflects the parsimony of the model. Values greater than .80 indicate good fit.

[d] CFI (Comparative Fit Index) provides a measure of the proportion of total covariance accounted for by a model. Values less than .90 indicate that the model can be substantially improved.

[e] PNFI(Parsimony Fit Index) is a ratio between covariance explained and number of parameters estimated. A good PNFI indicates that a large amount of variance is explained with only a few parameters. Values greater than .60 illustrate good fit.

[f] RMSEA (Root Mean Square Error of Approximation) represents the average of the residuals of the fitted covariance matrix from the observed covariance matrix and approximates the amount of error in the model. Should be less than .08 and cannot be used to compare models, only to illustrate fit.

for a theoretical model is found when it achieves the "best goodness of fit" relative to less or more complex rival models.

The structural model was tested by examining five nested alternative models. Each model was estimated using the covariance matrix of latent constructs derived from the item correlation matrix. The models were estimated in the following sequence. First, the structural null model (Model 1) was estimated (Anderson & Gerbing, 1988). This model restricted all relationships between latent constructs to 0. Next, the research model (Model 2) that included the proposed relationships between latent constructs was estimated. The next three models tested whether adding additional paths increased the models' fit. These models were estimated to test alternative explanations of the relationships between the constructs presented in the research model. Because personal innovativeness with IT, computer anxiety, and computer self-efficacy might have influenced computer usage, Model 3 added paths from these constructs to computer usage. Because cultural values might have influenced specific beliefs, Model 4 added paths from masculinity/femininity and individualism/collectivism to perceived ease of use and usefulness of IT. Finally, a nearly saturated model that included the direct and indirect effects examined in Models 2, 3, and 4 was estimated. To evaluate alternative models, methodologists suggest using parsimony as a decision rule (Anderson & Gerbing, 1988). Table 3 presents and explains goodness of fit measures for the structural models.

All five structural models demonstrated reasonably good fit with the observed data. Models 1 to 5 demonstrated comparable X^2 to degrees of freedom (DF) (1.53 to 1.72), AGFI's (.85 to .84) and RMSEA's (0.06). It is important to note that we did not meet the heuristic of .90 suggested by Gefen, Straub, and Boudreau (2000) for the GFI. Although the GFI's were not at an ideal level, they were sufficiently close to the .90 threshold (.88 to .86) to move forward with evaluating the model. Also, because we met the heuristics for

Figure 2. Research model results

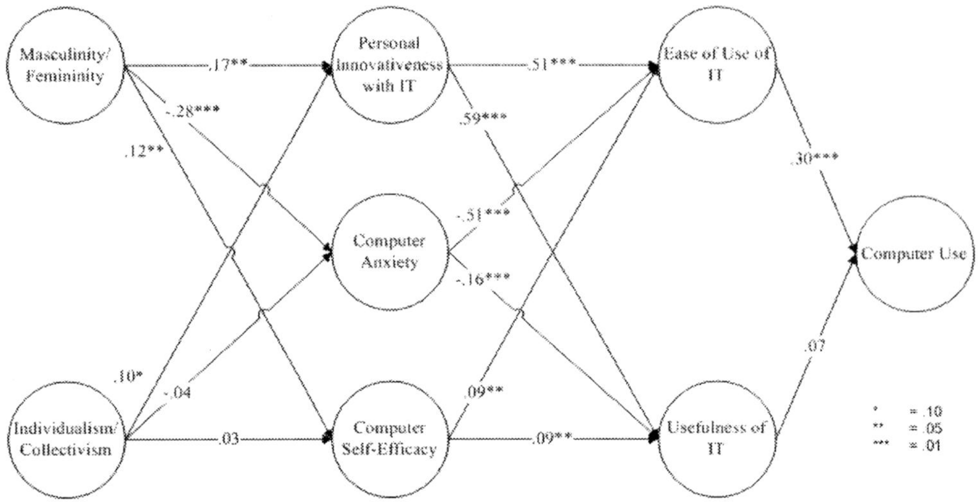

using the other measures, we were comfortable with the overall fit of the research model (Bollen, 1989; Gefen et al., 2000).

Because the nested models demonstrated comparable fit, a second way of comparing models is to identify which possesses the fewest number of insignificant paths (Kacmar et al., 1999). A review of the models revealed that paths added in Models 3, 4, and 5 were not significant. This suggests that the research model (Model 2) presents the most parsimonious explanation for the relationships between constructs examined in this study.

Analysis provides support for the research model. Figure 2 presents research model results. Beliefs about information technology explained moderate amount of variance in information technology use ($R^2 = .10$). Perceived ease of use was a strong positive predictor of IT use (H1b: $p < .01$). However, perceived usefulness did not demonstrate a direct effect on IT. This lack of support for the relationship between usefulness and use is interesting. Showing where well-supported theories do not hold up can provide insight complementary to showing where they are supported. It is possible that utility may not be a particularly strong driver with respect to students. They may use a computer for other reasons such as entertainment and communicating with friends and family.

Large amounts of variance were explained in the perceived ease of use ($R^2 = .62$) and perceived usefulness of IT ($R^2 = .33$). As hypothesized, personal innovativeness with IT demonstrated a strong positive relationship with perceived usefulness (H2a: $p < .05$) and perceived ease of use (H2b: $p < .05$). Computer anxiety showed a significant negative relationship with perceived usefulness (H3a: $p < .01$) and perceived ease of use (H3b: $p < .01$). Computer self-efficacy demonstrated a statistically significant relationship with perceived usefulness (H4a: $p < .05$) and perceived ease of use (H4b: $p < .05$).

Within-culture variance in values demonstrated a modest relationship to computer anxiety, computer self-efficacy, and personal innovativeness with IT. Cultural values explained a small amount of variance in computer anxiety ($R^2 = .07$) and minor amounts of variance in computer self-efficacy ($R^2 = .01$) and personal innovativeness with information technology ($R^2 = .03$). use (H1a: n.s.). Next we turn to discussing the implications of the results.

Masculinity/femininity was significantly related to personal innovativeness with information technology (H5a: $p < .05$), computer anxiety (H5b: $p < .01$), and computer self-efficacy (H5c: $p < .01$). Individualism/collectivism was not significantly related to computer anxiety (H6b: n.s.) or computer self-efficacy (H6c: n.s.) and demonstrated a weak relationship with personal innovativeness with information technology (H6a: $p < .10$).

DISCUSSION

Data analysis provided limited support for within-culture variance in values influencing IT-specific traits, beliefs, and behavior. Masculinity/femininity was found to influence the malleable traits (personal innovativeness with IT, computer avoidance, and computer self-efficacy). However, individualism/collectivism did not demonstrate significant relationships to these malleable traits. Personal innovativeness with IT, computer anxiety and computer self-efficacy influenced beliefs about information technology (perceptions of use and perceptions of ease of use). Perceptions of ease of use were found to influence use.

Our findings provide mixed support for relationships found in prior MIS research. Perceived ease of use (H1a: $p < .01$) positively influenced IT use. However, perceived usefulness of IT (H1b) did not significantly affect use. Our results contrast with findings in the broader IT diffusion literature that suggest perceived usefulness, not ease of use, is the most salient predictor of technology use (please see (Davis, 1989; Venkatesh et al., 2003)). Our findings may differ from prior research in that we focused respondents' attention on their mandated use of IT within an educational context. We speculate that when individuals have volitional control over IT use in these situations, ease of use, not perceived usefulness, might be the more salient predictor of IT use. Additional research is required to determine whether this is a consistent pattern in educational settings, or whether our findings are an anomaly.

Consistent with prior research, personal innovativeness with IT (H2a & H2b), computer anxiety (H3a & H3b), and computer self-efficacy (H4a & H4b) influenced beliefs about the perceived usefulness and ease of use of IT (Igbaria & Iivari, 1995; Venkatesh & Davis, 1996; Srite, 2000). Our results counter theory and research that suggests self-efficacy, not anxiety or innovativeness, is the primary predictor of beliefs leading to behavior (Bandura, 1997). A plausible explanation for this difference may lie in our research design. In this study, we measured computer self-efficacy, computer anxiety, and personal innovativeness at relatively broad levels. Although this is consistent with prior research (please see (Agarwal et al., 2000; Thatcher & Perrewe, 2002)), analysis of these relationships may differ when respondents' attention is directed to specific situations (Bandura, 1997). For example, if using a specific application to complete a task, situation-specific efficacy beliefs may exert greater influence than anxiety or innovativeness (Ghiselli et al., 1981; Agarwal et al., 2000). Hence, our findings provide support for the notion that the relative influence of efficacy may vary with the context considered by the researcher.

Our findings suggest cultural values may predispose individuals to report personal innovativeness with IT, computer self-efficacy, and computer anxiety. Each cultural dimension will be discussed in turn.

Masculinity/Femininity. Individuals who reported high levels of femininity were found to be less innovative with respect to IT (H5a: $p < .05$), to feel more computer anxiety (H5b: $p < .01$), and to express lower computer self-efficacy (H5c: $p < .01$) than individuals who reported high levels of masculinity. These results suggest culture influences the antecedents to individuals' beliefs about, and use of, information technology. When introducing new information technologies in culturally diverse environments, IT managers may want to pay attention to IT users' cultural values. For people with more feminine values, managers may want to stress the benefits of, and encourage, innovative behavior. Additional training to promote familiarity with, and reduce anxiety about, computers could prove beneficial for individuals who possess "feminine" values systems. Training could also increase levels of self-efficacy. For individuals with more masculine values, IT managers may want to reinforce existing dispositions to respond positively to IT. Alternatively, training on both masculinity and femininity could be provided to all employees to increase their understanding of this dimension's influence in the workplace. It is important to note that we are not suggesting that trainers use biological sex as a justification for providing different kinds of instruction, rather we are suggesting that they be sensitive to how cultural values may influence trainees' responses to IT instruction. Taken together, these findings suggest that an individual's place on the masculinity/femininity continuum influences malleable IT-specific traits.

Individualism/Collectivism. Results did not confirm our hypotheses linking individualism/collectivism to malleable IT-specific traits. Marginal support (H6a: $p < .10$) was found for individuals who reported greater individualism being more innovative with information technology. Because experimentation and other exploratory behavior linked to innovation may foster greater perceptions of ease of use and ultimately greater IT use, this finding suggests organizations that emphasize collectivist values may have to pro-actively encourage individual innovation with IT. Our results did not support a relationship between individualism/collectivism to computer anxiety (H6b) or computer self-efficacy (H6c). Although failing to reject a null hypothesis does not necessarily make the null hypothesis true (Levine et al., 1999), some conclusions can be drawn from this non-significant relationship. While acknowledging the potential limitations of our sample, we can conclude that respondents who were high in individualism were as likely to report similar levels of anxiety regarding computers and self-efficacy as individuals from collectivistic cultures.

LIMITATIONS

An important limitation of this study is the sample. Even though recent research has shown that students and workers essentially have the same values and beliefs (Voich, 1995), there have been several general criticisms of using students. Critics suggest that students might not be representative of the broader population. They tend to be more homogenous and consequently are difficult to generalize to a larger population (Fowler, 1988). However, we felt that college students were an appropriate population to examine because they frequently have significant experience with, and strongly held beliefs about, information technology. Within the domain of MIS, researchers have used student samples to examine a wide range of traits and beliefs linked to technology acceptance (Agarwal & Karahanna, 2000; Agarwal et al., 2000). In light of this research, we felt students were a good population to examine for the influence of within-culture differences on technology use.

To capture within-culture variance, our study sampled students from schools with geographic and demographic differences. In terms of geography, we drew our sample from schools that were in different states. By drawing a sample from widely separated schools, we hoped to capture variance that might be tied to geographic differences within a larger nation state. In terms of demographic differences, we sampled students from schools noted for their affiliation with different ethnic/regional groups with diverse demographic bases. Within the applied marketing literature, ethnic affiliation has been tied to willingness to adopt new technologies (African Americans and Hispanics Lead Mobile Culture, 2005). In light of our findings, we conducted a supplemental MANCOVA analysis to determine whether there was variation in the sample along ethnic lines. When controlling for gender, education, and computer experience, our analysis indicates that ethnicity was not a source of variation in computer use, perceived ease of use, perceived usefulness, computer self-efficacy, computer anxiety, personal innovativeness, masculinity/femininity, and individualism/collectivism. When controlling for different relevant characteristics, our study suggests that ethnicity is not a source of variance in beliefs about computing among students.

Despite our efforts to capture variance, we found within-culture differences among students to be weakly related to IT adoption variables. Our finding suggest that factors such as age, national origin (i.e., US nationality) or training (i.e., business education) may be more salient factors than within-culture variance in the influence of cultural values on technology adoption. For example, the relative widespread diffusion of cell-phone technologies amongst Hispanics and African-Americans may be attributed to the relative youth of the population, not to cultural differences, when compared to the broader US population (Morrison, 2006). Given the sample's homogeneity in terms of age and education and our limited results, future research should examine whether within-culture differences in technology use are more pronounced across more diverse age and educational groups.

It should also be noted that the use of the computer has been relatively well dispersed among student populations. Most students have access to a personal computer either at home or at a university computer lab. Our conclusions relating to the overall area of adoption and diffusion need to understood within this context. However, findings of this study could generalize to other less well-diffused technologies such as mobile computing via enhanced mobile phones. Additionally our dependent variable, computer use, focused on time spent at a computer. It did not address the issue of downtime, time waiting for the pc to startup, time spent waiting for downloads, etc. A future study might want to examine use at this finer level of granularity.

It is important to note that our findings may be an artifact of how we measured IT-related beliefs and behavior. TAM research typically focuses on specific information technologies (Davis, 1989). To ensure consistent target objects across research sites, we directed respondents' attention to beliefs about IT in general, rather than a specific technology. Due to this difference, we speculate that the network of relationships leading to peoples' use of specific information technologies may differ from those leading to use of information technology in general. This study also employed a single method to examine the research model. Although constructs covaried at different levels, future efforts at examining this relationship could use a variety of methodologies (interviews, qualitative methods, etc.) to yield additional insight into cultural links to technology acceptance. Further, values, traits, beliefs, and behaviors are not necessarily static, and a cross-sectional study, such as this one, might not fully capture the complexity of technology adoption. Longitudinal studies that examine how cultural values can influence the evolution of beliefs linked to innovation diffusion would extend our understanding of the influence of cultural values on perceptions and use of IT.

IMPLICATIONS

This study contributes to research and practice. In terms of research, this study makes two contributions to our understanding of technology acceptance and national culture. First, the study uses a theory driven approach to link within-culture variance in values to widely accepted constructs in the technology acceptance literature. We offer a theoretical explanation for how cultural dimensions should influence the development of important individual traits (i.e., personal innovativeness, computer anxiety, and computer self-efficacy) and consequently relate to IT-specific beliefs. Second, although we explained a relatively small amount of variance in our dependent variable, our analysis provides initial evidence that masculinity/femininity is a significant predictor of computer anxiety, computer self-efficacy, and personal innovativeness with information technology.

In light of the study's robust theoretical base, yet limited support for the research model, our findings suggest that future studies should examine how other cultural values relate to traits and beliefs linked to IT use. Research on culture and behavior in the workplace suggests that many aspects of broadly defined culture influence situation-specific beliefs and behaviors. For example, uncertainty avoidance has been linked to individuals reporting greater anxiety and stress (Peterson et al., 1995). It would be interesting to examine whether this relationship extends to individuals' beliefs and behavior within specific domains such as information technology. Although limited, this study does provide empirical evidence that cultural dimensions' may influence IT acceptance. In light of our findings, we suggest that research examine additional cultural values as potential sources of variation in technology acceptance and use. In addition, few studies have examined both technology acceptance and national culture (Gallivan & Srite, 2005; Srite & Karahanna, 2006; McCoy et al., 2007). This study provides a series of hypotheses that integrate cultural dimensions into an extended technology acceptance model. This integration is particularly relevant given the growing importance of global information technologies such as the Internet, the internationalization of markets, and the increasing use of dispersed teams operating across several time zones, countries, or continents.

It should also be noted that this study examined culture within a single country as opposed to much cultural research that compares and contrasts findings across multiple countries (Gallivan & Srite, 2005). As stated in the limitations section our findings show within-culture differences to be weakly related to IT adoption decisions. Although our subjects came from universities with different historical ethnic affiliations no attempt has been made, in this study, to examine differences in adoption across ethnicities. Such studies have implications within the overall issue of the digital divide. For example, Enoch and Soker's (2006) study in the Israeli university system indicates an age-, gender-, and ethnic-based digital divide exists. In order to bridge this gap, the authors suggest the continued promotion of IT use in the classroom combined with learning opportunities that will ensure equality among all students (Enoch and Soker, 2006).

Results from this study have direct managerial implications. Managers should recognize the cultural aspects of technology acceptance. This awareness may affect how a manager chooses to handle the planning, design, introduction, and implementation of new technologies. The support of peers with different national backgrounds and the reactions from subordinates from other cultures to new technologies can vary. Cultural awareness should be part of the training process for IT managers and planners. Reactions to IT implementations can have cultural variations. Resistance to a planned technology implementation may signal some cultural dimension that needs to be addressed. Strategies, that take culture into account, can be developed to overcome resistance and to learn from the different reactions. It may also be beneficial to consider different implementation strategies in different cultures. For instance, group-based training in the technology and roundtable discussions might be more appropriate in a culture high on femininity and/or collectivism while individual on-line training could work better in masculine and/or individualistic cultures.

A further practical implication of this study involves the design of IT training programs and their relationship with cross cultural training. Cross-cultural training facilitates effective interactions between people of different cultures by reducing the anxiety and disorientation a person feels when placed in a new environment i.e. culture shock. Perhaps with a lesser degree of intensity to culture shock but deserving of an equal degree of attention, there is the concept of subculture shock. Subculture shock is the term used when a person is sent to another part of their same country where cultural differences vary from that of their own region so much so that the person feels alienated. This is particularly prominent in cities that are shifting focuses (e.g. Charlotte, North Carolina) and must recruit skilled individuals to fill technology positions (Trauth et al., 2008). Individuals migrating to the area earlier are more likely to experience subculture shock; as time passes, this shock is diminished as the city becomes a melting pot of different cultures. For example, as noted by Deresky (2006) when someone from New York moved to Texas, "These differences exist within Texas, with cultures that range from roaming ranches and high technology to Bible-belt attitudes and laws and to areas with a mostly Mexican heritage" (p. 365). Hofstede's cultural dimensions widely cited in the literature apply to subcultures within the US to the degree that individuals are affected by the culture of their country of origin. "Living or working overseas or within a multicultural context in one's own home requires an individual to use interaction skills that transcend those that are effective when dealing with others from one's immediate in-group," (Black & Mendenhall, 1990).

Cross-cultural training increases the trainees' confidence in themselves and their ability to act effectively. As trainees receive either verbal or visual models of appropriate or inappropriate behaviors they create cognitive maps that increases their efficacy and outcome expectations (Black & Mendenhall, 1990). Adjusting to a cultural change, including that brought about by a new IT environment, involves the gradual development of familiarity, comfort, and proficiency regarding expected behavior and the values and assumptions inherent in the new culture, all of which are different than the native culture (Black & Mendenhall, 1990; Davidson, 2002; Walenta, 2004). Therefore, the more the trainee and trainer are able to understand and predict the behavior of each other, the better the relationship between them will be (Walenta, 2004). This can be seen to tie into the issue of trust. The prevailing view of trust in the IS literature is that trust has direct positive effects on cooperation and attitudes in a work environment. Trust is an intention or willingness to depend on another party. Individuals use their own preexisting dispositions and social categorizations about another person's initial trustworthiness. Trust affects how one assesses the future behavior of another party and how one interprets past behavior (Jarvenpaa et al., 2004).

FUTURE DIRECTIONS

Future research should examine sources of variance in cultural values such as subcultures or ethnic groups within single national states (Pineda & Whitehead, 1997). Subcultures within larger cultures could influence how individuals within organizations perceive artifacts such as IT and associated organizational structures (Pineda & Whitehead, 1997). As noted, "In pluralistic nations with more than one subculture, organizational members from different subcultures (also called ethnological groups) bring the values and norms of their respective ethnological groups into the organization" (Pineda & Whitehead, 1997). In order to examine this diversity, additional studies should compare ethnic groups within a single nation (Enoch and Soker, 2006). Additionally, the design of websites that work in multiple cultures or that contain elements to elicit responses from a specific culture is an area that has great potential for future research (please see (Zahedi et al., 2006)).

Also, although our findings suggest that broadly defined cultural values influence IT-specific beliefs and attitudes, this research should be considered a first step towards fully integrating the notion of cultural values into the domain of Management Information Systems. In the MIS literature, broadly defined personality traits such as extraversion have been more narrowly defined as personal innovativeness in the domain of IT

(Agarwal & Prasad, 1998). By more carefully defining and operationalizing the broad trait, MIS research has been able to more effectively account for personality's influence on beliefs and attitudes towards information technology (Thatcher & Perrewe, 2002). Consistent with this stream of research, our findings suggest that there might be value in developing IT-specific measures of culture, and examining whether they exert a greater influence on IT-related constructs than general measures of natural culture. Hence, in future research, academics might consider more narrowly focusing how they define and operationalize culture within the domain of MIS.

The limited findings of this study also suggest some avenues for future research. Greater effects of culture on technology acceptance variables could result from increased variability of the subjects sampled. Future studies may wish to examine participants from a wider variety of backgrounds or from multiple countries.

Finally, extensions of this research should use a more fine-grained approach to examining how individuals with different cultural orientations use specific technologies or engage in a range of activities with technology. For example, one might expect an individual from a collectivist culture to be more likely to join an on-line community. In contrast, one might expect an individual higher on individualist values to engage in more solitary activities such as "blogging" on the web. Although this study provides support for cultural values' influence on technology use, richer evidence for cultural dimensions' influence might be found through examining the relationship between specific cultural values and attributes of technologies.[1]

CONCLUSION

This study suggests cultural values can influence IT-related traits and beliefs. For IT implementation, this suggests resistance to a planned technology implementation may be rooted in extra-organizational cultural values. Strategies, that take cultural values into account, can be developed to overcome resistance and to learn from the different reactions to an IT. It may also be beneficial to consider adapting training programs to be consistent with participants' cultural values.

REFERENCES

Adams, D., Nelson, R., & Todd, P. (1992). Perceived Usefulness, Ease of Use, and Usage of Information Technology: A Replication. *MIS Quarterly*, 227–247. doi:10.2307/249577

African Americans and Hispanics Lead Mobile Culture. (2005). Retrieved July 28, 2006 from http://www.cellular-news.com/story/15030.php.

Agarwal, R., & Karahanna, E. (2000). Time Flies When You're Having Fun: Cognitive Absorption and Beliefs About Information Technology Usage. *MIS Quarterly*, *24*(4), 665–694. doi:10.2307/3250951

Agarwal, R., & Prasad, J. (1998). A Conceptual and Operational Definition of Personal Innovativeness in the Domain of Information Technology. *Information Systems Research*, *9*(2), 204–215. doi:10.1287/isre.9.2.204

Agarwal, R., Sambamurthy, V., & Stair, R. M. (2000). The Evolving Relationship between General and Specific Computer Self-Efficacy. *Information Systems Research*, *1*(4), 418–430. doi:10.1287/isre.11.4.418.11876

Ahuja, M. K. (2002). Women in the Information Technology Profession: A Literature Synthesis and Research Agenda. *European Journal of Information Systems*, *11*(1), 20–34. doi:10.1057/palgrave/ejis/3000417

Ajzen, I., & Fishbein, M. (1980). *Understanding Attitudes and Predicting Social Behavior*. Englewood Cliffs, NJ: Prentice-Hall.

Anderson, J. C., & Gerbing, D. W. (1988). Structural Equation Modeling in Practice: A Review and Recommended Two-Step Approach. *Psychological Bulletin, 103*(3), 411–423. doi:10.1037/0033-2909.103.3.411

Ashmore, R. D., Del Boca, F. K., & Wohlers, A. J. (1986). Gender Stereotypes. In R. D. Ashmore & F. K. Del Boca (Eds.), *The Social Psychology of Female-Male Relations: A Critical Analysis of Central Concepts*. New York: Academic Press.

Bagozzi, R. P., Davis, F., & Warshaw, P. R. (1992). Development and Test of a Theory of Technological Learning and Usage. *Human Relations, 45*(7), 659–686. doi:10.1177/001872679204500702

Bandura, A. (1977). Self-Efficacy: Towards a Unifying Theory of Behavioral Change. *Psychological Review, 84*, 191–215. doi:10.1037/0033-295X.84.2.191

Bandura, A. (1997). *Self-Efficacy: The Exercise of Control*. New York: W.H. Freeman.

Bandura, A., Adams, N. E., & Beyer, J. (1977). Cognitive Processes Mediating Behavioral Change. *Journal of Personality and Social Psychology, 35*(3), 125–139. doi:10.1037/0022-3514.35.3.125

Barling, J., & Beattie, R. (1983). Self-Efficacy Beliefs and Sales Performance. *Journal of Behavioral Management, 5*, 125–139.

Bentler, P. M., & Chou, C. P. (1987). Practical Issues in Structural Modeling. *Sociological Methods & Research, 16*, 78–117. doi:10.1177/0049124187016001004

Berry, J. W. (1979). Research in Multicultural Societies: Implications of Cross-Cultural Methods. *Journal of Cross-Cultural Psychology, 10*(4), 415–434. doi:10.1177/0022022179104002

Betz, N. E., & Hackett, G. (1981). The Relationship of Career-Related Self-Efficacy Expectations to Perceived Career Options in College Women and Men. *Journal of Counseling Psychology, 28*(5), 399–410. doi:10.1037/0022-0167.28.5.399

Black, J. S., & Mendenhall, M. (1990). Cross-Cultural Training Effectiveness: A Review and Theoretical Framework for Future Research. *Academy of Management Review, 15*(1), 113–136. doi:10.2307/258109

Bollen, K. A. (1989). *Structural Equations with Latent Variables*. New York: John Wiley and Sons.

Brosnan, M. J. (1999). Modeling Technophobia: A Case for Word Processing. *Computers in Human Behavior, 15*(2), 105–121. doi:10.1016/S0747-5632(98)00020-X

Brown, I., & Inouye, D. K. (1978). Learned Helplessness through Modeling: The Role of Perceived Similarity and Competence. *Journal of Personality and Social Psychology, 36*(8), 900–908. doi:10.1037/0022-3514.36.8.900

Brown, S., Fuller, R. M., & Vician, C. (2004). Who's Afraid of the Virtual World? Anxiety and Computer-Mediated Communication. *Journal of the Association of Information Systems, 5*(2), 79–107.

Burkhardt, M. E., & Brass, D. J. (1990). Changing Patterns or Patterns of Change: The Effects of a Change in Technology on Social Network Structure and Power. *Administrative Science Quarterly, 35*(1), 104–127. doi:10.2307/2393552

Chan, S., & Lu, M.-t. (2004). Understanding Internet Banking Adoption and Use Behavior: A Hong Kong Perspective. *Journal of Global Information Management, 12*(3), 21–43.

Chen, G., Gully, S. M., Whiteman, J.-A., & Kilcullen, R. N. (2000). Examination of Relationships among Trait-Like Individual Differences, State-Like Individual Differences, and Learning Performance. *The Journal of Applied Psychology, 85*(6), 835–847. doi:10.1037/0021-9010.85.6.835

Compeau, D., Higgins, C. A., & Huff, S. (1999). Social Cognitive Theory and Individual Reactions to Computing Technology: A Longitudinal Study. *MIS Quarterly, 23*(2), 145–158. doi:10.2307/249749

Compeau, D. R., & Higgins, C. A. (1995a). Application of Social Cognitive Theory to Training for Computer Skills. *Information Systems Research, 6*(2), 118–143. doi:10.1287/isre.6.2.118

Compeau, D. R., & Higgins, C. A. (1995b). Computer Self-Efficacy: Development of a Measure and Initial Test. *MIS Quarterly*, 189–211. doi:10.2307/249688

Crump, B. J., Logan, K. A., & McIlroy, A. (2007). Does Gender Still Matter? A Study of the Views of Women in the ICT Industry in New Zealand. *Gender, Work and Organization, 14*(4), 349–370. doi:10.1111/j.1468-0432.2007.00348.x

Cyr, D. (2008). Modeling Web Site Design Across Cultures: Relationships to Trust, Satisfaction, and E-Loyalty. *Journal of Management Information Systems, 24*(4), 47–72. doi:10.2753/MIS0742-1222240402

Cyr, D., Bonanni, C., Bowes, J., & Ilsever, J. (2005). Beyond Trust: Web Site Design Preferences across Cultures. *Journal of Global Information Management, 13*(4), 25–54.

Davidson, D. (2002). Cultural Complications of Erp. *Communications of the ACM, 45*(7), 109–111.

Davis, F. (1989). Perceived Usefulness, Perceived Ease of Use, and User Acceptance of Computing Technology. *MIS Quarterly, 13*(3), 319–339. doi:10.2307/249008

Davis, F. (1993). User Acceptance of Information Technology: System Characteristics, User Perceptions, and Behavioral Impacts. *International Journal of Management, 38*, 475–487.

Deresky, H. (2006). *International Management, Managing across Borders and Cultures*. Upper Saddle River, NJ: Pearson/Prentice Hall.

Dorfman, P. W., & Howell, J. (1988). Dimensions of National Culture & Effective Leadership Patterns: Hofstede Revisited. In E. G. McGowan (Ed.), *Advances in International Comparative Management* (pp. 127-149)... Greenwich, CT: JAI Press.

Draguns, J. G. (1979). Culture and Personality. In A. J. Marsella, T. Ciborowski & R. Tharp (Eds.), *Perspectives on Cross-Cultural Psychology* (pp. 179-207). New York: Academic Press.

Elbeltagi, I., McBride, N., & Hardaker, G. (2005). Evaluating the Factors Affecting DSS Usage by Senior Managers in Local Authorities in Egypt. *Journal of Global Information Management, 13*(2), 42–65.

Enoch, Y., & Soker, Z. (2006). Age, Gender, Ethnicity and the Digital Divide: University Students' Use of Web-Based Instruction. *Open Learning, 21*(2), 99–110. doi:10.1080/02680510600713045

Erez, M., & Early, C. P. (1993). *Culture, Self-Identity, and Work*. New York: Oxford University Press.

Fiske, A. P. (2002). Using Individualism and Collectivism to Compare Cultures - a Critique of the Validity and Measurement of the Constructs: Comment on Oysterman Et Al (2002). *Psychological Bulletin, 128*(1), 78–88. doi:10.1037/0033-2909.128.1.78

Fowler, F. J. (1988). *Survey Research Methods*. Newbury Park, CA: SAGE Publications, Inc.

Frayne, C. A., & Latham, G. P. (1987). The Application of Social Learning to Employee Self-Management of Attendance. *The Journal of Applied Psychology, 72*(3), 387–392. doi:10.1037/0021-9010.72.3.387

Gallivan, M., & Srite, M. (2005). Information Technology and Culture: Identifying Fragmentary and Holistic Perspectives of Culture. *Information and Organization, 15*(4), 295–338. doi:10.1016/j.infoandorg.2005.02.005

Gallupe, R. B., & Tan, F. B. (1999). A Research Manifesto for Global Information Management. *Journal of Global Information Management, 7*(3), 5–18.

Gefen, D. (2000). Gender Differences in the Perception and Adoption of E-Mail and Computer Mediated Communication Media: A Sociolinguistics Approach. In A. Kent (Ed.), *The Encyclopedia of Library and Information Science*. New York: Marcel Dekker.

Gefen, D., & Straub, D. (1997). Gender Difference in the Perception and Use of E-Mail: An Extension to the Technology Acceptance Model. *MIS Quarterly, 21*(4), 389–400. doi:10.2307/249720

Gefen, D., Straub, D. W., & Boudreau, M.-C. (2000). Structural Equation Modeling and Regression: Guidelines for Research and Practice. *Communications of the Association for Information Systems, 3*(1).

Ghiselli, E. E., Campbell, J. P., & Zedeck, S. (1981). *Measurement Theory for the Behavioral Science*. San Francisco, CA: W.H. Freeman.

Gist, M. E. (1989). The Influence of Training Method on Self-Efficacy and Idea Generation among Managers. *Personnel Psychology, 42*, 787–805. doi:10.1111/j.1744-6570.1989.tb00675.x

Hampden-Turner, C., & Trompenaars, F. (1993). *The Seven Cultures of Capitalism*. New York: Doubleday.

Heinssen, R. K., Glass, C. R., & Knight, L. A. (1987). Assessing Computer Anxiety: Development and Validation of the Computer Anxiety Rating Scale. *Computers in Human Behavior, 3*, 49–59. doi:10.1016/0747-5632(87)90010-0

Hill, N. D., Smith, D. B., & Man, M. F. (1986). Communicating Innovations: Convincing Computer Phobics to Adopt Innovative Technologies. In R. J. Lutz (Ed), *Advances in Consumer Research* (pp. 419-422). Provo, UT: Association for Consumer Research.

Hill, T., Smith, N. D., & Mann, M. F. (1987). Role of Efficacy Expectations in Predicting the Decision to Use Advanced Technologies: The Case of Computers. *The Journal of Applied Psychology, 72*(2), 307–313. doi:10.1037/0021-9010.72.2.307

Hoecklin, L. A. (1995). *Managing Cultural Differences: Strategies for Competitive Advantage*. Reading, MA: Addison-Wesley.

Hofstede, G. (1980). *Culture's Consequences: International Differences in Work-Related Values*. Beverly Hills, CA: Sage.

Hofstede, G. (1984). *Culture's Consequences: International Differences in Work-Related Values*. Newbury Park, CA: Sage.

Hofstede, G. (1991). *Organizations and Cultures: Software of the Mind*. London: McGraw-Hill.

Howard, G., Murphy, C. M., & Thomas, G. E. (1986). *Computer Anxiety Considerations for Design of Introductory Computer Courses*. Honolulu, HI: Decision Sciences Institute.

Hu, P. J., Chau, P. Y. K., Sheng, O. R. L., & Tam, K. Y. (1999). Examining the Technology Acceptance Model Using Physician Acceptance of Telemedicine Technology. *Journal of Management Information Systems, 16*(2), 91–112.

Igbaria, M., & Chakrabarti, A. (1990). Computer Anxiety and Attitudes Towards Microcomputer. *Behaviour & Information Technology, 9*(3), 229–241. doi:10.1080/01449299008924239

Igbaria, M., & Guimaraes, T., & Davis. (1995). Testing the Determinants of Microcomputer Usage Via a Structural Equation Model. *Journal of Management Information Systems, 11*(4), 87–114.

Igbaria, M., & Iivari, A. (1995). The Effects of Self-Efficacy on Computer Usage. *Omega, 23*(6), 587–605. doi:10.1016/0305-0483(95)00035-6

Igbaria, M., Parasuraman, S., & Baroudi, J. (1996). A Motivational Model of Computer Usage. *Journal of Management Information Systems, 13*(1), 127–143.

Igbaria, M., Pravir, F. N., & Huff, S. L. (1989). Microcomputer Applications: An Empirical Look at Usage. *Information & Management, 16*, 187–196. doi:10.1016/0378-7206(89)90036-0

Jackson, C. M., Chow, S., & Leitch, R. A. (1997). Toward an Understanding of the Behavioral Intention to Use an Information System. *Decision Sciences, 28*(2), 357–389. doi:10.1111/j.1540-5915.1997.tb01315.x

Jarvenpaa, S. L., Shaw, T. R., & Staples, D. S. (2004). Toward Contextualized Theories of Trust: The Role of Trust in Global Virtual Teams. *Information Systems Research, 15*(3), 250–267. doi:10.1287/isre.1040.0028

Jones, G. R. (1986). Socialization Tactics, Self-Efficacy, and Newcomer's Adjustments to Organizations. *Academy of Management Journal, 29*(2), 262–279. doi:10.2307/256188

Joreskog, K., & Sorbom, D. (2003). Lisrel, Scientific Software International Inc.

Kacmar, K. M., Bozeman, D. P., Carlson, D. S., & Anthony, W. P. (1999). An Examination of the Perceptions of Organizational Politics Model: Replication and Extension. *Human Relations, 52*(3), 383–416.

Karahanna, E., Evaristo, J., & Srite, M. (2005). Levels of Culture and Individual Behavior: An Integrative Perspective. *Journal of Global Information Management, 13*(2), 1–20.

Karahanna, E., & Straub, D. (1999). The Psychological Origins of Perceived Usefulness and Ease of Use. *Information & Management, 35*(4), 237–250. doi:10.1016/S0378-7206(98)00096-2

Karahanna, E., Straub, D., & Chervany, N. (1999). Information Technology across Time: A Cross-Sectional Comparison of Pre-Adoption and Post-Adoption Beliefs. *MIS Quarterly, 23*(2), 183–214. doi:10.2307/249751

Kase, S. E., & Trauth, E. M. (2003). Toward a Model of Women in the It Workplace. In *Proceedings of the Ninth Americas Conference on Information Systems, Atlanta, GA, Association for Information Systems*.

Keil, M., Beranek, P., & Konsynski, B. (1995). Usefulness and Ease of Use: Field Study Evidence Regarding Task Considerations. *Decision Support Systems, 13*(1), 75–91. doi:10.1016/0167-9236(94)E0032-M

Latham, G. P., & Frayne, C. A. (1989). Self-Management for Training for Increasing Job Attendance: A Follow-up and Replication. *The Journal of Applied Psychology, 7*(3), 411–416. doi:10.1037/0021-9010.74.3.411

Levine, D., Berenson, M., & Stephan, D. (1999). *Statistics for Managers: Using Microsoft Excel*. New Jersey: Prentice Hall.

Mao, E., Srite, M., Thatcher, J. B., & Yaprak, O. (2005). A Research Model for Mobile Phone Service Behaviors: Empirical Validation in the Us and Turkey. *Journal of Global Information Technology Management, 8*(4), 7.26.

Marakas, G. M., Yi, M. Y., & Johnson, R. D. (1998). The Multilevel and Multifaceted Character of Computer Self-Efficacy: Toward Clarification on the Construct and an Integrative Framework for Research. *Information Systems Research, 9*(2), 126–163. doi:10.1287/isre.9.2.126

Mathieson, K. (1991). Predicting User Intentions: Comparing the Technology Acceptance Model with the Theory of Reasoned Action. *Information Systems Research, 2*(3), 173–191. doi:10.1287/isre.2.3.173

McCoy, S., Galletta, D. F., & King, W. R. (2007). Applying TAM Across Cultures: The Need for Caution. *European Journal of Information Systems, 16*(1), 81–90. doi:10.1057/palgrave.ejis.3000659

Morris, M. G., & Venkatesh, V. (2000). Age Differences in Technology Adoption Decisions: Implications for a Changing Workforce. *Personnel Psychology, 53*(2), 375–403. doi:10.1111/j.1744-6570.2000.tb00206.x

Morrison, P. A. (2006). A Demographic Perspective on Our Nation's Future. *Population Matters* Retrieved June 28, 2006, from http://www.rand.org/pubs/documented_briefings/DB320/index.html.

Myers, M. D., & Tan, F. B. (2002). Beyond Models of National Culture in Is Research. *Journal of Global Information Management, 10*(1), 24–32.

Ndubisi, N., Gupta, O., & Ndubisi, G. (2005). The Moguls' Model of Computing: Integrating the Moderating Impact of Users' Persona into the Technology Acceptance Model. *Journal of Global Information Technology Management, 8*(1), 27–47.

Oysterman, D., Coon, H. M., & Kemmelmeir, M. (2002). Rethinking Individualism and Collectivism: Evaluation of Theoretical Assumptions and Meta-Analysis. *Psychological Bulletin, 128*(1), 3–72. doi:10.1037/0033-2909.128.1.3

Peterson, M. F., & Smith, P. B., & al, e. (1995). Role Conflict, Ambiguity, and Overload: A 21 Nation Study. *Academy of Management Journal, 38*(2), 429–452. doi:10.2307/256687

Pineda, R., & Whitehead, C. (1997). The Effect of Ethnic Group Culture on Managerial Task Activities. *Group & Organization Management, 22*(1), 31–52. doi:10.1177/1059601197221005

Redding, S., & Baldwin, E. (1991). *Managers for Asia/Pacific: Recruitment and Development Strategies*. Hong Kong: Business International.

Segev, E., Ahituv, N., & Barzilai-Nahon, K. (2007). Mapping Diversities and Tracing Trends of Cultural Homogeneity/Heterogeneity in Cyberspace. *Journal of Computer-Mediated Communication, 12*(4), 1269–1297. doi:10.1111/j.1083-6101.2007.00373.x

Spielberger, C. D., Gorsuch, R. L., & Lushene, R. E. (1970). *Manual for the State-Trait Anxiety Inventory*. Palo Alto, CA: Consulting Psychologists Press.

Srite, M. (2000). The Influence of National Culture on the Acceptance and Use of Information Technologies: An Empirical Study. Information and Management Sciences. Tallahassee, FL, Florida State University.

Srite, M., & Karahanna, E. (2006). The Role of Espoused National Cultural Values in Technology Acceptance. *MIS Quarterly, 30*(3), 1–26.

Steenkamp, J., Hofstede, F., & Wedel, M. (1999). A Cross-National Investigation into the Individual and National Cultural Antecedents of Consumer Innovativeness. *Journal of Marketing, 63*(2), 55–69. doi:10.2307/1251945

Stets, J. E., & Burke, P. J. (2000). Feminity/Masculinity. In E. F. Borgatta & R. J. V. Montgomery (Eds.), *Encyclopedia of Sociology* (pp. 997-1005). New York: MacMillan.

Stowers, G. N. L. (1995). Getting Left Behind? Gender Differences in Computer Conferencing. *Public productivity and management review, 19*(2), 143-195.

Straub, D., Loch, K., Evaristo, R., Karahanna, E., & Srite, M. (2002). Toward a Theory-Based Measurement of Culture. *Journal of Global Information Management*, Spring.

Straub, D. W., Limayen, M., & Karahanna-Evaristo, E. (1995). Measuring System Usage: Implications for Is Theory Testing. *Management Science, 41*(8), 1328–1342. doi:10.1287/mnsc.41.8.1328

Szajna, B. (1994). Software Evaluation and Choice: Predictive Validation of the Technology Acceptance Instrument. *MIS Quarterly, 18*(3), 319–325. doi:10.2307/249621

Szajna, B. (1996). Empirical Evaluation of the Revised Technology Acceptance Model. *Management Science, 42*(1), 85–92. doi:10.1287/mnsc.42.1.85

Tayeb, M. (1994). Organizations and National Culture: Methodology Considered. *Organization Studies, 15*(3), 429–446. doi:10.1177/017084069401500306

Taylor, M. S., Locke, E. A., Lee, C., & Gist, M. E. (1984). Type a Behavior and Faculty Research Productivity: What Are the Mechanisms. *Organizational Behavior and Human Decision Processes, 34*(3), 402–418.

Taylor, S., & Todd, P. (1995). Understanding Information Technology Usage: A Test of Competing Models. *Information Systems Research, 6*(2), 144–176. doi:10.1287/isre.6.2.144

Tellegen, A. (1985). Structures of Mood and Personality and Their Relevance to Assessing Anxiety with an Emphasis on Self-Report. In A. H. Tuma & J. D. Maser (Eds.), *Anxiety and Anxiety Disorders* (pp. 681-706). Hillsdale, N.J.: Erlbaum.

Thatcher, J., & Perrewe, P. L. (2002). An Empirical Examination of Individual Traits as Antecedents to Computer Anxiety and Computer Self-Efficacy. *MIS Quarterly, 26*(4), 381–396. doi:10.2307/4132314

Trauth, E. M. (1999). Leapfrogging an It Labor Force: Multinational and Indigenous Perspectives. *Journal of Global Information Management, 7*, 22–32.

Trauth, E. M. (2002). Odd Girl Out: An Individual Differences Perspective on Women in the It Profession. *Information Technology & People, 15*(2), 98–118. doi:10.1108/09593840210430552

Trauth, E. M., Quesenberry, J. L., & Yeo, B. (2008). Environmental Influences on Gender in the IT Workforce. *The Data Base for Advances in Information Systems, 39*(1), 8–32.

Venkatesh, V. (2000). Determinants of Perceived Ease of Use: Integrating Control, Intrinsic Motivation, and Emotion into the Technology Acceptance Model. *Information Systems Research, 11*(4), 342–365. doi:10.1287/isre.11.4.342.11872

Venkatesh, V., & Davis, F. (2000). A Theoretical Extension of the Technology Acceptance Model: Four Longitudinal Field Studies. *Management Science, 46*(2), 186–204. doi:10.1287/mnsc.46.2.186.11926

Venkatesh, V., & Davis, F. D. (1996). A Model of the Antecedents of Perceived Ease of Use: Development and Test. *Decision Sciences, 27*(3), 451–482. doi:10.1111/j.1540-5915.1996.tb01822.x

Venkatesh, V., & Morris, M. G. (2000). Why Don't Men Ever Stop and Ask for Directions? Gender, Social Influence, and Their Role in Technology Acceptance Usage Behavior. *MIS Quarterly*, *24*(1), 115–140. doi:10.2307/3250981

Venkatesh, V., Morris, M. G., Davis, G. B., & Davis, F. D. (2003). User Acceptance of Information Technology: Towards a Unified View. *MIS Quarterly*, *27*(3), 425–478.

Voich, D. (1995). *Comparative Empirical Analysis of Cultural Values and Perceptions of Political Economy Issues*. Westport, CT: Praeger.

Walenta, T. (2004). Managing Cross-Cultural Issues in Global Software Outsourcing. *Communications of the ACM*, *47*(4), 62–66. doi:10.1145/975817.975818

Webster, J., & Martocchio, J. J. (1992). Microcomputer Playfulness: Development of a Measure with Workplace Implications. *MIS Quarterly*, *16*(2), 201–266. doi:10.2307/249576

Webster, J., & Martocchio, J. J. (1993). Turning Work into Play: Implications for Microcomputer Software Training. *Journal of Management*, *19*(1), 127–146. doi:10.1177/014920639301900109

Wood, R., & Bandura, A. (1989). Social Cognitive Theory of Organizational Management. *Academy of Management Review*, *14*, 361–384. doi:10.2307/258173

Zahedi, M., van Pelt, W., & Srite, M. (2006). Web Documents' Cultural Masculinity and Femininity. *Journal of MIS*, *23*(1), 87–128.

ENDNOTE

1 We thank the associate editor for providing this interesting insight.

APPENDIX

Items and Sources

Computer Self-Efficacy – (Compeau & Higgins, 1995b)

For the following statements, imagine you are given a new software package that you have never used. For each condition described below, first indicate if you could use the software under the condition by circling YES or NO. For each condition that you answered "Yes", please rate your confidence about your ability to do the job, by writing in a number from 1 to 10, where 1 indicate "Not at all confident", and 10 indicates "Totally confident". You may only enter numbers between 1 and 10.

I could complete my assignments using the software if …

1. … There was no one around to tell me what to do.
2. … I had never used a package like it before.
3. … I had only the software manuals for reference.
4. … I had seen someone else using it before trying it myself.
5. … I could call someone for help if I got stuck.
6. … Someone else helped me get started.
7. ... I had a lot of time to finish the job for which it was provided.
8. … I had just the built-in help facility for assistance.
9. … Someone showed me how to do it first.
10. … I had used similar packages like this one before to do the job.

Computer Anxiety – (Heinssen et al., 1987)

Indicate the extent to which the following statements reflect your feelings when you think about computers.

1. Once I start working on the computer, I find it hard to stop.
2. I like working with computers.
3. I look forward to those aspects of this course that require me to use IT.
4. Using a computer is frustrating for me.
5. I get bored quickly when working on a computer.
6. I feel apprehensive about using computers.
7. It scares me to think that I could cause the computer to destroy a large amount of information by hitting the wrong key.
8. I hesitate to use a computer for fear of making mistakes that I cannot correct.
9. Computers are somewhat intimidating to me.
10. Computer terminology sounds like confusing jargon to me.

Personal Innovativeness – (Agarwal & Prasad, 1998)

1. Using computers improves my performance.
2. I like to experiment with new information technologies.
3. If I heard about a new information technology, I would look for ways to experiment with it.
4. In general, I am hesitant to try out new information technologies.
5. Among my peers, I am usually the first to try out new information technologies.

Masculinity/Femininity – (Hofstede, 1980); (Dorfman & Howell, 1988)

In general, I think that…

1. It is preferable to have a man in high level position rather than a woman.
2. It is more important for men to have a professional career than it is for women to have a professional career.
3. There are some jobs in which a man can always do better than a woman
4. Women do not value recognition and promotion in their work as much as men do.

Individualism/Collectivism – (Hofstede, 1980); (Dorfman & Howell, 1988); (Srite & Karahanna, 2006)

In general, I think that…

1. Being loyal **to a group** is more important than individual gain.
2. Being accepted as a member of a group is more important than having autonomy and independence on the job.
3. Group success is more important than individual success.
4. It is more important for a manager to encourage loyalty and a sense of duty in subordinates than it is to encourage individual initiative.
5. Individual rewards are not as important as group welfare.
6. I value my independence more than being accepted by others.
7. Being accepted as a member of a group is more important than being independent.
8. Group welfare is more important than individual rewards.

Perceived Usefulness – (Davis, 1989)

In general, I believe that…

1. Using computers enhances my productivity.
2. I find computers useful.
3. Using computers enhances my effectiveness

Perceived Ease of Use – (Davis, 1989)

1. It is easy for me to become skillful using computers.
2. I find computers easy to use.
3. I find it easy to get a computer to do what I want it to do.
4. Learning to operate a computer is easy for me.

Computer Use

In a typical week, I use a computer for

_____ hours for school
_____ hours for work
_____ hours for other activities

Demographic Information

1. Date of Birth
2. Sex
3. Ethnicity
4. Number of years at this university
5. Number of years of college education
6. Number of years of computer experience
7. Number of computer courses taken

Chapter 16
Mission-Critical Group Decision-Making:
Solving the Problem of Decision Preference Change in Group Decision-Making Using Markov Chain Model[1]

Huizhang Shen
Shanghai Jiaotong University, China

Jidi Zhao
University of New Brunswick, Canada

Wayne W. Huang
Ohio University, USA

ABSTRACT

Review on group decision support systems (GDSS) indicates that traditional GDSS are not specifically designed to support mission-critical group decision-making tasks that require group decision-making to be made effectively within short time. In addition, prior studies in the research literature have not considered group decision preference adjustment as a continuous process and neglected its impact on group decision-making. In reality, group members may dynamically change their decision preferences during group decision-making process. This dynamic adjustment of decision preferences may continue until a group reaches consensus on final decision. This article intends to address this neglected group decision-making research issue in the literature by proposing a new approach based on the Markov chain model. Furthermore, a new group decision weight allocation approach is also suggested. A real case example of New Orleans Hurricane Katrina is used to illustrate the usefulness and effectiveness of the proposed approaches. Finally, the article concludes with the discussion on the proposed approaches and presents directions for future research.

INTRODUCTION

Mission-critical events such as hurricanes, terrorist attacks, fires, and earthquakes require different governmental departments to work together to respond to those emerging crises and reach consensus quickly to make effective decisions within a short time period. Traditional group decision support systems (GDSS) have not specifically addressed this important issue in the research literature (Fjermestad & Hiltz 1999; Huang, 2003; Huang & Wei, 2000; Huang, Wei, & Lim, 2003; Tan, Wei, Huang, & Ng, 2000; Zigurs, DeSanctis, & Billingsley, 1991; Vogel, Martz, Nunamaker, Grohowski, & McGoff, 1990). A special type of GDSS, mission-critical GDSS (MC-GDSS), can be designed to support this group decision-making process.

Mission-critical group decision-making has some important characteristics that are different from conventional group decision-makings (Belardo & Wallace, 1989; Beroggi, Mendonça, & Wallace, 2003; Huang & Li, 2007; Limayem, Banerjee, & Ma, 2006; Mendonca, Beroggi, Gent, & Wallace, 2006; Wallace & DeBalogh, 1985): (1) decision-makers have to make nearly real-time decision. Decision-making on emergency response has to be made within a short time because of the nature of critical mission, (2) mission-critical decision-making problem is unstructured, fuzzy and unexpected in nature, and (3) information available to decision-makers is insufficient and not always accurate because complete information may not be collected in a short time, thus the decision makers can only rely on such incomplete information to making decisions. Therefore, conventional decision support approaches may not well solve decision problems of mission-critical events.

Prior research studies mission-critical decision-making from different perspectives. LaPorte and Consilini identify two emergency response patterns based on frequency and scene information respectively (LaPorte & Consilini, 1991). Ody thinks that crisis decision-making task, one type of mission-critical decision-making tasks, consists of three segments, pre-incident identification of hazards, the use of agreed communications, and the introduction of a third party to promote the coordination of decision makers (Ody, 1995). Wilkenfeld, Kraus, Holley, and Harris design a decision support system, GENIE, and demonstrate the usefulness of GENIE to help decision makers maximize their objectives in a crisis negotiation. Experimental results show that GENIE users, as compared to non-users, are more likely to identify utility maximization as their primary objective and to achieve higher utility scores (Wilkenfeld, Kraus, Holley, & Harris, 1995). Papazoglou and Christou propose a method on optimization of the short-term emergency response to nuclear accidents, which seeks an optimum combination of protective actions in the presence of a multitude of conflicting objectives and under uncertainty (Papazoglou & Christou, 1997). Bar-Eli and Tractinsky explore psychological performance crises under time pressure towards the end of basketball games (Bar-Eli & Tractinsky, 2000). Zografos, Vasilakis, and Giannouli present a methodological and unified framework for developing a decision support system (DSS) for hazardous materials emergency response operations (Zografos, Vasilakis, & Giannouli, 2000). Weisaeth, Knudsen, and Tonnessen discuss how psychological stress disturbs decision making during technological crisis and disaster, at an operative level of emergency response and at the strategic and political level respectively (Weisaeth, Knudsen, & Tonnessen, 2002). Chen, Sharman, and Rao et al. develop a set of supporting design concepts and strategic principles for an architecture for a coordinated multi-incident emergency response system based upon emergency response system requirement analysis (Chen, Sharman, & Rao et al., 2005).

As Arrow points out, based on the construction of group preference, group decision-making is a procedure of synthesizing the preferences of each decision-maker in a group and sorting decision alternatives or choosing the best decision alternative from a decision alternative set (Arrow, 1963). Group decision preference relation of a group should satisfy five rational terms: preference axiom, impossible axiom, completeness, Pareto optimization, and non-autarchy (Arrow, 1963). Prior studies by Arrow (1963), Dyer (1979), Keeney (1975), and French (1986), and so forth, provide a theoretical foundation on group decision preference relation analysis in group decision-making research literature. Group decision preference is a function of individual preferences on group decision-making issues. Preference is a term originally coming from economics. In group decision-making research literature, it is used to represent decision-makers' partiality on value (Dyer & Sarin, 1979). The procedure of forming individual preference is a decision-maker's meta-synthetic thinking procedure of perceiving all the information relating to expectation, information, sensibility, creativity, and so on, which is a extremely complex procedure (Bordly & Wolff, 1981). Some prior studies try to explore these complicated issues from different angles, including Weighted Average Method, Bordly Multiplication (Bordly & Wolff, 1981), Bayesian Integration Method (Keeney & Kirkwood, 1975), Entropy Method (French, 1986), and Fuzzy Cluster Analysis (Dyer & Sarin, 1979). Generally speaking, a decision-making group's decision preference on decision alternative sets will change as decision-makers adjust their decision preferences after communicating with other group decision-makers through group interactions, which could lead to group decision-marking preference convergence.

In this article, how a group reaches decision consensus quickly and effectively in group decision-making on emergency response is focused on. Emergency response, as one type of mission-critical group decision scenario, requires an MC-GDSS to collect group members' decision-making choice preferences automatically and quickly determine a group's overall decision choice preference. Further, group members may also dynamically change their decision preferences after seeing other group members' decision choice preferences during group decision-making process. This dynamic adjustment of decision preferences will continue until all the group members do not rectify their preferences. After a few rounds of group interactions with decision preference adjustment, group consensus may be reached on the group's final decision choice. Prior studies in the research literature have not considered the preference adjustment as a continuous procedure and neglected its impact on group decision-making. This article intends to address this important group decision-making research issue and proposes a new approach based on the Markov chain model.

In addition, one central element of group decision-making is decision weight. Prior main solutions to decision weight allocation in the research literature can be summarized. The first solution is the authority allocation method (Mallach, 2000). An authoritative decision maker allocates decision weight for each decision-maker, which may be biased. Another solution is the Nominal Group Technique (Potter & Balthazard, 2004; Shyur & Shih, 2006). Nominal Group Technique is a kind of anonymous survey which should be done for some rounds. Each member of a group endows weight to other decision members according to his/her own experience, value system, and personal judgment. The anonymous survey process will continue until all decision-making members' opinions converge. These two methods largely involve subjective judgment on decision weight allocation (Chen & Fu, 2005; Williams & Cookson, 2006), which is likely to lead to subjective biases as well. Other methods are based on forecasting each decision-maker's weight according to historical experience and data, such as entropy method and fuzzy cluster analysis (French, 1986), where two disadvantages exist. First, those require a lot of historical data, which is not easy to collect in reality. Second, the external environment of decision-making is changing fast. Therefore, historical successful experience may not provide a good indication for successful current and future decision-makings. This article proposes a new decision weight allocation approach, which can help address the problems of prior methods in terms of subjective biases and requiring substantial quantity of historical data.

The remainder of this article is organized as follows: The next section proposes a new decision weight allocation method. The third section presents a new approach to construct a Markov state transition matrix in group decision-making, addressing the neglected research issue of dynamically changed decision preference in the group decision-making process. A real case example of New Orleans Hurricane Katrina is used to illustrate the usefulness and effectiveness of the proposed approach. Finally, the article concludes with the discussion on the research results and presents directions for future research.

PROPOSING A NEW DECISION WEIGHT ALLOCATION APPROACH FOR MISSION-CRITICAL GROUP DECISION-MAKING

This section proposes a new decision weight allocation approach for mission-critical group decision-making. First, a group decision preference judgment matrix is defined, followed by a quantitative consistence indicator to measure decision-maker's decision consistence. Second, a clustering method to analyze the distances among decision preferences in a decision-making group is put forward. Finally, a decision weight is determined by both decision preference consistence indicator and decision preference distance indicator.

Group Decision Preference Judgment Matrix

In this article, the concept of preference utility value from economics literature to quantitatively represent preference, which describes preference direction or priority of a decision-maker is used. It would be difficult for a group member to accurately judge which decision choice is certainly the best among those alternative decision choices, especially for mission-critical problems. In reality, group decision-makers do pair wise comparisons *on each pair of two decision alternatives (or decision choices)* and give their decision preferences using fuzzy terms like "equal, a little better, better, much better, absolutely better." *Based upon this line of logic thinking, each decision-maker's preference utility value can be generated.* The definition of preference utility value $\theta_r(x^i, x^j)$ *and its quantificational values are given in Appendix A.1.*

Thus, according to the rth decision maker of a group, DM_r's pair wise comparison between each two alternatives on the set, we get a preference judgment matrix P_r. Apparently, it is a positive symmetrical matrix. Decision-makers only need to judge $s(s-1)/2$ times, which is equal to the amount of the elements of the upper or lower triangular matrix.

$$P_r = \begin{pmatrix} \theta_r(x^1,x^1) & \theta_r(x^1,x^2) & \cdots & \theta_r(x^1,x^s) \\ \theta_r(x^2,x^1) & \theta_r(x^2,x^2) & \cdots & \theta_r(x^2,x^s) \\ \cdots & \cdots & \cdots & \cdots \\ \theta_r(x^s,x^1) & \theta_r(x^s,x^2) & \cdots & \theta_r(x^s,x^s) \end{pmatrix} \tag{1}$$

Suppose there are l decision-makers, then there are l preference judging matrices altogether.

Decision Preference Consistence Indicator for a Preference Judgment Matrix

Although it is relatively easy for decision-makers to do pair wise comparisons and give the preference utility value, it may not be easy to derive sequential order of the decision alternatives from a preference judgment matrix. What is more, the derived order may often be self-contradictory. For example, analysis of a given preference judgment matrix may lead to a contradictory conclusion that A is more preferred than B, B is more preferred than C, and C is more preferred than A. This kind of contradiction indicates that a decision-maker may not always be consistent enough to make decision. As a result, a quantitative consistence indicator from AHP (Satty, 1988) is introduced to measure decision-maker's decision consistence. Let CI_r denote the rth decision maker DM_r's consistence indicator. The larger the indicator is, the worse the consistency of the preference judgment matrix becomes. Based on the theory of matrix, the preference utility value of DM_r on x^i, denoted by $\pi_r(x^i)$ can be derived and the consistence indicator from a matrix' characteristic vector and characteristic value, as illustrated in the Appendix A.2.

Clustering Analysis and Decision Preference Difference

Besides the individual carefulness measured by the consistence indicator, the differences among the individual preference and other's preferences (preference distance d_r) also play an important role in reaching consensus in group decision-making. As to an individual decision-maker, the larger the difference is, the extremer she is, and the less contribution she makes to the group consensus, and vice versa. In this section, firstly, a clustering method to classify the group decision-makers' preferences is introduced. Secondly, each decision-maker's preference distance to measure the extremenesses among the group members is computed. The clustering method and the definition of preference distance (d_r) are illustrated in Appendix B. The Euclidean preference distance (d_r) between the preference utility value vector of DM_r on X and the specified cluster center shows the preference distance of the decision-maker under the average criteria. The smaller d_r is, the lower the decision-maker's preference distance is, and the more contributions the decision-maker makes to group consensus.

As to those clusters that only contain one element, the distances between the element and the cluster centers of all the other clusters are calculated and the minimum distance is chosen to represent the corresponding decision-maker's preference distance.

The Optimization of Decision Weight Allocation

The decision weight allocation for group decision-makers can be described as the following optimization problem.

$$\min F(w) = \sum_{r=1}^{l} [CI_r + d_r] w_r^2 \qquad (2)$$

Subject to:

$$w_r \geq 0 \ (r = 1, 2, \cdots, l)$$

$$\sum_{r=1}^{l} w_r = 1$$

where $CI_r = (\frac{\lambda_{\max}^{(r)}}{s-1} - \frac{s}{s-1})$ denotes the consistency degree of decision-maker DM_r and $\sqrt{\sum_{k=1}^{s} |\pi_r(x^k) - \pi(x^k)|^2} = d_r$ denotes that person's preference distance. Equation (2) shows that the higher an expert's consistency is, the lower her/his extremeness is and the larger weight she/he should be assigned. A solution of the decision weight vector assigned to a group of decision-makers, $W = (w_1, w_2, \cdots, w_s)$ is given in the appendix C. Thus we have:

$$w_r = \frac{1}{[(CI_r + d_r) \bullet \sum_{r=1}^{l} \frac{1}{(CI_r + d_r)}]}$$

This approach of allocating decision weighs has at least two advantages over traditional approaches. First, it is less subjectively biased because as the decision weight allocation is based on individuals' current objective decision information with less subjective factors. Second, the allocation approach may be more accurate because it considers both individuals' decision preferences and the differences between individual decision preferences and others' decision preferences of a group.

PROPOSING A MISSION-CRITICAL GROUP DECISION-MAKING SUPPORT APPROACH USING MARKOV CHAIN MODEL

This section proposes a mission-critical group decision-making approach to address the issue of the impact of dynamic decision-making preference change on group decision-making. More specifically, the Markov state transition matrix is used to determine the dynamic nature of group decision-making preference changes, decision-making convergence, and decision preference distance. The section on group decision-making and Markov chains presents how to construct this Markov state transition matrix. Based upon that, an optimal group decision-making choice can be generated.

Group Decision-Making and Markov Chains

After the t rounds adjustment, the preference utility values in all the rounds for decision-maker DM_r are:

$$\pi_r = \begin{Bmatrix} \pi_r^1(x^1) & \pi_r^1(x^2) & \cdots & \pi_r^1(x^s) \\ \pi_r^2(x^1) & \pi_r^2(x^2) & \cdots & \pi_r^2(x^s) \\ \cdots & \cdots & \cdots & \cdots \\ \pi_r^t(x^1) & \pi_r^t(x^2) & \cdots & \pi_r^t(x^s) \end{Bmatrix}.$$

In this matrix, each row stands for the preference utility value vector in each round. Comparing the kth row with the $(k+1)^{th}$ row ($\{k = 1, 2, \cdots, t\}$), if there exists $\pi_r^{k+1}(x^i) \downarrow \Leftrightarrow \pi_r^{k+1}(x^j) \uparrow$, the state variable $E_{ij} = E_{ij} + 1$ is set, which shows that the decision-maker has ever changed her/his preference from the alternative x^i to x^j. For each decision-maker, there are at most $t - 1$ times of adjustment. Packing all the adjustment for the group together, we have:

$$T_r = \begin{bmatrix} 1-\sum_{j\neq 1}\frac{E_{1j}}{E_r} & \frac{E_{12}}{E_r} & \cdots\cdots & \frac{E_{1s}}{E_r} \\ \frac{E_{21}}{E_r} & 1-\sum_{j\neq 2}\frac{E_{2j}}{E_r} & \cdots\cdots & \frac{E_{2s}}{E_r} \\ \cdots\ \cdots\ \cdots & \cdots\ \cdots & \cdots\ \cdots & \cdots \\ \frac{E_{s1}}{E_r} & \frac{E_{s2}}{E_r} & \cdots\cdots & 1-\sum_{j\neq s}\frac{E_{sj}}{E_r} \end{bmatrix} \quad (3)$$

where T_r is the preference state transition matrix for decision-maker DM_r, E_{ij} denotes the preference transition times from x^i to x^j and $E_r = t - 1$ is the sample space for the state transition times.

For example, the preference utility value matrix for decision-maker DM_r is:

$$\Lambda_r = \begin{bmatrix} 0.1 & 0.3 & 0.2 & 0.4 \\ 0.2 & 0.2 & 0.3 & 0.3 \\ 0.2 & 0.3 & 0.2 & 0.3 \\ 0.2 & 0.4 & 0.2 & 0.2 \\ 0.3 & 0.3 & 0.2 & 0.2 \end{bmatrix}.$$

The first row of the matrix is the initial value and the sample space is $t - 1 = 5 - 1 = 4$.

Comparing the second row with the first row, we have $x^2 \rightarrow x^1, x^4 \rightarrow x^3$.

Comparing the third row with the second, we have $x^3 \rightarrow x^2$.

Comparing the fourth row with the third, we have $x^4 \to x^2$.

And, comparing the fifth row with the fourth, we have $x^2 \to x^1$.

According to Equation (9), we have the preference state transition matrix T_r for decision-maker DM_r is:

$$T_r = \begin{bmatrix} 1 & 0 & 0 & 0 \\ 0.5 & 0.5 & 0 & 0 \\ 0 & 0.25 & 0.75 & 0 \\ 0 & 0.25 & 0.25 & 0.5 \end{bmatrix}.$$

In this matrix, $\frac{E_{11}}{E_r} = 1$ shows that the decision-maker never changes her preference on x^1.

Define the overall state transition matrix of the decision-making group in the t rounds adjustment procedure as:

$$T = \frac{1}{l}\sum_{r=1}^{l} T_r. \tag{4}$$

In Appendix D, a review on discrete time Markov chains is given. It is also shown that the group decision-making procedure satisfies a Markov chain. Therefore, the Markov property can be used to predict adjustments of the decision-makers' preference.

Nine Implementation Steps of the Proposed Group Decision-Making Support Approach

The proposed approach for supporting mission-critical group decision-making works in following nine steps:

1. State a group decision-making problem and background information to each group member, including the mission-critical event, available information, constraints, decision alternatives, decision-making rules, the user handbook of a MC-GDSS that is being used, and so forth.
2. Each decision-maker gives her/his preference judgments between each two alternatives on the set of alternatives using the quantificational values given in Appendix A. The preference judgment values for decision-maker DM_r are presented in the matrix P_r. All the decision-makers can share their opinions, evidences, and explanations on the screen of the MC-GDSS system to support their view points.
3. Substituting the corresponding values into the approximate calculation algorithm presented in Appendix A yields the preference utility values for a decision-maker DM_r in the tth round, $\{\pi_r^t(x^1), \pi_r^t(x^2), \cdots, \pi_r^t(x^s)\}$. As stated, the individual preference adjustment in group decision-making is a continuous procedure in which the decision-makers adjust their preference in each round respectively based on the communications among the group members. The continuous adjustments make group decisions converge gradually. The preference utility values vector $\{\pi_r^t(x^1), \pi_r^t(x^2), \cdots, \pi_r^t(x^s)\}$ for the decision-maker is used for constructing the Markov state transition matrix in step (8).
4. With the preference values worked out in step (3), the preference utility values matrix Λ^t for the tth round are had. Using the Equation (-16), the preference distance d_{ij} between decision-maker DM_i and DM_j on X are had. Substituting these preference distances into Equation (17), the preference difference matrix D can be constucted. Furthermore, given $\varepsilon = \frac{\max d_{ij} - \min d_{ij}}{2}$, clustering analysis on the preference difference matrix D based on the definitions 3 and 4 can be done.
5. The MC-GDSS system displays the preference utility values and the clustering results on screen, which is a public communication space for group decision-makers to see and then maybe adjust their preferences. After that, members can go back to step (2) and begin another round of decision discussion

with further preference judgment as well.

6. Repeat the above procedure from step (2) to step (5) for $t = 7 \pm 2$ times. The choice of $t = 7 \pm 2$ is based on two reasons. First, conventional Delphi method usually repeats more than four times (Giunipero, Handfield, & Eltantawy, 2006; Lao, Dovrolis, & Sanadidi, 2006). Second, empirical research in psychology shows that 7 ± 2 is a common experienced value for human being's thinking-span (Myers, 2005; Murphy, Roodenrys, & Fox, 2006; Over, Hooge, & Erkelens, 2006). In addition, the value for t can also be determined by a group decision meeting organizer according to the meeting time limit and other factors.
7. Calculating the weight assigned to each decision-maker with the solution given in the appendix C yields the weight vector $W = (w_1, w_2, \cdots, w_s)$ for the group.
8. Constructing the Markov state transition matrix T using Equation (3) and (4) with the saved preference values $\{\pi_r'(x^1), \pi_r'(x^2), \cdots, \pi_r'(x^s)\}$.
9. Multiplying decision weight vector $W = (w_1, w_2, \cdots, w_s)$ by the preference matrix Λ in the last round, and then by the Markov state transition matrix T, we have Equation 5, seen in Box 1. Where $[x^1, x^2, \cdots, x^s]$ is the preference utility values vector on the decision alternative set X and $\max\{x^i\}$ $(i = 1, 2, \cdots, s)$ is the final decision made by the group.

Here some points on this group decision-making support approach are clarified:

1. The nine steps of group decision-making only need some interactions between group decision-makers and a MC-GDSS system, without additional interactions of group decision meeting's organizer as in traditional group decision-making setting. In this way, decision-making process may be sped up, which is important to mission-critical decision-making tasks.
2. Each decision maker can share her/his opinion, present her/his explanation, and browse other's opinions anonymously or with her/his identity.
3. The clustering analysis result of individual decision preference values in each decision round is displayed in public screen and used as a reference for decision preference adjustment for the next decision round.
4. Every decision-maker is encouraged to adjust her/his preference based upon the clustering analysis result of the previous decision round. If each decision-maker sticks to her/his initial decision position and does not adjust her/his decision preference at all in following decision rounds, the group will never reach consensus and such group decision-making makes no sense, which should be stopped. Otherwise, after a few rounds of group interactions, it could be possible for a group to reach consensus and final group decision can be achieved.

Box 1.

$$[w_1, w_2, \cdots, w_s] \begin{bmatrix} \pi_1(x^1) & \pi_1(x^2) & \cdots & \pi_1(x^s) \\ \pi_2(x^1) & \pi_2(x^2) & \cdots & \pi_2(x^s) \\ \cdots & \cdots & \cdots & \cdots \\ \pi_l(x^1) & \pi_l(x^2) & \cdots & \pi_l(x^s) \end{bmatrix} \begin{bmatrix} T_{11} & T_{12} & \cdots & T_{1s} \\ T_{21} & T_{22} & \cdots & T_{2s} \\ \cdots & \cdots & & \cdots \\ T_{s1} & T_{s2} & \cdots & T_{ss} \end{bmatrix} = [x^1 \quad x^2 \quad \cdots \quad x^s] \tag{5}$$

A Real Case Illustrating the Usefulness and Effectiveness of the Proposed Approach

Background Information

1. New Orleans is the largest city of the state of Louisiana in the USA and the second largest American port next to New York City. It is located at the southeast part of the state of Louisiana and at the lower part of Mississippi River near the sea. The city is next to Pontchartrain Lake in its north. The city is around 950 square kilometers with a population of 500,000. Moreover, the Great New Orleans District has a population of 1180,000.

In August 2005, Katrina, a category 5 hurricane called a "Perfect Hurricane" by meteorologists with its 280 kilometer-per-hour winds, lashed the city of New Orleans. New Orleans Mayor Ray Nagin of the city of New Orleans called for voluntary evacuation of the city's residents on August 27, 2005.

On August 28, New Orleans Mayor Ray Nagin sent down a compelling order of all-out evacuation of the city's residents and provided 10 refuges for the city's remaining residents. The Louisiana Superdome is assigned as an island refuge.

On August 29, Katrina made a landfall as a category 5 hurricane over the Gulf of Mexico and lashed Southern America. New Orleans's flood embankments could not withstand the ferocity of the hurricane and were breached at two sites. As a result, 80% of the city was flooded. In some parts of the city, the water continued to rise at a speed of one foot per hour.

Constraints

The New Orleans government assigned a 7000-people rescue army. For 700,000 refugees scattered in an area of 950 square kilometers, the rescuers were only one percent of the refugees.

The city was out of communication. Except the 10 refuges, the rescuers were not aware of the location or quantity of the refugees. The city was out of traffic transportation. The vehicles such as buses were not usable any more. Helicopters were the main transporters. Moreover, the city was out of clean water, power, and cooking. There have already appeared hostile looting and murders.

Decision Alternatives

x^1 (the first decision alternative for this mission-critical event): Search for the separated refugees. If the rescue is just in time, the death rate of the refugees can be reduced. Although people in refuges were besieged, they could be kept away from death.

x^2 (the second decision alternative for this mission-critical event): Evacuate those serious patients. Without clean water and power, they might die immediately.

x^3 (the third decision alternative for this mission-critical event): Evacuate people in refuges as there is no clean water, power, and cooking. Give up the search for separated refugees temporarily because they may not die in a reasonable time period.

x^4 (the fourth decision alternative for this mission-critical event): Arrest the looters in order to make the city safe, which can also help with the rescue work to be done in a safe context.

2. Assume that there are six decision-makers in the governmental rescue committee. Every decision-maker does pair wise judgments and gives her/his preference judgment according to the quantitative values given in Table 1 of the first section. The initial preference judgment matrix is illustrated in Table 1.
3. Substituting the corresponding values into the approximate calculation algorithm

Table 1. Pair wise preference judgments and preference utility values on a set of alternatives

DM_1	x^1	x^2	x^3	x^4	π	CI	DM_2	x^1	x^2	x^3	x^4	π	CI
x^1	1.00	0.33	3.00	0.33	0.17		x^1	1.00	5.00	2.00	1.00	0.38	
x^2	3.00	1.00	2.00	1.00	0.36		x^2	0.20	1.00	1.00	0.50	0.12	
x^3	0.33	0.50	1.00	0.50	0.12		x^3	0.50	1.00	1.00	0.17	0.11	
x^4	3.00	1.00	2.00	1.00	0.35	0.097	x^4	1.00	2.00	6.00	1.00	0.39	0.087
DM_3	x^1	x^2	x^3	x^4	π	CI	DM_4	x^1	x^2	x^3	x^4	π	CI
x^1	1.00	0.33	2.00	0.20	0.13		x^1	1.00	5.00	3.00	2.00	0.50	
x^2	3.00	1.00	3.00	1.00	0.37		x^2	0.20	1.00	2.00	2.00	0.20	
x^3	0.50	0.33	1.00	0.50	0.12		x^3	0.33	0.50	1.00	0.33	0.10	
x^4	5.00	1.00	2.00	1.00	0.38	0.075	x^4	0.50	0.50	3.00	1.00	0.20	0.123
DM_5	x^1	x^2	x^3	x^4	π	CI	DM_6	x^1	x^2	x^3	x^4	π	CI
x^1	1.00	0.33	6.00	5.00	0.34		x^1	1.00	5.00	4.00	0.33	0.33	
x^2	3.00	1.00	5.00	3.00	0.48		x^2	0.20	1.00	0.50	0.33	0.09	
x^3	0.17	0.20	1.00	2.00	0.10		x^3	0.25	2.00	1.00	0.50	0.15	
x^4	0.20	0.33	0.50	1.00	0.08	0.139	x^4	3.00	3.00	2.00	1.00	0.43	0.132

presented in the appendix A, we have the preference utility values for a decision-maker DM_r in the tth round, $\{\pi_r^t(x^1), \pi_r^t(x^2), \cdots, \pi_r^t(x^s)\}$. The preference utility values for the six decision-makers in the first round are shown in Table 2.

4. With the preference utility values worked out in step (3), we have the preference utility values matrix Λ^t for the tth round. Using Equation (16), we have the preference distance d_{ij} between decision-maker DM_i and DM_j on X. Substituting these preference distances into Equation (17), the preference difference matrix D can be constructed. The preference distances and the preference difference matrix are shown in Table 3.

Given $\varepsilon = \frac{\max d_{ij} - \min d_{ij}}{2}$, we have $\varepsilon^1 = 0.239$, as shown in Table 3 in bold font. Thus, we get $d_{31} \leq \varepsilon^1$, $d_{62} \leq \varepsilon^1$. According to the definitions 3 and 4, there are 4 clusters in this round, DM_1 and DM_3 belong to the same cluster in $\varepsilon^1 = 0.239$, so do the DM_2 and DM_6. DM_4 and DM_5 are independent clusters respectively. The cluster analysis result is shown in Figure 1. In Figure 1, the numbered black dots denote the current preference states of the decision-makers. The diameter of the circle is the clustering distance in this round, $\varepsilon^1 = 0.239$. All the dots that can be enclosed in a circle belong to a specific cluster, which shows that the decision-makers in the same cluster come to partial consensus in ε.

5. The preference judgment results can then feedback to all the decision-makers based upon the results as shown in Table 3 and Figure 1. Decision-makers can make adjustments after seeing the first round of deliberation. The group then begins another round of decision-making (i.e., repeating the decision-making process starting from step 2).
6. Repeat step (2) through step (5) for five times, t = 5.

Table 2. The preference value for every decision-maker in the first round

0.17	0.36	0.12	0.35
0.38	0.12	0.11	0.39
0.13	0.37	0.12	0.38
0.50	0.20	0.10	0.20
0.34	0.48	0.10	0.08
0.33	0.09	0.15	0.43

Figure 1. Clustering result of the individual preference utility values in the first round

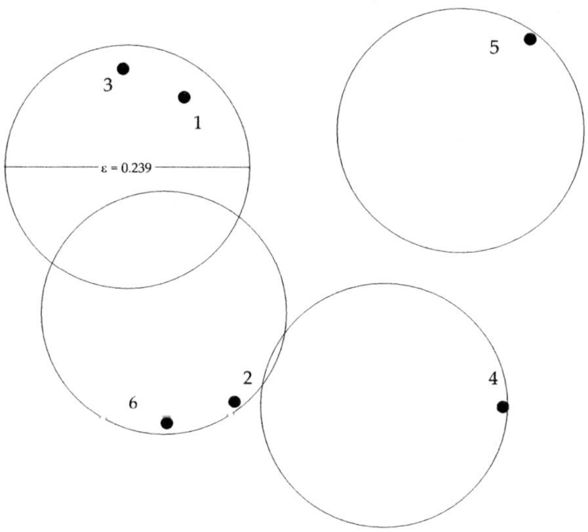

7. Different preference difference matrices in each round are gotten. Here the difference matrix in the last round are only presented, as shown in Figure 2 and Table 4. The scales in Figure 1 and Figure 2 are the same.

DM_1 and DM_3 belong to the same cluster in $\varepsilon^1 = 0.239$, so do the DM_2 and DM_6. DM_4 and DM_5.

As shown in Figure 2, the clustering distance in the fifth round is $\varepsilon^5 = 0.143$. It can be seen that the individual preferences are clustered into three clusters. DM_1, DM_3 and DM_4 belong to the same cluster, DM_3 and DM_5 belong to the same cluster, and DM_2 and DM_6 belong to the same cluster. In Figure 2, the diameter of the larger circle is the clustering distance in the first round ($\varepsilon^1 = 0.239$). From this figure, it is easy to see that if we use this distance to cluster the individual preferences, five decision-makers have come to consensus in $\varepsilon^1 = 0.239$, that is, DM_1, DM_2, DM_3, DM_4, and DM_6. Thus the clustering distance is reduced gradually in each round and shows the convergence of the group preference and the procedure of reaching consensus.

Substituting the values into the solution given in the appendix C yields the weight vector for the decision-making group $W = (0.131\ 0.264\ 0.163\ 0.165\ \ 0.113\ \ 0.162)$.

Table 3. Preference difference matrix in the first round

0					
0.313	0				
0.054	0.353	0			
0.393	0.245	0.446	0		
0.347	0.486	0.383	0.350	0	
0.321	**0.071**	0.354	0.307	0.532	0

8. Construct the Markov state transition matrix T using Equation (3) and (4) with the saved preference utility values $\{\pi_r^l(x^1), \pi_r^l(x^2), \cdots, \pi_r^l(x^n)\}$. In this example, if $\pi_r^k(x^i) - \pi_r^{k+1}(x^i) > 0.01$ and $\pi_r^{k+1}(x^j) - \pi_r^k(x^j) > 0.01$ occurs, it is considered as an one time transition $\pi_r^{k+1}(x^i)\downarrow \Leftrightarrow \pi_r^{k+1}(x^j)\uparrow$, let the state variable $E_{ij} = E_{ij} + 1$, thus it indicates that the decision-maker DM_r transits from alternative x^i to alternative x^j for one time. The final preference state transition matrix is

$$T = \begin{bmatrix} 0.333 & 0.417 & 0.0417 & 0.208 \\ 0.125 & 0.875 & 0 & 0 \\ 0.083 & 0 & 0.917 & 0 \\ 0.292 & 0.333 & 0.083 & 0.292 \end{bmatrix}.$$

Table 4. Preference difference matrix in the fifth round

0					
0.155	0				
0.098	0.215	0			
0.079	0.145	**0.091**	0		
0.211	0.318	**0.115**	0.186	0	
0.155	**0.060**	0.236	0.168	0.346	0

9. Multiply the weight vector $W = (w_1, w_2, \cdots, w_s)$ by the preference matrix Λ in the last round, and then by the Markov state transition matrix T, we have

$$\begin{bmatrix} 0.131 & 0.264 & 0.163 \\ 0.165 & 0.113 & 0.162 \end{bmatrix} \begin{bmatrix} 0.23 & 0.32 & 0.19 & 0.26 \\ 0.33 & 0.23 & 0.13 & 0.31 \\ 0.22 & 0.40 & 0.15 & 0.23 \\ 0.28 & 0.35 & 0.15 & 0.22 \\ 0.21 & 0.50 & 0.11 & 0.18 \\ 0.31 & 0.20 & 0.17 & 0.32 \end{bmatrix} = [0.273 \quad 0.314 \quad 0.148 \quad 0.262] \qquad (6)$$

$$\begin{bmatrix} 0.273 & 0.314 \\ 0.148 & 0.262 \end{bmatrix} \begin{bmatrix} 0.333 & 0.417 & 0.0417 & 0.208 \\ 0.125 & 0.875 & 0 & 0 \\ 0.083 & 0 & 0.917 & 0 \\ 0.292 & 0.333 & 0.083 & 0.292 \end{bmatrix} = [0.219 \quad 0.476 \quad 0.169 \quad 0.133]. \qquad (7)$$

[0.219 0.476 0.169 0.133] is the preference utility values vector on the set of alternatives X and the alternative x^2, corresponding to $\max\{x^i\}$ ($i = 1, 2, \cdots, s$) = 0.476, is the final alternative chosen by the decision-making group.

Comparing the result of Equation (6) with the result of (7), it can be seen that if the possible decision preference changes are not taken into account (the dynamic nature of group decision-making process), it will come to the static conclusion $x^2Rx^1Rx^4Rx^3$ as shown in Equation (6) (i.e., the

Figure 2. Clustering result in the fifth round

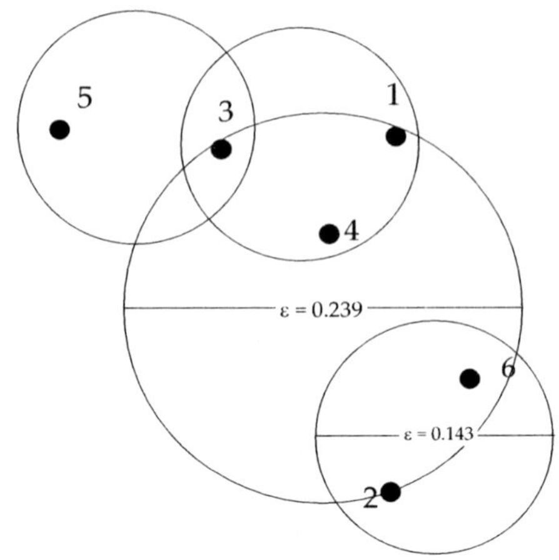

preferred decision alternatives are determined in following sequential order: the most preferred decision alternative x^2, followed by the decision alternatives x^1, x^4, and x^3). This conclusion is drawn by traditional meta-synthetic approaches on group decision-making, that is, after decision weights for every decision-maker are assigned and fixed, the group preference value on each decision alternative is determined by the sum of each decision-maker's decision weight multiplied by her/his *current preference value* of the alternative. Finally, all alternatives are sorted in the order of their preference values to derive the final group decision.

On the other hand, if the possible decision preference changes are not taken into account, the conclusion comes to the result $x^2Rx^1Rx^4Rx^3$ as shown in Equation (7), different from the result of Equation (6), which would be closer to group decision-making in reality. This difference shows the importance of considering dynamic decision preference change into group decision-making model.

The decision difference between traditional methods and the currently proposed one may not always ensure a better group decision result, which will be further discussed.

Box 2.

$$\begin{cases} [\pi_1 \quad \pi_2 \quad \pi_3 \quad \pi_4] = [\pi_1 \quad \pi_2 \quad \pi_3 \quad \pi_4] \begin{bmatrix} 0.333 & 0.417 & 0.0417 & 0.208 \\ 0.125 & 0.875 & 0 & 0 \\ 0.083 & 0 & 0.917 & 0 \\ 0.292 & 0.333 & 0.083 & 0.292 \end{bmatrix} \\ \pi_1 + \pi_2 + \pi_3 + \pi_4 = 1 \\ \pi_i > 0 \quad i = 1, \cdots, s \end{cases} \tag{10}$$

Considering an ergodic Markov chaie, let T be a probability matrix. If there exists a $m(m > 1, m \in Z)$, which makes all the elements of T^m positive, T is called a normal stochastic matrix. A probability vector π must exist, which makes

$$\pi = \pi T \text{ and } \pi_j = \lim_{n \to \infty} T_{ij}^{\,n} \textit{ for all } i \tag{8}$$

The probability vector π is called the steady state vector for the state transition matrix T.

It is easy to show that the preference state transition matrix in our example is a normal stochastic matrix. Thus there must exist a probability vector π, the steady state solution to the group decision-making problem on the alternative set. Therefore the following Equations are resolved.

$$\begin{cases} \pi = \pi T \\ \sum_{i=1}^{s} \pi_i = 1 \\ \pi_i > 0 \quad i = 1, \cdots, s \end{cases} \tag{9}$$

or see Box 2.

We have

$$\pi = [0.161014988 \quad 0.663345006 \quad 0.128267958 \quad 0.047323744] \tag{11}$$

The result shown in Equation (11) represents the decision preference order $x^2Rx^1Rx^4Rx^3$, the same result derived from Equation (7). Note that now this conclusion in Equation (11) has nothing to do with the decision weight vector W and decision preference value matrix Λ in the last round, and only depends on the decision preference state transition matrix T.

Comparing the Equations (6), (7), and (11), several conclusions can be drawn:

1. The traditional meta-synthetic approaches on group decision-making, neglecting the dynamic nature of decision preference adjustments/changes of group decision-makers, can lead to the loss of important decision element/information for group decision-making.
2. The dynamic nature of decision preference adjustment/change is one important part of group decision-making process, which should not be neglected.
3. The conclusion drawn on Equation (11) merely depends on the Markov state transition matrix, not on the decision weight vector W and decision preference value matrix Λ in the last round. This shows that if there would be enough time for a group to continue group decision-making process, group consensus will be reached in the form as shown in Equation (11).

4. The static conclusion $x^2 R x^1 R x^4 R x^3$ derived from Equation (6) can be considered as a transient result that will change as group decision-making process proceeds.
5. The dynamic decision-making conclusion $x^2 R x^1 R x^4 R x^3$ derived from Equation (7) can be considered as a stationary result that includes the developing trend of group decision-making process. That is that, as group decision-making rounds continue ($t > 5 \rightarrow \infty$), group decision result will come to the conclusion as shown Equation (11), the same as being derived from Equation (7).
6. As a result, it is shown that the group decision-making steps based on the Markov Chain, can help a group derive decision conclusion, as shown by Equation (11), which could otherwise be achieved by a big number of (or even infinite) group decision-making rounds. Therefore, in mission-critical group decision-making situation with short response time, the proposed approach could help a group reach consensus on final group decision within a few decision-making rounds (usually 5~9 rounds), rather than a big number of decision-making rounds (or infinite decision-making rounds), which may lead to more efficient and effective group decision-making.

DISCUSSION AND FUTURE RESEARCH

Discussion and Implications

This study contributes to the research literature in three aspects. First, prior research does not consider group decision-making preference being dynamic, which would be fixed and not be changed in group decision-making process, neglecting its existence and its impact on group decision-making. The proposed approach in this article solves this problem using the Markov Chain model. Further, the proposed approach can automatically determine and present group decision-makers' decision preference distances as well as similar decision preference clusters they belong to, which clearly shows similar and different positions of group decision-makers on a given mission-critical decision-making task in its first round and subsequent decision-making rounds, which in turn may support group decision-makers in more effectively adjusting their decision preferences/positions to help reach group final decision more efficiently and effectively. This is very important to mission-critical decision-making tasks. Future studies can use empirical research methodologies to examine this research issue.

Second, the proposed group decision weight allocation approach solves the problems of traditional methods that require substantial historical decision data and largely involve subjective judgment.

Third, the proposed approach provides a solution to Coudorcet's group decision paradox. One commonly used group decision rule is group concensus or majority rule (Nunamaker, Briggs, Mittleman, Vogel, & Balthazard, 1997; Huang & Wei, 1997; Huang, Wei, & Tan, 1999; Watson, DeSanctis, & Poole, 1988). When there are more than three decision alternatives, it may be possible to generate a group decision cyclic loop, which would be theoretically impossible to read a group consensus or majority rule (Coudorcet, 1785). For example, there are three decision-makers (DM_1, DM_2, DM_3) in a group and three alternatives (A, B, C). Table 5 shows possible decision results for each decision-maker.

It is so-called the Voting Paradox (also known as Condorcet's paradox) (Coudorcet, 1785; Deemen, 1999; Nanson, 1882), as shown in Figure 3.

Let the number of decision-makers in a group be l, P denotes the probability of generating group decision circular loop based on majority rule. Prior studies report the relationship between l and P, as shown in Table 6 (Niem & Weisberg, 1968);

Table 5. Decision result for each decision maker

Decision Maker	Preferences
DM_1	$A\ R_1\ B\ R_1\ C$
DM_2	$B\ R_2\ C\ R_2\ A$
DM_3	$C\ R_3\ A\ R_3\ B$

but when l is large, the relationship between the number of alternatives s and P is shown in Table 7 (Niem & Weisberg, 1968).

In this research, each decision-maker's decision preference judgment matrix based on pair wise comparisons are had and the characteristic vector from AHP is introduced to derive the sequential order of decision alternatives of each decision-maker. When decision-makers do pair wise comparisons on decision alternatives, which leads to a group decision preference judgment matrix, this matrix might result in group decision cyclic loops. However, this matrix is only used for determining group decision-makers' decision weights, not for determining group's final decision. So it will not lead to Condorcet's paradox. When a group comes to the final group decision, a group decision cyclic loop can be avoided because the group decision sequential order of decision alternatives from a decision-maker are gotten based upon the calculation of the characteristic vector of her preference judgment matrix, not the preference judgment matrix itself. Therefore, the group decision-making approach proposed in this research can avoid the possibility of group decision circular loop, which provides a solution to Condorcet's paradox in group decision-making.

In practice, incorporating the proposed approaches to an existing GDSS system, the system may have a potential to help a group reach group decision consensus faster and more effectively, which can be especially important to mission-critical decision-making tasks. While global terrorism currently becomes one major threat

Figure 3. Voting paradox

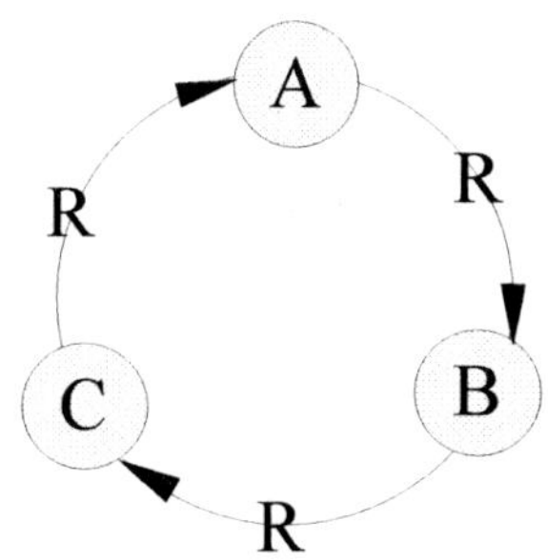

to all the countries of the world, and while more globalized world economy would possibly lead to one country's major economic problem quickly becoming an emerging mission-critical problem of other countries within days or sometimes hours, many of those cross-border mission-critical problems would require group decision-makers to respond quickly and make decisions quickly. The proposed approach provides a possible solution to those mission-critical group decision-making problems that may be faced by both developed and developing countries. Field studies can be conducted to further investigate the effectiveness of such proposed GDSS systems in the future.

Research Limitation

It should be noted that not all the Markov state transition matrices in group decision-making process, based on the Markov chain approach, would surely be normal stochastic ones, which can be shown in the example.

If decision preference adjustment only runs for a few rounds, for example, $t < 5$, the overall state transition matrix for a group can be shown in the matrix T:

$$T=\begin{bmatrix} 1 & 0 & 0 & 0 \\ 0.5 & 0.5 & 0 & 0 \\ 0 & 0.25 & 0.75 & 0 \\ 0 & 0.25 & 0.25 & 0.5 \end{bmatrix}.$$

Table 6. Relationship between l and P

l	*P*
3	0.0556
9	0.078
15	0.082
25	0.0843
…	…
∞	0.0877

Table 7. Relationship between s and P

s	*P*
3	0.0877
9	0.4545
15	0.082
25	0.7297
…	…
∞	1

It is clear that T is not a normal stochastic matrix, and its steady state solution can not be resolved using Equation (9). In this case, group decision-making result can be conducted derived from Equation (7) instead of Equations (8) ~ (11). As a result, the proposed approach, though being efficient and effective in most cases, may not be so in all cases. Future research can look at this limitation and provide further improvement.

REFERENCES

Arrow, K. J. (1963). *Social choice and individual values.* New York: JohnWiley & Sons.

Bar-Eli, M., & Tractinsky, N. (2000). Criticality of game situations and decision making in basketball-an application of performance crisis perspective. *Psychology of Sport and Exercise, 1*, 27-39.

Belardo, S., & Wallace, W. A. (1989). Gaming as a means for evaluating decision support systems for emergency management response. In J. Sullivan & R. Newkirk (Eds.), *Simulation in emergency management and technology, simulation series* (pp. 113-117).

Beroggi, G. E. G., Mendonça, D., & Wallace, W. A. (2003). Operational sustainability management for the infrastructure: The case of emergency response. In A. Sage (Ed.), *Encyclopedia of life support systems.* Oxford, UK: EOLSS Publishers Co. Ltd.

Bordley, R. F., & Wolff, R. W. (1981). On the aggregation of individual probability estimates. *Management Science, 27*(8), 959-964.

Chen, R., Sharman, R., Rao, H. R., et al. (2005). Design principles of coordinated multi-incident emergency response systems. *Lecture Notes in Computer Science, 3495*, 81-93.

Chen, S. Y., Fu, G. T. (2005). Combining fuzzy iteration model with dynamic programming to solve multiobjective multistage decision making problems. *Fuzzy Sets and Systems, 152*(3), 499-512.

Condorcet, M. D. (1785). Essai sur l' Application de l' Analyse à la Probabilité des Décisions Renduesà la Plurali té des Voix. Paris: L'imprimerie Royale.

Deemen, A. V. (1999). *The probability of the paradox of voting for weak preference orderings, social choice and welfare.* Berlin: Springer.

Dyer, J. S., & Sarin, R. K. (1979). Group preference aggregation rules based on strength of preference. *Management Science, 25*(9), 22-34.

Fjermestad, J., & Hiltz, S. R. (1999). An assessment of group support systems experimental research: Methodology and results. *Journal of Management Information Systems, 15*(3), 7-150.

French, S. (1986). *Decision theory: An introduction to the mathematics of rationality.* Chichester: Ellis Harwood.

Giunipero, L., Handfield, R. B., & Eltantawy, R. (2006). Supply management's evolution: key skill sets for the supply manager of the future. *International Journal of Operations & Production Management, 26*(7), 822-844.

Huang, W. (2003). Impacts of GSS generic structures and task types on group communication process and outcome: Some expected and unexpected research findings. *Behavior & Information Technology, 22*(1), 17-29.

Huang, W., & Li, D. (2007). Opening up the black box in GSS research: explaining group decision outcome with group process. *Computers in Human Behavior, 23*(1), 58-78.

Huang, W., & Wei, K. K. (2000). An empirical investigation of effects of GSS and task type on social interactions from an influence perspective. *Journal of Management Information Systems, 17*(2), 181-206.

Huang, W., & Wei, K. K. (1997). Task as a moderator for the effects of group support systems on group influence processes. *European Journal of Information Systems, December 6*, 208-217.

Huang, W., Wei, K. K., & Lim, J. (2003). Using GSS to support global virtual team-building: A theoretical framework. *International Journal of Global Information Management, 11*(1), 72-89.

Huang, W., Wei, K.K., and Tan, C.Y. (1999). Compensating effects of GSS on group performance. *Information & Management*, 35, 195-202.

Huang, W., Wei, K. K., Watson, R. T., & Tan, C. Y. (2003). Supporting virtual team-building with a GSS: An empirical investigation. *Decision Support Systems, 34*(4), 359-367.

Keeney, R. L., & Kirkwood, C. W. (1975). Group decision making using cardinal social welfare functions. *Management Science, 22*(4), 430-437.

Lao, L., Dovrolis, C., & Sanadidi, M. Y. (2006). The probe gap model can underestimate the available bandwidth of multihop paths. *Computer Communication Review, 36*(5), 29-34.

LaPorte, T., & Consilini, N. (1991). Working in practice but not in theory: theoretical challenges of "High Reliability Organizations". *Journal of Public Administration Research and Theory, 1*(1), 19-47.

Limayem, M., Banerjee, P., & Ma, L. (2006). Impact of GDSS: Opening the black box. *Decision Support Systems, 42*(2), 945-957.

Mallach, E. G. (2000). *Decision support and data warehouse systems*. New York: McGraw-Hill.

Mendonca, D., Beroggi, G. E. G., Gent, D. V., & Wallace, W. A. (2006). Designing gaming simulations for the assessment of group decision support systems in emergency response. *Safety Science, 44* (6), 523-535.

Murphy, K., Roodenrys, S., & Fox, A. (2006). Event-related potential correlates of the word length effect in working memory. *Brain Research, 1112*, 179-190.

Myers, D. G. (2005). *Social psychology*. New York: McGraw-Hill.

Nanson, E. J. (1882). Methods of election, transactions and proceedings of the royal society of Victoria, Vol. 18.

Niemi, R. G., & Weisberg, H. F. (1968). A mathematical solution for the probability of the paradox of voting. *Behavioral Science, 13*, 317.

Nunamaker, J. F., Briggs, R. O., Mittleman, D. D., Vogel, D. R., & Balthazard, P. A. (1997). Lesssons from a dozen years of group support systems research: A discussion of lab and field findings. *Journal of Management Information Systems, 13*(3), 163-207.

Ody, K. (1995). Facilitating the "right" decision in crisis-Supporting the crisis decision maker through analysis of their needs. *Safety Science, 20*, 125-133.

Over, E. A. B., Hooge, I. T. C., & Erkelens, C. J. (2006). A quantitative measure for the uniformity of fixation density: The Voronoi method. *Behavior Research Methods, 38*(2), 251-261.

Papazoglou, I. A., & Christou, M. D. (1997). Decision support system for emergency response to major nuclear accidents. *Nuclear Technology, 118*(2), 97-122.

Potter, R. E., & Balthazard, P. (2004). The role of individual memory and attention processes during electronic brainstorming. *MIS Quarterly, 28*(4), 621-643.

Saaty, T. L. (1988). *What is the analytic hierarchy process?* New York: Springer-Verlag Inc.

Shyur, H. J., & Shih, H. S. (2006). A hybrid MCDM model for strategic vendor selection. *Mathematical and Computer Modeling, 44*(7-8), 749-761.

Tan, B., Wei, K. K., Huang, W., & Ng, G. N. (2000). A dialogue technical to enhance electronic communication in virtual teams. *IEEE Transactions on Professional Communication, 43*(2), 153-165.

Vogel, D. R., Martz, W. B., Nunamaker, J. F., Grohowski, R. B., & McGoff, C. (1990). Electronic meeting system experience at IBM. *Journal of Management Information Systems, 6*(3), 25-43.

Wallace, W. A., & DeBalogh, F. (1985). Decision support systems for disaster management. *Public Administration Review, 45*, 134-146.

Watson, R. T., DeSanctis, G., & Poole, M. S. (1988). Using a GDSS to facilitate group consensus: some intended and unintended consequences. *MIS Quarterly, 12*(3), 463-478.

Weisaeth, L., Knudsen, O., & Tonnessen, A. (2002). Technological disasters, crisis management and leadership stress. *Journal of Hazardous Materials, 93*, 33-45.

Wilkenfeld, J., Kraus, S., Holley, K. M., & Harris M. A. (1995). GENIE: A decision support system for crisis negotiations. *Decision Support Systems, 14*, 369-391.

Williams, A. H., & Cookson, R. A. (2006). Equity-efficiency trade-offs in health technology assessment. *International Journal of Technology Assessment in Health Care, 22*(1), 1-9.

Zigurs, I., DeSanctis, G., & Billingsley, J. (1991). Adoption patterns and attitudinal development in computer-supported meetings: An exploratory study with SAMM. *Journal of Management Information Systems, 7*(4), 51-70.

Zografos, K. G., Vasilakis, G. M., & Giannouli, I. M. (2000). Methodological framework for developing decision support systems (DSS) for hazardous materials emergency response operations. *Journal of Hazardous Materials, 71*(1-3), 503-521.

ENDNOTE

1 This work is supported by the National Science Foundation of China (NSFC) under Grant 70671066.

APPENDIX A

A.1 Definition of Preference Utility Value and a Set of its Quantificational Values

Let G denote a decision-making group, DM_r be the rth decision-maker of the group with l decision-makers, then $G = \{DM_r | r \in \Omega\}(\Omega = \{1, 2, \cdots, l\}, 2 \leq l < +\infty)$. Let X be a set of alternatives, x^i be the ith alternative and there are s alternatives in the alternative set, then $X = \{x^i | i \in \Omega\}(\Omega = \{1, 2, \cdots, s\}, 2 \leq s < +\infty)$.

Definition 1. Preference utility value $\theta_r(x^i, x^j)$: *Let R_r denote the preference relation of DM_r on X. Let $x^i R_r x^j$ denote that comparing x^i with $x^j(x^i, x^j \in X)$, DM_r tends to choose x^i. According to the needs of the decision-making, let $\theta_r(x^i, x^j)$, a real number, denote the quantificational difference of DM_r's preference degrees on the two alternatives x^i and x^j.*

Let's define the quantificational values of $\theta_r(x^i, x^j)$ as in Table 5.

$\theta_r(x^i, x^j)$	the signification to DM_r
1	x^i and x^j has equal preference degree
3	Compared with x^j, x^i is a little better
5	Compared with x^j, x^i is better
7	Compared with x^j, x^i is much better
9	Compared with x^j, x^i is absolutely better
2, 4, 6, 8	The middle state's corresponding utility values of the judgments
reciprocal	Compared x^j with x^i, the utility value of preference $\theta_r(x^j,x^i) = 1 / \theta_r(x^i,x^j)$, $\theta_r(x^i,x^i) = 1$

A.2 The Solving Process of the Consistence Indicator CI_r

From the theory of matrix, the Equation $(P_r - \lambda I)\pi^T = 0$ has at least one group of solutions, where π^T is the characteristic vector, λ is the characteristic value. An approximate calculation algorithm is given to get the maximal characteristic value $\lambda_{max}^{(r)}$ and characteristic vector $\pi_r = (\pi_r(x^1), \pi_r(x^2), \cdots, \pi_r(x^s))$ of P_r in Appendix A.

1. Calculate the geometric mean of all the elements in each row of the matrix

$$\bar{\pi}_r(x^i) = \sqrt[s]{\prod_{j=1}^{s} \theta_r(x^i, x^j)} \quad i = 1,2,\cdots,s \tag{12}$$

We have $\bar{\pi}_r = (\bar{\pi}_r(x^1), \bar{\pi}_r(x^2), \cdots, \bar{\pi}_r(x^s))$

2. Normalize $\bar{\pi}_r(x^1)$

$$\pi_r(x^i) = \frac{\overline{\pi}_r(x^i)}{\sum_{j=1}^{s} \overline{\pi}_r(x^j)} \quad i = 1, 2, \cdots, s \tag{13}$$

Then $\pi_r = (\pi_r(x^1), \pi_r(x^2), \cdots, \pi_r(x^s))$ is the approximate solution of the characteristic vector. We call $\pi_r(x^1)$ the preference utility value of DM_r on x^1. The set $\{\pi_r(x^1), \pi_r(x^2), \cdots, \pi_r(x^s)\}$ denotes the preference utility values set of DM_r on the set of alternatives.

3. Calculate the maximal characteristic value $\lambda_{\max}^{(r)}$ of the matrix P_r

$$\lambda_{\max}^{(r)} = \sum_{i=1}^{s} \frac{(\mathrm{P}_r \pi_r)_i}{s \pi_r(x^i)} \tag{14}$$

where $(P_r \pi_r)_i$ is the ith element of the vector $P_r \pi_r$.

The consistency test index CI from AHP is introduced (Saaty, 1988)

$$CI_r = \frac{\lambda_{\max}^{(r)} - s}{s - 1} = \frac{\lambda_{\max}^{(r)}}{s - 1} - \frac{s}{s - 1} \tag{15}$$

Let CI_r denote the rth decision maker DM_r's preference judgment consistency. CI_r is an indicator to measure whether the decision maker's judgment is careful. The smaller CI_r is, the better it is. Especially, when $CI_r = 0$, the preference judgment matrix P_r is a complete consistency matrix, which represents the complete consistency of DM_r's preference judgment. However, when people do pair wise comparisons they cannot ensure their judgments are completely consistent because of the complexity of the objective reality and the limitation of human thoughts. There usually exists error of estimation which makes CI_r larger than 0. The larger CI_r is, the worse the consistency of P_r becomes.

APPENDIX B: CLUSTERING METHOD AND DEFINITION OF PREFERENCE DISTANCE

Packing all the preference values $\pi_r(x^1)$ ($1 \le i \le s$; $1 \le r \le l$) from the l decision-makers in the group, we have the $l \times s$ preference value matrix Λ

Definition 2. *The Euclidean preference distance between decision-maker DM_i and DM_j on a set of alternatives X is*

$$d_{ij} = \sqrt{\sum_{k=1}^{s} \left|\pi_i(x^k) - \pi_j(x^k)\right|^2}. \tag{16}$$

The Euclidean preference distance d_{ij} also denotes the difference of consensus between decision-maker DM_i and DM_j on X.

Packing the preference distances of all the l decision-makers, we have the $l \times l$ preference difference matrix,

$$D = \begin{bmatrix} 0 & & & & \\ d_{21} & 0 & & & \\ d_{31} & d_{32} & 0 & & \\ \cdots & \cdots & \cdots & 0 & \\ d_{l1} & d_{l2} & d_{l3} & \cdots & 0 \end{bmatrix} \tag{17}$$

where d_{ij} is nonnegative. The closer DM_i and DM_j are to each other, the smaller d_{ij} is. As $d_{ij} = d_{ij}$ and $d_{ij} = 0$, we have the matrix as shown in Equation (17).

Definition 3. *Let $C = \{c^\omega: \omega = 1, 2, \cdots, m\}$ be the preference cluster of the group G on a set of alternatives X, ε be the given clustering distance. If the distance between each two elements in c^ω satisfies the constraint $d_{ij} \leq \varepsilon \in c^\omega$, we call that c^ω is a cluster, that is, the sub-group comes to consensus in c^ω.*

Definition 4. *With respect to the decision-makers DM_i and DM_j, if $(d_{ij} \leq \varepsilon) \in c^\omega \subseteq C$, we call that DM_i and DM_j come to partial consensus in c^ω. As to $d_{rq} \leq \varepsilon^k \in c^k, (d_{ij} \leq \varepsilon^l) \in c^l$, if and only if $\varepsilon^k = \varepsilon^l = \varepsilon$ and $d_{ri} \leq \varepsilon$, $d_{rj} \leq \varepsilon$, $d_{iq} \leq \varepsilon$, $d_{jq} \leq \varepsilon$, we call $c^k = c^l$ is the same cluster.*

Example 1. *Suppose there is an initial preference utility value matrix as follows,*

$$\Lambda = \begin{bmatrix} 0.1 & 0.3 & 0.2 & 0.4 \\ 0.2 & 0.4 & 0.1 & 0.3 \\ 0.3 & 0.1 & 0.4 & 0.2 \\ 0.4 & 0.2 & 0.3 & 0.1 \\ 0.3 & 0.3 & 0.3 & 0.1 \\ 0.2 & 0.2 & 0.2 & 0.4 \end{bmatrix}. \tag{18}$$

Substituting the values into Equation (16), the consensus difference matrix (the preference difference matrix) as follows is had,

$$d = \begin{bmatrix} 0 & & & & & \\ 0.2 & 0 & & & & \\ 0.4 & 0.447 & 0 & & & \\ 0.447 & 0.4 & 0.2 & 0 & & \\ 0.374 & 0.316 & 0.245 & 0.141 & 0 & \\ 0.141 & 0.245 & 0.316 & 0.374 & 0.346 & 0 \end{bmatrix}. \tag{19}$$

1. Given $\varepsilon^1 \leq 0.15$ thus $d_{61} = d_{54} = 0.141 \leq \varepsilon^1$

The results DM_1, $DM_6 \in c^1$ and DM_4, $DM_5 \in c^2$ can be had. Although $d_{61} = d_{54} \leq \varepsilon^1$, $\min\{d_{65}, d_{64}, d_{51}, d_{41}\} = 0.346 > \varepsilon^1$ thus c^1, c^2 are not the same cluster according to Definition 4 and the two clusters come to partial consensus separately. DM_2 and DM_3 have not come to consensus with others as shown in Figure 3.

Figure 3.

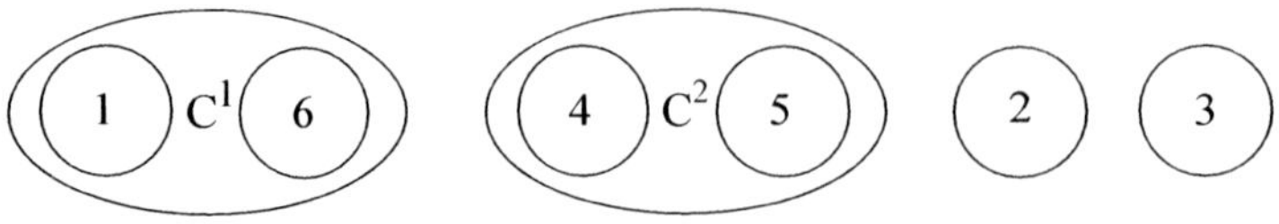

2. Given $\varepsilon^2 \leq 0.2$, we have $d_{21} = d_{43} = 0.2 \leq \varepsilon^2$ and $d_{61} = d_{54} = 0.141 \leq \varepsilon^1$, that is, $DM_1, DM_2 \in c^3$ and $DM_3, DM_4 \in c^4$ come to consensus respectively based on the consensus of $DM_1, DM_6 \in c^1$ and $DM_4, DM_5 \in c^2$. Here c^3 and c^4 are not the same cluster, as shown in Figure 4.

Figure 4.

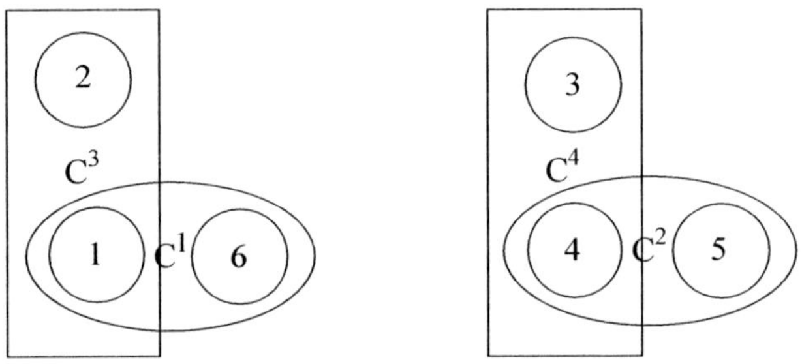

3. Given $\varepsilon^3 \leq 0.25$, we have $d_{61} = d_{54} = 0.141 \leq \varepsilon^1$, $d_{21} = d_{43} = 0.2 \leq \varepsilon^2$, and $d_{62} = d_{53} = 0.245 \leq \varepsilon^3$, that is, $DM_1, DM_2, DM_6 \in c^5$ come to consensus in c^5 and $DM_3, DM_4, DM_5 \in c^6$ come to consensus in c^6 as shown in Figure 5.

Figure 5.

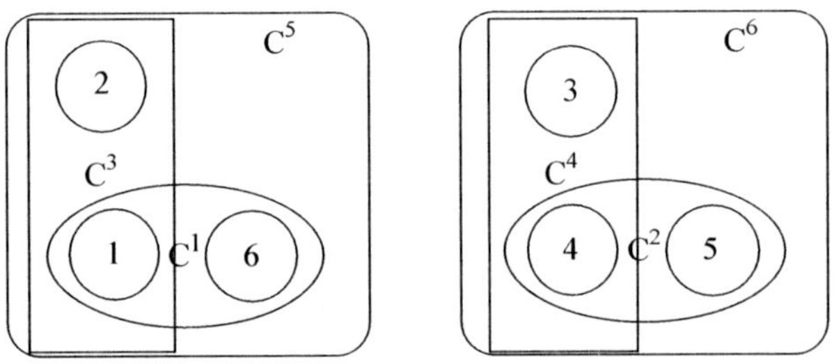

Assume k clusters are being sought after clustering with given ε and there are $\hat{l}$ elements in one of the k clusters, c^{ω}.

Definition 5. *To those clusters that have more than* 2 *elements, that is,* $2 \leq \hat{l} \leq s$, *the cluster center is defined as*

$$\hat{\pi} = \frac{1}{\hat{l}} \sum_{i=1}^{\hat{l}} \pi_i \,. \tag{20}$$

The Euclidean distance of preference between a decision-maker DM_r and the specified cluster center is then defined as

$$d_r = \sqrt{\sum_{k=1}^{s} \left|\pi_r(x^k) - \hat{\pi}(x^k)\right|^2}. \tag{21}$$

APPENDIX C: A SOLUTION OF THE DECISION WEIGHT VECTOR

Construct the Lagrange function for the optimization model,

$$L(w,\xi) = \sum_{r=1}^{l} [(\frac{\lambda_{\max}^{(r)}}{s-1} - \frac{s}{s-1}) + \sqrt{\sum_{k=1}^{s} (\pi_r(x^k) - \hat{\pi}(x^k))^2}\,] w_r^2 + 2\xi(\sum_{r=1}^{l} w_r - 1). \tag{22}$$

From the first-order condition of Equation (24), we have

$$\begin{cases} \dfrac{\partial L}{\partial w_r} = 2[(\dfrac{\lambda_{\max}^{(r)}}{s-1} - \dfrac{s}{s-1}) + \sqrt{\sum_{k=1}^{s} (\pi_r(x^k) - \hat{\pi}(x^k))^2}\,] w_r + 2\xi = 0 \\ \dfrac{\partial L}{\partial \xi} = \sum_{r=1}^{l} w_r - 1 = 0 \end{cases}$$

which implies that

$$\begin{cases} w_r - \dfrac{-\xi}{[(\dfrac{\lambda_{\max}^{(r)}}{s-1} - \dfrac{s}{s-1}) + \sqrt{\sum_{k=1}^{s} (\pi_r(x^k) - \hat{\pi}(x^k))^2}\,]} & (23) \\ \sum_{r=1}^{l} w_r = 1 & (24) \end{cases}$$

Thus, we have

$$\begin{cases} \xi = -\dfrac{1}{\sum_{r=1}^{l} 1 \Big/ [(\dfrac{\lambda_{\max}^{(r)}}{s-1} - \dfrac{s}{s-1}) + \sqrt{\sum_{k=1}^{s} (\pi_r(x^k) - \hat{\pi}(x^k))^2}\,]} & (25) \\ w_r = \dfrac{1}{[(\dfrac{\lambda_{\max}^{(r)}}{s-1} - \dfrac{s}{s-1}) + \sqrt{\sum_{k=1}^{s} (\pi_r(x^k) - \hat{\pi}(x^k))^2}\,] \bullet \sum_{r=1}^{l} 1 \Big/ [(\dfrac{\lambda_{\max}^{(r)}}{s-1} - \dfrac{s}{s-1}) + \sqrt{\sum_{k=1}^{s} (\pi_r(x^k) - \hat{\pi}(x^k))^2}\,]} & (26) \end{cases}$$

From Equation (26), the decision weight vector assigned to a group of decision-makers, $W = (w_1, w_2, \cdots, w_s)$ can be derived.

APPENDIX D: DISCRETE TIME MARKOV CHAINS AND MARKOV PROPERTY OF THE GROUP DECISION-MAKING PROCEDURE

A sequence of random variables $\{E_n\}$ is called a Markov chain if it has the Markov property:

$$T\{E_{n+1} = j \mid E_n = i, E_{n-1} = i_{n-1}, \ldots, E_0 = i_0\} = T\{E_{n+1} = j \mid E_n = i\}$$
$$T_{ij} = T\{E_{n+1} = j \mid E_n = i\} \tag{27}$$

Here, E_i is an event and T_{ij} is the probability to transit from state i to state j of the event. The property is called Memoryless. In other words, "Future" is independent of "Past" given "Present." Here the transition probabilities T_{ij} satisfy

$$T_{ij} \geq 0, \quad \sum_{j=0}^{\infty} T_{ij} = 1.$$

The Chapman-Kolmogorov Equation for a discrete-time Markov chain is as follows: If the distribution at time t_n is $\pi^{(n)}$, then the distribution at time t_{n+1} is given by

$$\pi^{(n+1)} \tag{28}$$

Because each decision-maker in the group independently puts forward her/his preference judgment matrix, the preference state E_n^r of decision-maker DM_r is independent of other decision-makers and the future preference state E_{n+1}^r is independent of other states except the current state E_n^r, thus the group decision-making procedure satisfies Equation (27).

Obviously, the transition probabilities T_{ij} constructed from Equation (3) satisfy

$$T_{ij} \geq 0, \quad \sum_{j=0}^{\infty} T_{ij} = 1.$$

Equation (4) shows that the overall state transition probabilities matrix is the mean value of the matrices of transition probabilities of each decision-maker, thus the group property is implied in the individual properties.

Therefore, the Chapman-Kolmogorov Equations, Equation (28) can be used to get $\pi^{(n+1)}$ at "time" t_{n+1} from $\pi^{(n)}$ at "time" t_n.

This work was previously published in the Journal of Global Information Management, Vol. 16, Issue 2, edited by F. Tan, pp. 35-57, copyright 2008 by IGI Publishing (an imprint of IGI Global).

Chapter 17
E-Business Strategy and Firm Performance

Jing Quan
Perdue School of Business, USA

ABSTRACT

Electronic business (e-business) has been popularly lauded as "new economy." As a result, firms are prompted to invest heavily in e-business related activities such as supplier/procurement and online exchanges. Whether the investments have actually paid off for the firms remain largely unknown. Using the data on the top 100 e-business leaders compiled by InternetWeek, this chapter compares the leaders with their comparable counterparts in terms of profitability and cost in both short-run and long-run. The authors find that while the leaders have superior performance based on most of the profitability measurements, such superiority is not observed when cost measurements are used. Based on the findings, this chapter offers managerial implications accordingly.

INTRODUCTION

The rapid expansion of e-business we witnessed in the late 1990s was nothing short of a spectacle. It seemed that almost everyone was talking about it, and every firm was eager to invest in it, hoping to take away a slice of the pie. Andy Grove, Chairman of Intel Corp, stated in 1998: "Within 5 years, all companies will be internet companies or they would not be companies." (Intel, 2000). Merely mentioning of the "e" word could mean multi-million dollars. The case at hand was Zapata Corp, a fish oil processing company, co-founded by former US President George H. W. Bush. The company announced on December 23, 1998 that it would transform itself into an internet portal to compete with Yahoo!, Lycos and alike. Immediately following the announcement, Zapata's stock price skyrocketed nearly 100% from 7.19 to 14.25 with trading volume at more than 2,000% higher than normal, according to Yahoo! Finance. Academic researchers rushed in and concluded that "a new economy was born."

DOI: 10.4018/978-1-60566-920-5.ch017

The potential benefits of e-business are well documented by academic researchers and practitioners alike (InternetWeek 2000/2001; Phan, 2003). Organizations that integrate e-business applications, such as shared online database and internet-based reporting in their business processes, can lead to reduced cost, increased efficiency and profitability, and better customer relationship management. Perhaps, one of the most significant contributions of e-business applications is its abilities to directly bring sellers and buyers together with little middleman's interventions.

Although the advantages of e-business exist in theory, little empirical work has been done to confirm them. Some study actually showed an inconclusive link between e-business and sustainable development (Digital Europe, 2003, p.1):

Our survey showed no conclusive evidence for companies that use a lot of e-business actually performing better than other companies on sustainable development, simply by virtue of their e-business use. There may be a relationship here - which could become more obvious as e-business applications are more fully integrated into companies' operations - but more research would be needed to prove a link.

Answering this call, researchers have attempted to build theoretical frameworks to pinpoint how e-business creates value. Using the technology-organization-environment (TOE) framework Zhu, Kraemer, Xu, and Dedrick (2004) found that technology readiness, firm size, global scope, financial resources, competition intensity, and regulatory environment may affect e-business value creation. Amit and Zott (2001) integrated several theoretical perspectives on entrepreneurship and strategic management to identify four interdependent dimensions: efficiency, complementarities, lock-in, and novelty as sources of value creation.

Despite the recent advancement of research in this area, the fundamental question regarding e-business remains unanswered, i.e., whether e-business creates value. This paper attempts to fill this vacuum by establishing a theoretical foundation to evaluating the linkage between e-business investments and firm performance in terms of profitability and cost savings. Confirmation or disconfirmation of the effectiveness of firms' investments in e-business will contribute to the knowledge accumulation in this area. It can also provide an insight for future investments.

We begin the paper by presenting our research framework grounded in the resource-based view (Barney, 1986; Barney, 1991; Conner, 1991; Rumelt, 1984). Resource-based view argues that firm-specific skills and resources that are rare and difficult to imitate or substitute are the main drivers of firm performance. We show how e-business initiatives create unique skills and resources for firms. Then we formulate our hypotheses, discuss the data set and methodology, and present estimation results. Finally, we provide discussion of the results and suggestions for future research.

RESEARCH FRAMEWORK: THE RESOURCE-BASED VIEW

Broadly speaking, e-business value is a subset of the business value of IT. The business value of IT investments in general has been long debated, which led to the birth of the famous term "productivity paradox." Some studies provide positive support for the business value of computer investments (Brynjolfsson 1993; Brynjolfsson and Hitt 1996; Hitt and Brynjolfsson 1996; Bharadwaj 2000; Stratopoulos and Dehning 2000). On the other hand, Strassmann (1997) argues that IT investments have no discernible effects on firm profitability measured in return on assets (ROA), return on equity (ROE), and economic value added (EVA).

In an attempt to explain the inconclusiveness, some researchers propose several theoretical models that examine the entire process needed for IT investments to make an impact on business value (Lucas 1993; Markus and Soh 1993). One of the dominate views is the resource-based view (RBV). Based on this view, IT investment itself does not provide any sustainable value because competitors can easily duplicate the investment by purchasing the same hardware and software. Rather, competitive advantages are derived from the manner in which firms deploy IT to generate a unique set of resources and skills that are difficult to duplicate (Clemons 1986, 1991; Clemons and Row 1991; Mata et al. 1995). This type of resources is firm specific, rare, imperfectly imitable, and not strategically substitutable by others create competitive advantages for firms (Barney, 1991). Grant (1991) extends the RBV by linking resources to organizational capabilities. Firms generate organizational capabilities by optimally assembling their resources. When these capacities are embedded in organizational processes, it makes firms deploy resources more effectively and efficiently than its competitors. In turn, competitive advantages are created.

Adopting this RBV, one can see that IT investments themselves do not necessarily generate sustained value because competitors can easily duplicate the action by investing in the same or equivalent hardware and software. In order to achieve competitive advantages of IT investments, firms must leverage their investments (resources) to create unique capacities that impact their overall effectiveness.

E-BUSINESS AND COMPETITIVE ADVANTAGE

Information systems researchers have classified key IT-based resources into three categories: (1) the physical IT infrastructure (the tangible resources); (2) the technical and managerial IT skills (the human resources); and (3) the intangible resources such as knowledge base, customer relations, and synergy (Bharadwaj, 2000; Grant, 1995). To be successful, e-business based firms need to invest in a new type of IT infrastructure that can provide real time responses 24/7 to customer inquiries. Some emerging infrastructures include XML, server farms, and dynamic storage. In addition, to protect the infrastructures and ensure the integrity of information, firms need to heavily invest in security. All these require IT and management staff to possess necessary skills for managing the new working environment. This allows the firms to acquire unique, rare and firm specific technical and managerial skills. With the infrastructure and management skills in place, the firms can manage their knowledge base better and create synergies between different working units. In the process, they can become truly customer oriented. Therefore, from the resource-based perspective, e-business initiatives help firms to obtain competitive advantage in the marketplace.

In this paper, we measure competitive advantage in terms of either higher profit or lower cost. As a result, we propose the following hypotheses:

H_1: *The average profit ratios of the e-business leader firms are higher than those of the non-leaders.*

H_2: *The average cost ratios of the e-business leader firms are lower than those of the non-leaders.*

METHODOLOGY

We adopt the "matched sample comparison group" method, which has been extensively used in previous research (Bharadwaj, 2000, Stratopoulos and Dehning 2000). In this methodology, there are two samples: the first sample is a treatment group and the second is a carefully selected control group that is matched to the treatment group by size and type. Then the levels of interest variables of these two samples are compared. In our case, the treatment group consists of the firms identified by the industry as e-business leaders while the control group consists of the matched firms in terms of size and type.

Dataset

In 2000 and 2001 InternetWeek published a special issue InternetWeek 100, in which 100 e-business leaders were identified for their effectiveness in using internet to achieve tangible business benefits (InternetWeek, 2000/2001). They were evaluated based on their e-business participation in customer-oriented activities, supplier/procurement activities, electronic marketplace, integration of front- and back-end systems, revenue growth, and cost cutting efforts.

In order to obtain a consistent sample, we restricted the selection of the companies that were identified as leaders in both years. In addition, firms must have complete financial data on Compustat for the period of 1999 to 2002. This process led to 46 companies in the treatment sample.

For the control sample, we first specified that a matching firm must be in the same industry as the leader based on the 4-digit primary Standard Industrial Classification (SIC) code. Second, the average sales of the matching firm must be within 70% to 130% of the leader firm's. When there were multiple matches, the firm with five-year average sales closest to that of the leader firm was selected. If a match couldn't be identified in this fashion, then the 4-digit SIC matching rule was relaxed to three- or two-digit SIC. This procedure has been used by previous studies such as Bharadwaj (2000) and Barber and Lyon (1996). Firms in both groups are listed in the Appendix.

Table 1 provides the descriptive statistics for the two groups. The t-test does not reveal any systematical differences between them in terms of size measures such as sales, total assets and number of employees.

Two categories of variables are collected for both treatment and control samples to test the aforementioned two hypotheses related to profit and cost. Five profit ratios include return on assets (ROA), return on sales (ROS), operating income to assets (OI/A), operating income to sales (OI/S), and operating income to employee (OI/E). Three cost ratios are total operating expenses to sales (OEXP/S), cost of goods sold to sales (COGS/S), and selling and general administrative expenses to sales (SG&A/S). Total operating expenses are defined as the sum of COGS and SG&A. The rational for those variables can be found in Bharadwaj (2000).

Statistical Tests and Outliers

Our primary interest is to test the hypotheses that the mean levels of operational performance variables of e-business leaders are better than those of non-leader firms. Traditional standard t-test would be used for this purpose. However, since the distributions of financial ratios, such as the variables defined above, tend to be non-normal, skewed and fat tailed, non-parametric test is preferred (Bharadwaj, 2000; Stratopoulos and Dehning, 2000). In this paper, we use the Wilcoxon signed rank test.

Another characteristic of financial data is that there are a significant number of outliers. As a data treatment, we followed a methodology suggested by Stratopoulos and Dehning (2000) by removing those data points that fall more than 1.5 times the interquartile range above the third quartile or below the first,.

RESULTS AND DISCUSSION

Table 2 provides the one-sided Wilcoxon signed rank results for the aforementioned profitability related variables between e-business leaders and control sample from 1999 and 2002. E-business leaders performed better in terms of all measures but one (OIE) in 1999, the year before they were identified as e-business leaders. This indicates that financial performance was one of the considerations for their selections. Most of the advantages

Table 1. Descriptive statistics

1999	**E-Business Leaders**		**Control Sample**		**Difference of Means**
	Mean	Median	Mean	Median	T
Sales (billion $)	20.84	11.27	18.56	10.28	1.326
Assets (billion $)	45.61	16.54	35.72	12.74	1.103
Number of Employees	82348	45504	120931	54450	-0.859
2000	E-Business Leaders		Control Sample		Difference of Means
	Mean	Median	Mean	Median	T
Sales (billion $)	23.05	12.26	20.78	11.42	1.207
Assets (billion $)	57.17	20.49	41.96	13.02	1.474
Number of Employees	89888	44000	121425	46546	-0.900
2001	E-Business Leaders		Control Sample		Difference of Means
	Mean	Median	Mean	Median	T
Sales (billion $)	21.69	12.81	20.72	11.33	0.531
Assets (billion $)	56.52	20.25	44.80	13.71	1.115
Number of Employees	85435	46800	121199	62175	-1.175
2002	E-Business Leaders		Control Sample		Difference of Means
	Mean	Median	Mean	Median	T
Sales (billion $)	21.66	11.92	20.38	11.45	0.605
Assets (billion $)	59.08	19.50	48.47	13.79	0.922
Number of Employees	83961	47480	101336	44323	-1.315

were maintained in 2000, except for ROA, while the leaders now performed better based on the OIE measurement. In 2001, however, there were no significant differences between the leaders and matched firms in all financial variables. In the last year of our sample, e-business leaders performed better than the control sample in terms of three out of 5 financial ratios. Based on the discussion above, we can conclude that overall our hypothesis #1 is partially supported.

Table 3 provides the one-sided Wilcoxon signed rank test results for the aforementioned cost related variables between the e-business leaders and the control sample from 1999 and 2002. Throughout all these years there were no significant differences between the leaders and the matched firms. This finding is largely consistent with other studies such as Bharadwaj (2000), and Mitra and Chaya (1996). Based on the results, we conclude that our hypothesis #2 is not supported.

CONCLUSION

As businesses rushed to invest in the "new" economy, pressured by either the thinking of a paradigm swift or peers during the internet boom, the payoff of such investments was not as important as making the move or taking action. Now that the bubble has burst, companies are forced to focus once again to justifying their IT investment decisions. This study aims to provide an assessment whether the investments made in e-business

Table 2. E-business and profitability

	1999			2000			2001			2002		
	Mean	Medi-an	Pr>Z	Mean	Medi-an	Pr>Z	Mean	Medi-an	Pr>Z	Mean	Medi-an	Pr>Z
ROA-leaders	5.145	4.508	0.06[c]	5.327	3.810	0.31	2.789	1.659	0.22	3.126	2.892	0.02[b]
ROA-control	3.876	2.726		4.067	3.457		1.452	1.513		1.384	2.031	
ROS-leaders	0.076	0.067	0.01[a]	0.066	0.070	0.04[b]	0.052	0.043	0.10[c]	0.029	0.032	0.49
ROS-control	0.051	0.045		0.052	0.049		0.020	0.032		0.021	0.032	
OIA-leaders	0.112	0.092	0.02[b]	0.097	0.089	0.02[b]	0.076	0.064	0.12	0.068	0.069	0.02[b]
OIA-control	0.085	0.068		0.067	0.064		0.059	0.049		0.045	0.046	
OIS-leaders	0.136	0.121	0.01[b]	0.132	0.121	0.01[a]	0.088	0.079	0.32	0.096	0.104	0.05[b]
OIS-control	0.104	0.089		0.095	0.085		0.092	0.068		0.074	0.069	
OIE-leaders	0.033	0.025	0.18	0.042	0.032	0.01[a]	0.028	0.023	0.21	0.027	0.021	0.33
OIE-control	0.027	0.018		0.024	0.016		0.023	0.011		0.021	0.014	

Notes:
[a] 1% level, [b] 5% level, [c] 10% level
ROA - return on assets;
ROS – return on sales;
OIA – operating income to assets;
OIS – operating income to sales;
OIE – operating income to employees.

during the boom period had actually paid off in terms of profitability and cost in both short- and long-runs. Using the e-business leaders identified by InternetWeek, we created a control sample that matched the leaders based on industry type and size. The performances, measured in profit and cost, of these two groups were compared using the Wilcoxon signed rank non-parameter test. The results indicate that in terms of profitability e-business leaders performed better than the control sample in the long-run but the superior performance fluctuated in the short-run. In terms of cost, there were no significant differences between the leaders and the control sample in

Table 3. E-business and cost

	1999			2000			2001			2002		
	Mean	Medi-an	Pr>Z	Mean	Medi-an	Pr>Z	Mean	Medi-an	Pr>Z	Mean	Medi-an	Pr>Z
COG/S-leaders	0.650	0.699	0.49	0.638	0.683	0.42	0.690	0.708	0.80	0.656	0.659	0.46
COG/S-control	0.653	0.669		0.644	0.650		0.670	0.683		0.679	0.683	
SGA/S-leaders	0.230	0.228	0.37	0.236	0.233	0.49	0.245	0.232	0.59	0.240	0.224	0.32
SGA/S-control	0.237	0.214		0.236	0.238		0.243	0.237		0.254	0.230	
OPEXP/S-leaders	1.086	0.788	0.13	1.227	0.952	0.33	1.208	0.956	0.25	1.263	1.238	0.22
OPEXP/S-control	1.223	1.301		1.175	1.234		1.229	1.316		0.909	1.315	

Notes:
COG/S – cost of goods sold to sales;
SGA/S – selling and general administration expense to sales;
OPEXP/S – operating expenses to sales.

both the short- and long-runs. The combination of leaders' higher profitability than and the same cost measures as the firms in the control sample is consistent with the observation by Bharadwaj (2000, p187) that "IT leaders do not necessarily have a cost focus, but tend to exploit IT for generating superior revenues."

Based on the findings in this study, we suggest that management should be very clear about the time horizon of the e-business, or IT in general, investments. The findings of this study demonstrate that the consistent superior financial performances of the e-business leaders are only observed in the long-run. In reality, management often fails to see the long-run benefits from new IT investments due to the cost concerns of new IT in the short-run. Dehning et al. (2005) suggest that management should take a long-term view because IT might allow a firm to form relationships with its customers and suppliers and reduce variability in cash flows and earning. The combined effect of such interactions between the other variables may easily make up for the temporary increase in cost and decline in competitive advantage.

This type of research using a third party ranking suffers a few limitations, such as causality, indirectness of measurements, inherent biases of leader firms, the selection of the control sample, as suggested by Bharadwaj (2000) and Stratopoulos and Dehning (2000). Those limitations may serve as the directions for future research.

Santhanam and Hartono (2003) suggest a different way of selecting the control sample. Instead of choosing a single benchmark firm for each e-business leader, one can consider all the firms in that industry for comparison. They argue that this method is more consistent with the procedure of selecting leaders, robust and general. Future research can consider adopting this approach of sample selection. Another logical follow-up study would be to extend the period beyond 2002 to examine the impact of e-business investment in the long term.

REFERENCES

Amit, R., & Zott, C. (2001). Value creation in e-business. *Strategic Management Journal, 22*, 493–520. doi:10.1002/smj.187

Barber, B. M., & Lyon, J. D. (1996). Detecting abnormal operating performance: the empirical power and specification of test statistics. *Journal of Financial Economics, 41*, 359–399. doi:10.1016/0304-405X(96)84701-5

Barney, J. B. (1986). Strategic factor markets: expectations, luck, and business strategy. *Management Science, 32*, 1231–1241. doi:10.1287/mnsc.32.10.1231

Barney, J. B. (1991). Firm resources and sustained competitive advantage. *Journal of Management, 17*, 99–120. doi:10.1177/014920639101700108

Barua, A., & Kriebel, C.H. & Mukhopadhyay. (1995). Information technologies and business value: an empirical investigation. *Information Systems Research, 6*(1), 3–23. doi:10.1287/isre.6.1.3

Bharadwaj, A. S. (2000). A resourced-based perspective on information technology capability and firm performance: an empirical investigation. *MIS Quarterly, 24*(1), 169–196. doi:10.2307/3250983

Brynjolfsson, E. (1993). The productivity paradox of information technology. *Communications of the ACM, 36*(12), 67–77. doi:10.1145/163298.163309

Brynjolfsson, E., & Hitt, L. (1996). Paradox lost? Firm-level evidence on the return to information systems spending. *Management Science, 42*(4), 541–558. doi:10.1287/mnsc.42.4.541

Clemons, E. K. (1986). Information systems for sustainable competitive advantage. *Information & Management, 11*(3), 131–136. doi:10.1016/0378-7206(86)90010-8

Clemons, E. K. (1991). Corporate strategy for information technology: a resource-based approach. *Computer*, *24*(11), 23–32. doi:10.1109/2.116848

Clemons, E. K., & Row, M. C. (1991). Sustaining IT advantage: the role of structural differences. *MIS Quarterly*, *15*(3), 275–294. doi:10.2307/249639

Conner, K. R. (1991). A historical comparison of the resource-based theory and five schools of thought within industrial organization economics: do I have a new theory of the firm? *Journal of Management*, *17*(1), 121–154. doi:10.1177/014920639101700109

Dehning, B., Richardson, V. J., & Stratopoulos, T. (2005). Information technology investments and firm value. *Information & Management*, *42*(7), 989–1008. doi:10.1016/j.im.2004.11.003

Digital Europe (2003). Is ebusiness good business? Survey key findings, May, DEESD IST-2000-28606

Grant, R. M. (1991). The resource-based theory of competitive advantage. *California Management Review*, *33*(3), 114–135.

Grant, R. M. (1995). Contemporary Strategy Analysis. Oxford, UK: Blackwell Publishers, Inc.

Hitt, L. M., & Brynjofsson, E. (1996). Productivity, business profitability, and consumer surplus: three different measures of information technology value. *MIS Quarterly*, *20*(2), 121–142. doi:10.2307/249475

Intel (2000). Retrieved January 23, 2004 from http://www.intel.com/ebusiness/estrategies/enabling/

InternetWeek. (2000). InternetWeek 100, Special Issue, June 8. http://internetweek.cmp.com/100/100-00.htm. Retrieved on February 18, 2004.

InternetWeek. (2001), InternetWeek 100, Special Issue, June 11. http://internetweek.cmp.com/100/100-01.htm. Retrieved on February 18, 2004.

Lucas, H. C. (1993). The business value of information technology: a historical perspective and thoughts for future research, in strategic information technology management: perspectives on organizational growth and competitive advantage. In R. Banker, R. Kauffman, and M.A. Mahmood (Eds.), *Strategic Information Technology Management: Perspectives on Organizational Growth and Competitive Advantage*. Hershey, PA: Idea Group Publishing.

Markus, M. L., & Soh, C. (1993). Banking on information technology: converting it spending into firm performance. In R. Banker, R. Kauffman, and M.A. Mahmood (Eds.), *Strategic Information Technology Management: Perspectives on Organizational Growth and Competitive Advantage*. Hershey, PA: Idea Group Publishing.

Mata, F. J., Fuerst, W. L., & Barney, J. B. (1995). Information technology and sustained competitive advantage: a resource-based analysis. *MIS Quarterly*, *19*(4), 487–505. doi:10.2307/249630

Mitra, S., & Chaya, A. K. (1996). Analyzing cost effectiveness of organizations: the impact of information technology spending. *Journal of Management Information Systems*, *13*(2), 29–57.

Phan, D. D. (2003). E-business development for competitive advantages: a case study. *Information & Management*, *40*(6), 581–590. doi:10.1016/S0378-7206(02)00089-7

Rumelt, R. P. (1984). Toward a strategic theory of the firm. In R. Lamb (Ed.), *Competitive strategic management* (pp. 556-570). Englewood Cliffs, NJ: Prentice-Hall.

Santhanam, R., & Hartono, E. (2003). Issues in linking information technology capability to firm performance. *MIS Quarterly*, *27*(1), 125–153.

Strassmann, P.A. (1997, September 15) Computers have yet to make companies more productive. *ComputerWorld.*

Stratopoulos, T., & Dehning, B. (2000). Does successful investment in information technology solve the productivity paradox? *Information & Management*, *38*(2), 103–117. doi:10.1016/S0378-7206(00)00058-6

Zhu, K., Kraemer, K. L., Xu, S., & Dedrick, J. (2004). Information technology payoff in e-business environment: an international perspective on value creation of e-business in the financial service industry. *Journal of Management Information Systems*, *21*(1), 17–54.

APPENDIX (TABLE 4)

Table 4. E-business leader firms and matched sample

E-Business Leaders	SIC	Control Sample	SIC
ANHEUSER-BUSCH COS INC	2082	KIRIN BREWERY LTD -ADR	2082
MILLER (HERMAN) INC	2520	HON INDUSTRIES	2522
KIMBERLY-CLARK CORP	2621	3M CO	2670
KNIGHT-RIDDER INC	2711	AMERICAN GREETINGS -CL A	2771
AIR PRODUCTS & CHEMICALS INC	2810	ROHM & HAAS CO	2821
DU PONT (E I) DE NEMOURS	2820	BAYER A G -SPON ADR	2800
DOW CHEMICAL	2821	AVENTIS SA -ADR	2834
EASTMAN CHEMICAL CO	2821	PRAXAIR INC	2810
BRISTOL MYERS SQUIBB	2834	ABBOTT LABORATORIES	2834
AVON PRODUCTS	2844	LAUDER ESTEE COS INC -CL A	2844
PPG INDUSTRIES INC	2851	COLGATE-PALMOLIVE CO	2844
GILLETTE CO	3420	CROWN HOLDINGS INC	3411
CISCO SYSTEMS INC	3576	SUN MICROSYSTEMS INC	3571
EMERSON ELECTRIC CO	3600	ELECTROLUX AB -ADR	3630
AMERICAN PWR CNVRSION	3620	ALTERA CORP	3674
WHIRLPOOL CORP	3630	KYOCERA CORP -ADR	3663
NORTEL NETWORKS CORP	3661	ERICSSON (L M) TEL -ADR	3663
INTEL CORP	3674	MOTOROLA INC	3663
DAIMLERCHRYSLER AG	3711	FORD MOTOR CO	3711
RAYTHEON CO	3812	NORTHROP GRUMMAN CORP	3812
CSX CORP	4011	NORFOLK SOUTHERN CORP	4011
UNION PACIFIC CORP	4011	BURLINGTON NORTHERN SANTA FE	4011
UNITED PARCEL SERVICE INC	4210	UNITED STATES POSTAL SERVICE	4210
CONSOLIDATED FREIGHTWAYS CP	4213	YELLOW CORP	4213
ALASKA AIR GROUP INC	4512	AMERICA WEST HLDG CP -CL B	4512
AMR CORP/DE	4512	BRITISH AIRWAYS PLC -ADR	4512
DELTA AIR LINES INC	4512	NORTHWEST AIRLINES CORP	4512
AT&T CORP	4813	DEUTSCHE TELEKOM AG -SP ADR	4813
COX COMMUNICATIONS -CL A	4841	BRITISH SKY BRDCSTG GP -ADR	4833
ARROW ELECTRONICS INC	5065	GENUINE PARTS CO	5013
AVNET INC	5065	TECH DATA CORP	5045
PENNEY (J C) CO	5311	TARGET CORP	5331
SEARS ROEBUCK & CO	5311	KMART HOLDING CORP	5331
OFFICE DEPOT INC	5940	TOYS R US INC	5945
STAPLES INC	5940	RITE AID CORP	5912
J P MORGAN CHASE & CO	6020	CITICORP	6020
MELLON FINANCIAL CORP	6020	BANCO COMERCIAL PORTGE -ADR	6020
SCHWAB (CHARLES) CORP	6211	BEAR STEARNS COMPANIES INC	6211

E-Business Leaders	SIC	Control Sample	SIC
HARTFORD FINL SVCS GRP INC	6331	MILLEA HOLDINGS INC -ADR	6331
HILTON HOTELS CORP	7011	STARWOOD HOTELS&RESORTS WLD	7011
MARRIOTT INTL INC	7011	INTERCONTINENTAL HOTELS -ADR	7011
INTL BUSINESS MACHINES CORP	7370	FUJITSU LTD -SPON ADR	7373
COMPUTER ASSOCIATES INTL INC	7372	KELLY SERVICES INC -CL A	7363
MICROSOFT CORP	7372	ADECCO S A -SPON ADR	7363
GENERAL ELECTRIC CO	9997	SIEMENS A G -SPON ADR	9997

Compilation of References

Abell, W., & Black, S. (1997). Business use of the internet in New Zealnad: a follow-up study. Retrieved June, 27, 2003, from http://www.lincoln.ac.nz/amac/publish/acms/followup.htm

ABI Research. (2003). *Not all RFID vendors ready for the Wal-Mart challenge*. Retrieved July 7, 2004, from http://www.abiresearch.com/abiprdisplay2.jsp?pressid=208

Abouzeedan, A., & Busler, M. (2002). Information technology (IT) impact on performance of small and medium-size enterprises (SMEs). In *Proceedings of RENT XVI, Research in Entrepreneurship and Small business, 16th Workshop 2* (pp. 127-156).

Abouzeedan, A., & Busler, M. (2006). Information technology (IT) and small and medium-sized enterprises (SMEs) management: The concept of firm impact sphere. *Global Business Review, 7*(2), 243–257. doi:10.1177/097215090600700204

Abrams, L. C., Cross, R., Lesser, E., & Levin, D. Z. (2003). Nurturing interpersonal trust in knowledge sharing networks. *The Academy of Management Executive, 17*(4), 64–76.

Accenture. (2004a). *High performance enabled through radio frequency identification accenture research on manufacturer perspectives*. Retrieved December 15, 2004, from http://www.accenture.com/xd/xd.asp?it=enweb&xd=services\rfid\insights

Accenture. (2004b). *High performance delivered from compliance to competitive impact through radio frequency identification*. Retrieved January 10, 2005, from http://www.accenture.com/xd/xd.asp?it=enweb&xd=services\rfid\insights

Accenture. (2004c). *High performance enabled through radio frequency identification-accenture research on Asia Pacific perspectives.* Retrieved January 2, 2005, from http://www.accenture.com/xd/xd.asp?it=enweb&xd=services\rfid\insights

Accounting, M. (1999). Top management complacent or uncertain about the implications of e-business? *Management Accounting, 77*(11), 4–5.

Adam, A., Howcroft, D., & Richardson, H. (2002). Guest Editorial. *Information Technology & People, 15*(2), 94–97.

Adams, D., Nelson, R., & Todd, P. (1992). Perceived Usefulness, Ease of Use, and Usage of Information Technology: A Replication. *MIS Quarterly*, 227–247. doi:10.2307/249577

Adams, J. C., Baichoo, S., & Bauer, V. (2006). Women Embrace Computing in Mauritius. In E.M. Trauth (Ed.), *Encyclopedia of Gender and Information Technology* (pp. 1258-1266). Hershey, PA: Idea Group Publishing.

Adams, J. C., Bauer, V., & Baichoo, S. (2003). An Expanding Pipeline: Gender in Mauritius. In *Proceedings of ACM SIGCSE Conference, Reno, Nevada, February 19-23, 2003* (pp. 59-63). New York: ACM Press.

African Americans and Hispanics Lead Mobile Culture. (2005). Retrieved July 28, 2006 from http://www.cellular-news.com/story/15030.php.

Agarwal, R., & Karahanna, E. (2000). Time Flies When You're Having Fun: Cognitive Absorption and Beliefs About Information Technology Usage. *MIS Quarterly, 24*(4), 665–694. doi:10.2307/3250951

Agarwal, R., & Prasa, J. (1998). A conceptual and operational definition of personal innovativeness in the domain of information technology. *Information Systems Research, 9*(2), 204-301.

Agarwal, R., Ferratt, T. W., Moore, J. E., & Brown, C. V. (1999). Observations from "the front": IT executives on practices to recruit and retain information technology professionals. In *Proceedings of the SIGCPR* (pp. 102-112).

Agarwal, R., Sambamurthy, V., & Stair, R. M. (2000). The Evolving Relationship between General and Specific Computer Self-Efficacy. *Information Systems Research, 1*(4), 418–430. doi:10.1287/isre.11.4.418.11876

Agarwal, V. (2001). *Assessing the benefits of auto-ID technology in the consumer industry* (MIT Auto-ID Center White Paper WH-003). Retrieved October 8, 2004, from http://www.autoidlabs.org/whitepapers/CAM-WH-003.pdf

Ahmed, P. K., Kok, L. K., & Loh, A. Y. E. (2002). *Learning through knowledge management.* Woburn, MA: Butterworth-Heinemann.

Ahn, J., & Chang, S. (2004). Assessing the contribution of knowledge to business performance: the KP^3 methodology. *Decision Support Systems, 36*, 403-416.

Ahuja, M. K. (2002). Women in the Information Technology Profession: A Literature Synthesis and Research Agenda. *European Journal of Information Systems, 11*(1), 20–34. doi:10.1057/palgrave/ejis/3000417

Aiken, M., Hwang, C., Magalhaes, R. D., & Jeanette, M. (1993). A comparison of Malaysian and American groups using a group decision support system. *Journal of Information Science, 19*(6), 489–491. doi:10.1177/016555159301900608

Aiken, M., Kim, D., Hwang, C., & Lu, L. (1995). A Korean group decision support system. *Information & Management, 28*(5), 303–310. doi:10.1016/0378-7206(95)00003-F

Aiken, M., Martin, J., Shirani, A., & Singleton, T. (1994). A group decision support system for multicultural and multilingual communication. *Decision Support Systems, 12*(2), 93–96. doi:10.1016/0167-9236(94)90009-4

Ajzen, I. (1985). From intentions to actions: A theory of planned behavior. In J. Kuhl & J. Beckmann (Eds.), *Springer series in social psychology* (pp. 11-39). Berlin: Springer.

Ajzen, I. (1991). The theory of planned behavior. *Organizational Behavior and Human Decision Processes, 50*(2), 179-211.

Ajzen, I., & Fishbein, M. (1980). *Understanding Attitudes and Predicting Social Behavior.* Englewood Cliffs, NJ: Prentice-Hall.

Ajzen, I., & Madden, T. J. (1986). Prediction of goal directed behaviour: Attitudes, attitudes, and perceived behavioral control. *Journal of Experimental Social Psychology, 22*, 453-474.

Alavi, M., & Leidner, D. E. (2001). Review: knowledge management and knowledge management systems: conceptual foundations and research issues. *MIS Quarterly, 25*(1), 107-136.

Alavi, M., Kayworth, T. D., & Leidner, D. E. (2005-2006). An empirical examination of the influence of organizational culture on knowledge management practices. *Journal of Management Information Systems, 22*(3), 191-224.

Albright, B. (2002).Will RFID be the answer people want it to be?. *Frontline Solutions, 12*(3), 8.

Alchian, A. A., & Demsetz, H. (1972). Production, information cost and economic organization. *American Economic Review, 62*(1), 777-792.

Alexander, K., Birkhofer, G., Gramling, K., Kleinberger, H., Leng, S., Moogimane, D., & Woods, M. (2002). *Focus on retail: Applying auto-ID to improve product availability at the retail shelf* (MIT Auto-ID Center White Paper BC-001). Retrieved July 8, 2003, from http://www.autoidcenter.org/publishedresearch

Ali, A. J., Lee, M., Hsieh, Y.-C., & Krishnan, K. (2005). Individualism and collectivism in Taiwan. *Cross Cultural Management, 12*(4), 3-16.

Allcock S, Webber S, & Yeates, R. (1999). *Business Information and the Internet: use of the Internet as an information resource for SMEs.*

Allen, D. B., Miller, E. D., & Nath, R. (1988). North America. In R. Nath (Ed.), *Comparative Management* (pp. 23-54). Cambridge, MA: Ballinger.

Allen, T. J. (1977). *Managing the Flow of Technology.* Cambridge: MIT Press.

Amit, R., & Zott, C. (2001). Value creation in e-business. *Strategic Management Journal, 22*, 493–520. doi:10.1002/smj.187

Amor, D. (2000). *The e-business (R)evolution: living and working in an interconnected world / Daniel Amor.* London: Upper Saddle River, NJ: Prentice Hall PTR.

Anderson, J. C. (1987). An approach for confirmatory measurement and structural equation modeling of organizational properties. *Management Science, 33*(4), 525-541.

Anderson, J. C., & Gerbing, D. W. (1982). Some methods for respecifying measurement models to obtain unidimensional construct measurement. *JMR, Journal of Marketing Research, 19*(4), 453–461. doi:10.2307/3151719

Anderson, J. C., & Gerbing, D. W. (1988). Structural equation modeling in practice: a review and recommended two-step approach. *Psychological Bulletin, 103*(3), 411-423.

Anderson, J. C., & Narus, J. A. (1990). A model of distributor firm and manufacturer firm working partnerships. *Journal of Marketing, 54*(1), 42–58. doi:10.2307/1252172

Anderson, K. V., Bjørn-Anderson, N., & Dedrick, J. (2003). Governance initiative creating a demand-driven e-commerce approach: The case of Denmark. *The Information Society, 19*, 95–105. doi:10.1080/01972240309475

Anderson, W. N., & Hiltz, S. R. (2001, January 3-6). *Culturally heterogeneous vs. culturally homogeneous groups in distributed group support systems: Effects on group process and consensus.* Paper presented at the 34th Hawaii International Conference on System Sciences (HICSS), Maui, HI.

Andres, P. (2002). A comparison of face-to-face and virtual software development teams. *Team Performance Management, 8*(1/2), 39-48.

Andrews, K. M., & Delahaye, B. L. (2000). Influences on knowledge processes in organizational learning: The psychosocial filter. *Journal of Management Studies, 37*(6), 797–810. doi:10.1111/1467-6486.00204

Andriole, S. J. (2006). The collaborate/integrated business technology strategy. *Communications of the ACM, 49*(5), 85-90.

Ang, S., & Slaughter, S. (2004). Turnover of information technology professionals: The effects of internal labour market strategies. *ACM SIGMIS Database, 35*(3), 11-27.

Angeles, R. (2005). RFID technologies: Supply-chain applications and implementation issues. *Information Systems Management, 22*(1), 51-65.

Anumba, C. J., & Ruikar, K. (2002). Electronic commerce in construction--trends and prospects. *Automation in Construction, 11*(3), 265–275. doi:10.1016/S0926-5805(01)00087-5

Applegate, L. M., McFarlan, F. W., & McKenney, J. L. (1996). *Corporate information systems management.* Irwin.

Application Development Trends. (2003). *DoD. Wal-Mart pushes RFID.* Retrieved July 25, 2004, from http://www.adtmag.com/article.asp?id=8542

Arbuckle, J. L., & Wothke, W. (1999). AMOS 4.0 [Computer software]. Chicago: Smallwasters.

Archer, N. P. (1990). A comparison of computer conferences with face-to-face meetings for small group business decisions. *Behavior & Information Technology, 9*(4), 307-317.

Arenius, P., Sasi, V., & Gabrielsson, M. (2006). Rapid internationalization enabled by the Internet: the case of a knowledge intensive company. *Journal of International Enterprise, 3*(4), 279–290. doi:10.1007/s10843-006-7856-x

Argote, L., McEvily, B., & Reagans, R. (2003). Managing knowledge in organizations: An integrative framework and review of emerging themes. *Management Science, 49*(4), 571-582.

Argyris, C. (1982). *Reasoning, Learning and Action.* San Francisco: Jossey-Bass

Armstrong, J. S., & Overton, T. S. (1977). Estimating nonresponse bias in mail surveys. *JMR, Journal of Marketing Research, 14*(3), 396–402. doi:10.2307/3150783

Arnett, K. P., & Schmidt, M. B. (2005). Busting the Ghost in the Machine. *Communications of the ACM, 48*(8), 92–95. doi:10.1145/1076211.1076246

Arnold, D., & Niederman, F. (2001). The Global Workforce. *Communications of the ACM, 44*(7), 31–33. doi:10.1145/379300.379306

Arora, A., & Fosfuri, A. (2000). Wholly owned subsidiary versus technology licensing in the worldwide chemical industry. *Journal of International Business Studies, 31*(4), 555-572.

Arrow, K. J. (1963). *Social choice and individual values*. New York: JohnWiley & Sons.

Ashmore, R. D., Del Boca, F. K., & Wohlers, A. J. (1986). Gender Stereotypes. In R. D. Ashmore & F. K. Del Boca (Eds.), *The Social Psychology of Female-Male Relations: A Critical Analysis of Central Concepts*. New York: Academic Press.

Atkinson, D., & Pervan, G. (1998, June 4-6). *Group support systems and productivity in four national cultures*. Paper presented at the Sixth European Conference on Information Systems, Aix-en-Provence, France.

Augier, M., Shariq, S. Z., & Vendelo, M. T. (2001). Understanding context: its emergence, transformation and role in tacit knowledge sharing. *Journal of Knowledge Management, 5*(2), 125–136. doi:10.1108/13673270110393176

Australian Bureau of Statistics. (2002). Special Tabulation. Unpublished. Cited in Staehr, L., Byrne, G. and Bell, E. (2006). Gender and the Australian IT Industry. In Trauth, E.M. (Ed.), *Encyclopedia of Gender and Information Technology* (pp. 467-473). Hershey, PA: Idea Group Publishing.

Australian Bureau of Statistics. (2004). Glossary. Retrieved July 9, 2004, from http://www.abc.net.au/eightdays/glossary/default.htm

Auto-ID Center. (2002). *Technology guide*. Retrieved July 12, 2004, from http://www.autoidcenter.org

Aycan, Z., & Fikret-Pasa, S. (2003, Winter). Career choices, job selection criteria, and leadership preferences in a transitional nation: The case of Turkey. *Journal of Career Development, 30*(2).

Bae, J., & Lawler, J. J. (2000). Organizational and HRM strategies in Korea: Impact on firm performance in an emerging economy. *Academy of Management Journal, 43*(3), 502-517.

Bae, J., Chen, S.-j., Wan, T. W. D., Lawler, J. J., & Walumbwa, F. O. (2003). Human resource strategy and firm performance in Pacific Rim countries. *International Journal of Human Resource Management, 14*(8), 1308-1332.

Bagozzi, R. P., & Phillips, L. W. (1982). Representing and testing organizational theories: A holistic construal. *Administrative Science Quarterly, 27*(3), 459-489.

Bagozzi, R. P., & Warshaw, P. R. (1989). User acceptance of computer technology: a comparison of two theoretical models. *Management Science, 38*(8), 982-1002.

Bagozzi, R. P., Davis, F., & Warshaw, P. R. (1992). Development and Test of a Theory of Technological Learning and Usage. *Human Relations, 45*(7), 659–686. doi:10.1177/001872679204500702

Bagozzi, R. P., Yi, Y., & Phillips, L. W. (1991). Assessing construct validity in organizational research. *Administrative Science Quarterly, 36*(3), 421-458.

Bagozzi, R. P., Yi, Y., & Surrendra, S. (1991). On the use of structural equation models in experimental designs: Two extensions. *International Journal of Research in Marketing, 8*(2), 125–140. doi:10.1016/0167-8116(91)90020-8

Bagozzi, R.P., Tybout, A.M., Craig, S., & Sternthal, B.(1979). The construct validity of the tripartite classification of attitudes. *Journal of Marketing Research* (pre-1986), *16*(1), 88-96.

Bahli, B., & Rivard, S. (2005). Validating measures of information technology outsourcing risk factors. *Omega, 33*, 175-187.

Baker, M. (1991). *Research in marketing*. London: MacMillan.

Bakker, E., Zheng, J., Knight, L., & Harland, C. (2008). Putting e-commerce adoption in a supply chain context. *International Journal of Operations & Production Management, 28*(4), 313–330. doi:10.1108/01443570810861543

Bandura, A. (1977). Self-Efficacy: Towards a Unifying Theory of Behavioral Change. *Psychological Review*, *84*, 191–215. doi:10.1037/0033-295X.84.2.191

Bandura, A. (1988). Organizational applications of social cognitive theory. *Australian Journal of Management*, *13*, 137-164.

Bandura, A. (1997). *Self-Efficacy: The Exercise of Control*. New York: W.H. Freeman.

Bandura, A., Adams, N. E., & Beyer, J. (1977). Cognitive Processes Mediating Behavioral Change. *Journal of Personality and Social Psychology*, *35*(3), 125–139. doi:10.1037/0022-3514.35.3.125

Barber, B. M., & Lyon, J. D. (1996). Detecting abnormal operating performance: the empirical power and specification of test statistics. *Journal of Financial Economics*, *41*, 359–399. doi:10.1016/0304-405X(96)84701-5

Barclay, D., Higgins, C., & Thompson, R. (1995). The partial least squares (PLS) approach to causal modeling: personal computer adoption and use as an illustration. *Technology Studies*, *2*, 285–309.

Bar-Eli, M., & Tractinsky, N. (2000). Criticality of game situations and decision making in basketball-an application of performance crisis perspective. *Psychology of Sport and Exercise*, *1*, 27-39.

Barling, J., & Beattie, R. (1983). Self-Efficacy Beliefs and Sales Performance. *Journal of Behavioral Management*, *5*, 125–139.

Barney, J. B. (1986). Strategic factor markets: expectations, luck, and business strategy. *Management Science*, *32*, 1231–1241. doi:10.1287/mnsc.32.10.1231

Barney, J. B. (1991). Firm resources and sustained competitive advantage. *Journal of Management*, *17*(1), 99–120. doi:10.1177/014920639101700108

Barrett, S., & Konsynski, B. (1982). Inter-organization information sharing systems. *MIS Quarterly*, (Special Issue), 93–105. doi:10.2307/248993

Bartels, A. (2000). The difference between e-business and e-commerce. *Computerworld*, *34*(44), 41.

Bartlett, C. A., & Ghoshal, S. (2002). Building competitive advantage through people. *Sloan Management Review*, *43*(2), 34-41.

Bartol, K. M., & Srivastava, A. (2002). Encouraging knowledge sharing: the role of organizational reward systems. *Journal of Leadership and Organizational Studies*, *9*(1), 64-76.

Barua, A., & Kriebel, C.H. & Mukhopadhyay. (1995). Information technologies and business value: an empirical investigation. *Information Systems Research*, *6*(1), 3–23. doi:10.1287/isre.6.1.3

Battin, R., Crocker, R., Kreidler, J., & Subramanian, K. (2001). Leveraging Resources in global software development. *IEEE Software*, *18*(2), 70-77.

Beatty, R. (1998). *An empirical investigation into the salient factors used by organisations in the adoption of Web site technology*: Mississippi State University, DBA.

Becerra-Fernandez, I., & Sabherwal, R. (2001). Organizational knowledge management: a contingency perspective. *Journal of Management Information System*, *18*(1), 23-55.

Begley, T. M., & Boyd, D. Y. (1986). Psychological Characteristics Associated with Entrepreneurial Performance. In R. Ronstadt (Ed.), *Frontiers of Entrepreneurship Research*.

Belardo, S., & Wallace, W. A. (1989). Gaming as a means for evaluating decision support systems for emergency management response. In J. Sullivan & R. Newkirk (Eds.), *Simulation in emergency management and technology, simulation series* (pp. 113-117).

Bell, K., Dyer, G., Hoopes, C., & Harris, S. (2004). Toward a model of effective knowledge management and directions for future research: Culture, leadership, and CKOs. *Journal of Leadership & Organizational Studies*, *10*(4), 26–43. doi:10.1177/107179190401000403

Benamati, J., & Lederer, A. L. (2001, Spring). Rapid information technology change, coping mechanisms, and the emerging technologies group. *Journal of Management Information Systems, 17*(4), pp. 183-202.

Bentle, P. M. (1990). Comparative fit indexes in structural models. *Psychological Bulletin*, *107*(2), 238–246. doi:10.1037/0033-2909.107.2.238

Bentler, P. M. (1990). Comparative fit indexes in structural models. *Psychological Bulletin*, *107*, 238-246.

Bentler, P. M., & Chou, C. P. (1987). Practical Issues in Structural Modeling. *Sociological Methods & Research*, *16*, 78–117. doi:10.1177/0049124187016001004

Berger, J., Fisek, M. H., Norman, R. Z., & Zelditch, M. (1977). *Status Characteristics and Social Interaction*. Amsterdam: North-Holland.

Beroggi, G. E. G., Mendonça, D., & Wallace, W. A. (2003). Operational sustainability management for the infrastructure: The case of emergency response. In A. Sage (Ed.), *Encyclopedia of life support systems*. Oxford, UK: EOLSS Publishers Co. Ltd.

Berry, J. W. (1979). Research in Multicultural Societies: Implications of Cross-Cultural Methods. *Journal of Cross-Cultural Psychology*, *10*(4), 415–434. doi:10.1177/0022022179104002

Betz, N. E., & Hackett, G. (1981). The Relationship of Career-Related Self-Efficacy Expectations to Perceived Career Options in College Women and Men. *Journal of Counseling Psychology*, *28*(5), 399–410. doi:10.1037/0022-0167.28.5.399

Bharadwaj, A. S. (2000). A Resource-based perspective on information technology capability and firm performance, an empirical investigation. *MIS Quarterly*, *24*(1), 169–196. doi:10.2307/3250983

Bharadwaj, A. S. (2000). A resourced-based perspective on information technology capability and firm performance: an empirical investigation. *MIS Quarterly*, *24*(1), 169–196. doi:10.2307/3250983

Bharadwaj, A. S., Sambamurthy, V., & Zmud, R. W. (1999). *IT Capabilities: theoretical perspectives and empirical operationalization*. Paper presented at 20th International Conferences on Information Systems, Charlotte, NC.

Bhatt, G. D. (2000). Exploring the relationship between information technology, infrastructure and business process re-engineering. *Business Process Management Journal*, *6*(2), 139–163. doi:10.1108/14637150010324085

Bhatt, G. D., & Grover, V. (2005). Types of information technology capabilities and their role in competitive advantage. *Journal of MIS*, *22*(3), 253–277.

Black, J. S., & Mendenhall, M. (1990). Cross-Cultural Training Effectiveness: A Review and Theoretical Framework for Future Research. *Academy of Management Review*, *15*(1), 113–136. doi:10.2307/258109

Blake, R. R., & Mouton, J. S. (1969). *Building a Dynamic Corporation through Grid Organization Development* Addison-Wesley Pub Co.

Blakeley, C. J., & Matsuura, J. H. (2004). The use of e-government to encourage e-commerce development. *International Conference on Information and Communication Technologies: From Theory to Applications*.

Bluedorn, A. C. (1982). The theories of turnover: Causes, effects, and meaning. In S. B. Bacharach (Ed.), *Research in the sociology of organizations* (Vol. 1, pp. 75-128). Greenwich, CT: JAI.

Bochner, S., & Hesketh, B. (1994). Power distance, individualism/collectivism and job-related attitudes in a culturally diverse work group. *Journal of Cross-Cultural Psychology*, *25*(2), 233-257.

Bock, G. W. & Kim, Y.-G. (2002). Breaking the myths of rewards: An exploratory study of attitudes about knowledge sharing. *Information Resources Management Journal*, *15*(2), 14-21.

Bock, G. W., Zmud, R. W., Kim, Y.-G., & Lee, J.-N. (2005). Behavioral intention formation in knowledge sharing: Examining the roles of extrinsic motivators, social-psychological forces, and organizational climate. *MIS Quarterly*, *29*(1), 87–111.

Boisot, M., & Child, J. (1999). Organizations as adaptive systems in complex environments: The case of China. *Organization Science*, *10*(3), 237–252. doi:10.1287/orsc.10.3.237

Bollen, K. A. (1989). A new incremental fit index for general structural models. *Sociological Methods & Research*, *17*, 303-316.

Bollen, K. A. (1989). *Structural Equations with Latent Variables*. New York: John Wiley and Sons.

Bollen, K.A. (1989b). A new incremental fit index for general structural models. *Social logical Methods & Research*, *17*(3), 303-316.

Bonoma, T. V. (1985). Case research in marketing: opportunities, problems, and a process. *JMR, Journal of Marketing Research, 22*(3), 199–208. doi:10.2307/3151365

Bordley, R. F., & Wolff, R. W. (1981). On the aggregation of individual probability estimates. *Management Science, 27*(8), 959-964.

Bouchard, T., & Hare, M. (1970). Size, performance, and potential in brainstorming groups. *The Journal of Applied Psychology, 54*(1), 51–55. doi:10.1037/h0028621

Boulle, C. (1996). HLSG report No. 2 barriers to electronic commerce in support of SMEs. Retrieved June, 23, 2003, from http://www.ict.etsi.fr/Activities/Documents/HLSG_Report2.pdf

Bowden, S., Clark, D., Patricia, C., Gibb, J., Kearins, K., & Pavolich, K. (2001). *Adoption and implementation of e-business in New Zealand: Preliminary results.* Paper presented at the 9th Annual Conference of the New Zealand Strategic Management Society.

Bowers, D. G., & Seashore, S. E. (1966). Predicting organizational effectiveness with a four-factor theory of leadership. *Administrative Science Quarterly, 11*(2), 238–263. doi:10.2307/2391247

Bozdağ, E. C., Kahraman, C., & Ruan, D. (2003). Fuzzy group decision making for selection among computer integrated manufacturing systems. *Computers in Industry, 51*(1), 13-29.

Brenner, B. (2005). Botnets are more menacing than ever. Retrieved September, 2005, from http://searchsecurity.techtarget.com/originalContent/0,289142,sid14_gci1068871,00.html

Bridge, S., O'Neill, K., & Cromie, S. (2003). *Understanding Enterprise, Entrepreneurship and small Business.* London: MacMillan Business.

Briggs, R. O., Balthazard, P. A., & Dennis, A. R. (1996). Graduate business students as surrogates in the evaluation of technology. *Journal of End User Computing, 8*(4), 11-17.

Briggs, R. O., de Vreede, G. J., & Reinig, B. A. (2003, January 6-9). *A theory and measurement of meeting satisfaction.* Paper presented at the 36th Hawaii International Conference on System Sciences (HICSS), Big Island, HI.

BroadBent, M., & Weill, P. (1997). Management by maxim: How business and IT managers can create IT infrastructures. *Sloan Management Review, 38*(3), 77–92.

Brock, D. L., Milne, T. P., Kang, Y. Y., & Lewis, B.(2002). *The physical markup language core components: Time and place* (MIT Auto-ID Center White Paper WH-005). Retrieved July 23, 2003, from http://www.autoidcenter.org/publishedresearch

Brockhaus, R. H. (1980). Risk Taking Propensity of Entrepreneurs. *Academy of Management Journal, 23*, 509–520. doi:10.2307/255515

Brosnan, M. J. (1999). Modeling Technophobia: A Case for Word Processing. *Computers in Human Behavior, 15*(2), 105–121. doi:10.1016/S0747-5632(98)00020-X

Brown, I., & Inouye, D. K. (1978). Learned Helplessness through Modeling: The Role of Perceived Similarity and Competence. *Journal of Personality and Social Psychology, 36*(8), 900–908. doi:10.1037/0022-3514.36.8.900

Brown, S. L., & Eisenhardt, K. M. (1997). The art of continuous change: Linking complexity theory and time-paced evolution in relentlessly shifting organizations. *Administrative Science Quarterly, 42*(1), 1-34.

Brown, S., Fuller, R. M., & Vician, C. (2004). Who's Afraid of the Virtual World? Anxiety and Computer-Mediated Communication. *Journal of the Association of Information Systems, 5*(2), 79–107.

Bruner, J. (1990). *Acts of meaning.* Cambridge, MA: Harvard University Press.

Bruque, S., & Moyano, J. (2007). Organisational determinants of information technology adoption and implementation in SMEs: The case of family and cooperative firms. *Technovation, 27*, 241–253. doi:10.1016/j.technovation.2006.12.003

Brynjolfsson, E. (1993). The productivity paradox of information technology. *Communications of the ACM, 36*(12), 67–77. doi:10.1145/163298.163309

Brynjolfsson, E., & Hitt, L. (1996). Paradox lost? Firm-level evidence on the return to information systems spending. *Management Science, 42*(4), 541–558. doi:10.1287/mnsc.42.4.541

Burger, C. J., Creamer, E. G., & Meszaros, P. S. (Eds.). (2007). *Reconfiguring the firewall: Recruiting women to information technology across cultures and continents.* Wellesley, MA: AK Peters Publishing.

Burke, K. (2005). The Impact of Firm Size on Internet Use in Small Businesses. *Electronic Markets, 15*(2), 79–93. doi:10.1080/10196780500083738

Burke, K., & Aytes, K. (1998). A longitudinal analysis of the effects of media richness on cohesion development and process satisfaction in computer-supported workgroups. In *Proceedings of the 31st Hawaii International Conference on Systems Sciences* (pp. 135-144).

Burke, K., & Chidambaram, L. (1996). How much bandwidth is enough? A longitudinal examination of media characteristics and media outcomes. *MIS Quarterly, 23*(4), 557-580.

Burkhardt, M. E., & Brass, D. J. (1990). Changing Patterns or Patterns of Change: The Effects of a Change in Technology on Social Network Structure and Power. *Administrative Science Quarterly, 35*(1), 104–127. doi:10.2307/2393552

Burns, T., & Stalker, G. M. (1961). *The management of innovation.* London: Tavistock.

Burnson, A. (1989). The perils of going global. *InfoWorld,* (August): 14, 39–40.

Burton, S. (2002). Where are all the shoppers? E-tailing lessons for the Asia Pacific. *Quarterly Journal of Electronic Commerce, 3*(4), 331-342.

Byrd, T. A., & Turner, D. E. (2000). Measuring the flexibility of information technology infrastructure, exploratory analysis of a construct. *Journal of Management Information Systems, 17*(1), 167–208.

Byrne, B. M. (2001). *Structural equation modeling with AMOS: Basic concepts, applications, and programming.* London: Lawrence Erlbaum Associates.

Cabrera, A., & Cabrera, E. F. (2002). Knowledge-sharing dilemmas. *Organization Studies, 23*(5), 687-710.

Calantone, R. J., Cavusgil, S. T., & Zhao, Y. (2002). Learning orientation, firm innovation capability, and firm performance. *Industrial Marketing Management, 31,* 515-524.

Caldeira, M. M., & Ward, J. M. (2002). Understanding the successful adoption and use of IS/IT in SMEs: an explanation from Portuguese manufacturing industries. *Information Systems Journal, 12*(2), 121–152. doi:10.1046/j.1365-2575.2002.00119.x

Calhoun, K. J., Teng, J. T. C., & Cheon, M. J. (2002). Impact of national culture on information technology usage behavior: An exploratory study of decision making in Korea and the USA. *Behaviour & Information Technology, 21*(4), 293–302. doi:10.1080/0144929021000013491

Camp, T. (2002). Reprints: The incredible shrinking pipeline. *ACM SIGCSE Bulletin, 34*(2), 129–134. doi:10.1145/543812.543846

Campbell, D. J. (1988). Task complexity: A review and analysis. *Academy of Management Review, 13*(1), 40–52. doi:10.2307/258353

Campbell, D. T., & Stanley, J. C. (1966). *Experimental and quasi-experimental designs for research.* Chicago: Rand McNally.

Capon, N., & Glazer, R. (1987). Marketing and technology, a strategic co alignment. *Journal of Marketing, 51*(3), 1–14. doi:10.2307/1251644

Carlsson, C., & Fuller, R. (2001). On possibilistic mean value and variance of fuzzy numbers. *Fuzzy Sets and Systems, 122,* 315-326.

Carmel, E. (2006). Building your information systems from the other side of the world: How Infosys manages time zone differences. *MIS Quarterly Executive, 5*(1), 43-53.

Carmel, E., & Nicholson, B. (2005). Small firms and offshore software outsourcing: High transaction costs and their mitigation. *Journal of global information management, 13*(3), 33-54.

Carneiro, A. (2000). How does knowledge management influence innovation and competitiveness? *Journal of Knowledge Management, 4*(2), 87-92.

Carpenter, M. A., & Fredrickson, J. W. (2001). Top management teams, global strategic posture and the moderating role of uncertainty. *Academy of Management Journal, 44*(3), 533-545.

Carter, C. R. (2000). Ethical issues in international buyer-supplier relationships: A dyadic examination. *Journal of Operations Management, 18*(2), 191-208.

Casimir, G., & Li, Z. (2005). Combinative aspects of leadership style: A comparison of Australian and Chinese followers. *Asian Business & Management, 4*, 271–291. doi:10.1057/palgrave.abm.9200132

Cass, S. (2006). Antipiracy software opens door to electronic intruders. *IEEE Spectrum, 43*(1), 12–13. doi:10.1109/MSPEC.2006.1572337

Castells, M. (2000). *The Information Age I-III*. Oxford: Oxford University Press.

Cavaye, A. L. M. (1996). Case study research: a multi-faceted research approach for IS. *Information Systems Journal, 6*, 227–242. doi:10.1111/j.1365-2575.1996.tb00015.x

Cavusgil, S. T. (1994). A quiet revolution in Australian exporters. *Marketing News, 28*, 18–21.

CCIDNet. (2006). *Increase rate at industrial informatization investment will reach 20% in 2006*: China Market Information Center. Retrieved from http://industry.ccidnet.com/art/7/20060217/431185_1.html

Chan, S., & Lu, M.-t. (2004). Understanding Internet Banking Adoption and Use Behavior: A Hong Kong Perspective. *Journal of Global Information Management, 12*(3), 21–43.

Chandler, A. D. (1962). *Strategy and structure*. Cambridge, MA: MIT Press.

Chandy, P. R., & Williams, T. G. E. (1994). The impact of journals and authors on international business. *Journal of International Business Studies, 25*(4), 715-728.

Chang, B. L. (2002). The social context of turnover among information technology professionals. In *Proceedings of SIGCPR* (pp. 145-153).

Chang, S. K. C. (1985). American and Chinese managers in U.S. companies in Taiwan. *California Management Review, 27*(4), 144-156.

Chang, T., & Grub, P. D. (1992). Competitive strategies of Taiwanese PC firms in their internationalization process. *Journal of Global Marketing, 6*(3), 5-27.

Chanopas, A., Krairit, D., & Khang, D. B. (2006). Managing information technology infrastructure: a new flexibility framework. *Management Research News, 29*(10), 632–651. doi:10.1108/01409170610712335

Chau, P. Y. K., & Tam, K. Y. (2000). Organizational adoption of open systems: a `technology-push, need-pull' perspective. *Information and Management, 37*(5), 229-239.

Chau, P., & Tam, K. Y. (1997). Factors affecting the adoption of open systems: an exploratory study. *MIS Quarterly, 21*(1), 1-21.

Chen, C. T. (2000). Extensions of the TOPSIS for group decision-making under fuzzy environment. *Fuzzy Sets and Systems, 114*, 1-9.

Chen, G., Gully, S. M., Whiteman, J.-A., & Kilcullen, R. N. (2000). Examination of Relationships among Trait-Like Individual Differences, State-Like Individual Differences, and Learning Performance. *The Journal of Applied Psychology, 85*(6), 835–847. doi:10.1037/0021-9010.85.6.835

Chen, L. Y., & Barnes, F. B. (2006). Leadership behaviors and knowledge sharing in professional service firms engaged in strategic alliances. *Journal of Applied Management and Entrepreneurship, 11*(2), 51–69.

Chen, M., Chen, A. N. K., & Shao, B. B. M. (2003). The Implications and Impacts of Web Services to Electronic Commerce Research and Practices. *Journal of Electronic Commerce Research, 4*(4), 128–139.

Chen, R., Sharman, R., Rao, H. R., et al. (2005). Design principles of coordinated multi-incident emergency response systems. *Lecture Notes in Computer Science, 3495*, 81-93.

Chen, S. Y., Fu, G. T. (2005). Combining fuzzy iteration model with dynamic programming to solve multiobjective multistage decision making problems. *Fuzzy Sets and Systems, 152*(3), 499-512.

Chew, S. B., & Chew, R. (2001). Public policy and entrepreneurship: The case of Singapore. *International Journal of Entrepreneurship and Innovation Management, 1*(2), 217.

Chidambaram, L. (1996). Relational development in computer-supported groups. *MIS Quarterly, 20*(2), 143-163.

Chidambaram, L., & Bostrom, R. (1993). Evolution of group performance over time: A repeated measures study of GDSS effects. *Journal of Organizational Computing, 3*(4), 443-469.

Child, J. (1972). Organizational structure, environment, and performance: The role of strategic choice. *American Journal of Sociology, 60*, 339-342.

Child, J. (1991). A foreign perspective on the management of people in China. *International Journal of Human Resource Management, 2*(1), 93–107.

Chin, W. W. (1998). Issues and opinion on structural equation modeling. *MIS Quarterly, 22*(1), vii-xvi.

Chin, W. W. (1998). Issues and opinion on structure equation modeling. *MIS Quarterly, 22*(1), vii–xvi.

Chin, W. W. (1998). The partial least squares approach to structural equation modeling In G. A. Marcoulids (Ed.), *Modern Methods for Business Research*. Mahwah, NJ: Lawrence Erlbaum Associates

Chin, W. W. (2001). *PLS-graph user's guide*. Soft Modeling Inc.

Chin, W. W., & Marcolin, B. L. (2001). Special issue on adoption, diffusion & infusion of IT. *The DATA BASE for Advances in Information Systems, 32*(3), 7-12.

Chin, W. W., & Newsted, P. R. (1999). Structural equation modeling analysis with small samples using partial least squares. In R. Hoyle (Ed.), *Statistical strategies for small sample research* (pp. 307-341). Sage Publications.

Chin, W. W., Marcolin, B. L., & Newsted, P. R. (2003). A partial least squares latent variable modeling approach for measuring interaction effects: Results from a Monte Carlo simulation study and an electronic-mail emotion/adoption study. *Information Systems Research, 14*(2), 189–217. doi:10.1287/isre.14.2.189.16018

China Top Target for Computer Attacks. Microsoft. Microsoft Security Report, November 3, 2008. Retrieved December 2, 2008 from http://www.spacewar.com/reports/China_top_target_for_computer_attacks_Microsoft_999.html.

China Will Become the Biggest Market for Electronic Information (1998, May 11). *People's Daily*.

ChinaLabs. (2004). China informatization report (2004 Q2, Chinese). Retrieved April 30, 2006

Chinese Culture Connection. (1987). Chinese values and the search for culture-free dimensions of culture. *Journal of Cross-Cultural Psychology, 18*(2), 143–164. doi:10.1177/0022002187018002002

Cho, B., Kwon, U., Gentry, J. W., Jun, S., & Kropp, F. (1999). Cultural values reflected in theme and execution: a comparative study of US and Korean television. *Journal of Advertising, 28*(4), 59–73.

Choi, B., & Lee, H. (2003). An empirical investigation of KM styles and their effect on corporate performance. *Information and Management, 40*, 403-417.

Choi, C. J., & Nailer, C. (2005). The China market and European companies: pricing and surviving the local competition. *European Business Review, 17*(2), 177-190.

Chong, S. (2001). *Electronic Commerce Adoption by Small- and Medium-sized Enterprises in Australia and Singapore*. Curtin University of Technology.

Choudhury, V., & Sabherwal, R. (2003). Portfolios of control in outsourced software development projects. *Information Systems Research, 14*(3), 291-314.

Chow, C. W., Deng, F. J., & Ho, J. L. (2000). The openness of knowledge sharing within organizations: A comparative study of the United States and the People's Republic of China. *Journal of Management Accounting Research, 12*, 65–95. doi:10.2308/jmar.2000.12.1.65

Chowdhury, S. (2005). The role of affect-and cognition-based trust in complex knowledge sharing. *Journal of Managerial Issues, 17*(3), 310–326.

Chung, K., & Adams, C. R. (1997). A study on the characteristics of group decision making behavior: Cultural difference perspective of Korea vs. US. *Journal of Global Information Management, 5*(3), 18–29.

Churchill, G. A. (1979). A Paradigm for developing better measures of marketing constructs. *JMR, Journal of Marketing Research, 16*, 64–73. doi:10.2307/3150876

Clapper, D. L., McLean, E. R., & Watson, R. T. (1991). *An experimental investigation of the effect of a group decision support system on normative influence in small groups*. Paper presented at the Twelfth Annual International Conference on Information Systems (ICIS), New York.

Clark, C. E., Cavanaugh, N. C., Brown, C. V., & Sambamurthy, V. (1997). Building change-readiness capabilities in the IS organization: insights from the Bell Atlantic experience. *MIS Quarterly, 21*(4), 425–456. doi:10.2307/249722

Clark, D. N., Bowden, S., & Corner, P. (2002). *Adoption and implementation of E-Business in New Zealand: Comparative empirical results, 2001 and 2002.* University of Waikato Management School Research Report.

Clarke, V. A., & Teague, G. J. (1994a). Encouraging girls to study computer science - Should we even try? *Australian Educational Computing, 9*(1), 17–22.

Clarke, V. A., & Teague, G. J. (1994b). A psychological perspective on gender differences in computing participation. In *Proceedings of the ACM SIGCSE 1994 Conference* (pp. 258-262). New York: ACM Press.

Clear, T., & Kassabova, D. (2005). *Motivational patterns in virtual team collaboration.* Paper presented at the 7th Australasian Conference on Computing Education, Newcastle.

Clemons, E. K. (1986). Information systems for sustainable competitive advantage. *Information & Management, 11*(3), 131–136. doi:10.1016/0378-7206(86)90010-8

Clemons, E. K. (1991). Corporate strategy for information technology: a resource-based approach. *Computer, 24*(11), 23–32. doi:10.1109/2.116848

Clemons, E. K., & Row, M. C. (1991). Sustaining IT advantage: the role of structural differences. *MIS Quarterly, 15*(3), 275–294. doi:10.2307/249639

Cloete, E., Courtney, S., & Fintz, J. (2002). Small Businesses' Acceptance and Adoption of E-Commerce in the Western-Cape Province of South-Africa. *Electronic Journal on Information Systems in Developing Countries, 10*(4), 1–13.

CMP. (2005). *Chinese enterprises' IT application demand and market research Report 2004-2005*: CMP Consulting. Retrieved from http://www.cmp.zikoo.com/?item=production&id=22

Collin, S. (1999). *Doing business on the Internet.* London: Kogan Page.

Collins, J. C., & Porras, J. I. (1996). Building your company's vision. *Harvard Business Review, 74*(5), 65-77.

Compeau, D. R., & Higgins, C. A. (1995a). Application of Social Cognitive Theory to Training for Computer Skills. *Information Systems Research, 6*(2), 118–143. doi:10.1287/isre.6.2.118

Compeau, D. R., & Higgins, C. A. (1995b). Computer Self-Efficacy: Development of a Measure and Initial Test. *MIS Quarterly*, 189–211. doi:10.2307/249688

Compeau, D., Higgins, C. A., & Huff, S. (1999). Social Cognitive Theory and Individual Reactions to Computing Technology: A Longitudinal Study. *MIS Quarterly, 23*(2), 145–158. doi:10.2307/249749

Comrey, A. L., & Lee, H. B. (1992). *A first course in factor analysis* (2nd ed.). Hillsdale, NJ: Lawrence Erlbaum Associates.

Condorcet, M. D. (1785). Essai sur l' Application de l' Analyse à la Probabilité des Décisions Renduesà la Plurali té des Voix. Paris: L'imprimerie Royale.

Conner, K. R. (1991). A historical comparison of the resource-based theory and five schools of thought within industrial organization economics: do I have a new theory of the firm? *Journal of Management, 17*(1), 121–154. doi:10.1177/014920639101700109

Conner, K. R., & Prahalad, C. K. (1996). A resource-based theory of the firm: Knowledge versus opportunism. *Organization Science, 7*(5), 477-501.

Connolly, T., Jessup, L. M., & Valacich, J. S. (1990). Effects of anonymity and evaluative tone on idea generation in computer-mediated groups. *Management Science, 36*(6), 689–703. doi:10.1287/mnsc.36.6.689

Constant, D., Keisler, S., & Sproull, L. (1994). What's mine is ours, or is it? A study of attitudes about information sharing. *Information Systems Research, 5*(4), 400-421.

Cook, D., & Luo, W. (2003). The role of third-party seals in building trust online. *E-Service Journal, 2*(3), 71-84.

Cook, J., & Wall, T. (1980). New work attitude measures of trust, organizational commitment and personal need non-fulfillment. *Journal of Occupational Psychology, 53*(1), 39–52.

Copeland, D. G., & McKenney, J. L. (1988). Airline reservations systems, lessons from history. *MIS Quarterly*, *12*(3), 353–371. doi:10.2307/249202

Cowles, D. L., Kiecker, P., & Little, M. W. (2002). Using key informant insights as a foundation for e-retailing theory development. *Journal of Business Research*, *55*(8), 629–636. doi:10.1016/S0148-2963(00)00203-4

Creamer, E. G., Lee, S., & Meszaros, P. S. (2007). Predicting women's interest and choice in a career in information technology: A statistical model. In C.J. Burger, E.G. Creamer & P.S. Meszaros (Eds.), *Reconfiguring the firewall: Recruiting women to information technology across cultures and continents*. Wellesley, MA: A K Peters, Ltd.

Crepeau, R. G., Crook, C. W., Goslar, M. D., & McMurtrey, M. E. (1992). Career anchors of information systems personnel. *Journal of Management Information Systems, 9*(2), 145-158.

Crisp, C. B. (2003). Control enactment in global virtual teams. *Dissertation Abstracts International*. (UMI No.)

Cronbach, L. J. (1951). Coefficient Alpha and the Internal Structure of Tests. *Psychometrica*, *16*(3), 297–334. doi:10.1007/BF02310555

Cronbach, L. J. (1970). Essentials of psychological testing (3rd ed.). New York: Harper & Row.

Cross, R., & Sproull, L. (2004). More than an answer: Information relationships for actionable knowledge. *Organization Science*, *15*(4), 446–462. doi:10.1287/orsc.1040.0075

Crum, M., Premkumar, G., & Ramamurthy, K. (1996). An assessment of motor carrier adoption, use, and satisfaction with EDI. *Transportation Journal, Summer*.

Crump, B. J., Logan, K. A., & McIlroy, A. (2007). Does Gender Still Matter? A Study of the Views of Women in the ICT Industry in New Zealand. *Gender, Work and Organization*, *14*(4), 349–370. doi:10.1111/j.1468-0432.2007.00348.x

Cummings, J. N. (2004). Work groups, structural diversity and knowledge sharing in a global organization. *Management Science*, *50*(3), 352–364. doi:10.1287/mnsc.1030.0134

Currall, S. C., & Judge, T. A. (1995). Measuring trust between organizational boundary role persons. *Organizational Behavior and Human Decision Processes*, *64*(2), 151–170. doi:10.1006/obhd.1995.1097

Cyr, D. (2008). Modeling Web Site Design Across Cultures: Relationships to Trust, Satisfaction, and E-Loyalty. *Journal of Management Information Systems*, *24*(4), 47–72. doi:10.2753/MIS0742-1222240402

Cyr, D., Bonanni, C., Bowes, J., & Ilsever, J. (2005). Beyond Trust: Web Site Design Preferences across Cultures. *Journal of Global Information Management*, *13*(4), 25–54.

Cyr, D., Bonanni, C., Bowes, J., & Ilsever, J. (2005). Beyond Trust: Web Site Design Preferences Across Cultures1. *Journal of Global Information Management*, *13*(4), 25.

Czarniawska-Joerges, B. (1995). Narration or science? Collapsing the division in organization studies. *Organization, 2*(1), 11-33.

D'Amico, E. (2002). Steering clear of new costs. *Chemical Week, 164*(36), 30-32.

D'Antoni, H. (2005, October 31). IT Security in China Shows Cracks. *InformationWeek,* 47-51.

Daft, R. L. (2003). *Management* (6th ed.). Mason, Ohio: South-Western.

Daft, R. L., & Lengel, R. H. (1986). Organizational information requirements, media richness and structural design. *Management Science*, *32*(5), 554–571. doi:10.1287/mnsc.32.5.554

Daft, R. L., & Weick, K. E. (1984). Toward a model of organizations as interpretation systems. *Academy of Management Review*, *9*(2), 284-295.

Daily, B. F., & Steiner, R. L. (1998). The Influence of Group Decision Support Systems on Contribution and Commitment Levels in Multicultural and Culturally Homogeneous Decision-Making Groups. *Computers in Human Behavior*, *14*(1), 147–162. doi:10.1016/S0747-5632(97)00037-X

Daily, B. F., Whatley, A., Ash, S. R., & Steiner, R. L. (1996). The effects of a group decision support system on culturally diverse and culturally homogeneous group decision making. *Information & Management, 30*(6), 281–289. doi:10.1016/S0378-7206(96)01062-2

Damaskopoulos, P., & Evgeniou, T. (2003). Adoption of New Economy Practices by SMEs in Eastern Europe. *European Management Journal, 21*(2), 133–145. doi:10.1016/S0263-2373(03)00009-4

Damian, D. E, Eberlein, A., Shaw, M. L. G., & Gaines, B. R. (2000). Using different communication media in requirements negotiation. *IEEE Software, 17*(3), 28-36.

Damian, D. E., & Zowghi, D. (2003). An insight into interplay between culture, conflict and distance in globally distributed requirement negotiations. In *Proceedings of the 36th Hawaii International Conference on System Sciences*.

Daniel, E., Wilson, H., & Myers, A. (2002). Adoption of e-commerce by SMEs in the UK. *International Small Business Journal, 20*(3), 253. doi:10.1177/0266242602203002

Datta, D. K., Guthrie, J. P., & Wright, P. M. (2005). Human resource management and labor productivity: Does industry matter? *Academy of Management Journal, 48*(1), 135-145.

Davenport, T. H., & Prusak, L. (1998). *Working Knowledge: How Organizations Manage What They Know*: Harvard Business School Press.

Davenport, T. H., De Long, D. W., & Beers, M. C. (1998). Successful knowledge management projects. *Sloan Management Review, 39*(2), 43-57.

David, H. B. N. L. (2004). Potential of critical e-applications for engaging SMEs in e-business: a provider perspective. *European Journal of Information Systems, 13*(1), 21. doi:10.1057/palgrave.ejis.3000480

David, M. (2003). Networks to unlock the value of RFID: Speeding the adoption & lowering the costs of RFID in the retail supply chain. *Cisco Systems, Important Notices & Privacy Statement*, 1-7.

Davidson, D. (2002). Cultural Complications of Erp. *Communications of the ACM, 45*(7), 109–111.

Davis, E. D., Bagozzi, R. R, & Warshaw, R. R. (1989). User acceptance of computer technology: A comparison of two theoretical models. *Management Science, 35*(8), 982-1003.

Davis, F. (1989). Perceived Usefulness, Perceived Ease of Use, and User Acceptance of Computing Technology. *MIS Quarterly, 13*(3), 319–339. doi:10.2307/249008

Davis, F. (1993). User Acceptance of Information Technology: System Characteristics, User Perceptions, and Behavioral Impacts. *International Journal of Management, 38*, 475–487.

Davis, F. D. (1986). *A technology acceptance model for empirically testing new end-user information system: Theory and results*. Unpublished doctoral dissertation, Sloan School of Management, Massachusetts Institute of Technology, Cambridge, MA.

Davis, F. D. (1989). Perceived usefulness, perceived ease of use, and user acceptance of information technology. *MIS Quarterly, 13*(3), 319-339.

Davis, H. E., & Luehlging, M. H. (2004). Radio frequency identification: The wave of the future. *Journal of Accountancy; 198*(5), 43-49.

Davison, R. (1996). National cultures, organisational forms and group support systems Retrieved September 28, 2004, from http://www.is.cityu.edu.hk/Research/WorkingPapers/paper/9607.pdf

Davison, R. (2002). Cultural complications of ERP. *Communications of the ACM, 45*(7), 109–111. doi:10.1145/514236.514267

De Vreede, G., Jones, N., & Mgaya, B. J. (1999). Exploring the application and acceptance of group support systems in Africa. *Journal of Management Information Systems, 15*(3), 197–234.

Dedrick, J., & Kraemer, K. L. (2001). China IT Report. *Electronic Journal on Information Systems in Developing Countries, 6*(2), 1–10.

Deemen, A. V. (1999). *The probability of the paradox of voting for weak preference orderings, social choice and welfare*. Berlin: Springer.

Dehning, B., Richardson, V. J., & Stratopoulos, T. (2005). Information technology investments and firm value. *Information & Management, 42*(7), 989–1008. doi:10.1016/j.im.2004.11.003

Deluga, R. J. (1995). The relation between trust in the supervisor and subordinate organizational citizenship behavior. *Military Psychology, 7*(1), 1–16. doi:10.1207/s15327876mp0701_1

Dennis, A. R. (1994). Electronic support for large groups. *Journal of Organizational Computing, 4*(2), 177–197. doi:10.1080/10919399409540222

Dennis, A. R., & Wixon, B. H. (2001). Investigating the moderators of the group support systems use with meta analysis. *Journal of Management Information Systems, 18*(3), 235–257.

Dennis, A. R., Aronson, J. E., Heninger, W. G., & Walker, E. D. (1999). Structuring Time and Task in Electronic Brainstorming. *MIS Quarterly, 23*(1), 95–108. doi:10.2307/249411

Dennis, A. R., Hilmer, K. M., & Taylor, N. J. (1998). Information exchange and use in GSS and verbal group decision making: Effects of minority influence. *Journal of Management Information Systems, 14*(3), 61–88.

Department of Trade and Industry. (2000). Business in the information age: international benchmarking study 2000. Retrieved June 24, 2004, from http://www.idgl.lu/library/pdf-files/DTI-ecommerce-bench-Oct2000.pdf

Deresky, H. (2006). *International Management, Managing across Borders and Cultures*. Upper Saddle River, NJ: Pearson/Prentice Hall.

Dex, S. (1991). *Life and work history analyses.* London: Routledge.

Dhar, S., & Balakrishnan, B. (2006). Risks, benefits, and challenges in global IT outsourcing: perspectives and practices. *Journal of Global Information Management, 14*(3), 39-69.

Dhillon, G., & Backhouse, J. (2000). Information System Security Management in the New Millennium. *Communications of the ACM, 43*(7), 125–128. doi:10.1145/341852.341877

Dhungana, B. P. (2003). *Strengthening the competitiveness of small and medium enterprises in the globalization process: prospects and challenges.* Investment Promotion and Enterprise Development Bulletin for Asia and the Pacific.

Digital Europe (2003). Is ebusiness good business? Survey key findings, May, DEESD IST-2000-28606

Dillard, K. (2005). Rootkit battle: Rootkit Revealer vs. Hacker Defender. Retrieved from http://wwwSearchWindowsSecurity.com

DiMaggio, P. J., & Powell, W. W. (1983). The iron cage revisited: Institutional isomorphism and collective rationality in organizational fields. *American Sociological Review, 48*(2), 147–160. doi:10.2307/2095101

Dipboye, R. L., & Flanagan, M. F. (1979). Research setting in industrial and organization psychology: Are findings in the field more generalizable than in laboratory. *American Psychologist, 34*(2), 141-150.

Dixon, N. M. (1990). Organizational learning: A review of the literature with implications for HRD professionals. *Human Resource Development Quarterly, 3*(1), 29-49.

Dodgsom, M. (1993). Learning, trust and technological collaboration. *Human Relations, 46*(1), 77–95. doi:10.1177/001872679304600106

Dodgson, M. (1993). Organizational learning: A review of some literatures. *Organization Studies, 14*(3), 375-394.

Doh, J. (2005). Offshore Outsourcing: Implications for International Business and Strategic Management Theory and Practice. *Journal of Management Studies, 42*(3), 695-701.

Doney, P. M., Cannon, J. P., & Mullen, M. R. (1998). Understanding the influence of national culture on the development of trust. *Academy of Management Review, 23*(3), 601-620.

Dorfman, P. W., & Howell, J. (1988). Dimensions of National Culture & Effective Leadership Patterns: Hofstede Revisited. In E. G. McGowan (Ed.), *Advances in International Comparative Management* (pp. 127-149)... Greenwich, CT: JAI Press.

Dornheim, M. A. (2002). Port security. *Aviation Week & Space Technology, 157*(7), 17.

Douglas, S. P., & Craig, C. S. (1983). *International Marketing Research.* Englewood Cliffs, NJ: Prentice-Hall.

Dow, D. (2006). Adaptation and performance in foreign markets: evidence of systematic under-adaptation. *Journal of International Business Studies, 37*(2), 212–226. doi:10.1057/palgrave.jibs.8400189

Downie, R., Dryburgh, H., McMullin, J., & Ranson, G. (2004). A profile of information technology in Canada. *Workforce Aging in the New Economy International Report, Number One*. Retrieved from http://www.wane.ca/PDF/IR1.pdf.

Draguns, J. G. (1979). Culture and Personality. In A. J. Marsella, T. Ciborowski & R. Tharp (Eds.), *Perspectives on Cross-Cultural Psychology* (pp. 179-207). New York: Academic Press.

Dubois, D., & Prade, H. (1992). Putting rough sets and fuzzy sets together. In R. Slowinski (Ed.), *Intelligent decision support: Handbook of applications and advances of the rough sets theory* (pp. 203-232). Dordrecht: Kluwer Academic Publishers.

Duncan, N. B. (1995). Capturing flexibility of information technology infrastructure: A study of resource characteristics and their measure. *Journal of Management Information Systems, 12*(2), 37–57.

Dunteman, E. A., & Bass, B. M. (1963). Supervisory and engineering success associated with self, interaction, and task orientation scores. *Personnel Psychology, 16*, 13–21. doi:10.1111/j.1744-6570.1963.tb01250.x

Durndell, A., Haag, Z., & Laithwaite, H. (2000). Computer selfefficacy and gender: A cross-cultural study of Scotland and Romania. *Personality and Individual Differences, 28*, 1037–1044. doi:10.1016/S0191-8869(99)00155-5

Dyer, J. S., & Sarin, R. K. (1979). Group preference aggregation rules based on strength of preference. *Management Science, 25*(9), 22-34.

Earl, M. (2001). Knowledge management strategies: Toward a taxonomy. *Journal of Management Information System, 18*(1), 215-233.

Earley, P. C. (1993). East meets west meets mid-east: Further explorations of collectivistic and individualistic work groups. *Academy of Management Journal, 36*(2), 319-348.

Earley, P. C. (1994). Self or group? Cultural effects of training on self-efficacy and performance. *Administrative Science Quarterly, 39*(1), 89–117. doi:10.2307/2393495

Ebert, C., & De Neve, P. (2001). Surviving global software development. *IEEE Software, 18*(2), 62-69.

Ecevit, Y., Gündüz-Hoşgőr, A., & Tokluoğlu, C. (2003). Professional women in computer programming occupations: The case of Turkey. *Career Development International, 8*(2), 78–87. doi:10.1108/13620430310465480

Eduard, T. (2001). Adding clicks to bricks. *Consulting to Management, 12*(4), 10.

Edvinsson, L., & Malone, M. S. (1997). *Intellectual capital: Realizing your company's true value by finding its hidden brainpower.* NY: Harper Business.

Edwards, K., & Sridhar, V. (2005). Analysis of software requirements engineering exercises in a global virtual team setup. *Journal of Global Information Management, 13*(2), 21-41.

Egelhoff, W. (1982). Strategy and structure in multinational corporations: an information processing approach. *Administrative Science Quarterly, 27*(3), 435-458.

Eidelman, L., & Hazzan, O. (2005). Factors influencing the shrinking pipeline in high schools: A sector-based analysis for the Israeli high school system. In the *Proceedings of the ACM SIGCSE Conference, St. Louis, MS, February 23-27, 2005* (pp. 406-410). New York: ACM Press.

Eidelman, L., & Hazzan, O. (2006). The shrinking pipeline in Israel high schools. In E. M. Trauth (Ed.), *Encyclopedia of gender and information technology* (pp. 1092-1098). Hershey, PA: Idea Group Publishing.

Eisenhardt, K. M. (1989). Building Theories From Case Study Research. *Academy of Management Review, 14*(4), 532–551. doi:10.2307/258557

Eisenhardt, K. M. (1989). Making fast strategic decisions in high-velocity environments. *Academy of Management Journal, 32*(3), 543-576.

Eisenhardt, K. M., & Martin, J. A. (2000). Dynamic capabilities: What are they? *Strategic Management Journal, 21,* 1105-1121.

Eisenhardt, K. M., & Santos, F. M. (2002). Knowledge-based view: A new theory of strategy? In A. Pettigrew, H. Thomas, & R. Whittington (Eds.), *Handbook of strategy and management* (pp. 139-164). London: Sage.

Eisenhartd, K. M., & Schoonboven, C. B. (1996). Resource-based view of strategic alliance formation: strategic and social effects in entrepreneurial firms. *Organization Science, 7*(2), 136–151. doi:10.1287/orsc.7.2.136

El Sawy, O. A., & Pavlou, P. A. (2008). IT-enabled business capabilities for turbulent environments. *MIS Quarterly Executive, 7*(3), 139–150.

Elbeltagi, I., McBride, N., & Hardaker, G. (2005). Evaluating the Factors Affecting DSS Usage by Senior Managers in Local Authorities in Egypt. *Journal of Global Information Management, 13*(2), 42–65.

Elliott, R. K., & Pallais, D. M. (1997). First: Know your market. *Journal of Accountancy, July,* 56-63.

Elliott, R., & Boshoff, C. (2007). The influence of the owner-manager of small tourism businesses on the success of internet marketing. *South African Journal of Business Management, 38*(3), 15–27.

El-Shinnawy, M., & Vinze, A. S. (1997). Technology, culture and persuasiveness: A study of choice-shifts in group settings. *International Journal of Human-Computer Studies, 47*(3), 473–496. doi:10.1006/ijhc.1997.0138

Enoch, Y., & Soker, Z. (2006). Age, Gender, Ethnicity and the Digital Divide: University Students' Use of Web-Based Instruction. *Open Learning, 21*(2), 99–110. doi:10.1080/02680510600713045

Erez, M., & Early, C. P. (1993). *Culture, Self-Identity, and Work.* New York: Oxford University Press.

Ernst, D. (2003). *The new mobility of knowledge: Digital information systems and global flagship networks.* Unpublished manuscript.

Erramilli, M. K. (1996). Nationality and subsidiary ownership patterns in multinational corporations. *Journal of International Business Studies, 27*(2), 225-248.

Ettlie, J. E. (1990). What makes a manufacturing firm innovative? *Academy of Management Executive, 4*(4), 7–20.

European Commission. (1999). *The Wider Picture: Enlargement and Cohesion in Europe*. Seville, Spain.

Eylon, D.,&Au, K. Y. (1999). Exploring empowerment cross-cultural differences along the power distance dimension. *International Journal of Intercultural Relations, 23,* 373-385.

Falk, R. F., & Miller, N. B. (1992). *A primer for soft modeling.* OH: University of Akron Press.

Favela, J., & Pena-Mora, F. (2001). An experience in collaborative software engineering education. *IEEE Software, 18*(2), 47-53.

Feeney, D. F., & Willcocks, L. P. (1998). Core IS capabilities for exploiting information technology. *Sloan Management Review, 39*(3), 9-21.

Feeny, D. F., & Willcocks, L. P. (1998b). Re-designing the IS function around core capabilities. *Long Range Planning, 31*(3), 354–367. doi:10.1016/S0024-6301(98)80003-4

Fertuck, L. (1992). *Systems Analysis and Design with CASE Tools.* Wm. C. Dubuque, Iowa: Brown Communications Inc.

Fichman, R. G. (1992, December). Information technology diffusion: a review of empirical research. In *Proceedings of the Thirteenth International Conference on Information Systems (ICIS)* (pp. 195-206). Dallas

Filley, A. C., House, R. J., & Kerr, S. (1976). *Managerial Process and Organizational Behavior.* Glenview. Illinois: Scott, Foresman & Co.

Fink, L., & Neumann, S. (2007). Gaining agility through IT personnel capabilities: the mediating role of IT infrastructure capabilities. *Journal of the Assocation for Information Systems, 8*(8), 440–462.

Finkenzeller, K. (2003). *RFID-Handbook: Fundamentals and applications in contact-less smart cards and identification* (2nd ed.). New York: John Wiley &Sons.

Finquelievich, S. (2003). Civil society and the new economy. Social Science Research Council. Retrieved from http://www.ssrc.org/programs/itic/publications/knowledge_report/memos/finquelievichmemo2.pdf

Fisher, B. M. & Edwards, J. E. (1988). Consideration and initiating structure and their relationships with leader effectiveness: A meta-analysis. *Academy of Management Proceedings*, 201-205.

Fiske, A. P. (2002). Using Individualism and Collectivism to Compare Cultures - a Critique of the Validity and Measurement of the Constructs: Comment on Oysterman Et Al (2002). *Psychological Bulletin, 128*(1), 78–88. doi:10.1037/0033-2909.128.1.78

Fjermestad, J., & Hiltz, S. R. (1999). An assessment of group support systems experimental research: Methodology and results. *Journal of Management Information Systems, 15*(3), 7-150.

Fjermestad, J., & Hiltz, S. R. (1999). An assessment of group support systems experimental research methodology and results. *Journal of Management Information Systems, 15*(3), 7–149.

Fleishman, E. A. (1973). *Current Developments in the Study of Leadership.* Carbondale: Southern Illinois University Press.

Fleishman, E. A., & Harris, E. F. (1962). Patterns of leadership behavior related to employee grievances and turnover. *Personnel Psychology, 15*, 43–56. doi:10.1111/j.1744-6570.1962.tb01845.x

Forcinio, H. (2002). Packaging advances showcases. *Pharmaceutical Technology North America, 26*(8), 22-30.

Ford, D. P., Connelly, C. E., & Meister, D. B. (2003). Information systems research and Hofstede's culture's consequences: An uneasy and incomplete partnership. *IEEE Transactions on Engineering Management, 50*(1).

Fornell, C., & Bookstein, F. L. (1982). Two structural equation models: LISREL and PLS applied to consumer exit-voice theory. *JMR, Journal of Marketing Research, 19*, 440–452. doi:10.2307/3151718

Fornell, C., & Larcker, D. F. (1981). Evaluating structural equation models with unobservable variables and measurement error. *JMR, Journal of Marketing Research, 18*(1), 39–50. doi:10.2307/3151312

Forrest, Cummings, & Johnson. (1977). Organizational participation: A critique and model. *Academy of Management Review, 2,* 586-601.

Foster, S., & Franz, C. (1999). User involvement in information systems development: A comparison of analyst and user perceptions of system acceptance. *Journal of Engineering Technology Management, 16*(3-4), 329-348.

Fowler, F. J. (1988). *Survey Research Methods.* Newbury Park, CA: SAGE Publications, Inc.

Frayne, C. A., & Latham, G. P. (1987). The Application of Social Learning to Employee Self-Management of Attendance. *The Journal of Applied Psychology, 72*(3), 387–392. doi:10.1037/0021-9010.72.3.387

Fredendall, L. D., & Emery, C. R. (2003). Productivity increases due to the use of teams in service garages. *Journal of Managerial Issues, XV*(2), 221–242.

French, S. (1986). *Decision theory: An introduction to the mathematics of rationality.* Chichester: Ellis Harwood.

Fried, Y., & Ferris, G. (1987). The validity of the job characteristics model: A review and meta-analysis. *Personnel Psychology, 40,* 287-322.

Frieze, C., Hazzan, O., Blum, L., & Dias, M. B. (2006). Culture and environments as determinants of women's participation in computing: Revealing the "women-CS" fit. In *Proceedings of the ACM SIGCSE Conference, Houston, TX, March 1-5, 2006* (pp. 22-26). New York: ACM Press.

Fu, P. P., & Tsui, A. S. (2003). Utilizing printed media to understand desired leadership attributes in the People's Republic of China. *Asia Pacific Journal of Management, 20*, 423–446. doi:10.1023/A:1026373124564

Fulk, J., Schmitz, J., & Steinfield, C. (1990). A social influence model of technology use. In J. Fulk & C. Steinfield (Eds.), *Organizations and Communication Technology* (pp. 117-142). Newbury Park, CT: Sage.

Fygensen, M. (2006). Understanding and predicting electronic commerce adoption: An extension of the theory of planned behavior. *MIS Quarterly, 30*(1), 115-143.

Gable, G. G., & Raman, K. S. (1992). Government initiatives for IT adoption in small businesses: experiences of the Singapore Small Enterprise Computerization Programme. *International Information Systems*, *1*(1), 68–93.

Galbraith, J. (1973). *Designing Complex Organizations.* Reading, MA: Addison-Wesley Publishing Co.

Galletta, D. F., Henry, R. M., McCoy, S., & Polak, P. (2006). When the wait isn't so bad: The interacting effects of website delay, familiarity, and breadth. *Information Systems Research*, 20-37.

Gallivan, M., & Srite, M. (2005). Information technology and culture: identifying fragmentary and holistic perspectives of culture. *Information and Organization*, *15*, 295–338. doi:10.1016/j.infoandorg.2005.02.005

Gallupe, R. B., & Tan, F. B. (1999). A Research Manifesto for Global Information Management. *Journal of Global Information Management*, *7*(3), 5–18.

Gallupe, R. B., Bastianutti, L. M., & Cooper, W. H. (1991). Unlocking brainstorms. *The Journal of Applied Psychology*, *76*(1), 137–142. doi:10.1037/0021-9010.76.1.137

Gallupe, R. B., Dennis, A. R., Cooper, W. H., Valacich, J. S., Bastianutti, L. M., & Nunamaker, J. F. Jr. (1992). Electronic brainstorming and group size. *Academy of Management Journal*, *35*(2), 350–369. doi:10.2307/256377

Gallupe, R. B., DeSanctis, G., & Dickson, G. W. (1988). Computer-based support for group problem-finding: An experimental investigation. *MIS Quarterly*, *12*(2), 277–298. doi:10.2307/248853

Galpin, V. (2002). Women in computing around the world. *ACM SIGSCE Bulletin*, *34*(2), 94–100. doi:10.1145/543812.543839

Garfield, M. J., & Watson, R. T. (1998). Differences in national information infrastructures: the reflection of national cultures. *Journal of Strategic Information Systems*, *6*, 313-337.

Gatignon, H., & Robertson, T. S. (1989). Technology diffusion: an empirical test of competitive effects. *Journal of Marketing*, *53*(1), 35–49. doi:10.2307/1251523

Gauvin, S., & Sinha, R. K. (1993). Innovativeness in industrial organizations: a two-stage model of adoption. *International Journal of Research in Marketing*, *10*,165-183.

Gefen, D. (2000). Gender Differences in the Perception and Adoption of E-Mail and Computer Mediated Communication Media: A Sociolinguistics Approach. In A. Kent (Ed.), *The Encyclopedia of Library and Information Science*. New York: Marcel Dekker.

Gefen, D. (2000). Structural equation modeling and regression: Guidelines for research practice. *Communications of AIS*, *4*(7), 1–77.

Gefen, D., & Heart, T. (2006). On the need to include national culture as a central issue in e-commerce trust beliefs. *Journal of Global Information Management*, *14*(4), 1-30.

Gefen, D., & Straub, D. (1997). Gender Difference in the Perception and Use of E-Mail: An Extension to the Technology Acceptance Model. *MIS Quarterly*, *21*(4), 389–400. doi:10.2307/249720

Gefen, D., & Straub, D. (2005). A practical guide to factorial validity using PLS-Graph: Tutorial and annotated example. *Communications of the AIS*, *16*, 91–109.

Gefen, D., Karahanna, E., & Straub, D. W. (2003). Trust and TAM in online shopping: an integrated model. *MIS Quarterly*, *27*(1), 51–90.

Gefen, D., Karahanna, E., & Straub, D. W. (2003b). Inexperience and experience with online stores: The importance of TAM and trust. *IEEE Transactions on Engineering Management*, *50*(3), 307-321.

Gefen, D., Straub, D. W., & Boudreau, M.-C. (2000). Structural Equation Modeling and Regression: Guidelines for Research and Practice. *Communications of the Association for Information Systems*, *3*(1).

Geng, Q., Townley, C., Huang, K., & Zhang, J. (2005). Comparative knowledge management: A pilot study of Chinese and American universities. *Journal of the American Society for Information Science and Technology*, *56*(10), 1031–1044. doi:10.1002/asi.20194

Gengatharen, D. E., & Standing, C. (2005). A framework to assess the factors affecting success or failure of the implementation of government-supported regional e-marketplaces for SMEs. *European Journal of Information Systems*, *14*(4), 417–433. doi:10.1057/palgrave.ejis.3000551

George, J. F. (2004). The theory of planned behavior and internet purchasing. *Internet Research*, *14*(3), 198-212.

George, J. F., Easton, G., Nunamaker, J. F., & Northcraft, G. (1990). A study of collaborative group work with and without computer-based support. *Information Systems Research*, *1*(4), 394–415. doi:10.1287/isre.1.4.394

Gerbing, D. W., & Anderson, J. C. (1988). An updated paradigm for scale development incorporating unidimensionality and its assessment. *Journal of Marketing Research*, *25*(2), 186-192.

Ghiselli, E. E., Campbell, J. P., & Zedeck, S. (1981). *Measurement Theory for the Behavioral Science*. San Francisco, CA: W.H. Freeman.

Gibbs, J. L., & Kraemer, K. L. (2004). A cross-country investigation of the determinants of scope of e-commerce use: An institutional approach. *Electronic Markets*, *14*(2), 124–137. doi:10.1080/10196780410001675077

Gibbs, J., Kraemer, K. L., & Dedrick, J. (2003). Environment and policy factors shaping global e-commerce diffusion: a cross-country comparison. *The Information Society*, *19*(1), 5–18. doi:10.1080/01972240309472

Gibbs, M. (2005, November 14). More on Sony's rootkit. *New World (New Orleans, La.)*, *22*, 82.

Gibson, R. (1994). Global information technology architectures. *Journal of Global Information Management*, *2*(1), 28–39.

Gionfriddo, J., & Dhingra, L. (2000, May/Jun). *Human Resource Management International Digest* *8*(4), 9-11.

Gist, M. E. (1989). The Influence of Training Method on Self-Efficacy and Idea Generation among Managers. *Personnel Psychology*, *42*, 787–805. doi:10.1111/j.1744-6570.1989.tb00675.x

Gist, M. E., & Mitchell, T. R. (1992). Self-efficacy: A theoretical analysis of its determinants and malleability. *Academy of Management Review*, *17*, 183-211.

Giunipero, L., Handfield, R. B., & Eltantawy, R. (2006). Supply management's evolution: key skill sets for the supply manager of the future. *International Journal of Operations & Production Management*, *26*(7), 822-844.

Gold, A. H., Malhortra, A., & Segars, A. H. (2001). Knowledge management: an organizational capabilities perspective. *Journal of Management Information System*, *18*(1), 185-214.

Goodhue, D. L. (1995). Understanding user evaluations of information systems. *Management Science*, *41*(12), 1827-1844.

Goodhue, D. L., & Straub, D. W. (1989). *Security Concerns of System Users: A Proposed Study of User Perceptions of the Adequacy of Security Measures*. Paper presented at the Proceedings of the Twenty-Second Annual Hawaii International Conference on System Science (HICSS), Kailua-Kona, HI.

Goodhue, D. L., & Thompson, R. L. (1995).Task-technology fit and individual performance. *MIS Quarterly*, *19*(2), 213-236.

Gordon, L. A., Loeb, M. P., Lucyshyn, W., & Richardson, R. (2004). *2004 CSI/FBI Computer Crime and Security Survey*.

Gordon, M., Slade, L., & Schmitt, N. (1986). The "science of the sophomore" revisited: From conjecture to empiricism. *Academy of Management Review*, *11*, 91-207.

Grabowski, M., & Lee, S. (1993). Linking information systems application portfolios and organizational strategy. In R. D. Banker, R. J. Kauffman & M.A. Mahmood (Eds.), *strategic information technology management: Perspectives on organizational growth and competitive advantage* (pp. 33-54). Hershey, PA: Idea Group Publishing.

Graham, J. (2005, November 16). Copy-protected-CD flap raises questions. *USA Today*.

Grant, R. M. (1991). The resource-based theory of competitive advantage. *California Management Review*, *33*(3), 114–135.

Grant, R. M. (1995). Contemporary Strategy Analysis. Oxford, UK: Blackwell Publishers, Inc.

Grant, R. M. (1996a). Prospering in dynamically-competitive environments: Organizational capability as knowledge integration. *Organization Science*, *7*(4), 375-387.

Grant, R. M. (1996b). Toward a knowledge-based theory of the firm. *Strategic Management Journal*, *17*, 109-122.

Gray, P., & Olfman, L. (1989). The user interface in group decision support systems. *Decision Support Systems*, *5*(2), 119–137. doi:10.1016/0167-9236(89)90002-X

Grewal, R., Comer, & J.M., Mehta, R. (2001). An investigation into the antecedents of organizational participation in business-to-business electronic markets. *Journal of Marketing*, *65*(3), 17–34. doi:10.1509/jmkg.65.3.17.18331

Grewal, R., Johnson, J., & Sarker, S.(2007). Crises in Business Markets: Implications for Interfirm Linkages. *Journal of the Academy of Marketing Science*.

Griffith, T. L. (1998). Cross-cultural and cognitive issues in the implementation of new technology: Focus on group support systems and Bulgaria. *Interacting with Computers*, *9*(4), 431–447. doi:10.1016/S0953-5438(97)00033-7

Groeschl, S., & Doherty, L. (2000). Conceptualizing culture. *Cross Cultural Management -. International Journal (Toronto, Ont.)*, *7*(4), 12–17.

Grossman, R. B., & Packer, M. B. (1989). Betting the business, strategic programs to rebuild core information systems. *Information Technology & People*, *5*(4), 235–244. doi:10.1108/EUM0000000003537

Grover, V. (1993). An empirically derived model for the adoption of customer-based interorganizational systems. *Decision Sciences*, *24*(3), 603-640.

Grover, V., & Davenport, T. H. (2001). General perspectives on knowledge management: fostering a research agenda. *Journal of Management Information Systems*, *18*(1), 5-21.

Grover, V., & Goslar, M. D. (1993). The initiation, adoption, and implementation of telecommunications technologies in U.S. organizations. *Journal of Management Information Systems*, *10*(1), 141-163.

Grover, V., Segars, A. H., & Durand, D. (1994). Organizational practice, information resource deployment and systems: a cross-cultural survey. *Journal of Strategic Information Systems*, *3*(2), 85-106.

Guan, S. U., Tan, S. L., & Hua, F. (2004). A modularized electronic payment system for agent-based e-commerce. *Journal of Research and Practice in Information Technology*, *36*(2), 67–87.

Guinea, A. O. d., Kelley, H., & Hunter, M. G. (2005). Information systems effectiveness in small businesses: Extending a Singaporean model in Canada. *Journal of Global Information Management*, *13*(3), 55–79.

Gupta, A. J., & Govindarajan, V. (2000). Knowledge management's social dimension: Lessons from Nucor Steel. *Sloan Management Review*, *42*(1), 71-80.

Guthrie, J. P., Spell, C. S., & Nyamori, R. O. (2002). Correlates and consequences of high involvement work practices: The role of competitive strategy. *International Journal of Human Resource Management*, *13*(1), 183-197.

Haenlein, M., & Kaplan, A. M. (2004). A beginner's guide to partial least squares analysis. *Understanding Statistics*, *3*(4), 283–297. doi:10.1207/s15328031us0304_4

Hage, J., & Aiken, M. (1967). Relationship of centralization to other structural properties. *Administrative Science Quarterly*, *12*(2), 72-92.

Hair, J. F., Anderson, R. E., Tatham, R. L., & Black, W. C. (1998). *Multivariate Data Analysis*. Upper Saddle River, NJ: Prentice-Hall.

Haley, G. (2002). E-commerce in China: changing business as we know it. *Industrial Marketing Management*, *31*(2), 119–124. doi:10.1016/S0019-8501(01)00183-3

Hall, E. T., & Hall, M. R. (1990). *Understanding Cultural Differences*. Yarmouth, ME: Intercultural Press.

Halpin, A. W. (1957). *Manual for the Leader Behavior Description Questionnaire*. Columbus, Ohio: The Ohio State University.

Hamel, G., & Prahalad, C. K. (1989). Strategic intent. *Harvard Business Review*, *67*(3), 63-76.

Hamel, G., & Prahalad, C. K. (1993). Strategy as stretch and leverage. *Harvard Business Review, 71*(2), 75-84.

Hampden-Turner, C. M., & Trompenaars, F. (2000). *Building cross-cultural competence: How to create wealth from conflicting values.* New York: Wiley.

Hampden-Turner, C., & Trompenaars, F. (1993). *The Seven Cultures of Capitalism*. New York: Doubleday.

Hannon, J. M., Huang, I. C., & Jaw, B. S. (1995). International human resources strategy and its determinants: the case of subsidiaries in Taiwan. *Journal of International Business Studies*, 531-554.

Hardin, A. M., Fuller, M. A., & Davison, R. M. (2007). I Know I Can, But Can We? *Small Group Research, 38*(1), 130–155. doi:10.1177/1046496406297041

Hare, A. P. (1981). Group size. *The American Behavioral Scientist, 24*, 695–708. doi:10.1177/000276428102400507

Hartwick, J., & Barki, H. (1994). Explaining the role of user participation in information system use. *Management Science, 40*(4), 440-465.

Harvie, C., & Lee, H. H. (2003). Export-led industrialization and growth: Korea's economic miracle, 1962-1989. *Australian Economic History Review, 43*(3), 256–286. doi:10.1046/j.1467-8446.2003.00054.x

Hasan, H., & Ditsa, G. (1999). The impact of culture on the adoption of IT: An interpretive study. *Journal of Global Information Management, 7*(1), 5–15.

Hauschild, S., Licht, T., & Stein, W. (2001). Creating a knowledge culture. *The McKinsey Quarterly, 1*, 74-81.

Hawk, S. (2004). A Comparison of B2C E-Commerce in Developing Countries. *Electronic Commerce Research, 4*(3), 181. doi:10.1023/B:ELEC.0000027979.91972.36

Hazari, S. I. (2005). Perceptions of end-users on the requirements in personal firewall software: An exploratory study. *Journal of Organizational and End User Computing, 17*(3), 47-65.

He, X. (2004). The ERP challenge in China: a resource-based perspective. *Information Systems Journal, 14*(2), 153–167. doi:10.1111/j.1365-2575.2004.00168.x

Hedberg, B. (1981). How organizations learn and unlearn. In P. C. Nystrom & W. H. Starbuck (Eds.), *Handbook of organizational design* (pp. 3-27). NY: Oxford University Press.

Heijden, H. V. D. (2000). Measuring IT core capabilities for electronic commerce, results from a confirmatory factor analysis. *Proceedings of the 21st ICIS, December.*

Heinssen, R. K., Glass, C. R., & Knight, L. A. (1987). Assessing Computer Anxiety: Development and Validation of the Computer Anxiety Rating Scale. *Computers in Human Behavior, 3*, 49–59. doi:10.1016/0747-5632(87)90010-0

Helfat, C. E. (1997). Know-how and asset complementarity and dynamic capability accumulation: The case of R&D. *Strategic Management Journal, 18*, 339-360.

Hembry, O., & Presley, A. (2006). IT proves to be a turnoff for women. Retrieved from http://www.nzherald.co.nz/topic/story.cfm?c_id=498&objectid=10370311

Hemphill, J. K., & Coons, A. E. (1957). *Development of the Leader Behavior Description Questionnaire*. Ohio: Bureau of Business Research, Ohio State University.

Henderson, J. C., & Venkatraman, N. (1993). Strategic alignment, Leveraging information technology for transforming organizations. *IBM Systems Journal, 32*(1), 40–64.

Hersh, M. (2000). The changing position of women in engineering worldwide. *IEEE Transactions on Engineering Management, 47*(3), 345–359. doi:10.1109/17.865903

Heung, V. C. S. (2003). Barriers to implementing E-commerce in the travel industry: a practical perspective. *International Journal of Hospitality Management, 22*(1), 111–118. doi:10.1016/S0278-4319(02)00075-0

Hill, N. D., Smith, D. B., & Man, M. F. (1986). Communicating Innovations: Convincing Computer Phobics to Adopt Innovative Technologies. In R. J. Lutz (Ed), *Advances in Consumer Research* (pp. 419-422). Provo, UT: Association for Consumer Research.

Hill, T., Smith, N. D., & Mann, M. F. (1987). Role of Efficacy Expectations in Predicting the Decision to Use Advanced Technologies: The Case of Computers. *The Journal of Applied Psychology, 72*(2), 307–313. doi:10.1037/0021-9010.72.2.307

Hinings, C. R., & Greenwood, R. (1987). *The normative prescription of organizations*. MA: Ballinger.

Hitt, L. M., & Brynjofsson, E. (1996). Productivity, business profitability, and consumer surplus: three different measures of information technology value. *MIS Quarterly*, *20*(2), 121–142. doi:10.2307/249475

HKPC. (2003). *E-business adoption in Hong Kong*. Hong Kong Productivity Council.

Ho, T., Raman, K., & Watson, R. (1989, December 4-6). *Group decision support systems: The cultural factor.* Paper presented at the Tenth Annual International Conference on Information Systems, Boston, MA.

Hoecklin, L. A. (1995). *Managing Cultural Differences: Strategies for Competitive Advantage*. Reading, MA: Addison-Wesley.

Hoffer, J., George, J., & Valacich, J. (1999). *Modern systems analysis and design*. Reading, MA: Addison Wesley.

Hofstede, G. (1980). *Culture's Consequences: International Differences in Work-Related Values*. Beverly Hills, CA: Sage.

Hofstede, G. (1984). *Culture's Consequences: International Differences in Work Related Values*. London: Sage Publications.

Hofstede, G. (1991). *Cultures and Organizations: Software of the Mind*. Berkshire, England: McGraw-Hill Book Company Europe.

Hofstede, G. (1991). *Cultures and organizations: software of the mind*. New York: McGraw Hill.

Hofstede, G. (1991). *Organizations and Cultures: Software of the Mind*. London: McGraw-Hill.

Hofstede, G. (1993). Cultural constraints in management theories. *Academy of Management Executive*, *7*(1), 81-94.

Hofstede, G. (1998). Attitudes, values and organizational cultures: disentangling the concepts. *Organization Studies*, *19*(3), 477–492. doi:10.1177/017084069801900305

Hofstede, G. (2001). *Culture's Consequences*: Sage Publications Newbury Park London

Hofstede, G. (2003). Cultural Dimensions. Retrieved August 12, 2006, from http://www.geert-hofstede.com/geert_hofstede_resources.shtml

Hofstede, G. H. (1984). *Culture's consequences: international differences in work-related values*. Beverly Hills: Sage Publications.

Hofstede, G. H. (1997). *Cultures and organizations: software of the mind.* New York: McGraw-Hill.

Hofstede, G. H. (2001). *Culture's consequences: Comparing values, behaviors, institutions and organizations across nations*. Thousand Oaks, CA: Sage Publications.

Hofstede, G. H., & Hofstede, G. J. (2005). *Cultures and organizations: software of the mind.* New York: McGraw-Hill.

Hoglund, G. (2006). The Definition of a Rootkit. Retrieved February 17, 2006, from http://www.rootkit.com/blog.php?newsid=440

Hollenstein, H. (2005). Determinants of international activities: are SMEs different? *Small Business Economics*, *24*(5), 431–450. doi:10.1007/s11187-005-6455-x

Holmstrom, H., Fitzgerald, B., Agerfalk, P., & Conchuir, E. (2006). Agile practices reduce distance in global software development. *Information Systems Management*, *23*(3), 7-18.

Holsapple, C. W., & Joshi, K. D. (2000). An investigation of factors that influence the management of knowledge in organizations. *Journal of Strategic Information Systems*, *9*, 235-261.

Holsapple, C. W., & Joshi, K. D. (2002). Knowledge manipulation studies: results of a Delphi study. *Information and Management*, *39*, 477-490.

Holste, J. S., & Fields, D. (2005). The relationship of affect and cognition based trust with sharing and use of tacit knowledge. *Academy of Management Best Conference Paper* (MED: B1).

Hom, P. W., Caranikas-Walker, F., Prussia, G. E., & Griffeth, R. W. (1992). A meta-analytical structural equations analysis of a model of employee turnover. *Journal of Applied Psychology*, *77*, 890-909.

Hong, W. Y., & Zhu, K. (2006). Migrating to internet-based e-commerce: Factors affecting e-commerce adoption and migration at the firm level. *Information & Management, 43*(2), 204–221. doi:10.1016/j.im.2005.06.003

Hornby, G., Goulding, P., & Poon, S. (2002). Perceptions of Export Barriers and Cultural Issues: The SME E-Commerce Experience. *Journal of Electronic Commerce Research, 3*(4), 213–226.

House, R. J., Hanges, P., Mansour, J., Dorfman, P., & Gupta, V. (2004). *Culture, leadership and organizations: The globe study of 62 societies.* Thousand Oaks, CA: Sage.

House, R., Javidan, M., Hanges, P., & Dorfman, P. (2002). Understanding cultures and implicit leadership theories across the globe: An introduction to project GLOBE. *Journal of World Business, 37*, 3–10. doi:10.1016/S1090-9516(01)00069-4

Howard, G., Murphy, C. M., & Thomas, G. E. (1986). *Computer Anxiety Considerations for Design of Introductory Computer Courses.* Honolulu, HI: Decision Sciences Institute.

Howcroft, D., & Trauth, E. M. (2008). The implications of a critical agenda in gender and IS research. *Information Systems Journal, 18*(2), 185–202. doi:10.1111/j.1365-2575.2008.00294.x

Hsu, I.-C. (2005, August 5-10). *Developing a model of knowledge management from a human capital perspective—preliminary thoughts.* Paper presented at the 2005 Academy of Management Meeting, Honolulu, Hawaii, U.S.

Hsu, I.-C. (2006). Enhancing employee tendencies to share knowledge—case studies of nine company cases in Taiwan. *International Journal of Information Management, 26*(4), 326-338.

Hsu, J. (2003). Chinese cultures and e-commerce. In T. Thanasankit (Ed.), *E-commerce and cultural values* (pp. 268-289). Hershey, PA: Idea Group Publishing.

Hsu, M., Ju, T. L., Yen, C., & Chang C. (2007). Knowledge sharing behavior in virtual communities: The relationship between trust, self-efficacy, and outcome expectations. *International Journal of Human-Computer Studies, 65*, 153-169.

Hu, P. J., Chau, P. Y. K., Sheng, O. R. L., & Tam, K. Y. (1999). Examining the Technology Acceptance Model Using Physician Acceptance of Telemedicine Technology. *Journal of Management Information Systems, 16*(2), 91–112.

Huang, H. (2006). The cross-cultural dimension of gender and information technology. In E. M. Trauth (Ed.), *Encyclopedia of gender and information technology* (pp. 147-153). Hershey, PA: Idea Group Publishing.

Huang, H., & Trauth, E. M. (2006) Cultural diversity challenges: Issues for managing globally distributed knowledge workers in software development. In P. Yoong & S. Huff (Eds.), *Managing IT professionals in the Internet age* (pp. 254-276). Hershey, PA: Idea Group, Inc.

Huang, L., Lu, M.-T., & Wong, B. K. (2003). The impact of power distance on email acceptance: Evidence from The PRC. *Journal of Computer Information Systems*, (Fall): 93–101.

Huang, W. (2003). Impacts of GSS generic structures and task types on group communication process and outcome: Some expected and unexpected research findings. *Behavior & Information Technology, 22*(1), 17-29.

Huang, W., & Li, D. (2007). Opening up the black box in GSS research: explaining group decision outcome with group process. *Computers in Human Behavior, 23*(1), 58-78.

Huang, W., & Wei, K. K. (1997). Task as a moderator for the effects of group support systems on group influence processes. *European Journal of Information Systems, December 6*, 208-217.

Huang, W., & Wei, K. K. (2000). An empirical investigation of effects of GSS and task type on social interactions from an influence perspective. *Journal of Management Information Systems, 17*(2), 181-206.

Huang, W., Wei, K. K., & Lim, J. (2003). Using GSS to support global virtual team-building: A theoretical framework. *International Journal of Global Information Management, 11*(1), 72-89.

Huang, W., Wei, K. K., Watson, R. T., & Tan, C. Y. (2003). Supporting virtual team-building with a GSS: An empirical investigation. *Decision Support Systems, 34*(4), 359-367.

Huang, W., Wei, K.K., and Tan, C.Y. (1999). Compensating effects of GSS on group performance. *Information & Management*, 35, 195-202.

Hulin, C. L., Roznowski, M., & Hachiya, D. (1985). Alternative opportunities and withdrawal decisions: Empirical and theoretical discrepancies and integration. *Psychological Bulletin, 97,* 233-250.

Hunter, M. G., & Beck, J. E. (1996). A Cross-cultural comparison of "excellent" systems analysts. *Information Systems Journal, 6*(4), 261-281.

Hunter, M.G. (2004). Information system and small business: research issues. *Journal of Global Information Management,* Oct-Dec, *12*(4),1-6.

Hunton, J. E., Benford, T., Arnold, V., & Sutton, S. (2000). The impact of electronic commerce assurance on financial analysts' earnings forecasts and stock price estimates. *Auditing: A Journal of Practice & Theory,* 19 (Supplement), 5-22.

Husted, K., & Michailova, S. (2002). Diagnosing and fighting knowledge-sharing hostility. *Organizational Dynamics*, *31*(1), 60-73.

Huyer, S. (2005, June 12-14). Women, ICT and the information society: Global perspectives and initiatives. In *Proceedings of the International Symposium on Women and ICT: Creating Global Transformation,* Baltimore, MD. New York: ACM Press.

Hyvarinen, L. (1990). Innovativeness and Its Indicators in Small and Medium-sized Industrial Enterprises. *International Small Business Journal*, *9*(1), 65–79.

Iacovou, C. L., Benbasat, I., & Dexter, A. S. (1995). Electronic data interchange and small organisations: Adoption and impact of technology. *MIS Quarterly*, *19*(4), 465–485. doi:10.2307/249629

Iacovou, C., Benbasat, I., & Dexter, A. (1995). Electronic data interchange and small organizations: Adoption and impact of technology. *MIS Quarterly*, *19*(4), 465-485.

IDTechEx. (2005). *RFID case study analysis.* Retrieved December 25, 2005, from http://www.idtechex.com/knowledgebase/en/breakdown.asp

Igbaria, M., & Chakrabarti, A. (1990). Computer Anxiety and Attitudes Towards Microcomputer. *Behaviour & Information Technology*, *9*(3), 229–241. doi:10.1080/01449299008924239

Igbaria, M., & Guimaraes, T., & Davis. (1995). Testing the Determinants of Microcomputer Usage Via a Structural Equation Model. *Journal of Management Information Systems*, *11*(4), 87–114.

Igbaria, M., & Iivari, A. (1995). The Effects of Self-Efficacy on Computer Usage. *Omega*, *23*(6), 587–605. doi:10.1016/0305-0483(95)00035-6

Igbaria, M., Parasuraman, S., & Badawy, M. K. (1994, June). Work experiences, job involvement, and quality of work life among information systems personnel. *MIS Quarterly, 18*(2), 175-197.

Igbaria, M., Parasuraman, S., & Baroudi, J. (1996). A Motivational Model of Computer Usage. *Journal of Management Information Systems*, *13*(1), 127–143.

Igbaria, M., Pravir, F. N., & Huff, S. L. (1989). Microcomputer Applications: An Empirical Look at Usage. *Information & Management*, *16*, 187–196. doi:10.1016/0378-7206(89)90036-0

Im, G. P., & Baskerville, R. L. (2005). A Longitudinal Study of Information System Threat Categories: The Enduring Problem of Human Error. *The Data Base for Advances in Information Systems*, *36*(4), 68–79.

Information Technology Association of America (ITAA). (2005). *Untapped talent: Diversity, competition, and America's high tech future – Executive summary.* Retrieved from: http://www.itaa.org/eweb/upload/execsummdr05.pdf

Inmon, W. H. (1989). *Data architecture, The information paradigm.* Wellesley, MA, QED Information Sciences.

Intel (2000). Retrieved January 23, 2004 from http://www.intel.com/ebusiness/estrategies/enabling/

InternetWeek. (2000). InternetWeek 100, Special Issue, June 8. http://internetweek.cmp.com/100/100-00.htm. Retrieved on February 18, 2004.

InternetWeek. (2001), InternetWeek 100, Special Issue, June 11. http://internetweek.cmp.com/100/100-01.htm. Retrieved on February 18, 2004.

Irwin, L. (2000). Gender inequities in technology in developing nations: Females and computers in traditional cultures. *Intercultural Education, 11*(2), 195–200. doi:10.1080/713665242

ISIC. (2004). The measuring and comparative research of regional imformatization level from 1999 to 2001 of China. *Statistical Research, 3*, 3–11.

ISIC. (2009). Regional differences in informatization development level. Retrieved from http://www.zgxxb.com.cn/news.asp?id=14960

Jackson, C. M., Chow, S., & Leitch, R. A. (1997). Toward an Understanding of the Behavioral Intention to Use an Information System. *Decision Sciences, 28*(2), 357–389. doi:10.1111/j.1540-5915.1997.tb01315.x

Jackson, L. A., Zhao, Y., Qiu, W., Kolenic, A., Fitzgerald, H. E., Harold, R., & von Eye, A. (2008). Culture, gender and information technology use: A comparison of Chinese and US children. Comput. *Human Behavior, 24*(6), 2817–2829. doi:10.1016/j.chb.2008.04.007

Jaeger, A. M. (1986). Organization development and national culture: Where's the fit? *Academy of Management Review, 11,* 178-190.

Jago, A. G. (1982). Leadership: Perspectives in theory and research. *Management Science, 28*(3), 315–336. doi:10.1287/mnsc.28.3.315

Janis, I. L. (1971). Groupthink. *Psychology Today, 5*(6), 43–76.

Janis, I. L. (1972). *Victims of Groupthink*. Boston, MA: Houghton Mifflin.

Jarillo, J. C., & Martinez, J. L. (1990). Different roles for subsidiaries: the case of multinational corporations in Spain, *Strategic Management Journal, 11*, 501-512.

Jarvenpaa, S. L., & Staples, D. S. (2000). The use of collaborative electronic media for information sharing: an exploratory study of determinants. *Journal of Strategic Information Systems, 9*, 129-154.

Jarvenpaa, S. L., & Staples, D. S. (2001). Exploring perceptions of organizational ownership of information and expertise. *Journal of Management Information Systems, 18*(1), 151-183.

Jarvenpaa, S. L., & Tractinsky, N. (2003). Consumer trust in an Internet store: A cross-cultural validation. In C. Steinfeld (Ed.), *New directions in research on e-commerce* (pp.33-63). West Lafayette, IN: Purdue University Press.

Jarvenpaa, S. L., Shaw, T. R., & Staples, D. S. (2004). Toward Contextualized Theories of Trust: The Role of Trust in Global Virtual Teams. *Information Systems Research, 15*(3), 250–267. doi:10.1287/isre.1040.0028

Jarvenpaa, S., & Ives, B. (1994). The global network organization of the future: information management opportunities and challenges. *Journal of Management Information Systems, 10*(4), 25-57.

Jarvenpaa, S., & Leidner, D. (1999). Communication and trust in global virtual teams. *Organization Science, 10*(6), 791-815.

Jarvenpaa, S., Knoll, K., & Leidner, D. (1998). Is anybody out there? Antecedents of trust in global virtual teams. *Journal of Management Information Systems, 14*(4), 29-64.

Javidan, M., Stahl, G. K., Brodbeck, F., & Wilderom, C. P. M. (2005). Cross-border transfer of knowledge: Cultural lessons from project GLOBE. *The Academy of Management Executive, 19*(2), 59–76.

Jessup, L. M., Connolly, T., & Galegher, J. (1990). The effects of anonymity on GDSS group process with an idea-generating task. *MIS Quarterly, 14*(3), 313–321. doi:10.2307/248893

Jiang, B., & Prater, E. (2002). Distribution and logistics development in China:The revolution has begun. *International Journal of Physical Distribution & Logistics Management, 32*(9), 783–798. doi:10.1108/09600030210452459

Jiang, J. J., & Klein, G. (2002). A discrepancy model of information system personnel turnover. *Journal of Management Information Systems, 19*(2), 240-272.

Johnson, J. E. (2004). Factors influencing the early internationalization of high technology start-ups: U.S. and U.K. evidence. *Journal of International Entrepreneurship, 2*(2), 139–152. doi:10.1023/B:JIEN.0000026910.87323.4e

Jones, G. R. (1986). Socialization Tactics, Self-Efficacy, and Newcomer's Adjustments to Organizations. *Academy of Management Journal, 29*(2), 262–279. doi:10.2307/256188

Jones, M. C., Arnett, K. P., Tang, J. T. E., & Chen, N. S. (1993). Perceptions of computer viruses a cross-cultural assessment. *Computers & Security, 12*, 191–197. doi:10.1016/0167-4048(93)90101-A

Jones, S., Wilikens, M., Morris, P., & Masera, M. (2000). Trust requirements in e-business. *Communications of the ACM, 43*(12), 80-87.

Jöreskog, K. G., & Sörbom, D. (1988). *LISREL 7, A Guide to the program and applications.* Chicago, IL: SPSS Inc.

Joreskog, K., & Sorbom, D. (2003). Lisrel, Scientific Software International Inc.

Judge, T. A., Piccolo, R. F., & Ilies, R. (2004). The forgotten ones? The validity of consideration and initiating structure in leadership research. *The Journal of Applied Psychology, 89*(1), 36–51. doi:10.1037/0021-9010.89.1.36

Kacmar, K. M., Bozeman, D. P., Carlson, D. S., & Anthony, W. P. (1999). An Examination of the Perceptions of Organizational Politics Model: Replication and Extension. *Human Relations, 52*(3), 383–416.

Kalling, T. (2003). Knowledge management and the occasional links with performance. *Journal of Knowledge Management, 7*(3), 67-81.

Kambayashi, N., & Scarbrough, H. (2001). Cultural influences on IT use amongst factory mangers: a UK-Japanese comparison. *Journal of Information Technology Cases and Applications, 16*, 221–236.

Kankanhalli, A., Tan, B. C. Y., & Wei, K.-K. (2005). Contributing knowledge to electronic knowledge repositories: An empirical investigation. *MIS Quarterly, 29*(1), 113-143.

Karahanna, E., & Straub, D. (1999). The Psychological Origins of Perceived Usefulness and Ease of Use. *Information & Management, 35*(4), 237–250. doi:10.1016/S0378-7206(98)00096-2

Karahanna, E., Evaristo, J., & Srite, M. (2005). Levels of Culture and Individual Behavior: An Integrative Perspective. *Journal of Global Information Management, 13*(2), 1–20.

Karahanna, E., Straub, D., & Chervany, N. (1999). Information Technology across Time: A Cross-Sectional Comparison of Pre-Adoption and Post-Adoption Beliefs. *MIS Quarterly, 23*(2), 183–214. doi:10.2307/249751

Karimi, J., & Konsynski, B. R. (1991). Globalization and information management strategies, *Journal of Management Information Systems, 7*(4), 7-26.

Karkkainen, M.(2003). Increasing efficiency in the supply chain for short shelf life goods using RFID tagging. *International Journal of Retail & Distribution Management, 31*(10), 529-536.

Kase, S. E., & Trauth, E. M. (2003). Toward a Model of Women in the It Workplace. In *Proceedings of the Ninth Americas Conference on Information Systems, Atlanta, GA, Association for Information Systems.*

Kashlak, R. J., Chandran, R., & Benedetto, C. (1998). Reciprocity in internal business: a study of telecommunications alliances and contracts. *Journal of International Business Studies, 29*(2), 281-304.

Kearns, G. S., & Lederer, A. L. (2003). A resource-based view of strategic IT alignment: How knowledge sharing creates competitive advantage. *Decision Sciences, 34*(1), 1–29. doi:10.1111/1540-5915.02289

Keen, P. G. W. (1991). *Shaping the future, business design through information technology.* Boston: Harvard Business School Press.

Keen, P., & Mackintosh, R. (2001). *The freedom economy: Gaining the m-commerce edge in the era of the wireless Internet.* New York: McGraw-Hill.

Keeney, R. L., & Kirkwood, C. W. (1975). Group decision making using cardinal social welfare functions. *Management Science, 22*(4), 430-437.

Keil, M., Beranek, P., & Konsynski, B. (1995). Usefulness and Ease of Use: Field Study Evidence Regarding Task Considerations. *Decision Support Systems, 13*(1), 75–91. doi:10.1016/0167-9236(94)E0032-M

Kern, C. (1999). RFID-technology- recent development and future requirements. In *Proceedings of the European*

Conference on Circuit Theory & Design ECCTD99 (pp. 25-28). Stresa

Khalifa, M., & Davison, R. M. (2006). SME adoption: The case of electronic trading systems. *IEEE Transactions on Engineering Management, 53*(2), 275–284. doi:10.1109/TEM.2006.872251

Kim, B. O. (1994). Business process reengineering: building a cross-functional information architecture. *Journal of Systems Management, December,* 30-35.

Kim, K., Park, H., & Suzuki, N. (1990). Reward allocations in the United States, Japan and Korea: A comparison of individualistic and collectivistic cultures. *Academy of Management Journal, 33*(1), 188–198. doi:10.2307/256358

Kim, M. K., & Jee, K. Y. (2007). Factors influencing strategic use of informationt technology and its impact on business performance of SMEs. *ETRI Journal, 29*(4), 497–506. doi:10.4218/etrij.07.0106.0303

Kim, U., Triandis, H. C., Kagitcibasi, C., Choi, S. C., & Yoon, G. (1994). *Individualism and Collectivism: Theory, Methods and Applications.* Thousand Oaks, CA: Sage Publications.

Kimery, K., & McCord, M. (2002). Third-party assurances: Mapping the road to trust in e-tailing. *Journal of Information Technology Theory and Application, 4*(2), 63-82.

King, R. C., & Sethi, V. (1998). The impact of socialization on the role adjustment of information systems professionals. *Journal of Management Information Systems, 14*(4), 195-217.

Kircsh, L. J. (1996). The management of complex tasks in organizations: Controlling the systems development process. *Organizational Science, 7*(1), 1-21.

Kircsh, L., Sambamurthy, V., Ko, D., & Purvis, R. (2002). Controlling information systems development projects: The view from the client. *Management Science, 48*(4), 484-498.

Kirk, A. R. (2000). *E-commerce for the individual or small business owner.* Wellington, New Zealand: Capital Letters Pub.

Kirschenbaum, A., & Mano-Negrin, R. (1999). Underlying labour market dimensions of opportunities: The case of employee turnover. *Human Relations, 52*(10), 1233-1255.

Kirton, M. J. (1976). Adaptors and innovators: a description and measure. *The Journal of Applied Psychology, 61*(5), 622–629. doi:10.1037/0021-9010.61.5.622

Kirton, M. J. (1984). Adaptors and innovators-why new initiatives get blocked. *Long Range Planning, 17*(2), 137–143. doi:10.1016/0024-6301(84)90145-6

Kittikanya, C. (2000). E-commerce: Internet slow to make inroads. In P. Chantranontwong (Ed.), *Bangkok post: 2000 Mid-year economic review* (pp. 32-35).

Klaus, T., LeRouge, C., & Blanton, J. E. (2003). An examination of the relationships between select nature of work characteristics and organizational commitment of IT professionals. In *Proceedings of SIGMIS Conference* (pp. 147-149).

Kliem, R. (2004). Managing the risks of offshore IT development projects. *Information systems management, 21*(3), 22-27.

Kluckhohn, C. (1962). *Culture and Behavior.* New York: The Free Press of Glencoe.

Knight, G. A., & Cavusgil, S. T. (2004). Innovation, organizational capabilities, and the born-global firms. *Journal of International Business Studies, 35*(2), 124–141. doi:10.1057/palgrave.jibs.8400071

Knott, A. M. (2004). Persistent heterogeneity and sustainable innovation. *Strategic Management Journal, 24*(8), 687-705.

Ko, A. (1995). Towards an understanding of Overseas Chinese management. *Journal of Management systems, 7*(1), 13-28.

Kogut, B., & Singh, H. (1988). The effect of national culture on the choice of entry mode. *Journal of International Business Studies, 19,* 411-432.

Koh, J., & Kim, Y. G. (2004). Knowledge sharing in virtual communities: an e-business perspective. *Expert Systems with Applications, 26,* 155–166. doi:10.1016/S0957-4174(03)00116-7

Kolekofski, K. E., & Heminger, A. R. (2003). Beliefs and attitudes affecting intentions to share information in an organizational setting. *Information & Management, 40*, 521–532. doi:10.1016/S0378-7206(02)00068-X

Komiak, S. Y. X., & Benbasat, I. (2006). The effects of personalization and familiarity on trust and adoption of recommendation agents. *MIS Quarterly, 30*(4), 941–960.

Korsgaard, M. A., Schweiger, D. M., & Sapienza, H. J. (1995). Building commitment, attachment, and trust in strategic decision-making teams: The role of procedural justice. *Academy of Management Journal, 38*(1), 60–84. doi:10.2307/256728

Kotlarsky, J., & Oshri, L. (2005). Social ties, knowledge sharing and successful collaboration in globally distributed system development projects. *European Journal of Information Systems, 14*, 37–48. doi:10.1057/palgrave.ejis.3000520

Kouzes, J. M., & Posner, B. Z. (1995). *The Leadership Challenge*. San Francisco: CA: Jossey- Bass.

Kovar, S. E., Burke, K. G., & Kovar, B. R. (2000). Consumer responses to the CPA WebTrust assurance. *Journal of Information Systems, 14*(1), 17-35.

Kraemer, K., Gibbs, J., & Dedrick, J. (2002). *Environment and policy facilitators shaping e-commerce diffusion: A cross-country comparison*. Paper presented at the Proceedings of the Twenty-Third International Conference on Information System, Barcelona, Spain.

Kumar, R. L. (2004). A framework for assessing the business value of information technology infrastructures. *Journal of Management Information Systems, 21*(2), 11–32.

Kundu, S. K., & Katz, J. A. (2003). Born-International SMEs: BI-level impacts of resources and intenstions. *Small Business Economics, 20*(1), 25–48. doi:10.1023/A:1020292320170

Kunene, K. N. (2005). A Field Experiment on the Effect of Task Decomposition on the Quality of Decision in a Group Support Environment. *International Journal of Computers. Systems and Signals, 6*(2), 13–25.

Kvasny, L. (2003). Triple jeopardy: Race, gender and class politics of women in technology. In M. Mandviwalla & E.M. Trauth (Eds.), *Proceedings of the 2003 ACM SIGMIS Conference on Computer Personal Research, Philadelphia, Pennsylvania, USA* (pp. 112-116). New York: ACM Press.

Kvasny, L., Trauth, E. M., & Morgan, A. (2009). Power relations in IT education and work: The intersectionality of gender, race and class. *Journal of Information. Communication and Ethics in Society Special Issue on ICTs and Social Inclusion, 7*(2/3), 96–118.

Kyobe, M. E. (2004). Investigating the strategic utilization of it resources in the small and medium-sized firms of the eastern free state province. *International Small Business Journal, 22*(2), 131–158. doi:10.1177/0266242604041311

Kyriakidou, O. (2004). Developing a knowledge sharing culture. *Management Services, 48*(6), 22–23.

Laarhoven, P. J. M., & Pedrycz, W. (1983). A fuzzy extension of Saaty's priority theory. *Fuzzy Sets System, 3*, 229-241.

Lai, C. T. C., Liu, X., & Shaffer, M. A. (2004). Interpersonal citizenship behavior of employees in greater China: A social capital perspective, Business Research Centre Paper on Cross-Cultural Management (Vol. 2004-02,34, pp. http://net2.hkbu.edu.hk/~brc/CCMP200402.PDF)

Lai, V. (2001). Issues of international information systems management: a perspective of affiliates. *Information and Management, 38*, 253-264.

Lai, V., & Floyd, S. (1998). The impact of transborder data flow restrictions on international information systems management. *Decision Support Systems, 22*, 121-134

Lai, V., & Guynes, J. (1997). An assessment of the influence of organizational characteristics on information technology adoption decision: A discriminative approach. *IEEE Transactions on Engineering Management, 44*(2), 146-157.

Lai, V., & Mahapatra, R. (2004). Re-engineering the organization: an evaluation of the role of information system function. *Internal Journal of Production Research, 42*(12), 2357-2382.

Lai, V., & Wong, B. (2003). The moderating effect of local environment on a foreign affiliate's global IS strategy-effectiveness relationship. *IEEE Transactions on Engineering Management*, *50*(3), 352-361.

Lambe, C. J., Spekman, R. E., & Hunt, S. D. (2002). Alliance competence, resources, and alliance success: conceptualization, measurement, and initial test. *Journal of the Academy of Marketing Science*, *30*(2), 141–158. doi:10.1177/03079459994399

Langrish, J. (1972). *Wealth from knowledge: Studies of innovation in industry*. London: Macmillan.

Lao, L., Dovrolis, C., & Sanadidi, M. Y. (2006). The probe gap model can underestimate the available bandwidth of multihop paths. *Computer Communication Review*, *36*(5), 29-34.

LaPorte, T., & Consilini, N. (1991). Working in practice but not in theory: theoretical challenges of "High Reliability Organizations". *Journal of Public Administration Research and Theory*, *1*(1), 19-47.

Latham, G. P., & Frayne, C. A. (1989). Self-Management for Training for Increasing Job Attendance: A Follow-up and Replication. *The Journal of Applied Psychology*, *7*(3), 411–416. doi:10.1037/0021-9010.74.3.411

Lawrence, P. R., & Lorsch, J. (1967). *Organization and environment*. Boston: Harvard University.

Lee, A. S., & Baskerville, R. L. (2003). Generalizing generalizability in information systems research. *Information Systems Research*, *14*(3), 221–243. doi:10.1287/isre.14.3.221.16560

Lee, D. M. S., Trauth, E., & Farwell, D. (1995). Critical skills and knowledge requirements of is professionals: A joint academic/industry investigation. *MIS Quarterly*, *19*(3), 313–340. doi:10.2307/249598

Lee, D. M. S., Trauth, E., & Farwell, D. (1995). Critical skills and knowledge requirements of IS professionals: A joint academic/industry investigation. *MIS Quarterly*, *19*(3), 313-335.

Lee, H., & Choi, B. (2003). Knowledge management enablers, processes, and organizational performance: an integrative view and empirical examination. *Journal of Management Information Systems*, *20*(1), 179-228.

Lee, K. C., Lee, S., & Kang, I. W. (2005). KMPI: measuring knowledge management performance. *Information and Management*, *42*, 469-482.

Lee, T. W., & Mitchell. T. R. (1994). An alternative approach: The unfolding model of voluntary employee turnover. *The Academy of Management Review*, *19*(1), 51-79.

Leidner, D. E., & Kayworth, T. (2006). A review of culture in information systems research: Toward a theory of information technology culture conflict. *MIS Quarterly*, *30*(2), 357-399.

Leidner, D., & Jarvenpaa, S. (1995). The Use of Information Technology to Enhance Management School Education: A Theoretical View. *MIS Quarterly*, *19*(3), 265–291. doi:10.2307/249596

Leonard-Barton, D. (1995). *Wellsprings of knowledge: Building and sustaining the sources of innovation*. Boston: Harvard Business School.

Lepak, D. P., & Snell, S. A. (1999). The human resource architecture: Toward a theory of human capital allocation and development. *Academy of Management Review*, *24*(1), 31-48.

Levin, D. Z., & Cross, R. (2004). The strength of weak ties you can trust: The mediating role of trust in effective knowledge transfer. *Management Science*, *50*(11), 1477–1490. doi:10.1287/mnsc.1030.0136

Levin, R., & Rosse, J. (2001). *Talent flow: A strategic guide to keeping good employees, helping them grow and letting them go*. San Francisco: Jossey-Bass.

Levine, D., Berenson, M., & Stephan, D. (1999). *Statistics for Managers: Using Microsoft Excel*. New Jersey: Prentice Hall.

Levine, J. M., & Russo, E. M. (1987). Majority and Minority Influence. In C. Hendrick (Ed.), *Group Processes* (pp. 13-54). Newbury Park, CA: Sage.

Levine, J., Grizzard, J., & Owen, H. (2004). A methodology to detect and characterize kernel level rootkit exploits involving redirection of the system call table. In *Proceedings of the Second IEEE International Information Assurance Workshop*, 2004.

Levy, M., & Powell, P. (2003). Exploring SME Internet Adoption: Towards a Contingent Model. *Electronic Markets*, *13*(2), 173–181. doi:10.1080/1019678032000067163

Levy, M., Loebbecke, C., & Powell, P. (2003). SMEs, co-opetition and knowledge sharing: the role of information systems. *European Journal of Information Systems*, *12*(1), 3–17. doi:10.1057/palgrave.ejis.3000439

Lewin, A., & Volberda, H. (1999). Prologomena on co-evolution: A framework for research on strategy and new organizational forms. *Organization Science*, *10*(5), 519-534.

Lewis, J. D., & Weigert, A. (1985). Trust as a social reality. *Social Forces*, *63*(4), 967–985. doi:10.2307/2578601

Li, F. (1998). Same Kentucky Chicken, Different Taste: Cross-cultural Leadership Studies at KFC in Beijing. Unpublished Master Thesis, Blacksburg, Virginia.

Li, H., & Atuahene-Gima, K. (2001). Production innovation strategy and the performance of new technology ventures in China. *Academy of Management Journal*, *44*(6), 1123–1134. doi:10.2307/3069392

Li, N., & Kirkup, G. (2007). Gender and cultural differences in Internet use: A study of China and the UK. *Computers & Education*, *48*(2), 301–317. doi:10.1016/j.compedu.2005.01.007

Li, X. C. (2008). National Economy: Steady and Fast Growth in the First Three Quarters of 2008. National Bureau of Statistics of China. Retrieved December 2, 2008 from http://www.stats.gov.cn.

Li, Z., Murray, L., & Efendioglu, A. (2002). Marketing PCs to China. *Business Horizons, 45*(6), 60-66.

Liang, H., Xue Y., Boulton, W., & Byrd, T. A. (2004). Why Western vendors don't dominate China's ERP market. *Communications of the ACM, 47*(7) 69-72.

Liebeskind, J. P. (1996). Knowledge, strategy, and the theory of the firm. *Strategic Management Journal*, *17*, 93-107.

Liebowitz, J. & Chen, Y. (2001). Developing knowledge-sharing proficiencies: Building a supportive culture for knowledge-sharing. *Knowledge Management Review*, *3*(6), 12-15.

Light, R. J., Singer, J. D., & Willett, J. B. (1990). *By Design: Planning Research on Higher Education*, Cambridge, MA: Harvard University Press.

Limayem, M., Banerjee, P., & Ma, L. (2006). Impact of GDSS: Opening the black box. *Decision Support Systems*, *42*(2), 945-957.

Lin, C., Standing, C., & Liu, Y. (2008). A model to develop effective virtual teams. *Decision Support Systems*, *45*(4), 1031–1045. doi:10.1016/j.dss.2008.04.002

Lin, H.-F., & Lee, G.-G. (2004). Perception of senior managers toward knowledge sharing behavior. *Management Decision*, *42*(1), 108–125. doi:10.1108/00251740410510181

Lin, L., & Kwok, L. (2006). Challenges to KM at Hewlett Packard China. *Knowledge Management Review*, *9*(1), 20-23.

Lin, W., & Shao, B. (2000). A relationship between user participation and system success: A simultaneous contingency approach. *Information & Management*, *37*(6), 283-295.

Lind, M. (1999). The gender impact of temporary virtual work groups. *IEEE Transactions on Professional Communication*, *42*(4), 276-285.

Liu, C., Marchewka, J. T., & Ku, C. (2004). American and Taiwanese perceptions concerning privacy, trust and behavioral intentions in electronic commerce. *Journal of Global Information Management*, *12*(1), 18-40.

Liu, S. J., Huang, T. L., & Chen, Q. H. (1998). International development of Taiwan's information industry: an empirical study on human resource strategy of overseas subsidiaries. *IEEE Transactions on Engineering Management*, *45*(3), 296-310.

Llewellyn, D., & Usselman, M. (2001). *Ethnic differences in female applicants to engineering and IT majors.* American Educational Research Association Conference (AERA), Seattle, Washington.

Locke, E. A. (1986). *Generalizing from laboratory to field setting: Research finding from industrial organization, organization behavior, and human resource management.* Lexington, MA: Lexington Books.

Lohmoller, J. B. (1989). *Latent variable path modeling with partial least squares*. New York: Springer-Verlag.

Lok, P., & Crawford, J. (2004). The effect of organisational culture and leadership style on job satisfaction and organisational commitment A cross-national comparison. *Journal of Management Development, 3*(4), 321–338. doi:10.1108/02621710410529785

Love, P. E. D., Irani, Z., Standing, C., Lin, C., & Burn, J. M. (2005). The enigma of evaluation: benefits, costs and risks of IT in Australian small-medium-sized enterprises. *Information & Management, 42*(7), 947–964. doi:10.1016/j.im.2004.10.004

Love, Peter, E.D., & Irani, Z. (2004). An exploratory study of information technology evaluative and benefits management practices of SMEs in the construction industry. *Information & Management, 42*(1), 227–242.

Lowry, P. B., & Nunamaker, J. F. Jr. (2003). Using Internet-based, distributed collaborative writing tools to improve coordination and group awareness in writing teams. *IEEE Transactions on Professional Communication, 46*(4), 277–297. doi:10.1109/TPC.2003.819640

Lu, H. P., & Wang, J. Y. (1997). The relationship between management styles, user participation, and system success over MIS growth stages. *Information & Management, 32*, 203–213. doi:10.1016/S0378-7206(97)00021-9

Lu, L. T., & Lee, Y. H. (2005). The effect of culture on the management style and performance of international joint ventures in China: The perspective of foreign parent firms. *International Journal of Management, 22*(3), 452–462.

Lucas, H. C. (1993). The business value of information technology: a historical perspective and thoughts for future research, in strategic information technology management: perspectives on organizational growth and competitive advantage. In R. Banker, R. Kauffman, and M.A. Mahmood (Eds.), *Strategic Information Technology Management: Perspectives on Organizational Growth and Competitive Advantage*. Hershey, PA: Idea Group Publishing.

Luftman, J., & McLean, E. R. (2004). Key Issues for IT Executives. *MIS Quarterly Executive, 3*(2), 89–104.

Lukas, B. A., Hult, G. T. M., & Ferrell, O. C. (1996). A theoretical perspective of the antecedents and consequences of organizational learning in marketing channels. *Journal of Business Research, 36*(3), 233-244.

Luo, Y. (2003). Market-seeking MNEs in an emerging market: How parent-subsidiary links shape overseas success. *Journal of International Business Studies, 34*, 290-309.

Lurey, J., & Raisinhgani, M. (2001). An Empirical study of best practices in virtual teams. *Information & Management, 38*(8), 523-544.

Lynn, G. S. (1998). New product team learning: developing and profiting from your knowledge capital. *California Management Review, 40*(4), 74-93.

MacKay, N., Parent, M., & Gemino, A. (2004). A model of electronic commerce adoption by small voluntary organizations. *European Journal of Information Systems, 13*(2), 147. doi:10.1057/palgrave.ejis.3000491

Madan, P. (2004). *Voluntary turnover: A study of IS professionals*. B. Comp. Honours Thesis, National University of Singapore.

Madapusi, A., & D'Souza, D. (2005). Aligning ERP systems with international strategies. *Information Systems Management, 22*(1), 7-17.

Madsen, T. K., Rasmussen, E., & Servais, P. (2000). Differences and similarities between born globals and other types of exporters. *Advances in International Marketing, 10*(2), 247–265. doi:10.1016/S1474-7979(00)10013-4

Mahler, V., & Rogers, E. M. (1999). The diffusion of interactive communication innovations and the critical mass: the adoption of telecommunications services by German banks. *Telecommunication Policy, 23*(10-11), 719-740.

Makrakis, V., & Sawada, T. (1996). Gender, computers and other school subjects among Japanese and Swedish students. *Computers & Education, 26*(4), 225–231. doi:10.1016/0360-1315(95)00085-2

Mallach, E. G. (2000). *Decision support and data warehouse systems*. New York: McGraw-Hill.

Mallett, T. (2000). *E-business update: internet use among small and medium-sized firms.*

Malone, P. (2002). The Benefits of Doing Business Electronically - eBusiness. Retrieved September, 2, 2003, from http://www.noie.gov.au/projects/ebusiness/Advancing/benefits/index.htm

Mao, E., Srite, M., Thatcher, J. B., & Yaprak, O. (2005). A Research Model for Mobile Phone Service Behaviors: Empirical Validation in the Us and Turkey. *Journal of Global Information Technology Management, 8*(4), 7.26.

Marakas, G. M., Yi, M. Y., & Johnson, R. D. (1998). The Multilevel and Multifaceted Character of Computer Self-Efficacy: Toward Clarification on the Construct and an Integrative Framework for Research. *Information Systems Research, 9*(2), 126–163. doi:10.1287/isre.9.2.126

March, J. G., & Simon, H. A. (1958). *Organizations.* New York: Wiley.

Margolis, J., & Fisher, A. (2002). *Unlocking the clubhouse: Women in computing.* Cambridge, MA: MIT Press.

Mario, C., Ryan, G., Franziska, H., Kim, M., Chris, N., Natasha, S. et al. (2002). *RFID a week long survey on the technology and its potential.* Retrieved November 12, 2004, from http://www.interaction-ivrea.it/

Markus, H. R., & Kitayama, S. (1991). Culture and the self: Implications for cognition, emotion and motivation. *Psychological Review, 98,* 224-253.

Markus, M. L., & Soh, C. (1993). Banking on information technology: converting it spending into firm performance. In R. Banker, R. Kauffman, and M.A. Mahmood (Eds.), *Strategic Information Technology Management: Perspectives on Organizational Growth and Competitive Advantage.* Hershey, PA: Idea Group Publishing.

Markus, M. L., & Soh, C. (1993). Banking on information technology: Converting IT spending into firm performance. In R. D. Banker, R. J. Kauffman & M.A. Mahmood (Eds.), *Strategic information technology management: Perspectives on organizational growth and competitive advantage* (pp. 375-403). Hershey, PA: Idea Group Publishing

Martinez, Z. L., & Ricks, D. A. (1989). Multinational parent companies' influence over human resources decisions of affiliates: U.S. firms in Mexico. *Journal of International Business Studies, 20*(3), 465-487.

Martinsons, M. G. (1991). Management philosophy and IT assimilation: the East-West divide. *Journal of Technology Management, 18*(3), 207–218.

Martinsons, M. G., & Westwood, R. I. (1997). Management information systems in the Chinese business culture: An explanatory theory. *Information & Management, 32*(5), 215–228. doi:10.1016/S0378-7206(96)00009-2

Mata, F. J., Fuerst, W. L., & Barney, J. B. (1995). Information technology and sustained competitive advantage: a resource-based analysis. *MIS Quarterly, 19*(4), 487–505. doi:10.2307/249630

Mathews, J. A. (2001). National systems of economic learning: The case of technology diffusion management in East Asia. *International Journal of Technology Management, 22*(5/6), 455-479.

Mathieson, K. (1991). Predicting user intentions: Comparing the technology acceptance model with the theory of planned behavior. *Information Systems Research, 2*(3), 173-191.

Matti, K., & Andrew, U. (2004). The relationship between quality of service perceived and delivered in mobile Internet communications. *Information Systems and eBusiness Management, 2*(4), 309.

May, P. (2000). *The Business of E-Commerce From Corporate Strategy To Technology* (1st ed.). London: Cambridge University Press.

Mayer, R. C., & Davis, J. H. (1995). An integrative model of organizational trust. *Academy of Management Review, 20*(3), 709–734. doi:10.2307/258792

McAllister, D. J. (1995). Affect- and cognition-based trust as foundations for interpersonal cooperation in organizations. *Academy of Management Journal, 38*(1), 24–59. doi:10.2307/256727

McCoy, S., Galletta, D. F., & King, W. R. (2007). Applying TAM Across Cultures: The Need for Caution. *European Journal of Information Systems, 16*(1), 81–90. doi:10.1057/palgrave.ejis.3000659

McCracken, G. (1988). *The long interview.* New York: Sage.

McDermott, R. (1999). Why information technology inspired but cannot deliver knowledge management. *California Management Review, 41*(4), 103-117.

McDermott, R. (2000). Building a support structure for your communities. *Knowledge Management Review, 3*(3), 5.

McDonough, E., Kahn, K., & Barczak, G. (2001). An investigation of the use of global, virtual, and collocated new product development teams. *The Journal of Product Innovation Management, 18*(2), 110-120.

McFarlan, W. F. (1984). Information technology changes the way you compete. *Harvard Business Review, May-June*, 98-103.

McGahnan, A. M., & Porter. M. E. (1999). The persistence of shocks to profitability. *The Review of Economics and Statistic, 81*(1), 143-153.

McGrath, J. (1984). *Groups: Interaction and performance*. Upper Saddle River, NJ: Prentice Hall.

McInerney, C. (2002). Knowledge management and the dynamic nature of knowledge. *Journal of the American Society for Information Science and Technology, 53*(12), 1009–1018. doi:10.1002/asi.10109

McKenney, J. L. (1995). *Waves of Change, Business Evolution through information technology.* Cambridge, MA: Harvard Business School Press.

McKenzie, J. & van Winkelen, C. (2004). *Understanding the knowledgeable organization: Nurturing knowledge competence*. London: Thomson Learning.

McKinsey & Company. (1993) *Emerging exporters: Australia's high value-added manufacturing exporters*. Melbourne: McKinsey and Company and the Australian manufacturing council.

McKnight, D., & Chervany, N. (2001). What trust means in e-commerce customer relationships: An interdisciplinary conceptual typology. *International Journal of Electronic Commerce, 6*(2), 35-39.

McKnight, D., Choudhury, V., & Kacmar, C. (2002). Developing and validating trust measures for e-commerce: An integrative typology. *Information Systems Research, 13*(3), 334-359.

McLaren, T., & Head, M. M. (2004). *Strategic fit of supply chain management information systems: A measurement model.* Paper presented at the Twenty-Fifth International Conference on Information Systems.

McMillan, V. (2002, September 4). Little Asia. *The Independent.*

Medeiros, C. B. (2005, June 12-14). From subject of change to agent of change – Women and IT in Brazil. In *Proceedings of the International Symposium on Women and ICT: Creating Global Transformation,* Baltimore, MD. New York: ACM Press.

Mehrtens, J., Cragg, P. B., & Mills, A. M. (2001). A model of Internet adoption by SMEs. *Information & Management, 39*(3), 165–176. doi:10.1016/S0378-7206(01)00086-6

Mejias, R. J., Shepherd, M. M., Vogel, D. R., & Lazaneo, L. (1997). Consensus and perceived satisfaction levels: A cross-cultural comparison of GSS and non-GSS outcomes within and between the United States and Mexico. *Journal of Management Information Systems, 13*(3), 137–161.

Mejias, R. J., Vogel, D. R., & Shepherd, M. M. (1997, January 7-10). *GSS meeting productivity and participation equity: A US and Mexico cross-cultural field study.* Paper presented at the Thirtieth Hawaii International Conference on System Sciences (HICSS), HI.

Melville, N., Kraemer, K., & Gurbaxani, V. (2004). Review: Information technology and organizational performance: An integrative model of IT business value. *MIS Quarterly, 28*(2), 283–322.

Mendo, F., & Fitzgerald, G. (2005). A multidimensional framework for SME e-business progression. *Journal of Enterprise Information Management, 18*(6), 678–696. doi:10.1108/17410390510628382

Mendonca, D., Beroggi, G. E. G., Gent, D. V., & Wallace, W. A. (2006). Designing gaming simulations for the assessment of group decision support systems in emergency response. *Safety Science, 44* (6), 523-535.

Merritt, A. (2000). Culture in the cockpit—Do Hofstede's dimensions replicate? *Journal of Cross-Cultural Psychology, 31*(3), 283-301.

Meszaros, P. S., Lee, S., & Laughlin, A. (2007). Information processing and information technology career interest and choice among high school students. In C.J. Burger, E.G. Creamer, and P.S. Meszaros (Eds.), *Reconfiguring the firewall: Recruiting women to information technology across cultures and continents.* Wellesley, MA: AK Peters Publishing.

Michailova, S. & Husted, K. (2003). Knowledge sharing hostility in Russian firms. *California Management Review, 45*(3), 59-77.

Mieszkowicz-Rolka, A., & Rolka, L. (2004). Variable precision fuzzy rough sets. In J. F. Peters et al. (Eds.), *Transactions on rough sets I, LNCS (3100)* (pp. 144-160). Berlin Heidelberg: Springer-Verlag.

Miles, R. E., & Snow, C. C. (1978). *Organizational strategy, structure, and process.* NY: McGraw-Hill.

Miles, R. E., Snow, C. C., Mathews, J. A., Miles, G., & Coleman, H. J., Jr. (1997). Organizing in the knowledge age: Anticipating the cellular form. *Academy of Management Executive, 11*(4), 7-20.

Miller, D. (1988). Relating Porter's business strategies to environments and structure: Analysis and performance implications. *Academy of Management Journal, 31*(2), 280-308.

Miller, D., & Friesen, P. H. (1978). Archetypes of strategy formulation. *Management Science, 24,* 921-933.

Miller, D., & Friesen, P. H. (1983). Strategy-making and environment: The third link. *Strategic Management Journal, 4,* 221-235.

Minguez, A. M. (2005, June 12-14). New technologies as social fact: Gender and digital divide in Spain in compared perspective. In *Proceedings of the International Symposium on Women and ICT: Creating Global Transformation,* Baltimore, MD. New York: ACM Press.

Ministry of Economic Affairs. (2003). *White paper on small and medium enterprises in Taiwan.* Ministry of Economic Affairs, Taiwan: Small and Medium Enterprise Administration.

Ministry of Economic Development. (2000). *E-commerce: a guide for New Zealand business.* Wellington, N.Z.: Ministry of Economic Development.

Mintchell, G. (2002). It's automatic: automation shifts transmission assembly into high gear. *Control Engineering, 49*(6), 12.

Mintzberg, H. (1973). Strategy making in three modes. *California Management Review, 16,* 44-58.

Miranda, S., & Saunders, C. (2003). The Social Construction of Meaning: An Alternative Perspective on Information Sharing. *Information Systems Research, 14*(1), 87–106. doi:10.1287/isre.14.1.87.14765

Mirchandani, A. A., & Motwani, J. (2001). Understanding small business electronic commerce adoption: an empirical analysis. *Journal of Computer Information Systems,* (Spring): 70–73.

Mitra, S., & Chaya, A. K. (1996). Analyzing cost effectiveness of organizations: the impact of information technology spending. *Journal of Management Information Systems, 13*(2), 29–57.

Mobile Internet in Taiwan. (2005). *RFID leads the way for the implementation of U-Taiwan.* Retrieved November 1, 2005, from http://www.find.org.tw/mit/200506/200506e/200506-008.htm

Mobley, W. H. (1977). Intermediate linkages in the relationship between job dissatisfaction and employee turnover. *Journal of Applied Psychology, 62,* 237-240.

Mobley, W. H., Griffeth, R. W., Hand, H. H., & Meglino, B. M. (1979). Review and conceptual analysis of the employee turnover process. *Psychological Bulletin 86*(3), 493-522.

Moen, O., & Servais, P. (2002). Born Global or Gradual Global? Examining the export behavior of small and medium-sized enterprises. *Journal of International Marketing, 10*(3), 49–72. doi:10.1509/jimk.10.3.49.19540

Moenaert, R. K., & Souder, W. E. (1996). Context and Antecedents of information utility at the R&D/marketing interface. *Management Science, 42*(11), 1592-1610.

Montazemi, A. R. (2006). How they manage IT: SMEs in Canada and the U.S. *Communications of the ACM, 49*(12), 109–112. doi:10.1145/1183236.1183240

Montoya-Weiss, M. M., Massey, A. P., & Song, M. (2001). Getting it together: Temporal coordination and conflict management in global virtual teams. *Academy of Management Journal*, *44*(6), 1251–1262. doi:10.2307/3069399

Mooradian, T., Renzl, B., & Matzler, K. (2006). Who trusts? Personality, trust and knowledge sharing. *Management Learning*, *37*(4), 523–540. doi:10.1177/1350507606073424

Moore, G. C., & Benbasat, I. (1991). Development of an instrument to measure the perceptions of adopting an information technology innovation. *Information Systems Research*, *2*(3), 192-222.

Moore, G. C., & Benbasat, I. (1996). Integrating diffusion of innovations & theory of reasoned action models to predict utilization of information technology by end- users. In K. Kautz & J. Pries-Heje (Eds.), *Diffusion & adoption of information technology* (pp.132-146). London: Chapman & Hall.

Moorman, C., & Miner, A. S. (1998). Organizational improvisation and organizational memory. *Academy of Management Review*, *23*(4), 132-142.

Morales, B., Moriera, H., & Vogel, D. R. (1995, January 4-7). *Group support for regional development in Mexico.* Paper presented at the 28th Hawaii International Conference on System Sciences (HICSS), HI.

Moran, P. (1998). Personality characteristics and growth-orientation of the small business owner-manager. *International Small Business Journal*, *16*(3), 17. doi:10.1177/0266242698163001

Morgan, A. J., Quesenberry, J. L., & Trauth, E. M. (2004). Exploring the importance of social networks in the IT workforce: Experiences with the 'boy's club.' In J. Luftman (Ed.), *Proceedings of the Americas Conference on Information Systems, New York* (pp. 1313-1320).

Morgan, N. A., Kaleka, A., & Katsikeas, C. S. (2000). Antecedents of export venture performance: a theoretical model and empirical assessment. *Journal of Marketing*, *68*(1), 90–108. doi:10.1509/jmkg.68.1.90.24028

Morosini, P., Shane, S., & Singh, H. (1998). National cultural distance and cross-border acquisition performance. *Journal of International Business Studies*, *29*(1), 137-158.

Morris, M. G., & Venkatesh, V. (2000). Age Differences in Technology Adoption Decisions: Implications for a Changing Workforce. *Personnel Psychology*, *53*(2), 375–403. doi:10.1111/j.1744-6570.2000.tb00206.x

Morrison, P. A. (2006). A Demographic Perspective on Our Nation's Future. *Population Matters* Retrieved June 28, 2006, from http://www.rand.org/pubs/documented_briefings/DB320/index.html.

Morrow, P. (1993). *The theory and measurement of work commitment.* Greenwich, CT: JAI Press.

Moscovici, S., & Zavalloni, M. (1969). The group as a polarizer of attitudes. *Journal of Personality and Social Psychology*, *12*, 125–135. doi:10.1037/h0027568

Mulligan, P. (2002). Specification of a capability-based IT classification framework. *Information & Management*, *39*(8), 647. doi:10.1016/S0378-7206(01)00117-3

Munro, H., & Noori, H. (1988). Measuring commitment to new manufacturing technology: integrating technological push and marketing pull concepts. *IEEE Transactions on Engineering Management*, *35*(2), 63-70.

Murphy, K., Roodenrys, S., & Fox, A. (2006). Event-related potential correlates of the word length effect in working memory. *Brain Research*, *1112*, 179-190.

Myers, D. G. (2005). *Social psychology.* New York: McGraw-Hill.

Myers, M. D., & Tan, F. B. (2002). Beyond Models of National Culture in Is Research. *Journal of Global Information Management*, *10*(1), 24–32.

Nahaipet, J., & Ghoshal, S. (1998). Social capital, intellectual capital, and the organizational advantage. *Academy of Management Review*, *23*(2), 242–266. doi:10.2307/259373

Nair, K. G. K., & Prasad, P. N. (2004). Offshore outsourcing: A SWOT analysis of a state in India. *Information systems management*, *21*(3), 34-40.

Nambisan, S., & Wang, Y.-M. (1999). Roadblocks to Web technology adoption? *Association for Computing Machinery. Communications of the ACM*, *42*(1), 98. doi:10.1145/291469.291482

Nanson, E. J. (1882). Methods of election, transactions and proceedings of the royal society of Victoria, Vol. 18.

Naryayan, U. (1998). Essence of culture and a sense of history: A feminist critique of cultural essentialism. *Hypatia: A Journal of Feminist Philosophy, 13*(2), 86-107.

National Association of Software and Service Companies. (2005). *Indian IT industry*. Retrieved March 3, 2005, from http://www.nasscom.org/

Ndubisi, N., Gupta, O., & Ndubisi, G. (2005). The Moguls' Model of Computing: Integrating the Moderating Impact of Users' Persona into the Technology Acceptance Model. *Journal of Global Information Technology Management, 8*(1), 27–47.

Neo, B. S. (1991). Information technology and global competition: a framework for analysis. *Information and Management, 20*, 151-160.

New Zealand Ministry of Economic Development. (2000). *E-commerce: building the strategy for New Zealand.*

Ng, K. (2000). The new e-commerce horizon. *The Hong Kong Accountant, May*, 24-28.

Ng, K. Y., & Chua, R. Y. J. (2006). Do I contribute more when I trust more? Different effects of cognition- and affect-based trust. *Management and Organization Review, 2*(1), 43–66. doi:10.1111/j.1740-8784.2006.00028.x

Ngai, E. W. T., & Wat, F. K. T. (2005). Fuzzy decision support system for risk analysis in e-commerce development. *Decision Support Systems, 40*(2), 235-255.

Ngai, E. W. T., Cheng, T. C. E., Au, S., & Lai, K. H. (2007). Mobile commerce integrated with RFID technology in a container depot. *Decision Support Systems, 43*, 62-76.

NIEC. (2005). *Top500 of Chinese enterprise informatization*. National Informatization Evaluation Center.

NIEC. (2008, 3-24). 2007 Survey report of top 500 informatization enterprises in China. *China Economy Weekly, 11*.

Niederman, F. (1997). Facilitating computer-supported meetings: an exploratory comparison of U.S. and Mexican facilitators. *Journal of Global Information Management, 5*(1), 17–26.

Nielsen, S., von Hellens, L. A., Greenhill, A., & Pringle, R. (1998). Conceptualising the influence of cultural and gender factors on students' perception of IT studies and careers. In *Proceedings of the 1998 ACM SIGCPR Conference,* Boston, MA, (pp. 86-95). New York: ACM Press.

Nielsen, S., von Hellens, L., Pringle, R., & Greenhill, A. (1999). Students' perceptions of information technology careers: Conceptualising the influence of cultural and gender factors for IT education. *GATES, 5*(1), 30–38.

Niemi, R. G., & Weisberg, H. F. (1968). A mathematical solution for the probability of the paradox of voting. *Behavioral Science, 13*, 317.

Noe, R. A., Hollenbeck, J. R., Gerhart, B., & Wright, P. M. (2003). *Human resource management: Gaining a competitive advantage* (4th ed.). Boston: McGraw-Hill.

Noe, R. A., Hollenbeck, J. R., Gerhart, B., & Wright, P. M. (2004). *Fundamentals of human resource management.* Boston: Irwin.

NOIE, & Young, E. (2001). Advancing with e-commerce: a summary of 34 case studies of small business e-commerce ventures. Retrieved September, 3, 2003, from http://www.noie.gov.au/projects/CaseStudies/Ecommerce/SummaryReport/index.htm

Nolan, R. L. (1979). Managing the crises in data processing. *Harvard Business Review*, (March-April): 115–126.

Nonaka, I. (1991). The knowledge creating company. *Harvard Business Review, 69*(6), 96-104.

Nonaka, I. (1994). A dynamic theory of organizational knowledge creation. *Organization Science, 5*(1), 14–37.

Nonaka, I., & Konno, N. (1998). The concept of 'Ba': Building a foundation for knowledge creation. *California Management Review, 40*(3), 40-54.

Nonaka, I., & Takeuchi, H. (1995). *The knowledge creating company.* NY: Oxford University Press.

Nonaka, I., & Takeuchi, H. (1995). *The knowledge-creating company, how Japanese companies create the dynamics of innovation.* New York: Oxford University Press.

Nugent, P. D., & Abolafia, M. Y. (2006). The creation of trust through interaction and exchange. *Group & Organization Management, 31*(6), 628–650. doi:10.1177/1059601106286968

Nunamaker, J. F., Briggs, R. O., Mittleman, D. D., Vogel, D. R., & Balthazard, P. A. (1997). Lesssons from a dozen years of group support systems research: A discussion of lab and field findings. *Journal of Management Information Systems, 13*(3), 163-207.

Nunnally, J. C. (1978). *Psychometric Theory.* New York: McGraw Hill, Inc.

Nunnally, J.C., & Bernstein, I.H. (1994). *Psychometric theory* (3rd ed.). McGraw-Hill.

NZIER. (2008). Asian Investment in New Zealand. Retrieved November, 28, 2008, from http://www.asianz.org.nz/our-work/knowledge-research/research-reports/business-research#businessresearch

NZIS. (2004). Statistics of residence decisions by financial year. Retrieved July, 2004, from http://www.immigration.govt.nz/NR/rdonlyres/EC5C8D0E-BCB7-4382-A35C-44CE16EE38DC/0/R1.xls

O'Kane, P., & Hargie, O. (2004). Technology Travels: Can national culture impact upon attitudes toward communication-technology? *Journal of Intercultural Communication Research, 33*(1), 49–62.

Ody, K. (1995). Facilitating the "right" decision in crisis-Supporting the crisis decision maker through analysis of their needs. *Safety Science, 20,* 125-133.

OECD. O. f. E. C.-o. a. D. (1998). *Small and medium-sized enterprises and electronic commerce.* Paper presented at the Ministerial Conference on Electronic Commerce, Ottawa, Canada.

Okazaki, S. (2004). Do multinationals standardise or localise? The cross-cultural dimensionality of product-based Web sites. *Internet Research, 14*(1), 81–94. doi:10.1108/10662240410516336

Ölçer, A. I., & Odabasi, A. Y. (2005). A new fuzzy multiple attributive group decision making methodology and its application to propulsion/maneuvering system selection problem. *European Journal of Operational Research, 1,* 93-114.

Organ, D. W. (1988). *Organizational Citizenship Behavior: The Good Soldier Syndrome* Lexington, MA: Lexington Books.

Organization for Economic Co-operation and Development (OECD). (2007). ICTs and gender. Retrieved from: http://www.oecd.org/dataoecd/16/33/38332121.pdf

Over, E. A. B., Hooge, I. T. C., & Erkelens, C. J. (2006). A quantitative measure for the uniformity of fixation density: The Voronoi method. *Behavior Research Methods, 38*(2), 251-261.

Oviatt, B. M., & McDougall, P. P. (1994). Toward a theory of international new ventures. *Journal of International Business Studies, 25*(1), 45–64. doi:10.1057/palgrave.jibs.8490193

Oviatt, B. M., & McDougall, P. P. (1999). Challenges for internationalization process theory: the case of international new ventures. *Management International Review, 37*(1), 85–99.

Oysterman, D., Coon, H. M., & Kemmelmeir, M. (2002). Rethinking Individualism and Collectivism: Evaluation of Theoretical Assumptions and Meta-Analysis. *Psychological Bulletin, 128*(1), 3–72. doi:10.1037/0033-2909.128.1.3

Özsomer, A., Calantone, R. J., & Benedetto, A. D. (1997). What makes firms more innovative? A look at organizational and environmental factors. *Journal of Business and Industrial Marketing, 12*(6), 400-416.

Padmanabhan, P., & Cho, K. R. (1996). Ownership Strategy for a foreign affiliate: an empirical investigation of Japanese firms. *Management International Review, 36,* 45-65.

Palmer, J. W., Bailey, J. P., & Faraj, S. (2003). Intermediaries and trust on the Internet: The use and prominence of trusted third parties and privacy statements. In C. Steinfeld (Ed.), *New directions in research on e-commerce* (pp. 128-146). West Lafayette, IN: Purdue University Press.

Pande, R. (2006). Digital divide, gender and the Indian experience in IT. In E.M. Trauth, (Ed.), *Encyclopedia of gender and information technology* (pp. 191-199). Hershey, PA: Idea Group Reference.

Panteli, N., & Sockalingam, S. (2005). Trust and conflict within virtual inter-organizational alliances: a frame work for facilitating knowledge sharing. *Decision Support Systems, 39*, 599–617. doi:10.1016/j.dss.2004.03.003

Papanastassiou, M., & Pearce, R. (1997). Technology sourcing and the strategic roles of manufacturing subsidiaries in the U.K.: local competences and global competitiveness. *Management International Review, 17*(1), 5-25.

Papazoglou, I. A., & Christou, M. D. (1997). Decision support system for emergency response to major nuclear accidents. *Nuclear Technology, 118*(2), 97-122.

Park, S. H., & Ungson, G. R. (1997). The effect of national culture, organizational complementary, and economic motivation on joint venture dissolution. *Academy of Management Journal, 40*(2), 279-307.

Parks, C. D., & Hulbert, L. G. (1995). High and low trusters' responses to fear in a payoff matrix. *The Journal of Conflict Resolution, 39*(4), 718–730. doi:10.1177/0022002795039004006

Pavlou, P. A. (2003). Consumer acceptance of electronic commerce: Integrating trust and risk with the technology acceptance model. *International Journal of Electronic Commerce, 7*(3), 101-134.

Pawlyna, A. (2000). The seal of approval. *The Hong Kong Accountant, May*, 20-23.

Penley, L. E., & Hawkins, B. (1985). Studying interpersonal communication in organizations: A leadership application. *Academy of Management Journal, 28*(2), 309–326. doi:10.2307/256203

Peppard, J., & Ward, J. (2004). Beyond strategic information systems: towards an IS capability. *The Journal of Strategic Information Systems, 13*(2), 167–194. doi:10.1016/j.jsis.2004.02.002

Peszynski, K. J. (2003). Trust in B2C e-commerce: the New Zealand Māori Internet shopper. In T. Thanasankit (Ed.), *E-commerce and cultural values* (pp. 169-198). Hershey, PA: Idea Group Publishing.

Peter, H., & Raghu, D. (2005). *RFID forecasts, players & opportunities 2005-2015*. IDTechEx.

Peterson, M. F., & Smith, P. B., & al, e. (1995). Role Conflict, Ambiguity, and Overload: A 21 Nation Study. *Academy of Management Journal, 38*(2), 429–452. doi:10.2307/256687

Pfeffer, J. (1994). *Competitive advantage through people: Unleashing the power of the workforce*. Boston: Harvard Business School.

Pfeffer, J., & Salancik, G. (1978). *The external control of organizations: a resource dependence perspective*. New York: Harper & Row.

Phan, D. D. (2003). E-business development for competitive advantages: a case study. *Information & Management, 40*(6), 581–590. doi:10.1016/S0378-7206(02)00089-7

Piccoli, G., & Ives, B. (2003). Trust and the unintended effects of behavior control in virtual teams. *MIS Quarterly, 27*(3), 365-395.

Pineda, R., & Whitehead, C. (1997). The Effect of Ethnic Group Culture on Managerial Task Activities. *Group & Organization Management, 22*(1), 31–52. doi:10.1177/1059601197221005

Png, I. P. L., Tan, B. C. Y., & Wee, K. L. (2001). dimensions of national culture and corporate adoption of IT infrastructure. *IEEE Transactions on Engineering Management 48*(1), 36-45.

Podsakoff, P. M., & Organ, D. W. (1986). Self-reports in organizational research: Problems and prospects. *Journal of Management, 12*(4), 531–544. doi:10.1177/014920638601200408

Podsakoff, P. M., MacKenzie, S. B., Paine, J. B., & Bachrach, D. G. (2000). Organizational citizenship behaviors: A critical review of the theoretical and empirical literature and suggestions for future research. *Journal of Management, 26*(3), 513–563. doi:10.1177/014920630002600307

Politis, J. D. (2001). The relationship of various leadership styles to knowledge management. *Leadership and Organization Development Journal, 22*(8), 354–364. doi:10.1108/01437730110410071

Politis, J. D. (2003). The connection between trust and knowledge management: What are its implications for team performance. *Journal of Knowledge Management, 7*(5), 55–66. doi:10.1108/13673270310505386

Poole, M. S., Seibold, D. R., & McPhee, R. D. (1985). Group decision-making as a structural process. *The Quarterly Journal of Speech, 71*, 74–102. doi:10.1080/00335638509383719

Porter, L. W., & Steers, R. M. (1973). Organizational, work and personal factors in employee turnover and absenteeism. *Psychological Bulletin, 80,* 151-176.

Porter, M. E. (1980). *Competitive advantage: Techniques for analyzing industries and competitors.* NY: Free Press.

Porter, M. E. (1990). *The competitive advantage of nations.* New York: Free Press.

Potter, R. E., & Balthazard, P. (2004). The role of individual memory and attention processes during electronic brainstorming. *MIS Quarterly, 28*(4), 621-643.

Powell, A., Piccoli, G., & Ives, B. (2004). Virtual teams: A review of current literature and directions for future research. *The DATABASE for Advances in Information Systems, 35*(1), 6-36.

Powell, T. C., & Dent-Micallef, A. (1997). Information technology as competitive advantage, The role of human, business, and technology resources. *Strategic Management Journal, 18*(5), 375–405. doi:10.1002/(SICI)1097-0266(199705)18:5<375::AID-SMJ876>3.0.CO;2-7

Prahalad, C. K., & Doz, Y. L. (1987). *The multinational mission: balancing local demands and global vision.* New York: Free Press.

Prahalad, C. K., & Hamel, G. (1990). The core competence of the corporation. *Harvard Business Review, 68*(3), 79-91.

Prahalad, C. K., & Hamel, G. (1994). Strategy as a field of study: Why search for a new paradigm? *Strategic Management Journal, 15,* 5-16.

Prasad, V. K., Ramamurthy, K., & Naidu, G. M. (2001). The influence of Internet-marketing integration on marketing competencies and export performance. *Journal of International Marketing, 9*(4), 82–111. doi:10.1509/jimk.9.4.82.19944

Premkumar, G., & King, W. R. (1992). An empirical assessment of information systems planning and the role of information systems in organizations. *Journal of Management Information Systems, 9,* 299-125.

Premkumar, G., & Potter, M. (1995). Adoption of computer aided software engineering (CASE) technology: an innovation adoption perspective. *DATA BASE, 26*(2&3), 105-124.

Premkumar, G., & Ramamurthy, K. (1995). The role of interorganizational and organizational factors on the decision mode for adoption of interorganizational systems. *Decision Sciences, 26*(3), 303–336. doi:10.1111/j.1540-5915.1995.tb01431.x

Prescott, M. B., & Conger, S. A. (1995). Information technology innovations: a classification by IT locus of impact & research approach. *DATA BASE, 26*(2&3), 20-41.

Price, J. L., & Mueller, C. W. (1981). A casual model for turnover for nurses. *Academy of Management Journal, 24,* 543-565.

PriceWaterhouseCoopers. (1999). *SME Electronic Commerce Study.* Paper presented at the Asia Pacific Economic Cooperation (APEC) Telecommunications Working Group.

Prooijen, J. W. V., & Kloot, V. D. (2001). Confirmatory analysis of explanatively obtained factor structures. *Educational and Psychological Measurement, 61*(5), 777–792. doi:10.1177/00131640121971518

Pruitt, D. G. (1971). Choice shifts in group discussion: an introductory review. *Journal of Personality and Social Psychology, 20*, 339–360. doi:10.1037/h0031922

Punj, C., & Stewart, D. W. (1983). Cluster analysis in marketing research: review and suggestions for application. *Journal of Marketing Research, 20,* 134-148.

Purao, S., & Campbell, B. (1998). Critical concerns for small business electronic commerce: some reflections based on interviews of small business owners. In *Proceedings of the Association for Information Systems Americas Conference* (pp. 325-327).

Pye, L. (1985). *Asian Power and Politics: The Cultural Dimensions of Authority.* Cambridge, MA: Harvard University Press.

Qu, Z. H., & Brocklehurst, M. (2003). What will it take for China to become a competitive force in offshore outsourcing? An analysis of the role of transaction costs in supplier selection. *Journal of information technology, 18*(1), 53-67.

Quaddus, M. A., & Tung, L. L. (2002). Explaining cultural differences in decision conferencing. *Communications of the ACM, 45*(8), 93–98. doi:10.1145/545151.545157

Quesenberry, J. L., & Trauth, E. M. (2005). The role of ubiquitous computing in maintaining work-life balance: Perspectives from women in the IT workforce. In C. Sorensen, Y. Youngjin, K. Lyytinen, & J.I. DeGross (Eds.), *Designing ubiquitous information environments: Socio-technical issues and challenges* (pp. 43-55). New York, Springer.

Quesenberry, J. L., & Trauth, E. M. (2007). What do women want?: an investigation of career anchors among women in the IT workforce. In *Proceedings of the ACM SIGMIS Computer Personnel Research Conference, St. Louis, Missouri, April* (pp. 122-127). New York: ACM Press.

Quesenberry, J. L., & Trauth, E. M. (2008). Revisiting career path assumptions: The case of women in the IT workforce. In *Proceedings of the International Conference on Information Systems* (Paris, France, December).

Quesenberry, J. L., Trauth, E. M., & Morgan, A. J. (2006). Understanding the 'mommy tracks': A framework for analyzing work-family issues in the IT workforce. *Information Resources Management Journal, 19*(2), 37–53.

Quigley, N. R., Tesluk, P. E., Locke, E. A., & Bartol, K. M. (2007). A multilevel investigation of the motivational mechanisms underlying knowledge sharing and performance. *Organization Science, 18*(1), 71-88.

Quinn, J. B., Anderson, P., & Finkelstein, S. (1996). Leveraging intellect. *Academy of Management Executive, 10*(3), 7-26.

Rahim, M. A. (1983). A measure of styles of handling interpersonal conflict. *Academy of Management Journal, 26*(2), 368–376. doi:10.2307/255985

Rai, A. S., Lang, S., & Welker, R. B. (2002). Assessing the validity of IS success models: An empirical test & theoretical analysis. *Information Systems Research, 13*(1), 50-69.

Ranganathan, C., Dhaliwal, J. S., & Teo, T. S. H. (2004). Assimilation and diffusion of Web technologies in supply-chain management: An examination of key drivers and performance impacts. *International Journal of Electronic Commerce, 9*(1), 127–161.

Rao, S. S., Metts, G., & Monge, C. A. M. (2003). Electronic commerce development in small and medium sized enterprises: A stage model and its implications. *Business Process Management, 9*(1), 11–32. doi:10.1108/14637150310461378

Ray, G., Muhanna, W. A., & Barney, J. B. (2005). Information technology and the performance of the customer service process: A resource-based analysis. *MIS Quarterly, 29*, 625–652.

Raymond, L. (1990). Organizational context and information systems success: a contingency approach. *Journal of Management Information Systems, 6*(4), 5-20.

Raymond, L., & Pare, G. (1992). Measurement of information technology sophistication in small manufacturing business. *Information Resource Management Journal*, 4-16.

Raymond, L., Pare, G., & Bergeron, F. (1994). Matching information technology and organizational structure: an empirical study with implications for performance. *European Journal of Information Systems, 4*(1), 3-16.

Reader, J. A. (1987). Motivating Chinese employees in joint ventures in the PRC: Appalachian State University, April.

Redding, S. G. (1993). *The spirit of Chinese capitalism.* Berlin: Walter de Gruyter.

Redding, S. G., & Richardson, S. (1986). Participative management and its varying relevance in Hong Kong and singapore. *Asia Pacific Journal of Management, 3*(2), 76–98. doi:10.1007/BF01733215

Redding, S. G., Norman, A., & Schlander, A. (1994). The nature of individual attachment to the organization: A review of east Asian variations. In H. C. Triandis, M. Dunnette, & L. Hough (Eds.), *Handbook of industrial and organizational psychology* (2nd ed., Vol. 4, pp. 557-607). Palo Alto, CA: Consulting Psychologists Press.

Redding, S., & Baldwin, E. (1991). *Managers for Asia/Pacific: Recruitment and Development Strategies*. Hong Kong: Business International.

Reid, F. (2003). Creating a knowledge-sharing culture among diverse business units. *Employment Relations Today, 30*(3), 43–49. doi:10.1002/ert.10097

Reik, W. R., Patrick, A., Snell, C. F. A., & Timothy, P. B. (2004). *RFID explained.* Robert W, Baird & Co. Incorporated, 12-13.

Reimers, K. (2002). *Implementing ERP systems in China.* Paper presented at the Proceedings of the 35th Hawaii International Conference on System Sciences.

Reinig, B. A., & Mejias, R. J. (2003, January 6-9). *An investigation of the influence of national culture and group support systems on group processes and outcomes.* Paper presented at the 36th Annual Hawaii International Conference on System Sciences (HICSS), Big Island, HI.

Remus, W. E. (1986). An empirical test of the use of graduate students as surrogates for managers in experiments on business decision making. *Journal of Business Research, 14*(1), 19-25.

Rennie, M. W. (1993). Global competitiveness, Born Global. *The McKinsey Quarterly* Number 4, 45-52.

Rice, R. E., & Love, G. (1987). Electronic emotion: Socio-emotional content in a computer-mediated communication network. *Communication Research*, 14(1), 85-108.

Richardson, R. (2008). *2008 CSI/FBI Computer Crime and Security Survey.*

Ridgeway, C. L., Berger, J., & Smith, L. (1985). Nonverbal cues and status: An expectation states approach. *American Journal of Sociology, 90*(5), 955–978. doi:10.1086/228172

Riquelme, H. (2002). Commercial Internet adoption in China: comparing the experience of small, medium and large businesses. *Internet Research: Electronic Networking Applications and Policy, 12*(3), 276–286. doi:10.1108/10662240210430946

Rizzoni, A. (1991). Technological innovation and small firms: a taxonomy. *International Small Business Journal, 9*(3), 31–42. doi:10.1177/026624269100900302

Robbins, S. P. (1997). *Organization Behavior* (7th ed.). Prentice-Hall International.

Robeiro, F. L., & Love, P. E. D. (2003). Value creation through an e-business strategy: implication for SMEs in construction. *Construction Innovation, 3*(1), 3–14.

Robert, C., Probst, T. M., Martocchio, J. J. Drasgow, F., & Lawler, J. J. (2000). Empowerment and continuous improvement in the United States, Mexico, Poland and India: Predicting fit on the basis of the dimensions of power distance and individualism. *Journal of Applied Psychology, 85,* 643-658.

Roberts, C. M. (2006). Radio frequency identification (RFID). *Computers and Security, 25,* 18-26.

Roberts, P. F. (2005, October 17). Rootkits sprout on networks. *eWeek, 22,* 25.

Robichaux, B. P., & Cooper, R. B. (1998). GSS participation: A cultural examination. *Information & Management, 33*, 287–300. doi:10.1016/S0378-7206(98)00033-0

Rockart, J. F., Earl, M. J., & Ross, J. W. (1996). Eight imperatives for the new IT organization. *Sloan Management Review, 38*(1), 43–56.

Rodgers, J., Yen, D., & Chou, D. (2002). Developing e-busienss: a strategic approach. *Information Management & Computer Security, 10*(4), 184–192. doi:10.1108/09685220210436985

Roepke, R., Agarwal, R., & Ferratt, T. W. (2000). Aligning the IT human resource with business vision: the leadership initiative at 3M. *MIS Quarterly, 24*(2), 327–353. doi:10.2307/3250941

Rogers, E. M. (1962). *Diffusion of innovations.* New York: Free Press.

Rogers, E.M. (1983). *The Diffusion of Innovations.* New York: The Free Press

Ronen, S. (1994). An understanding of motivational needs taxonomies: A cross-cultural conformation. In H. C. Triandis, M. D. Dunnette, & L. M. Hough (Eds.),

Handbook of industrial and organizational psychology (2nd ed, Vol. 4, pp. 241-270). Palo Alto, CA: Consulting Psychologists Press.

Ronen, S., & Shenkar, O. (1985). Clustering countries on attitudinal dimensions: A review and synthesis. *Academy of Management Review, 10*(3), 435-454.

Roos, J., Roos, G., Edvinsson, L., & Dragonetti, N. C. (1998). *Intellectual capital: Navigating in the new business landscape*. NY: New York University Press.

Rosencrance, L., & Vijayan, J. (2005, March 21). University Computers Hacked on Each Coast. *Computerworld, 39*, 57.

Rosenzweig, P. M., & Nohria, N. (1994). Influences on human resource management practices in multinational corporations, *Journal of International Business Studies, 25*(2), 229-251.

Ross, I. C., & Zander, A. (1957). Need satisfaction and employee turnover. *Personnel Psychology, 10*, 327-338.

Ross, J. W., Beath, C. M., & Goodhue, D. L. (1996). Develop long-term competitiveness through IT assets. *Sloan Management Review, 38*(1), 31 33.

Rosse, J. G., & Hulin, C. L. (1985). Adaptation to work: An analysis of employee health, withdrawal and change. *Organizational Behavior and Human Decision Processes, 36*, 324-347.

Rosser, S. V. (2005, June 12-14). Women and ICT: Global issues and actions. In *Proceedings of the International Symposium on Women and ICT: Creating Global Transformation*, Baltimore, MD. New York: ACM Press.

Roth, K., & Morrison, A. L. (1992). Implementing global strategy: characteristics of global subsidiary mandates. *Journal of International Business Studies, 23*(4), 715-735.

Roth, K., & O'Donnell, S. (1996). Foreign subsidiary compensation strategy: an agency theory perspective. *Academic Management Journal, 39*(3), 678-703.

Rottman, J. W. (2006). Successfully outsourcing embedded software development. *IEEE Computer, 39*(1), 55-61.

Ruggles, R. (1998). The state of notion: Knowledge management in practice. *California Management Review, 40*(3), 80-89.

Rumelt, R. P. (1984). Toward a strategic theory of the firm. In R. Lamb (Ed.), *Competitive strategic management* (pp. 556-570). Englewood Cliffs, NJ: Prentice-Hall.

Ryu, S., Ho, S. H., & Han, I. (2003). Knowledge sharing behavior of physicians in hospitals. *Expert Systems with Applications, 25*(1), 113–122. doi:10.1016/S0957-4174(03)00011-3

Saar, S., & Thomas, V. (2003). Toward trash that thinks product tags for environmental management. *Journal of Industrial Ecology, 6*(2), 133-146.

Saaty, T. L. (1988). *What is the analytic hierarchy process?* New York: Springer-Verlag Inc.

Sabherwal, R. (1999). The relationship between information system planning sophistication and information system success, An empirical assessment. *Decision Sciences, 30*(1), 137–168. doi:10.1111/j.1540-5915.1999.tb01604.x

Sabherwal, R., & Becerra-Fernandez, I. (2005). Integrating specific knowledge: Insights from the Kennedy Space Center. *IEEE Transactions on Engineering Management, 52*(3), 301-315.

Sabherwal, R., & Kirs, P. (1994). The alignment between organizational critical success factors and information technology capability in academic institutions. *Decision Sciences, 25*(2), 301–331. doi:10.1111/j.1540-5915.1994.tb01844.x

Sabherwal, R., & Sabherwal, S. (2005). Knowledge management using information technology: Determinants of short-term impact on firm value. *Decision Sciences, 36*(4), 531-566.

Sabo, D. (2003). Electronic Commerce barriers survey results. Retrieved September, 18, 2003, from http://www.itaa.org/software/research/indpulse/bartext.htm

Saffu, K., Walker, J. H., & Hinson, R. (2008). Strategic value and electronic commerce adoption among small and medium-sized enterprises in a transitional economy. *Journal of Business and Industrial Marketing, 23*(6), 395–404. doi:10.1108/08858620810894445

Samarah, I., Paul, S., Mykytyn, P., & Seetharaman, P. (2003, January 6-9). *The collaborative conflict management style and cultural diversity in DGSS supported fuzzy tasks: An experimental investigation.* Paper presented at the 36th Annual Hawaii International Conference on System Sciences (HICSS), Big Island, HI.

Sambamurthy, V., & Zmud, R. W. (1992). *Managing IT for success, The empowering business partnership.* Morristown, NJ: Financial Executives Research Foundation.

Sambamurthy, V., & Zmud, R. W. (1994). *IT management competency assessment: A tool for creating business value through IT.* Morristown, NJ: Financial Executives Research Foundation.

Sambamurthy, V., Bharadwaj, A., & Grover, V. (2003). Shaping agility through digital options: Reconceptualizing the role of information technology in contemporary firms. *MIS Quarterly, 27*(2), 237–263.

Sambharya, R. B., & Phatak, A. (1990). The effect of transborder data flow restrictions on American multinational corporations. *Management International Review, 30*(3), 267-289.

Sanders, J. (2005, June 12-14). Gender and technology in education: What the research tells us. In *Proceedings of the International Symposium on Women and ICT: Creating Global Transformation,* Baltimore, MD. New York: ACM Press.

Santhanam, R., & Hartono, E. (2003). Issues in linking information technology capability to firm performance. *MIS Quarterly, 27*(1), 125–153.

Sarkar, S., & Sahay, S. (2002). Information systems development by US-Norwegian virtual teams: Implications of time and space. In *Proceedings of the 35th Annual Hawaii International Conference on System Sciences* (pp. 1-10).

Sarker, S., Valacich, J., & Sarker, S. (2003). Virtual team trust: instrument development and validation in an IS educational environment. *Information Resources Management Journal, 16*(2), 35–55.

Saunders, C. S. (2000). *Virtual Teams: Piecing Together the Puzzle.* In R.W. Zmud (Ed.), *Framing the Domains of IT Management: Projecting the Future through the Past.* Cincinnati, OH: Pinnaflex.

Scarbrough, H., Swan, J., & Preston, J. (1999). *Knowledge management and the learning organization.* London: IPD.

Schienstock, G. (1999). *Social exclusion in the learning economy.* Presented at the European Socio-Economic Research Conference, Brussels. Retrieved from http://www.uta.fi/laitokset/tyoelama/sowing/report/SocExcLearningEcon.pdf

Schimdt, J. B., Montoya-Weiss, M. M., & Massey, A. P. (2001). New product development decision-making effectiveness: Comparing individuals, face-to-face teams and virtual teams. *Decisions Sciences, 32*(4), 575-600.

Schinzel, B. (1999, July 29-31). The contingent construction of the relationship between gender and computer science. In *Proceedings of International Symposium on Technology and Society: Women and Technology,* New Brunswick, NJ, (pp. 299-311).

Schmidt, M. B., & Arnett, K. P. (2005). Spyware: A Little Knowledge is a Wonderful Thing. *Communications of the ACM, 48*(8), 67–70. doi:10.1145/1076211.1076242

Schmidt, M. B., Johnston, A. C., & Arnett, K. P. (2006). An Empirical Investigation of Rootkit Awareness. *Business Research Yearbook: Global Business Perspectives, 13,* 153–158.

Schon, D. (1967). *Technology & social change.* New York: Delacorte.

Schriesheim, C. A. (1982). The great high consideration-high initiating structure leadership myth: evidence on its generalizability. *The Journal of Social Psychology, 116,* 221–228.

Scott, W. R. (1995). *Institutions and organizations.* London: Sage Publications.

Scupola, A. (2002). *Adoption Issues of Business-to-Business Internet Commerce in European SMEs.* Paper presented at the 35th Hawaii International Conference on System Sciences, Hawaii, USA.

Segars, A. H., & Hendrickson, A. R. (2000). Value, knowledge, and the human equation: Evolution of the information technology function in modern organizations. *Journal of Labor Research, 21*(3), 431-445.

Segev, E., Ahituv, N., & Barzilai-Nahon, K. (2007). Mapping Diversities and Tracing Trends of Cultural Homogeneity/Heterogeneity in Cyberspace. *Journal of Computer-Mediated Communication, 12*(4), 1269–1297. doi:10.1111/j.1083-6101.2007.00373.x

Seltzer, L. (2005). Rootkits: The Ultimate Stealth Attack. *PC Magazine, 24*, 76.

SETEL. (1999). Pathways to Electronic Commerce: Getting Australian Small Business Online. Retrieved September 4, 2003, from http://www.smallbusiness.org.au/sbc/pathways/

Sethi, V., & King, W. R. (1991). Construct measurement in Information systems research, An illustration in strategic systems. *Decision Sciences, 22*(3), 455–472. doi:10.1111/j.1540-5915.1991.tb01274.x

Sexton, D. L., & Bowman, N. B. (1984). *The Effects of Pre-Existing Psychological Characteristics on New Venture Initiations.* Paper presented at the annual meeting of the Academy of Management, Boston.

Shackleton, V. J., & Ali, A. H. (1990). Work-related values of managers: A test of the Hofstede model. *Journal of Cross-Cultural Psychology 21*(1), 109-118.

Shah, A. C., Sterrett, J. C., & Wilmore, J. (2001). Meeting the need for employee development in the 21st century. *Advanced Management Journal, 66*(2), 22-28.

Sharda, R., Barr, S. H., & McDonnell, J. C. (1988). Decision support system effectiveness: A review and an empirical test. *Management Science, 34*(2), 139-157.

Sheh, S. W. (2001). Chinese cultural values and their implication to Chinese management. *Singapore Management Review, 23*(2), 75-83.

Shen, C. Y., & Ge, J. (2005, June 12-14). Women and ICT: from the Chinese perspective. In *Proceedings of the International Symposium on Women and ICT: Creating Global Transformation,* Baltimore, MD. New York: ACM Press.

Shen, Q., & Jensen, R. (2004). Selecting informative features with fuzzy-rough sets and its application for complex systems monitoring. *Pattern Recognition, 37*, 1351-1363.

Shenkar, O., & Glinow, M. A. v. (1994). Paradoxes of organizational theory and research: Using the case of China to illustrate national contingency. *Management Science, 40*(1), 56–71. doi:10.1287/mnsc.40.1.56

Sher, P. J., & Lee, V. C. (2004). Information technology as a facilitator for enhancing dynamic capabilities through knowledge management. *Information and Management, 41*, 933-945.

Sheu, C., Yen, H. R., & Krumwiede, D. W. (2003). The effects of national differences on multinational ERP implementation: an exploratory study. *TQM and Business Excellence, 14*(6), 641-657.

Shih, D. H., Sun, P. L., & Chiu, Y. W. (2004, October). Barriers to radio frequency identifier. In *Proceedings of the 1st Conference of Service Management and Innovation,* Taiwan.

Shih, E., Kraemer, K. L., & Dedrick, J. (2008). IT diffusion in developing countries. *Communications of the ACM, 51*(2), 43–48. doi:10.1145/1314215.1340913

Shiva, V. (1989). *Staying Alive: Women, Development, and Ecology in India.* London: Zed Press.

Shore, B. (2006). Enterprise integration across the globally distributed service organization. *Communications of the ACM, 49*(6), 102-106.

Short, J., Williams, E., & Christie, B. (1976). *The Social Psychology of Telecommunication.* London, England: John Wiley and Sons.

Shrivastava, P. (1983). A typology of organizational learning systems. *Journal of Management Studies, 20*(1), 7-28.

Shyu, J. Z., & Chiu, Y.-C. (2002). Innovation policy for developing Taiwan's competitive advantages. *R&D Management, 32*(4), 369-374.

Shyur, H. J., & Shih, H. S. (2006). A hybrid MCDM model for strategic vendor selection. *Mathematical and Computer Modeling, 44*(7-8), 749-761.

Siddiqui, H. N. *(2008).* Investigation of intention to use e-commerce in the Arab countries: A comparison of self-efficacy, usefulness, culture, gender, and socioeconomic status in Saudi Arabia and the United Arab Emirates. *Doctoral Thesis.*

Silin, R. (1976). *Leadership and values.* Cambridge, MA: Harvard University Press.

Silvestro, R., & Westley, C. (2002. Challenging the paradigm of the process enterprise: a case study analysis of BPR implementation. *Omega, 30*(3), 215-225.

Sinclair, J. (1992). *Collins Co-build English language dictionary.* London: Collins.

Singh, N., Kumar, V., & Baack, D. (2004). Adaptation of cultural content: evidence from B2C e-commerce firms. *European Journal of Marketing, 39*(1/2), 71–86. doi:10.1108/03090560510572025

Siponen, M. T. (2000). A Conceptual Foundation for Organizational Information Security Awareness. *Information Management & Computer Security, 8*(1), 31–41. doi:10.1108/09685220010371394

Sitkin, S. B., & Roth, N. L. (1993). Explaining the limited effectiveness of legalistic "remedies" for trust/distrust. *Organization Science, 4*(3), 367–392. doi:10.1287/orsc.4.3.367

Siu, W., Fang, W., & Lin, T. (2004). Strategic marketing practices and the performance of Chinese small and medium-sized enterprises Taiwan. *Entrepreneurship and Regional Development, 16*(2), 161–178. doi:10.1080/08985620410001677862

Smith, H. A., & Konsynski, B. (2003). Developments in practice X: radio frequency identification (RFID)—an Internet for physical objects. *Communications of the Association for Information Systems, 12*, 301-311.

Smith, H. A., & McKeen, J. D. (2002). *Instilling a knowledge-sharing culture* (Vol. Learning and Capabilities). Paper presented at the Proceedings of the Third European Conference on Organizational Knowledge, ALBA: Athens, Greece.

Sondergaard, M. (1990). Hofstede's consequences: A study of reviews, citations and replications. *Organization Studies 15*(3), 447-456.

Song, M., Nason, R. W., & Di Benedetto, C. A. (2008). Distinctive marketing and information technology capabilities and strategic types: A cross-national investigation. *Journal of International Marketing, 16*(1), 4–38. doi:10.1509/jimk.16.1.4

Souren, P., Priya, S., Imad, S., & Mykytyn, P. P. (2004). Impact of heterogeneity and collaborative conflict management style on the performance of synchronous global virtual teams. *Information & Management, 41*(3), 303–321. doi:10.1016/S0378-7206(03)00076-4

Southon, F. C. G., Todd, R. J., & Seneque, M. (2002). Knowledge management in three organizations: An exploratory study. *Journal of the American Society for Information Science and Technology, 53*(12), 1047–1059. doi:10.1002/asi.10112

Spector, P. E., Cooper, C. L., & Sparks, K. (2001). An international study of the psychometric properties of the Hofstede values survey module 1994: A comparison of individual and country/province level results. *Applied Psychology, 50*(2), 269-281.

Spencer, R. A. (1985). Information Architecture. *Journal of Systems Management, 36*(11), 34–42.

Spielberger, C. D., Gorsuch, R. L., & Lushene, R. E. (1970). *Manual for the State-Trait Anxiety Inventory.* Palo Alto, CA: Consulting Psychologists Press.

Sridhar, V., Nath, D., & Malik, A. (in press). Analysis of user involvement and participation on the quality of IS planning projects: An exploratory study. *Journal of Organizational and End User Computing.*

Srite, M. (2000). The Influence of National Culture on the Acceptance and Use of Information Technologies: An Empirical Study. Information and Management Sciences. Tallahassee, FL, Florida State University.

Srite, M., & Karahanna, E. (2006). The role of espoused national cultural values in technology acceptance. *MIS Quarterly, 30*(3), 679-704.

Srite, M., & Karahanna, E. (2006). The Role of Espoused National Cultural Values in Technology Acceptance. *MIS Quarterly, 30*(3), 1–26.

Srivastava, A., & Bartol, K. M. (2006). Empowering leadership in management teams: Effects on knowledge sharing, efficacy, and performance. *Academy of Management Journal*, *49*(6), 1239–1251.

Stafford, T. F. (2005). Spyware. *Communications of the ACM*, *48*(8), 34–35. doi:10.1145/1076211.1076235

Standbridge, J., & Autrey, R. (2001). Rapid skill obsolescence in an IT company: A case study of Acxiom corporation. *Journal of Organizational Excellence, 20*(3), 3-9.

Staples, S. D., & Zhao, L. (2006). The effects of cultural diversity in virtual teams versus face-to-face teams. *Group Decision and Negotiation*, *15*, 389–406. doi:10.1007/s10726-006-9042-x

Statistics New Zealand. (2001). Information Technology Use in New Zealand: 2001. Retrieved Oct. 26, 2003

Statistics New Zealand. (2003). National Asian Population Projections (2001(base) - 2021) - Media Release. Retrieved July 10, 2004, from http://www.stats.govt.nz/domino/external/pasfull/pasfull.nsf/web/Media+Release+National+Asian+Population+Projections+2001(base)+-+2021?open

Steenkamp, J., Hofstede, F., & Wedel, M. (1999). A Cross-National Investigation into the Individual and National Cultural Antecedents of Consumer Innovativeness. *Journal of Marketing*, *63*(2), 55–69. doi:10.2307/1251945

Steers, R., & Mowday, R. (1981). Employee turnover and post decision accommodation processes. *Research in Organizational Behavior, 3,* 235-281.

Steinbart, P. J., & Nath, R. (1992). Problems and issues in the management of international data communications networks: the experiences of American companies. *MIS Quarterly*, *16*(1), 55-76.

Steiner, I. D. (1972). *Group Processes and Productivity*. New York: Academic Press.

Stets, J. E., & Burke, P. J. (2000). Feminity/Masculinity. In E. F. Borgatta & R. J. V. Montgomery (Eds.), *Encyclopedia of Sociology* (pp. 997-1005). New York: MacMillan.

Stevenson, W., & McGrath, E. W. (2004). Differences between on-site and off-site teams: Manager perceptions. *Team Performance Management, 10*(5/6), 127-132.

Stopford, J., & Wells, L. (1972). *Managing the multinational enterprise*. New York: Basic Books.

Stowers, G. N. L. (1995). Getting Left Behind? Gender Differences in Computer Conferencing. *Public productivity and management review, 19*(2), 143-195.

Strassmann, P.A. (1997, September 15) Computers have yet to make companies more productive. *ComputerWorld.*

Stratopoulos, T., & Dehning, B. (2000). Does successful investment in information technology solve the productivity paradox? *Information & Management*, *38*(2), 103–117. doi:10.1016/S0378-7206(00)00058-6

Straub, D. (1989). Validating instruments in MIS research. *MIS Quarterly*, *13*(2), 147–169. doi:10.2307/248922

Straub, D. W. (1994). The effect of culture on IT diffusion: e-mail and fax in Japan and the U.S. *Information Systems Research*, *5*(1), 23-47.

Straub, D. W., & Welke, R. J. (1998). Coping With Systems Risk: Security Planning Models for Management Decision Making. *MIS Quarterly*, *22*(4), 441–469. doi:10.2307/249551

Straub, D. W., Limayen, M., & Karahanna-Evaristo, E. (1995). Measuring System Usage: Implications for Is Theory Testing. *Management Science*, *41*(8), 1328–1342. doi:10.1287/mnsc.41.8.1328

Straub, D., Hoffman, D., Weber, B., & Steinfield, C. (2002). Toward new metrics for net-enhanced organizations. *Information Systems Research*, *13*(3), 227–238. doi:10.1287/isre.13.3.227.80

Straub, D., Keil, M., & Brenner, W. (1997). Testing the technology acceptance model across cultures: a three country study. *Information and Management*, *33*, 1-11.

Straub, D., Loch, K., Evaristo, R., Karahanna, E., & Srite, M. (2002). Toward a Theory-Based Measurement of Culture. *Journal of Global Information Management*, *10*(1), 13–23.

Subramaniam, M., & Youndt, M. A. (2005). The influence of intellectual capital on the types of innovative capabilities. *Academy of Management Journal*, *48*(3), 450-463.

Sullivan, C. H., Jr. (1982). Rethinking computer systems architecture. *Computerworld extra,* XVI, 5-10.

Sullivan, D. (1992/3).Organization in American MNCs: The perspective of the European regional headquarters. *Management International Review*, *32*(3), 237-250.

Swanson, E. B. (1994). Information systems innovation among organizations. *Management Science*, *40*(9), 1069–1092. doi:10.1287/mnsc.40.9.1069

Swap, W., Leonard, D., Shields, M., & Abrams, L. (2001). Using mentoring and storytelling to transfer knowledge in the workplace. *Journal of Management Information Systems, 18*(1), 95-114.

Swedberg, C. (2006, September 12). Wal-Mart's on track to hit target. *RFID Journal.* Retrieved September 30, 2006, from http://www.rfidjournal.com/article/articleview/2649/

Szajna, B. (1994). Software Evaluation and Choice: Predictive Validation of the Technology Acceptance Instrument. *MIS Quarterly*, *18*(3), 319–325. doi:10.2307/249621

Szajna, B. (1996). Empirical Evaluation of the Revised Technology Acceptance Model. *Management Science*, *42*(1), 85–92. doi:10.1287/mnsc.42.1.85

Szulanski, G. (1996). Exploring internal stickiness: Impediments to the transfer of best practice within the firm. *Strategic Management Journal*, *17*, 27-43.

Taggart, J. H. (1997). An evaluation of the integration-responsiveness framework: MNC manufacturing subsidiaries in the UK. *Management International Review*, *37*(4), 295-318.

Taipei Rapid Transit Corporation Annual Report. (2003). *Corporate overviews.* Retrieved September 30, 2004, from http://www.trtc.com.tw/img/all/A61/report2002-2003.pdf

Taiwan Investment Biweekly. (2005). *U Taiwan: RFID called second IT revolution.* Retrieved October 15, 2006, from http://investintaiwan.nat.gov.tw/en/news/200504/2005042902.html

Tan, B. C. Y., Wei, K. K., Watson, R. T., & Walczuch, R. M. (1998). Reducing status effects with computer-mediated communication: Evidence from two distinct national cultures. Journal *of Management Information Systems, 15*(1), 119-141.

Tan, B. C. Y., Wei, K. K., Watson, R. T., Clapper, D. L., & McLean, E. R. (1998). Computer-mediated communication and majority influence: Assessing the impact in an individualistic and a collectivistic culture. *Management Science, 44*(9), 1263-1278.

Tan, B. C. Y., Wei, K.-K., Watson, R. T., & Walczuch, R. M. (1998). Reducing Status Effects with Computer-Mediated Communication: Evidence from Two Distinct National Cultures. *Journal of Management Information Systems*, *15*(1), 119–142.

Tan, B. C. Y., Wei, K.-K., Watson, R. T., Clapper, D. L., & McLean, E. R. (1998). Computer-Mediated Communication and Majority Influence: Assessing the Impact in an Individualistic and a Collectivistic Culture. *Management Science*, *44*(9), 1263–1278. doi:10.1287/mnsc.44.9.1263

Tan, B., Wei, K. K., Huang, W., & Ng, G. N. (2000). A dialogue technical to enhance electronic communication in virtual teams. *IEEE Transactions on Professional Communication*, *43*(2), 153-165.

Tan, F. B., & Hunter, M. G. (2003, January 6-9). Using narrative inquiry in a study of information systems professionals. In *Proceedings of the 36th Hawaii International Conference on Systems Sciences (Hicss-36).*

Tan, F. B., & Sutherland, P. (2004). Online consumer trust: A multi-dimensional model. *Journal of Electronic Commerce in Organizations*, *2*(3), 40-58.

Tan, H. H., & Chee, D. (2005). Understanding interpersonal trust in a Confucian-influenced society: An exploratory study. *International Journal of Cross Cultural Management*, *5*(2), 197–212. doi:10.1177/1470595805054493

Tan, Z., & Ouyang, W. (2004). Diffusion and impacts of the Internet and e-commerce in China. *Electronic Markets*, *14*(1), 25–35. doi:10.1080/1019678042000175270

Tang, P., Powell, D., Worlock, K., & Bingham, J. (2000). *The impact of electronic commerce on the competitiveness of SMEs in the EU*: The STOA Programme.

Tanriverdi, H. (2005). Information technology relatedness, knowledge management capability, and performance of multibusiness firms. *MIS Quarterly, 29*(2), 311-334.

Tayeb, M. (1994). Organizations and National Culture: Methodology Considered. *Organization Studies, 15*(3), 429–446. doi:10.1177/017084069401500306

Taylor, M. S., Locke, E. A., Lee, C., & Gist, M. E. (1984). Type a Behavior and Faculty Research Productivity: What Are the Mechanisms. *Organizational Behavior and Human Decision Processes, 34*(3), 402–418.

Taylor, S., & Todd, R. A. (1995). Understanding information technology usage: A test of competing models. *Information Systems Research, 6*(2), 144-176.

Taylor, S., Beechler, S., & Napier, N. (1996). Toward an integrative model of strategic international human resource management. *Academy of Management Review, 21*(4), 959-985.

Teague, J. (2002). Women in computing: What brings them to it, what keeps them in it? *SIGCSE Bulletin, 34*(2), 147–158. doi:10.1145/543812.543849

TechWeb. (2005). Retrieved October 29, 2005 from http://www.techweb.com/encyclopedia/

Teece, D. J. (1998). Capturing value from knowledge assets: the new economy, markets for know-how, and intangible assets. *California Management Review, 40*(3), 55-79.

Teece, D. J., & Pisano, G. (1994). The dynamic capabilities of firms: an introduction. *Industrial and Corporate Change, 3*, 537-556.

Teece, D. J., Pisano, G., & Shuen, A. (1997). Dynamic capabilities and strategic management. *Strategic Management Journal, 18*, 509-533.

Tellegen, A. (1985). Structures of Mood and Personality and Their Relevance to Assessing Anxiety with an Emphasis on Self-Report. In A. H. Tuma & J. D. Maser (Eds.), *Anxiety and Anxiety Disorders* (pp. 681-706). Hillsdale, N.J.: Erlbaum.

Teo, H. H., Wei, K. K., & Benbasat, I. (2003). Predicting intention to adopt interorganizational linkages: An institutional perspective. *MIS Quarterly, 27*(1), 19–49.

Teo, T. S. H. & Tan, M. (1997-1998). A contingency model of Internet adoption in Singapore. *International Journal of Electronic Commerce, 2*(2), 95-118.

Teo, T. S. H., & King, W. R. (1997). An assessment of perceptual differences between informants in information systems research. *Omega, 25*(5), 557–566. doi:10.1016/S0305-0483(97)00031-5

Teo, T. S. H., & King, W. R. (1997). Integration between business planning and information systems planning: An evolutionary-contingency perspective. *Journal of Management Information Systems, 14*(1), 185-214.

Tesluk, P. E., & Mathieu, J. E. (1999). Overcoming roadblocks to effectiveness: Incorporating management of performance barriers into models of work group effectiveness. *Journal of Applied Psychology, 84*(2), 200-217.

Tett, R., & Meyer, J. P. (1993). Job satisfaction, organizational commitment, turnover intention, and turnover: Path analyses based on meta-analysis findings. *Personnel Psychology, 46*(2), 259-280.

Tezuka, S., & Niwa, K. (2004). knowledge sharing in inter-organizational intelligence: R&D-based venture alliance community cases in Japan. *International Journal of Technology Management, 28*(7/8), 714–728. doi:10.1504/IJTM.2004.005779

Thatcher, J., & Perrewe, P. L. (2002). An Empirical Examination of Individual Traits as Antecedents to Computer Anxiety and Computer Self-Efficacy. *MIS Quarterly, 26*(4), 381–396. doi:10.2307/4132314

Thatcher, S. M. B., & Foster, W. (2003). *B2B e-commerce adoption decisions in Taiwan: The interaction of organizational, industrial, governmental and cultural factors.* Paper presented at the Proceedings of the 36th Annual Hawaii International Conference on System Sciences (HICSS'03)

Thatcher, S. M. B., Foster, W., & Zhu, L. (2006). B2B e-commerce adoption decisions in Taiwan: The interaction of cultural and other institutional factors. *Electronic Commerce Research and Applications, 5*(2), 92–104. doi:10.1016/j.elerap.2005.10.005

The Whole-View Scanning of the Electronic Information Industries in China. (1998, August 10, 1998). *People's Daily.*

Theron. (2004). *Voluntary turnover: A study of IS professionals.* B. Comp. Honours Thesis, National University of Singapore.

Thompson, C. J. (1997). Interpreting consumers: A hermeneutical framework for deriving marketing insights from the texts of consumers' consumption stories. *Journal of Marketing Research, 34,* 438-455.

Thompson, J. D. (1967). *Organization in action.* NY: McGraw Hill.

Thong, J. Y. L. (1999). An integrated model of information systems adoption in small businesses. *Journal of Management Information Systems, 15*(4), 187.

Tihanyi, L., Griffith, D. A., & Russell, C. J. (2005). The effect of cultural distance on entry mode choice, international diversification, and MNE performance: a meta-analysis. *Journal of International Business Studies, 36*(3), 270-283.

Ting-Toomey, S. (1994). Managing intimate conflict in intercultural personal relationships. In D. D. Cahn (Ed.), *Intimate conflict in personal relationships.* Hillsdale, NJ: Erlbaum.

Tippins, M. J., & Sohi, R. S. (2003). IT competency and firm performance: Is organizational learning a missing link? *Strategic Management Journal, 24*(8), 745–761. doi:10.1002/smj.337

To, M. L., & Ngai, E. W. T. (2006). Predicting the organisational adoption of B2C e-commerce: an empirical study. *Industrial Management & Data Systems, 106*(8), 1133–1147. doi:10.1108/02635570610710791

Tom, S. (2003). *Understanding RFID: A practical guide for supply chain professionals.* Retrieved September 10, 2004, http://www.tompkinsinc.com, 6-7.

Torgerson, W. S. (1967). *Theory and methods of scaling.* New York: Wiley.

Tornatzky, L. G., & Fleischer, M. (1990). *The processes of technological innovation.* Lexington, MA: Lexington Books.

Tornatzky, L.G., & Klein, R. J. (1982). Innovation characteristics & innovation adoption-implementation: a meta-analysis of findings. *IEEE Transactions on Engineering Management, 29,* 28-45.

Townsend, A., DeMarie, A. M., & Hendrickson, A. R. (1998). Virtual teams: Technology and the workplace of the future. *Academy of Management Executive, 12*(3), 17-29.

Tractinsky, N., & Jarvenpaa, S. L. (1995). Information systems design decisions in a global versus domestic context. *MIS Quarterly, 19*(4), 507-529.

Trauth, E. M. (1995). Women in Ireland's information industry: Voices from inside. *Eire-Ireland, 30*(3), 133–150.

Trauth, E. M. (1999). Leapfrogging an IT labor force: Multinational and indigenous perspectives. *Journal of Global Information Management, 7*(2), 22–32.

Trauth, E. M. (2000). *The culture of an information economy: Influences and impacts in the Republic of Ireland.* Dordrecht, The Netherlands: Kluwer Academic Publishers.

Trauth, E. M. (2001). Mapping information-sector work to the workforce: The lessons from Ireland. *Communications of the ACM. Special Issue on The Global IT Workforce, 44*(7), 74–75.

Trauth, E. M. (2002). Odd girl out: An individual differences perspective on women in the IT profession. *Information Technology & People, 15*(2), 98–118. doi:10.1108/09593840210430552

Trauth, E. M. (2006). Theorizing gender and information technology research. In E.M. Trauth (Ed.), *Encyclopedia of gender and information technology* (pp. 1154-1159). Hershey, PA: Idea Group Publishing.

Trauth, E. M., & Howcroft, D. (2006). Critical empirical research in IS: An example of gender and IT. *Information Technology & People, 9*(3), 272–292. doi:10.1108/09593840610689859

Trauth, E. M., & Quesenberry, J. (2006). Are women an underserved community in the information technology profession? In *Proceedings of the International Conference on Information Systems, Milwaukee, Wisconsin, December.*

Trauth, E. M., & Quesenberry, J. L. (2005, June, 23-24). Individual inequality: Women's responses in the IT profession. In G. Whitehouse (Ed.), *Proceedings of the Women, Work and IT Forum, Brisbane, Queensland, Australia.*

Trauth, E. M., & Quesenberry, J. L. (2007). Gender and the information technology workforce: issues of theory and practice. In P. Yoong & S. Huff (Eds.), *Managing IT professionals in the Internet age* (pp. 18-36). Hershey, PA: Idea Group Publishing.

Trauth, E. M., Huang, H., Morgan, A. J., Quesenberry, J. L., & Yeo, B. (2006a). Investigating the existence and value of diversity in the global IT workforce: An analytical framework. In F. Niederman & T. Ferratt (Eds.), *Managing information technology human resources* (pp. 331-360). Hershey, PA: Information Science Reference.

Trauth, E. M., Nielsen, S. H., & von Hellens, L. A. (2003). Explaining the IT gender gap: Australian stories for the new millennium. *Journal of Research and Practice in IT, 35*(1), 7–20.

Trauth, E. M., Quesenberry, J. L., & Morgan, A. J. (2004). Understanding the under representation of women in IT: Toward a theory of individual differences. In M. Tanniru, & S. Weisband (Eds.), *Proceedings of the 2004 ACM SIGMIS Conference on Computer Personal Research, Tucson, Arizona, USA* (pp. 114-119). New York: ACM Press.

Trauth, E. M., Quesenberry, J. L., & Yeo, B. (2005). The influence of environmental context on women in the IT workforce. In *Proceedings of the ACM SIGMIS Computer Personnel Research Conference, Atlanta, Georgia, April* (pp. 24-31).

Trauth, E. M., Quesenberry, J. L., & Yeo, B. (2008). Environmental Influences on Gender in the IT Workforce. *The Data Base for Advances in Information Systems, 39*(1), 8–32.

Trauth, E. M., Quesenberry, J., & Huang, H. (2006b, April 13-15). Cross-cultural influences on women in the IT workforce. In *Proceedings of the 2006 ACM SIGMIS CPR Conference, Claremont, California, USA* (pp. 12-19). New York: ACM Press.

Trauth, E. M., Quesenberry, J., & Huang, H. (2008a). A multicultural analysis of factors influencing career choice for women in the information technology workforce. *Journal of Global Information Management, 16*(4), 1–23.

Trauth, E. M., Quesenberry, J., & Yeo, B. (2008b). Environmental influences on gender in the IT workforce. *The Data Base for Advances in Information Systems, 39*(1), 8–32.

Trevor, C. O. (2001). Interactive effects among actual case of movement determinants and job satisfaction in the prediction of voluntary turnover. *Academy of Management Journal, 44,* 621-638.

Triandis, H. (1972). *An Analysis of Subjective Culture.* New York: John Wiley & Sons.

Triandis, H. C. (1989). The self and social behavior in differing culture contexts. *Psychological Review, 96*(3), 506-520.

Triandis, H. C. (1995). *Individualism and collectivism.* Boulder, CO: Westview.

Triandis, H. C., Hall, E. R., & Ewen, R. B. (1965). Member homogeneity and dyadic creativity. *Human Relations, 18,* 33–54. doi:10.1177/001872676501800104

Triandis, H. C., McCusker, C., & Hui, C. H. (1990). Multimedia probes of individualism and collectivism. *Journal of Personality and Social Psychology, 59*(5), 1006-1020.

Trompenaars, F., & Hampden-Turner, C. (1998). *Riding the waves of culture: Understanding cultural diversity in global business* (2nd ed.). New York: McGraw-Hill.

Tsai, K., & Wang, J. (2004). The innovation policy and performance of innovation in Taiwan's technology-intensive industries. *Problems and Perspectives in Management, 1,* 62-75.

Tsao, H. Y., Lin, K. H. C., & Lin, C. (2004). An investigation of critical success factors in the adoption of B2BEC by Taiwanese companies. *Journal of American Academy of Business, Cambridge.*

Tsoukas, H., & Vladimirou, E. (2001). What is organizational Knowledge? *Journal of Management Studies, 38*(7), 973-993.

Tucker, L. R., & Lewis, C. (1973). A reliability coefficient for maximum likelihood factor analysis. *Psychometrika*, *38*(1), 1–10. doi:10.1007/BF02291170

Tulving, E. (1972). *Organization of memory.* New York: Academic Press.

Tung, L. L., & Quaddus, M. A. (2002). Cultural differences explaining the differences in results in GSS: Implications for the next decade. *Decision Support Systems*, *33*, 177–199. doi:10.1016/S0167-9236(01)00143-9

Tung, R. (1995). Strategic human resource challenge: Managing diversity. *International Journal of Human Resource Management*, *6*(3), 482–494.

Tunzelana, S., & Technikon, C. (2003). *Obstacles for e-business implementation for SMEs.* South Africa. UK online for busienss. (2003). what is UK online for business. Retrieved Oct.12, 2003, from http://www.ukonlineforbusiness.gov.uk/cms/template/popup-content2.jsp?id=310478

Turban, E., Leidner, D., McLean, E., & Wetherbe, J. (2006). *Information Technology For Management* (5th Ed.). NJ: John Wiley & Sons.

Turner, J. C. (1987). *Rediscovering the Social Group: A Self-Categorization Theory.* Oxford, UK: B. Blackwell.

Ulrich, D. (1998). Intellectual capital = competence x commitment. *Sloan Management Review*, *39*(2), 15-26.

USHER. (2003). The current and future barriers to SMe-volution. Retrieved September,18, 2003, from http://www.usherproject.org.uk/support/scenarios/barriers.pdf

Usunier, J. C. (1998). *International and Cross-Cultural Management Research.* Thousand Oaks, CA: SAGE Publications.

Uzzi, B. (1997). Social structure and competition in interfirm networks: The paradox of embeddedness. *Administrative Science Quarterly*, *42*(1), 35–67. doi:10.2307/2393808

Valacich, J., Wheeler, B., Mennecke, B., & Wachter, R. (1995). The effects of numerical and logical size on computer-mediated idea generation. *Organizational Behavior and Human Decision Processes*, *62*(3), 318–329. doi:10.1006/obhd.1995.1053

Van de Vijver, F., & Leung, K. (1997). *Methods and data analysis for cross-cultural research.* Thousand Oaks, CA: Sage.

Varma, R. (2007). Changing borders and realities: Emigration of Indian scientists and engineers to the United States. *Perspectives on Global Development and Technology*, *6*(4), 1–18. doi:10.1163/156914907X253224

Varma, R., Prasad, A., & Kapur, D. (2006). Confronting 'socialization' barrier: Cross-ethnic differences in undergraduate women's preference for IT education. In J. McGrath Cohoon & W. Aspray (Eds.) *Women and information technology: research on underrepresentation* (pp. 301-323). Cambridge, MA: MIT Press.

Venaik, S., Midgley, D., & Devinney, T. (2004). A new perspective on the integration-responsiveness pressures confronting multinational firms. *Management International Review*, *44*(1), 15-48.

Vendelo, M. T. (1998). Narrating corporate reputation: Becoming legitimate through storytelling. *International Journal of Management and Organization, 28*(3), 120-137.

Venkatesh, V. (2000). Determinants of Perceived Ease of Use: Integrating Control, Intrinsic Motivation, and Emotion into the Technology Acceptance Model. *Information Systems Research*, *11*(4), 342–365. doi:10.1287/isre.11.4.342.11872

Venkatesh, V., & Davis, F. D. (1996). A Model of the Antecedents of Perceived Ease of Use: Development and Test. *Decision Sciences*, *27*(3), 451–482. doi:10.1111/j.1540-5915.1996.tb01822.x

Venkatesh, V., & Davis, F. D. (2000). A theoretical extension of the technology acceptance model: four longitudinal field studies. *Management Science*, *46*(2), 186-204.

Venkatesh, V., & Morris, M. G. (2000). Why Don't Men Ever Stop and Ask for Directions? Gender, Social Influence, and Their Role in Technology Acceptance Usage Behavior. *MIS Quarterly*, *24*(1), 115–140. doi:10.2307/3250981

Venkatesh, V., & Ramesh, V. (2006). Web and wireless site usability: Understanding differences and modeling use. *MIS Quarterly*, *30*(1), 181-2006.

Venkatesh, V., Morris, M. G., Davis, G. B., & Davis, F. D. (2003). User Acceptance of Information Technology: Towards a Unified View. *MIS Quarterly, 27*(3), 425–478.

Venkatraman, N. (1989). Strategic orientation of business enterprises: The construct, dimensionality, and measurement. *Management Science, 35*(8), 942–962. doi:10.1287/mnsc.35.8.942

Venkatraman, N. (1991). *IT-related business reconfiguration*. New York: Oxford University Press.

Verhoef, C. (2005). Quantitative aspects of outsourcing deals. *Science of computer programming, 56*(3), 275-313.

Vestring, T., Rouse, T., & Reinert, U. (2005). Hedge your offshoring bets. *MIT Sloan Management Review, Spring*, 27-29.

Vick, R. M. (1998). Perspectives on and problems with computer-mediated teamwork: current groupware issues and assumptions. *Journal of Computer Documentation, 22*(2), 3–22. doi:10.1145/291391.291392

Voelpel, S. C., & Han, Z. (2005). Managing knowledge sharing in China: The case of Siemens sharenet. *Journal of Knowledge Management, 9*(3), 51–63. doi:10.1108/13673270510602764

Vogel, D. R., Martz, W. B., Nunamaker, J. F., Grohowski, R. B., & McGoff, C. (1990). Electronic meeting system experience at IBM. *Journal of Management Information Systems, 6*(3), 25-43.

Vogel, D., Davison, R., & Shroff, R. (2001). Sociocultural learning: A perspective on GSS-enabled global education. *Communications of AIS, 7*(9), 1–41.

Vogel, D., Van Genuchten, M., Lou, D., Verveen, S., Van Eekout, M., & Adams, A. (2001). Exploratory research on the role of national and professional cultures in a distributed learning project. *IEEE Transactions on Professional Communication, 44*(2), 114–125. doi:10.1109/47.925514

Voich, D. (1995). *Comparative Empirical Analysis of Cultural Values and Perceptions of Political Economy Issues*. Westport, CT: Praeger.

Voordijk, H., & Stegee, R. (2005). ERP and the changing role of IT in engineering consultancy firms. *Business Process Management Journal, 11*(4), 418-430.

Wade, M., & Hulland, J. (2004). Review: The resource-based view and information systems research: Review, extension, and suggestions for future research. *MIS Quarterly, 28*(1), 107–143.

Wagner, J. A., III. (1995). Studies of individualism-collectivism: Effects on cooperation in groups. *Academy of Management Journal, 38*(1), 152-172.

Walder, A. G. (1995). China's transitional economy: Interpreting its significance. *The China Quarterly, 144*, 963–979. doi:10.1017/S0305741000004689

Walenta, T. (2004). Managing Cross-Cultural Issues in Global Software Outsourcing. *Communications of the ACM, 47*(4), 62–66. doi:10.1145/975817.975818

Wallace, W. A., & DeBalogh, F. (1985). Decision support systems for disaster management. *Public Administration Review, 45*, 134-146.

Walther, J. (1995). Relational aspects of computer-mediated communication: Experimental observations over time. *Organization Science, 6*(2), 186-203.

Walther, J. B. (1997). Group and interpersonal effects in international computer-mediated collaboration. *Human Communication Research, 23*(3), 342–369. doi:10.1111/j.1468-2958.1997.tb00400.x

Wang, C., Xu, L., Liu, X., & Qins, X. (2005). ERP research, development and implementation in China: an overview. *International Journal of Production Research, 43*(18), 3915–3932. doi:10.1080/13629390500124556

Wang, E., Klein, G., & Jiang, J. (2006). ERP misfit: Country of origin and organizational factors. *Journal of Management Information Systems, 23*(1), 263-292.

Wang, J., & Guan, J. (2005). The analysis and evaluation of knowledge efficiency in research groups. *Journal of the American Society for Information Science and Technology, 56*(11), 1217–1226. doi:10.1002/asi.20225

Wang, Li., & Alam, P. (2007). Information technology capability: firm valuation, earnings uncertainty, and forecast accuracy. *Journal of Information Systems, 21*(2), 27–48. doi:10.2308/jis.2007.21.2.27

Wang, P. (1993). Information systems solutions for trans-border data flow problems for multinational companies. *International Journal of Information Management*, *13*(1), 29-41.

Wang, Y., & Yao, Y. (2002). Market reforms, technological capabilities and the performance of small enterprises in China. *Small Business Economics*, *18*(2), 197–211.

Warkentin, M., Luo, X., & Templeton, G. F. (2005). A Framework for Spyware Assessment. *Communications of the ACM*, *48*(8), 79–84. doi:10.1145/1076211.1076244

Watson, R. T. (1987). *A study of group decision support system use in three and four person groups for a preference allocation decision.* Unpublished doctoral dissertation, University of Minnesota, Minneapolis, MN.

Watson, R. T., DeSanctis, G., & Poole, M. S. (1988). Using a GDSS to facilitate group consensus: some intended and unintended consequences. *MIS Quarterly*, *12*(3), 463-478.

Watson, R., Ho, T., & Raman, K. (1994). Culture: A fourth dimension of group support systems. *Communications of the ACM*, *37*(10), 44–55. doi:10.1145/194313.194320

Webster, J., & Martocchio, J. J. (1992). Microcomputer Playfulness: Development of a Measure with Workplace Implications. *MIS Quarterly*, *16*(2), 201–266. doi:10.2307/249576

Webster, J., & Martocchio, J. J. (1993). Turning Work into Play: Implications for Microcomputer Software Training. *Journal of Management*, *19*(1), 127–146. doi:10.1177/014920639301900109

Weil, M. M., & Rosen, L. D. (1995). The psychological impact of technology from a global perspective: A study of technological sophistication and technophobia in university students from twenty-three countries. *Computers in Human Behavior*, *11*(1), 95–133. doi:10.1016/0747-5632(94)00026-E

Weill, P., Broadbent, M., & Butler, C. (1996). Exploring how firms view IT infrastructure. Working Paper.

Weir, D., & Hutchings, K. (2005). Culture embeddedness and contextual constraints: Knowledge sharing in Chinese and Arab cultures. *Knowledge and Process Management*, *12*(2), 89–98. doi:10.1002/kpm.222

Weisaeth, L., Knudsen, O., & Tonnessen, A. (2002). Technological disasters, crisis management and leadership stress. *Journal of Hazardous Materials*, *93*, 33-45.

Wenger, E. C., & Snyder, W. M. (2000). Communities of practice: The organizational frontier. *Harvard Business Review*, *78*(1), 139-145.

Werb, J., & Sereiko, P. (2002). More than just tracking. *Frontline Solutions*, *3*(11), 42.

Westwood, R. (1997). Harmony and patriarchy: The cultural basis for 'paternalistic headship' among the overseas Chinese. *Organization Studies*, *18*(3), 445–480. doi:10.1177/017084069701800305

Whitman, M. E. (2003). Enemy at the Gate: Threat to Information Security. *Communications of the ACM*, *46*(8), 91–95. doi:10.1145/859670.859675

Widen-Wulff, G., & Ginman, M. (2004). Explaining knowledge sharing in organizations through the dimensions of social capital. *Journal of Information Science*, *30*(5), 448-458.

Wilkenfeld, J., Kraus, S., Holley, K. M., & Harris M. A. (1995). GENIE: A decision support system for crisis negotiations. *Decision Support Systems*, *14*, 369-391.

Willcocks, L. P., & Feeny, D. (2006). IT outsourcing and core IS capabilities: Challenges and lessons at Dupont. *Information Systems Management*, *23*(1), 49-56.

Willcocks, L., Sauer, C., Feeny, D., Basu, K., Moore, K., Ruddle, K., et al. (2000). *Moving to E-Business, the ultimate practical guide to effective e-business.* London: Random House Business Books.

Williams, A. H., & Cookson, R. A. (2006). Equity-efficiency trade-offs in health technology assessment. *International Journal of Technology Assessment in Health Care*, *22*(1), 1-9.

WITSA. (2001). International Survey of Electronic Commerce - 2000: World Information Technology and Services Alliance. Retrieved July 16, 2004, from http://www.witsa.org/papers/EComSurv.pdf

Women and Minorities in Information Technology Forum. (1999). *Causes and Solutions for Increasing the Numbers in the Workforce Pipeline*. Women and Minorities in Information Technology Forum, Old Dominion University, Hampton Virginia.

Wong, J., Wong, P. N. K., & Li, H. (2007). An investigation of leadership styles and relationship cultures of Chinese and expatriate managers in multinational construction companies in Hong Kong. *Construction Management and Economics*, *25*, 95–106. doi:10.1080/01446190600632573

Wong, Y., Maher, T. E., Wang, J. L., & Long, F. (2001). Exploring Taiwan's competitive advantages: Present and future. *Management Research News*, *24*(6/7), 17-24.

Wood, R., & Bandura, A. (1989). Social cognitive theory of organizational management. *Academy of Management Review*, *14*(3), 361-384.

Workforce Aging in the New Economy (WANE). (2004). *Europe, phase one: A selection of initial findings on employment diversity*. Retrieved from http://www.wane.ca/PDF/EUBriefing.pdf

Woszczynski, A., Myers, M., Beise, C., & Moody, J. (2004, August 5-8). Diversity within the ranks: How ethnicity affects choices in IT. In *Proceedings of the Tenth Americas Conference on Information Systems (AMCIS)*. New York.

Wright, P. M., McMahan, G. C., McCormick, B., & Sherman, W. S. (1998). Strategy, core competence and HR involvement as determinants of HR effectiveness and refinery performance. *Human Resource Management*, *37*(1), 17-29.

WSIS. (2003). Benchmarking e-business policies for SMEs: The approach. Retrieved September, 18, 2003, from http://www.cio.gv.at/WSIS/events/austria/perspectives/wg2/Beitrag_Technopolis.pdf

Wu, J. H., & Wang, S. C. (2005). What drives mobile commerce? An empirical evaluation of the revised technology acceptance model. *Information & Management*, *42*(5), 719-729.

Wu, N. C., Nystrom, M. A., Lin, T. R., & Yu, H. C. (2006). Challenges to global RFID adoption. *Technovation*, *26*, 1317-1323.

Wu, P. (2004) HRM in Taiwan. In P. Budhwar (Ed.), *Managing human resources in Asia-Pacific* (pp. 93-112). London: Routledge.

Wu, S., & Hsu, F. B.-M. (2001). Toward a knowledge-based view of OEM relationship building—sharing of industrial experiences in Taiwan. *International Journal of Technology Management*, *22*(5/6), 203-223.

Wynekoop, J. L., & Walz, D. B. (1998). Revisiting the perennial question: Are IS people different? *Database for Advances in Information Systems*, *29*(2), 62-72.

Xie, G., Zhang, J. L., & Lai, K. K. (2005). A group decision-making model of risk evasion in software project bidding based on VPRS. (*LNAI 3642*, 530-538). Springer-Verlag GmbH.

Xu, S., Zhu, K., & Gibbs, J. (2004). Global technology, local adoption: A cross-country investigation of internet adoption by companies in the United States and China. *Electronic Markets*, *14*(1), 13–24. doi:10.1080/1019678042000175261

Xue, Y., Liang, H., Boulton, W., & Snyder, C. (2005). ERP implementation failures in China: case studies with implications for ERP vendors. *International Journal of Production Economics*, *97*, 279-295.

Yang, K. (2005). Chinese social orientation: A social interactional approach. In Y. Yang (Ed.), *Chinese Social Psychological Review* (Vol. 1). Beijing: Social Science Academic Press (China).

Yap, A., Das, J., Burbridge, J., & Cort, K. (2006). A composite-model for e-commerce diffusion: integrating cultural and socio-economic dimensions to the dynamics of diffusion. *Journal of Global Information Management*, *14*(3), 17-38.

Yau, O. H. M. (1988). Chinese cultural values: their dimensions and marketing implications. *European Journal of Marketing*, *22*(5), 44–57. doi:10.1108/EUM0000000005285

Yeung, J. H. Y., Shim, J. P., & Lai, A. Y. K. (2003). Current progress of e-commerce adoption: Small and medium enterprises in Hong Kong. *Communications of the ACM*, *46*(9ve), 227. doi:10.1145/903893.903941

Yin, R. K. (1989). *Case study research--design and methods (revised edition)*. Newbury Park: Sage Publications.

Young, J. (2000). *The career paths of computer science and information systems major graduates*. Unpublished doctoral dissertation, University of Tasmania.

Yu, T. F.-L. (2001). The Chinese family business as a strategic system: An evolutionary perspective. *International Journal of Entrepreneurial Behaviour and Research*, *7*(1), 22-40.

Yukl, G. (1992). Theory and research on leadership in organizations. *Handbook of Industrial and Organizational Psychology*, 3, 147-198.

Zahedi, M., van Pelt, W., & Srite, M. (2006). Web Documents' Cultural Masculinity and Femininity. *Journal of MIS*, *23*(1), 87–128.

Zaheer, A., McEvily, B., & Perrone, V. (1998). Does trust matter? Exploring the effects on inter-organizational and interpersonal trust on performance. *Organization Science*, *9*(2), 141–159. doi:10.1287/orsc.9.2.141

Zakaria, N., Amelinckx, A., & Wilemon, D. (2004). Working together apart? Building a knowledge sharing culture for global virtual teams. *Creativity and Innovation Management*, *13*(1), 15–29. doi:10.1111/j.1467-8691.2004.00290.x

Zakour, A. B. (2004, Feb. 27-28). *Cultural differences and information technology acceptance.* Paper presented at the 7th Annual Conference of the Southern Association for Information Systems, Savannah, Georgia.

Zaltman, G., Duncan, R., & Holbek, J. (1973). *Innovations and organizations.* NY: Wiley.

Zhang, D., & Lowry, P. B. (2008). Issues, Limitations, and Opportunities in Cross-Cultural Research on Collaborative Software in Information Systems. *Journal of Global Information Management*, *16*(1), 61–92.

Zhang, D., Lowry, P. B., Fu, X., Zhou, L., Adipat, B., & Ran, T. (2006, January 4-7). *Culture, social presence, and media effects on group decision making under majority influence.* Paper presented at the 39th Annual Hawai'i International Conference on System Sciences (HICSS), Kauai, HI.

Zhang, D., Lowry, P. B., Zhou, L., & Fu, X. (2007). The Impact of Individualism-Collectivism, Social Presence, and Group Diversity on Group Decision Making Under Majority Influence. *Journal of Management Information Systems*, *23*(4), 53–80. doi:10.2753/MIS0742-1222230404

Zhang, H. (2004). Trust-promoting seals in electronic markets: Impact on online shopping decisions. *Journal of Information Technology Theory and Application*, *6*(4), 29-40.

Zhang, Y., & Tang, Y. (2002). Challenges facing SMEs in China: A preliminary analysis. In Shaw, R., Adam, S., McDonald H. (Eds), *Proceedings of the Australia New Zealand Marketing Academy Conference.*

Zhang, Z., Lee, M., Huang, P., Zhang, L., & Huang, X. (2005). A framework of ERP systems implementation success in China: an empirical study. *International Journal of Production Economics*, *98*, 56-80.

Zheng, J. (2005). China's GDP Grows 9.5% In First Half [Electronic Version]. *National Bureau of Statistics (NBS).* Retrieved May 1, 2006 from http://www.china-embassy.org/eng/gyzg/t204319.htm

Zhu, K. (2004). The complementarity of information technology infrastructure and e-commerce capability: A resource-based assessment of their business value. *Journal of Management Information Systems*, *21*(1), 167–202.

Zhu, K., & Kraemer, K. (2005). Post-adoption variations in usage and value of e-business by organizations: cross-country evidence from the retail industry. *Information Systems Research*, *16*(1), 61-84.

Zhu, K., Kraemer, K. L., & Xu, S. (2002). *A cross-country study of electronic business adoption using the technology-organization-environment framework.* Paper presented at the Twenty-Third International Conference on Information Systems.

Zhu, K., Kraemer, K. L., Xu, S., & Dedrick, J. (2004). Information technology payoff in e-business environment: an international perspective on value creation of e-business in the financial service industry. *Journal of Management Information Systems*, *21*(1), 17–54.

Zhu, K., Kraemer, K., & Xu, S. (2003). Electronic business adoption by European firms: a cross-country assessment of the facilitators and inhibitors. *European Journal of Information Systems*, *12*(4), 251-268.

Ziarko, W. (1993) Variable precision rough sets model. *Journal of Computer and System Sciences, 46*, 39-59.

Zigurs, I., DeSanctis, G., & Billingsley, J. (1991). Adoption patterns and attitudinal development in computer-supported meetings: An exploratory study with SAMM. *Journal of Management Information Systems*, *7*(4), 51-70.

Zigurs, I., Poole, M. S., & DeSanctis, G. (1988). A study of influence in computer-mediated group decision making. *MIS Quarterly*, *12*(4), 625–644. doi:10.2307/249136

Zmud, R. W. (1984). An examination of push-pull theory applied to process innovation in knowledge work. *Management Science*, *30*(6), 727-738.

Zografos, K. G., Vasilakis, G. M., & Giannouli, I. M. (2000). Methodological framework for developing decision support systems (DSS) for hazardous materials emergency response operations. *Journal of Hazardous Materials*, *71*(1-3), 503-521.

Zou, S. M., & Cavusgil, S. T. (2002). The GMS: A broad conceptualization of global marketing strategy and its effect on firm performance. *Journal of Marketing*, *66*(Oct), 40–56. doi:10.1509/jmkg.66.4.40.18519

Zou, S. M., Taylor, C. R., & Osland, G. E. (1998). The EXPERF Scale: A cross-national generalized export performance measure. *Journal of International Marketing*, *6*(3), 37–58.

Zucker, L. G. (1987). Institutional theories of organization. *Annual Review of Sociology*, *13*, 443–464. doi:10.1146/annurev.so.13.080187.002303

About the Contributors

M. Gordon Hunter is a professor in information systems in the Faculty of Management at The University of Lethbridge. Dr. Hunter has held academic positions in Canada, Hong Kong, and Singapore and visiting positions in Australia, Monaco, Germany, USA and New Zealand. Dr. Hunter is an associate editor of the Journal of Global Information Management. He has published articles in MIS Quarterly, Information Systems Research, The Journal of Strategic Information Systems, The Journal of Global Information Management, Information Systems Journal, and Information, Technology and People. His current research interests relate to the productivity of information systems professionals with emphasis upon the personnel component, including cross-cultural aspects.

Felix B. Tan is professor of information systems, director of research management and head of the University Research Office at AUT University, New Zealand. He serves as the editor-in-chief of the Journal of Global Information Management and sits on the council of the Information Resources Management Association. He was on the council of the association for information systems from 2003-2005. Dr. Tan's current research interests are in electronic commerce, global information management, business-IT alignment, and the management of IT. He actively uses cognitive mapping and narrative inquiry methods in his research. Dr. Tan has published in MIS Quarterly, Information & Management, Journal of Information Technology, IEEE Transactions on Engineering Management, Information Systems Journal as well as other journals and refereed conference proceedings. Dr. Tan has over 20 years experience in information systems management and consulting with large multinationals, as well as University teaching and research in Singapore, Canada and New Zealand.

* * *

Monica Adya received her PhD from Case Western Reserve University. She researches in the area of knowledge management systems, particularly for business forecasting. She also conducts research on IT workforce issues and virtual team management. Her work appears in Human Resource Management, Journal of Managerial Psychology, Information Systems Research, Information Technology & People, International Journal of Forecasting, and Journal of Forecasting among others. She was recently a co-recipient of a grant from 3M Foundation for examining the impact of IT outsourcing on American education.

Kirk P. Arnett is Professor of Management Information Systems at Mississippi State University. He was previously the College of Business and Industry Outstanding Faculty Member and the National Association of Academic Advisors Outstanding Academic Advisor. He has been a member of the academic community for more than 20 years and has multiple publications in the Communications of the ACM, Information and Management, the Journal of Computer Information Systems, Man-Machine Studies and other journals. More than 80 doctoral students have worked with Dr. Arnett for their dissertations. Prior to his full time academic career, Dr. Arnett worked with several US companies for more than 15 years in the information systems arena. In addition to academic credentials Dr. Arnett is a certified computing professional (CCP) from the Institute for Certification of Computing Professionals and holds a Global Information Assurance Certificate from SANS Institute.

She-I Chang received his MS and PhD degrees in computer science and information systems management from Bond University and Queensland University of Technology (Australia), respectively. He is currently an assistant professor at the Department of Accounting and Information Technology, National Chung Cheng University. His research focusing on ERP systems, with a particular emphasis on the issues, challenges and benefits realization associated with ERP life cycle-wide implementation, management and support. He also has methodological interest in the Delphi survey methodology. He has presented and published his research at several IS journals and conferences.

Jihong Chen is a PhD candidate in the Department of Management Systems, University of Waikato Management School, New Zealand, where she received a master's degree in System Management (2005). Her research interests are in the areas of knowledge transfer, outsourcing, cross-cultural issues, electronic business adoption and implementation.

Jim Q. Chen is Chairperson and Professor of Business Computer Information Systems at St. Cloud State University. He received his Ph.D. in Management Information Systems in 1995 from University of Nebraska-Lincoln. His current research interests include Web application development methodologies, E-commerce, and computer database security. His recent publications appeared in Information Systems Management, Communications of the ACM, Decision Support Systems, Journal of Internet Commerce, Journal of Computer Information Systems, Systems Development Management, among other journals.

Tao Chen is a PhD candidate of the School of Management, HUST. His main interests focus on managing IT investment risk from a real options perspective, software development process model, and security in mobile e-commerce.

Yuh-Wen Chiu is doctoral student of information management at National Yunlin University of Science & Technology and instructor of information management at Far East University, Taiwan. She received her BS and MS degrees in information management. Her research interests include e-commerce, e-learning and issues related to IS/IT adoption.

Guodong Cong is a PhD candidate of the School of Management, Huazhong University of Science and Technology (HUST). His main research interests focus on IT outsourcing risk management, knowledge discovery algorithm based on fuzzy rough set, IT media management. He has published several papers in international refereed journals on the above areas.

Lili Cui received the B.S. and M.S. degrees from East China Normal University, Shanghai, China, and the Ph.D. degree in Management Science & Engineering from School of Management, Fudan University, Shanghai, China. She worked as a senior analyst in shanghai municipal internet economy consulting center from 2002 to 2008. During this period, she experienced the dramatic spread of information technology in China and generated the interest in information systems research. She is currently a lecturer at E-Commerce department, School of Information Management & Engineering, Shanghai University of Finance & Economics. Her research interests include organizational IT adoption and usage in developing countries, and e-government. She actively applies an empirical study method in her research in organizational contexts. Her papers have been published in Journals like Electronic Markets, Journal of Global Information Management and various conference proceedings like Hawaii International Conference of System Science, Academy of Management Annual Meeting, IFIPC8.6 and PACIS.

Robert Davison is an associate professor of information systems at the City University of Hong Kong. His current research focuses on virtual knowledge management and collaboration in the Chinese context, specifically in the context of SMEs. His work has appeared in such journals as Chinese Management Studies, Communications of the ACM, Communications of the AIS, Decision Support Systems, IEEE Transactions on Engineering Management, IEEE Transactions on Professional Communication, Information & Management, Information Systems Journal, Information Technology & People, Journal of Global Information Management, Journal of Management Information Systems, MIS Quarterly and Small Group Research, as well as in a variety of international conferences. Robert is the Editor-in-Chief of the Electronic Journal of Information Systems in Developing Countries, Senior Editor for the Information Systems Journal, Regional Editor of Information Technology & People and Associate Editor of MIS Quarterly. He has also edited special issues of the IEEE Transactions on Engineering Management (Cultural Issues and IT Management), the Communications of the ACM (Global Application of Collaborative Technologies), Information Technology & People (Virtual Work, Teams and Organisations) and the Information Systems Journal (Information Systems in China).

Edith Galy is an Assistant Professor of Management Information Systems at the University of Texas at Brownsville. She holds a PhD in International Business from the University of Texas-PanAmerican. Her current research interests are in Organizational Learning, Absorptive Capacity of Information Technologies, Cross-Cultural Influences of IT Adoption, and Change Management. She has published articles in the Journal of International Technology and Information Management, the International Journal of Knowledge, Culture and Change Management, and the Journal of Applied Management and Entrepreneurship.

James Gaskin is an Information Systems Ph.D. student at Weatherhead School of Management with research interests in immersive play and cognitive absorption, motivation at the desk, virtual teams, and improving software design for enjoyable usage. James received his Bachelors and Masters degree in Information Systems Management from Brigham Young University, where he also completed the IS Ph.D. Preparation Program. James's work experience includes game design, business processes automation programming, and information security.

Robert R. Greenberg is professor of accounting at Washington University in Pullman, Washington. Professor Greenberg's research interests include cross-cultural differences and their effects on business behavior and decisions, implementation of Sarbanes-Oxley and its effects on decisions and behavior, the effects of administrative controls on behavior, and the behavioral effects associated with the use of accounting information and systems. Journals where his research has been published include The Journal of Accounting Research, Journal of Accounting, Auditing, and Finance, Advances in Management Accounting, Journal of Cost Analysis, Issues in Accounting Education.

Jibao Gu is an associate professor in University of Science and Technology of China. His research mainly focuses on organizational strategy management. His work has appeared in many Chinese core management journals, e.g. Forecasting and China Soft Science Magazine. He is also the director of the MBA Center of University of Science and Technology of China.

I-Chieh Hsu received his PhD degree at Manchester Business School, UK. He is currently an Associate Professor at the Department of Business Administration, National Changhua University of Education, Taiwan. He has also been a visiting scholar at the Institute of Labor and Industrial Relations, University of Illinois at Urbana Champaign for the first seven months of 2007. Dr. Hsu's areas of interest include knowledge management, intellectual capital management and organizational diversity management. He is a member of an integrative research program, Taiwan Intellectual Capital Study, initiated by National Science Council, Taiwan. This program seeks to develop Taiwan as an important country in studies of intellectual capital through collaborative, interdisciplinary research efforts.

Haiyan Huang is a doctoral candidate at the College of Information Sciences and Technology at the Pennsylvania State University. Her research and teaching interests include global information systems development, global IT offshore outsourcing, virtual teams, computer supported cooperative work and learning, knowledge management, knowledge economy, and global IT workforce development. She has published journal articles, book chapters and conference papers in these areas.

Qian Huang is a PhD student of City University of Hong Kong – University of Science and Technology of China Joint Research Center in Suzhou. She received her bachelor's degree from Anhui University of Finance & Economics, majoring in international trade. She then moved to the University of Science and Technology of China to study for her Masters degree, majoring in Management Science. In 2005, she was admitted to Joint Research Center. Her PhD research focuses on the knowledge sharing issue in China.

Wayne W. Huang is a professor at the Department of Management Information Systems, College of Business, Ohio University. His main research interests include group support systems (GSS), electronic commerce, eEducation, and software engineering. He has published papers in leading international information systems journals including Journal of Management Information Systems (JMIS), IEEE Transactions on Systems, Man, and Cybernetics; Communications of ACM; Information & Management (I&M); IEEE Transactions on Professional Communication; Decision Support Systems (DSS); European Journal of Information Systems (EJIS). He was a faculty member in School of Information Systems, University of New South Wales, Sydney, Australia and Chinese University of Hong Kong, Hong Kong. He has been a visiting scholar in the Terry College of Business of the University of Georgia. He is on the editorial boards of the International Journal of Information & Management (I&M), Global Information Management (JGIM), and Journal of Data Management (JDM).

Allen Johnston is an Assistant Professor in the School of Business at the University of Alabama Birmingham. He holds a BS from Louisiana State University in Electrical Engineering as well as an MSIS and PhD in Information Systems from Mississippi State University. His works can be found in such outlets as Communications of the ACM, Journal of Global Information Management, Journal of Organizational and End User Computing, Information Resources Management Journal, Journal of Information Privacy and Security, and the Journal of Internet Commerce. The primary focus of his research has been in the area of information assurance and security, with a specific concentration on the behavioral aspects of information security and privacy.

Kin-Keung Lai received his PhD at Michigan State University. He is currently the chair professor of management science at the City University of Hong Kong and the associate dean of the Faculty of Business. Professor Lai's main areas of research interests are operations and supply chain management, financial and business intelligent modeling. He has extensively published in international refereed journals on the above areas. He is the chief-editor of the International Journal of Computational Science. He also serves on the editorial board for the International Abstracts in Operations Research, etc. He is the member of the International Advisory Committee of the Journal of Operational Research Society of UK, Council of International Federation of Operational Research Societie, etc. He has actively engaged in management consultant projects for corporations and organizations in Hong Kong and China, on sales forecasting, manpower scheduling, material flow planning, marketing research, inventory control and investment appraisals.

Vincent S. Lai is a professor in MIS at the Chinese University of Hong Kong. His research focuses on IS adoption and diffusion, virtual collaboration, electronic commerce, and global IS strategy. His articles on these topics have been published in IEEE Transactions on Engineering Management, Communications of The ACM, Journal of MIS, Decision Support Systems, Information and Management, European Journal of Information Systems, European Journal of Operational Research, Journal of Information Technology, among others.

Suicheng Li is vice dean and professor of School of Business Administration at Xi'an University of Technology in China. He received his Ph. D. in Management Science and Engineering in 2005 from Northwestern Polytechnical University in China. His current research interests include supply chain management and strategic management. His recent publications appeared in Journal of Industrial Engineering and Engineering Management (in Chinese), Science Research Management (in Chinese), Industrial Engineering Journal (in Chinese), among other journals.

Hefu Liu is a Ph.D. Candidate in the Information Systems Department at the City University of Hong Kong-University of Science and Technology of China Joint Advanced Research Center, Suzhou Campus programme. He has published in the Journal of Global Information Management and in the academic conference PACIS. His research also has been accepted by Decision Support Systems. His current research focuses on the knowledge management, supply chain management and firms Inter-organizational systems adoption.

Paul Benjamin Lowry is an Assistant Professor of Information Systems at the Marriott School, Brigham Young University and a Kevin and Debra Rollins Faculty Fellow, where he also directs the

IS Ph.D. Preparation Program. His research interests include Human-Computer Interaction (HCI) (collaboration, culture, communication, adoption, entertainment), e-business (privacy, security, trust, branding, electronic markets), and scientometrics of Information Systems research. He received his Ph.D. in Management Information Systems (MIS) from the University of Arizona. He has articles published in the Journal of Management Information Systems; Journal of the Association for Information Systems; Communications of the ACM; Communications of the Association for Information Systems; Decision Support Systems; IEEE Transactions on Systems, Man, and Cybernetics; IEEE Transactions on Professional Communication; Small Group Research; Information Sciences; Journal of Business Communication; and others. He serves as an associate editor at AIS Transactions on HCI and at Communications of the AIS.

Gladie Lui is an associate professor at Department of Accountancy, Lingnan University, Hong Kong. She is also the associate director of the business program office at Lingnan University. Dr. Lui's current research interests are in behavioral accounting, information management, financial accounting and accounting education. She has published in Behavioral Research in Accounting, Issues in Accounting Education, Chinese Economy and Management and Accounting Research. Dr. Lui has over 15 years experience in University teaching and research at Hong Kong, China and Canada.

Amit Malik is a doctoral candidate in information management at the Management Development Institute, India. He has received bachelor's degree in computer engineering from National Institute of Technology, India. He has over 3 years of professional experience in software design and development, process designing and implementation. His research interests include virtual teams, software development off-shoring, and knowledge management.

Jim McCullough is George F. Jewett Distinguished Professor of International Business and Director of the School of Business and Leadership at the University of Puget Sound in Tacoma, Washington. His research interests include International Marketing and Information Technology issues in East and Southeast Asia.

Robert J. McQueen is professor of electronic commerce technologies at the Waikato Management School, University of Waikato. He holds a PhD from Waikato, a MBA from the Harvard Business School, and a BApSc in electrical engineering from the University of Waterloo. His research interests are in electronic commerce, computer mediated group communication, and technology support for tacit knowledge building in individuals.

Dhruv Nath is professor and chairman of the doctoral program at the Management Development Institute (MDI), Gurgaon, India. Earlier, he was senior vice president at NIIT Ltd, a leading software and education company. Prof. Nath holds a BTech in electrical engineering and a PhD in the area of computer science, both from IIT Delhi. He has conducted Top Management Workshops in IT and has been a consultant in the area to several organizations such as Glaxo, Unilever, Gillette, Nestle, etc. He has published research papers in international journals such as the IEEE transactions on Computers, and has written two books on managing IT.

Jing Quan is an Assistant Professor in the Department of Information and Decision Sciences in Perdue School of Business at Salisbury University. He holds a Ph.D. from the University of Florida. His research interests include Information technology (IT) and organizations, IT professional and personnel issues, and e-commerce. His work has appeared in such journals as Journal of Management Information Systems, Communications of ACM, Communications of AIS, Information Resources Management Journal, International Journal of Information Management and Journal of Computer Information Systems. He presented papers at national and international conferences on information systems and technology.

Jeria L. Quesenberry is an Assistant Teaching Professor in the Information Systems Program at Carnegie Mellon University. Her doctoral dissertation examined career values and motivations of women in the information technology (IT) workforce and the influence these factors have on their career retention decisions. Her current research interests are directed at investigations of the demands and motivations of IT human capital, and the comparison of how these professionals react to their workplace environment, administrative structures, technologies and policies that accommodate them. She received her Ph.D. from the College of Information Sciences and Technology at the Pennsylvania State University.

Suprateek Sarker is an Associate Professor (Information Systems) at Washington State University, Pullman. His research has appeared in outlets such as the Journal of the AIS, Journal of MIS, IEEE Transactions on Engineering Management, European Journal of Information Systems, Decision Support Systems, IEEE Transactions on Professional Communication, Journal of the Academy of Marketing Science, Information & Management, Information Systems Journal, DATABASE, Journal of Strategic Information Systems, Communications of the ACM, Communications of the AIS, and ICIS Proceedings. He is a recipient of the Stafford Beer Medal from the OR Society, UK, and currently serves as an Associate Editor of MIS Quarterly.

Mark B. Schmidt is an Associate Professor of IS and the director of the Center for Information Assurance Studies in the G.R. Herberger College of Business at St. Cloud State University. He has a Bachelors of Science degree in Business Administration and Agri-Business from Southwest State University, a Masters in Business Administration from St. Cloud State University, and Masters and Ph.D. degrees in Business Information Systems from Mississippi State University. He has works published in the Communications of the ACM, Journal of Computer Information Systems, Journal of Global Information Management, Journal of End User Computing, Mountain Plains Journal of Business and Economics, Business Research Yearbook, Mississippi Business Journal, Proceedings of the National Decision Sciences Institute, Proceedings of the Americas Conference on Information Systems, Proceedings of the Information Resources Management Association, Proceedings of the Security Conference, and in the Proceedings of the ISOneWorld International Conference. His research focuses on information security, end-user computing, and innovative information technologies.

Huizhang Shen received the PhD degree in management science and engineering from Tian Jin University in 1999. He is professor of IT and IS at the Department of Management Information Systems, College of Economics & Management, Shanghai Jiao Tong University. His teaching and research interests include system architecture, system design, group decision support system, group decision making, emergency response, data mining, electronic commerce and information security. He has published over 60 research papers in journals and international conferences.

Dong-Her Shih received his PhD degree in electrical engineering from the National Cheng Kung University, Taiwan, in 1986. He is currently a senior professor in the Department of Information Management, National Yunlin University of Science and Technology, Douliu, Yunlin, Taiwan. He was the chair of the Department of Information Management during 1991–1994 and director of the Computer Center during 1997–2002. His current researches include network security, intrusion detection, wireless network, RFID and peer-to-peer network. He has published over 30 journal articles in related area.

Varadharajan Sridhar is Professor in Information Management at the Management Development Institute, India. He received his PhD from the University of Iowa, USA. Dr. Sridhar's primary research interests are in the area of telecommunication management and policy and Global Software Development. He has published his research work in European Journal of Operational Research, Telecommunication Systems, International Journal of Business Data Communications and Networking, Applied Econometrics and International Development, Information Resource Management Journal, Journal of Global Information Management, Journal of Regional Analysis and Policy, and Journal of Information System Security. He was the recipient of the Nokia Visiting Fellowship awarded by the Nokia Research Foundation. He is an associate editor of the International Journal of Business Data Communications and Networking and is on the editorial board of the Journal of Global Information Management.

Mark Srite is an Associate Professor in the Management Information Systems area at the University of Wisconsin – Milwaukee's Sheldon B. Lubar School of Business. He received his PhD from Florida State University in 2000. His research interests include the acceptance, adoption, and use of information technologies, cross-cultural IT issues, and group decision making. His work has been published in MIS Quarterly, the Journal of MIS, Decision Support Systems, Information and Organization, the Journal of Global Information Management, the Journal of Global of Information Technology Management, the Journal of Computer Information Systems, and elsewhere.

Bernard C.Y. Tan (http://www.comp.nus.edu.sg/~btan) is professor and head of the Department of Information Systems at the National University of Singapore (NUS). He has won research awards and teaching awards at NUS. He has been a Visiting Scholar at Stanford University and University of Georgia. He has served as council member for the Association for Information Systems. He is on the editorial boards of MIS Quarterly (senior editor emeritus), Journal of the AIS (senior editor), IEEE Transactions on Engineering Management (department editor), Management Science, Journal of Management Information Systems, Information and Management and Journal of Global Information Management. His current research interests are knowledge management, virtual communities, and information privacy.

Jason Bennett Thatcher is an Assistant Professor in the Department of Management at Clemson University. Dr. Thatcher's research examines the influence of individual beliefs and characteristics on the use of information technology. He also studies strategic and human resource management issues related to the application of technologies in organizations. Dr. Thatcher's work has appeared in, or is forthcoming in, MIS Quarterly, Communications of the ACM, Journal of Management Information

Systems, IEEE Transactions on Engineering Management, American Review of Public Administration, and the Journal of Applied Psychology.

Eileen M. Trauth is Associate Dean for Diversity, Outreach and International Engagement, and Professor of Information Sciences and Technology at the Pennsylvania State University. During 2008 she held the Universität Klagenfurt Fulbright Distinguished Chair in Gender Studies. Her research is concerned with societal, cultural and organizational influences on information technology and the information technology professions with a special focus on the role of diversity within the field. During 2008 she held the Universität Klagenfurt Fulbright Distinguished Chair in Gender Studies. She was also a Fulbright Scholar in Ireland where she undertook a multi-year investigation of socio-cultural influences on the emergence of Ireland's information economy. She has analyzed cultural, economic, infrastructure and public policy influences on the development of information technology occupational clusters in the U.S. Dr. Trauth has investigated gender under representation in the information technology professions in Austria, Australia, Ireland, New Zealand, South Africa and the United States with grants from the National Science Foundation and Science Foundation Ireland. In addition to her work on gender, she has published papers and books on qualitative research methods, critical theory, global informatics, information policy, information management and information systems skills.

Yi-Shun Wang is an associate professor in the Department of Information Management at National Changhua University of Education, Taiwan. He received his PhD in MIS from National Chengchi University, Taiwan. His current research interests include IT/IS adoption strategy, IS success measures, customer relationship management, and e-learning. Dr. Wang's research has appeared or is forthcoming in Information Systems Journal, Information & Management, Journal of Global Information Management, Government Information Quarterly, Computers in Human Behavior, Computers & Education, British Journal of Educational Technology, CyberPsychology & Behavior, Journal of Computer Information Systems, Journal of End User Computing, Journal of Electronic Commerce Research, International Journal of Electronic Business, International Journal of Service Industry Management, and others. He is currently an editorial board member of the International Journal of Applied Decision Sciences.

Bernard Wong-On-Wing is professor of accounting at Washington State University. At different stages of this study, he was a visiting research scholar at the Southwestern University of Finance and Economics in Chengdu, China. Professor Wong-On-Wing's research interests include the study of cross-cultural differences and their implications for business practices, judgment and decision making. His research has been published in journals such as Accounting, Organizations and Society, Auditing: A Journal of Practice and Theory, Behavioral Research in Accounting, Decision Sciences, and Journal of Information Systems.

David C. Yen is a Raymond E. Glos professor in business and professors of MIS of the Department of Decision Sciences and Management Information Systems at Miami University. He received a PhD in MIS and MSc in computer science from the University of Nebraska. Professor Yen is active in research, he has published three books and many articles which have appeared in Communications of the ACM, Decision Support Systems, Information & Management, International Journal of Information Management, Information Sciences, Journal of Computer Information Systems, Interfaces, Telematics and Informatics, Computer Standards and Interfaces, Information Society, Omega, International

Journal of Organizational Computing and Electronic Commerce, Communications of AIS, and Internet Research among others.

Cheng Zhang (corresponding author zhangche@fudan.edu.cn) received the B.S. degree from MIS department, FuDan University, Shanghai, China, and the Ph.D. degree in Information systems from department of Information Systems, National University of Singapore, Singapore. He is an assistant professor at MIS department, Fudan University. His research interests include information sharing strategy, Information Technology diffusion and e-business. His works have appeared in journals like Omega, Journal of Global Information Management, Electronic Markets, Simulation Modeling Practice and Theory, and conference proceedings like International Conference of Information Systems, European Conference of Information Systems, Academy of Management Annual Meeting, IFIP, DSI and AMCIS.

Dongsong Zhang is an Associate Professor in the Department of IS at University of Maryland, Baltimore County. His current research interests include context-aware mobile computing, computer-mediated collaboration and communication, knowledge management, and e-Business. His work has been published or will appear in journals such as Communications of the ACM (CACM), Journal of Management Information Systems (JMIS), IEEE Transactions on Knowledge and Data Engineering (TKDE), IEEE Transactions on Software Engineering, IEEE Transactions on Multimedia, IEEE Transactions on Systems, Man, and Cybernetics, IEEE Transactions on Professional Communication, Decision Support Systems, Information & Management, Communications of the AIS, Journal of the American Society for Information Science and Technology, among others. He has received research grants and awards from NIH, Google Inc., and Chinese Academy of Sciences.

Jinlong Zhang received his PhD at HUST. He is currently the dean of the School of Management at the HUST. Professor Zhang's main areas of research interests are modern management theory, information system, electronic commerce, materials flow, managerial innovation and decision-making. He has published over 120 papers in international refereed journals on the above areas. He is the chief-editor of the Chinese Journal of Management. He also serves on the editorial board for the Management Review, etc. He is the member of the Advisory Committee of the Institute of Chinese Soft Science, etc. He has actively engaged in management consultant projects for corporations and organizations in China, on strategy management, material flow planning, inventory control and investment appraisals.

Man Zhang is an Assistant Professor (International Business) at Bowling Green State University, Bowling Green, Ohio. Her Research has appeared in outlets such as the Multinational Business Review, Information Systems Journal, Journal of International Business and Economics, Journal of Academy of Business and Economics and ICIS proceeding.

Jidi Zhao is a PhD candidate in management science and engineering at Shanghai Jiao Tong University. Her current research interests focus on group decision making, data mining and electronic commerce.

Index

H

I

U

V

W